W9-AXU-849

TWELFTH EDITION

Modern
Real Estate
Practice

FILLMORE W. GALATY
WELLINGTON J. ALLAWAY
ROBERT C. KYLE

**Real Estate
Education Company**
a division of Dearborn Financial Publishing, Inc.

© 1959, 1963, 1965, 1968, 1971, 1973, 1975, 1978, 1982, 1985, 1988, 1991 by Dearborn Financial Publishing, Inc.

Published by Real Estate Education Company/Chicago
a division of Dearborn Financial Publishing, Inc.

All rights reserved. The text of this publication, or any part thereof, may not be reproduced in any manner whatsoever without written permission in writing from the publisher. Printed in the United States of America.

92 93 10 9 8 7 6 5 4

While a great deal of care has been taken to provide accurate and current information, the ideas, suggestions, general principles and conclusions presented in this text are subject to local, state and federal laws and regulations, court cases and any revisions of same. The reader is thus urged to consult legal counsel regarding any points of law—this publication should not be used as a substitute for competent legal advice.

Library of Congress Cataloging-in-Publication Data

Galaty, Fillmore W.
    Modern real estate practice / Fillmore W. Galaty, Wellington J.
Allaway, Robert C. Kyle. — 12th ed.
        p.   cm.
    Includes index.
    ISBN 0-7931-0098-4 (paper)
    1. Real estate business—Law and legislation—United States.
2. Vendors and purchasers—United States.   3. Real property—United
States.   4. Real estate business—United States.   I. Allaway,
Wellington J.   II. Kyle, Robert C.   III. Title.
KF2042.R4G34   1990
346.7304'37—dc20
[347.306437]
                                                                90-46291
                                                                CIP

Acquisitions Editor: Margaret M. Maloney
Project Editor: Joan McLaughlin
Cover and Internal Design: James A. Buddenbaum

Contents

Preface

Since its first printing in 1959, *Modern Real Estate Practice* has provided hundreds of thousands of people with valuable real estate information. Whether they were using the book to prepare for taking a state licensing examination, or for a college or university program, or just for their own personal knowledge, they knew that *Modern Real Estate Practice* set the standard for contemporary information in an easy-to-read format.

In response to extensive research, this twelfth edition contains many changes, all made so that the book will be as sensitive as possible to the needs of the reader. The text has been condensed to eliminate unnecessary explanatory notes but still includes the latest information for the reader. The glossary has been expanded to accommodate the most-recent terminology, particularly in the areas of finance and appraising, both of which have received increased coverage in the text. The end-of-chapter questions have been rewritten and adapted for use not only as benchmarks for reader understanding, but also as study material for state licensing examinations. There now are two 80-question sample examinations in the text to allow the reader to gauge his or her progress at the end of the book. Commentary has been added regarding agency relationships and stigmatized properties, and there is an appendix on environmental considerations. This is in addition to the Mathematics Review and the Residential Construction Appendix. So this twelfth edition is an excellent tool for those who possess a sincere interest in real estate.

The text, however, is still *only* a tool. It will start the reader on an educational path for which the reader must assume responsibility. The reader is encouraged to talk with professionals in the field: brokers, salespeople, mortgage lenders, appraisers, public officials and others to obtain a feel for the impact this business has on his or her community. The reader also is encouraged to read as much as possible about the specialty areas of the business; the publisher has more than 100 additional titles available. The classroom instructor is encouraged to bring additional material into the classroom to supplement the concepts brought out in the text: state and local contract forms, deeds, financing documents, sample appraisals, closing statements, subdivision reports, environmental reports, etc. This type of "personalization" of the text materials makes the instructor so much more effective in the classroom, familiarizes the students with the documents and reduces student anxiety both in the examination situation and in the field. Because education is a continuous process, reader and instructor alike must enhance that process through their active participation in it.

Supplements for *Modern Real Estate Practice* have been developed for more than 30 states, detailing laws, principles and practices specific to the real estate business in those particular states. A *Study Guide for Modern Real Estate Practice* contains additional review questions and study problems to further assist the student in his or her real estate education. In addition, a comprehensive *Instructor's Manual*, a computerized test bank and transparencies are available to instructors as companions to this text. Contact Real Estate Education Company for further details about these materials.

Comments always are appreciated; they assist in evaluating the current edition and formulating policy for future editions. Any comments should be directed to Anita Constant, Senior Vice-President, Real Estate Education Company, a division of Dearborn Financial Publishing, Inc., 520 North Dearborn, Chicago, Illinois 60610.

Acknowledgments

The authors would like to thank Terrence M. Zajac, DREI, of Scottsdale, Arizona, who served as development writer for the Twelfth Edition of *Modern Real Estate Practice*. The authors also would like to thank the following people, who served as topic specialists for the twelfth edition: Lawrence Sager, Madison Area Technical College—Chapter 5; Vern Hoven, Vern Hoven Tax Seminars—Chapters 10, 14 and 15; Gerald R. Cortesi, Triton College—Chapters 14 and 15; Floyd M. Baird, RPA/MSA, Manager, Trust Real Estate, The First National Bank and Trust Company of Tulsa—Chapter 17; Martha R. Williams, J.D., University of San Francisco, Paralegal Studies Program—Chapter 18; Gaylon E. Greer, Fogelman Chair of Excellence in Real Estate, Memphis State University—Chapters 19 and 20; Edith Lank, charter member, Real Estate Educators Association—Chapters 11–14, 21–23; Stephen J. Martin, Executive Director, National Association of Environmental Risk Auditors—environmental issues appendix; Nick A. Tillema, J.D., general counsel, National Association of Environmental Risk Auditors—environmental issues appendix. The authors also thank the following reviewers for their valuable assistance:

Frank Adams, Blue Ridge Community College
Michael J. Ahern III, University of Toledo
Thomas E. Anderson, Northwestern Connecticut Community College
Nancy L. Artz, Moraine Park Technical College
Mary Jane Balazs, John Carroll University
Elyse Berns, ERA Real Estate Institute
Dean Bishop, Omaha School of Real Estate
Ed Bjork, C.B. 1st Minot Realty, Minot High School
Morton J. Blumenthal, J.D., CCIM, Remax Professionals, New Hampshire College
William R. Bowles, Esquire, New Haven Real Estate School
William D. Bramble, Northern Kentucky University
Shirley Branson, Carl Albert Junior College
Frances Mills Brintley, Germanna Community College, Rappahannock Community College
Lois Burdette, Thomas Nelson Community College
Alvin G. Busch, Busch Bros. Realtors, Moraine Valley Community College
Rose Mary Chambers, First Institute of Real Estate
Richard Cohn, Coldwell Banker School of Real Estate
Tracey A. Cooper, Bill Miller School of Real Estate, Inc.
Charles E. Cuson, University of Arizona

John C. Davis, Howard Community College
Lee E. Dillenbeck, Elgin Community College
Michael Dominguez, National Institue of Real Estate, Capstone Realty, Inc.
John Donahue, National Institute of Real Estate
Jerry Duggan, Iowa Western Community College
R. Stephen Elliott, Ph.D., Northwestern State University of Louisiana
Emma T. Fabbri, Triton College
David L. Finley, Better Homes Academy of Real Estate
Tom Fisher, GRI, CRB, Southern Ohio College
Charles F. Floyd, University of Georgia
Ronald Forman, Century-21 Forman Reality, Montgomery College, George
    Washington University
H. Janet Frandsen, Truckee Meadows Community College
Paul W. Gainer, Preferred Properties of Summerville Inc., Charleston Trident Board
    of Realtors
Edward A. Geswein, Century-21 Mennen Real Estate
Joe Giacoma, Jr., Neosho County Community College, Broken Wagon Wheel
    Land Agency
Louis Pete Gikas, Bill Miller School of Real Estate, Inc., Discover Real
    Estate, Inc.
Norma L. Good, DREI, GRI, Malone College
Andrew J. Grod, South Suburban College
Donald E. Harris, Oakton Community College
E. Ray Henry, Flagstaff, Arizona
Hank Hoesli, Western State College
Joseph C. Holbrook, T. C. Williams High School
N. Wayne Horine, Thrust School of Real Estate
Eric Howard, UNLV
Carl R. Hurst, Southern Institute of Technology
Don T. Johnson, Western Illinois University
Mary Ellen Johnson, Sally McMahon School of Real Estate
Jerald C. Juliano, M.S.A, Indiana Vocational Technical College, Northwest
Kristine A. Jung, Century 21 John Jung Real Estate Inc., McHenry County College
Lois Kadosh, REALTOR®
Tom Karras, Montgomery College
P. Leslie Kepner, Danville Area Community College, Danville Area Board
    of Realtors
Lenora E. Key, Bill Miller School of Real Estate, Inc.
Fred Kuhn, CRS, GRI, Fred Kuhn Realty
Thomas B. Lally, Broker Associate
Melvin S. Lange, National Institute of Real Estate
Vincent C. Lopez, Truman College
Wanda R. Manz, Eau Claire Chippewa Board of Realtors, Chippewa Valley
    Technical College
Joseph H. Martin, MAI, CRE, SREA, ASA, Martin, Benner, Pintinalli,
    Hedden, Inc.
Ralph De Martino, JRI, Sirk & Co. Realtors, Paducah Community College
Joanne Matzke, College of DuPage
Robert McAvey, GRI, Anoka Ramsey Community College
Bob McConnell, Metropolitan Kansas City Board of Realtors
Diane F. McDonald, DREI, Real Estate Career Trainers
Rose McDonald, Institute for Development of Sales Potential
Dwight J. McFarland, Lincolnland Community College
Jerry Melchionna, Quinnipiac College

Leslie C. Michigan, ERA Questarr Properties

Joyce Mikitka, Coldwell Banker School of Real Estate

Jerome M. Morgan, William Carey College

Kenneth H. Morrison, Real Estate Development Institute

Joseph J. Nadolny, Wauwatosa Real Estate Institute, Inc.

Carl Edward Neeley, South Carolina School of Real Estate

Edward Norris, Norris School of Real Estate

Margaret Offenberger, Northeast Career Institute

Henry J. Olivieri, Jr., Attorney-at-Law, Real Estate Education Company

Paul Olsen, Wesley College

Anthony W. Palazzolo, Xavier University

Raye N. Parks, CRB, The Real Estate Academy, Inc.

Jens A. Pedersen, Bill Miller School of Real Estate

Lawrence F. Perreault, Real Estate Academy of Huntsville, Century-21
    Ambassador Realty, Inc.

George N. Plavac, Ph.D., Cuyahoga Community College

Marilyn J. Popa, Realty One Boebinger, Kent State University

Roger Poulos, University of Southern Mississippi

Tom Quade, National Institute of Real Estate

John Reilly, J.D., Dinman, Nakamura, Elisha & Nakatani

Elmer E. Remsen, Princeton School of Real Estate

John D. Rinchart, The Real Estate Institute of York County, Inc.

Darren E. Roach, Career Education Systems, Inc.

David S. Roberts, O'Conor, Piper & Flynn

K. Michael Schulz, University of Evansville

Bryna D. Seliq, ERA, Mimi Seliq Homes, Inc.

Gary L. Shepard, Central Virginia School of Real Estate

David Sirota, Real Estate Consultant

Kathryn "Tootie" Smith, Smith Real Estate School

Monroe Smith, Chattahoochee Valley State Community College

Martie Stegall, Rock Island Board of Realtors

Dawn M. Svenningsen, Dabbs Academy of Real Estate, Inc.

Robert L. Tabler, Jr., Carroll Community College

Paul J. Thiel, South Carolina School of Real Estate

Wayne Tomlinson, Wayne Tomlinson Real Estate, Spoon River Junior College

Randall S. van Reken, Southern Nevada School of Real Estate

Frank E. Van Vlierbergen, Attorney-at-Law, Village Real Estate Corp.

James A. Walsh, Tidewater Community College

John M. Ware, GSH Referral Company

Wilma "Billie" Watteau, Indiana Vocational Technical College

Alfred P. Werbner, ASA, CRA, Manchester Community College

Mary Lou Wood, Arkansas State University, White Realty Better Homes
    and Garden

Dale P. Zahn, Dabbs Academy of Real Estate, Century-21 Dabbs Corporation

Thanks also are extended to the many real estate professionals who have contributed to earlier editions of the book. Each new edition builds on the foundation they have helped us develop.

Furthermore, special credit is extended to the following people or groups for permission to use materials or forms: Floyd M. Baird; Kermit Burton, Alpha Enterprises; Diane Flannigan, Founders Title Insurance Agency, Inc.; Yvette Fleeger, Peter Cook Mortgage Company; The Forms Committee, Arizona Association of REALTORS®; National Association of Environmental Risk Auditors; Robert Rucker,

Arizona Regional Multiple Listing Service; William L. Ventolo, Jr.; Vista Environmental Information, Inc.; and Martha R. Williams. The sample forms may not be applicable to all jurisdictions and are subject to pertinent changes in the law.

Finally, the authors would like to extend their appreciation to the entire staff of Real Estate Education Company for their execution of this Twelfth Edition. Special assistance has been provided by Margaret Maloney, Acquisitions Editor; Joan McLaughlin, Project Editor; Lucy Jenkins, Art and Design Manager.

Fillmore W. Galaty
Wellington J. Allaway
Robert C. Kyle

Part One
Principles

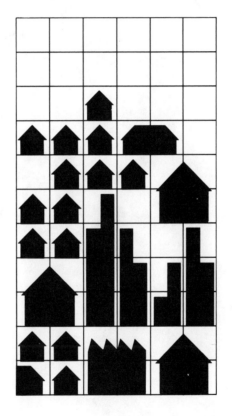

1

The Real Estate Business

The Real Estate Business Is "Big" Business

Billions of dollars' worth of real estate is sold each year in the United States. Adding to this great volume of sales are rental collections by real estate management firms, appraisals of properties ranging from vacant land to modern office and apartment buildings and the lending of money through mortgage loans on real estate.

Millions of people depend on some aspect of the real estate business for their livelihood. As the technical aspects of real estate activities become more complex, real estate offices require an increasing number of people properly trained to handle such transactions. Many professional and business people and organizations, such as attorneys, banks, trust companies, abstract and title insurance companies, architects, surveyors, accountants and tax specialists, also depend on the real estate specialist.

Real Estate—A Business of Many Specializations

Despite the size and complexity of the real estate business, many people think of it as being composed only of brokers and salespeople. Actually today's real estate industry employs millions of knowledgeable individuals who are well trained in areas of specialization such as appraisal, property management, financing, subdivision and development, counseling and education. Each of these is a business unto itself, but every real estate professional must have a basic knowledge of all of these specializations to be successful.

Real Estate Professions

Brokerage. Brokerage is the bringing together of people in a real estate transaction. Usually the **broker** acts as an agent who negotiates the sale, purchase or rental of property on behalf of others for a fee or commission; in any transaction there may be a **salesperson** working on behalf of the broker. The commission is generally a percentage of the amount of the transaction. It is usually paid by the seller in a sale or the owner in a rental transaction. Brokerage is further discussed in Chapter 4.

Appraisal. Appraisal is the process of estimating a property's value. Although brokers must have some understanding of valuation as part of their training, qualified appraisers are employed when property is financed or sold by court order. Appraisers must have sound judgment and detailed knowledge of the methods of valuation, and most must meet state licensing or certification requirements. Appraisal is covered in Chapter 18.

Property management. Someone who operates property for its owner is involved in property management. The property manager's basic responsibility is to protect the value of the owner's investment while maximizing the owner's return on that investment. In that role the property manager might be responsible for soliciting tenants, collecting rents, altering or constructing new space for tenants, ordering repairs and generally maintaining the property. Property management is discussed in Chapter 17.

Financing. Financing is the business of providing funds for a real estate transaction. Most transactions are financed by means of a mortgage loan or a trust deed loan secured by the property. Financing is examined in Chapters 14 and 15.

Subdivision and development. Subdivision entails splitting a large parcel of real estate into smaller ones. The subdivider must survey the land, both before and after the splitting is done, and draft a map of the newly created parcels in the subdivision, often referred to as a *plat map*. Development relates to the construction of improvements on land. These improvements fall into two categories. Offsite improvements, such as water lines and storm sewers under city streets, are made on public lands. On-site improvements, such as a new home or a swimming pool, are made on individual parcels. While subdivision and development normally are related—particularly in the area of new housing—they are independent processes that can occur separately. Subdividing and the development process are discussed further in Chapters 19 and 20.

Counseling. Counseling involves providing clients with competent independent advice based on sound judgment. The counselor attempts to give the client direction in choosing among alternative courses of action regarding the purchase, use and investment of property. Increasing the client's knowledge is every counselor's function.

Education. Education is the provision of information to both the real estate practitioner and the consumer. Colleges and universities, private schools and trade organizations conduct courses and seminars on all aspects of the business, from the principles of a prelicensing program to the technical aspects of tax and exchange law.

Other areas. Many other people are also a part of the real estate business, such as those associated with mortgage banking firms and those who negotiate mortgages for banks and savings and loan associations, people in property management firms and real estate departments of corporations and officials and employees of such government agencies as zoning boards and assessing offices.

Professional Organizations

The real estate business has many trade organizations, the largest being the National Association of REALTORS® (NAR). NAR sponsors various affiliate organizations that offer professional designations to brokers, salespeople and others who complete required courses. Members subscribe to a code of ethics and are entitled to be known as REALTORS® or Realtor-Associates.

Among the many other professional associations is the National Association of Real Estate Brokers (NAREB), whose members also subscribe to a code of ethics. Members of NAREB are known as Realtists.

Types of Real Property

Just as there are areas of specialization within the real estate industry, there are different types of property in which to specialize. Real estate can generally be classified as follows.

1. Residential—all property used for housing, from acreage to small city lots, both single-family and multifamily, in urban, suburban and rural areas.
2. Commercial—business property, including office space, shopping centers, storefronts, theaters, hotels and parking facilities.
3. Industrial—warehouses, factories, land in industrial districts and power plants.
4. Agricultural—farms, timberland, ranches and orchards.
5. Special-purpose—churches, schools, cemeteries and government-held lands.

The market for each of these types of properties can be further subdivided into the sale market, which involves the transfer of title, and the rental market, which involves the transfer of space on a rental basis.

In Practice . . .

Although a real estate firm or person can, in theory, perform all the services listed above and handle all classes of property, this is rarely done except in small towns. Most firms tend to specialize to some degree, especially in urban areas. In some cases a licensee may perform only one service for one type of property. Residential property brokers and industrial property appraisers are two examples of such specialization.

The Real Estate Market

In literal terms a **market** is a place where goods can be bought and sold, where value for those goods can be established and where it is advantageous for buyers and sellers to trade. The function of the market is to facilitate this exchange by providing a setting in which the supply and demand forces of the economy can establish market value.

Supply and Demand

The economic forces of **supply** and **demand** continually interact in the market to establish and maintain price levels. Essentially, *when supply goes up, prices will drop as more producers compete for buyers; when demand increases, prices will rise as more buyers compete for the product.*

Supply and demand in the real estate market. Real estate is not a standardized product; no two parcels can ever be exactly alike. The apparent exceptions to this are in some developments where a number of units may be built to the same specifications. But even where this condition exists, each parcel of real estate is unique because it has its own geographic location.

Because real estate is fixed in nature (immobile), it cannot be moved from area to area to satisfy the pressures of supply and demand. Property buyers are also generally limited in their mobility—retirees are a major exception in regard to residences. For these reasons the real estate business has tended toward local markets where offices can maintain detailed familiarity with market conditions and available units.

Because of real estate's characteristics of uniqueness and immobility, the real estate market is generally relatively slow to adjust to the forces of supply and demand. To a certain extent the product can be removed from the market (as when a home offered for resale is withdrawn), yet an oversupply usually results in a lowering of price levels. Development and construction of real estate take a long time from conception to completion, so increases in demand may not be met immediately. Building and housing construction may occur in uneven spurts of activity due to such factors.

Factors affecting supply. Factors that tend to affect supply in the real estate market include the labor force, construction costs, government controls and financial policies.

Labor force and construction costs. A shortage of labor in the skilled building trades, an increase in the cost of building materials or a scarcity of materials will tend to decrease the amount of housing built. The impact of the labor force on price levels depends on the extent to which higher costs can be passed on to the buyer or renter in the form of higher purchase prices or rents. Technological advances that result in cheaper materials and more efficient means of construction may tend to counteract some price increases.

Government controls and financial policies. Government monetary policy can have a substantial impact on the real estate market. The Federal Reserve Board, as well as such government agencies as the Federal Housing Administration (FHA), the Government National Mortgage Association (GNMA) and the Federal Home Loan Mortgage Corporation (FHLMC), can affect the amount of money available to lenders for mortgage loans (see Chapter 15).

The government also can influence the amount of money available for real estate investment through its fiscal and monetary policies. Such policies include the amount of money taken out of circulation through taxation and other methods and the amount of money the government puts into circulation through spending programs ranging from welfare to farm subsidies.

At the local level real estate taxation is one of the primary sources of revenue for government. Policies on taxation of real estate can have either positive or negative effects. Tax incentives have been one way for communities to attract new businesses and industries to their areas. And, of course, along with these enterprises come increased employment and expanded residential real estate markets.

Local governments also can affect market operations and the development and construction of real estate by applying land-use controls. Communities use building codes and zoning ordinances to control and stimulate the highest potential use of land, thereby stabilizing real estate values and markets. Efficient governmental policies, as well as community amenities such as churches, schools and parks, influence the real estate market.

Factors affecting demand. Factors that tend to affect demand in the real estate market include population and employment and wage levels.

Population. Shelter, in the form of owned or rented property, is a basic human and family need, so the general need for housing will grow as the population grows. Even though the total population of the country may continue to increase, some areas are growing faster than others. The Sunbelt still attracts businesses, retirees and others, but effective local controls can make northern areas attractive for newcomers as well. There also are areas of no growth or rapidly decreasing population, where the exhaustion of natural resources, the termination of an industrial operation or the closing of a military installation has resulted in a mass exodus.

Demographics. The makeup of the population— demographics—affects demand as strongly as simple numbers. Family size and the ratio of adults to children, the number of people moving into retirement care facilities and retirement communities, the effect of "doubling up" (two or more families using one housing unit) and the changing number of single-parent households all contribute to the amount and type of housing needed. Also of concern are the number of young people who would prefer to rent or own their own residences but have roommates or remain in their parents' homes for economic reasons.

Employment and wage levels. Decisions on home ownership and rental are closely related to ability to pay. Employment opportunities and wage levels in a small community can be affected drastically by decisions made by major employers in the area. Individuals involved in the real estate market in such communities must keep themselves well informed about the business plans of local employers.

Key Terms

broker
demand
market

salesperson
supply

Summary

Although selling is the most widely recognized activity of the real estate business, the industry also involves many other services, such as appraisal, property management, property development, counseling, property financing and education. Most real estate firms specialize in only one or two of these areas. However, the highly complex and competitive nature of our society requires that a real estate person be an expert in a number of fields.

Real property can be classified according to its general use as either residential, commercial, industrial, agricultural or special-purpose. Although many brokers deal with more than one type of real property, they usually specialize to some degree.

A market is a place where goods and services can be bought and sold and price levels established. Because of its unique characteristics, real estate is relatively slow to adjust to the forces of supply and demand.

The supply of and demand for real estate are affected by many factors, including changes in population numbers and demographics, wage and employment levels, construction costs and availability of labor and governmental monetary policy and controls.

Questions

1. Commercial real estate includes all of the following *except:*

   a. office buildings for sale.
   b. apartments for rent.
   c. retail space for lease.
   d. fast-food restaurants.

2. In general, when the supply of a certain commodity increases:

   a. prices tend to rise.
   b. prices tend to drop.
   c. demand tends to rise.
   d. demand tends to drop.

3. All of the following factors tend to affect supply *except:*

   a. the labor force.
   b. construction costs.
   c. government controls.
   d. employment and wage levels.

4. Which of the following is an example of special-purpose real estate?

   a. A private school
   b. A public library
   c. A shopping center
   d. An industrial park

Real Property and the Law

Characteristics of Real Estate

Licensees must understand the seven characteristics that define the nature of real estate and affect its use. These characteristics fall into two broad categories—economic characteristics and physical characteristics (see Figure 2.1).

Economic Characteristics

The economic characteristics of land are the factors that influence its value as an investment.

Scarcity. Although land is not thought of as a rare commodity, the total supply of land is fixed. While a considerable amount is still not used or inhabited, the supply in a given location or of a particular quality can be limited.

Improvements. The building of an improvement on one parcel of land has an effect on the value and utilization of neighboring tracts and can have a direct bearing on whole communities. For example, the improvement of a parcel by the construction of a shopping center or the selection of a site for the building of an atomic reactor can directly influence a large area.

Permanence of investment. Once land has been improved, the capital and labor used to build the improvement represent a large fixed investment. Although even a well-built structure can be razed to make way for a newer building or other use of the land, improvements such as drainage, electricity, water and sewerage remain, because they generally cannot be dismantled or removed economically. The return on such investments will tend to be long-term and relatively stable.

Area preference. This economic characteristic, sometimes called *situs*, does not refer to a geographical location but rather to people's choices and preferences for a given area. It is the unique quality of people's preferences that results in different valuations being attributed to similar units. *Area preference is the most important economic characteristic of land.*

Physical Characteristics

Land also has certain physical characteristics that set it apart from other commodities.

Land is immobile. It is true that some of the substances of land are removable and that topography can be changed, but *the geographical location of any given parcel of land can never be changed*. It is fixed.

Figure 2.1
Characteristics of
Real Estate

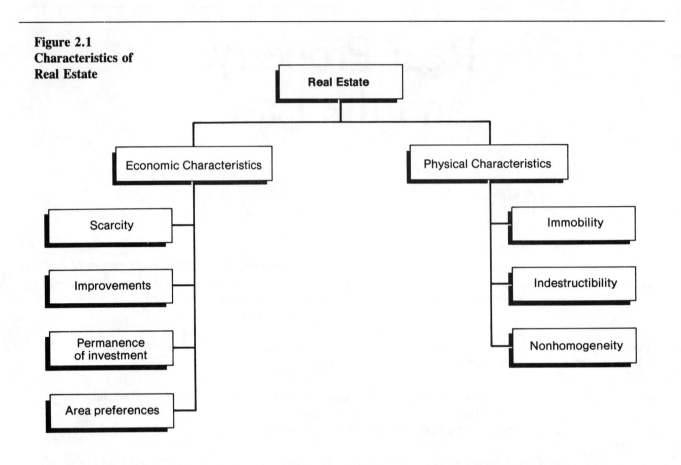

Land is indestructible. Land is also *indestructible*. This permanence of land, coupled with the long-term nature of the improvements placed on it, has tended to stabilize investments in land.

Land is unique. No two parcels of land are ever exactly the same. Although there may be substantial similarity, *all parcels differ geographically*, as each parcel has its own location. The uniqueness of land is also referred to as its *heterogeneity* or *nonhomogeneity*.

Ownership of
Real Property

The unique nature of real estate has given rise to a unique set of laws and rights. Even the simplest of real estate transactions brings into play a body of complex laws, and licensees must understand not only the effect of the law but also how the law defines real property. Real property is often described as a **bundle of legal rights.** In other words, a purchaser of real estate is actually buying the rights of ownership held by the seller. The rights of ownership (see Figure 2.2) include the right of possession, the right to control the property within the framework of the law, the right of enjoyment (to use the property in any legal manner), the right of exclusion (to keep others from entering or using the property) and the right of disposition (to sell, will or otherwise dispose of the property).

The concept of a bundle of rights comes from old English law. When the populace could not commonly read and write, a seller transferred property by giving

**Figure 2.2
The Bundle of
Legal Rights**

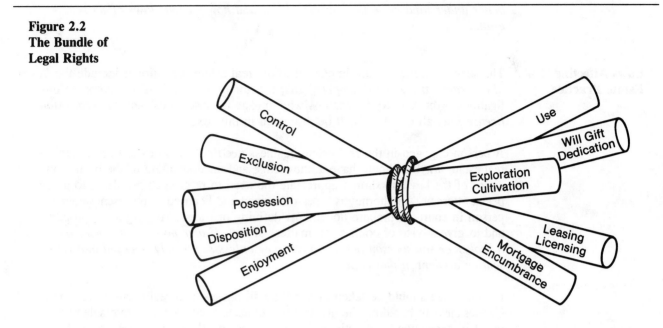

the purchaser a bundle of bound sticks from a tree on the property. This process was referred to as a *livery of seisin*. The purchaser who held the bundle also owned the tree from which the sticks came and the land to which the tree was attached. Because the rights of ownership can be separated and individually transferred, the sticks became symbolic of those rights.

A person who acquires real estate owns the property subject to any rights the seller retains and also to any rights in the property that other persons have or acquire. For example, a person may sell real estate while retaining the rights to certain minerals or natural resources located on or beneath the surface of the land. Likewise, a lending institution that holds a mortgage on real estate has the right to force a sale of the property if the loan is not repaid. The various rights in real estate will be discussed in detail later in the text.

Buying or selling real estate is usually the biggest financial transaction of a person's life. The buyer typically pays out more cash, undertakes more debt and has a deeper personal interest in this transaction than in any other purchase made during his or her lifetime. The real estate also is likely to have been the seller's biggest single investment in terms of money and work. Although there are people for whom the sale or purchase of real estate is a routine matter, for most it is a very important, emotional and complicated affair. Therefore the real estate licensees aiding in this transaction must pay strict attention to the applicable laws to ensure successful transfer of the property.

Real Estate Law   The average citizen generally thinks of laws as rules laid down by the state to govern conduct. *Real estate brokers and salespeople must have a broader and* *better understanding of the sources of law and how various laws affect real estate.*

Laws Affecting Real Estate Practice   The specific areas that are important to the real estate practitioner include the *law of contracts*, the *general property law*, the *law of agency* (which covers the obligations of brokers to the persons who engage their services) and the *real estate license law*, all of which will be discussed in this text.

A person engaged in the real estate business need not be an expert on all areas of real estate law but should have a knowledge and understanding of the basic principles of the law and should appreciate the need to refer such problems to a competent attorney. An attorney is a person trained and licensed to represent another person in court, to prepare documents defining or transferring rights in property and to give advice or counsel on matters of law. *Under no circumstances may a broker or salesperson act as an attorney unless separately licensed and representing a client in that capacity.*

Extreme care should be taken in handling all phases of a real estate transaction. Carelessness in handling the documents connected with a real estate sale can result in expensive legal actions. In many cases costly court actions could have been avoided if the parties handling negotiations had exercised greater care and employed competent legal counsel.

Real estate license laws. Because brokers and salespeople are engaged in a business that involves other people's real estate and money, the need for regulation of their activities has long been recognized. To protect the public from fraud, dishonesty or incompetence in the buying and selling of real estate, all 50 states, the District of Columbia and all Canadian provinces have passed laws that require real estate brokers and salespeople to be licensed. The license laws of the various states are similar in many respects but differ in some details.

Under these laws a person must obtain a license to engage in the real estate business. In most cases applicants must possess certain stated personal and educational qualifications and must pass an examination to prove an adequate knowledge of the business. In addition, to qualify for license renewal and continue in business licensees must follow certain prescribed standards of conduct in the operation of their business. Some states also require licensees to complete continuing education courses. Chapter 13 describes more fully the state license laws and the required standards.

Land, Real Estate and Real Property   The words *land, real estate* and *real property* are often used interchangeably. However, for a full understanding of the nature of real estate and the laws that affect it, licensees need to be aware of the subtle yet important differences in meaning.

Land   **Land** is defined as *the earth's surface extending downward to the center of the earth and upward to infinity, including things permanently attached by nature, such as trees and water* (see Figure 2.3).

The term *land* thus refers not only to the surface of the earth but also to the underlying soil and things that are naturally attached to the land, such as boulders and growing things. Land also includes the minerals and substances below the earth's surface together with the airspace above the land up to infinity. The surface, subsurface and airspace can be owned as surface rights, subsurface rights and air rights.

Real Estate

Real estate is defined as *land at, above and below the earth's surface, including all things permanently attached to it, whether natural or artificial* (see Figure 2.3). The term *real estate* is thus somewhat broader than the term *land* and includes not only the physical components of the land provided by nature but also all permanent improvements on and to the land. An **improvement** is any artificial thing attached to land, such as a building or fence. Land is also referred to as *improved* when streets, utilities, sewers and other additions make it suitable for building.

Real Property

Real property is defined as *the interests, benefits and rights inherent in the ownership of real estate* (see Figure 2.3).

The term *real property* is thus broader still. It includes the physical surface of the land, what lies below it, what lies above it and what is permanently attached to it, as well as the *bundle of legal rights* discussed earlier.

**Figure 2.3
Land, Real Estate and
Real Property**

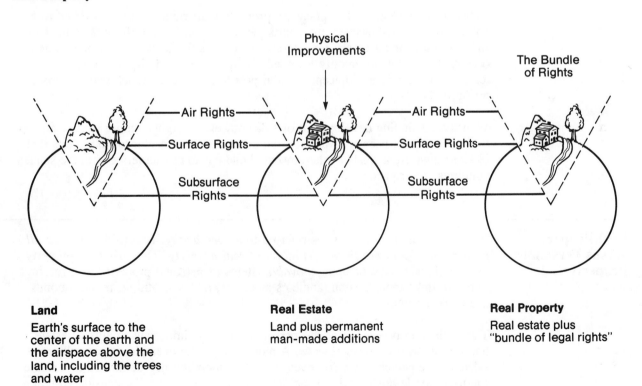

Land
Earth's surface to the center of the earth and the airspace above the land, including the trees and water

Real Estate
Land plus permanent man-made additions

Real Property
Real estate plus "bundle of legal rights"

In Practice . . .   *When people talk about buying or selling houses, office buildings, land and the like, they usually call all of these things* real estate. *For all practical purposes the term is synonymous with* real property, *as defined here. Thus in everyday usage* real estate *includes the legal rights of ownership specified in the definition of real property. Sometimes the term* realty *is used instead.*

Subsurface and air rights. Surface rights are simply the rights to use the surface of the earth. But real property ownership can also include **subsurface rights,** which are the rights to the natural resources lying below the earth's surface. A transfer of surface rights may, however, be accomplished without transfer of subsurface rights.

For example, a landowner could sell the rights to any oil and gas found in the land to an oil company. The landowner could then sell his or her remaining interest, reserving the rights to all coal found in the land. After the sale three parties would have ownership interests in the real estate: the oil company would own all oil and gas, the seller would own all coal and the new landowner would own the rights to all the rest of the real estate.

The rights to use the air above the land also may be sold or leased independently of the land. Such **air rights** are an increasingly important part of real estate, particularly in large cities, where air rights over railroads have been purchased to construct huge office buildings like the Pan-Am Building in New York City and the Merchandise Mart in Chicago. To construct such a building the developer must purchase not only the air rights but also numerous small portions of the land's surface for the building's foundation supports, called *caissons.*

Until the development of airplanes, a property's air rights were considered to be unlimited. Today, however, the courts permit reasonable interference with these rights, such as is necessary for aircraft, as long as the owner's right to use and occupy the land is not unduly lessened. Governments and airport authorities often purchase air rights adjacent to an airport to provide approach patterns for air traffic.

With the continuing development of solar power, air rights—more specifically, *sun rights*—have been redefined by the courts. They consider tall buildings that block sunlight from smaller solar-powered buildings to be interfering with the smaller buildings' sun rights.

Real Property versus Personal Property   **Personal property,** sometimes referred to as *personalty,* is considered to be *all property that does not fit the definition of real property.* Thus personal property has the characteristic of being *movable.* Items of personal property, also referred to as **chattels,** include such tangibles as chairs, tables, clothing, money, bonds and bank accounts.

The distinction between real and personal property, important to all real estate transactions, is not always obvious. A mobile home, for example, is generally considered to be personal property even though its mobility may be limited to a single trip to a mobile-home park. A mobile home may, however, be considered real property if it is permanently affixed to land, as prescribed by state law. Real estate licensees should be familiar with local laws before attempting to market mobile homes. In some states mobile homes may be sold only by mobile-home dealers.

Trees and crops generally fall into one of two classes. Trees, perennial bushes and grasses that do not require annual cultivation (*fructus naturales*—fruits of nature) are considered real property. Annual crops of wheat, corn, vegetables and fruit, known as *emblements* (*fructus industriales*—fruits of industry), are generally considered personal property. But as long as an annual crop is growing, it will be transferred as part of the real property if no special provision is made in the sales contract. A tenant may reenter land, if necessary, to harvest crops that result from the tenant's labor.

It is possible to change an item of real property to personal property by **severance.** For example, a growing tree is real estate until the owner cuts down the tree and thereby severs it from the earth. Similarly, an apple becomes personal property once it is picked from a tree, and a crop of wheat becomes personal property once it is harvested.

It is also possible to change personal property into real property. If a landowner buys cement, stones and sand and constructs a concrete walk on the land, the component parts of the concrete, which were originally personal property, are converted into real property. They have become a permanent improvement on the land. This process is called *annexation.*

Classification of Fixtures

In considering the differences between real property and personal property, it is important to be able to distinguish between a *fixture* and personal property.

Fixtures. *An article that was once personal property but has been so affixed to land or a building that the law construes it to be part of the real estate is a* **fixture.** Examples of fixtures are heating plants, elevator equipment in high-rise buildings, radiators, kitchen cabinets, light fixtures and plumbing fixtures. As a matter of fact, almost any item that has been added as a *permanent part* of a building is considered a fixture.

Legal tests of a fixture. Courts apply four basic tests to determine whether an item is a fixture (and therefore part of the real property) or personal property:

1. The intention of the annexor: Did the person who installed the item intend it to remain permanently or to be removable?
2. The method of annexation: How permanently was the item attached? Can it be removed without causing damage?
3. The adaptation to real estate: Is the item being used as real property or personal property?
4. The existence of an agreement: Have the parties agreed to the nature of the item, whether real or personal?

Although these tests seem simple, court decisions have not been consistent regarding what constitutes a fixture. Articles that appear to be permanently affixed have sometimes been held by the courts to be personal property, while items that do not appear to be permanently attached have been held to be fixtures.

In the sale of property the one certain way to avoid confusion over the nature of an article is to make *a written agreement between the parties* establishing which items are considered part of the real property. The real estate broker or salesperson should ensure that a sales contract includes a list of all articles that are being included in the sale, particularly if there is any doubt as to whether they are permanently attached fixtures. Articles that might cause confusion include television satellite dishes, built-in appliances, built-in bookcases and wall-to-wall carpeting.

Trade fixtures. An article owned by a tenant and attached to a rented space or building for use in conducting a business is a **trade fixture** or a *chattel fixture*. Examples of trade fixtures are bowling alleys, store shelves, bars and restaurant equipment. Agricultural fixtures, such as chicken coops and toolsheds, are also included in this definition. Trade fixtures must be removed on or before the last day the property is rented. The tenant is responsible for any damage caused by removal of a fixture. Trade fixtures that are not removed become the real property of the landlord. Acquiring the property in this way is known as **accession.**

Trade fixtures differ from fixtures generally in these ways:

1. Fixtures are part of the real property and belong to the owner of that property. Trade fixtures are usually owned and installed by a tenant for his or her use and are the tenant's personal property.

2. Fixtures are considered a permanent part of a building, but trade fixtures are removable. Trade fixtures may be attached to a building as are other fixtures. Due to the relationship of the parties (landlord and tenant), however, the law gives a tenant the right to remove trade fixtures provided the removal is completed before the term of the lease expires and the rented space restored to approximately its original condition.

3. Because fixtures are legally construed to be real property, they are included in any sale or mortgage of the real property. Trade fixtures are not included in the sale or mortgage of real property except by special agreement.

Key Terms

accession	real estate
air rights	real estate license law
bundle of legal rights	real property
chattel	severance
fixture	subsurface rights
improvement	surface rights
land	trade fixture
personal property	

Summary

The special nature of land as an investment is apparent in both its economic and physical characteristics. The economic characteristics are controlled by such factors as scarcity, improvements, permanence of investment and area preferences. Physically, land is immobile, indestructible and unique.

Even the simplest real estate transactions reflect a complex body of laws. A purchaser of real estate actually purchases from the seller the legal rights to use the land in certain ways.

Every state and Canadian province has some type of licensing requirement for real estate brokers and salespeople. Students should become familiar with the licensing requirements of their states.

Although most people think of land as the surface of the earth, land is the earth's surface and also the mineral deposits under the earth and the air above it. The term real estate further expands this definition to include all natural and man-made improvements attached to the land. Real property is the term used to describe the "bundle of legal rights" associated with ownership of real estate.

The different rights to the same parcel of real estate may be owned and controlled by different parties, one owning the surface rights, one owning the air rights and another owning the subsurface rights.

All property that does not fit the definition of real estate is classified as personal property, or chattels. When articles of personal property are permanently affixed to land, they may become fixtures and as such are considered a part of the real estate. Personal property attached to real estate by a tenant for the purpose of his or her business is classified as a trade, or chattel, fixture and remains personal property.

Questions

1. Which of the following best defines *real estate?*
   a. Land and the air above it
   b. Land and the buildings permanently affixed to it
   c. Land and all things permanently affixed to it
   d. Land and the mineral rights in the land

2. Emblements are:
   a. *fructus naturales.*
   b. *fructus industriales.*
   c. fixtures.
   d. trade fixtures.

3. The term *nonhomogeneity* refers to:
   a. scarcity.
   b. immobility.
   c. uniqueness.
   d. indestructibility.

4. The bundles of legal rights is included in:
   a. land.
   b. real estate.
   c. real property.
   d. trade fixtures.

5. The bundle of legal rights includes all of the following *except:*
   a. the right to exclude someone from the property.
   b. the right to enjoy the property within the framework of the law.
   c. the right to sell or otherwise convey the property.
   d. the right to use the property for any purpose, legal or otherwise.

6. All of the following would be considered real estate *except:*
   a. fences.
   b. buildings.
   c. growing trees.
   d. farm equipment.

7. All of the following would be considerations for an item being real property *except:*
   a. the cost of the item when it was purchased.
   b. the method of its attachment to other real property.
   c. the intended use of the item by its owner.
   d. the manner in which the item is actually used with other real property.

8. Which of the following is *not* an economic characteristic of real estate?
   a. Indestructibility
   b. Improvements
   c. Area preferences
   d. Scarcity

9. Real property can be converted into personal property through:
   a. severance.
   b. accession.
   c. conversion.
   d. inference.

10. M is renting a single-family home under a one-year lease. Two months into the lease she installs awnings over the building's front windows to keep the sun away from some delicate hanging plants. Which of the following is true?
    a. M must remove the awnings before the rental period is over.
    b. Because of their nature, the awnings are considered personal property.
    c. The awnings are considered fixtures.
    d. Because of the nature of the property, the awnings are considered trade fixtures.

11. G purchases a parcel of land and sells the rights to minerals located in the ground to an exploration company. This means that G now owns all but which of the following with regard to this property?
    a. Air rights
    b. Surface rights
    c. Subsurface rights
    d. Air and subsurface rights

Concepts of Home Ownership

Home Ownership　To many people home ownership represents financial stability, a psychological and emotional pride in ownership and a sense of belonging to the community. It also can be a form of investment. Some of the expenses of home ownership, including mortgage interest and property tax payments, are offset partially by a reduction in federal income tax.

Traditionally the residential real estate market was composed predominantly of single-family dwellings. The typical buyer was a married couple, usually with small children. Today, however, social changes, demographic shifts and economic considerations have altered the market considerably. For example, many real estate buyers today are *single* men and women; many are *empty nesters,* married couples whose housing needs change after their children move away from home; and many are married couples who choose not to have children or unmarried couples living together.

Types of Housing　As the residential market evolves, the needs of its buyers become more specialized. The following paragraphs describe the types of housing available to meet those needs.

Apartment complexes, groups of apartment buildings with any number of units in each building, continue to be popular. The buildings may be low-rise or high-rise, and the amenities may include parking as well as clubhouses, swimming pools and even golf courses.

The *condominium* is a popular form of residential ownership, particularly for people who want the security of owning property but not the responsibilities of caring for and maintaining a house. Owners of condominium apartments or townhouses—which share party walls with other units—share ownership of common facilities, such as halls, elevators and surrounding grounds. Management and maintenance of building exteriors and grounds are provided by agreement, with expenses paid out of monthly assessments charged to owners. Office buildings and shopping centers may also be established as condominiums, allowing businesses to build equity in the space they occupy while avoiding unpredictable rent increases. The condominium form of ownership is discussed in detail in Chapter 7.

A *cooperative* is very similar to a condominium in that it involves units within a larger building with common walls and facilities. An owner of a cooperative unit, however, owns not the unit itself but shares of stock in the corporation that holds title to the building. In return for stock, the owner receives a *proprietary lease,* which entitles him or her to occupancy of a particular unit in the building. Each unit owner must pay his or her share of the building's expenses in the same way that a condominium unit owner does. Cooperatives are discussed further in Chapter 7.

Planned unit developments (PUDs), sometimes called master-planned communities, are zoned under special cluster zoning ordinances that allow them to make maximum use of open space by reducing lot sizes and street areas. A community association formed as a corporation maintains common areas through fees paid by homeowners, but the owners have no direct ownership interest in the common areas.

Converted-use properties are existing structures, such as factories, office buildings, hotels, schools and churches, that have been converted to residential use. Usually such buildings had been abandoned by their original owners or tenants. Rather than demolish them, developers often find it both aesthetically and economically appealing to renovate them for use as rental or condominium units. An abandoned warehouse may be transformed into luxury loft condominium units, a closed hotel may become an apartment building and an old factory may become a shopping complex.

Retirement communities, often structured as PUDs, may provide shopping, recreational opportunities and health care facilities in addition to residential units. These communities often arise in areas of temperate climate.

High-rise developments, sometimes called mixed-use developments (MUDs), combine office space, stores, theaters and apartment units. MUDs usually are self-contained, offering laundry facilities, restaurants, food stores, valet shops, beauty parlors, barbershops, swimming pools and other attractive and convenient features. The most successful developments also effectively use natural assets such as rivers, lakes and forest preserves.

Mobile homes are one of the housing industry's fastest-growing areas in times of high-priced housing. Once considered useful only as temporary residences or for travel, mobile homes now are often used as principal residences or stationary vacation homes. Their relatively low cost, coupled with the increased living space available in the newer, double-wide and triple-wide models, has made mobile homes an attractive alternative to conventionally constructed residences. The increase in sales has resulted in growing numbers of mobile-home parks, which offer complete residential environments with permanent community facilities as well as semipermanent foundations and hookups for gas, water and electricity.

Modular homes, prefabricated structures that arrive on-site in units preassembled at the factory, are also gaining popularity as the price of newly constructed homes rises. Each preassembled room is lowered into place on the building site by a crane; workers later finish the structure and connect plumbing and wiring. Entire developments can be built at a fraction of the time and cost of conventional construction.

Through *time-shared occupancy* a number of individual purchasers share ownership of one vacation home. A share entitles each owner to occupy the property for a certain period of time each year, usually one week. Each owner pays the purchase price plus an annual maintenance fee. Due to high initial marketing costs and the uncertain resale market for time-share interests, time-share resale prices are usually significantly lower than their original purchase prices.

Factors Influencing Home Ownership

After 35 years of steady advances the percentage of housing units occupied by their owners has fluctuated during the 1980s. The high inflation of the 1970s caused housing prices to rise rapidly, but individual incomes failed to keep pace. As a result the average home price in some markets is now beyond the means of many single wage earners and even some two-income households.

Home ownership has declined most severely among the young. First-time purchasers often have difficulty saving the ten to 20 percent down payment needed for a conventional loan. The government-sponsored programs that traditionally have helped first-time purchasers have more stringent requirements now than in the past, and higher down payments and fees may be required in the near future.

Certainly not all people should own homes. Home ownership involves substantial commitment and responsibility, and the flexibility of renting suits some individuals' needs. People whose work requires frequent moves or whose financial position is uncertain will particularly benefit from renting. Renting also provides more leisure time by freeing tenants from management and maintenance.

Those who choose the responsibilities of home ownership must evaluate many factors before they make a final decision to purchase a particular property.

Mortgage Terms

Liberalization of mortgage terms and payment plans since the 1920s has helped make home ownership a reality for many. The amount of a conventional mortgage loan in relation to the value of the property (the loan-to-value ratio) has increased from 40 percent in the 1920s to more than 90 percent today. Payment periods also have been extended from 15 years to 30 years.

Small-down-payment mortgage loans are available under programs sponsored by the Federal Housing Administration (FHA) and the Department of Veteran Affairs (commonly called *VA*, in deference to the original Veterans Administration). In addition, private mortgage insurance companies offer programs to assist loan applicants in receiving higher loan-to-value ratios from private lenders than they could otherwise obtain. Mortgage lending is discussed in Chapter 15.

Ownership Expenses and Ability to Pay

Home ownership obviously entails expenses for basic support services such as utilities (electricity, natural gas, water), trash removal, sewer charges and maintenance and repairs. It also, however, imposes the obligation to pay for real estate taxes and property insurance, as well as the interest due on the mortgage loan.

To determine whether a prospective buyer can afford a certain purchase, lenders traditionally have used the "rule of thumb" formula that the monthly cost of buying and maintaining a home (mortgage payments plus tax and insurance impounds) should not exceed 28 percent of gross (pretax) monthly income. They also require that payments on all debts not exceed 38 percent of monthly income. How strictly these formulas are applied, however, depends on the borrower's age, earnings, credit history, number of dependents and other factors.

Investment Considerations

Besides satisfying the basic need for shelter, purchasing a home offers several financial advantages. For example, the owner may eventually realize a long-term gain due to increased value (appreciation) when the home is sold. In the meantime, the homeowner is also building **equity** in the property. Equity, the owner's financial interest in the property, is the difference between the value of the property and the amount of any outstanding debt against it. As the mortgage debt is decreased by monthly payments, the owner's interest increases. Equity can also increase through appreciation.

Homeowners also may deduct from their income for tax purposes some or all of the mortgage interest paid. In fact tax considerations are among the most important in any decision to purchase a home.

Tax Benefits

To encourage home ownership the federal government allows homeowners certain income tax advantages. Besides mortgage interest, a homeowner may deduct real estate taxes and certain other expenses from gross income. A homeowner may even defer or eliminate tax liability on the profit received from the sale of a home. (See the listing of these benefits in Table 3.1.)

Tax deductions. Homeowners may deduct from their gross income:

1. mortgage interest payments on first and second homes, subject to limitations described below;

2. real estate taxes (but not interest paid on overdue taxes);

3. certain loan origination fees;

4. certain loan discount points; and

5. loan prepayment penalties.

Deductions for "qualified residence interest" are limited as follows: For a principal residence, second residence or both, the aggregate amount of acquisition indebtedness cannot exceed a total of $1 million. Acquisition indebtedness is defined as the debt incurred in acquiring, constructing or substantially improving the principal residence or second residence [or both] of the taxpayer, where the debt is secured by such property. Home equity loans—loans secured by the property and in amounts less than the difference between fair market value and outstanding

Table 3.1 Homeowners' Tax Benefits	**Income Tax Deductions**	**Age 55 or Older**
	Loan interest on first and second homes, subject to limitation	Once in lifetime, homeowner may exclude up to $125,000 of profit on sale of home owned and used as principal residence for at least three years during last five years before sale
	Loan origination fees	
	Some loan discount points	
	Loan prepayment penalties	
	Real estate taxes	
	Deferment of Tax on Profit	
	Tax on some or all of profit on sale postponed if another residence is purchased within 24 months before or after sale	

mortgage loan balance—cannot exceed $100,000. Home equity indebtedness is defined as that debt which is secured by the taxpayer's residence(s) that does not exceed the fair market value of such residences less the amount of acquisition indebtedness.

Capital gain. Capital gain is the *profit* realized from the sale or exchange of an asset, including real property. To stimulate investment in the economy, Congress at various times has allowed part of a taxpayer's capital gain to be free from income tax.

Deferment of tax on capital gain. All or part of the gain (profit) on the sale of a personal residence is exempt from immediate taxation if another residence is bought and occupied within 24 months before or 24 months after the sale of the old residence. The capital gains tax is *deferred* until the property is sold later in a taxable transaction (such as when another home is not purchased).

If the next home is of value equal to or greater than that of the house sold, the entire gain may be deferred.

55 or older exclusion. Taxpayers aged 55 or older are entitled to a one-time exclusion from taxation of up to $125,000 of profit from the sale or exchange of property used as the taxpayer's principal residence for at least three of the last five years preceding the sale or exchange.

Each homeowner may elect to exclude gains from taxation under this provision *only once in a lifetime,* even if the total gain excluded is less than the $125,000 limit. When this exclusion is taken by a married couple selling a home, the tax laws hold that *both parties* have given up their once-in-a-lifetime exclusion. In the case of divorce or death and remarriage the individual is not entitled to a second exclusion even if his or her new spouse has not claimed the exclusion.

In Practice . . .   *The Internal Revenue Service, a certified public accountant or some other tax specialist should be consulted for further information on these and other income tax issues. IRS regulations are subject to frequent revision and official interpretation. A real estate licensee should not attempt to give tax advice or legal advice to clients or customers.*

Homeowner's Insurance

Because home ownership represents a large financial investment for most purchasers, homeowners usually protect their investment by taking out insurance on the property. Although it is possible for a homeowner to obtain individual policies for each type of risk, most residential owners take out insurance in the form of a packaged **homeowner's insurance policy.** These policies insure holders against the destruction of their property by fire or windstorm, injury to others if it occurs on the property and theft from the premises of any personal property owned by the insured or members of the insured's family.

The package homeowner's policy also includes **liability coverage** for personal injuries to others resulting from the insured's acts or negligence, voluntary medical payments and funeral expenses for accidents sustained by guests or resident employees on the property of the owner and physical damage to the property of others caused by the insured. Voluntary medical payments will cover injuries to a resident employee but will not cover benefits due under any workers' compensation or occupational disease law.

Characteristics of Homeowners' Packages

Although coverage provided may vary among policies, all homeowners' policies have three common characteristics.

First, they all have *fixed ratios of coverage*. That is, each type of coverage in a homeowner's policy must be maintained at a certain level. The amount of coverage on household contents and other items must be a fixed percentage of the amount of insurance on the building itself. While the amount of contents coverage may be increased, it cannot be reduced below the standard percentage.

Second, homeowners' policies have an *indivisible premium*, which means the insured receives coverage for all the perils included in the policy for a single rate and may not choose to exclude certain perils from coverage.

Finally, *first- and third-party insurance* is the liability coverage discussed above. It covers not only damage or loss to the insured's property or its contents but also the insured's legal liability for losses or damages to another's property as well as injuries suffered by another party while on the owner's property.

There are four major forms of homeowners' policies. The basic form provides property coverage against:

- fire or lightning;
- glass breakage;
- windstorm or hail;
- explosion;
- riot or civil commotion;
- damage by aircraft;
- damage from vehicles;
- damage from smoke;
- vandalism and malicious mischief;
- theft; and
- loss of property removed from the premises when endangered by fire or other perils.

A broad-form policy also covers:

- falling objects;
- weight of ice, snow or sleet;
- collapse of the building or any part of it;
- bursting, cracking, burning or bulging of a steam or hot water heating system or of appliances used to heat water;
- accidental discharge, leakage or overflow of water or steam from within a plumbing, heating or air-conditioning system;

- freezing of plumbing, heating and air-conditioning systems and domestic appliances; and

- injury to electrical appliances, devices, fixtures and wiring from short circuits or other accidentally generated currents.

Further coverage is made possible by use of policies that cover almost all possible perils.

Other policies include a broad-form policy designed specifically for apartment renters and a broad-form policy for condominium owners. Apartment and condominium policies generally provide fire and windstorm, theft and public liability coverage for injuries or losses sustained within the unit but do not usually extend to cover losses or damages to the structure. The structure is insured by either the landlord or the condominium owners' association (except, in condominium ownership, for additions or alterations made by the unit owner and not covered by the association's master policy).

Claims

Most homeowners' insurance policies contain a **coinsurance clause.** This provision usually requires the owner to maintain insurance equal to at least 80 percent of the **replacement cost** of the dwelling (not including the price of the land). If the owner carries such a policy, a claim may be made for the full cost of the repair or replacement of the damaged property.

For example, a home that has a replacement cost of $100,000 is damaged by fire, and the estimated cost to repair the damage is $71,000. If the homeowner carries at least $80,000 insurance on the dwelling (80% of $100,000) he or she can file a claim for the full $71,000.

If the homeowner carries coverage of less than 80 percent of the full replacement cost, however, the loss will be either settled for the **actual cash value** (replacement cost less depreciation) or prorated by dividing the percentage of replacement cost actually covered by the policy by the minimum coverage requirement (usually 80 percent). For example, if a building is insured for only 60 percent of its value, the policy will pay only 75 percent of any claim filed (60% ÷ 80% = 75%). Therefore, the insurance company will pay only $53,250 of the $71,000 loss (75% of $71,000).

In any event, *the total settlement cannot exceed the face value of the policy*. Because of coinsurance clauses, it is important for homeowners to review all policies periodically to be certain that the coverage is equal to at least 80 percent of the current replacement cost of their homes.

Most policies also have a **subrogation clause,** which provides that if the insured collects for damage from the insurance company, any rights the insured may have to sue the person who caused the damage will be assigned to the insurance company. A subrogation clause allows the insurer to pursue legal action to collect the amount paid out from the party at fault and prevents the insured from collecting twice for the same damage.

Federal Flood Insurance Program

The National Flood Insurance Act of 1968 was authorized by Congress to help owners of property located in flood-prone areas by subsidizing flood insurance. Such property owners must obtain flood damage insurance on properties financed by mortgages or other loans, grants or guarantees obtained from federal agencies and federally insured or regulated lending institutions.

The Department of Housing and Urban Development (HUD), which administers the flood program, has maps prepared by the Army Corps of Engineers that identify specific flood-prone areas throughout the country. Property owners in the designated areas who do not obtain flood insurance (either because they don't want it or because they don't qualify as a result of their communities' not having properly entered the program) are unable to obtain federal and federally related financial assistance.

Key Terms

capital gain
coinsurance clause
equity
homeowner's insurance policy

liability coverage
replacement cost
subrogation

Summary

In addition to single-family homes, current trends in home ownership include apartment complexes, condominiums, cooperatives, planned unit developments, retirement communities, high-rise developments, converted-use properties, modular homes, mobile homes and time-shared occupancy of vacation homes.

In considering the purchase of a home a prospective buyer should be aware of both the advantages and disadvantages of home ownership. While a homeowner gains financial security and pride of ownership, the costs of ownership—both the initial price and the continuing expenses—must be considered.

One of the income tax benefits available to homeowners allows them to deduct mortgage interest payments (with certain limitations) and property taxes from their federal income tax returns. Income tax on the gain from a sale may be deferred if the homeowner purchases and occupies another residence within 24 months before or after the sale. Homeowners aged 55 or older are given additional benefits.

To protect their investment in real estate most homeowners purchase insurance. A standard homeowner's insurance policy covers fire, theft and liability and can be extended to cover many types of less common risks. Another type of insurance, which covers personal property only, is available to people who live in apartments and condominiums.

If a homeowner carries insurance issued by more than one company, any benefits paid out will be prorated according to the insured amount under each policy.

A subrogation clause enables an insurer to sue the party responsible for damage to the insured's property.

In addition to homeowner's insurance, the federal government makes flood insurance mandatory for people living in flood-prone areas who wish to obtain federally regulated or federally insured mortgage loans.

Many homeowners' policies contain a coinsurance clause that requires the policyholder to maintain insurance in an amount equal to 80 percent of the replacement cost of the home. If this percentage is not met, the policyholder may not be reimbursed for the full repair costs if a loss occurs.

Questions

1. The real cost of owning a home includes certain costs or expenses that many people tend to overlook. Which one of the following is *not* a cost or expense of owning a home?

    a. Interest paid on borrowed capital
    b. Homeowner's insurance
    c. Maintenance and repairs
    d. Taxes on personal property

2. When a person buys a house using a mortgage loan, the difference between the amount owed on the property and its market value represents the homeowner's:

    a. tax basis.   c. replacement cost.
    b. equity.   d. capital gain.

3. A building that is remodeled into residential units and is no longer used for the purpose for which it was originally built is a(n):

    a. converted-use property.
    b. example of urban homesteading.
    c. planned unit development.
    d. modular home.

4. In a homeowner's insurance policy *coinsurance* refers to:

    a. the specific form of policy purchased by the owner.
    b. the stipulation that the homeowner must purchase insurance coverage equal to at least 80 percent of the replacement cost of the structure to collect the full insured amount in the event of a loss.
    c. the stipulation that the homeowner must purchase fire insurance coverage equal to at least 70 percent of the replacement cost of the structure to collect the full insured amount in the event of a loss.
    d. Both a and b

5. Federal income tax laws do *not* allow a homeowner to deduct which of the following expenses from gross income?

    a. Mortgage origination fees
    b. Real estate taxes
    c. Home improvements
    d. Mortgage prepayment penalties

6. A town house may be associated with which of the following types of housing?

    a. High-rise development
    b. Condominium
    c. Mobile home
    d. Ranch house

7. V , age 38, sells his home of eight years and realizes a $25,000 gain from the sale. Income tax on the profit from the sale of his home may be:

    a. eliminated by claiming a once-in-a-lifetime exclusion.
    b. deferred by purchasing another home of equal or greater value.
    c. reduced by the amount of mortgage interest paid over the life of the property's ownership.
    d. Either a or b

8. F, age 62, sells the home she has occupied for the last 15 years and realizes a $52,000 gain from the sale. Income tax on the profit from the sale of her home may be:

    a. eliminated by claiming a once-in-a-lifetime exclusion.
    b. deferred by purchasing another home of equal or greater value.
    c. reduced by the amount of mortgage interest paid over the life of the property's ownership.
    d. Either a or b

9. A typical homeowner's insurance policy covers all of the following *except:*

    a. the cost of medical expenses for a person injured in the policyholder's home.
    b. theft.
    c. vandalism.
    d. flood damage.

Real Estate Brokerage

Agency Defined

An **agent** is a person who represents the interests of someone called a **principal** in dealings with third persons. The relationship of agent and principal is called an **agency.** An agent may be authorized by the principal to use the assistance of others in carrying out the purpose of the agency. Those persons would act as **subagents** of the principal.

Brokerage Defined

Brokerage is the business of bringing buyers and sellers together in the marketplace. Buyers and sellers in many fields employ the services of brokers to facilitate complex business transactions. In the real estate business a broker is defined as a person who is licensed to buy, sell, exchange or lease real property for others and to charge a fee for his or her services. A brokerage—the broker's business—may be established as a sole proprietorship, a corporation or a partnership with another broker. The real estate salesperson works on behalf of and is licensed to represent the broker.

The principal who employs the broker may be a seller, a prospective buyer, an owner who wishes to lease his or her property or a person seeking property to rent. The real estate broker acts as the agent of the principal, and the salesperson usually acts as the subagent. When the broker successfully performs the service for which he or she was employed, the principal usually compensates the broker with a commission. That service generally is negotiating a transaction with a prospective purchaser, seller, lessor or lessee who is ready, willing and able to complete the contract.

In a typical real estate listing contract the seller will authorize the broker to use salespeople employed by the broker as well as other, cooperating brokers. Co-operating brokers act as subagents of the principal and may, in turn, employ their own salespeople. The relationship of a salesperson to an employing broker is also an agency. The salesperson is thus the agent of the broker in addition to being the subagent of the principal. (In some states a licensed broker may choose to work for another broker as an associate broker and would have the same agency status to the client as a salesperson.)

Law of Agency

In the typical real estate transaction, the broker is hired by a seller to market the seller's real estate. In this situation the broker is an *agent* of the seller; the seller is the broker's *client*. Unless there has been another agreement, a buyer who contacts the broker to review properties listed with his or her firm is merely the broker's *customer*. Though obligated to deal fairly with all parties to a transaction, the broker is strictly accountable *only to the principal*—in this case, the seller.

The role of a broker as the agent of the principal is a fiduciary relationship. A **fiduciary** is one who is placed in a position of trust and confidence and normally is responsible for the money and/or property of another. The body of law that governs the rights and duties of principal, agent and third persons is the **law of agency.**

Types of Agent

An agent may be classified as a general agent or special agent, based on the nature of his or her authority.

A **general agent** is empowered to represent the principal in a *range of matters* and may bind the principal to any contracts within the scope of his or her authority. This type of agency can be created by a *general power of attorney*, which makes the agent an *attorney-in-fact* as opposed to simply an *attorney-at-law*.

A **special agent** is authorized to represent the principal in *one specific transaction or business activity only*. A real estate broker is generally a special agent, hired by a seller to find a ready, willing and able buyer for the seller's property. A *special power of attorney* is another means of authorizing an agent to carry out only a specified act or acts.

Creation of Agency

An agency relationship is created by an oral or written agreement of the parties. The real estate broker–seller relationship normally is created by an employment contract, commonly referred to as a **listing agreement.**

Principal and agent may make an **express agreement,** in which the parties state the contract's terms and express their intention either orally or in writing. Although a written listing agreement is usually preferred, it is not necessary in all states. Some states construe an oral agreement as binding.

An agency may also be created by **implied agreement**—when principal and agent, without formally agreeing to the agency, act as if one exists.

When someone claims to be an agent but there is no agreement, the "principal" can establish an agency by **ratification,** by performing any act that accepts the conduct of the agent as that of an agent.

An agency relationship may be created by **estoppel** if someone states incorrectly that another person is his or her agent. If a third person relies on that representation in dealing with the "agent," the "principal" cannot later deny the existence of an agency.

By using a *multiple-listing agreement* a principal can authorize the broker to use the members of the broker's multiple-listing service. This and other provisions of listing agreements will be discussed in greater detail in Chapter 5.

Termination of Agency

An agency may be terminated at any time (except in the case of an agency coupled with an interest, discussed below), for any of the following reasons:

1. Death or incapacity of either party (notice of death is not necessary)
2. Destruction or condemnation of the property by eminent domain
3. Expiration of the terms of the agency
4. Mutual agreement to terminate the agency
5. Breach by one of the parties, such as abandonment by the agent or revocation by the principal (The breaching party might be liable for damages.)
6. By operation of law, as in a bankruptcy of the principal (since title to the property would be transferred to a court-appointed receiver)
7. Completion or fulfillment of the purpose for which the agency was created

An **agency coupled with an interest** is an agency relationship in which the agent is given an interest in the subject of the agency (such as the property being sold). Such an agency *cannot be revoked by the principal, nor can it be terminated upon the principal's death.* For example, a broker might supply the financing for a condominium development, provided the developer agrees to give the broker the exclusive right to sell the completed condo units. Since this is an agency coupled with an interest, the developer would not be able to revoke the listing agreement after the broker provided the financing.

Buyer as Principal

Sometimes a potential buyer hires a broker to find a parcel of real estate that has certain characteristics or is usable for specific purposes. Buyers seeking commercial or industrial property are particularly likely to hire their own brokers. In this situation the broker and the buyer usually draw up a *buyer agency agreement,* which sets forth in detail the nature of the property desired and the amount of the broker's compensation.

Agent's Responsibilities to Principal

Whether an employment agreement exists between broker and seller or broker and buyer, it usually authorizes the broker to act for the principal but does not carry with it a guarantee that the broker will be able to perform. As an agent of the principal, however, the broker is obligated to make a reasonable effort to carry out the assumed agency duties successfully. In fact, as an agent the broker owes the principal certain and specific duties. These duties are not simply moral or ethical; they are the law—the *law of agency.* The *fiduciary relationship* that the agent has to the principal is one of trust and confidence that carries with it the duties of *care, obedience, accounting, loyalty* and *disclosure,* easily remembered by the acronym COALD (see Figure 4.1).

Care. The broker must exercise a reasonable degree of care and skill while transacting the business of the principal. Such care and skill includes being knowledgeable about the transaction, such as knowing the physical characteristics of the property being transferred and the type of financing being used. A broker who does not make a reasonable effort to properly represent the interests of the principal could probably be found negligent. The broker is liable to the principal for any loss resulting from the broker's negligence or carelessness.

**Figure 4.1
Agent's
Responsibilities**

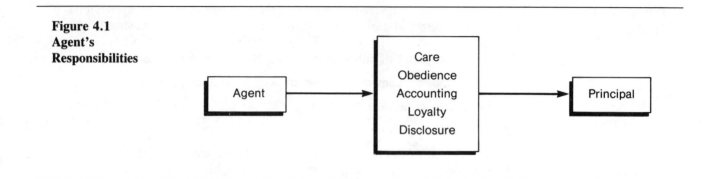

Obedience. The broker is at all times obligated to act in good faith and in conformity with the principal's instructions and authority. A broker is liable for any losses incurred by the principal due to any acts the broker performs that are not within the broker's authority. The broker is bound to obey the instructions of the principal, but only if those instructions are legal and relevant to their relationship (in accordance with the terms of the contract). For example, if the principal tells the listing broker that she will not sell to a member of a particular minority group, the broker cannot obey the principal's wishes as doing so would violate the law. The broker may disobey a principal or perform unauthorized acts in an emergency, as long as the broker's actions are in the principal's best interests.

Accounting. The broker must be able to report the status of all funds received from or on behalf of the principal. Most state real estate license laws require brokers to give accurate copies of all documents to all parties affected by them and to keep copies of such documents on file for a specified period of time. In addition, the license laws generally require the broker to deposit immediately, or within 24 to 48 hours, all funds entrusted to him or her in a special trust, or escrow, account. It is illegal for the broker to *commingle* such monies with personal funds.

Loyalty. The broker owes the principal 100 percent loyalty and must always place the principal's interests above those of the other persons with whom the broker deals. Thus an agent cannot disclose such information as the principal's financial condition, the fact that the principal (if the seller) will accept a price lower than the listing price for the offered real estate or any similar confidential facts that might harm the principal's bargaining position.

The duty of loyalty also requires the agent to act without self-interest, unless with the principal's knowledge and consent. All states forbid brokers or salespeople to buy property listed with them for their own accounts, or for accounts in which they have a personal interest, without first notifying the principal of such interest and receiving the principal's consent. Likewise, by law neither brokers nor salespeople may sell property in which they have a personal interest without informing the purchaser of that interest.

Disclosure. Along with these four responsibilities goes the duty of disclosure, sometimes called *notice*. It is the broker's duty to keep the principal fully informed at all times of all facts or information the broker obtains that could affect the transaction. A broker who fails to disclose such information, such as the fact that the purchaser does not qualify for low down payments, may be held liable for any damages that result.

The real estate agent may also be liable for facts he or she *should have known* and revealed to the principal but did not. This *duty of discovery* includes facts favorable or unfavorable to the principal's position, even if the disclosure of those facts would "kill the deal."

Agent's Responsibilities to Third Parties

Even though an agent's primary responsibility is to the principal, the agent also has duties to third parties. The duties of the seller's agent to the buyer include:

1. reasonable care and skill in performance of the agent's duties;

2. honest and fair dealing; and

3. disclosure of all facts known to the agent that materially affect the value or desirability of the property and that are not known to the buyer.

In recent years the doctrine of caveat emptor ("let the buyer beware") has been changed by both public awareness and the legal system. Society has accepted that the purchase of real estate is the largest investment a person will make and that therefore purchasers should be afforded some public protection. Many states now have statutes regarding disclosures to prospective buyers, prepurchase structural inspections, termite infestation reports and other protective documentation.

In dealing with a buyer, a broker, as an agent of the seller, must exercise extreme caution and be aware of the laws and ethical considerations that affect this relationship. For example, brokers must be careful about the statements they or their staff members make about a parcel of real estate. Statements of opinion are permissible as long as they are offered as opinions and without any intention to deceive.

Statements of fact, however, must be accurate. Statements that exaggerate a property's benefits are called **puffing.** While puffing is legal, brokers and salespeople must ensure that none of their statements can be interpreted as involving **fraud.** Fraud is the *intentional* misrepresentation of a material fact in such a way as to harm or take advantage of another person. In addition to false statements about a property, the concept of fraud covers intentional concealment or nondisclosure of important facts. If a contract to purchase real estate is obtained as a result of fraudulent misstatements made by a broker or by that broker's salespeople, the contract may be disaffirmed or renounced by the purchaser. In such a case the broker will lose a commission. If either party suffers loss because of a broker's misrepresentations, the broker can be held liable for damages. If the broker's misstatements are based on the owner's own inaccurate statements to the broker, however, and the broker had no independent duty to investigate their accuracy, the broker may be entitled to a commission even if the buyer rescinds the sales contract.

A seller is also responsible for revealing to a buyer any hidden, or latent, defects in a building. *A latent defect is one that is known to the seller but not to the buyer and that is not discoverable by ordinary inspection.* Buyers have been able to either rescind the sales contract or receive damages when such defects had not been revealed. Examples of such circumstances are cases in which a house was built over a ditch that was covered with decaying timber, a buried drain tile caused water to accumulate or a driveway was built partly on adjoining property. Cases in which the seller neglected to reveal violations of zoning or building codes also have been decided in favor of the buyer.

Stigmatized properties. In the past few years brokers have started to encounter stigmatized properties, those properties that society has branded as undesirable because of events that occurred there. Such properties are typically stigmatized by a criminal event: a homicide or suicide, a shooting, illegal drug manufacturing, gang-related activity or some other event that renders the property socially unmarketable to most of the population. Environmental concerns—such as toxic waste dumping, contaminated soil and water and proximity to chemical or nuclear facilities—can also stigmatize property. Because of the potential liability of a broker for inadequately researching the facts concerning a property's physical condition, and the inherent responsibility of a broker to disclose material facts to a prospective buyer, brokers are cautioned to seek competent counsel when dealing with such property. Brokers are also urged to obtain advice from the state and local authorities responsible for regulating the environmental factors that can render these properties unsalable.

In Practice . . .   *Because real estate licensees have, under the law, enormous exposure to liability, some brokers purchase what is known as* errors and omissions insurance *policies for their firms. Operating similarly to malpractice insurance in the medical field, such policies generally cover liabilities for errors, mistakes and negligence in the usual listing and selling activities of a real estate office or escrow company.*

Dual Agency   In dealing with buyers the broker must be careful of any situation that might be considered a **dual agency.** Sometimes a broker may have the opportunity to receive compensation from both buyer and seller in a transaction. Theoretically, however, an agent cannot be loyal to two or more distinct principals in the same transaction. Thus most state real estate license laws prohibit a broker from representing and collecting compensation from both parties to a transaction without their prior mutual knowledge and written consent. Although the courts tend to accept this *informed consent exception,* many reluctantly do so, and others reject the exception altogether because of public policy considerations. Many brokers today believe in what is known as the *single agency* concept, which strictly holds that a broker can effectively be a principal to only one party at a time in a given transaction.

In Practice . . .   *Before entering into a listing agreement a licensee should fully explain to a seller/ principal the nature of the agency relationship and the provisions of the document that creates it. Also, the licensee should inform each buyer/customer that he or she represents the seller and owes the seller 100 percent loyalty. However, giving this information does not relieve the licensee from dealing fairly and honestly with the buyer/customer.*

Broker's Compensation   The broker's compensation is specified in the listing agreement, management agreement or other contract with the principal. Compensation is usually made in the form of a **commission** or brokerage fee computed as a *percentage of the total amount of money involved.* Such commission is usually due at the closing of the sale or other transaction. Most sales commissions are payable when the sale is consummated by *delivery of the seller's deed,* and this provision is customarily included in the listing agreement or real estate sales contract.

To be entitled to collect a commission an agent must be a licensed real estate broker, have been employed by the principal under a valid contract and have been the procuring cause of the transaction. To be considered the **procuring cause** of sale the broker must have taken action to start or cause a chain of events that resulted in the sale. A broker who causes or completes such action without a contract to promise to be paid is termed a *volunteer* and has no legal claim to compensation. The state license law may stipulate that claims for commissions are legally enforceable only when a written listing agreement exists.

Once a seller accepts an offer from a ready, willing and able buyer, the seller is technically liable for the broker's commission. A **ready, willing and able buyer** is one who is *prepared to buy on the seller's terms and ready to take positive steps toward consummation of the transaction*. But even if the transaction is *not* consummated, the broker may still be entitled to a commission when the seller:

• has a change of mind and refuses to sell;

• has a spouse who refuses to sign the deed;

• has a title with uncorrected defects;

• commits fraud with respect to the transaction;

• is unable to deliver possession within a reasonable time;

• insists on terms not in the listing (for example, the right to restrict the use of the property); or

• has a mutual agreement with the buyer to cancel the transaction.

In other words, *a broker is generally due a commission if a sale is not consummated because of the principal's default.*

The rate of a broker's commission is *negotiable in every case*. For members of the profession to attempt, however subtly, to impose uniform commission rates would be a clear violation of state and federal antitrust laws (discussed later in this chapter). Yet a broker is free to set the minimum rate that is acceptable. The important point is for broker and client to agree on a rate before the agency relationship is established. If no amount or percentage rate of commission is stated in the listing contract and a legal action results, the court may determine a reasonable amount of commission by evidence of the custom in a particular community.

Most (but not all) license laws make it illegal for a broker to share a commission with someone (other than the buyer or seller) who is not licensed as a salesperson or broker. This has been construed to include the giving of certain items of personal property (for instance, a broker giving a new TV to "a friend" for providing a valuable lead) and other premiums (vacations and the like) as well as finder's fees and portions of the commission.

Salesperson's Compensation

The compensation of a salesperson is set by mutual agreement between the broker and the salesperson. The broker may agree to pay the salesperson a salary or a share of the commissions from transactions originated by the salesperson. A salesperson may have a drawing account against his or her earned share of commissions. Some brokers require salespeople to pay all or part of the expenses of advertising listed properties.

A recent innovation in salespeople's compensation is the *100 percent commission plan*, in which all salespeople who achieve a predetermined sales quota pay a monthly service charge to the broker (to cover the costs of office space, telephones and supervision) and receive 100 percent of the commissions from the sales they negotiate.

However the salesperson's compensation is structured, it may come only from the employing broker. The salesperson cannot receive any fee or other compensation initiating from a seller, a buyer or an outside broker unless the employing broker first agrees in writing to the payment.

Legal Rights and Obligations

As each contract is prepared for signature during a real estate transaction, the broker should advise the parties of the desirability of securing legal counsel to protect their interests. As mentioned earlier, *while real estate brokers and salespeople do bring buyers and sellers together, only an attorney can offer the parties legal advice.*

Still, state supreme courts have uniformly recognized that a real estate broker must have the authority to secure some form of agreement between a buyer and seller, documenting the transaction and providing for payment of the broker's commission. As a result, in many states a special form of sales contract that must be used by real estate brokers has been approved by the bar associations and real estate commissions. Not only are brokers prohibited from using any other form of contract, in some instances, a broker who does so can have his or her license revoked.

Antitrust Laws

The real estate industry is subject to federal and state **antitrust laws.** Generally these laws prohibit monopolies and contracts, combinations and conspiracies that unreasonably restrain trade. The most common antitrust violations that can occur in the real estate business are price-fixing and allocation of customers or markets.

Illegal *price-fixing* occurs when brokers conspire to set prices (sales commissions, management rates) for the services they perform rather than let those prices be established through competition in the open market. Any discussion of commission rates with a competitor is dangerous and should be scrupulously avoided.

Allocation of customers or markets involves an agreement between brokers to divide their markets and refrain from competing for each other's business. Allocations may take place on a geographic basis, with brokers agreeing to specific territories within which they will operate exclusively. The division may also take place along other lines; for example, two brokers may agree that one will handle only residential properties under $100,000 in value while another will handle residential properties over $100,000 in value.

The penalties for such acts are severe. For example, under the Sherman Antitrust Act people who fix prices or allocate markets may be found guilty of a felony punishable by a maximum $100,000 fine and three years in prison. For corporations the penalty may be as high as $1 million. In a civil suit a person who has suffered a loss because of the antitrust activities of a guilty party may recover triple the value of the actual damages plus attorney's fees and costs.

| **Nature of the Brokerage Business** | Whether affiliated with any national franchise or marketing organization or not, a real estate broker is an independent businessperson who sets the policies of his or her own office. A broker engages employees and salespeople, determines their compensation and directs their activities. A broker is free to accept or reject agency relationships with principals. This is an important characteristic of the brokerage business: *a broker has the right to reject agency contracts that in the broker's judgment violate the ethics or high standards of the office.* However, once a brokerage relationship has been established, the broker represents a principal and owes that person all the duties discussed earlier. |

Broker-Salesperson Relationship

A person licensed to perform real estate activities on behalf of a licensed real estate broker is known as a *real estate salesperson. A salesperson licensed under a broker is responsible only to that broker* and can carry out only those responsibilities assigned by that broker. For example, a salesperson may fill out a listing contract with a seller, but is doing so only as an representative of the broker and may not take the listing upon leaving the broker's firm. A salesperson has no authority to make contracts or receive compensation directly from a principal. *All of a salesperson's activities must be performed in the name of the supervising broker.*

Independent contractor vs. employee. The agreement between a broker and a salesperson should be set down in a written contract that defines the obligations and responsibilities of the relationship. In defining legal responsibilities, state license laws generally treat the salesperson as the employee of the broker whether the salesperson is considered, for tax purposes, an employee or an independent contractor. The broker is thus liable for all acts performed by the salesperson within the "scope" of the salesperson's employment—that is, the real estate business. Whether a salesperson is treated as an employee or an independent contractor will, however, affect the structure of the salesperson's work responsibilities and the broker's liability to pay and withhold taxes from the salesperson's earnings (see Figure 4.2).

The broker can exercise certain *controls* over salespeople who are employees. The broker may require an **employee** to adhere more strictly to regulations concerning working hours and office routine. As an employer a broker is required by the federal government to withhold social security tax and income tax from wages paid to employees. The broker is also required to pay unemployment compensation tax on wages paid to one or more employees, as defined by state and federal laws. In addition, a broker may provide employees with such benefits as health insurance, profit-sharing plans, and workers' compensation.

A broker's relationship with an independent contractor is very different. As an **independent contractor** a salesperson operates more independently than an employee, and the broker may not control the salesperson's activities in the same way. Basically the broker may control *what* the independent contractor will do but not *how* it will be done. An independent contractor assumes responsibility for paying his or her own income and social security taxes. An independent contractor receives from the broker nothing that could be construed as an employee benefit (such as health insurance).

In Practice . . .

The Internal Revenue Service often investigates the independent contractor/employee situation in real estate offices. Under the "qualified real estate agent" category

Figure 4.2
Independent
Contractor vs.
Employee

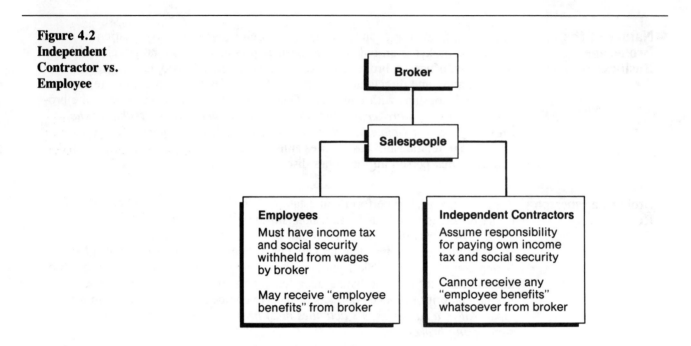

in the Internal Revenue Code, meeting three requirements can establish an independent contractor status: (1) The individual must have a current real estate
license. (2) He or she must have a written contract with the broker containing
the following clause: "The salesperson will not be treated as an employee with
respect to the services performed by such salesperson as a real estate agent for
federal tax purposes." (3) Ninety percent or more of the individual's income as
a licensee must be based on sales production and not on the number of hours
worked. The broker should have a standardized agreement drawn or reviewed
by an attorney to assure its compliance with these federal dictates. The broker
should also be aware that written agreements mean little to an IRS auditor if
the actions of the parties are contrary to the document's provisions.

Key Terms

agency   implied agreement
agency coupled with an interest   independent contractor
agent   law of agency
antitrust laws   listing agreement
commission   principal
dual agency   procuring cause
employee   puffing
estoppel   ratification
express agreement   ready, willing and able buyer
fiduciary   special agent
fraud   subagent
general agent

Summary

Real estate brokerage is the bringing together, for a fee or commission, of people
who wish to buy, sell, exchange or lease real estate. An important part of real

estate brokerage is the law of agency. A real estate broker is the agent, usually hired by the seller but occasionally by a buyer, to sell or find a particular parcel of real estate. The person who hires the broker is the principal. The principal and the agent have a fiduciary relationship, under which the agent owes the principal the duties of care, obedience, accounting, loyalty and disclosure.

The broker's compensation in a real estate sale ordinarily takes the form of a commission, which usually is a percentage of the real estate's selling price. The broker is considered to have earned a commission when he or she procures a ready, willing and able buyer for a seller.

A broker may hire salespeople to assist in this work. The salesperson works on the broker's behalf as either an employee or an independent contractor.

State and federal antitrust laws prohibit brokers from conspiring to fix prices or allocate customers or markets.

Missed —4

Questions

1. A person who has the authority to enter into contracts concerning all business affairs of another is called a(n):
   a. general agent.
   b. secret agent.
   c. special agent.
   d. attorney.

2. The term *fiduciary* refers to:
   a. the sale of real property.
   b. principles by which a real estate seller must conduct his or her business.
   c. one who has legal power to act on behalf of another.
   d. the principal-agent relationship.

3. The legal relationship between broker and seller is generally a:
   a. special agency.
   b. general agency.
   c. secret agency.
   d. universal agency.

4. A real estate broker acting as the agent of the seller:
   a. is obligated to render faithful service to the seller.
   b. can make a profit if possible in addition to the commission.
   c. can agree to a change in price without the seller's approval.
   d. can accept a commission from the buyer without the seller's approval.

5. The statement "to recover a commission for brokerage services, a broker must be employed" means that:
   a. the broker must work in a real estate office.
   b. the seller must have made an agreement to pay a commission to the broker for selling the property.
   c. the broker must have asked the seller the price of the property and then found a ready, willing and able buyer.
   d. the broker must have a salesperson employed in the office.

6. A broker is entitled to collect a commission from both the seller and the buyer:
   a. when the broker holds a state license.
   b. when the buyer and the seller are related.
   c. when both parties agree to such a transaction.
   d. when both parties have attorneys.

7. An agency relationship may be terminated by all *but* which of the following means?
   a. The owner decides not to sell the house.
   b. The broker discovers that the market value of the property is such that he or she will not make an adequate commission.
   c. The owner dies.
   d. The broker secures a ready, willing and able buyer for the seller's property.

8. Under the law of agency, a real estate broker owes all of the following to the principal *except:*
   a. care.
   b. obedience.
   c. disclosure.
   d. advertising.

9. A broker may lose the right to a commission in a real estate transaction if he or she:
   a. did not advertise the property.
   b. was not licensed when employed as an agent.
   c. did not personally market and sell the listing.
   d. accepted a commission from another licensee.

10. A real estate broker hired by an owner to sell a parcel of real estate must comply with:
    a. any instructions of the owner.
    b. any instructions of the buyer.
    c. the concept of caveat emptor.
    d. the law of agency.

11. While in the employ of a real estate broker a salesperson has the authority to:

    a. act as an agent for the seller.

    b. assume responsibilities assigned by the broker.

    c. accept a commission from another broker.

    d. advertise the property on his or her own behalf.

12. M, a real estate broker, learns that her neighbor V wishes to sell his house. M knows the property well and is able to persuade E to make an offer for the property. M then asks V if she can present an offer to him, and V agrees. At this point:

    a. V is not obligated to pay M a commission.

    b. E is obligated to pay M for locating the property.

    c. V must pay M a commission.

    d. M has become a subagent of V.

no listing agreement was signed

13. A real estate broker who engages salespeople as independent contractors must:

    a. withhold income tax from all commissions earned by them.

    b. require them to participate in office insurance plans offered to other salespeople hired as employees.

    c. withhold social security from all commisions earned by them.

    d. refrain from controlling how the salesperson conducts his or her business activities.

14. Salesperson T was listing seller J's house. J informed T that he would not sell to a member of a particular religious sect. T would be wise to do any of the following *except:*

    a. accept the listing and ignore J's comment.

    b. attempt to convince J to change his mind.

    c. discuss the situation with his broker.

    d. refuse the listing.

15. Broker D lists K's residence for $87,000. K's employer has transferred her to another state, and she must sell her house quickly. To expedite the sale D tells a prospective purchaser that K will accept at least $5,000 less for the property. Based on these facts, all of the following statements are true *except:*

    a. D has violated his agency responsibilities to K.

    b. D should not have disclosed this information regardless of its accuracy.

    c. D should have disclosed only the lowest price that K would accept.

    d. D has a special agency relationship with K.

16. A broker would have the right to dictate which of the following to an independent contractor who was working for him?

    a. The number of hours that the person would have to work

    b. The schedule that the person would have to follow

    c. The minimum acceptable dress code for the office

    d. The commission rate that the person would earn

5

Listing Agreements

Just as a supermarket without any inventory will have no customers, the real estate broker with no inventory will have no customers and thus no business. To acquire inventory most brokers obtain listings of properties for sale (although some work with properties for lease, rent, exchange or option).

As discussed in Chapter 4, a listing agreement creates a special agency relationship between the principal (usually the seller) and the broker (the agent), wherein the agent is authorized to represent the principal and the principal's property to third parties, including securing and submitting offers for the property.

The listing agreement is an **employment contract** rather than a real estate contract. It involves the hiring of the broker to represent the principal but does not necessarily involve the transfer of real estate. As the listing is a contract for the personal professional services of the broker, some jurisdictions do not require to be in writing. However, most states require the listing to be in writing to be enforceable in court, either by their statute of frauds or by specific rule from their real estate licensing authority.

Under the provisions of the state real estate license laws, only a broker can act as agent to list, sell or rent another person's real estate. Throughout this chapter, unless otherwise stated, the terms *broker, agent* and *firm* are intended to include both the broker and a salesperson working under the broker. However, only the broker has the authority to list, lease and sell property and provide other services to a principal, and state real estate license laws stipulate that these acts must be done in the name and under the supervision of the broker.

Types of Listing Agreements

The types of listing agreements generally used are discussed below.

Exclusive-Right-to-Sell Listing

In an **exclusive-right-to-sell listing** one broker is appointed as the sole agent of the seller and is given the exclusive right, or *authorization,* to market the seller's property. Under this form of contract the seller must pay the broker a commission *regardless of who sells the property* if it is sold while the listing is in effect. In other words, if the seller finds a buyer without the broker's assistance, the seller must *still* pay the broker a commission. This is the most popular form of listing agreement among brokers. Because it offers the broker the greatest opportunity to receive a commission, the broker feels freer to spend money for multiple-listing service fees, advertising, brochures, fliers, open house expenses, etc.

Exclusive-Agency Listing

In an **exclusive-agency listing** *only one broker* is authorized to act as the exclusive agent of the principal. However, the seller under this form of agreement *retains the right to sell the property by himself or herself* without obligation to the broker. The seller is obligated to pay a commission to the broker if the broker has been the procuring cause of a sale *or* if any other broker sells the property as a subagent of that broker.

Open Listing

In an **open listing** (also known in some areas as a *nonexclusive listing* or a *general listing*), the seller retains the right to employ any number of brokers as agents. The brokers can act simultaneously, and the seller is obligated to pay a commission only to that broker who successfully produces a ready, willing and able buyer. If the seller personally sells the property *without the aid of any of the brokers*, the seller is not obligated to pay any commission. A listing contract ordinarily creates an open listing unless wording that specifically provides otherwise is included. An advertisement of property ''for sale by owner'' may indicate ''brokers protected'' or in some other way invite offers brought by brokers. Such an invitation does not by itself create any form of listing agreement. The terms of even an open listing would still need to be negotiated.

Special Listing Provisions

Multiple listing. A *multiple-listing clause* may be included in an exclusive listing. A **multiple-listing service** (MLS) is a marketing organization whose broker members make their own exclusive listings available through other brokers and gain access to other brokers' listed properties as well.

A multiple-listing service offers advantages to both the broker and the seller. Brokers develop a sizable inventory of properties to be sold and are assured a portion of the commission if they list a property or participate in the sale of another broker's listing. Sellers gain because their property is exposed to a larger market.

In Practice . . .

Through computers most MLSs offer instant access to information on which properties are on and off the market. They are equally helpful to the agent or broker who needs to make a competitive market analysis to determine the value of a particular property and thus arrive at a listing price for it. Computerization also helps the buyer select a property that is in the community that best fulfills the buyer's needs.

The contractual obligations among the member brokers of a multiple-listing organization vary widely. Most provide that upon sale of the property *the commission is divided between the listing broker and the selling broker*. Terms for division of the commission are agreed upon by the brokers.

Under most MLS contracts the broker who secures a listing is not only authorized but *obligated* to turn the listing over to the multiple-listing service within a specific period of time so that it can be distributed to the other member brokers. The length of time during which the listing broker can offer the property exclusively without notifying the other member brokers varies but usually is less than 72 hours.

Under the provisions of most multiple-listing services a participating broker agrees to offer unilateral subagency to any other brokers who attempt to sell the listing broker's property. To offer such subagency the broker must have the written consent of the seller. If a broker specifically chooses to represent a buyer for a property in the multiple-listing service, that broker *should* notify the listing broker in writing before any other communication takes place. Otherwise the buyer's broker might be considered a dual agent.

Net listing. A **net listing** provision specifies that the seller will receive a net amount of money from any sale, with the excess being given to the listing broker as commission. Thus the broker is free to offer the property at any price higher than that net amount. However, because of the question of the propriety of the broker's actions and the potential for fraud, net listings are illegal in many states and discouraged by real estate licensing authorities and trade associations in most others.

Option listing. An **option listing** provision gives the broker the right to purchase the listed property. Use of an option listing may open the broker to charges of fraud unless the broker is scrupulous in fulfilling all obligations to the property owner. In some states a broker who chooses to exercise such an option must first inform the property owner of the broker's profit in the transaction and secure *in writing* the owner's agreement to it.

Termination of Listings	A listing agreement may be terminated for any of the following reasons: (1) fulfillment of the purpose of the listing; (2) expiration of the time period stated in the agreement; (3) breach or cancellation by one of the parties, although that party may be liable to the other for damages; (4) transfer of title to the property by operation of law, as in a bankruptcy; (5) mutual consent; (6) death or incapacity of either party; (7) destruction of the property or a change in property use by outside forces (such as a change in zoning or condemnation by eminent domain).

Remember that a listing agreement is a *personal service contract*. As such its success depends on the personal efforts of the broker who is a party to the agreement. The broker cannot turn the listing over to another broker without the principal's written consent. If the broker abandons the listing by failing to perform any work toward its fulfillment, or revokes the agreement, the property owner cannot force the broker to comply with it. The property owner can, however, sue the broker for damages.

The property owner could fail to fulfill the terms of the agreement by refusing to cooperate with reasonable requests of the broker (such as allowing tours of the property by prospective buyers) or refusing to proceed with a sales contract. The property owner could also simply cancel the listing agreement. In either case the property owner could be liable for damages to the broker.

Expiration of Listing Period	All listings should specify a definite period of time during which the broker is to be employed. *In most states failure to specify a definite termination date in a listing is grounds for suspension or revocation of the agent's real estate license.*

The use of automatic extensions of time in exclusive listings has been discouraged by the courts and outlawed in some states. Many listing contract forms specifically provide that there can be no automatic extensions of the agreement. An example of an automatic extension is a listing that provides for a base period of 90 days and "continues thereafter until terminated by either party hereto by 30 days' notice in writing." Some court decisions have held that such an extended period is to be considered an open listing rather than part of the original exclusive-agency listing.

Some listing contracts contain a "broker protection clause," which provides that the property owner will pay the listing broker a commission if, within a specified number of days after the listing expires, the owner sells, rents, leases, exchanges or options the property to someone the owner originally met or made contact with through the broker. This clause protects a broker who introduced the parties and was the procuring cause, only to have the parties enter into a contract and complete the transaction after the listing has expired. The times for such clauses usually parallel the terms of the listing agreement; for example, a six-month listing would probably carry a broker protection clause of six months after the listing's expiration. However, to protect the owner and prevent any liability of the owner for two separate commissions, most of these clauses stipulate that they cannot be enforced if the property is relisted under a new contract either with the original listing broker or with another broker.

Listing Property

Probably the most critical concern of a prospective seller in giving a listing to a broker is the selling price of the property and the net amount that the seller will receive upon sale.

Pricing the Property

While it is the responsibility of the broker or salesperson to advise and assist, it is ultimately the *seller* who must determine the listing price for the property. Because the average seller does not usually have the background to make an informed decision about a listing price, however, real estate agents must be prepared to offer their knowledge, information and expertise in this area.

A broker or salesperson can help the seller determine a listing price for the property by means of a **competitive market analysis (CMA).** Essentially this is a comparison of the prices of recently sold properties that are similar in location, style and amenities to the property of the listing seller. If no such comparisons can be made, or if the seller feels his or her property is unique in some way, a real estate appraisal—a detailed estimate of a property's value by a professional appraiser— may be warranted.

Whether a CMA or a formal appraisal is used, the figure sought is the property's market value. **Market value,** discussed in Chapter 18, is the most probable price property would bring in an arm's-length transaction under normal conditions on the open market. A broker performing a CMA will estimate market value as likely to fall within a range of figures (for example, $135,000 to $140,000).

While it is the property owner's privilege to set whatever listing price he or she chooses, a broker should reject any listing in which the price is substantially exaggerated or severely out of line with the indications of the CMA.

✱   *Look it over*

| **Math Concept: Calculating Sales Prices, Commissions and Nets to Seller** | When a property sells, the sales price is equal to 100% of the money being transferred. Therefore, if a broker is receiving a 6% commission, 94% would be left for the seller's other expenses and equity. |

To calculate a commission using a sales price of $80,000 and a commission rate of 6% (.06 as a decimal), multiply the sales price by the commission rate:

$$\$80,000 \times 6\% = \quad \$80,000 \times .06 = \quad \$4,800 \text{ commission}$$

To calculate a sales price using a commission of $4,550 and a commission rate of 7% (.07 as a decimal), divide the commission by the commission rate:

$$\$4,550 \div 7\% = \quad \$4,550 \div .07 = \quad \$65,000 \text{ sales price}$$

To calculate a commission rate using a commission of $3,200 and a sales price of $64,000, divide the commission by the sales price:

$$\$3,200 / \$64,000 = \quad .05 \text{ as a decimal} = \quad 5\% \text{ commission rate}$$

To calculate the net to the seller using a sales price of $85,000 and a commission rate of 8% (.08 as a decimal), multiply the sales price by *100% minus the commission rate:*

$$\$85,000 \times (100\% - 8\%) = \$85,000 \times .92 = \quad \$78,200$$

The same result could be achieved by calculating the commission ($85,000 × .08 = $6,800) and deducting it from the sales price ($85,000 − $6,800 = $78,200). However, this involves extra calculations that aren't necessary.

Sales price × commission rate = commission

Commission ÷ commission rate = sales price

Commission ÷ sales price = commission rate

Sales price × (100% − commission rate) = net to seller

Information Needed for Listing Agreements

Once the real estate licensee and the owner have agreed that the property can be marketed for a listing price consistent with the owner's wishes and what the market will bear, the licensee must obtain specific detailed information on the property. Obtaining as much factual information on the property as possible assures that most contingencies can be anticipated and provided for. This is particularly important when the listing will be shared with other brokers through a multiple-listing service and other licensees must rely on the information taken by the lister.

Information about the property that appears in the listing agreement (see Figure 5.1 on pages 48–49) generally includes:

1. the names and relationships, if any, of the owners;

2. the street address of the property;

3. the size of the improvements (residence, garage, carport, patio, etc.);

4. the age of the improvements and their type of construction;

5. the number and the sizes of the rooms ("room count"); *only finished space*

6. the size of the lot, including its dimensions; *only finished space*

✱ 7. information on any existing loans, including the name and address of each lender, the type of loan, the loan number, the loan balance, the interest rate, the monthly payment and what it includes (principal, interest, real estate tax impounds, hazard insurance impounds, mortgage insurance premiums), whether the loan may be assumed by the buyer and under what circumstances, whether the loan may be prepaid without penalty, etc.;

8. the possibility of seller financing;

9. the amount of any outstanding special assessments and whether they will be paid by the seller or assumed by the buyer;

10. the zoning classification of the property;

11. the current (or most recent year's) property taxes;

12. information concerning the neighborhood of the property (schools, parks and recreational areas, churches, public transportation, etc.);

You can make copies of public info on schoolschools and show them. You can not tell verbally tell them

13. any real property to be removed from the premises by the seller and any personal property to be included in the sale for the buyer (both the listing contract and the subsequent purchase contract should be explicit on these points);

14. any additional information that would make the property more appealing and marketable; and

15. any required disclosures concerning agency representation, property condition, etc.

In Practice . . .   *Some brokers use a separate information sheet (also known as a* profile *or* data sheet) *for recording many of the foregoing property features, including room sizes, lot sizes and taxes. In these firms listing agreements contain mainly the specific contract terms—listing price, duration of the agreement, signatures of the parties and so forth.*

The Listing Contract Form

A wide variety of listing contract forms is available today. Some brokers draft their own contracts, some use forms prepared by their multiple-listing service and some use forms produced by their state real estate licensing authority. Some have the property data on one form and "wed" it to a second form that contains the contractual obligations between the seller and the broker; others use a single form. But no matter which form is used, most listing contracts require similar information because the same considerations arise in almost all real estate transactions. Some of these considerations are discussed below.

The type of agency created. Is the contract an exclusive-right-to-sell listing (the most common type of listing), an exclusive-agency listing or an open listing? This is the section of the contract in which the principal gives the broker the authority to act on the principal's behalf. A major consideration is whether the broker will be allowed to authorize subagents through a multiple-listing service.

The broker's authority. According to the terms of the contract, will the broker be able to place a sign on the property, advertise and market the property using the broker's best efforts, submit the contract to a multiple-listing service, show the property at reasonable times and upon reasonable notice to the seller, place a lockbox on the property and accept earnest money deposits on behalf of the seller? Without the written consent of the seller, the broker cannot undertake any of these or similar activities.

**Figure 5.1
Sample Listing
Agreement**

**EXCLUSIVE AUTHORIZATION AND RIGHT TO SELL
RESIDENTIAL**

This is Intended to be a Legally Binding Contract

Type **ER**

Legal I.D. 347954

1. **Exclusive Right to Sell.** In consideration of the acceptance by the undersigned licensed Arizona real estate broker ("Broker") of the terms of
2. this Contract and Broker's promise to endeavor to effect a sale of the property described below (the "Property"), I or we, as owner(s) (the
3. "Owner"), employ and grant Broker the exclusive and irrevocable right commencing on _____ , 19 _____ , and expiring at
4. midnight on _____ , 19 _____ to sell, exchange, option or rent the Property described in lines 5 through 8.

5. **The Property.** For purposes of this Contract, the "Property" means the real property in _____ County, Arizona described
6. below, plus all fixtures and improvements thereon, all appurtenances incident thereto and all personal property described in lines 11 through 17.

7. _____
                     Legal Description

8. _____
                     Street Address

9. **Price.** The listing price shall be $ _____ , to be paid as described in the Owner's Data Entry Form, or such other price
10. and terms as are accepted by Owner.

11. **Fixtures and Personal Property.** Except as provided in the Data Entry Form, the property includes the following fixtures or personal property:
12. All existing storage sheds, heating and cooling equipment, built-in appliances, light fixtures, window and door screens, sun screens, storm
13. windows and doors, towel, curtain and drapery rods, attached carpeting, draperies and other window coverings, fireplace equipment, pool
14. and spa equipment (including any mechanical or other cleaning systems), garage door openers and controls, irrigation systems, fire
15. warning and security systems, fences, ceiling fans and attached antennas.

16. **Additional Property and Leased Equipment.** The property may include additional personal property and exclude leased equipment as
17. described in the Data Entry Form.

18. **Access and Lockbox.** Owner authorizes Broker to install and use a Lockbox containing a key to the Property. ☐ yes ☐ no. Owner
19. acknowledges that a Lockbox and any other keys left with or available to Broker will permit access to the Property by Broker, Broker's
20. subagents and buyers' agents, together with potential purchasers, even when Owner is absent; that neither the Arizona Regional Multiple
21. Listing Service ("ARMLS"), nor any Board of REALTORS®, nor any broker is insuring Owner against theft, loss or vandalism resulting from any
22. such access; that Owner is responsible for obtaining appropriate insurance; and that Owner will obtain and provide to Broker written per-
23. mission from the occupant of the Property, if it is a person other than Owner.

24. **Sign.** Broker is authorized to place Broker's "For Sale" and "Sold" Signs, as appropriate, on the Property.

25. **Home Protection Plan.** Owner acknowledges that home protection plans are available and that such plans may provide additional protection
26. and benefits to Owner and any purchaser of the Property. Owner agrees to provide at his expense a home protection plan promptly after
27. the execution of this Contract ☐ yes ☐ no.

28. **Additional Terms.** _____
29. _____
30. _____

31. **Compensation to Broker.** Owner agrees to compensate Broker as follows:

32. a. If Broker produces a ready, willing and able purchaser in accordance with this Contract, or if a sale or exchange of the Property is made
33. by Owner or through any other agent, or otherwise, during the term of this exclusive listing, for services rendered, Owner agrees to pay
34. Broker a commission of _____
35. The same amount of commission shall be payable to Broker if, without the consent of Broker, the Property is withdrawn from this listing,
36. otherwise withdrawn from sale, or transferred or conveyed by Owner.

37. b. Owner agrees not to rent the Property during the term of this Contract without Broker's prior knowledge and consent and, if the Property
38. is rented, Owner agrees to pay Broker a rental commission of _____ .
39. If during the terms of such rental or within _____ after its termination, the tenant, or any of such tenant's heirs, executors, or assigns
40. shall buy the Property from Owner, the commission described in line 34 shall be deemed as earned by and payable to Broker.

41. c. If within _____ days after the expiration of this Contract, a sale, exchange or option is made by Owner to any person to
42. whom the Property has been shown by Broker or any agent of Broker, or with whom Broker or any agent of Broker has negotiated
43. concerning the sale of the Property, the same fee shall be payable unless this Contract has been renewed or the Property has been relisted
44. on an exclusive basis with another real estate broker.

45. d. Owner authorizes Broker to cooperate with other brokers and to divide with other brokers all such compensation in any manner acceptable
46. to Broker.

47. e. Owner will instruct the escrow company to pay all such commissions to Broker as a condition to closing and irrevocably assigns Owner's
48. proceeds to Broker at close of escrow to the extent necessary therefor. If completion of the sale is prevented by default of Owner, or with
49. the consent of Owner, the entire fee shall be paid directly by Owner. If the earnest deposit is forfeited for any other reason, Owner shall
50. pay a brokerage fee equal to one-half of the earnest deposit, provided such payment shall not exceed the full amount of the fee. Nothing in
51. this paragraph shall be construed as limiting applicable provisions of law relating to when commissions are earned or payable.

52. **TERMS ON REVERSE.** THE TERMS AND CONDITIONS ON THE REVERSE SIDE HEREOF PLUS ALL INFORMATION ON THE DATA
53. ENTRY FORM ARE INCORPORATED HEREIN BY REFERENCE.

54. **Receipt of Copy.** Broker and Owner acknowledge receipt of a copy of this Contract.

55. COMMISSIONS PAYABLE FOR THE SALE, LEASING OR MANAGEMENT OF PROPERTY ARE NOT SET BY ANY BOARD OF REALTORS®
56. OR MULTIPLE LISTING SERVICE OR IN ANY MANNER OTHER THAN BY NEGOTIATION BETWEEN THE BROKER AND THE CLIENT.

57. _____
   Owner   Address   Date

58. _____
   Owner   City/Zip   Phone

59. In consideration of Owner's representations and promises in this Contract, Broker agrees to endeavor to effect a sale, exchange or option
60. in accordance with this Contract and further agrees to file this listing for publication by a local Board of REALTORS® and dissemination to the
61. Users of ARMLS.

62. _____
   Listing Office   By (Signature)   Phone

63. Accepted by: _____ Date: _____
                     Broker

64. Broker's File/Log No. _____ Manager's Initials _____ Broker's Initials _____ Date _____

NO REPRESENTATION IS MADE AS TO THE LEGAL VALIDITY OR ADEQUACY OF ANY PROVISION OR THE TAX CONSEQUENCES THEREOF. IF YOU DESIRE LEGAL OR TAX ADVICE, CONSULT YOUR ATTORNEY OR TAX ADVISOR.

Copyright © 1989 by Arizona Regional Multiple Listing Service   FOR USE WITH DATA ENTRY FORM NUMBER 1, 2 & 3

                                              7/89

BROKER

**Figure 5.1
(continued)**

65. **Multiple Listing Service.** Broker is a member of a local Board of REALTORS®, which is a member of ARMLS. This listing information will be
66. provided to ARMLS to be published and disseminated to its Users. Broker is authorized to offer subagency and to appoint subagents and to
67. report the sale, exchange, option or rental of the Property, and its price, terms and financing, to a local Board of REALTORS® for dis-
68. semination to and use by authorized ARMLS Users and to the public.

69. **Role of Broker.** Owner acknowledges that Broker is not responsible for the custody or condition of the Property or for its management,
70. maintenance, upkeep or repair.

71. **Title.** Owner agrees to furnish marketable title by warranty deed and an Owner's policy of title insurance in the full amount of the
72. purchase price.

73. **Cooperation by Owner.** Owner agrees to make available to Broker and prospective purchasers all data, records and documents pertaining
74. to the Property, to allow Broker, and any other broker who is a subagent of Broker to show the Property at reasonable times and upon
75. reasonable notice and to commit no act which might tend to obstruct Broker's performance hereunder. Owner shall not deal directly with any
76. prospective purchaser of the Property during the term of this Contract and shall refer all prospective purchasers to Broker during the term
77. hereof. Owner agrees to cooperate with Broker on any offers to purchase the Property. Owner also authorizes Broker to permit a broker who
78. is a buyer's agent to show the Property at such times and on such terms as are acceptable to Owner or Broker.

79. **Warranties by Owner.** Owner represents and warrants, as follows:

80. a. Owner is the Owner of record of the Property and has full authority to execute this Contract.

81. b. All information concerning the Property in this Contract, including the Data Entry Form relating to the Property, or otherwise provided by
82. Owner to Broker or any purchaser or prospective purchaser of the Property is, or will be at the time made, and shall be at the closing, true,
83. correct and complete. Owner agrees to notify Broker promptly if there is any material change in such information during the term of
84. this Contract.

85. c. Except as otherwise provided in this Contract, Owner warrants that Owner shall maintain and repair the Property so that, at the earlier of
86. possession or the close of escrow: the property shall be at least in substantially the same condition as on the effective date of this Contract;
87. the roof will be water-tight; all heating, cooling, plumbing and electrical systems and built-in appliances will be in working condition; and
88. if the Property has a swimming pool and/or spa, the motors, filter systems (and heaters, if so equipped) will be in working condition. Owner
89. warrants that prior to the close of escrow, payment in full will have been made for all labor, materials, machinery, fixtures or tools furnished
90. within the 120 days immediately preceding the close of escrow in connection with the construction, alteration or repair of any structure on
91. or improvement to the Property. Prior to the close of escrow, Owner shall grant the purchaser or purchaser's representatives reasonable
92. access to enter and inspect the Property.

93. d. The information in this Contract, if any, pertaining to a public sewer system, septic tank or other sanitation system is correct.

94. e. Owner will disclose to any potential purchaser all facts known to him concerning adverse conditions or latent defects in, to or affecting
95. the Property.

96. f. At his expense, Owner will place in escrow a wood-infestation inspection report by a licensed pest control contractor which, when considered
97. in its entirety, indicates that all residences and buildings attached to the Property are free from evidence of current infestation by any
98. wood-destroying organisms.

99. **Indemnification.** Owner agrees to indemnify and hold Broker, all Boards of REALTORS®, ARMLS, and all other cooperating brokers harmless
100. against any and all claims, liability, damage or loss arising from any misrepresentation or breach of warranty by Owner in this Contract, any
101. incorrect information supplied by Owner and any facts concerning the Property not disclosed by Owner, including without limitation, any
102. facts known to Owner relating to adverse conditions or latent defects.

103. **Attorneys Fees.** In any action or proceeding to enforce any provision of this Contract, or for damages sustained by reason of its breach, the
104. prevailing party shall be entitled to reasonable attorneys fees, as set by the court or arbitrator and not by a jury, and to all other related
105. expenses, such as expert witness fees, fees paid to investigators and court costs. Additionally, if any Broker reasonably hires an attorney to
106. enforce the collection of any commission payable pursuant to this Contract, and is successful in collecting some or all of such commission
107. without commencing an action or proceeding, Owner agrees to pay such Broker's reasonable attorneys fees and costs.

108. **Deposits.** Owner authorizes Broker to accept earnest deposits on behalf of Owner and to issue receipts for such earnest deposits.

109. **Recommendations.** If any broker recommends a builder or contractor or any other person or entity to Owner for any purpose, such recom-
110. mendation will be independently investigated and evaluated by Owner, who hereby acknowledges that any decision to enter into any
111. contractual arrangements with any such person or entity recommended by any Broker will be based solely upon such independent investiga-
112. tion and evaluation.

113. **FIRPTA.** Upon Broker's request, Owner agrees to complete, sign and deliver to escrow company a certificate concerning whether Owner is a
114. foreign person or nonresident alien pursuant to the Foreign Investment in Real Property Tax Act of 1980 (FIRPTA).

115. **Subsequent Offer.** Upon Owner's acceptance of an offer with respect to the Property, Owner waives his right to receive any subsequent offer
116. with respect to the Property until after forfeiture by the offeror or other nullification of the contract with the offeror.

117. **Entire Agreement.** This Contract, any attached exhibits and any addenda or supplements signed by the parties, shall constitute the entire
118. agreement between Owner and Broker and supersede any other written or oral agreements between Owner and Broker. This Contract can be
119. modified only by a writing signed by Owner and Broker.

120. **Equal Opportunity.** The Property is offered without respect to ancestry, race, religion, color, sex, handicap, marital status, familial status, age
121. or national origin.

122. **Construction of Language.** The language of this Contract shall be construed according to its fair meaning and not strictly for or against
123. either party. Words used in the masculine, feminine or neuter shall apply to either gender or the neuter, as appropriate. All singular and plural
124. words shall be interpreted to refer to the number consistent with circumstances and context.

The names of all parties to the contract. Anyone having an interest in the property must be identified and should sign the listing for it to be valid. If the property is owned under one of the forms of concurrent ownership discussed in Chapter 7, that fact should be clearly established. If one or more of the owners is married, it is wise to obtain the spouse's consent and signature on the contract to release the appropriate marital rights. If the property is in the possession of a tenant, that should be disclosed along with instructions on how the property is to be shown to a prospective buyer.

The brokerage firm. The firm, the employing broker and, if appropriate, the salesperson taking the listing must all be identified in the contract.

The broker's responsibilities. This section identifies the obligations the broker promises to fulfill, such as advertising, showing the property, submitting the contract to a multiple-listing service, accounting for funds received on behalf of the seller, etc.

The listing price. This is the proposed gross sales price, and the seller should understand that any outstanding obligations such as unpaid real estate taxes, special assessments and mortgage and trust deed debts remain the seller's responsibility and must be paid from the proceeds of the sale (unless otherwise agreed to by the buyer in the contract).

Real property and personal property. This section expands on the items of personal property that will be left with the real estate when it is sold and what items of real property the seller expects to remove at the time of the sale. Each item should be explicitly identified (brand name, serial number, color) even though some of these items may later become points of negotiation should a ready, willing and able buyer be found for the property. Typical items to consider: major appliances, swimming pool and spa equipment, fireplace accessories, storage sheds, stacked firewood, stored heating oil and so on.

Leased equipment. Is any leased equipment—security systems, cable television boxes, water softeners, special antennas—going to be left with the property? If so, the seller is responsible for notifying the lessor of such items of the change of property ownership.

The description of the premises. In addition to the street address, both the legal description and tax parcel number may be required for future insertion into a purchase offer.

The proposed dates for the closing and for the buyer's possession. These should be based on an anticipated sale date, with adequate time allowed for the paperwork involved (including the buyer's qualification for any financing) and the physical moves to be arranged by the seller and the buyer.

The closing. Who will handle the closing of the transaction? Will the designated party complete the settlement statements and disburse the funds? Will he or she file the proper forms, such as documents to be recorded, documents to be sent the Internal Revenue Service and documents to be submitted for registering foreign owners?

The evidence of ownership. How will the title be transferred to the buyer? Most commonly used are a warranty deed and either a title insurance policy or an abstract and legal opinion.

Encumbrances. What liens will be paid in full at the closing by the seller and what liens will be assumed by the buyer?

Homeowner warranty program. Is a homeowner warranty plan available? Is the seller willing to pay for it? If not, will it be available to the buyer at the buyer's expense?

The commission. Under what circumstances will a commission be paid: only upon the sale of the property or upon any transfer of interest created by the broker? Will it be a percentage or a flat fee? When will it be paid? Will it be paid directly by the seller or by the party handling the closing?

The termination of the contract. What circumstances will terminate the contract? Can the seller arbitrarily refuse to sell or cooperate with the listing broker?

The broker protection clause. Under what circumstances will the broker still be entitled to a commission, and how long will such a clause remain in effect after the listing expires?

Warranties by the owner. Is the property suitable for its intended purpose? Does it comply with the appropriate local building and zoning codes? Will it be transferred to the buyer in essentially the same condition as it was originally presented, considering repairs or alterations to be made as provided for in a purchase contract? Are there any known defects?

Indemnification ("hold harmless") wording. Do the seller and the broker agree to hold each other harmless for incorrect information supplied by one to the other, regardless of whether such inaccuracies were intentional or unintentional?

Nondiscrimination ("equal opportunity") wording. Does the seller understand that the property must be shown and offered without respect to the race, color, creed or religious preference, national origin, sex, sexual orientation, age, handicap, source of income, etc., of the prospective buyer?

Antitrust wording. Does the contract indicate that all commissions are negotiable between the seller and the broker and that they are not set by any regulatory agency or trade association?

The signatures of the parties. All parties identified in the contract must sign it.

The date the contract is signed. This date may differ from the date the contract actually becomes effective, particularly if a salesperson is taking the listing and must subsequently have his or her broker sign the contract to accept employment under its terms.

Anyone taking a listing should use *only* the appropriate documents as provided by the broker. Most brokers are conscientious enough to utilize only documents that have been carefully drafted or reviewed by an attorney so that their construction and legal language comply with the appropriate federal, state and local laws. Such contracts should also give consideration to local customs, such as closing dates and the proration of income and expenses, with which most real estate attorneys would be familiar.

Key Terms

competitive market analysis (CMA)   multiple-listing service
employment contract   net listing
exclusive-agency listing   open listing
exclusive-right-to-sell listing   option listing
market value

Summary

To acquire an inventory of property to sell, brokers must obtain listings. Types of listings include exclusive-right-to-sell listings, exclusive-agency listings and open listings.

With an exclusive-right-to-sell listing the seller employs only one broker and must pay that broker a commission regardless of whether it is the broker or the seller who finds a buyer—provided the buyer is found within the listing period.

Under an exclusive-agency listing the broker is given the exclusive right to represent the seller, but the seller can avoid paying the broker a commission by selling the property without the broker's help.

An open listing is one in which, to obtain a commission, the broker must find a buyer before the property is sold by the seller or another broker.

A multiple-listing provision may appear in an exclusive-right-to-sell or an exclusive-agency listing and gives the broker the additional authority and obligation to distribute the listing to other members of the broker's multiple-listing organization. A net listing, which is outlawed in some states and considered unethical in most areas, is based on the net price the seller will receive if the property is sold. The broker under a net listing is free to offer the property for sale at the highest available price and will receive as his or her commission any amount over and above the seller's stipulated net. An option listing, which also must be handled with caution, gives the broker the option to purchase the listed property.

A listing agreement may be terminated for the same reasons as any other agency relationship.

Missed 6 Wrong

Questions

1. A listing taken by a real estate salesperson belongs to the:

   a. broker.
   b. seller.
   c. salesperson.
   d. salesperson and broker equally.

2. Which of the following is a similarity between an exclusive-agency listing and an exclusive-right-to-sell listing?

   a. Under both types of listings the seller retains the right to sell the real estate without the broker's help and without paying the broker a commission.
   b. Under both the seller authorizes only one particular salesperson to show the property.
   c. Both give the responsibility of representing the seller to one broker only.
   d. Both are open listings.

3. All of the following would terminate a listing *except* the:

   a. expiration of the contract.
   b. death or incapacity of the broker.
   c. nonpayment of the commission by the seller.
   d. destruction of the improvements on the property.

4. Seller M has his property under an exclusive-agency listing with broker K. If M sells his property himself during the term of the listing without using K's services, he will owe K:

   a. no commission.
   b. the full commission.
   c. a partial commission.
   d. only reimbursement for broker K's costs.

5. A broker sold a residence for $88,000 and received $6,160 as her commission in accordance to the terms of the listing. What percentage of the sales price was the broker's commission?

   a. six percent
   b. 6.5 percent
   c. seven percent
   d. 7.5 percent

6. A seller's residence is listed with a broker, and the seller stipulates that she wants to receive $85,000 from the sale but the broker can sell the property for as much as possible and keep the difference as the commission. The broker agrees. This type of listing would be a(n):

   a. exclusive-right-to-sell listing.
   b. exclusive-agency listing.
   c. open listing.
   d. net listing.

7. All of the following provisions are usually found in a listing agreement *except:*

   a. the rate of commission.
   b. the monthly utility bill.
   c. the price the seller wants.
   d. the contract expiration date.

8. The listed price for a property should be based on:

   a. the net to the seller.
   b. the appraised value.
   c. what the seller chooses.
   d. the maximum of a range of values.

9. A listing contract:

   a. is an employment contract for the personal and professional services of the broker.
   b. obligates the seller to convey the property if the broker procures a ready, willing and able buyer.
   c. obligates the broker to work diligently for both the seller and the buyer.
   d. automatically requires the payment of a commission while the broker protection clause is in effect.

10. Seller W hired broker N under the terms of an open listing. While that listing was still in effect. W—without informing N—hired broker F under an exclusive-right-to-sell listing for the same property. If broker N produces a buyer for the property whose offer seller W accepts, then seller W must pay a:
    a. full commission only to broker N.
    b. full commission only to broker F.
    c. full commission to both broker N and broker F.
    d. half commission to both broker N and broker F.

11. Seller G listed her residence with broker D. Broker D brought an offer at full price and terms of the listing from buyers who are willing and able to pay cash for the property. However, seller G changed her mind and rejected the buyers' offer. In this situation seller G:
    a. must sell her property.
    b. owes a commission to broker D.
    c. is liable to the buyers for specific performance.
    d. is liable to the buyers for compensatory damages.

12. Which of the following is a similarity between an open listing and an exclusive-agency listing?
    a. Under both the seller avoids paying the broker a commission if the seller sells the property unassisted by the broker.
    b. Both grant a commission to any broker who procures a buyer for the seller's property.
    c. Under both the broker earns a commission regardless of who sells the property as long as it is sold within the listing period.
    d. Both grant an exclusive right to sell to whatever broker procures a buyer for the seller's property.

13. The parties to the listing contract are:
    a. the seller and the buyer.
    b. the seller and the broker.
    c. the seller and the salesperson.
    d. the broker and the salesperson.

14. A competitive market analysis:
    a. is the same as an appraisal.
    b. can help the seller price the property.
    c. by law must be completed for each listing taken.
    d. should not be retained in the property's listing file.

15. A property was listed with a broker who belonged to a multiple-listing service and was sold by another member broker for $53,500. The total commission was six percent of the sale price. The selling broker received 60 percent of the commission, and the listing broker received the balance. What was the listing broker's commission?
    a. $1,284   c. $1,926
    b. $1,464   d. $2,142

6

Interests in Real Estate

Government Powers

Although an individual has maximum rights to the land he or she owns, these ownership rights are subject to certain powers, or rights, held by federal, state and local governments. Because they are for the general welfare of the community, these limitations on the ownership of real estate supersede the rights of the individual and can affect any interest in real property held by the individual. Such government rights include the following.

Police power. This is the power vested in a state to establish legislation to preserve order, protect the public health and safety and promote the general welfare. There is no federal **police power** as such—it exists on the state level only. A state's police power is passed on to municipalities and counties through legislation called *enabling acts*.

The use and enjoyment of property is subject to restrictions authorized by such legislation, such as environmental protection laws, zoning ordinances, building codes and regulations governing the use, occupancy, size, location, construction and rental of real estate. These laws, along with the licensing laws and departmental rules also created for the protection of the public, affect each licensee's day-to-day work. See Chapter 19 for more information on police power.

Eminent domain. Through what is called a *condemnation suit* a government may exercise the right to acquire privately owned real estate for public use. While **eminent domain** refers to the governmental power, condemnation is the process through which that power can be exercised. The proposed use must be declared by the court to be a public use, just compensation must be paid to the owner and the rights of the property owner must be protected by due process of law. The exercise of decision making under the right of eminent domain is generally granted by state laws to quasi-public bodies, such as land-clearance commissions and public housing or redevelopment authorities, as well as to publicly held companies such as railroads, public utilities and mining companies.

Public agencies acquire real property through direct negotiation with and purchase from the owner. Condemnation proceedings are instituted only when the owner's consent cannot be obtained. In some instances an owner will dedicate the property to the government for the particular use being sought by the agency, such as a site for a school, park or library.

Taxation. **Taxation** is a charge on real estate to raise funds to meet the public needs of a government. See Chapter 9 for more information on real estate taxes.

Escheat. While escheat is not actually a limitation on ownership, state laws provide for ownership of real estate to revert, or **escheat**, to the state when an owner dies and leaves no heirs and no will designating the disposition of the real estate. In some states real property will escheat to the county the land is located in rather than to the state.

Estates in Land

The degree, quantity, nature and extent of interest that a person has in real property is an **estate in land.**

Estates in land are divided into freehold estates and leasehold (less-than-freehold) estates (those involving tenants). The various estates and interests in real estate are illustrated in Figure 6.1.

Freehold estates are *estates of indeterminable duration,* such as those existing for a lifetime or forever. These include fee simple, defeasible fee, conventional life estate and legal life estate. The first two of these estates continue for an indefinite period and are inheritable by the heirs of the owner. The third and fourth terminate upon the death of the person on whose life they are based.

Leasehold estates are *estates for a fixed term of years.* These are estate for years, estate from period to period, estate at will and estate at sufferance. Leasehold estates are covered in Chapter 16.

Fee Simple Estate

An estate in fee simple is the *highest type of interest in real estate recognized by law.* It is complete ownership. Because this estate is of unlimited duration, upon the death of its owner it will pass to his or her heirs or as provided in the owner's will. A fee simple estate is thus an *estate of inheritance.* It is, like all estates, subject to the governmental powers previously explained.

Fee simple absolute. If there are no limitations on fee simple ownership (other than the governmental powers), it is a **fee simple absolute.** In common usage the terms *fee* and *fee simple* are used interchangeably with *fee simple absolute.*

Fee simple defeasible. A fee simple defeasible estate (or defeasible fee estate) is qualified and may be lost on the occurrence or nonoccurrence of a specified event. Such an estate may have a *special limitation* or may be subject to a *condition subsequent.*

A fee simple estate with a special limitation, also called a *fee simple determinable, base fee* or *fee simple on condition precedent,* ends automatically upon the owner's failure to comply with that limitation. The former owner (the person who created or transferred the limitation) has the possibility of reverter and can reacquire the title. This type of estate is frequently used when property is being given for a specific purpose and is sometimes referred to as a "must do" estate. The deed creating the limitation must contain wording such as "so long as" or "while" or "during" for the limitation to be created or transferred. For example, someone might grant property to his church "so long as" the land is used exclusively for religious purposes. If the church uses the land for a nonreligious purpose, title automatically reverts to the grantor (or the grantor's heirs or assigns).

**Figure 6.1
Estates and Interests
in Real Estate**

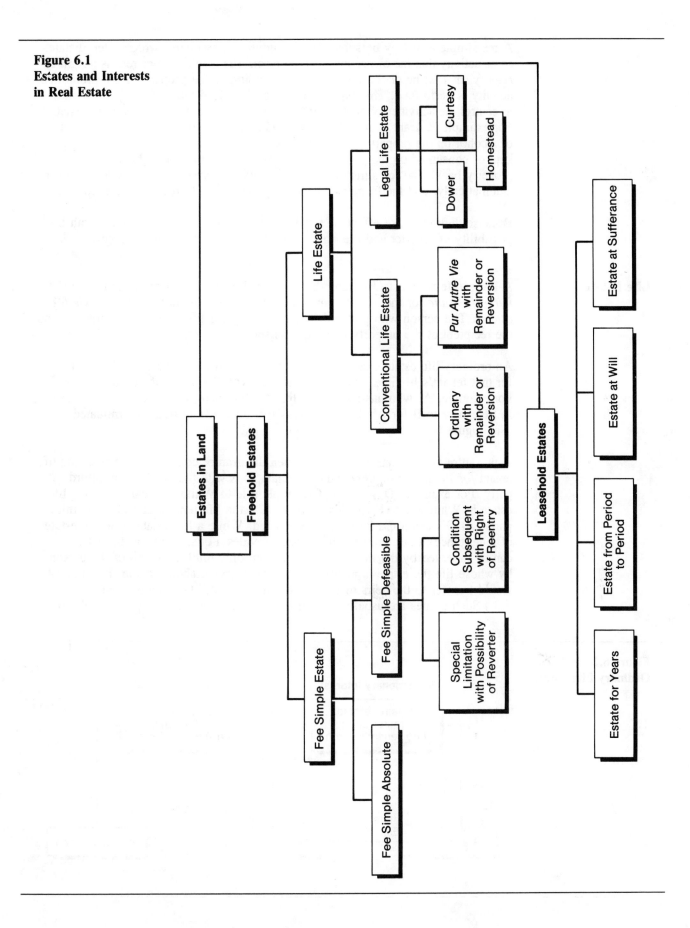

A fee simple also may be subject to a condition subsequent, which often dictates some activity that the owner must *not* perform. The former owner retains a *right of reentry;* that is, he or she can recover possession of the property if the prohibited activity is performed. This type of estate is often used when one person wishes to control the activities of another and is sometimes called a "must *not* do" estate. For example, a grant of land "on the condition that" there is no consumption of alcohol on the property is a fee simple on condition subsequent. If alcohol is kept or consumed on the property, the former owner has the right to get the property back. The fee simple on condition subsequent does *not,* however, revert automatically, and the former owner *is* required to act to recover the property.

Because they will take effect, if at all, only at some time in the future, both the possibility of reverter and the right of reentry are termed **future interest.**

Life Estate

A **life estate** is an estate in land that is limited to the life of the owner (an *ordinary life estate*) or the life of some other designated person (a *pur autre vie life estate*). The person who grants the deed creating the life estate is the grantor, and the recipient of the property is the life tenant.

An ordinary life estate exists when the grantor conveys property to the life tenant for that tenant's lifetime, and the estate ends with the death of the life tenant. For example, A, who has fee simple title to Blackacre, can convey a life estate in Blackacre to B for B's lifetime. At B's death the life estate is terminated. (See Figure 6.2.)

A pur autre vie life estate is created when the grantor conveys property to the life tenant *for the life of another,* and the estate ends with the death of that third party. For example, D, who has fee simple title to Whiteacre, can convey a life estate in Whiteacre to E for G's lifetime. E is the life tenant, and G is the third party. At G's death E's interest is terminated. While a life estate is not an estate of inheritance, a pur autre vie life estate provides a qualified right in that it can be inherited by the life tenant's heirs, but only until the death of the person by whose life the estate is measured. In this example, should E die, E's interest would transfer to the heirs of the estate, but only until G's death. (See Figure 6.3.) Such estates are usually created in favor of someone who is physically or

Figure 6.2
Ordinary Life Estate

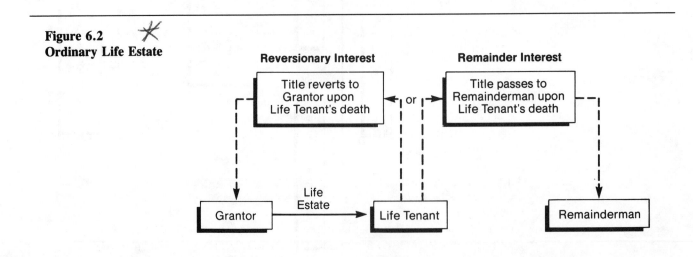

Figure 6.3
Pur Autre Vie Life
Estate

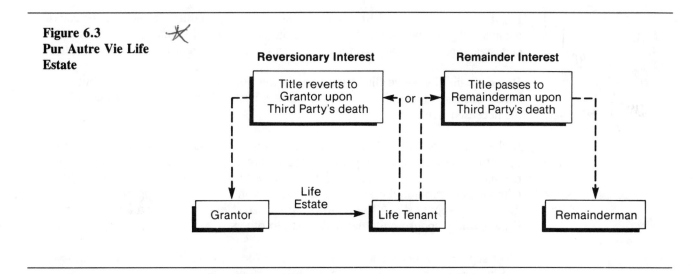

mentally incapacitated, and the estate can provide an incentive for someone else to care for them.

A life tenant's interest in real property is a true ownership interest, but his or her rights are not absolute. The life tenant cannot perform any acts that would permanently injure the property, such as destroy any improvements to the property or allow them to deteriorate. Such injury to real estate is called *waste* in legal terms. In such a situation those having any future interest in the property could sue to obtain an injunction against the life tenant.

A life tenant is entitled to all income and profits arising from the property during the life tenancy. The life tenant is also responsible for not committing waste by maintaining the property and paying for such utilities as are necessary to maintain the property. A life interest can be sold, leased or mortgaged, but such interest will always terminate upon the death of the person by whose life the estate is measured.

Remainder and reversion. A fee simple owner who creates a life estate must also consider the disposition of the property after the termination of the life estate. The future interest can take one of two forms:

1. Remainder interest: If the document that creates a life estate names someone to whom title will pass at the termination of the life estate, that person (the remainderman) owns a remainder interest. Such a remainder interest is a nonpossessory estate—a future interest.

2. Reversionary interest: If a life estate does not convey a remainder interest, then upon its termination the ownership returns to the original fee simple owner (or that owner's heirs or assigns). This estate is a reversionary interest and is also a future interest.

Thus upon the termination of the life estate the holder of the future interest, whether remainder or reversionary, will become the owner of a fee simple estate.

Conventional life estate. A conventional life estate is created by the owner of a fee simple estate. The owner retains a reversionary interest in the property or names a remainderman.

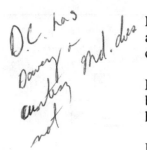

Legal life estate. A legal life estate is one created by statute. It becomes effective automatically, by operation of law, upon the occurrence of certain events. Dower, curtesy and homestead are the forms of legal life estate currently used in some states.

Dower is the life estate that a wife has in the real estate of her deceased husband. **Curtesy** is a similar life interest that a husband has in the real estate of his deceased wife.

In the few states where they are still used, dower and curtesy usually provide that upon the death of the owning spouse the nonowning spouse has a right to a one-half or a one-third interest in the real estate for the rest of his or her life. The purpose is to provide the nonowning spouse with a means of support after the owning spouse dies. The nonowning spouse is entitled to such a right even if the owning spouse wills the real estate to others.

Most separate property states have abolished the common law concepts of dower and curtesy in favor of the Uniform Probate Code, and the provisions of community property law are such that community property states never used dower and curtesy.

In Practice . . .

Because of the possibility that a nonowning spouse might claim an interest in the future even where one does not exist, it is important that both spouses sign the proper documents when real estate is conveyed. Usually the nonowning spouse's signature releases any potential statutory or common law interests in the property being transferred.

A **homestead** *is a parcel of property owned and occupied as the family home.* In those states that have homestead exemption laws a portion of the area or value of such land is protected, or exempt, from certain judgments for unsecured debts. An unsecured debt is one in which there is no collateral as security for payment of the loan, such as a charge account or personal loan. The homestead exemption would not apply to real estate taxes levied against the property or to a mortgage for purchase money or the cost of improvements. A family can have only one homestead at any one time.

Homestead laws vary from state to state and are not uniform in their wording or scope but generally include the following requirements: To create a homestead one must first *establish a family.* (In some states a single person may establish a homestead.) The family must *occupy the premises as its residence.* The head of the family must *own or lease the property.* In some states the homestead interest attaches by operation of law, but in others the family must protect its homestead interest by filing a notice as required by local statute.

In a few states the entire homestead is exempt from being sold. Usually the homestead merely reserves a certain amount of money for the family in the event of a court sale. For example, if the state homestead exemption is $25,000 and a court sale brings $40,000 for a property, the homeowner would receive the first $25,000 of the proceeds and the remaining $15,000 would be applied to the homeowner's debts. This basic example assumes that there are no unpaid taxes, mortgage liens or mechanics' liens (all of which are exceptions to homestead protection). If such debts were outstanding, they would be paid before the family received any share. A sale would not be ordered if the amount to be realized would cover no more than debts secured by the home (such as a mortgage) and the amount of the exemption.

Encumbrances

An **encumbrance** is *anything* that affects title to real estate (see Figure 6.4). It is a right or an interest held by a party who is not the fee owner of the property. An encumbrance may lessen the value or obstruct the use of the property, but it does not necessarily prevent a transfer of title. Encumbrances include liens, restrictions, easements and other interests.

Liens

A **lien** *is a charge against property that provides security for a debt or obligation of the property owner.* If the obligation is not repaid, the lienholder, or creditor, has the right to have it paid out of the debtor's property, usually from the proceeds of a court-ordered sale. Real estate taxes, mortgages and trust deeds, judgments and mechanics' liens (for people who have furnished labor or materials in the construction or repair of real estate) all represent possible liens against an owner's real estate. Liens are discussed in detail in Chapter 9.

Restrictions

Deed restrictions (also referred to as *covenants, conditions* and *restrictions*) are private agreements that affect the use of land. They are usually imposed by an owner of real estate when property is sold and are included in the seller's deed to the buyer. Typically deed restrictions are imposed by a developer or subdivider to maintain specific standards in a subdivision, and they are listed in the original development plans for the subdivision filed in the public record. Deed restrictions are discussed further in Chapter 19.

Easements

An **easement** *is the right to use the land of another for a particular purpose.* An easement right may be in any portion of land, including the airspace above a parcel.

Appurtenant easement. An easement that is annexed to the ownership of one parcel and allows this owner the use of a neighbor's land is called an appurtenant

Figure 6.4
Encumbrances

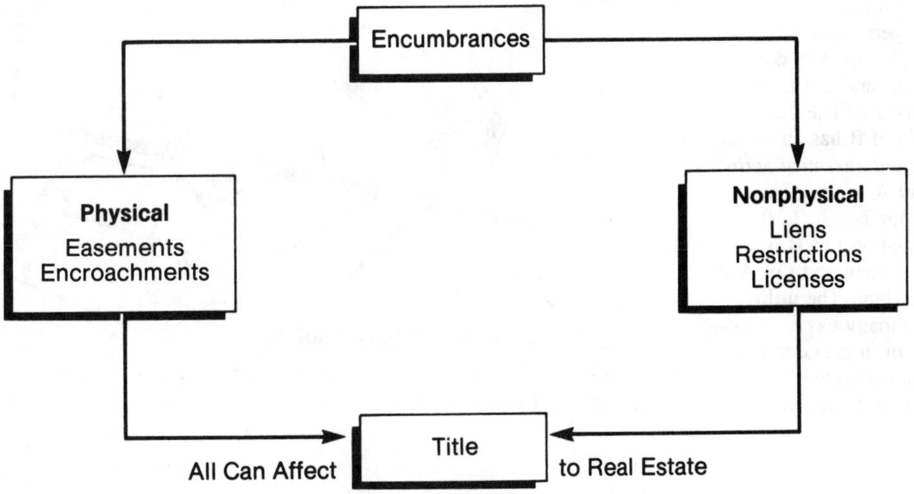

easement. For such an easement to exist there must be two adjacent tracts of land owned by different parties. The tract over which the easement runs is known as the *servient tenement;* the tract that benefits is known as the *dominant tenement.*

For example, if A and B own properties in a lake resort community and only A's property borders the lake, A may grant B an easement across A's property to give B access to the beach (see Figure 6.5). A's property is the servient tenement, and B's property is the dominant tenement. Conversely, B may grant A an easement across B's property so that A can have access to the road. In this situation B's property is the servient tenement and A's property is the dominant tenement.

An appurtenant easement is part of the dominant tenement, and if the dominant tenement is conveyed to another party the easement transfers with the title. An easement is said to run with the land. That is, it is an encumbrance on property, and unless the holder of the dominant tenement somehow releases that right it will transfer with the deed of the dominant tenement forever.

Party wall easements. A **party wall** can be an exterior wall of a building that straddles the boundary line between two owners' lots, with half of the wall on each lot, or it can be merely a commonly shared partition wall between two properties. Each lot owner owns the half of the wall on his or her lot, and each has an appurtenant easement in the other half of the wall. A written party wall agreement must be used to create the easement rights. Expenses to build and maintain the wall are usually shared. A party driveway shared by and partly on the land of adjoining owners must also be created by written agreement, specifying responsibility for expenses.

Figure 6.5
Easements

The owner of Lot A has an *appurtenant easement* across Lot B to gain access to his property from the paved road. Lot A is dominant, and Lot B is servient. The owner of Lot B has an *appurtenant easement* across Lot A to gain access to the beach. In this situation Lot B is dominant and Lot A is servient. The utility company has an *easement in gross* across both parcels of land for its power lines.

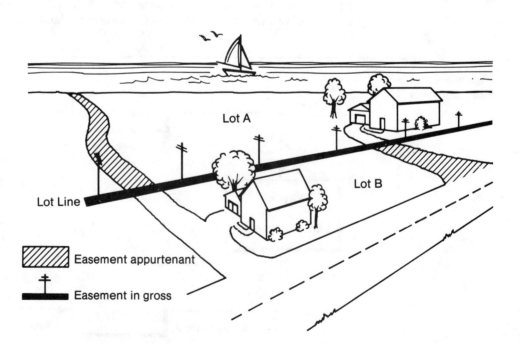

Easement in gross. *A mere personal interest* in or right to use the land of another is an **easement in gross.** Examples are the easement rights a railroad has in its right-of-way or the right-of-way for a utility company's pipeline or power line. Commercial easements in gross may be assigned or conveyed. However, personal easements in gross usually are not assignable and terminate upon the death of the easement owner. Easements in gross are often confused with the similar personal privilege of license, discussed later in this chapter.

Creating an easement. An easement is commonly created by written agreement between the parties establishing the easement right. Easements may also be created by *express grant* in a deed from the owner of the property over which the easement will run or by *express reservation* by the grantor in a deed of conveyance reserving an easement over the sold land. Three other ways that an easement can be created are discussed below.

An **easement by necessity** or *easement by operation of law* arises because owners should have rights of ingress to and egress from their property—they cannot be landlocked (without permanent access). The easement is usually implied over an adjoining parcel owned by the person who sold or gave the landlocked parcel or, if that is not possible, over an adjoining parcel that provides the most efficient road access.

When a claimant has made use of another's land for a period of time defined by state law usually from ten to 20 years, an **easement by prescription** or *prescriptive easement* can be acquired. The claimant's use must have been continuous, exclusive and without the owner's approval. Also, the use must have been visible, open and notorious so that the owner could readily learn of it.

Successive periods of continuous occupation by different parties may be tacked on, or combined, to reach the prescriptive period so that a party not in possession of the property for the entire statutory period can successfully establish a claim for an easement by prescription. However, the parties must have been successors in interest, such as an ancestor and his or her heir, a landlord and tenant or a seller and buyer.

The concept of an easement by prescription is based on state statutes relating to adverse possession, under which a claimant can obtain title to property rather than just an easement. Adverse possession is discussed in detail in Chapter 11.

An easement by condemnation is acquired by operation of law for a public purpose, such as pipeline location, through the power of eminent domain. As with any exercise of eminent domain, the owner of the servient tenement must be compensated for any loss in property value.

Terminating an easement. Easements may be terminated:

1. when the owner of either the dominant or the servient tenement becomes the owner of both and the properties are merged under one legal description (termination by merger);

2. when the owner of the dominant tenement releases the easement right to the owner of the servient tenement;

3. when the owner of the dominant tenement physically abandons the easement (the intention of the parties is the determining factor);

4. by nonuse of a prescriptive easement by its owner;

5. by adverse possession of the dominant tenement by the owner of the servient tenement;

6. by destruction of the servient tenement (such as the demolition of a party wall);

7. by court decision under a suit to quiet title against someone claiming an easement; or

8. by excessive use (such as when a residential use is converted to a commercial use).

Licenses

A personal privilege to enter the land of another for a specific purpose is a **license.** Examples include permission to park in a neighbor's driveway or erect a billboard, and the privileges that are granted by the purchase of a ticket for the theater or a sporting event. A license differs from an easement in that *it can be terminated or canceled.* If a right to use another's property is given orally or informally, it will generally be considered a license rather than a personal easement in gross. A license ceases upon the death of either party and is revoked by the sale of the land by the licensor.

Encroachments

When a building (or some portion of it) or a fence or driveway illegally *extends beyond the land of its owner* and covers some land of an adjoining owner or a street or alley, an **encroachment** occurs. Encroachments are usually disclosed by either a physical inspection of the property or a spot survey. (A spot survey shows the location of all improvements located on a property and whether any improvements extend over the lot lines.) If the building on a lot encroaches on neighboring land, the neighbor may be able either to recover damages or to secure removal of the portion of the building that encroaches. Encroachments of long standing (for the prescriptive period) may give rise to easements by prescription.

In Practice . . .

Because an undisclosed encroachment could make a title unmarketable, such an encroachment should be noted in a listing agreement and the sales contract. Encroachments are not disclosed by the usual title evidence provided in a real estate sale unless *a survey is submitted while the title examination is being made.*

Water Rights

The ownership of water and the land adjacent to it is determined by either the doctrines of riparian and littoral rights or the doctrine of prior appropriation.

Riparian Rights

Many states subscribe to the common law doctrine of **riparian rights.** These rights are granted to owners of land located along the course of a river, stream or lake. Such an owner has the unrestricted right to use the water, provided such use does not interrupt or alter the flow of the water or contaminate the water. In addition, an owner of land that borders a nonnavigable waterway owns the land under the water to the exact center of the waterway. Land adjoining navigable rivers is usually owned to the water's edge, with the state holding title to the submerged land (see Figure 6.6). Navigable waters are considered public highways in which the public has an easement or right to travel. The laws governing and defining riparian rights differ from state to state.

Figure 6.6
Riparian Rights

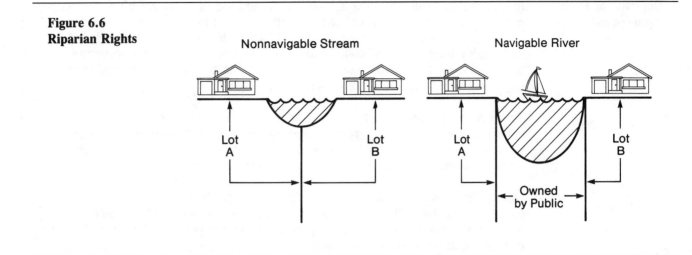

Littoral Rights

Closely related to riparian rights are the **littoral rights** of owners whose land borders on large, navigable lakes, seas and oceans. Owners with littoral rights enjoy unrestricted use of available waters but own the land adjacent to the water only up to the mean ("average") high-water mark (see Figure 6.7). All land below this point is owned by the government.

Riparian and littoral rights are appurtenant (attached) to the land and cannot be retained when the property is sold. The right to use the water belongs to whoever owns the bordering land and cannot be retained by a former owner after the land is sold.

Where land adjoins streams or rivers, an owner is entitled to all land created through **accretion**—increases in the land resulting from the deposit of soil by the natural action of the water. (Such deposits are called *alluvion* or *alluvium*.) If water recedes, new land is acquired by *reliction*.

Likewise, an owner may lose land through *erosion*, the gradual and imperceptible wearing away of the land caused by flowing water (or other natural forces). This contrasts with **avulsion,** the sudden removal of soil by an act of nature.

Figure 6.7
Littoral Rights

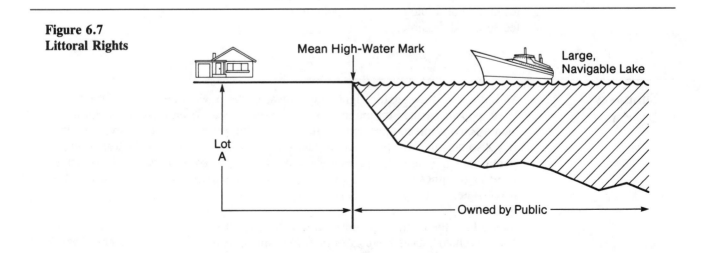

Doctrine of Prior Appropriation

In states where water is scarce the ownership and use of water are often determined by the doctrine of **prior appropriation.** Under this doctrine *the right to use any water, with the exception of limited domestic use, is controlled by the state rather than by the adjacent landowner.* Ownership of the land bordering bodies of water in states recognizing this doctrine is generally determined in the same way as riparian and littoral ownership.

To secure water rights a person must show a beneficial use for the water, such as crop irrigation, and obtain a permit from the proper state department. Although statutes governing prior appropriation vary from state to state, the priority of water rights is usually determined by the oldest recorded permit date.

Once granted, water rights may be perfected through the legal processes prescribed by the individual state. When the water right is perfected, it generally becomes attached to the land of the person holding the permit. The permit holder may sell such a water right to another party.

Issuance of a water permit does not grant access to the water source. All access rights-of-way over the land of another (easements) must be obtained from the property owner.

Key Terms

accretion	freehold estate
avulsion	future interest
curtesy	homestead
deed restrictions	leasehold estate
dower	license
easement	lien
easement by necessity	life estate
easement by prescription	littoral rights
easement in gross	party wall
eminent domain	police power
encroachment	prior appropriation
encumbrance	remainder
escheat	reversion
estate in land	riparian rights
fee simple absolute	taxation
fee simple defeasible	

Summary

An individual's ownership rights are subject to the powers held by government. These powers include the police power, by which states can enact legislation such as environmental protection laws and zoning ordinances. The government may also acquire privately owned land for public use through the power of eminent domain. Real estate taxes are imposed to raise government funds. When a property becomes ownerless, ownership of the property may revert, or escheat, to the state.

An estate is the degree, quantity, nature and extent of interest a person holds in land. Freehold estates are estates of indeterminate length. Less-than-freehold estates are called leasehold estates, and they concern tenants.

A freehold estate may be a fee simple estate or a life estate. A fee simple estate can be absolute or defeasible upon the happening of some event. A conventional life estate is created by the owner of a fee estate; a legal life estate is created by law. Legal life estates include curtesy, dower and homestead.

Encumbrances against real estate may be in the form of liens, deed restrictions, easements, licenses and encroachments.

An easement is the right acquired by one person to use another's real estate. Easements are classified as interests in real estate but are not estates in land. Appurtenant easements involve two separately owned tracts. The tract benefited is known as the dominant tenement; the tract that is subject to the easement is called the servient tenement. An easement in gross is a personal right, such as that granted to utility companies to maintain poles, wires and pipelines.

Easements may be created by agreement, express grant or reservation in a deed, necessity, prescription or condemnation. They can be terminated by merger of both interests, by release or by abandonment of the easement, by nonuse of a prescriptive easement, adverse possession, destruction, excessive use or a lawsuit.

A license is permission to enter another's property for a specific purpose. A license is usually created orally, is temporary and can be revoked.

An encroachment is an unauthorized use of another's real estate.

Ownership of land encompasses not only the land itself but also the right to use the water on or adjacent to it. Many states subscribe to the common law doctrine of riparian rights, which gives the owner of land adjacent to a nonnavigable stream ownership of the stream to its midpoint. Littoral rights are held by owners of land bordering large lakes and oceans and include rights to the water and ownership of the land up to the high-water mark. In states where water is scarce water use is often decided by the doctrine of prior appropriation. Under prior appropriation water belongs to the state and it is allocated to users who have obtained permits.

−6

Questions

1. The right of a governmental body to take ownership of real estate for public use is called:

   a. escheat.
   b. eminent domain.
   c. condemnation.
   d. police power.

2. A purchaser of real estate learned that his ownership rights will continue forever and that no other person claims to be the owner or has any ownership control over the property. This person owns a:

   a. fee simple interest.
   b. life estate.
   c. determinable fee estate.
   d. fee simple on condition subsequent.

3. J owned the fee simple title to a vacant lot adjacent to a hospital and was persuaded to make a gift of the lot. She wanted to have some control over its use, so her attorney prepared her deed to convey ownership of the lot to the hospital "so long as it is used for hospital purposes." After completion of the gift the hospital will own a:

   a. fee simple absolute estate.
   b. license.
   c. fee simple determinable.
   d. leasehold estate.

4. After D had purchased his house and moved in, he discovered that his neighbor regularly used D's driveway to reach a garage located on the neighbor's property. D's attorney explained that ownership of the neighbor's real estate includes an easement over the driveway. D's property is properly called:

   a. the dominant tenement.
   b. a freehold.
   c. a leasehold.
   d. the servient tenement.

5. A *license* is an example of a(n):

   a. easement.
   b. encroachment.
   c. encumbrance.
   d. restriction.

6. Which one of the following best describes a life estate?

   a. An estate conveyed to A for the life of Z
   b. An estate held by A and B in joint tenancy
   c. An estate without condition
   d. A fee simple estate

7. When a homeowner who is entitled by state law to a homestead exemption is sued by his or her creditors, the creditors:

   a. can have the court sell the home and apply the full proceeds of sale to the debts.
   b. have no right to have the debtor's home sold.
   c. can force the debtor to sell the home to pay them.
   d. can request a court sale and apply the sale proceeds, in excess of the statutory exemption and secured debts, to the unsecured debts.

8. If the owner of real estate does not take action against a trespasser before the statutory period has passed, the trespasser may acquire:

   a. an easement by necessity.
   b. a license.
   c. an easement by implication of law.
   d. a prescriptive easement.

9. Many states determine water use by allocating water to users who hold recorded beneficial-use permits. This type of water use privilege is called:

   a. riparian rights.
   b. littoral rights.
   c. the doctrine of prior appropriation.
   d. the doctrine of highest and best use.

10. All of the following are powers of the government *except:*

    a. condemnation.
    b. police power.
    c. eminent domain.
    d. taxation.

11. Property deeded to a school "for educational purposes only" conveys a:

    a. fee simple absolute.
    b. fee simple on condition precedent.
    c. leasehold interest.
    d. fee simple on condition subsequent.

12. T has the legal right to pass over the land owned by his neighbor. This is an:

    a. estate in land.   c. emblement.

    b. easement.   d. encroachment.

13. All of the following are legal life estates *except:*

    a. leasehold.   c. homestead.

    b. curtesy.   d. dower.

14. A father conveys ownership of his residence to his daughter but reserves for himself a life estate in the residence. The interest the daughter owns during her father's lifetime is:

    a. pur autre vie.   c. a reversion.

    b. a remainder.   d. a leasehold.

15. K has fenced his property. The fence extends one foot over his lot line onto the property of a neighbor, M. The fence is an example of:

    a. a license.

    b. an encroachment.

    c. an easement by necessity.

    d. an easement by prescription.

16. A homeowner may be allowed certain protection from judgments of creditors as a result of his state's:

    a. littoral rights.   c. homestead rights.

    b. curtesy rights.   d. dower rights.

17. K has permission from X to hunt on X's property during dove season. K has:

    a. an easement by necessity.

    b. an easement by condemnation.

    c. riparian rights.

    d. a license.

18. Encumbrances on real estate:

    a. include easements, encroachments and licenses.

    b. make it impossible to sell the encumbered property.

    c. must all be removed before the title can be transferred.

    d. are of no monetary value to those who own them.

19. A tenant in an apartment holds a:

    a. tenancy in common.

    b. tenancy by the entirety.

    c. freehold interest.

    d. leasehold interest.

How Ownership Is Held

Forms of Ownership

A fee simple estate may be held in **severalty,** where title is held by one owner, in concurrent ownership or co-ownership, where title is held by two or more persons, or in **trust,** where title is held by a third person for the benefit of another.

Form of ownership is important to the real estate broker's work because *when a property is sold it determines who must sign the various documents involved* (listing contract, acceptance of offer to purchase, deed). Also *the purchaser must determine in what form to take title.* For example, if there are two or more purchasers, they may take title as tenants in common or as joint tenants. (Married purchasers' choices are governed by state laws.)

The forms of ownership available are controlled by the laws of the state in which the land is located. When questions about these forms are raised by the parties to a transaction, the real estate broker should recommend that the parties seek legal advice. Table 7.1 shows the forms of ownership recognized by each of the states.

Ownership in Severalty

When title to real estate is *vested in* (presently owned by) one individual (a natural person) or one organization (a legal person), that person owns the property *in severalty* (as the owner is "severed" or "cut off" from other owners). That person is also referred to as the *sole owner.* Various states have special laws that affect title held in severalty by either a husband or a wife. In some states, when either the husband or wife owns property in severalty, it is still necessary for the nonowning spouse to sign documents to release dower or curtesy rights in states that have such rights, to release homestead rights in states that provide a homestead exemption for homeowners or when the nonowning spouse is a minor. In other states only the owner's signature is needed.

Co-Ownership

When title to one parcel of real estate is vested in two or more persons, those parties are said to be *co-owners,* or *concurrent owners,* of the property. The forms of co-ownership most commonly recognized by the various states, each with unique legal characteristics, are tenancy in common, joint tenancy, tenancy by the entirety, community property and partnership property.

Table 7.1
Chart of Ownership

State	Forms of Ownership						
	Severalty	Concurrent					
	Individual	Tenancy in Common	Joint Tenancy	Tenancy by the Entirety	Community Property	Trust	Condominium
Alabama	•	•	•			•	•
Alaska	•	•		•		•	•
Arizona	•	•	•		•	•	•
Arkansas	•	•	•	•		•	•
California	•	•	•		•	•	•
Colorado	•	•	•			•	•
Connecticut	•	•	•			•	•
Delaware	•	•	•	•		•	•
District of Columbia	•	•	•	•		•	•
Florida	•	•	•	•		•	•
Georgia	•	•	•			•	•
Hawaii	•	•	•	•		•	•
Idaho	•	•	•		•	•	•
Illinois	•	•	•			•	•
Indiana	•	•	•	•		•	•
Iowa	•	•	•			•	•
Kansas	•	•	•			•	•
Kentucky	•	•	•	•		•	•
Louisiana[1]						•	•
Maine	•	•	•			•	•
Maryland	•	•	•	•		•	•
Massachusetts	•	•	•	•		•	•
Michigan	•	•	•	•		•	•
Minnesota	•	•	•			•	•
Mississippi	•	•	•	•		•	•
Missouri	•	•	•	•		•	•
Montana	•	•	•			•	•
Nebraska	•	•	•			•	•
Nevada	•	•	•		•	•	•
New Hampshire	•	•	•			•	•
New Jersey	•	•	•	•		•	•
New Mexico	•	•	•		•	•	•
New York	•	•	•	•		•	•
North Carolina	•	•	•			•	•
North Dakota	•	•	•			•	•
Ohio[2]	•	•		•		•	•
Oklahoma	•	•	•	•		•	•
Oregon	•	•		•		•	•
Pennsylvania	•	•	•	•		•	•
Rhode Island	•	•	•	•		•	•
South Carolina	•	•	•		•	•	•
South Dakota	•	•	•			•	•
Tennessee	•	•	•			•	•
Texas	•	•	•			•	•
Utah	•	•	•	•		•	•
Vermont	•	•	•	•		•	•
Virginia	•	•	•	•		•	•
Washington	•	•	•		•	•	•
West Virginia	•	•	•	•		•	•
Wisconsin[3]	•	•	•			•	•
Wyoming	•	•	•	•		•	•

[1]In Louisiana, real estate can be owned by one person and by two or more persons, but these ownership interests are created by Louisiana statute. There are no estates comparable to those of joint tenancy, tenancy by the entirety, or community property, nor is there any statutory estate giving surviving co-owners the right of survivorship. Two or more persons may be co-owners under indivision, or joint, ownership.
[2]Ohio does not recognize joint tenancy, but permits a special form of survivorship by deed through an instrument commonly called a "joint and survivorship deed."
[3]As of 1986, Wisconsin recognizes "marital property" that is similar to community property.

Tenancy in Common

A parcel of real estate may be owned by two or more people as **tenants in common.** The ownership interest of a tenant in common is an **undivided interest;** there is a *unity of possession* between the **co-owners.** Although a tenant in common may hold, say, a one-half or one-third interest in a property, it is impossible to distinguish physically which specific half or third of the property the tenant in common owns. It is the *ownership* interest and *not* the property that is divided. The deed creating a tenancy in common may or may not state the fractional interest held by each co-owner; if no fractions are stated, the tenants are presumed to hold equal shares. For example, if five people hold title, each would own an undivided one-fifth interest.

Each owner in a tenancy in common can sell, convey, mortgage or transfer his or her interest without consent of the other co-owners. Upon the death of a co-owner that tenant's undivided interest passes to his or her heirs (see Figure 7.1).

When two or more people acquire title to real estate and the deed does not stipulate the tenancy, then by operation of law the new owners usually acquire title as tenants in common. But if the deed is made to a husband and wife with no further explanation, this assumption may not apply. In some states a deed made to a husband and wife creates a tenancy by the entirety; in others, community property; and in at least one state, a joint tenancy. It is therefore important to know the legal interpretation of such a situation under your state law.

Joint Tenancy

Most states recognize some form of **joint tenancy** in property owned by two or more people. The feature that distinguishes a joint tenancy from a tenancy in common is the **right of survivorship.** The death of one of the joint tenants does not destroy the ownership unit; it only reduces by one the number of people who make up the unit. The joint tenancy continues until there is only one owner, who then holds title in severalty. The last surviving joint tenant has the same rights to dispose of the property as any sole owner (see Figure 7.2).

Note that the right of survivorship refers to the rights of the co-owners of the joint tenancy, not to their heirs. As each successive joint tenant dies, the surviving joint tenant(s) acquire(s) the interest of the deceased joint tenant. The last survivor takes title in severalty and then has all of the rights of individual ownership, including the right to have the property pass to his or her heirs.

Figure 7.1
Tenancy in Common

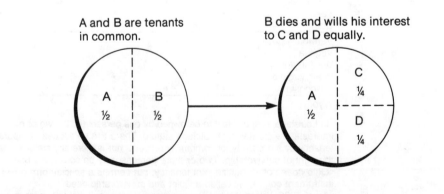

A and B are tenants in common.

B dies and wills his interest to C and D equally.

Figure 7.2
Joint Tenancy with
Right of Survivorship

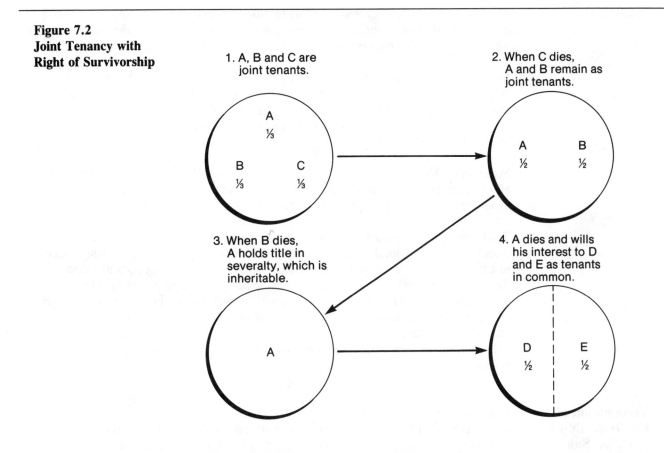

1. A, B and C are joint tenants.

A
⅓

B
⅓

C
⅓

2. When C dies, A and B remain as joint tenants.

A
½

B
½

3. When B dies, A holds title in severalty, which is inheritable.

A

4. A dies and wills his interest to D and E as tenants in common.

D
½

E
½

In Practice . . .

The form under which title is to be taken (particularly by a married couple) should always be discussed with an attorney. Joint tenancy should not be used as a substitute for a will.

Creating joint tenancies. A joint tenancy can be created only by grant or purchase (with a deed) or by devise (by will). It cannot be implied or created by operation of law. The deed must specifically state the parties' intention to create a joint tenancy, and the parties must be explicit identified as joint tenants. For example, typical wording in a deed creating a joint tenancy would be ''to A and B as joint tenants and not as tenants in common.'' Some states, however, have abolished the right of survivorship as the distinguishing characteristic of joint tenancy. In these states the deed must also explicitly indicate the intention to create the right of survivorship for that right to exist. In such cases appropriate wording might be ''to A and B and to the survivor of them, his or her heirs and assigns, as joint tenants.''

Four ''unities'' are required to create a joint tenancy. There must be:

1. unity of *possession*—all joint tenants holding an undivided right to possession;

2. unity of *interest*—all joint tenants holding equal ownership interests;

3. unity of *time*—all joint tenants acquiring their interests at the same time; and

4. unity of *title*—all joint tenants acquiring their interests by the same document.

The four unities (PITT) are present when title is acquired by *one deed, executed and delivered at one time and conveying equal interests to all of the parties, who hold undivided possession of the property as joint tenants.*

In many states, if real estate is owned in severalty by a person who wishes to create a joint tenancy between himself or herself and others, the owner will have to convey the property to an intermediary (usually called a *nominee,* or *straw man*), and the nominee must convey it back, naming all the parties as joint tenants in the deed.

Some states have eliminated this "legal fiction" by allowing an owner in severalty to execute a deed to himself or herself and others "as joint tenants and not as tenants in common" and thereby create a valid joint tenancy.

Terminating joint tenancies. A joint tenancy is destroyed when any one of the essential unities of joint tenancy is terminated. Thus, while a joint tenant is free to convey his or her interest in the jointly held property, doing so will destroy the unity of interest and, in turn, the joint tenancy as it applied to the conveying tenant. Rights of other joint tenants will be unaffected. For example, if *A, B* and *C* hold title as joint tenants and *A* conveys her interest to *D*, then *D* will own an undivided one-third interest as a tenant in common with *B* and *C*, who will continue to own their undivided two-thirds interest as joint tenants (see Figure 7.3).

Termination of Co-Ownership by Partition Suit

Concurrent owners who wish to terminate their co-ownership may file in court a suit to **partition** the land. The right of partition is a legal way to dissolve co-ownership when the parties do not voluntarily agree to its termination. If the court determines that the land cannot be divided physically into parts, it will order the real estate sold and divide the proceeds of the sale among the co-owners according to their fractional interests.

Ownership by Married Couples

Tenancy by the entirety. Some states allow **tenancy by the entirety,** a special form of tenancy in which the owners are husband and wife. Each spouse has an equal, undivided interest in the property. Upon the death of one spouse the

**Figure 7.3
Combination of
Tenancies**

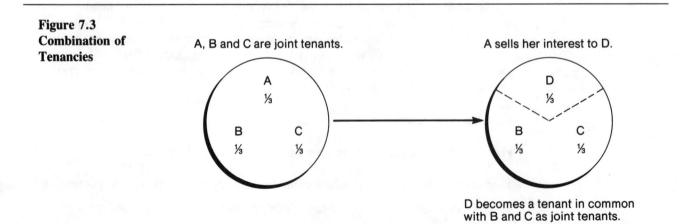

A, B and C are joint tenants.

A sells her interest to D.

D becomes a tenant in common
with B and C as joint tenants.

tenancy operates like a joint tenancy—full title automatically passes to the surviving spouse.

In a tenancy by the entirety the owners must be husband and wife, and they have rights of survivorship. During the owners' lives title can be conveyed *only by a deed signed by both parties* (one party cannot convey a one-half interest). Generally there is no right to partition. Under early common law a husband and wife were considered one legal person, so real estate owned by a husband and wife as tenants by the entirety is considered to be owned by one indivisible unit.

Under the common law a grant to husband and wife created a tenancy by the entirety even when no form of ownership was specified. Some states that recognize it now require that the intention to create a tenancy by the entirety be specifically stated. If it is not stated in the original document, a tenancy in common can result in many states.

A tenancy by the entirety may be terminated by the death of either spouse, divorce (leaving the parties as tenants in common), mutual agreement or execution proceedings in favor of a *joint* creditor of husband and wife.

Community property rights. The concept of community property originated in Spanish law rather than English common law and was adopted by Arizona, California, Idaho, Louisiana, Nevada, New Mexico, Texas and Washington. The community property laws of these states vary widely.

Community property laws are based on the concept that a husband and wife, rather than merging into one entity, are equal partners in the marriage. Thus any property acquired during a marriage is considered to be obtained by mutual effort. Community property states recognize two kinds of property. **Separate property** is that owned solely by either spouse before the marriage or acquired by gift or inheritance during the marriage. Separate property also includes any property purchased with separate funds during the marriage. Any income earned from a person's separate property generally remains part of his or her separate property. Property classified as sole and separate can be mortgaged or conveyed by the owning spouse without the signature of the nonowning spouse.

Community property consists of all other property, real and personal, acquired by either spouse during the marriage. Any conveyance or encumbrance of community property requires the signatures of *both* spouses. Upon the death of one spouse the survivor automatically owns one-half of the community property. The other half is distributed according to the decedent's will. If the decedent died without a will, the other half is inherited by the surviving spouse or by the decedent's other heirs, depending on state law. Community property does *not* automatically provide survivorship as joint tenancy does.

Examples of Co-Ownership

To clarify the concepts of co-ownership further, note the following examples of co-ownership arrangements:

1. A deed conveys title to A and B. The intention of the parties is not stated, so generally ownership as tenants in common is created. If A dies, her one-half interest will pass to her heirs.

2. A deed conveying title one-third to C and two-thirds to D creates a tenancy in common, with each owner having the fractional interest specified.

3. A deed to H and W as husband and wife creates a tenancy by the entirety, community property or other interests between the husband and wife as provided by state law.

4. A conveyance of real estate of two people (not husband and wife) by such wording as "to Y and Z, as joint tenants and not as tenants in common" may create a joint tenancy ownership. Upon the death of Y the title to the property usually passes to Z by right of survivorship. In those states that do not recognize the right of survivorship, additional provisions are required (such as "and to the survivor and his or her heirs and assigns").

Trusts

In most states title to real estate can be held in a trust. For a trust to be created the title to the real estate involved must be conveyed by the trustor (the person originating the trust) to a trustee, who will own the property for one or more people or legal entities, called beneficiaries (see Figure 7.4). The trustee is a *fiduciary*, one who acts in confidence or trust, and has a special legal relationship with the beneficiary or beneficiaries. The trustee can be either an individual or a corporation, such as a trust company. The trustee has only as much power and authority as is given by the document that creates the trust. Such a document may be a trust agreement, will or deed in trust. Ownership can be held under living or testamentary trusts or land trusts. In addition, real estate may be owned by investors in a *real estate investment trust*, which is discussed in Chapter 22.

Living and Testamentary Trusts

Property owners may provide for their own financial care and/or that of their families by establishing a trust. Such trusts may be created by agreement during a property owner's lifetime (living) or established by will after his or her death (testamentary).

The trustor makes an agreement with a trustee (usually a corporate trustee) by which the trustor conveys assets (real and/or personal property) to the trustee with the understanding that the trustee will assume certain duties. Those duties may include the care and investment of the trust assets to produce an income. After payment of operating expenses and trustee's fees the income is paid to or used for the benefit of the beneficiary. The trust may continue for the lifetime of the beneficiary, or the assets can be distributed when the beneficiary reaches a predetermined age or when other conditions of the trust agreement are met.

Figure 7.4
Trust Ownership

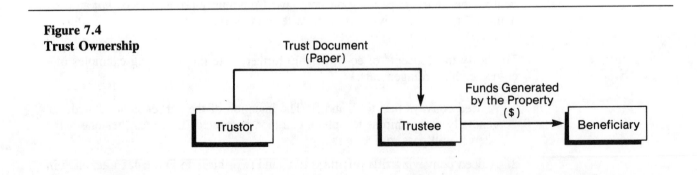

Land Trusts

A few states permit the establishment of land trusts in which real estate is the only asset. As in all trusts, the title to the property is conveyed to a trustee and the beneficial interest belongs to the beneficiary, who, in the case of land trusts, is usually also the trustor. While the beneficial interest is *personal property,* the beneficiary retains management and control of the real property and has the right of possession and the right to any income or proceeds from its sale.

The term *trust deed* can be used to mean both a deed *in* trust (which relates to the creation of a living, testamentary or land trust) and a deed *of* trust (which is a financing document similar to a mortgage). Because these documents are *not* interchangeable, licensees should exercise caution in using the term *trust deed* to avoid misunderstanding.

One of the distinguishing characteristics of a land trust is that the *public records usually do not indicate the beneficiary's identity.* A land trust may thus be used for secrecy when assembling separate parcels, and there are other benefits as well. A beneficial interest can be transferred by assignment, making the formalities of a deed unnecessary. A collateral assignment can be made (the property pledged as security for a loan) without having a mortgage recorded. Real property is subject to the laws of the state in which it is located. But since the beneficiary's interest is personal, it will pass at the beneficiary's death under the laws of the state in which the beneficiary resided. If the deceased owned property in several states, additional probate costs and inheritance taxes can thus be avoided.

Usually only individuals create land trusts, but corporations as well as individuals can be beneficiaries. A land trust ordinarily continues for a definite term, such as 20 years. If the beneficiary does not extend the trust term when it expires, the trustee is usually obligated to sell the real estate and return the net proceeds to the beneficiary.

Ownership of Real Estate by Business Organizations

A business organization is an entity that exists independently of the people who are its members. Ownership by a business organization makes it possible for many people to hold an interest in the same parcel of real estate. Investors may be organized to finance a real estate project in various ways. Some provide for the real estate to be owned by the entity; others provide for direct ownership by the investors.

Partnerships

An association of two or more people to carry on a business as co-owners and share in the business's profits and losses is a **partnership.** In a **general partnership** all partners may participate to some extent in the operation and management of the business and may be held personally liable for business losses and obligations. A **limited partnership** includes one or more general partners as well as limited partners. The business is run by the general partner or partners. The limited partners are not legally permitted to participate, and each can be held liable for business losses *only* to the extent of his or her investment. The limited partnership is a popular method of organizing investors in a real estate project.

Under common law a partnership is not a legal entity and cannot own real estate. Title must be vested in the partners as individuals in a tenancy in common or joint tenancy, not in the partnership. Most states, however, have adopted the *Uniform Partnership Act,* under which realty may be held in the partnership name, and the *Uniform Limited Partnership Act,* which establishes the legality of the limited partnership form and also provides that realty may be held in the partnership name. Still, profits and losses are passed through the partnership to the partners, whose individual tax situations determine their tax liabilities.

General partnerships are dissolved and must be reorganized if one partner dies, withdraws or goes bankrupt. In a limited partnership the agreement creating the partnership may provide for the continuation of the organization upon the death or withdrawal of one of the partners.

Corporations

A **corporation** is a legal or artificial person created under the laws of the state from which it receives its charter. A corporation is managed and operated by its *board of directors.* The charter sets forth the powers of the corporation, including its right to buy and sell real estate after passage of a resolution to that effect by its board of directors. Some charters permit a corporation to purchase real estate for any purpose; others limit such purchases to land that is needed to fulfill the entity's corporate purpose.

As a legal entity a corporation exists in perpetuity until it is formally dissolved. The death of one of the officers or directors does not affect title to property owned by the corporation.

Individuals participate, or invest, in a corporation by purchasing stock. Because stock is *personal property,* stockholders do not have a direct ownership interest in real estate owned by a corporation. Each stockholder's liability for the corporation's losses is usually limited to the amount of his or her investment.

One of the main disadvantages of corporate ownership of income property is that the profits are subject to double taxation. As a legal entity a corporation must file an income tax return and pay tax on its profits. The portions of the remaining profits distributed to stockholders as dividends are taxed again as part of the stockholders' individual incomes.

Syndicates

Generally speaking, a **syndicate** is a *joining together of two or more people or firms to make and operate a real estate investment.* A syndicate is not in itself a legal entity; however, it may be organized into a number of ownership forms, including co-ownership (tenancy in common, joint tenancy), partnership, trust or corporation. A *joint venture* is a form of partnership in which two or more people or firms carry out a *single business project.* Joint ventures are characterized by a time limitation resulting from the fact that the joint venturers do not intend to establish a permanent relationship. These organizations are discussed further in Chapter 22.

co op — you own stock

Cooperatives, Condominiums and Time-Shares

During the first half of this century the nation's population grew rapidly and concentrated in the large urban areas. This concentration led to multiple-unit housing—high-rise apartment buildings in the center city and low-rise apartment complexes in adjoining suburbs. Initially these buildings were occupied by tenants under the traditional rental system. But the urge to ''own a part of the land,'' together with certain tax advantages that accrue to such ownership, led to *cooperative* ownership and, more recently, to the *condominium* form of ownership of multiple-unit buildings.

Cooperative Ownership

Under the usual **cooperative** arrangements title to land and building is held by a *corporation* or land trust. The building management sets a price for each unit in the building, and when a purchaser pays the agreed-upon price for a unit he or she receives stock in the corporation. The purchaser then becomes a stockholder and, *by virtue of that stock ownership, receives a proprietary* ("owner's") *lease* to his or her unit for the life of the corporation.

The cooperative building's real estate taxes are assessed against the corporation as owner. The mortgage note is signed by the corporation, creating one lien on the entire parcel of real estate. Taxes, mortgage interest and principal, and operating and maintenance expenses on the property are shared by the tenant/shareholders in the form of monthly assessments.

Thus, while the cooperative tenant/owners do not actually own an interest in real estate (they own stock, which is *personal property*), for all practical purposes they control the property through their stock ownership and their voice in the management of the corporation. For example, the bylaws of the corporation generally provide that each prospective purchaser of an apartment lease must be approved by an administrative board.

One disadvantage of cooperative ownership is particularly evident and must be considered. If enough owner/occupants become financially unable to make prompt payment of their monthly assessments, the corporation might be forced to allow mortgage and tax payments to go unpaid. Through such defaults the entire property could be ordered sold by court order in a foreclosure suit. Such a sale would usually destroy the interests of all occupant/shareholders, even those who have paid their assessments. These limitations have diminished the appeal of this form of ownership and resulted in greater preference for the condominium form. Another disadvantage is that some cooperatives provide that a tenant/owner can sell his or her interest back to the cooperative only at the original purchase price so that the cooperative gains any profits made on the resale. Sometimes the owner can sell to someone other than the cooperative, but the cooperative reserves the right to approve the sale.

In Practice . . .

In most states real estate brokers are prohibited from listing or selling cooperative interests in the open market because the owners own only personal property. Brokers who participate in these transactions must have a securities license that is appropriate for the type of cooperative interest involved.

Condominium Ownership

The **condominium** form of occupant ownership was popular in Europe for many years before gaining acceptance in the United States. Condominium laws, often called *horizontal property acts*, have been enacted in every state. Under these laws the owner of each unit holds a *fee simple title* to the unit and also a specified share of the indivisible parts of the building and land, known as the **common elements** (see Figure 7.5). The individual unit owners in a condominium own these common elements together as *tenants in common*. (State law usually provides that unit owners have *no right to partition*.)

The condominium form of ownership is usually used for residential buildings, though it is also used for commercial property, office buildings and multiuse buildings that contain offices and shops as well as residential units. Residential condominiums range from freestanding high-rise buildings to town houses, and the common ele-

**Figure 7.5
Condominium
Ownership**

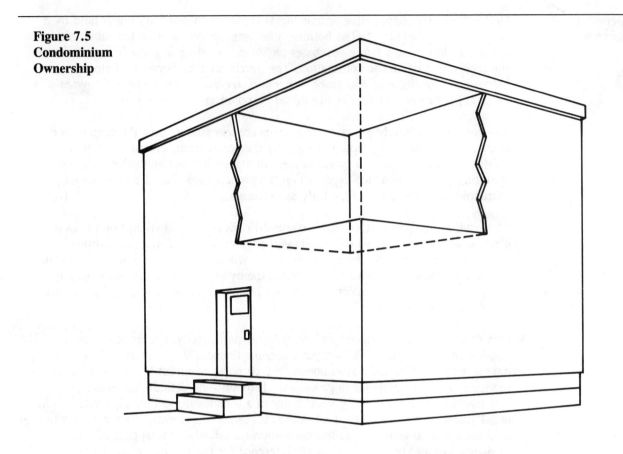

ments include such items as the land, exterior structure, hallways, elevators, stair-
ways and roof. In some instances (particularly with town house developments)
lawns and recreational facilities such as swimming pools, clubhouses, tennis courts
and golf courses may also be considered common elements.

Creation of a condominium. State laws usually specify that a condominium is
created when the owners or developers of the property execute and record a
declaration of its creation in the county where the property is located. The items
that must, by state law, be contained in or attached to the declaration generally
include a legal description of the land, a plat map illustrating and identifying each
unit, a list of the values of the land and of each unit, a list of the percentages
of undivided interest in all common areas and facilities assigned to each unit, a
copy of the condominium's bylaws and provisions for the establishment of a
condominium owners' association.

Ownership. Once the property is established as a condominium, each unit becomes a separate parcel of real estate that is *owned in fee simple and may be
held by one or more people in any type of ownership or tenancy recognized by
state law.* As such each unit may be dealt with in the same way as any other
parcel of real property. For example, unlike a cooperative, a condominium unit
can usually be sold or transferred to whomever the owner chooses, without approval of the condominium association. Some condominium properties, however,
provide for a "right of first refusal." An owner who wants to sell his or her
unit can list it with a real estate broker or offer it to the public directly. But if

the owner receives and accepts an offer, the owner must offer the unit at the same price to the other owners in the condominium project (and perhaps even the association). They have the right either to purchase the unit at the accepted price or to refuse it and allow the sale to be completed.

Real estate taxes are assessed and collected on each unit as an individual property. Default in the payment of taxes or a mortgage loan by one unit owner may result in a foreclosure sale of that owner's unit but does not affect the ownership of the other unit owners.

Operation and administration. The condominium property generally is administered by an association of unit owners according to the bylaws set forth in the declaration. The association may be governed by a board of directors or other official entity, manage the property on its own or engage a professional property manager to perform this function.

Acting through its board of directors or other officers, the association must enforce any rules it adopts regarding the cooperation and use of the property. The association is responsible for the maintenance, repair, cleaning and sanitation of the common elements and structural portions of the property. It must also maintain fire and extended-coverage insurance as well as liability insurance for those portions of the property.

Expenses incurred in fulfilling the association's responsibilities are paid by the unit owners in the form of monthly assessments collected by the owners' association. Such fees are assessed each unit owner. They are due monthly, quarterly, semiannually or annually, depending on the provisions of the bylaws. If the assessments are not paid, the association usually may seek a court-ordered judgment to have the property sold to cover the outstanding amount.

Time-Shared Ownership

Time-sharing allows multiple purchasers to buy interests in real estate—usually in a resort property—with each purchaser receiving the right to use the facilities for a certain period of time. A time-share estate includes a real property interest, while a time-share use does not.

A time-share estate consists of a fee simple interest. Once the property has been developed and sold, the owner's occupancy and use of the property is limited to the contractual period purchased; for example, the 17th complete week Sunday through Saturday of each calendar year. The owner is assessed for maintenance and common area expenses based on the relationship of his or her ownership period to the total number of ownership periods in the property. Time-share estates theoretically never end because of the real property interest; however, the physical life of the improvements is limited and must be looked at carefully when considering such a purchase.

The principal difference between a time-share estate and a time-share use lies in the interest transferred to an owner by the developer of the project. A time-share use consists of the right to occupy and use the facilities for a certain number of years (30 years is a common period); at the end of such time any rights in the property held by the owner terminate. In effect the developer has sold only a right of occupancy and use to the owner and not a fee simple interest.

Some time-sharing programs specify certain months or weeks of the year during which the owner can use the property. Others provide a rotation system under which the owner can occupy the unit during different times of the year in different years. Some include a "swapping" privilege for transferring the ownership period to another property to provide some variety for the owner. Time-shared properties typically are used for 50 weeks each year, with the remaining two weeks reserved for the maintenance of the improvements.

Membership camping is similar to a time-share use in that the owner has the right to use the facilities of the developer. However, there is usually an open range area available with minimal improvements (such as camper/trailer hookups and restrooms). Normally the owner is not limited to a specific time for use of the property; use is limited only by weather and access.

In Practice . . .   *The laws governing the development and sale of time-share units are generally complex and vary substantially from state to state. In many states time-share properties are now subject to subdivision requirements. Familiarity with such provisions of real estate statutes helps brokers minimize problems when dealing with such specialized properties.*

Key Terms

common elements	right of survivorship
community property	separate property
condominium	severalty
cooperative	syndicate
corporation	tenancy by the entirety
general partnership	tenancy in common
joint tenancy	time-share
limited partnership	trust
partition	undivided interest
partnership	

Summary

Sole ownership, or ownership in severalty, indicates that title is held by one natural or legal person. Under co-ownership title can be held concurrently by more than one person in several ways.

Under tenancy in common each party can hold a separate title but shares possession with other tenants. An individual owner may sell his or her interest. Upon death a tenant in common's interest passes to the tenant's heirs. There are no special requirements to create this interest. When two or more parties hold title to real estate, they will hold title as tenants in common unless another intention is expressed. Joint tenancy indicates two or more owners with the right of survivorship. The intention of the parties to establish a joint tenancy with right of survivorship must be stated clearly. The four unities of possession, interest, time and title must be present.

Tenancy by the entirety, in those states where it is recognized, is actually a joint tenancy between husband and wife. It gives the husband and wife the right of survivorship in all lands acquired by them during marriage. During their lives both must sign the deed for any title to pass to a purchaser. Community property rights exist only in certain states and pertain only to land owned by husband and wife. Usually the property acquired by combined efforts during the marriage is community property and one-half is owned by each spouse. Properties acquired by a spouse before the marriage and through inheritance or gifts during the marriage are termed separate property.

Real estate ownership may also be held in trust. In creating a trust, title to the property involved is conveyed to a trustee, who owns and manages the property.

Various types of business organizations may own real estate. A corporation is a legal entity and can hold title to real estate in severalty. While a partnership is technically not a legal entity, the Uniform Partnership Act and the Uniform Limited Partnership Act, adopted by most states, enable a partnership to own property in the partnership's name. A syndicate is an association of two or more people or firms to make an investment in real estate. Many syndicates are joint ventures and are organized for only a single project. A syndicate may be organized as a co-ownership trust, corporation or partnership.

Cooperative ownership indicates title in one entity (corporation or trust) that must pay taxes, mortgage interest and principal, and all operating expenses. Reimbursement comes from shareholders through monthly assessments. Shareholders have proprietary, long-term leases entitling them to occupy their apartments. Under condominium ownership each owner/occupant holds fee simple title to a unit plus a share of the common elements. Each unit owner receives an individual tax bill and may mortgage the unit. Expenses for operating the building are collected by an owners' association through monthly assessments. A variation of condominium ownership called time-sharing enables multiple purchasers to own an estate or use interest in real estate, with the right to use it for a part of each year.

−4

Questions

1. The four unities of possession, interest, time and title are associated with which of the following?

   a. Tenancy by the entirety
   b. Severalty ownership
   c. Tenants in common
   d. Joint tenancy

2. A parcel of property was purchased by K and Z. The deed they received from the seller at the closing conveyed the property "to K and Z" without further explanation. Therefore, K and Z most likely took title as:

   a. joint tenants.
   b. tenants in common.
   c. tenants by the entirety.
   d. community property owners.

3. M, B and F are joint tenants with rights of survivorship in a tract of land. F conveys her interest to V. Which of the following statements is true?

   a. M and B are joint tenants.
   b. M, B and V are joint tenants.
   c. M, B and V are tenants in common.
   d. V now has severalty ownership.

4. Individual ownership of an individual unit and common ownership of the common area best describes:

   a. a cooperative.
   b. a condominium.
   c. a time-share.
   d. membership camping.

5. In a trust the person in whom the title is vested is the:

   a. trustor.   c. beneficiary.
   b. trustee.   d. straw man.

6. D and S are getting married. Under the laws of their state any real property that either owns at the time of the marriage will remain separate property. And any real property acquired by either during the marriage, except by gift or inheritance, will belong to both of them equally. This form of ownership is called:

   a. a partnership.
   b. joint tenancy.
   c. tenancy by the entirety.
   d. community property.

7. E, J and Q were concurrent owners of a parcel of real estate. J died, and his interest passed according to his will to become part of his estate. J was a:

   a. joint tenant.
   b. tenant in common.
   c. tenant by the entirety.
   d. severalty owner.

8. A legal arrangement under which the title to real property is held to protect the interests of a beneficiary is a:

   a. trust.
   b. corporation.
   c. limited partnership.
   d. general partnership.

9. A condominium is created when:

   a. the construction of the improvements is completed.
   b. the owner files a declaration in the public record.
   c. the condominium owners' association is established.
   d. all of the unit owners file their documents in the public record.

10. Ownership that allows possession for only a specific time each year is a:

    a. cooperative.   c. time-share.
    b. condominium.   d. trust.

11. A corporation may own real estate in all of the following manners *except:* in

    a. trust.   c. partnership.
    b. severalty.   d. joint tenancy.

married couple — Tenants by entirety

12. All of the following are forms of concurrent ownership *except:*

    a. tenancy by the entirety.
    b. community property.
    c. tenancy in common.
    d. severalty.

13. The right of survivorship is associated with:

    a. severalty ownership.
    b. community property.
    c. tenancy in common.
    d. joint tenancy.

14. All of the following involve a fee simple interest *except:*

    a. a condominium.
    b. a time-share use.
    c. a tenancy by the entirety.
    d. a tenancy in common.

15. If property is held by two or more owners as tenants in common, the interest of a deceased co-tenant will pass to the:

    a. surviving owner or owners.
    b. heirs of the deceased.
    c. state by the law of escheat.
    d. trust under which the property was owned.

16. Which of the following best evidences the ownership of a cooperative?

    a. A tax bill for the individual unit
    b. The existence of a reverter clause
    c. A shareholder stock certificate
    d. A right of first refusal

17. A proprietary lease is characteristic of the ownership of a:

    a. condominium unit.
    b. cooperative unit.
    c. time-share estate.
    d. membership camping interest.

18. Which of the following statements applies to both joint tenancy and tenancy by the entirety?

    a. There is no right to file a partition suit.
    b. The survivor becomes a severalty owner.
    c. A deed signed by one owner will convey a fractional interest.
    d. A deed will not convey any interest unless signed by both spouses.

19. T owns a fee simple interest in Unit 9 and five percent of the common elements. T owns a:

    a. membership camping interest.
    b. time-share estate.
    c. cooperative unit.
    d. condominium unit.

20. If property is held by two or more owners as joint tenants, the interest of a deceased co-tenant will be passed to the:

    a. surviving owner or owners.
    b. heirs of the deceased.
    c. state under the law of escheat.
    d. trust under which the property was owned.

8

Legal Descriptions

Describing Land	In everyday life we often refer to real estate by its street address, such as ''1234 Main Street'' or ''the two-story house at the corner of Oak and Main.'' However, such a reference is not accurate enough to be used in the practice of real estate. Documents such as sales contracts, deeds, mortgages and trust deeds must identify the exact location of a parcel of property according to an established system. This identification is referred to as the property's **legal description.** Courts have held that the description of a parcel of real estate is legally sufficient if a competent surveyor can locate the parcel using that description.
	Typically ownership of a parcel of property has been transferred many times, and upon each transfer the legal description used in the documents should be identical to the one used in prior transfers. Legal problems can be minimized or prevented if this practice is followed.
Methods of Describing Real Estate	The methods used to describe real estate are metes and bounds, rectangular (government) survey and lot and block (recorded plat). Although each method can be used independently, the methods may be combined in some situations. Figure 8.1 shows the types of legal descriptions historically used in the United States.
Metes-and-Bounds Method	A **metes-and-bounds description,** the earliest type of legal description used, makes use of the boundaries and measurements of the parcel in question. The description starts at a designated place on the parcel called the **point of beginning (POB)** and proceeds around the outside of the tract by reference to linear measurements and directions. A metes-and-bounds description always ends at the POB so that the tract being described is completely enclosed.
	Monuments are fixed objects used to establish real estate boundaries. Natural objects such as stones, large trees, lakes and streams, as well as man-made objects like streets, highways and markers placed by surveyors, are commonly used as monuments. Measurements often include the words ''more or less''; the location of the monuments is more important than the distance stated in the wording. The actual distance between monuments takes precedence over linear measurements set forth in the description if the two measurements differ.
	An example of a metes-and-bounds description of a parcel of land (pictured in Figure 8.2) follows:

**Figure 8.1
Public Land Survey
Systems of the United
States**

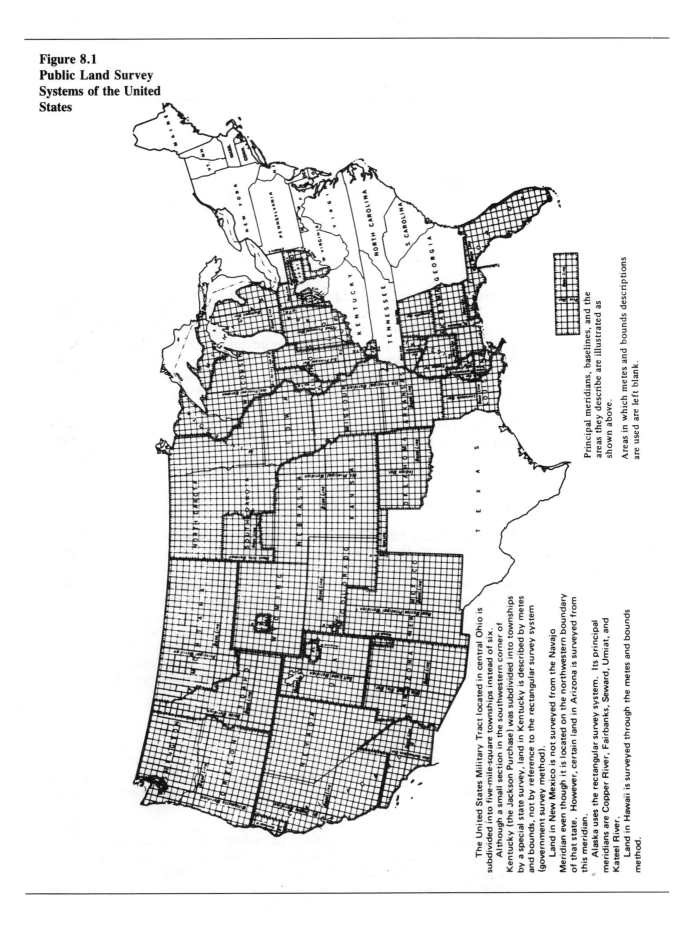

The United States Military Tract located in central Ohio is subdivided into five-mile-square townships instead of six.

Although a small section in the southwestern corner of Kentucky (the Jackson Purchase) was subdivided into townships by a special state survey, land in Kentucky is described by metes and bounds, not by reference to the rectangular survey system (government survey method).

Land in New Mexico is not surveyed from the Navajo Meridian even though it is located on the northwestern boundary of that state. However, certain land in Arizona is surveyed from this meridian.

Alaska uses the rectangular survey system. Its principal meridians are Copper River, Fairbanks, Seward, Umiat, and Kateel River.

Land in Hawaii is surveyed through the metes and bounds method.

Principal meridians, baselines, and the areas they describe are illustrated as shown above.

Areas in which metes and bounds descriptions are used are left blank.

**Figure 8.2
Metes-and-Bounds
Tract**

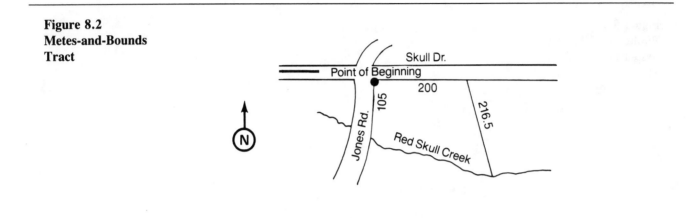

"A tract of land located in Red Skull, Boone County, Virginia, described as follows: Beginning at the intersection of the east line of Jones Road and the south
line of Skull Drive; then east along the south line of Skull Drive 200 feet; then
south 15° east 216.5 feet, more or less, to the center thread of Red Skull Creek;
then northwesterly along the center line of said creek to its intersection with the
east line of Jones Road; then north 105 feet, more or less, along the east line of
Jones Road to the point of beginning."

When used to describe property within a town or city, a metes-and-bounds description may begin as follows:

"Beginning at a point on the southerly side of Kent Street, 100 feet easterly from
the corner formed by the intersection of the southerly side of Kent Street and
the easterly side of Broadway; then. . . ."

In this description the POB is given by reference to the corner intersection. *The
description must close by returning to the POB.*

Metes-and-bounds descriptions can be complex and problematic. When they include detailed compass directions or concave and convex lines, they can be difficult to understand. Natural deterioration or destruction (usually by vandalism)
of the monuments in a description can make boundaries difficult to identify.
And in some parts of the country the colloquialisms and slang that they contain
have made some very early metes-and-bounds descriptions colorful but incom-
prehensible to people not familiar with that area. In such situations the advice of
a surveyor should be obtained.

**Rectangular
(Government)
Survey System**

The **rectangular survey system,** sometimes called the *government survey system,*
was established by Congress in 1785, soon after the federal government was
organized. The system was developed as a standard method of describing all lands
conveyed to or acquired by the federal government, including the extensive area
of the Northwest Territory.

The rectangular survey system is based on two sets of intersecting lines: principal
meridians and base lines. The **principal meridians** run north and south, and
the **base lines** run east and west. Both are located by reference to degrees of lon-
gitude and latitude. Each principal meridian has a name or number and is crossed

Figure 8.3
Township Lines

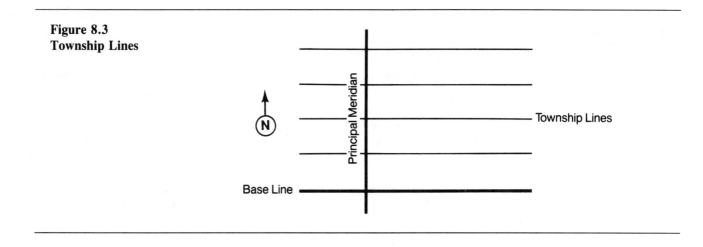

Figure 8.4
Range Lines

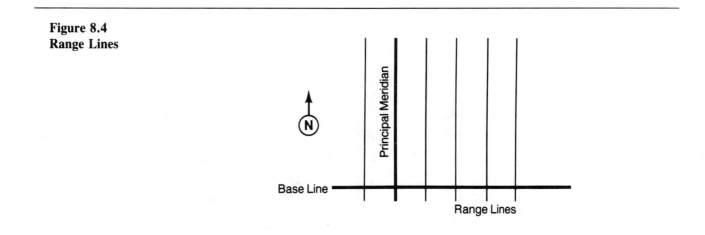

by a base line. These lines are pictured in Figure 8.1. Each principal meridian and its corresponding base line are used to survey a definite area of land, indicated on the map by boundary lines.

Each principal meridian affects or controls *only* the specific area of land shown by the boundaries in Figure 8.1. No parcel of land is described by reference to more than one principal meridian, and the meridian used may not necessarily be the nearest one.

Further divisions—township lines, ranges, section lines and quarter-section lines—are used in the same way as monuments in the metes-and-bounds method.

Townships. Lines running east and west, parallel with the base line and six miles apart, are referred to as **township strips,** and they form *strips* of land (or **tiers**) called **townships** (see Figure 8.3). These tiers of townships are designated by consecutive numbers north or south of the base line. For instance, the strip of land between six and 12 miles north of a base line is Township 2 North.

Ranges. The land on either side of a principal meridian is divided into *six-mile-wide strips* by lines that run north and south, parallel to the meridian. These north–south strips of land are called **range strips** (see Figure 8.4). They are designated by consecutive numbers east or west of the principal meridian. For example, Range 3 East would be a strip of land between 12 and 18 miles east of its principal meridian.

The township squares formed by the intersecting township and range lines are the basic units of the rectangular survey system (see Figure 8.5). Theoretically townships are six miles square and contain 36 square miles (23,040 acres). Note that *although a township square is part of a township strip, the two terms do not refer to the same thing.* In this discussion the word *township* used by itself refers to the township square.

Each township is given a legal description by using the designation of the township strip in which the township is located, the designation of the range strip and the name or number of the principal meridian for that area. For example, in Figure 8.5, the township marked *X* is described as Township 3 North, Range 4 East of the Principal Meridian. That township is the third strip, or tier, north of the base line. This strip (or tier) designates the township number and direction. The township is also located in the fourth range strip (those running north and south) east of the Principal Meridian. Finally, reference is made to the Principal Meridian because the land being described is within the boundary of land surveyed from that meridian. This description is abbreviated as *T3N, R4E Principal Meridian.*

Sections. Each township contains 36 **sections**, each one square mile, or *640 acres.* Sections are numbered one through 36, as shown in Figure 8.6. Section 1 is always in the northeast, or upper right-hand, corner. By law each section number 16 has been set aside for school purposes and is referred to as a *school section.* The sale or rental proceeds from this land were originally available for township school use, and the schoolhouse was usually located in this section so that it would be centrally located for all of the students in the township.

Sections (see Figure 8.7) are divided into *halves* (320 acres), *quarters* (160 acres) and halves and quarters of those divisions. The southeast quarter of a section, which is a 160-acre tract, is abbreviated SE¼. The SE¼ of SE¼ of SE¼ of Section 1 would be a ten-acre square in the lower right-hand corner of Section 1. Sometimes this description is written without the word *of* as a comma means *of:* SE¼, SE¼, SE¼ Section 1. It is possible to combine portions of a section, as NE¼ of SW¼ and N½ of NW¼ of SE¼ of Section 1, which could also

Figure 8.5
Townships in the
Rectangular Survey
System

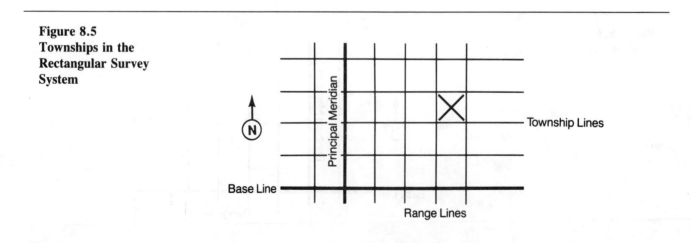

**Figure 8.6
Sections in a
Township**

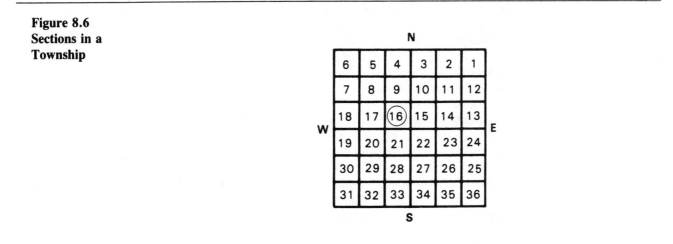

16=School Section

be written NE¼, SW¼; N½, NW¼, SE¼ of Section 1. A semicolon means *and*. Notice that because of the word *and* in this description the area is 60 acres.

Correction lines. Due to the curvature of the earth, the convergence of the range lines, which run north and south, must be compensated for. All range lines continually approach each other and, if extended northward, would eventually meet at the North Pole. An accurate survey of a township would show its north line to be about 50 feet shorter than its south line. In the case of the fourth township

**Figure 8.7
A Section**

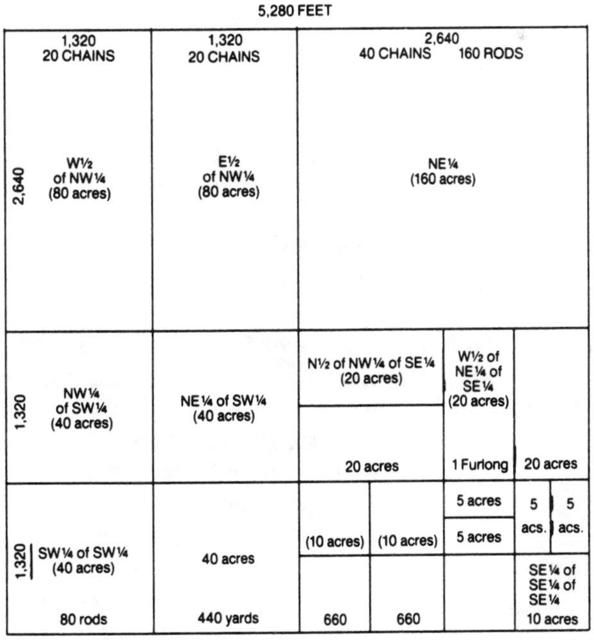

north of the base line the difference is four times as great, or about 200 feet. The rectangular survey system compensates for the resulting shortages with **correction lines** (see Figure 8.8). Every fourth township line both north and south of the base line is designated a correction line, and on each correction line the range lines are measured to the full distance of six miles apart. Guide meridians run north and south at 24-mile intervals from the principal meridian. A **government check** is the area bounded by two guide meridians and two correction lines, approximately 24 miles square. Because of the curvature of the earth and the crude instruments used in early days, in practice few townships are exactly six-mile squares or contain exactly 36 square miles.

Because most townships do not contain exactly 36 square miles, surveyors follow well-established rules in adjusting such errors. These rules provide that any overage or shortage in a township be adjusted in those sections adjacent to its north and west boundaries (Sections 1, 2, 3, 4, 5, 6, 7, 18, 19, 30 and 31). These are called *fractional sections* (discussed below). All other sections are exactly one square mile and are known as *standard sections*. These provisions for making corrections explain some of the variations in township and section acreage under the rectangular survey system of legal description.

Fractional sections and government lots. Undersized or oversized sections are classified as **fractional sections** and may occur for a number of reasons. For example, part of a section may be submerged under water. In some areas the rectangular survey was made by separate crews and may have resulted in gaps less than a section wide being left when the surveys met. Other errors may have resulted from the physical difficulties encountered in the actual survey.

Areas smaller than full quarter-sections were numbered and designated as **government lots** by government surveyors. An overage or shortage was corrected whenever possible by placing the government lots in the north or west portions of the fractional sections. For example, a government lot might be described as Government Lot 2 in the northwest quarter of fractional section 18, Township 2 North, Range 4 East of the Salt Lake Meridian.

In Practice . . .   *When reading a government survey description of land, read from the end of the description to the beginning to determine the location and size of the property. For example, consider the following description:*

"The S½ of the NW¼ of the SE¼ of Section II, Township 8 North, Range 6 West of the Fourth Principal Meridian."

To locate this tract of land from this citation alone, first search for the Fourth Principal Meridian on a map of the United States. Then, on a regional map, find the township in which the property is located by counting six range strips west of the Fourth Principal Meridian and eight townships north of its corresponding base line. After locating Section II you would divide the section into quarters, the SE¼ into quarters and then the NW¼ of that into halves. The S½ of that NW¼ contains the property in question.

In computing the size of this tract of land, first determine that the SE¼ of the section contains 160 acres (640 acres divided by 4). The NW¼ of that quarter-section contains 40 acres (160 acres divided by 4), and the S¼ of that quarter-section—the property in question—contains 20 acres (40 acres divided by 2).

Figure 8.8
Correction Lines and
Guide Meridians

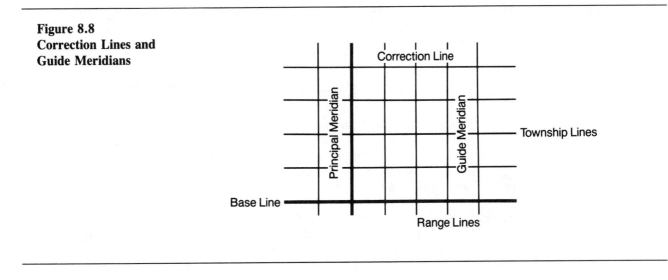

In general, *if a rectangular survey description does not use the conjunction* and *or a semicolon (indicating various parcels are combined),* the *longer the description,* the *smaller the tract of land it describes.*

Metes-and-bounds descriptions within the rectangular survey system. Land in states using the rectangular survey system may also require a metes-and-bounds description. This usually occurs in describing an irregular tract, a tract too small to be described by quarter-sections or a tract that does not follow either the lot or block lines of a recorded subdivision or section, quarter-section or other fractional section lines. An example of a combined metes-and-bounds and rectangular survey system description is as follows (see Figure 8.9):

"That part of the northwest quarter of Section 12, Township 10 North, Range 7 West of the Third Principal Meridian, bounded by a line described as follows: Commencing at the southeast corner of the northwest quarter of said Section 12, then north 500 feet; then west parallel with the south line of said section 1,000 feet; then south parallel with the east line of said section 500 feet to the south line of said northwest quarter; then east along said south line to the point of beginning."

Figure 8.9
Metes and Bounds
with Rectangular
Survey

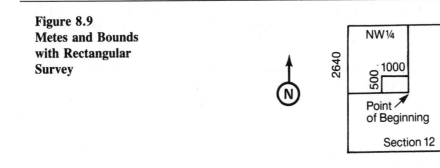

"Section 12, TN10, R7W, Third Principal
Meridian"

**Lot-and-Block
System**

The third method of legal description is the **lot-and-block (recorded plat) system.** This system uses *lot-and-block numbers* referred to in a **plat map** placed in the public records of the county where the land is located.

Initially, a large parcel of land is described either by metes and bounds or by rectangular survey. Once this large parcel is surveyed, it is broken down into smaller parcels, so the lot-and-block legal description is always based on a reference to a prior metes-and-bounds or rectangular survey description. For each parcel described under the lot-and-block system the lot refers to the numerical designation of any particular parcel and the block refers to the name of the subdivision under which the map is recorded. The block reference is drawn from the early 1900s, when a city block was the most common type of subdivided property.

The lot-and-block system starts with the preparation of a *survey plat*—by a licensed surveyor or an engineer—as illustrated in Figure 8.10. On this plat the land is divided into numbered or lettered lots and blocks, and streets or access roads for public use are indicated. Lot sizes and street details must be indicated completely and must comply with all local ordinances and requirements. When properly signed and approved, the subdivision plat is recorded in the county in which the land is located; it thereby becomes part of the legal description. In describing a lot from a recorded subdivision plat, the lot and block number, name or number of the subdivision plat and name of the county and state are used. For example:

"Lot 71, Happy Valley Estates 2, located in a portion of the southeast quarter of Section 23, Township 7 North, Range 4 East of the Seward Principal Meridian in _____ County, _____ [state]."

Anyone wishing to locate this parcel would start with the map of the Seward Principal Meridian to locate the township and range reference; then consult the township map of Township 7 North, Range 4 East; then the section map of Section 23; then the quarter-section map of the southeast quarter, which would refer to the plat map for the subdivision known as the second unit (second parcel subdivided) under the name of Happy Valley Estates.

Some subdivided lands are further divided by a later resubdivision. For example, if one developer (in this example, "Western View") purchased a large parcel from a second developer ("Homewood") and resubdivided this into different-sized parcels, the resulting legal description might be as follows:

"Lot 4, Western View Resubdivision of the Homewood Subdivision, located in a portion of west half of Section 19, Township 10 North, Range 13 East of the Black Hills Principal Meridian, _____ County, _____ [state]."

The lot-and-block system is the newest form of legal description and is now used to some degree in all states. Some states have passed plat acts that specify the smallest parcel that may be sold without a subdivision plat map being prepared, approved and recorded. For example, in some states the minimum size is five acres; in others it is one acre.

**Preparation and
Use of a Survey**

Legal descriptions should not be changed, altered or combined without adequate information from a competent authority, such as a surveyor or title attorney. Legal descriptions should *always* include the name of the county and state in which

Figure 8.10
Subdivision Plat Map

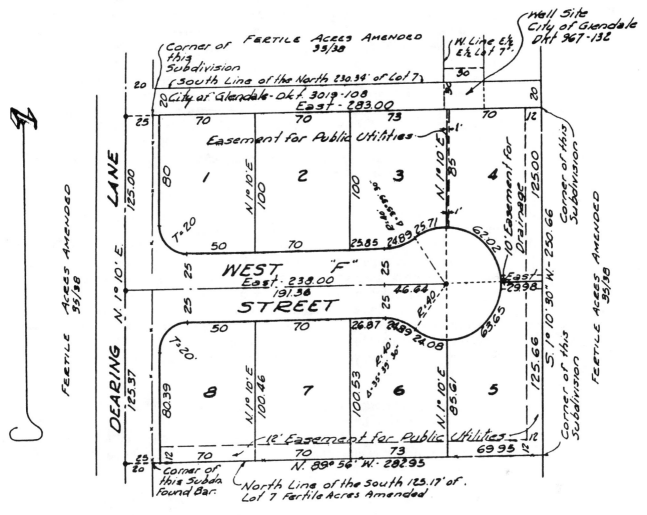

the land is located because meridians often relate to more than one state and occasionally relate to two base lines. For example, the description "the southwest quarter of Section 10, Township 4 North, Range 1 West of the Fourth Principal Meridian" could refer to land in either Illinois or Wisconsin.

A licensed surveyor is trained and authorized to locate a given parcel of land and determine its legal description. The surveyor does this by preparing a *survey,* which sets forth the legal description of the property, and a *survey sketch,* which shows the location and dimensions of the parcel. When a survey also shows the location, size and shape of buildings located on the lot, it is referred to as a *spot survey.* Surveys are required in many real estate transactions, such as when conveying a portion of a given tract of land, conveying real estate as security for a mortgage loan, showing the location of new construction, locating roads and highways, determining the legal description of the land on which a particular building is located and determining if there are any encroachments.

In Practice . . .   *Because legal descriptions of newly subdivided land, once recorded, affect title to real estate, they should be prepared only by a surveyor. Real estate licensees who attempt to draft legal descriptions create potential risks for themselves and their clients and customers. Further, legal descriptions should be copied with care. An incorrectly worded legal description in a sales contract may obligate the seller to convey or the buyer to purchase more or less land than intended. Title problems can arise for the buyer who seeks to convey the property at a future date. Even if the contract can be corrected by the parties involved before the sale is closed, the licensee runs the risk of losing a commission and may be held liable for damages suffered by an injured party because of an improperly worded legal description.*

Measurements   Surveyors must properly and accurately mark the survey points they have established. In doing so they use *monuments* and **benchmarks.**

The term *monument* refers to any item used to mark a corner or an angle in a survey. It could be a marker set in concrete, a piece of steel reinforcing bar (''rebar'') or pipe driven into the soil or simply a wooden one- by two-inch stake placed in the dirt. Monuments are traditionally used to mark only surface measurements between points, and their accuracy can be suspect. Also, a monument is at best informal and subject to the whims of nature and vandals. Therefore, surveyors rely most heavily on benchmarks to mark their work accurately and permanently.

Elevations. Benchmarks (see Figure 8.11) are permanent reference points that have been established throughout the United States. They are usually embossed brass markers set into solid concrete or asphalt bases. While used to some degree for surface measurements, their principal reference use is for marking datums.

A **datum** *is a point, line or surface from which elevations are measured or indicated.* For the purpose of the United States Geological Survey (USGS), *datum* is defined as the mean sea level at New York Harbor. It is of special significance to surveyors in determining the height of structures, establishing the grades of street and so on.

All large cities have established a local official datum that is used in place of the USGS datum. For instance, the official datum for Chicago is known as the *Chicago City Datum* and is a horizontal plane below the surface of the city. This plane was established in 1847 as corresponding to the low-water level of Lake Michigan in that year and is considered to be at zero elevation.

A surveyor's measurement of elevation based on the USGS datum will differ from one computed according to a local datum. A surveyor can always translate an elevation based on a local datum to the elevation based on the USGS.

Cities with local datums also have designated local benchmarks, which are given official status when assigned a permanent identifying number. Local benchmarks simplify surveyors' work, for measurements may be based on them rather than on the basic benchmark, which may be miles away.

Figure 8.11
Benchmark

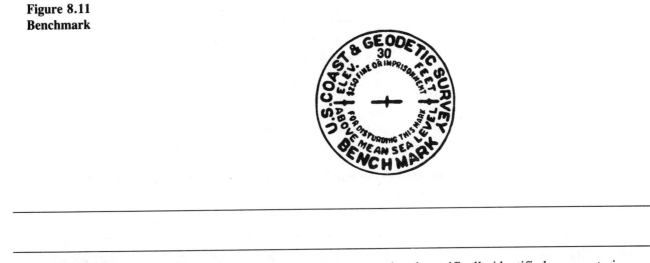

Air Rights and Subsurface Rights

Just as surface rights must be surveyed and specifically identified, so must air rights and subsurface rights. The owner of a parcel of land may subdivide the air above his or her land into **air lots.** Air lots are composed of airspace within specific boundaries located over a parcel of land. This type of description is found in titles to tall buildings located on air rights, generally over railroad tracks. Similarly a surveyor, in preparing a subdivision plat for condominium use, describes each condominium unit by reference to the elevation of the floors and ceilings on a vertical plane above the city datum.

The condominium laws passed in all states (see Chapter 7) require that a registered land surveyor prepare a plat map showing the elevations of floor and ceiling surfaces and the vertical boundaries of each condominium unit with reference to an official datum. Typically a separate plat will be prepared for each floor in the condominium building.

The following is an example of the legal description of a condominium apartment unit that includes a fractional share of the common elements of the building and land:

"UNIT _____ as delineated on survey of the following described parcel of real estate (hereinafter referred to as Development Parcel): The north 99 feet of the west ½ of Block 4 (except that part, if any, taken and used for street), in Sutton's Division Number 5 in the east ½ of the southeast ¼ of Section 24, Township 3 South, Range 68 West of the Sixth Principal Meridian, in Denver County, Colorado, which survey is attached as Exhibit A to Declaration made by Colorado National Bank as Trustee under Trust No. 1250, recorded in the Recorder's Office of Denver County, Colorado, as Document No. 475637; together with an undivided _____% interest in said Development Parcel (excepting from said Development Parcel all the property and space comprising all the units thereof as defined and set forth in said Declaration and Survey)."

Subsurface rights can be legally described in the same manner as air rights. However, they are measured *below* the datum rather than above it. Subsurface rights are used not only for coal mining, petroleum drilling and utility line location but also for multistory condominiums—both residential and commercial—that have several floors below ground level. In urban areas this type of land planning affords

Table 8.1 Units of Land Measurement	Unit	Measurement
	mile	5,280 feet; 1,760 yards; 320 rods
	rod	16.5 feet; 5.50 yards
	sq. mile	640 acres
	acre	43,560 sq. feet; 160 sq. rods
	sq. yard	9 sq. feet
	sq. foot	144 sq. inches
	chain	66 feet; 4 rods; 160 links

a practical solution to the problem of imposing skylines, and in extreme climates it can reduce utility bills.

Land Units and Measurements

It is important to understand land units and measurements because they are an integral part of legal descriptions. Some commonly used measurements are listed in Table 8.1. Remember that a *section* of land is one square mile and contains 640 acres; a *quarter-section* contains 160 acres; a *quarter of a quarter-section* contains 40 acres. A *circle* contains 360 degrees; a *quarter-segment* of a circle contains 90 degrees; a *half-segment* of a circle contains 180 degrees. One *degree* (1°) can be subdivided into 60 minutes (60′), each of which contains 60 seconds (60″). One-and-a-half degrees would be written 1°30′0″.

Key Terms

air lot	monument
base line	plat map
benchmark	point of beginning (POB)
correction line	principal meridian
datum	range strip
fractional section	rectangular (government) survey system
government check	section
government lot	tier
legal description	township
lot-and-block (recorded plat) system	township strip
metes-and-bounds description	

Summary

A legal description is a precise method of identifying a parcel of land. There are three methods of legal description: metes and bounds, rectangular (government) survey system and lot-and-block system. A property's description should always be the same as the one used in previous documents.

In a metes-and-bounds description the actual location of monuments takes precedence over the written linear measurement in a document. When property is being described by metes and bounds, the description must always enclose a tract of land; that is, the boundary line must end at the point at which it started.

The rectangular (government) survey system is used in 30 states. It involves surveys based on 35 principal meridians. Under this system each principal merid-

Math Concept: Land Acquisition Costs	To calculate the cost of purchasing land you must calculate using the same unit in which the cost is given. Costs quoted per square foot must be multiplied by the proper number of square feet, costs quoted per acre must be multiplied by the proper number of acres, and so on.

To calculate the cost of a parcel of land of 3 acres at $1.10 per square foot, convert the acreage to square feet before multiplying:

43,560 square feet per acre × 3 acres = 130,680 square feet

130, 680 square feet × $1.10 per square foot = $143,748

To calculate the cost of a parcel of land of 17,500 square feet at $60,000 per acre, convert the cost per acre into the cost per square foot before multiplying by the number of square feet in the parcel:

$60,000 per acre / 43,560 square feet per acre = $1.38 (rounded) per square foot;

17,500 square feet × $1.38 per square foot = $24,150

Note: when land calculations are made, additional land cannot be "created." Therefore, all land calculations must be rounded *down* to the nearest unit of measurement (acre, square yard, square foot, etc.).

ian and its corresponding base line are specifically located. Any particular parcel of land is surveyed from only one principal meridian and its base line.

East and west lines parallel with the base line form six-mile-wide strips called township strips or tiers. North and south lines parallel with the principal meridian form range strips. The resulting squares are 36 square miles in area and are called townships. Townships are designated by their township and range numbers and their principal meridian—for example, Township 3 North, Range 4 East of the _____ Meridian. Townships are divided into 36 sections of one square mile each.

When a tract is irregular or its boundaries do not coincide with a section, regular fractions of a section or a boundary of a lot or block in a subdivision, a surveyor can prepare a combination rectangular survey and metes-and-bounds description.

Land in every state can be subdivided into lots and blocks by means of a plat map. An approved plat of survey showing the division into blocks, giving the size, location and designation of lots and specifying the location and size of streets to be dedicated for public use is filed for record in the recorder's office of the county in which the land is located. A subdivision plat will give the legal description of a building site in a town or city by lot, block and subdivision in a section, township and range of a principal meridian in a county and state.

Air lots, condominium descriptions and other measurements of vertical elevations may be computed from the United States Geological Survey datum, which is the mean sea level in New York harbor. Most large cities have established local survey datums for surveying within the area. The elevations from these datums are further supplemented by reference points, called benchmarks, placed at fixed intervals from the datums.

Questions

1. What is the proper description of the following shaded area?

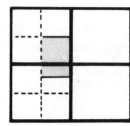

  a. SW¼ of the NE¼ and the N½ of the SE¼ of the SW¼
  b. N½ of the NE¼ of the SW¼ and the SE¼ of the NW¼
  c. SW¼ of the SE¼ of the NW¼ and the N½ of the NE¼ of the SW¼
  d. S½ of the SW¼ of the NE¼ and the NE¼ of the NW¼ of the SE¼

2. When surveying land, a surveyor refers to the principal meridian that is:
  a. nearest the land being surveyed.
  b. in the same state as the land being surveyed.
  c. not more than 40 townships or 15 ranges distant from the land being surveyed.
  d. within the rectangular survey system area in which the land being surveyed is located.

3. The N½ of the SW¼ of a section contains:
  a. 40 acres.   c. 160 acres.
  b. 20 acres.   d. 80 acres.

4. In describing real estate, the system that uses feet, degrees and natural markers as monuments is:
  a. rectangular survey.
  b. metes and bounds.
  c. government survey.
  d. lot and block.

Questions 5 through 8 refer to the following illustration of a whole township and parts of the adjacent townships:

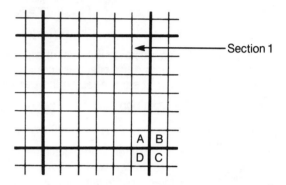

5. The section marked A is which of the following?
  a. School section   c. Section 31
  b. Section 36   d. Government lot

6. Which of the following is Section 6?
  a. D   c. B
  b. C   d. A

7. The section directly below C is:
  a. Section 12.   c. Section 30.
  b. Section 25.   d. Section 7.

8. Which of the following is Section D?
  a. Section 36   c. Section 1
  b. Section 31   d. Section 6

9. Which of these shaded areas depicts the NE¼ of the SE¼ of the SW¼?

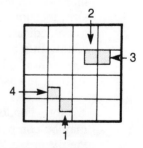

  a. Area 1   c. Area 3
  b. Area 2   d. Area 4

10. An acre contains: *98*
    a. 160 square feet.
    b. 43,560 square feet.
    c. 640 square feet.
    d. 360 degrees.

11. How many acres are there in the tract described
    as "Beginning at the NW corner of the
    SW¼, then south along the west line to the
    SW corner of the section, then east along
    the south line of the section 2,640 feet, more
    or less, to the SE corner of the said SW¼,
    then in a straight line to the POB"?

    a. 100 acres   c. 90 acres
    b. 160 acres   d. 80 acres

12. The proper description of the shaded township
    area in this illustration is:

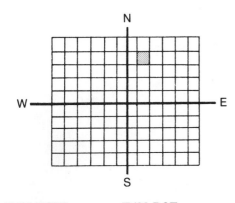

    a. T4N R2W.   c. T4N R2E.
    b. T2W R4N.   d. T2E R4N.

13. If a farm described as "the NW¼ of the SE¼
    of Section 10, Township 2 North, Range 3
    West of the 6th. P.M." sold for $1,500 an
    acre, what would the sales price be?

    a. $30,000   c. $45,000
    b. $15,000   d. $60,000

14. The legal description "The northwest ¼ of the
    southwest ¼ of Section 6, Township 4 North,
    Range 7 West" is defective because there is
    no reference to:

    a. lot numbers.
    b. boundary lines.
    c. a principal meridian.
    d. a record of survey.

15. To keep the principal meridian and range lines   *92*
    as near six miles apart as possible, a correction
    known as a *government check* is made every

    a. one mile.   c. six miles.
    b. three miles.   d. 24 miles.

16. Fractional sections in the rectangular survey   *92*
    system that are less than a quarter-section in
    area are known as:

    a. fractional parcels.
    b. government lots.
    c. hiatus.
    d. fractional townships.

17. A woman purchased 4.5 acres of land for   *99*
    which she paid $78,400. An adjoining owner
    wants to purchase a strip of her land measuring
    150 feet by 100 feet. What should this strip
    cost the adjoining owner if the woman sells it
    for the same price she originally paid for it?

    a. $3,000.   c. $7,800
    b. $6,000.   d. $9,400.

18. How many acres are contained in the parcel
    defined as "Beginning at the NE corner of
    the SW¼ of Section 23; then one mile, more
    or less, in a northerly direction to the NW
    corner of the SE¼ of Section 14; then one
    mile, more or less, in a southeasterly direction
    to the NW corner of the SE¼ of Section 24;
    then one mile, more or less, in a westerly
    direction to the point of beginning"?

    a. 160   c. 640
    b. 320   d. 1,280

19. A property contained ten acres. How many   *98*
    50-foot by 100-foot lots could be subdivided
    from the property if 26,000 square feet were
    dedicated for roads?

    a. 80   c. 82
    b. 81   d. 83

20. A parcel of land is 400 feet by 640 feet. The   *98*
    parcel is cut in half diagonally by a stream.
    How many acres are there in each half of the
    parcel?

    a. 2.75   c. 5.51
    b. 2.94   d. 5.88

21. What is the shortest distance between Section
    4 and Section 32 in the same township?

    a. 3 miles   c. 5 miles
    b. 4 miles   d. 6 miles

always 16

22. A man owns the NW¼ and the SW¼ of Section 17, and his neighbor owns the NE¼ and the SE¼ of Section 18. If they agree that each will install one half of a common fence, how many rods of fence would each install?

    a. 0   c. 320
    b. 160   d. 440

23. The section due west of Section 18, Township 5 North, Range 8 West, is

    a. Section 19, T5N, R8W.
    b. Section 17, T5N, R8W.
    c. Section 13, T5N, R9W.
    d. Section 12, T5N, R7W.

24. An owner is considering building a patio in her backyard. The 60-foot by 15-foot by 4-inch slab would cost $78.40 per cubic yard of concrete, and the finishing would cost $.38 per square foot. The total cost would be

    a. $875.33   c. $1,182.13
    b. $1,045.33   d. $1,213.11

25. In any township the section designated as the school section is section:

    a. 1.   c. 25.
    b. 16.   d. 36.

26. The least acceptable method for identifying real property is:

    a. rectangular survey.
    b. metes and bounds.
    c. street address.
    d. lot and block.

Real Estate Taxes and Other Liens

A lien is a charge against property that provides security for a debt of the property owner. In case of a default a lien allows a creditor to force the sale of property given as security by the debtor to satisfy the debt. A lien does not constitute ownership; it is a type of *encumbrance*—a charge or burden on a property that may diminish its value. Note that all liens are encumbrances, but not all encumbrances are liens.

Generally liens are enforced by court order. A creditor must take legal action and request the court to order the sale of the property in question for full or partial satisfaction of the debt.

Liens can be categorized on several levels (see Figure 9.1). They are classified as to how they are created: a lien can be voluntary or involuntary. A **voluntary lien** is created by the debtor's action, such as when someone takes out a mortgage loan to buy real estate. An **involuntary lien** is created by law and can be either statutory or equitable. A **statutory** lien is created by statute. A real estate tax lien, for example, is an involuntary, statutory lien; it is created by statute without any action by the property owner. An **equitable lien** arises out of common law and may be created by a court under the concept of "fairness." A court-ordered judgment requiring payment of the balance on a delinquent charge account would be an involuntary, equitable lien on the debtor's property.

Liens may also be classified as to the property they affect. **General liens** include judgments, estate and inheritance taxes, debts of a decedent, corporation franchise taxes and Internal Revenue Service taxes, and they affect all the property, real and personal, of a debtor. **Specific liens** are secured by specific property and affect only that particular property. Specific liens on real estate include mechanics' liens, mortgage liens, tax liens and liens for special assessments and utilities. (Specific liens can also secure personal property, such as when a vendor's lien is placed on a car to secure payment of a car loan.)

Effects of Liens on Title	Although a fee simple estate can be reduced in value by the lien rights of others, the owner of the real estate is still free to convey his or her title to a willing purchaser. The purchaser will, however, buy the property subject to any liens and encumbrances. Once properly established, a lien will bind successive owners if it is not cleared.

Remember, specific liens attach to property, not to the property owner. Thus, although a purchaser who buys real estate under a specific lien is not responsible for payment of the debt secured by the lien, he or she faces possible loss of the property if the creditors take court action to enforce payment of their liens.

Priority of liens. Real estate taxes and special assessments generally take **priority** over all other liens, regardless of date. This means that if the property goes through a sale (usually court-ordered) to satisfy unpaid debts or obligations, outstanding real estate taxes and special assessments will be paid from the proceeds *first*. The remainder of the proceeds will be used to pay other outstanding liens in the order of their priority, which is established (with the exception of mechanics' liens, discussed later in this chapter) from the date of recording in public records of the county where the property is located.

For example, if the courts ordered a parcel of land sold to satisfy a judgment lien entered in the public record on February 7, 1991 subject to a first mortgage lien recorded January 22, 1988, and to this year's unpaid real estate taxes, the proceeds of the sale would be distributed in the following order:

1. To the taxing bodies for this year's real estate taxes.

2. To the mortgage lender for the entire amount of the mortgage loan outstanding as of the date of the sale.

3. To the creditor named in the judgment lien (if any proceeds remain after paying the first two items).

4. To the foreclosed-on landowner (if any proceeds remain after paying the first three items).

Figure 9.1
Types of Liens

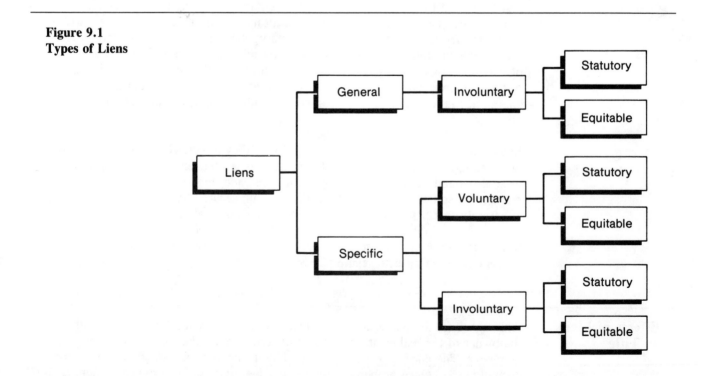

Subordination agreements are written agreements between lienholders to change the priority of mortgage, judgment and other liens under certain circumstances. Priority and recording of liens will be discussed in detail in Chapter 12.

Real Estate Tax Liens

As discussed in Chapter 6, the ownership of real estate is subject to certain government powers. One of these is the right of state and local governments to impose **tax liens** for the support of their functions. Because the location of real estate is permanent, the government can levy taxes with a high degree of certainty that the taxes will be collected. The annual taxes levied on real estate usually have priority over previously recorded liens, so they may be enforced by a court-ordered sale.

There are two types of real estate taxes; both are levied against specific parcels of property and automatically become liens on those properties.

General Tax (Ad Valorem Tax)

The first type of real estate tax, the general real estate tax or **ad valorem tax**, is made up of the taxes levied on real estate by various governmental agencies and municipalities. These include states, counties, cities, towns and villages. Other taxing bodies are school districts (including local elementary and high schools, junior colleges and community colleges), drainage districts, water districts and sanitary districts. Municipal authorities operating recreational preserves such as forest preserves and parks are also authorized by the legislatures of the various states to levy real estate taxes.

General real estate taxes are levied for the *general operation* of the governmental agency authorized to impose the levy. These taxes are known as *ad valorem* (Latin for "according to value") taxes because the amount of the tax is based on the *value of the property being taxed.* Ad valorem taxes are specific, involuntary, statutory liens.

Exemptions from general taxes. Under most state laws certain real estate is exempt from real estate taxation. For example, property owned by cities, various municipal organizations (such as schools, parks and playgrounds), the state and federal governments, religious organizations, hospitals or educational institutions is tax-exempt. The property must be used for tax-exempt purposes.

Many state laws also allow special exemptions to reduce real estate tax bills for certain property owners or land uses. *Homeowners* and *senior citizens* are frequently granted set reductions in the assessed values of their homes. Some states offer real estate tax reductions to attract industries, and many states offer tax reductions for agricultural land.

Assessment. Real estate is valued, or assessed, for tax purposes by county or township assessors or appraisers. The land is usually appraised separately from the buildings or other improvements. Some states require assessments to be a certain percentage of market value. State laws may provide for property to be reassessed periodically.

Property owners who claim that errors were made in determining the assessed value of their property may present their objections, usually to a local board of appeal or board of review. Protests or appeals regarding tax assessments may ultimately be taken to court.

Equalization. In some jurisdictions, when it is necessary to correct general inequalities in statewide tax assessments, uniformity may be achieved by use of an **equalization factor.** Such a factor may be provided for use in counties or districts where the assessments are to be raised or lowered. The assessed value of each property is multiplied by the equalization factor, and the tax rate is then applied to the equalized assessment. For example, the assessments in one county are determined to be 20 percent lower than the average assessments throughout the rest of the state. This underassessment can be corrected by decreeing the application of an equalization factor of 125 percent to each assessment in that county. Thus, a parcel of land assessed for tax purposes at $98,000 would be taxed on an equalized value of $122,500 ($98,000 × 1.25 = $122,500).

Tax rates. The process of arriving at a real estate tax rate begins with the *adoption of a budget* by each taxing district. Each budget covers the financial requirements of the taxing body for the coming fiscal year, which may be the January to December calendar year or some other 12-month period designated by statute. The budget must include an estimate of all expenditures for the year and indicate the amount of income expected from all fees, revenue sharing and other sources. The net amount remaining to be raised from real estate taxes is then determined from these figures.

The next step is *appropriation,* the action taken by each taxing body that authorizes the expenditure of funds and provides for the sources of such monies. Appropriation generally involves the adoption of an ordinance or the passage of a law setting forth the specifics of the proposed taxation.

The amount to be raised from the general real estate tax is then imposed on property owners through a *tax levy,* the formal action taken to impose the tax, by a vote of the taxing district's governing body.

The *tax rate* for each individual taxing body is computed separately. To arrive at a tax rate the total monies needed for the coming fiscal year are divided by the total assessments of all real estate located within the jurisdiction of the taxing body. For example, a taxing district's budget indicates that $300,000 must be raised from real estate tax revenues, and the assessment roll (assessor's record) of all taxable real estate within this district equals $10,000,000. The tax rate is computed thus:

$$\$300,000 \div \$10,000,000 = .03, \text{ or } 3\%$$

The tax rate may be stated in a number of different ways. In many areas it is expressed in mills. A **mill** is *1/1,000 of a dollar, or $.001.* The tax rate may be expressed as a mill ratio, in dollars per hundred or in dollars per thousand. The tax rate computed in the example above could be expressed as:

30 mills

or

$3 per $100 of assessed value

or

$30 per $1,000 of assessed value

Tax bills. A property owner's tax bill is computed by applying the tax rate to the assessed valuation of the property. For example, on property assessed for tax purposes at $90,000, at a tax rate of 3 percent, or 30 mills, the tax will be $2,700 ($90,000 × .030 = $2,700). If an equalization factor is used, the computation with an equalization factor of 120 percent would be as follows:

$$\$ 90,000 \times 1.20 = \$108,000$$
$$\$108,000 \times .030 = \$ \ 3,240 \text{ tax}$$

Generally one tax bill that incorporates all real estate taxes levied by the various taxing districts is prepared for each property. In some areas, however, separate bills are prepared by each taxing body. Sometimes the real estate taxing bodies may operate on different budget years so that the taxpayer receives separate bills for various taxes at different times during the year.

Due dates for tax payments are usually set by statute. Taxes may be payable in two installments (semiannually), four installments (quarterly) or 12 installments (monthly). In some areas taxes become due at the beginning of the current tax year and must be paid in advance (1991 taxes paid at the beginning of 1991). In others they are payable during the year after the taxes are levied (1991 taxes paid throughout 1991). And in still others a partial payment is due in the year of the tax with the balance due in the following year (1991 taxes payable during 1991 and 1992). Knowledge of local tax payment schedules is critical in computing the real estate taxes owed when a property is sold.

Some states offer discounts to encourage prompt payment of real estate taxes. Penalties in the form of monthly interest charges are added to all taxes that are not paid when due. The due date may also be called the *penalty date*.

Enforcement of tax liens. To be enforceable real estate taxes must be valid, which means they must be levied properly, used for a legal purpose and applied equitably to all affected property. Real estate taxes that have remained delinquent for the period of time specified by state law can be collected by the tax collecting officer through either tax foreclosure (similar to mortgage foreclosure) or **tax sale.** While there are substantial differences in the methods and details of the various states' tax sale procedures, the results are the same.

Tax sales are usually held according to a published notice after a court has rendered a judgment for the tax and penalties and ordered that the property be sold. Because a specific amount of delinquent tax and penalty must be collected, the purchaser at a tax sale must pay at least this amount. A defaulted taxpayer may have the right of **redemption** (the right to buy back the real estate), so in some areas the bidding at a tax sale is based on the interest rate the defaulted taxpayer would have to pay to redeem the property. That is, the person bidding the lowest redemption interest rate (the one most beneficial for the taxpayer) becomes the successful bidder; that interest rate theoretically would be the easiest for the taxpayer to meet and thus redeem the property. A *certificate of sale* is usually given to the successful bidder when he or she pays the delinquent tax amount.

Generally the delinquent taxpayer can redeem the property at any time before the tax sale by paying the delinquent taxes plus interest and charges (any court costs or attorney's fees); this is known as an *equitable right of redemption*. Some state laws also grant a period of redemption *after the tax sale* during which the defaulted owner or creditors of the defaulted owner may redeem the property by paying the amount paid at the tax sale plus interest and charges (including any taxes levied since the sale); this is known as the *statutory right of redemption*. (The right of redemption is discussed further in Chapter 14.) If the property is not redeemed within the statutory period, the certificate holder can apply for a *tax deed*. The quality of the title conveyed by a tax deed varies from state to state.

In some states tax-delinquent land is sold or conveyed to the state or a taxing authority. At the expiration of the redemption period title to such land is sold at auction to the highest bidder(s). The tax deed issued to the purchasers is regarded as conveying good title, because it is considered a conveyance by the state of state-owned land. In some jurisdictions tax-delinquent land that is not sold at a tax sale due to lack of buyers is forfeited to the state. The state may then either use the land for its own purposes or sell it later.

Special Assessments (Improvement Taxes)

Special assessments, the second category of real estate taxes, are special taxes levied on real estate for public improvements to that real estate. Property owners in the area of the improvements are required to pay for them because their properties benefit directly from the improvements. The installation of paved streets, curbs, gutters, sidewalks, storm sewers and street lighting increases the values of the affected properties, so the owners are, in effect, merely reimbursing the levying authority for that increase. However, dollar-for-dollar increases in value are rarely the result.

Special assessments are always specific and statutory, but they can be either involuntary or voluntary liens. Improvements initiated by a public agency create involuntary liens. However, when property owners petition the local government to install a public improvement for which the owners agree to pay, the assessment lien is voluntary.

Whether the lien is voluntary or involuntary, typically each property in the improvement district will be charged a prorated share of the total amount of the assessment, either on a fractional basis (four houses may equally share the cost of one streetlight) or on a cost-per-front-foot basis (wider lots will incur a greater cost than narrower lots for street paving and curb and sidewalk installation).

Special assessments are usually due in equal annual installments over a period of five to ten years, with the first installment usually due during the year following the public authority's approval of the assessment. The first bill will include one year's interest on the property owner's share of the entire assessment; subsequent bills will include one year's interest on the unpaid balance. Property owners have the right to prepay any or all installments to avoid future interest charges.

Today strict subdivision regulations have almost eliminated the concept of special assessments in some parts of the country. Most items for which assessments have traditionally been levied are now required to be installed as part of a subdivision's approval by the state real estate authority.

Other Liens on Real Property

Aside from real estate tax and special assessment liens, the following types of liens may also be charged against real property.

Mortgage Liens and Deed of Trust Liens

In general a **mortgage lien** or a trust deed lien is a voluntary lien on real estate given to a lender by a borrower as security for a real estate loan. It becomes a lien on real property when the funds are disbursed and the lender files or records the documents in the office of the proper official of the county where the property is located. Lenders generally require a preferred lien, referred to as a *first lien;* this means that (aside from real estate taxes), no other liens against the property will take priority over their lien. (Mortgages and deeds of trust are discussed in detail in Chapter 14.)

Mechanics' Liens

The purpose of the **mechanic's lien** is to *give security to those who perform labor or furnish material in the improvement of real property*. A mechanic's lien is a specific, involuntary lien and is available to contractors, subcontractors, architects, equipment lessors, surveyors, laborers and others. This type of lien is filed when the owner has not fully paid for the work or when the general contractor has been paid but has not paid the subcontractors or suppliers of materials. However, statutes in some states prohibit subcontractors from placing liens directly on certain types of property, such as owner-occupied residences.

To be entitled to a mechanic's lien the person who did the work must have had a contract (express or implied) with the owner or the owner's authorized representative. If improvements that were not ordered by the property owner have commenced, the property owner should execute a document called a *notice of nonresponsibility* to relieve himself or herself from possible mechanics' liens. By posting this notice in some conspicuous place on the property and recording a verified copy of it in the public record, the owner gives notice that he or she will not be responsible for the work done.

A person claiming a mechanic's lien must file a notice of lien in the public record of the county where the property is located within a certain period of time after the work has been completed. According to state law, priority of a mechanic's lien may be established as of the date the construction began or materials were first furnished, the date the work was completed, the date the individual subcontractor's work was either commenced or completed, the date the contract was signed or work ordered or the date a notice of the lien was recorded, filed, posted or served. In some states, mechanics' liens may be given priority over previously recorded liens (such as mortgages).

In most states, while a mechanic's lien takes priority from the time it attaches, a claimant's notice of lien will not be filed in the public records until some time after that. A purchaser of property that has been recently constructed, altered or repaired should therefore be cautious about possible unrecorded mechanics' liens against the property.

Judgment Liens

A *judgment* is a *decree issued by a court* at the end of a lawsuit. When the decree provides for the awarding of money and sets forth the amount owed by the debtor (defendant) to the creditor (plaintiff), the judgment is referred to as a *money judgment*.

A judgment lien is a *general, involuntary, equitable lien on both real and personal property* owned by the debtor. A judgment differs from a mortgage in that a *specific* parcel of real estate was not given as security at the time that the debtor-creditor relationship was created. Because a lien usually covers only property located within the county in which the judgment is issued, a notice of the lien must be filed in any county to which a creditor wishes to extend the lien coverage. To enforce a judgment the creditor must obtain from the court a *writ of execution* directing the sheriff to levy upon and sell as much of the debtor's property as is necessary to pay the debt and the expenses of the sale.

A judgment lien's priority is established by one or a combination of the following (as provided by state law): the date the judgment was entered by the court, the date the judgment was filed for record in the recorder's office or the date a writ of execution was issued. When property is sold to satisfy a debt, the debtor should demand a legal document known as a *satisfaction of judgment,* or *satisfaction piece,* which should be filed with either the clerk of the court or, in some states, the recorder of deeds so that the record will be cleared of the judgment.

Attachments. To prevent a debtor from conveying title to previously unsecured real estate while a court suit is being decided, a creditor may seek a writ of **attachment.** By this writ the court retains custody of the property until the suit is concluded. The creditor must first post a surety bond or deposit with the court sufficient to cover any possible loss or damage the debtor may sustain during the period the court has custody of the property, in case the judgment is not awarded to the creditor.

Lis pendens. Generally there is a considerable time lag between the filing of a lawsuit and the rendering of a judgment. When any suit is filed that affects title to a specific parcel of real estate (such as a foreclosure suit), a notice known as a *lis pendens* (Latin for "litigation pending") is recorded, or registered. A lis pendens is not a lien but rather a *notice of a possible future lien.* Recording of the lis pendens gives notice to all interested parties, such as prospective purchasers and lenders, and establishes a priority for the later lien, which is dated back to the date the lis pendens was recorded.

Estate and Inheritance Tax Liens

Federal **estate taxes** and state **inheritance taxes** (as well as the debts of decedents) are *general, statutory, involuntary liens* that encumber a deceased person's real and personal property. These are normally paid or cleared in probate court proceedings. Probate and issues of inheritance are discussed in Chapter 11.

Vendors' Liens

A vendor's lien is a *seller's claim* against the title of property conveyed to a buyer; it occurs in cases where the seller did not receive the full, agreed-on purchase price. This is a *specific, equitable, involuntary lien* for the amount of the unpaid balance due the seller. It is often used when personal property is sold using seller financing or when property is not returned from consignment.

Vendees' Liens

A vendee's lien is a *buyer's claim* against a seller's property in cases where the seller failed to deliver title. This usually occurs when property is purchased under an installment contract (also called a *contract for deed* or an *agreement of sale*) and the seller fails to deliver title after all other terms of the contract have been satisfied. A vendee's lien is a *specific, equitable, involuntary lien* for any money paid plus the value of any improvements made to the property by the buyer.

Liens for Municipal Utilities

Municipalities are generally given the right to a *specific, equitable, involuntary lien* on the property of an owner who refuses to pay bills for water or other municipal utility service.

Bail Bond Lien   A real estate owner charged with a crime for which he or she must face trial may choose to put up real estate instead of cash as surety for bail. The execution and recording of such a bail bond creates a *specific, statutory, voluntary lien* against the owner's real estate. This lien is enforceable by the sheriff or another court officer if the accused person does not appear in court as required.

Corporation Franchise Tax Lien   State governments generally levy a corporation franchise tax on corporations as a condition of allowing them to do business in the state. Such a tax is a *general, statutory, involuntary lien* on all property, real and personal, owned by the corporation.

IRS Tax Lien   An Internal Revenue Service (IRS) tax lien results from a person's failure to pay any portion of IRS taxes, such as income and withholding taxes. A federal tax lien is a *general, statutory, involuntary lien* on all real and personal property held by the delinquent taxpayer. Its priority, however, is based on the date of filing or recording; it does not supersede previously recorded liens.

A summary of the real estate–related liens discussed in this chapter appears in Table 9.1.

Key Terms

ad valorem tax	priority
attachment	redemption
equalization factor	special assessment
equitable lien	specific lien
estate taxes	statutory lien
general lien	subordination agreement
inheritance taxes	tax lien
involuntary lien	tax sale
mechanic's lien	trust deed lien
mill	voluntary lien
mortgage lien	

Summary   Liens are claims of creditors or taxing authorities against the real and personal property of a debtor. A lien is a type of encumbrance. Liens are either general, covering all real and personal property of a debtor/owner, or specific, covering only identified property. They are also either voluntary (arising from an action of the debtor) or involuntary—created by statute (statutory) or based on the concept of fairness (equitable).

With the exception of real estate tax liens and mechanics' liens, the priority of liens is generally determined by the order in which they are placed in the public record of the county in which the property is located.

Real estate taxes are levied annually by local taxing authorities and are generally given priority over other liens. Payments are required before stated dates, after which penalties accrue. An owner may lose title to property for nonpayment of

**Table 9.1
Real Estate–Related
Liens**

	General	Specific	Voluntary	Involuntary
General Real Estate Tax (Ad Valorem Tax) Lien		XX		XX
Special Assessment (Improvement Tax) Lien		XX	XX . . . . .or. XX	
Mortgage Lien		XX	XX	
Trust Deed Lien		XX	XX	
Mechanic's Lien		XX		XX
Judgment Lien	XX			XX
Estate Tax Lien	XX			XX
Inheritance Tax Lien	XX			XX
Debts of a Decedent	XX			XX
Vendor's Lien		XX		XX
Vendee's Lien		XX		XX
Municipal Utilities Lien		XX		XX
Bail Bond Lien		XX	XX	
Corporation Franchise Tax Lien	XX			XX
Income Tax Lien	XX			XX

taxes, because such tax-delinquent property can be sold at a tax sale. Some states allow a time period during which a defaulted owner can redeem his or her real estate from a tax sale.

Special assessments are levied to allocate the cost of public improvements to the specific parcels of real estate that benefit from them. Assessments are usually payable annually over a five- or ten-year period, together with interest due on the balance of the assessment.

Mortgage liens and trust deed liens are voluntary, specific liens given to lenders to secure payment for real estate loans.

Mechanics' liens protect general contractors, subcontractors and material suppliers whose work enhances the value of real estate.

A judgment is a court decree obtained by a creditor, usually for a monetary award from a debtor. A judgment lien can be enforced by court issuance of a writ of execution and sale by the sheriff to pay the judgment amount and costs.

Attachment is a means of preventing a defendant from conveying property before completion of a suit in which a judgment is sought.

Lis pendens is a recorded notice of a lawsuit that is awaiting trial in court and may result in a judgment that will affect title to a parcel of real estate.

Federal estate taxes and state inheritance taxes are general liens against a deceased owner's property.

Vendors' liens and vendees' liens are liens against specific property. A vendor's lien is a seller's claim against a purchaser who has not paid the entire purchase price, and a vendee's lien is a purchaser's claim against a seller under an installment contract who has not conveyed title.

Liens for water charges or other municipal utilities and bail bond liens are specific liens, while corporation franchise tax liens are general liens against a corporation's assets.

Internal Revenue Service tax liens are general liens against the property of a person who is delinquent in payment of IRS taxes.

Questions

1. Which of the following best refers to the type of lien that affects all real and personal property of a debtor?
   a. Specific lien
   b. Voluntary lien
   c. Involuntary lien
   d. General lien

2. *Priority of liens* refers to which of the following?
   a. The order in which a debtor assumes responsibility for payment of obligations
   b. The order in which liens will be paid if property is sold to satisfy a debt
   c. The dates liens are filed for record
   d. The fact that specific liens have greater priority than general liens

3. A lien on real estate made to secure payment for specific municipal improvements is which of the following?
   a. Mechanic's lien
   b. Special assessment
   c. Ad valorem
   d. Utility lien

4. Which of the following is classified as a general lien?
   a. Vendor's lien
   b. Bail bond lien
   c. Debts of a deceased person
   d. Real estate taxes

5. Which of the following liens would usually be given highest priority?
   a. A mortgage dated last year
   b. The current real estate tax
   c. A mechanic's lien for work started before the mortgage was made
   d. A judgment rendered yesterday

6. A specific parcel of real estate has a market value of $80,000 and is assessed for tax purposes at 25 percent of market value. The tax rate for the county in which the property is located is 30 mills. The tax bill will be:
   a. $50.
   b. $60.
   c. $600.
   d. $700.

7. Which of the following is used to distribute the cost of public services among real estate owners?
   a. Personal property tax
   b. Sales tax
   c. Real property tax
   d. Special assessment

8. A mechanic's lien claim arises when a general contractor has performed work or provided material to improve a parcel of real estate on the owner's order and the work has not been paid for. Such a contractor has a right to:
   a. tear out his or her work.
   b. record a notice of the lien.
   c. record a notice of the lien and file a court suit within the time required by state law.
   d. have personal property of the owner sold to satisfy the lien.

9. What is the annual real estate tax on a property that is valued at $135,000 and assessed for tax purposes at $47,250 with an equalization factor of 125 percent, when the tax rate is 25 mills?
   a. $1,418
   b. $1,477
   c. $945
   d. $1,181

10. Which of the following is a voluntary, specific lien?
    a. IRS tax lien
    b. Mechanic's lien
    c. Mortgage lien
    d. Vendor's lien

11. Seller W sold buyer T a parcel of real estate. Title has passed, but to date T has not paid the purchase price in full as originally agreed on. If W does not receive payment, which of the following would she be entitled to enforce?
    a. Attachment
    b. Vendee's lien
    c. Lis pendens
    d. Vendor's lien

12. A general contractor is going to sue a homeowner for nonpayment; the suit will be filed in two weeks. The contractor just learned that the homeowner has listed the property for sale with a real estate broker. In this situation, which of the following will be used by the contractor and his attorneys to protect his interest?
    a. Vendor's lien
    b. Vendee's lien
    c. Assessment
    d. Attachment

13. Special assessment liens:
    a. are general liens.
    b. are paid on a monthly basis.
    c. take priority over mechanics' liens.
    d. cannot be prepaid in full without penalty.

14. Which of the following is a lien on real estate?
    a. An easement running with the land
    b. A recorded and unpaid mortgage
    c. An attachment
    d. An encroachment

15. Both a mortgage lien and a judgment lien:
    a. must be entered by the court.
    b. involve a debtor-creditor relationship.
    c. are general liens.
    d. are involuntary liens.

16. A mechanic's lien would be available to all of the following *except* a:
    a. subcontractor.
    b. contractor.
    c. surveyor.
    d. broker.

17. The right of a defaulted taxpayer to recover his or her property prior to its sale for unpaid taxes is the:
    a. statutory right of reinstatement.
    b. equitable right of appeal.
    c. statutory right of assessment.
    d. equitable right of redemption.

18. Which of the following is a specific, involuntary lien? — specific property
    a. A real estate tax lien
    b. An income tax lien
    c. An estate tax lien
    d. A judgment lien

19. Taxes levied for the operation of the government are called:
    a. assessment taxes.
    b. ad valorem taxes.
    c. special taxes.
    d. improvement taxes.

20. All of the following probably would be exempt from real estate taxes *except:*
    a. a medical research facility.
    b. a public golf course.
    c. a community church.
    d. an apartment building.

Real Estate
Contracts

Contract Law

Brokers and salespeople use many types of contracts and agreements to carry out their responsibilities to sellers, buyers and the general public. The general body of law that governs the operations of such agreements is known as *contract law*. A **contract** can be defined as a voluntary agreement between legally competent parties to perform or refrain from performing some legal act, supported by legal consideration.

Depending on the situation and the nature or language of the agreement, a contract may be categorized in several ways.

Express and Implied Contracts

Depending on how a contract is created, it may be express or implied. In an express contract the parties state the terms and show their intentions in words. An express contract may be either oral or written. In an implied contract the agreement of the parties is demonstrated by their acts and conduct. The patron who orders a meal in a restaurant has implied a promise to pay for the food.

Bilateral and Unilateral Contracts

Contracts also may be classified as either bilateral or unilateral. In a **bilateral contract** both parties promise to do something; one promise is given in exchange for another. A real estate sales contract is a bilateral contract because the seller promises to sell a parcel of real estate and deliver title to the property to the buyer, who promises to pay a certain sum of money for the property. "I will do this, *and* you will do that." "Okay."

A **unilateral contract,** however, is a one-sided agreement whereby one party makes a promise to induce a second party to do something. The second party is not legally obligated to act; however, if the second party does comply, the first party is obligated to keep the promise. An offer of a reward would be an example of a unilateral contract. Under this agreement a law enforcement agency offers a monetary payment to anyone who can aid in the capture of a criminal. "I will do this *if* you will do that." Only if someone *does* aid in the capture is the reward paid.

Executed and Executory Contracts

A contract may be classified as either executed or executory, depending on whether the agreement is performed. An **executed contract** is one in which all parties have fulfilled their promises and thus performed the contract. (This usage is not to be confused with the use of *execute* to refer to the signing of a contract.) An

executory contract exists when something remains to be done by one or both parties.

Validity of Contracts

A contract can be described as either valid, void, voidable, or unenforceable (see Table 10.1), depending on the circumstances.

A **valid contract** contains all the essential elements (which will be discussed later in this chapter) and is binding and enforceable on both parties.

A **void contract** is one that has no legal force or effect because it does not contain the essential elements of a contract. One of the essential conditions for a contract to be valid is that it be for a legal purpose; thus a contract to commit a crime would be void.

A **voidable contract** is one that seems on the surface to be valid but may be rescinded by one of the parties. For example, a contract entered into with a minor usually is voidable; a minor generally is permitted to rescind a real estate contract within a reasonable time after reaching legal age. A voidable contract is considered by the courts to be valid if the party who has the option to rescind the agreement does not do so within a prescribed period of time.

An **unenforceable contract** also seems on the surface to be valid; however, neither party can sue the other to force performance. Unenforceable contracts are said to be "valid as between the parties" because if both desire to go through with it they can do so.

Elements Essential to a Valid Contract

The essentials of a valid contract vary somewhat from state to state. The elements that are uniformly required are described below.

1. **Legally competent parties:** All parties to the contract must be of legal age and have sufficient mental capacity. In most states 18 is the age of contractual capacity. In some states a contract with a minor is statutorily void; in other states it is voidable by the minor. In most jurisdictions the following are considered legally incompetent: minors (except for legally married or emancipated minors), wards of the state (the mentally deficient and others for whom the state has assumed responsibility) and people under the influence

Table 10.1 Legal Effects of Contracts

Type of Contract	Legal Effect	Example
Valid	Binding and Enforceable on Both Parties	Agreement Complying with Essentials of a Valid Contract
Void	No Legal Effect	Contract for an Illegal Purpose
Voidable	Valid, but May Be Disaffirmed by One Party	Contract with a Minor
Unenforceable	Valid Between the Parties, but Neither May Force Performance	Certain Oral Agreements

of drugs (including alcohol) or under duress (which is very difficult to prove) at the time the contract is created.

2. **Offer and acceptance:** This requirement, also called *mutual assent,* means that there must be a meeting of the minds. The wording of the contract must express all the agreed-on terms and must be clearly understood by the parties.

3. **Consideration:** The agreement must be based on good or valuable consideration. Consideration is what the parties promise in the agreement to give to or receive from each other, and it may consist of legal tender, exchange of value, love and affection, or a promise to act or to refrain from some act. The price or amount must be definitely stated and payable in exchange for the deed or right received.

4. **Legality of object:** To be valid and enforceable a contract must not involve a purpose that is illegal or against public policy.

Absence of undue influence, duress and misrepresentation. Contracts signed by a person under duress or undue influence are voidable (may be canceled) by that person or by a court. Extreme care should be taken when one or more of the parties to a contract is elderly, sick, in great distress or under the influence of drugs or alcohol. To be valid every contract must be signed as the free and voluntary act of each party. Misrepresentation or fraud could render a contract voidable by the injured party.

Agreement in writing. Not all contracts need to be in writing to be enforceable; however, every state has adopted the **statute of frauds,** which requires certain types of contracts to be in writing to be enforceable in a court of law. The **parol evidence** rule states that a written contract takes precedence over oral agreements or promises.

In Practice . . .   *Contracts for the sale of real estate and leases for more than one year must be in writing.*

Legal description. A real estate sales contract also must contain an adequate description of the property being conveyed.

Signatures. A real estate sales contract requires the signatures of the buyer and seller. In some states the seller's spouse may also be required to sign to release potential marital or homestead rights. An agent may sign for a principal when proper authority, such as a power of attorney, has been granted. When sellers are co-owners, all co-owners must sign if the entire ownership is being transferred.

Performance of Contract

Occasionally a contract may call for a specific time at or by which the agreed-on acts must be completely performed. In addition, many contracts provide that **"time is of the essence."** This means that the contract must be performed within the time limit specified and any party who has not performed on time is guilty of a breach of contract. The phrase "time is of the essence" is a two-edged sword and brokers should leave its use to attorneys.

When a contract does not specify a date for performance, the acts it requires should be performed within a reasonable time. What is interpreted as reasonable will depend on the situation.

In Practice . . .

In the most common situation a real estate sale contract stipulates a target date and place for closing. If that date comes and goes without settlement, the contract is void unless all parties agree to its validity. But should one party decide to withdraw from the contract, that party can do so because the original agreement was neither promptly nor contractually performed. Either party may later make time of the essence; again, that action should be taken only with a lawyer's advice.

Assignment and Novation

Often, after a contract has been signed one party may want to withdraw without actually terminating the agreement. This may be accomplished through either assignment or novation.

Assignment refers to a transfer of rights and/or duties under a contract. Generally rights may be assigned to a third party unless the agreement forbids it. Obligations also may be assigned, but the original obligor remains secondarily liable for them (after the new obligor) unless he or she is specifically released from this responsibility. Most contracts include a clause that either permits or forbids assignment.

A contract also may be performed by **novation,** or the substitution of a new contract for an existing agreement. The new agreement may be between the same parties, or a new party may be substituted for either (this is *novation of the parties*).

In Practice . . .

For example, when a borrower refinances the loan on his or her property to reduce the interest rate, the original contract with the lender will be replaced (novated) by a new contract carrying the lower interest rate.

Discharge of Contract

A contract may be completely performed, with all terms carried out, or it may be breached (broken) if one of the parties **defaults.** Other methods by which a contract may be discharged (canceled) include the following.

1. *Partial performance* of the terms along with a written acceptance by the person for whom acts have not been done or to whom money has not been paid.

2. *Substantial performance,* in which one party has substantially performed the contract but does not complete all the details exactly as the contract requires. Such performance may be sufficient to force payment with certain adjustments for any damages suffered by the other party.

3. *Impossibility of performance,* in which an act required by the contract cannot be legally accomplished.

4. *Mutual agreement* of the parties to cancel.

5. *Operation of law,* as in the voiding of a contract by a minor, as a result of fraud, the expiration of the statute of limitations or a contract's being altered without the written consent of all parties involved.

Default—breach of contract. A breach of contract is a violation of any of the terms or conditions of a contract without legal excuse, as when a seller breaches a sales contract by not delivering title to the buyer under the conditions stated in the agreement.

If the seller defaults, the buyer has three alternatives:

1. The buyer may *rescind, or cancel, the contract* and recover the earnest money.

2. The buyer may file a court suit, known as an action for **specific performance,** to force the seller to perform the contract (*i.e.,* convey the property).

3. The buyer may *sue the seller for compensatory damages.*

A suit for damages seldom is used in this instance, however, because in most cases the buyer would have difficulty proving the extent of damages.

If the *buyer defaults,* the seller may pursue one of the following courses:

1. The seller may *declare the contract forfeited.* The right to forfeit usually is provided in the terms of the contract, and the seller usually is entitled to retain the earnest money and all payments received from the buyer.

2. The seller may *rescind the contract,* that is, cancel or terminate the contract as if it had never been made. In this case the seller must return all payments the buyer has made.

3. The seller may *sue for specific performance.* This may require the seller to offer, or tender, a valid deed to the buyer to show the seller's compliance with the contract terms.

4. The seller may *sue for compensatory damages.*

Statute of limitations. The law of every state allows a specific time limit during which parties to a contract may bring legal suit to enforce their rights. The **statute of limitations** varies for different legal actions, and any rights not enforced within the applicable time period will be lost.

Contracts Used in the Real Estate Business	The written agreements most commonly used by brokers and salespeople are listing agreements, real estate sales contracts, option agreements, contracts for deed, leases and escrow agreements.

Broker's Authority To Prepare Documents	In many states specific guidelines have been drawn, whether by state real estate officials, court decision or statute, regarding the authority of real estate licensees to prepare contracts for their clients and customers. As a rule a licensed real estate broker is not authorized to practice law—that is, to prepare legal documents such as deeds and mortgages. A broker or salesperson may, however, be permitted to fill in the blanks on certain approved preprinted documents (such as sales contracts and leases), provided the licensee does not charge a separate fee for completing such forms.

Contract forms. *Printed forms* are used for all kinds of contracts because most transactions are basically similar in nature. The use of printed forms raises three problems: what to *fill in the blanks,* what printed matter is not applicable to a particular sale and is to be *ruled out* by drawing lines through the unwanted words and what additional clauses or agreements (called *riders or addenda*) are to be *added.* All changes and additions are usually initialed in the margin or on the rider by both parties when a contract is executed.

In Practice . . .	*To gain familiarity with the forms used in a local area students should ask brokers or real estate companies for copies of their sales contract, listing agreement and other forms. Title or abstract companies and some banks and savings and loan associations are other sources, or they may be purchased at local office supply and stationery stores.*
In Practice . . .	*The parties to a real estate transaction should be advised, before signing them, to have sales contracts and other legal documents examined by their attorneys to ensure that the agreements accurately reflect their intentions. Whenever preprinted forms do not sufficiently cover special provisions, the parties should be encouraged to have an attorney draft a sales contract that properly covers those provisions.*

Listing Agreements

Listing agreements are contracts that establish the rights of the broker as agent and of the buyer or seller as principal.

Some states suggest or require the use of specific forms of listing contracts. Oral listing contracts for a period of less than one year are recognized in some states, while in others only written listing contracts are recognized.

In Practice . . .	*If there is any ambiguity in a contract, the courts generally will interpret the agreement against the party who prepared it. For example, a broker usually prepares a listing agreement. If there is any doubt as to whether a listing agreement is an exclusive agency or an exclusive right to sell, a court will probably construe it to be an exclusive agency, ruling against the broker who prepared the document.*

Sales Contracts

A real estate sales contract sets forth all details of the agreement between a buyer and a seller for the purchase and sale of a parcel of real estate. Depending on the state or locality, this agreement may be known as an *offer to purchase, a contract of purchase and sale, a purchase agreement, an earnest money agreement, a deposit receipt* or some other variation.

Whatever the contract is called, when it has been prepared and signed by the purchaser it is an offer to purchase the subject real estate. Later, if the document is accepted and signed by the seller, it becomes, or "ripens into," a contract of sale. Figure 10.3 (on pages 127–129) provides an example of a real estate sales contract.

The contract of sale is the most important document in the sale of real estate because it sets out in detail the agreement between the buyer and the seller and establishes their legal rights and obligations. It is more important than the deed, because *the contract, in effect, dictates the contents of the deed.*

Details to be included in a real estate sales contract are the price, terms, legal description of the land, kind and condition of the title, form of deed the seller will deliver, kind of title evidence required, who will provide title evidence and how defects in the title, if any, are to be eliminated. The contract must state all the terms and conditions of the agreement and spell out all contingencies (discussed later in the chapter).

Figure 10.1
Offer and Acceptance

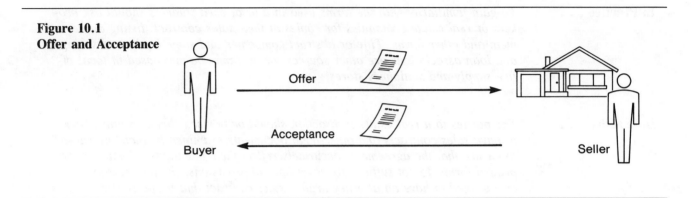

Buyer — Offer → Seller

← Acceptance

The following pages discuss some of the contingencies and other issues that arise as an offer to purchase ripens into a contract of sale.

Offer. A broker lists an owner's real estate for sale at the price and conditions set by the owner. When a prospective buyer is found, an offer to purchase is drawn up, signed by the prospective buyer and presented by the broker to the seller (see Figure 10.1). This is an *offer.*

Earnest money deposits. It is customary, but not essential, for a purchaser to provide a cash deposit when making an offer to purchase real estate. This cash deposit, commonly referred to as an **earnest money deposit,** *gives evidence of the buyer's intention to carry out the terms of the contract.* It is given to the broker, and the sales contract typically provides that the broker will hold the deposit for the parties. In some areas it is common practice for deposits to be held in escrow by the seller's attorney. If the offer is not accepted, the earnest money deposit is returned to the would-be buyer immediately.

The amount of the deposit is a matter to be agreed on by the parties. Under the terms of most listing agreements a real estate broker is required to accept a reasonable amount as earnest money. Generally the deposit should be sufficient to discourage the buyer from defaulting, compensate the seller for taking the property off the market and cover any expenses the seller might incur if the buyer defaults. A purchase offer with no earnest money, however, is valid. Most contracts provide that the deposit becomes the seller's property if the buyer defaults. The seller might also claim further damages.

Earnest money held by a broker must be held in a special *trust,* or *escrow, account.* This money cannot be *commingled,* or mixed, with a broker's personal funds. A broker may not use such funds for personal use; this illegal act is known as *conversion.* A broker need not open a special escrow account for each earnest money deposit received but may deposit all such funds in one account. A broker should maintain full, complete and accurate records of all earnest money deposits. Under no circumstances does the money belong to the broker, who must maintain it in his or her trust account. This uncertain nature of earnest money deposits makes it absolutely necessary that such funds be properly protected pending a final decision on their disbursement.

Binder. In a few localities it is customary to prepare a shorter document, known as a *binder,* for the purchaser to sign. This document states the essential terms of the purchaser's offer and acknowledges receipt of the deposit. It also provides that the parties agree to have a more formal and complete contract of sale drawn up by an attorney upon the seller's acceptance and signing of the binder. Throughout the country a binder receipt might be used in any situation where the details of the transaction are too complex for the standard sales contract form.

Mirror image offer. On rare occasion a broker will obtain a purchase offer for a client's property that exactly matches the specifications outlined in the listing contract. Such an offer is called a *mirror image offer*. If the seller rejects the offer and refuses to sell the property, in most cases the broker will be entitled to receive a commission, based on the wording in the listing, because the broker has obtained a ready, willing and able buyer who met the terms of the seller. Most listings consider this performance of the contract.

Counteroffer. Any attempt by the seller to change the terms proposed by the buyer creates a **counteroffer.** The buyer is relieved of his or her original offer because the seller has, in effect, rejected it. The buyer can accept the seller's counteroffer or can reject it and, if desired, make another counteroffer. Any change in the last offer made results in a counteroffer until one party finally agrees to the other party's last offer and both parties sign the final contract (see Figure 10.2).

An offer or counteroffer *may be revoked at any time before it has been accepted* (even if the person making the offer or counteroffer agreed to keep the offer open for a set period of time).

Acceptance. If the seller agrees to the original offer or a later counteroffer *exactly as it was made* and signs the contract, the offer has been *accepted* (see Figure 10.1) and the contract is *valid*. The broker then must advise the buyer of the seller's acceptance, obtain lawyers' approval if the contract calls for it and deliver a duplicate original of the contract to each party.

An offer is not considered accepted until the person making the offer has been *notified of the other party's acceptance*. When the parties are communicating through an agent or at a distance, questions may arise regarding whether an acceptance, a rejection or a counteroffer has effectively occurred. The real estate broker or salesperson must transmit all offers, acceptances or other responses as soon as possible to avoid such problems.

Equitable title. When a buyer signs a contract to purchase real estate, he or she does not receive title to the land; only a deed can actually convey title. However, after both buyer and seller have executed a sales contract, the buyer acquires

**Figure 10.2
Counteroffer and
Acceptance**

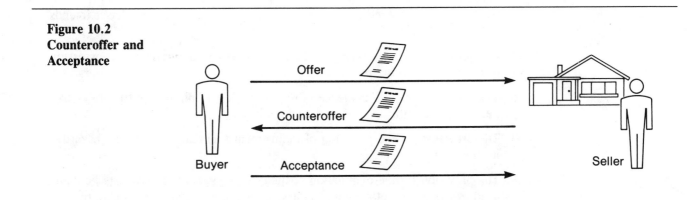

an interest in the land known as **equitable title.** Rights of a holder of equitable title vary from state to state. Acquisition of equitable title may give the buyer an insurable interest in the property. If the parties decide not to go through with the purchase and sale, the buyer may be required, to release the equitable interest in the land, to give the seller a quitclaim deed. (Quitclaim deeds are discussed in Chapter 11.)

Destruction of premises. In many states, once the sales contract is signed by both parties but before the deed is delivered (and unless the contract provides otherwise), the buyer must bear the loss of any damage to or destruction of the property by fire or other casualty. Through laws and court decisions, however, a growing number of states have placed the risk of any such loss on the seller. Many of these states have adopted the *Uniform Vendor and Purchaser Risk Act,* which specifically provides that the seller bears any loss that occurs before the title passes or the buyer takes possession.

Liquidated damages. Liquidated damages are an amount of money, agreed to in advance by buyer and seller, that will serve as compensation if one party does not live up to the contract. If a sales contract specifies that the earnest money deposit is to serve as liquidated damages in case of default by the buyer, the seller will be entitled to keep the deposit if the buyer refuses to perform for no good reason. The seller who does choose to keep the deposit as liquidated damages may not sue for any further damages.

Parts of a sales contract. All real estate sales contracts can be divided into a number of general parts. Although each form of contract will contain these divisions, their location within a particular contract may vary. The information generally required will include at least the following items:

1. The identification of the purchaser and the statement of the purchaser's obligation to purchase the property, including an indication of how the purchaser intends to take title to the property.

2. The legal description of the property and, if appropriate, the street address.

3. The identification of the seller and the statement of the type of deed the seller agrees to give, including the covenants, conditions and restrictions to which the deed will be subject.

4. The statement of the purchase price and how the purchaser intends to pay for the property, including earnest money deposits, additional cash from the purchaser and the conditions of any mortgage financing the purchaser intends to obtain or assume.

5. The provision for the closing of the transaction and the transfer of possession of the property to the purchaser.

6. The provision for title evidence (abstract and legal opinion, certificate of title, Torrens certificate, title insurance policy).

7. The provision for the proration of (adjustment for) real estate taxes, hazard insurance, rents, fuel, etc.

8. The provision for the completion of the contract should the property be damaged or destroyed between the signing of the contract and the closing of the transaction.

9. The provision for remedies available should either party default on the contract (including liquidated damages, the right to sue, etc.).

10. The provision for any contingencies (such as delays in obtaining or inability to obtain financing, inability of the purchaser to sell a previously owned property, inability of the seller to acquire another desired property, inability of the seller to clear the title, etc.).

11. Any miscellaneous provisions (discussed below).

12. The dated signatures of all parties (the signature of a witness is not essential to a valid contract).

Miscellaneous provisions. Among the more common considerations in many sales contracts are:

1. the identification of any personal property to be left with the premises for the purchaser (such as major appliances, lawn and garden equipment);

2. the identification of any real property to be removed by the seller prior to the closing (such as storage sheds);

3. the transfer of any applicable warranties on items such as heating and cooling systems, built-in appliances, etc.;

4. the identification of any leased equipment that must be transferred to the purchaser or returned to the lessor (such as security systems, cable television boxes, water softeners);

5. the appointment of a closing or settlement agent;

6. the generation of closing or settlement instructions;

7. the transfer of any impound or escrow account funds;

8. the transfer of the hazard insurance policy or the issuance of a new one;

9. the transfer or payment of any outstanding special assessments;

10. the provision by either party for a homeowner warranty program;

11. the purchaser's need to secure a specific type of loan;

12. if the property is to be financed with a new FHA or VA loan, the provision that the contract can be voided by the purchaser if the property is appraised for less than the contracted sales price;

13. the purchaser's right to a satisfactory structural engineering report, pest/insect infestation report or habitability report within a specified few days;

14. the purchaser's right to inspect the property shortly before the closing or settlement (often called the *walk-through*);

15. the purchaser's right to have a family member or an attorney approve the contract within a specified few days;

16. the agreement as to what documents will be provided by each party and when and where they will be delivered; and

17. the purchaser's right to sell a presently owned home before purchasing the next residence under this contract.

Math Concept: Sharing Commissions

A commission might be shared by many people: the listing broker, the listing salesperson, the selling broker and the selling salesperson. Drawing a diagram can help you determine which person is entitled to receive what amount of the total commission.

Salesperson E, while working for broker H, took a listing on a $73,000 house at a 6% commission rate. Salesperson T, while working for broker M, found the buyer for the property. If the property sold for the listed price, the listing broker and the selling broker shared the commission equally, and the selling broker kept 45% of what he received, how much did salesperson T receive? (If the broker retained 45% of the total commission that he received, his salesperson would receive the balance: 100% − 45% = 55%)

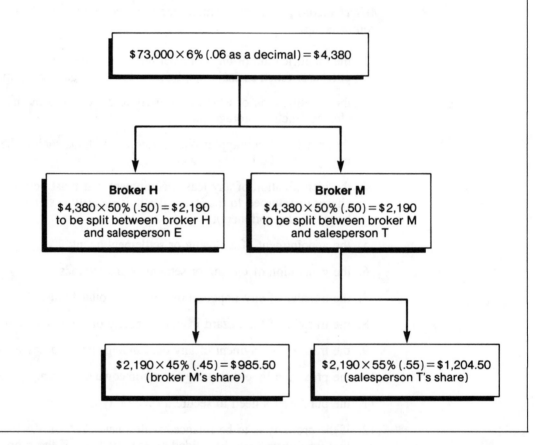

The last provision is known as a **contingency.** When the purchaser has another home that must be sold first, the seller may insist on an escape clause. Such a provision allows the seller to look at a more favorable offer, with the original purchaser retaining the right—if challenged—either to firm up the first sales contract by eliminating the contingency or to void the contract.

Option Agreements

An **option** is a *contract by which an* optionor *(generally an owner) gives an* optionee *(a prospective purchaser or lessee) the right to buy or lease the owner's property at a fixed price within a stated period of time.* The optionee pays a fee (the agreed-on consideration) for this option right and assumes no other obligation until he or she decides, within the specified time, to exercise the option right (to buy or lease the property) or allow the option right to expire. The owner may be bound to sell; the optionee is not bound to buy. A common application is a lease

Figure 10.3
Real Estate Sales Contract

RESIDENTIAL
REAL ESTATE PURCHASE CONTRACT AND RECEIPT FOR DEPOSIT

REALTOR®

THE PRINTED PORTION OF THIS CONTRACT HAS BEEN APPROVED BY THE ARIZONA ASSOCIATION OF REALTORS®. THIS IS INTENDED TO BE A BINDING CONTRACT. NO REPRESENTATION IS MADE AS TO THE LEGAL VALIDITY OR ADEQUACY OF ANY PROVISION OR THE TAX CONSEQUENCES THEREOF. IF YOU DESIRE LEGAL OR TAX ADVICE, CONSULT YOUR ATTORNEY OR TAX ADVISOR.

RECEIPT

1. **Received From:** ______________________________ ("Buyer")
2. **Title:** Buyer will take title as: ☐ **Determined before Close of Escrow** ☐ **Community Property** ☐ **Joint Tenants with Right of Survivorship** ☐ **Sole and Separate Property** ☐ **Tenants In Common** ☐ **Other:**

3. **Earnest Money Deposit:** Earnest money shall be held by Broker named in Line 7 until offer is accepted, subject to prior sale. Upon acceptance, Broker is
4. authorized to deposit the earnest money with the escrow company to which the check is payable. If the check is payable to Broker, Broker may deposit in
5. Broker's trust account or endorse the check without recourse and deposit it with a duly licensed escrow company. All earnest money is subject to collection
6. and is considered to be part of the purchase price for the Premises described below.

a. Amount of Deposit $ **b.** Form of Earnest Money: ☐ Personal Check ☐ Other: **c.** Deposited With: ☐ Broker's Trust Account ☐ Escrow Company:

7. **Received By:** ______________________________
Firm Name Agent's Signature Mo/Da/Yr

OFFER

8. **Property Description & Offer:** Buyer agrees to purchase the real property and all fixtures and improvements thereon and appurtenances incident thereto,
9. plus personal property described below (collectively the "Premises")

10. Property Address: ______________ Assessor's#: ______________
11. City: ______________ County: ______________ AZ, Zip Code: ______________
12. Legal Description:

13. **Fixtures and Personal Property:** All existing storage sheds; heating and cooling equipment; built-in appliances; light fixtures; ceiling fans; window and
14. door screens; sun screens; storm windows and doors; towel, curtain and drapery rods; draperies and other window coverings; attached carpeting; attached
15. fireplace equipment; pool and spa equipment (including any mechanical or other cleaning systems); garage door openers and controls; and attached TV
16. antennas, excluding satellite dishes, shall be left upon and included with the Premises.

17. **Additional Personal Property Included:** ______________________________
18. **Fixtures and Leased Equipment NOT Included:** ______________________________
19. **Terms and Conditions Include:** ☐ Government Financing Addendum ☐ Financing Addendum ☐ Addendum: ☐ None

20. $ ______________ **Full purchase price**, payable as follows:
21. $ ______________ Earnest deposit as indicated above.
22. $ ______________________________
23. $ ______________________________
24. ______________________________
25. ______________________________
26. ______________________________
27. ______________________________
28. **Assumption of Existing Loans:** The balance of any encumbrance being assumed is approximate. Any difference shall be reflected in the
29. ☐ Cash down payment ☐ Seller Carryback ☐ Other: Buyer shall reimburse Seller for any impounds transferred to Buyer.
30. **Close of Escrow:** Seller and Buyer will comply with all terms and conditions of this Contract and close escrow on or before:
31. Seller and Buyer hereby agree that close of escrow shall be defined as recordation of the documents. If escrow does not close by such date, this Contract
32. is subject to cancellation as provided on lines 147-154.
33. **Possession:** Possession shall be delivered to Buyer at ☐ Close of Escrow ☐ Other:
34. **Assessments:** The amount of any assessment which is a lien as of the close of escrow shall be ☐ Paid in Full by Seller ☐ Prorated and Assumed by Buyer
35. Any assessment that becomes a lien after close of escrow is the Buyer's responsibility.
36. **Proration and Costs:** Taxes, homeowner association fees, and irrigation fees, and if assumed, insurance premiums, interest on assessments and interest
37. on encumbrances shall be prorated as of ☐ Close of Escrow ☐ Other:

Figure 10.3
(continued)

38. **Home Protection Plan:** A home protection plan will be obtained for the Premises at close of escrow ☐ Yes ☐ No   The plan will be obtained at the
39. expense of the ☐Seller ☐Buyer   Name of Plan:_____ Type of Plan or Maximum Cost:_____
40. **Fire and Extended Insurance Coverage:** ☐A new policy to be issued   ☐ Existing policy to be assumed   ☐Determined in escrow .
41. **Escrow Instructions:** ☐ Separate escrow instructions will be executed   ☐ This Contract will be used as escrow instructions
42.   The escrow company shall be:
43. **Time for Acceptance:** This offer must be accepted by Seller on or before_____. Written acceptance of this Contract
44. given to the Broker named on Line 7 of this Contract shall be notice to Buyer.
45. COMMISSIONS PAYABLE FOR THE SALE, LEASING OR MANAGEMENT OF PROPERTY ARE NOT SET BY ANY BOARD OR ASSOCIATION OF
46. REALTORS® OR MULTIPLE LISTING SERVICE OR IN ANY MANNER OTHER THAN BETWEEN THE BROKER AND CLIENT.
47. **Terms on Reverse:** THE TERMS AND CONDITIONS ON THE REVERSE SIDE HEREOF ARE INCORPORATED HEREIN BY REFERENCE.
48. **Agency Confirmation:** Unless otherwise disclosed in writing, Buyer and Seller understand and agree that Brokers represent the Seller only, and have a
49. duty to treat fairly all parties to the transaction.
50. The undersigned agree to purchase the Premises on the terms and conditions herein stated and acknowledge receipt of a copy hereof.
51. _____   _____
    (Buyer's Signature)   Mo/Da/Yr   (Buyer's Signature)   Mo/Da/Yr
52. _____   _____
    Street   City   State   Zip

ACCEPTANCE

53. Seller agrees to sell the Premises as stated herein and for services rendered, agrees to pay a brokerage fee as follows:
54. _____ to _____("Broker named in Line 7")
55. _____ to _____("Listing Broker")
56. Seller instructs escrow company to pay such fee to Brokers in cash as a condition to closing and, to the extent necessary, irrevocably assigns Seller's
57. proceeds to Brokers at close of escrow. If completion of the sale is prevented by default of Seller, or with the consent of Seller, the entire brokerage fee
58. shall be paid directly by Seller. If the earnest deposit is forfeited for any reason, Seller shall pay a brokerage fee equal to one-half of the earnest deposit,
59. provided such payment shall not exceed the full amount of the brokerage fee. Nothing in this paragraph shall be construed as limiting applicable provisions
60. of law or any listing agreement relating to when commissions are earned or payable. UPON ACCEPTANCE OF THIS CONTRACT, SELLER HEREBY
61. WAIVES HIS RIGHT TO RECEIVE ANY SUBSEQUENT OFFER TO PURCHASE THE PREMISES UNTIL AFTER FORFEITURE BY BUYER OR OTHER
62. CANCELLATION OF THIS CONTRACT.
63. **Seller Receipt of Copy:** The undersigned acknowledge receipt of a copy hereof and grant permission to Broker in Line 7 to deliver a copy to Buyer.
64. ☐ **Counter Offer** is attached, which is incorporated herein by reference. If there is a conflict between this Contract and the Counter Offer, the provisions of
65. the Counter Offer shall be controlling. (NOTE: If this box is checked, Seller must sign both Contract and Counter Offer.)

66. _____   _____
    (Seller's Signature)   Mo/Da/Yr   (Seller's Signature)   Mo/Da/Yr
67. _____   _____
    (Print Name of Seller)   (Print Name of Seller)
68. _____   _____
    Street   City   State   Zip

For Broker Use Only | Brokerage File/Log No._____ Manager's Initials_____ Broker's Initials_____ Date_____

ᶜArizona Association of REALTORS® 1990 **This Form Available Through Your Local Board of REALTORS®**   FORM RREPCRD 4/90

**Figure 10.3
(continued)**

69. **Time of Essence:** Time is of the essence.

70. **Permission:** Buyer and Seller grant Brokers permission to advise the public of the sale upon execution of this Contract, and Brokers may disclose
71. price and terms herein after close of escrow.

72. **Entire Agreement:** This Contract, any attached exhibits and any addenda or supplements signed by the parties, shall constitute the entire agreement
73. between Seller and Buyer. and shall supersede any other written or oral agreement between Seller and Buyer. This Contract can be modified only by
74. a writing signed by Seller and Buyer. A fully executed facsimile copy of the entire agreement shall be treated as an original Contract.

75. **Title and Title Insurance:** Seller hereby instructs the escrow company to obtain and distribute to Buyer a preliminary title report together with
76. complete and legible copies of all documents which will remain as exceptions to Buyer's policy of title insurance. Title to the real property described
77. in Lines 8-12 of this Contract shall be conveyed by a general warranty deed. Title to the personal property described in Lines 13-17 of this Contract
78. shall be transferred free and clear of any liens or encumbrances. Seller shall furnish to Buyer, at Seller's expense, a Standard Owner's Title
79. Insurance Policy in the full amount of the purchase price issued by a title insurance company, showing good and marketable title to the real property
80. vested in Buyer free from defects and encumbrances except as follows: (1) liens and other matters described in this Contract, (2) building, use and
81. other restrictive covenants of record, (3) claims, title or rights to water (4) zoning regulations, (5) easements and rights-of-way for roadways,
82. canals, laterals, ditches and public utilities, (6) taxes, paving, irrigation and other assessments not delinquent as of the close of escrow, (7) rights of
83. tenants in possession, if any. (8) rights and minerals reserved in patents or otherwise by any entity, (9) printed exceptions contained in the Standard
84. Owner's Title Insurance Policy. If title to the real property otherwise is defective at the time set for close of escrow, Buyer may elect, as Buyer's sole
85. option, either to accept title subject to defects which are not cured or to cancel this Contract whereupon all money paid by Buyer pursuant to this
86. Contract shall be returned to Buyer. Buyer shall furnish to Seller. at Buyer's expense, a Standard Loan Policy in the full amount of any loan carried
87. back by Seller and secured by the real property described in Lines 8-12 of this Contract. Such Standard Loan Policy shall show that Seller's lien has
88. the priority agreed to by the parties. If applicable Seller agrees to complete, sign and deliver to escrow company a certificate indicating whether
89. Seller is a foreign person or non-resident alien pursuant to the Foreign Investment in Real Property Tax Act. (FIRPTA)

90. **Documents and Escrow:** (1) If Seller and Buyer elect to execute escrow instructions to fulfill the terms hereof, they shall deliver the same to escrow
91. company within 15 days of the acceptance of this Contract. (2) All documents necessary to close this transaction shall be executed promptly by
92. Seller and Buyer in the standard form used by escrow company. Seller and Buyer hereby instruct escrow company to modify such documents to the
93. extent necessary to be consistent with the Contract. (3) If any conflict exists between this Contract and any escrow instructions executed pursuant
94. hereto, the provisions of this Contract shall be controlling. (4) All closing and escrow costs shall be allocated between Seller and Buyer in accordance
95. with local custom and applicable laws and regulations. (5) Escrow company is hereby instructed to send to Brokers copies of all notices and
96. communications directed to Seller or Buyer and shall provide to such Brokers access to escrowed materials and information about the escrow upon
97. request. (6) Any documents necessary to close the escrow may be signed in counterparts, each of which shall be effective as an original upon
98. execution and all of which together shall constitute one and the same instrument.

99. **Default and Remedies:** If Buyer defaults in any respect on any material obligations under this Contract, Seller may elect to be released from the
100. obligation to sell the Premises to Buyer. Seller may proceed against Buyer upon any claim or remedy which he may have, in law or equity, or
101. because it would be difficult to fix actual damages in case of Buyer's default, the amount of the earnest deposit may be deemed a reasonable
102. estimate of the damages; and Seller may, at his option retain the earnest deposit, subject to the brokerage fee as provided herein, as his sole right to
103. damages. If Buyer or Seller files suit against the other to enforce any provision of this Contract or for damages sustained by reason of its breach, all
104. parties prevailing in such action, on trial and appeal, shall receive their reasonable attorneys' fees and costs as awarded by the court. In
105. addition, both Seller and Buyer agree to indemnify and hold harmless all Brokers against all costs and expenses, which any Broker may incur or
106. sustain in connection with any lawsuit arising from this Contract and will pay the same on demand unless the court shall grant judgment in such
107. action against the party to be indemnified. Costs shall include, without limitation: attorneys' fees, expert witness fees, fees paid to investigators and
108. court costs.

109. **Warranties:** Except as otherwise provided in this Contract, Seller warrants and shall maintain and repair the Premises so that, at the earlier of
110. possession or the close of escrow: (1) the Premises shall be in substantially the same condition as on the effective date of this Contract, (2) the roof
111. has no known leaks, (3) all heating, cooling, mechanical, plumbing and electrical systems and built-in appliances will be in working condition, (4) if the
112. Premises has a swimming pool and/or spa, the motors, filter systems, cleaning systems, and heaters, if so equipped, will be in working condition.
113. The Seller grants Buyer or Buyer's representative reasonable access to enter and inspect the Premises for the purpose of satisfying Buyer that the
114. items warranted by Seller are in working condition. Buyer shall keep the Premises free and clear of any liens; indemnify and hold Seller and Brokers
115. harmless from all liability, claims, demands and costs; and repair all damages to the Premises caused by said inspection. At the earlier of
116. possession or close of escrow, Buyer acknowledges that all warranties concerning the Premises have been satisfied or extinguished. Any personal
117. property included herein shall be transferred IN AS IS CONDITION AND SELLER MAKES NO WARRANTY of any kind, express or implied (including,
118. without limitation, ANY WARRANTY OF MERCHANTABILITY). Brokers are hereby relieved of any and all liability and responsibility from everything
119. stated in this paragraph and the following paragraph.

120. **Warranties That Survive Closing:** Prior to the close of escrow, Seller warrants that, payment in full will have been made for all labor, professional
121. services, materials, machinery, fixtures or tools furnished within the 120 days immediately preceding the close of escrow in connection with the
122. construction, alteration or repair of any structure on or improvement to the Premises. Seller warrants that the information in the current listing
123. agreement, if any, regarding connection to a public sewer system, septic tank or other sanitation system is correct to the best of his knowledge.
124. Seller warrants that he has disclosed to Buyer and Brokers all material latent defects concerning the Premises that are known to Seller. Seller further
125. warrants that he has disclosed to all parties any information, excluding opinions of value, that he possesses which materially and adversely affects the
126. consideration to be paid by Buyer.

127. **Representations and Releases:** By signing this Contract, Buyer represents that he has or will have prior to close of escrow conducted all
128. independent investigations desired by Buyer of any and all matters concerning this purchase and by closing accepts the Premises. Seller and Buyer
129. hereby release all Brokers from all responsibility and liability regarding the condition, square footage, lot lines or boundaries, value, rent rolls,
130. compliance with building codes or other governmental regulations, or other material matters relating to the Premises; and neither Seller, Buyer, nor
131. any Broker shall be bound by any understanding, agreement, promise or representation, express or implied, not specified herein.

132. **Wood Infestation Report:** Seller will, at his expense, place in escrow a wood infestation report by a qualified licensed pest control operator, which,
133. when considered in its entirety, indicates that all residences and buildings attached to the Premises are free from evidence of current infestation and
134. damage from wood-destroying pests or organisms. Seller agrees to pay up to one percent of the purchase price for the treatment and repair of the
135. damage caused by infestation and correct any conditions conducive to infestation. If such costs exceed one percent of the purchase price: (1)
136. Buyer may elect to cancel this Contract unless Seller agrees in writing to pay such costs, or (2) Seller may elect to cancel this contract unless Buyer
137. agrees in writing to either accept the Premises or to pay such costs in excess of one percent that the Seller has agreed to pay.

138. **Recommendations:** If any Broker recommends a builder, contractor, or any other person or entity to Seller or Buyer for any purpose, such
139. recommendation will be independently investigated and evaluated by Seller or Buyer, who hereby acknowledge that any decision to enter into any
140. contractual arrangements with any person or entity recommended by any Broker will be based solely upon such independent investigation and
141. evaluation. Seller and Buyer understand that said contractual arrangement may result in a commission or fee to Broker.

142. **Risk of Loss:** If there is any loss or damage to the Premises between the date hereof and the close of escrow, by reason of fire, vandalism, flood,
143. earthquake or act of God. the risk of loss shall be on the Seller, provided. however, that if the cost of repairing such loss or damage would exceed
144. ten percent of the purchase price. (1) Buyer may elect to cancel this Contract unless Seller agrees in writing to pay the cost of repairing all such loss
145. or damage, or (2) Seller may elect to cancel this Contract unless Buyer agrees in writing to accept the Premises and to pay the cost of repair in
146. excess of ten percent of the purchase price that the Seller has agreed to pay.

147. **Cancellation:** Any party who wishes to cancel this Contract because of any breach by another party, or because escrow fails to close by the agreed
148. date, and who is not himself in breach of this Contract. except as occasioned by a breach by the other party, may cancel this Contract by delivering a
149. notice to either the breaching party or to the escrow company stating the nature of the breach and that this Contract shall be cancelled unless the
150. breach is cured within 13 days following the delivery of the notice. If this notice is delivered to the escrow company, it shall contain the address of
151. the party in breach. Any notice delivered to any party must be delivered to the Brokers and the escrow company. Within three days after receipt of
152. such notice, the escrow company shall send the notice by United States Mail to the party in breach at the address contained in the notice. No further
153. notice shall be required. In the event that the breach is not cured within 13 days following the delivery of the notice to the party in breach or to the
154. escrow company, this Contract shall be cancelled.

155. **Brokers' Rights:** If any Broker hires an attorney to enforce the collection of the commission payable pursuant to this Contract, and is successful in
156. collecting some or all of such commission, Seller agrees to pay such Broker's costs including, but not limited to: attorneys' fees, expert witness fees,
157. fees paid to investigators. and court costs. The parties agree that any monies deposited in the trust account of the Broker named in line 7 pursuant
158. to this Contract may earn interest. and that the Broker shall be entitled to all of the interest from said interest-bearing trust account as additional
159. compensation. The Seller and the Buyer acknowledge that the Brokers are third-party beneficiaries of this Contract.

160. **FHA or VA:** If applicable, the current language prescribed by FHA and VA pertaining to the value of the Premises shall be incorporated in this
161. Contract by reference as if set forth in full herein, and Seller and Buyer agree to execute any appropriate FHA or VA supplements to this Contract.
162. Buyer is entitled to a return of the earnest deposit if, after a diligent and good faith effort, Buyer does not qualify for a VA or FHA Loan. Buyer
163. acknowledges that prepaid items paid separately from earnest money are not refundable.

164. **Buyer's Loan:** If Buyer is seeking a new loan or an assumption of an existing loan that requires qualification in connection with this transaction.
165. Buyer agrees to file a substantially complete loan application within five business days after the acceptance of this Contract and to promptly supply all
166. documentation required by the lender.

167. **Severability:** If a court of competent jurisdiction makes a final determination that any term or provision of this Contract is invalid or unenforceable, all
168. other terms and provisions shall remain in full force and effect, and the invalid or unenforceable term or provision shall be deemed replaced by a term
169. or provision that is valid and enforceable and comes closest to expressing the intention of the invalid term or provision.

170. **Construction of Language:** The language of this Contract shall be construed according to its fair meaning and not strictly for or against either party.
171. Words used in the masculine, feminine or neuter shall apply to either gender or the neuter, as appropriate. All singular and plural words shall be
172. interpreted to refer to the number consistent with circumstances and context.

This form is available for use by the entire real estate industry. The use of this form is not intended to identify the user as a REALTOR, REALTOR is a registered collective membership mark which may be used only by real estate licensees who are members of the NATIONAL ASSOCIATION OF REALTORS and who subscribe to its Code of Ethics

Arizona Association of REALTORS 1990 **This Form Available Through Your Local Board of REALTORS**   FORM RREPCRD 4/90

that includes an option for the tenant to purchase the property. Options must contain all the terms and provisions required for a valid contract of sale.

Land Contracts

A real estate sale can be made under a **land contract,** sometimes called *a contract for deed,* an **installment contract** or *articles of agreement for warranty deed.* Under a typical land contract the seller, also known as the *vendor,* retains fee ownership while the buyer, known as the *vendee,* secures possession and an equitable interest in the property. The buyer agrees to give the seller a down payment and pay regular monthly installments of principal and interest over a number of years. The buyer also agrees to pay real estate taxes, insurance premiums, repairs and upkeep on the property. Although the buyer obtains possession when the contract is signed by both parties, *the seller is not obligated to execute and deliver a deed to the buyer until the terms of the contract have been satisfied.* This frequently occurs when the buyer has made a sufficient number of payments to obtain a mortgage loan and pay off the balance due on the contract.

Real estate is occasionally sold with the new buyer assuming an existing land contract from the original buyer/vendee. Generally the seller/vendor must approve the new purchaser.

In Practice . . .

Land contracts require extensive input from lawyers experienced in real estate matters. The broker who negotiates a land contract should consult attorneys for both parties at every step of the way and refrain from specifying any detailed terms in the agreement.

Rescission

With contracts for the purchase of some types of personal property, the buyer has three days in which to reconsider and *rescind* (cancel) the contract. No such right of rescission applies to contracts for the purchase of real estate.

Key Terms

assignment	liquidated damages
bilateral contract	novation
breach of contract	offer and acceptance
consideration	option
contingency	parol evidence rule
contract	specific performance suit
counteroffer	statute of frauds
default	statute of limitations
earnest money deposit	time is of the essence
equitable title	unenforceable contract
executed contract	unilateral contract
executory contract	valid contract
installment contract	void contract
land contract	voidable contract

Summary

A contract is defined as a legally enforceable promise or set of promises that must be performed and, if a breach occurs, for which the law provides a remedy.

Contracts must be in writing.

Contracts may be classified according to whether the parties' intentions are express or are implied by their actions. They may also be classified as bilateral, when both parties have obligated themselves to act, or unilateral, when one party is obligated to perform only if the other party acts. In addition, contracts may be classified according to their legal enforceability as either valid, void, voidable or unenforceable.

Many contracts specify a time for performance. In any case all contracts must be performed within a reasonable time. An executed contract is one that has been fully performed. An executory contract is one in which some act remains to be performed.

The essentials of a valid contract are legally competent parties, offer and acceptance, legality of object and consideration. A valid real estate contract must include a description of the property, and it should be in writing and signed by all parties to be enforceable in court.

In many types of contracts either of the parties may transfer his or her rights and obligations under the agreement by assignment of the contract or novation (substitution of a new contract).

Contracts usually provide that the seller has the right to declare a sale canceled if the buyer defaults. If either party has suffered a loss because of the other's default, he or she may sue for damages to cover the loss. If one party insists on completing the transaction, he or she may sue the defaulter for specific performance of the terms of the contract; a court can order the other party to comply with the agreement.

Contracts frequently used in the real estate business include listing agreements, sales contracts, options, land contracts (installment contracts) and leases.

A real estate sales contract binds a buyer and a seller to a definite transaction as described in detail in the contract. The buyer is bound to purchase the property for the amount stated in the agreement. The seller is bound to deliver title, free from liens and encumbrances (except those identified in the contract).

Under an option agreement the optionee purchases from the optionor, for a limited time period, the exclusive right to purchase or lease the optionor's property. A land contract, or installment contract, is a sales/financing agreement under which a buyer purchases a seller's real estate on time. The buyer takes possession of and responsibility for the property but does not receive the deed immediately.

Questions

1. A legally enforceable agreement under which two parties agree to do something for each other is known as a(n):
   a. escrow agreement.
   b. legal promise.
   c. valid contract.
   d. option agreement.

2. D drives into a filling station and tops off her gas tank. She is obligated to pay for the fuel through what kind of contract?
   a. Express   c. Oral
   b. Implied   d. Voidable

3. A contract is said to be *bilateral* if:
   a. one of the parties is a minor.
   b. the contract has yet to be fully performed.
   c. only one party to the agreement is bound to act.
   d. all parties to the contract are bound to act.

4. A seller gave an open listing to several brokers, specifically promising that if one of the brokers found a buyer for the seller's real estate the seller would be obligated to pay a commission to that broker. This offer by the seller is a(n):
   a. executed agreement.
   b. discharged agreement.
   c. implied agreement.
   d. unilateral agreement.

5. During the period of time after a real estate sales contract is signed but before title actually passes, the status of the contract is:
   a. voidable.   c. unilateral.
   b. executory. d. implied.

6. A contract for the sale of real estate that does not state the consideration to be paid for the property and is not signed by the parties is considered to be:
   a. voidable.   c. void.
   b. executory. d. enforceable.

7. The statute of frauds requires that a contract must be in writing for:
   a. all real estate sales.
   b. all real estate contracts of any sort.
   c. all contracts.
   d. bilateral contracts only.

8. The seller told the buyer she would leave the washing machine but instead took it with her. The written contract made no mention of the washing machine. The buyer has no right to complain because of the rule of:
   a. partial performance.
   b. novation.
   c. undue influence.
   d. parol evidence.

9. A suit for specific performance of a real estate contract asks for:
   a. money damages.
   b. a new contract.
   c. a deficiency judgment.
   d. a forced sale or purchase.

10. If a real estate sales contract does not state that time is of the essence and the stipulated date of transfer comes and goes without a closing, the contract is:
    a. binding for only 30 more days.
    b. novated.
    c. still valid.
    d. automatically void.

11. In filling out a sales contract someone crossed out several words and inserted others. To eliminate future controversy as to whether the changes were made before or after the contract was signed, the usual procedure is to:
    a. write a letter to each party listing the changes.
    b. have each party write a letter to the other approving the changes.
    c. redraw the entire contract.
    d. have both parties initial or sign in the margin near each change.

12. A real estate purchaser is said to have *equitable title:*

 a. when the sales contract is signed by both buyer and seller.
 b. when the transaction is closed.
 c. when escrow is opened.
 d. when a contract for deed is paid off.

13. The sales contract says J will purchase only if his wife flies up and approves the sale by the following Saturday. Mrs. J's approval is a:

 a. contingency.   c. warranty.
 b. reservation.   d. consideration.

14. When the buyer promises to purchase only if he can sell his own present home, the seller gains some protection from an:

 a. escrow.   c. equitable title.
 b. option.   d. escape clause.

15. An option to purchase binds:

 a. the buyer only.
 b. the seller only.
 c. neither buyer nor seller.
 d. both buyer and seller.

16. Which of the following best describes a land contract, or installment contract?

 a. A contract to buy land only
 b. A mortgage on land
 c. A means of conveying title immediately while the purchaser pays for the property in installments
 d. A method of selling real estate whereby the purchaser pays in regular installments while the seller retains title

17. The purchaser of real estate under an installment contract:

 a. generally pays no interest charge.
 b. receives title immediately.
 c. is not required to pay property taxes for the duration of the contract.
 d. is called a vendee.

18. Under the statute of frauds all contracts for the sale of real estate must be:

 a. originated by a real estate broker.
 b. on preprinted forms.
 c. in writing.
 d. accompanied by earnest money deposits.

19. The Fs offer in writing to purchase a house for $120,000, including its draperies, with the offer to expire on Saturday at noon. The Ws reply in writing on Thursday, accepting the $120,000 offer but excluding the draperies. On Friday, while the Fs are considering this counteroffer, the Ws decide to accept the original offer, draperies included, and state that in writing. At this point, the Fs:

 a. must buy the house and have the right to insist on the draperies.
 b. are not bound to buy and can forget the whole situation.
 c. must buy the house but are not entitled to the draperies.
 d. must buy the house and can deduct the value of the draperies from the $120,000.

20. Q makes an offer to purchase certain property listed with broker M and leaves a deposit with the broker M to show good faith. M should:

 a. immediately apply the deposit to the listing expenses.
 b. put the deposit in an account as provided by state law.
 c. give the deposit to the seller when the offer is presented.
 d. put the deposit in her checking account.

21. T has a contract to buy property but would rather let his friend M buy it instead. If the contract allows, M can take over T's obligation by the process known as:

 a. assignment.
 b. substantial performance.
 c. subordination.
 d. mutual consent.

22. Broker J has found a buyer for G's home. The buyer has indicated in writing his willingness to buy the property for $1,000 less than the asking price and has deposited $5,000 earnest money with broker J. G is out of town for the weekend, and J has been unable to inform him of the signed document. At this point, the buyer has signed a(n):

 a. voidable contract.
 b. offer.
 c. executory agreement.
 d. implied contract.

11

Transfer of Title

Title

The term *title* has two functions. **Title** to real estate means the right to or ownership of the land; it represents the "bundle of rights" the owner possesses. Title also represents the *evidence* of ownership; it denotes the facts that, if proven, would enable a person to recover or retain ownership or possession of a parcel of real estate.

A parcel of real estate may be transferred *voluntarily* by sale or gift, or it may be taken *involuntarily* by operation of law. In addition, it may be transferred by the living or by will or descent after a person has died.

Voluntary Alienation

Voluntary alienation (transfer) of title may be made by either gift or sale. To transfer title by voluntary alienation during his or her lifetime an owner must use some form of deed of conveyance.

A **deed** is a *written instrument by which an owner of real estate intentionally conveys his or her right, title or interest in a parcel of real estate to another*. All deeds must be in writing in accordance with the requirements of the statute of frauds. The owner is referred to as the **grantor,** and the one who acquires title is called the **grantee.** A deed is executed (signed) by the grantor.

Requirements for a Valid Conveyance

Although the formal requirements for a valid deed are not uniform in all states, certain requirements are basic:

1. A *grantor* having the legal capacity to execute (sign) the deed

2. A *grantee* named with reasonable certainty so that he or she can be identified

3. A recital of *consideration*

4. A *granting clause* (words of conveyance)

5. A habendum clause (to define ownership taken by the grantee)

6. Designation of any *limitations* on the conveyance of a full fee simple estate

7. An accurate *legal description* of the property conveyed

8. *Exceptions and reservations,* if any, affecting the title

9. The *signature of the grantor,* sometimes with a seal

10. *Delivery* of the deed and *acceptance* by the grantee to pass title

Grantor. A grantor must be of sound mind and of lawful age. A **minor,** generally a person under 18 years old, usually does not have legal capacity to transfer title. Any attempted conveyance by a minor is considered voidable (see Chapter 10). A grantor generally is held to have sufficient mental capacity to execute a deed if he or she is capable of understanding the action. A deed executed by a person while mentally impaired (as by intoxication) is only *voidable*—it is not void. A deed executed by a person who has been judged legally incompetent is considered to be void. Court authority must be secured before real estate owned by a legally incompetent person can be conveyed.

In some states a grantor's spouse is required to sign any deed of conveyance so as to waive any marital and/or homestead rights. This requirement varies according to state law and the manner in which the title to real estate is held, as discussed in Chapters 6 and 7.

It is important that a grantor's name be spelled correctly and that there be no variation in its spelling throughout the deed. If for any reason a grantor's name has been changed from that by which title was acquired originally, as when a woman changes her name by marriage, both names should be shown as, for example, ''Mary Smith, formerly Mary Jones.''

Grantee. To be valid a deed must name a grantee and do so in such a way that the grantee is readily identifiable.

Consideration. To be valid all deeds must contain a clause acknowledging the grantor's receipt of a consideration. In most states the amount of consideration must be stated in dollars. When a deed conveys real estate as a gift to a relative, ''love and affection'' may be sufficient consideration, but it is customary in most states to recite a *nominal* consideration, such as ''$10 and other good and valuable consideration.'' The full dollar amount of consideration is seldom set forth in the deed, except when the instrument is executed by a corporation or trustee or pursuant to court order by an executor or administrator.

Granting clause (words of conveyance). A deed must state, in the **granting clause,** the grantor's intention to convey the property. Depending on the type of deed and the obligations agreed to by the grantor, the wording generally is either ''convey and warrant,'' ''grant,'' ''grant, bargain and sell'' or ''remise, release and quitclaim.'' Deeds that convey the entire fee simple interest of the grantor usually contain wording such as ''to Jacqueline Smith and to her heirs and assigns forever.'' If the grantor is conveying less than his or her complete interest, such as a life estate, the wording must indicate this limitation; for example, ''to Jacqueline Smith for the duration of her natural life.''

If more than one grantee is involved, the granting clause should specify their rights in the property. The clause might state, for example, that the grantees will take title as joint tenants or tenants in common. This section is especially important because specific wording is necessary to create a joint tenancy.

Habendum clause. When it is necessary to define or explain the ownership to be enjoyed by the grantee, a **habendum clause** follows the granting clause. The habendum clause begins with the words "to have and to hold." Its provisions must agree with those set down in the granting clause. For example, when conveying a time-share interest or an interest less than fee simple absolute, the habendum clause would specify the rights that the owner is entitled to as well as how they are limited (timeframe, prohibited activity, etc.).

Legal description of real estate. To be valid a deed must contain an adequate legal description of the real estate conveyed. Land is considered adequately described if a competent surveyor can locate the property using the description.

Exceptions and reservations. A grantor may reserve some right in the land for his or her own use (an easement, for instance). A grantor also may place certain restrictions on a grantee's use of the property. A developer, for example, can restrict the number of houses that may be built on a one-acre lot in a subdivision. Such restrictions may be stated in the deed or contained in a previously recorded document (such as the subdivider's master deed) that is expressly cited in the deed.

A deed should specifically note any encumbrances, reservations or limitations that affect the title being conveyed. Such exceptions to clear title may include mortgage liens, taxes, restrictions and easements that run with the land.

Signature of grantor. To be valid a deed must be signed by *all grantors* named in the deed. As discussed previously, in some states the spouse must also sign the deed to release marital or other rights. Some states also require witnesses to the grantor's signature. Most states permit an attorney-in-fact to sign for a grantor. The attorney must be acting under a *power of attorney,* the specific written authority to execute and sign one or more legal instruments for another person. Usually the power of attorney must be recorded in the county where the property is located. Because the power of attorney terminates upon the death of the person granting such authority, adequate evidence must be submitted that the grantor was alive at the time the attorney-in-fact signed the deed.

A grantor who is unable to write is permitted to sign by *mark* in most states. With this type of signature two persons other than the notary public taking the acknowledgment (discussed below) usually must witness the grantor's execution of the deed and sign as witnesses.

In some states it is still necessary for a seal or the word *seal* to be written or printed after an individual grantor's signature. The corporate seal should always be used by corporations.

Acknowledgment. An acknowledgment is a form of declaration made voluntarily by a person who is signing a formal, written document before a notary public or an authorized public officer, such as a judge, justice of the peace, court clerk, county clerk or one of certain officers in the military as prescribed by state law. An acknowledgment usually states that the person signing the deed or other document is known to the officer or has produced sufficient identification and that the person signing is doing so as his or her own *free and voluntary act.* The acknowledgment provides evidence that the signature is genuine. The form of the certificate of acknowledgment authorized by the state where the property is located should be used even if the party signing is a resident of another ("foreign") state.

Although it is customary to acknowledge the execution of a deed to real estate, such acknowledgment is not essential to the *validity* of the deed unless state statutes require it. From a purely practical point of view a deed that is not acknowledged is not a satisfactory instrument. In some states an unacknowledged deed is not eligible for recording.

Delivery and acceptance. A transfer of title by conveyance cannot take effect until actual delivery of the deed by the grantor and either actual or implied acceptance by the grantee. Delivery may be made by the grantor to the grantee personally or to a third party, commonly known as an *escrow* (discussed in Chapter 23), for ultimate delivery to the grantee upon the fulfillment of certain requirements. *Title is said to pass when a deed is delivered.* The effective date of the transfer from the grantor and to the grantee is the date of delivery of the deed itself. When a deed is delivered in escrow, the date of delivery of the conveyance generally is ("relates back" to) the date that it was deposited with the escrow agent. (However, when the real estate is registered under the Torrens system, as discussed in Chapter 12, title does not pass until the deed has been examined and accepted for registration).

Execution of Corporate Deeds

The laws affecting corporations' rights to convey real estate vary from state to state. Some basic rules include the following:

1. A corporation can convey real estate only by authority granted in its *bylaws* or upon a proper resolution passed by its *board of directors*. If all or a substantial portion of a corporation's real estate is being conveyed, usually a resolution authorizing the sale must be secured from the *stockholders*.

2. Deeds to real estate can be *signed only by an authorized officer*.

3. The corporate *seal* must be affixed to the conveyance.

Rules pertaining to religious corporations and not-for-profit corporations vary widely. Because the legal requirements must be followed strictly, it is advisable to consult an attorney for all corporate conveyances.

Types of Deeds

The most common forms of deeds are:

1. general warranty deed;

2. special warranty deed;

3. bargain and sale deed;

4. quitclaim deed;

5. deed in trust;

6. trustee's deed;

7. reconveyance deed; and

8. deed executed pursuant to a court order.

General warranty deed. A **general warranty deed** provides a purchaser of real estate the *greatest protection* of any deed. It is called a *general warranty deed* or simply a *warranty deed* because the grantor is legally bound by certain covenants

**Figure 11.1
Sample Deeds**

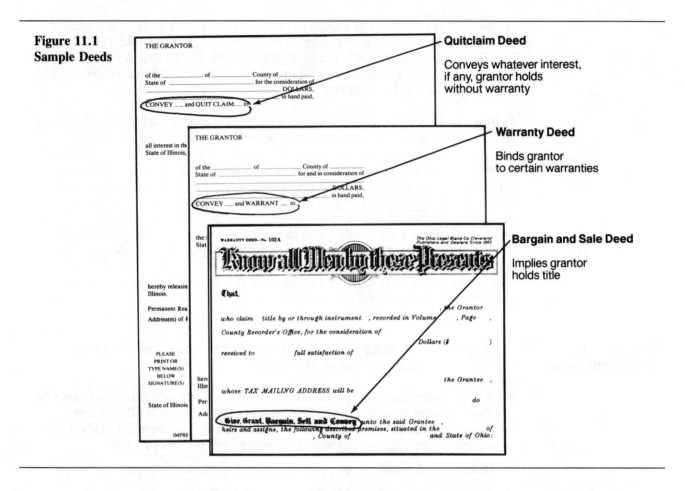

Quitclaim Deed

Conveys whatever interest,
if any, grantor holds
without warranty

Warranty Deed

Binds grantor
to certain warranties

Bargain and Sale Deed

Implies grantor
holds title

or warranties. In most states the warranties are usually implied by the use of certain words specified in the state statutes. Each state law should be examined, but some of the specific words include "convey and warrant," "warrant generally" and, in some states, "grant, bargain and sell." In some localities the grantor's warranties are expressly written into the deed itself. These are the basic warranties:

1. *Covenant of seisin:* The grantor warrants that he or she is the owner of the property and has the right to convey title to it. The grantee may recover damages up to the full purchase price if this covenant is broken.

2. *Covenant against encumbrances:* The grantor warrants that the property is free from liens or encumbrances except those specifically stated in the deed. Encumbrances generally include mortgages, mechanics' liens and easements. If this covenant is breached, the grantee may sue for expenses to remove the encumbrance.

3. *Covenant of quiet enjoyment:* The grantor guarantees that the grantee's title will be good against third parties who might bring court actions to establish superior title to the property. If the grantee's title is found to be inferior, the grantor is liable for damages.

4. *Covenant of further assurance:* The grantor promises to obtain and deliver any instrument needed to make the title good. For example, if the grantor's spouse has failed to sign away dower rights, the grantor must deliver a quitclaim deed (discussed below) executed by the spouse to clear the title.

5. *Covenant of warranty forever:* The grantor guarantees that if the title fails at any time in the future, he or she will compensate the grantee for the loss sustained.

These covenants in a general warranty deed are not limited to matters that occurred during the time the grantor owned the property; they extend back to its origins.

Special warranty deed. A conveyance that carries only one covenant is a **special warranty deed,** also called a *limited warranty deed* or, in some areas a *bargain and sale deed with covenant.* The grantor warrants *only* that the property was not encumbered during the time he or she held title except as noted in the deed. Special warranty deeds generally contain the words "remise, release, alienate and convey" in the granting clause. Any additional warranties must be specifically stated in the deed.

A special warranty deed may be used by a fiduciary such as an estate representative or trustee and will usually state the full consideration for the property. A special warranty deed may also be used by a corporation and sometimes by a grantor who has acquired title at a tax sale.

Bargain and sale deed. Deeds using the words "grant and release" or "grant, bargain and sell" in the granting clause are usually **bargain and sale deeds.** A bargain and sale deed contains no warranties against encumbrances; however, it does *imply* that the grantor holds title and possession of the property. Because the warranty is not specifically stated, the grantee has little legal recourse if defects later appear in the title. In some areas this deed is used in foreclosures and tax sales. The buyer would purchase title insurance for protection.

Quitclaim deed. A **quitclaim deed** provides the grantee with the least protection. It carries no covenant or warranties and conveys only any interest the grantor may have when the deed is delivered. Through a quitclaim deed the grantor only "remises, releases and quitclaims" his or her interest in the property to the grantee.

If the grantor has no interest in the property, the grantee will acquire neither title nor any claim against the grantor. A quitclaim deed can convey title as effectively as a warranty deed if the grantor has good title when he or she delivers the deed, but it provides no guarantees.

A quitclaim deed commonly is used for simple transfers within a family and for property transferred during divorce settlements. It also can be used to clear a cloud on a title when persons who may or may not have some claim to property are asked to "sign off."

Deed in trust. A **deed in trust** is the means by which a *trustor* conveys real estate to a *trustee* for the benefit of a *beneficiary.* The real estate is held by the trustee to fulfill the purpose of the trust.

Trustee's deed. A deed of conveyance executed by a trustee is a **trustee's deed** and is used when a trustee named in a will, trust agreement or trust deed conveys the trust real estate to anyone other than the trustor. The trustee's deed sets forth the fact that the trustee is executing the instrument in accordance with the powers and authority granted to him or her by the trust instrument.

Reconveyance deed. A **reconveyance deed** is used by a trustee under a deed of trust (a financing document) to return title to the trustor. For example, when a loan secured by a deed of trust has been fully paid, the beneficiary notifies the trustee, who then reconveys the property to the trustor. As with any document of title, a reconveyance deed should be recorded to prevent future title problems.

Deed executed pursuant to court order. This classification covers such deed forms as executors' (or administrators') deeds, masters' deeds, sheriffs' deeds and many others. These statutory deed forms are used to convey title to property that is transferred by court order or by will. The forms of such deeds must conform to the laws of the state where the property is located.

One characteristic of such instruments is that the *full consideration* is usually stated in the deed. Instead of $10 and other valuable consideration, the deed would list the actual sales price.

Transfer Tax Stamps

Most states have enacted laws providing for a tax, usually referred to as the state **transfer tax,** on conveyances of real estate. In these states the tax is usually payable when the deed is recorded, through the purchase of *stamps* (sometimes called *documentary stamps*) from the county recorder of the county in which the deed is recorded. The stamps are then affixed to deeds and conveyances before the document can be recorded.

The *transfer tax is usually paid by the seller*. The *tax rate* varies from state to state; examples are rates of 50¢ for each $500, or $1.50 for each $1,000 or fraction thereof of taxable consideration.

In many states a *transfer declaration form (or transfer statement* or *affidavit of real property value)* must be signed by both the buyer and the seller or their agents. This form usually requires such information as the full sales price of the property; the legal description of the property; the address, date and type of deed; and the type of improvement. The form also must specify when a transfer is being made between relatives or in accordance with a court order.

Certain deeds may be *exempted* from the tax, such as gifts of real estate; deeds not made in connection with a sale (such as a change in the form of co-ownership); conveyances to, from or between governmental bodies; deeds by charitable, religious or educational institutions; deeds securing debts or releasing property as security for a debt; partitions; tax deeds; deeds pursuant to mergers of corporations; and deeds from subsidiary to parent corporations for cancellations of stock.

Involuntary Alienation

Title to property can be transferred by **involuntary alienation,** that is, without the owner's consent (see Figure 11.2). Such transfers are usually carried out by operation of law and range from government condemnation of land for public use to the sale of property to satisfy delinquent tax or mortgage liens. When a person dies intestate and leaves no heirs, the title to his or her real estate passes to the state by the state's power of escheat.

Federal, state and local governments, school boards, some government agencies and certain public and quasi-public corporations and utilities (railroads and gas and electric companies) have the power of *eminent domain*. Under this power private property may be taken for public use through a *suit for condemnation*. Eminent domain may be exercised only when a court determines that the use is for the benefit of the public; that an equitable amount of compensation, as set by the court, will be paid to the owner; and that the rights of the property owner will be protected by due process of law.

Land may also be transferred without an owner's consent to satisfy debts contracted by the owner. In such cases the debt is foreclosed, the property is sold and the proceeds of the sale are applied to pay off the debt. Debts that could be foreclosed include mortgage loans, real estate taxes, mechanics' liens and general judgments against the property owner.

In addition to the involuntary transfer of land by legal processes, land may be transferred by natural forces. As discussed in Chapter 6, owners of land bordering on rivers, lakes and other bodies of water may acquire additional land through the process of *accretion,* the slow accumulation of soil, rock or other matter deposited by the movement of water on an owner's property. The opposite of accretion is *erosion,* the gradual wearing away of land by the action of water and wind. In addition, property may be lost through *avulsion,* the sudden tearing away of land by such natural means as earthquakes or tidal waves.

Adverse possession is another means of involuntary transfer. An owner who does not use his or her land or does not inspect it for a number of years may lose

Figure 11.2
Involuntary Alienation

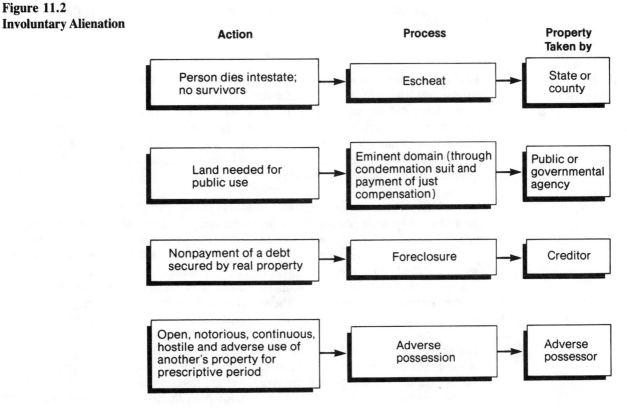

title to another person who makes some claim to the land, takes possession and, most importantly, uses the land. Through adverse possession the law recognizes that the use of land is an important function of its ownership. Usually the possession of the claimant must be open, notorious, continuous (uninterrupted for the number of years set by state law—as long as 20 years in some states), hostile and adverse to the true owner's possession. Through the principle of *tacking,* successive periods of different adverse possession by different adverse possessors can be combined, enabling a person who is not in possession for the entire required time to establish a claim of adverse possession. A claimant who does not receive title may acquire an easement by prescription (see Chapter 6).

In Practice . . .   *Because the right of adverse possession is statutory, and state requirements must be followed carefully to establish ownership, the parties to a transaction that might involve adverse possession should seek legal counsel.*

Transfer of a Deceased Person's Property

A person who dies **testate** has prepared a will indicating the way his or her property will be disposed of after death. Every state has a law known as the *statute of descent and distribution.* When a person dies **intestate** (without having left a will), the decedent's real estate and personal property pass to the decedent's heirs according to this statute.

Legally, when a person dies, title to the real estate owned by that person immediately passes either to the heirs by descent or to the persons named in the will. Before the heirs can take possession of the property, however, the estate must be probated and all claims against it must be satisfied.

Probate Proceedings

Probate is a legal process by which a court determines the assets of a deceased person and who will inherit those assets. When a person dies testate, the court rules on the validity of the will. If the will is upheld, the property is distributed according to the will's provisions. When a person dies intestate, the court determines who inherits by reviewing a *proof of heirship.* This statement, usually prepared by an attorney, gives personal information regarding the decedent's spouse, children and other relatives.

To initiate probate proceedings, the custodian of the will, an heir or another interested party must petition the court in the county where the real estate in question is located. If for any reason the will is declared invalid by the court, any property owned by the decedent will pass by the laws of descent. Once the heirs are established, the court will appoint an *administrator* (called an *administratrix* if a woman) to oversee the administration and distribution of the estate (if no *executor (executrix)* was named in the will). In some states the person who oversees an estate is called the *personal representative,* however appointed.

The court gives the administrator or executor the authority to appraise the assets of the estate and satisfy all debts owed by the decedent. The estate representative is also responsible for paying federal estate taxes and, in most states, state inheritance taxes. Once all these liens against the property have been satisfied, the executor distributes the remaining assets of the estate according to the provisions of the will or the state law of descent.

In Practice . . .   *A broker entering into a listing agreement with the executor or administrator of an estate in probate should be aware that the amount of commission will be fixed by the court and that such commission is payable only from the proceeds of the sale. The broker will not be able to collect a commission unless the court approves the sale.*

Transfer of Title by Will   A **will** is an instrument made by an owner to convey title to property after the owner's death. A will takes effect only after death; until that time, any property covered by the will can be conveyed by the owner and thus be removed from the owner's estate.

The gift of real property by will is known as a *devise,* and a person who receives property by will is known as a *devisee.*

A will cannot supersede the state laws of dower and curtesy, which were enacted to protect the inheritance rights of the surviving spouse. In a case where a will does not provide a spouse with the minimum statutory inheritance, the surviving spouse may demand it from the estate.

A will differs from a deed in that a deed conveys a present interest in real estate during the lifetime of the grantor, while a will conveys no interest in the property until after the death of the testator. To be valid a deed *must* be delivered during the lifetime of the grantor. The parties named in a will have no rights or interests as long as the party who has made the will is alive; they acquire interest or title only after the owner's death. For title to pass to the devisees, state laws usually require that upon the death of a testator the will be filed with the court and *probated.*

Legal requirements for making a will. Because a will must be valid and admitted to probate to effectively convey title to real estate, it must be executed and prepared in accordance with the laws of the state where the real estate is located. A **testator** must have legal capacity to make a will (see Figure 11.3). Usually a person must be of *legal age* and of *sound mind.* There are no rigid tests to determine the capacity to make a will. Generally, the courts hold that to make a valid will the testator must have sufficient mental capacity to understand the nature and extent of the property owned, the identity of natural heirs and that at the testator's death the property will go to those named in the will. The drawing of a will must be a voluntary act, free of any undue influence by other people.

**Figure 11.3
Requirements for a
Valid Will**

WILL

1. Legal Age
2. Sound Mind
3. Proper Wording
4. No Undue Influence
5. Witnesses

In most states, a written will must be signed by its testator before two or more witnesses, who must also sign the document. The witnesses should not be people who are named as devisees in the will.

The testator may modify the will. A modification of, an amendment of or an addition to a previously executed will is called a *codicil*.

A *holographic will* is one that is in the testator's handwriting but is not witnessed or acknowledged. A *nuncupative will* is one that is given orally by a testator. Certain states do not permit the use of holographic and/or nuncupative wills to convey title to property.

Transfer of Title by Descent

By law the title to real estate and personal property of a person who dies intestate passes to the decedent's heirs. Under the **descent** statutes the primary heirs of the deceased are the spouse and close blood relatives, such as children, parents, brothers, sisters, aunts, uncles and, in some cases, first and second cousins.

The right to inherit under laws of descent varies from state to state, and intestate property is distributed according to the laws of the state in which the property is located.

Key Terms

adverse possession	minor
bargain and sale deed	probate
deed	quitclaim deed
deed in trust	reconveyance deed
descent	special warranty deed
general warranty deed	testate
grantee	testator
granting clause	title
grantor	transfer tax
habendum clause	trustee's deed
intestate	voluntary alienation
involuntary alienation	will

Summary

Title to real estate is the right to, and evidence of, ownership of the land. It may be transferred in four ways: by voluntary alienation, involuntary alienation, will and descent.

The voluntary transfer of an owner's title is made by a deed, executed (signed) by the owner as grantor to the purchaser or donee as grantee.

Among the most common requirements for a valid deed are a grantor with legal capacity to contract, a readily identifiable grantee, a granting clause, a legal description of the property, a recital of consideration, exceptions and reservations on the title and the signature of the grantor. In addition, the deed should be acknowledged before a notary public or other officer to provide evidence that the signature is genuine and to allow recording. Title to the property passes when the grantor delivers a deed to the grantee and it is accepted. The obligation of a grantor is determined by the form of the deed.

A general warranty deed provides the greatest protection of any deed by binding the grantor to certain covenants or warranties. A special warranty deed warrants only that the real estate is not encumbered except as stated in the deed. A bargain and sale deed carries with it no warranties but implies that the grantor holds title to the property. A quitclaim deed carries with it no warranties whatsoever and conveys only the interest, if any, the grantor possesses in the property.

An owner's title may be transferred without his or her permission by a court action, such as a foreclosure or judgment sale, a tax sale, condemnation under the right of eminent domain, adverse possession or escheat. Land may also be transferred by the natural forces of water and wind, which either increase property by accretion or decrease it through erosion or avulsion.

The real estate of an owner who makes a valid will (who dies testate) passes to the devisees through the probating of the will. The title of an owner who dies without a will (intestate) passes according to the provisions of the law of descent of the state in which the real estate is located.

Questions

1. The basic requirements for a valid conveyance are governed by:
   a. state law.
   b. local custom.
   c. national law.
   d. law of descent.

2. It is essential that every deed be signed by the:
   a. grantor.
   b. grantee.
   c. grantor and grantee.
   d. devisee.

3. H, age 15, recently inherited many parcels of real estate from his late father and has decided to sell one of them to pay inheritance taxes. If H entered into a deed conveying his interest in the property to a purchaser, such a conveyance would be:
   a. valid.
   b. void.
   c. invalid.
   d. voidable.

4. An instrument authorizing one person to act for another is called a(n):
   a. power of attorney.
   b. release deed.
   c. quitclaim deed.
   d. acknowledgment.

5. The grantee receives greatest protection with what type of deed?
   a. Quitclaim
   b. Warranty
   c. Bargain and sale with covenant
   d. Executor's

6. Determination of the type of deed used in conveying title can be made by examining the:
   a. grantor's name.
   b. grantee's name.
   c. granting clause.
   d. acknowledgment.

7. Which of the following best describes the covenant of quiet enjoyment?
   a. The grantor promises to obtain and deliver any instrument needed to make the title good.
   b. The grantor guarantees that if the title fails in the future he or she will compensate the grantee.
   c. The grantor warrants that he or she is the owner and has the right to convey title to it.
   d. The grantor assures that the title will be good against the title claims of third parties.

8. Which of the following types of deeds most often recites the full, actual consideration paid for the property?
   a. Warranty deed
   b. Quitclaim deed
   c. Deed of conveyance
   d. Deed executed pursuant to court order

9. Which of the following types of deeds implies but does not specifically warrant that the grantor holds good title to the property?
   a. Special warranty deed
   b. Bargain and sale deed
   c. Quitclaim deed
   d. Trustee's deed

10. Title to property transfers at the moment a deed is:
    a. signed.
    b. acknowledged.
    c. delivered and accepted.
    d. recorded.

11. Consideration in a deed refers to:
    a. gentle handling of the document.
    b. something of value given by each party.
    c. the habendum clause.
    d. the payment of transfer tax stamps.

12. A declaration before a notary or other official providing evidence that a signature is genuine is an:
    a. affidavit.
    b. acknowledgment.
    c. affirmation.
    d. estoppel.

13. R executes a deed to P as grantee, has it acknowledged and receives payment from the buyer. R holds the deed, however, and arranges to meet P the next morning at the courthouse to deliver the deed to her. In this situation at this time:
    a. P owns the property because she has paid for it.
    b. title to the property will not officially pass until P has been given the deed the next morning.
    c. title to the property will not pass until P has received the deed and recorded it the next morning.
    d. P will own the property when she has signed the deed the next morning.

14. Title to real estate may be transferred during a person's lifetime by:
    a. devise.
    b. descent.
    c. involuntary alienation.
    d. escheat.

15. F bought acreage in a distant county, never went to see the acreage and did not use the ground. H moved his mobile home onto the land, had a water well drilled and lived there for 22 years. H may become the owner of the land if he has complied with the state law regarding:
    a. requirements for a valid conveyance.
    b. adverse possession.
    c. avulsion.
    d. voluntary alienation

16. Which of the following is *not* one of the manners in which title to real estate may be transferred by involuntary alienation?
    a. Eminent domain
    b. Escheat
    c. Erosion
    d. Seisin

17. The acquisition of land through deposit of soil or sand washed up by water is called:
    a. accretion.
    b. avulsion.
    c. erosion.
    d. condemnation.

18. Local transfer taxes on real estate conveyances are usually paid:
    a. by the grantee.
    b. to the state real estate commission.
    c. by the grantor.
    d. by the real estate agent.

19. A person who has died leaving a valid will is called a(n):
    a. devisee.
    b. testator.
    c. legatee.
    d. intestate.

20. Title to real estate can be transferred at death by which of the following documents?
    a. Warranty deed
    b. Special warranty deed
    c. Trustee's deed
    d. Will

21. J, a bachelor, died owning real estate that he devised by his will to his niece, K. In essence at what point does title pass to his niece?
    a. Immediately upon J's death
    b. After his will has been probated
    c. After K has paid all inheritance taxes
    d. When K executes a new deed to the property

22. An owner of real estate who was adjudged legally incompetent made a will during his stay at a nursing home. He later died and was survived by a wife and three children. His real estate will pass:
    a. to his wife.
    b. to the heirs mentioned in his will.
    c. according to the state laws of descent.
    d. to the state.

Title Records

Public Records and Recording

For the protection of real estate owners, taxing bodies, creditors and the general public, public records are maintained in every city, county, parish or borough in the United States. Such records help to establish official ownership, give notice of encumbrances and establish priority of liens. The placing of documents in the public record is known as **recording.**

Public records are maintained by the recorder of deeds, county clerk, county treasurer, city clerk and collector and clerks of various courts of record. Records involving taxes, special assessments, ordinances and zoning and building records also fall into this category. All these records are open for public inspection.

Necessity for Recording

Before buying a parcel of property, a potential purchaser wants to know that the seller can convey good title to the property as well as what liens and encumbrances affect that title. Through the recording process, documents that affect property ownership are readily available as matters of public record. Thus, a person can inspect the documents that affect a property before making a decision about purchasing it.

For example, a purchaser offering cash for a property might want to be sure that the seller has paid in full, before the settlement takes place, all of the debts outstanding against the property. By inspecting the recorded document the purchaser could determine what debts encumber the property.

Recording Acts

Under the recording acts, to serve as public notice all documents affecting any estate, right, title or interest in land *must be recorded in the county where the land is located*. Everyone interested in the title to a parcel of property can thus receive notice of the various interests of all other parties. From a practical point of view the recording acts may give legal priority to those interests that are recorded first.

To be *eligible for recording* a document must be drawn and executed in conformity with the provisions of the recording statutes of the state in which the real estate is located. Many states require that the names be typed below the signatures and that the document be acknowledged before a notary public or other officer. In a few states the document must also be witnessed. A number of states require that the name of the attorney who prepared the document appear on it.

Notice

Through the legal maxim of **caveat emptor** (''let the buyer beware'') the courts charge a prospective real estate buyer or lender with the responsibility for inspecting the property and searching the public records to determine the interests of other parties. **Constructive notice** means simply that the information has been made available; the buyer or lender could find it out and is therefore responsible for learning it.

In contrast, **actual notice** means the person has been given the information and actually knows it (see Figure 12.1). After an individual has searched the public records and inspected the property, he or she has actual notice, or knowledge, of the information learned.

Priority. Many complicated situations can arise that affect the priority of rights in a parcel of real estate. For example, a purchaser may receive a deed and take possession of the property but not record the deed. By taking possession, the purchaser gives constructive notice of an interest in the land. His or her rights would be considered superior to the rights of a subsequent purchaser who acquired a deed from the original owner at a later date and recorded the deed but did not inspect the property to determine who was in possession. How the courts rule in any situation depends, of course, on the specific facts of the case. These are strictly legal questions that should be referred to the parties' attorneys.

Documents That Are Not Recorded

Real estate taxes and special assessments are direct liens on specific parcels of real estate and need not be recorded. Other liens, such as inheritance taxes and franchise taxes, are placed by statutory authority against all real estate owned either by a decedent at the time of death or by a corporation at the time the franchise tax became a lien; these liens are not recorded either.

Foreign Language Documents

Deeds or mortgages written in a foreign language, although valid between the parties to a transaction, usually do not impart constructive notice when recorded. Recorded documents must be in the English language. An official translation by a consulate of the country in which the language is used, when attached to a foreign language document, may meet state recording requirements. Both the original document and the translation are then recorded and become part of the public record.

**Figure 12.1
Notice**

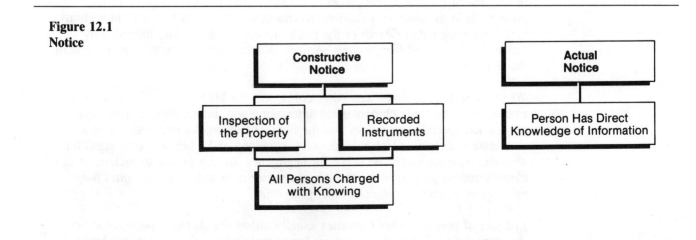

Chain of Title
The **chain of title** shows the record of ownership of the property over a period of time, depending on the length of the title search. An **abstract of title** is a condensed history of all the documents affecting a particular parcel of land. Through the chain of title the ownership of the property can be traced from its origin to its present owner. If this cannot be done, it is said that there is a *gap* in the chain. In such cases it is usually necessary to establish ownership by a court action called a **suit to quiet title** or by the simpler procedure of obtaining any relevant quitclaim deeds.

Evidence of Title
Under the terms of the usual real estate sales contract the seller is required to deliver **marketable title** to the buyer at the closing. To be marketable a title must be free from any significant liens and encumbrances, disclose no serious defects and not depend on doubtful questions of law or fact to prove its validity, not expose a purchaser to the hazard of litigation or threaten the quiet enjoyment of the property and convince a reasonably well-informed and prudent person, acting on business principles and knowledge of the facts that he or she could, in turn, sell or mortgage the property.

Although an unmarketable title (one that does not meet these requirements) may still be transferable, it contains *certain defects that may limit or restrict ownership of the property.* A buyer cannot be forced to accept a conveyance that is materially different from the one bargained for in the sales contract. Questions of marketable title must be raised by a buyer (or the buyer's broker or attorney) prior to acceptance of the deed. Once a buyer has accepted a deed with unmarketable title, the only available legal recourse is to sue the seller under the covenants of warranty (if any) contained in the deed.

Proper **evidence of title** is proof that title is, in fact, marketable. A deed by itself is not considered sufficient evidence of title; while it conveys the interest of the grantor, even a warranty deed contains no proof of the condition of the grantor's title. The only effective proof is based on an adequate search of the public records. A buyer can be satisfied that evidence of title exists by acquiring an abstract of title, a certificate of title, a title insurance policy or a Torrens certificate.

Abstract of Title
An abstract of title is a brief history of the documents appearing in the public record that affect title to the parcel in question. The legal description of the property is in the abstract's caption. Abstracts usually consist of several sections, each beginning with a search of the public record from the date immediately following the date of the previous section. Without this continuity a gap exists in the abstract.

When an abstract is first prepared or continued, the abstractor lists and summarizes each document in chronological order along with information relative to taxes, judgments, special assessments and the like. The abstractor concludes with a certificate indicating which records were examined and when and then signs the abstract. Abstractors can be liable for negligence for any failure to include or accurately record all pertinent data. An *abstractor does not, however, pass judgment on or guarantee the condition of the title.*

In a sale of land the seller's attorney usually orders the abstract continued to cover the current date. When the abstractor has completed the abstract, it is submitted to the buyer's attorney, who must *examine the entire abstract*. This means that the lawyer must examine each section from the origin of that title. Following a detailed examination, the attorney must evaluate all the facts and material to prepare a written report for the purchaser on the condition of the ownership; this report is called an **attorney's opinion of title.**

As transfers of title accumulate through the years, the abstract of title to a particular parcel becomes more and more voluminous and the time an attorney will need to examine the abstract increases.

Certificate of Title

In some localities a **certificate of title** is used, and no abstract is prepared. A title examiner checks the public records and prepares a certificate of title stating the property's owner of record and listing any present encumbrances—usually without an attorney's opinion.

In many ways use of an abstract examination and opinion or a certificate of title is imperfect and open to objection. For example, it is difficult to detect forged deeds or false statements, including incorrect marital information and transfers involving incompetent parties or minors. Or an honest mistake could be made against which the owner of real estate has no recourse. To provide purchasers with protection against this type of error and to provide defense of the title, title insurance is now widely used.

Title Insurance

A **title insurance** policy (see Table 12.1) is a contract by which a title insurance company agrees, subject to the terms of its policy, to indemnify (to compensate or reimburse) the insured (the owner, mortgagee or other interest holder) against any losses sustained as a result of defects in that title other than those exceptions listed in the policy. A title insurance policy may also be used in addition to an abstract or certificate of title.

A *standard-coverage* policy usually insures against defects that may be found in the public records plus such items as forged documents, documents of incompetent grantors, incorrect marital statements and improperly delivered deeds. The *extended coverage* provided by an **American Land Title Association (ALTA) policy** includes all the protection of a standard policy plus protection against risks that may be discovered only through inspection of the property, including rights of persons in actual possession of the land, even if unrecorded, or that

Table 12.1 Owner's Title Insurance Policy	Standard Coverage	Extended Coverage	Not Covered by Either Policy
	1. Defects found in public records 2. Forged documents 3. Incompetent grantors 4. Incorrect marital statements 5. Improperly delivered deeds	Standard coverage plus defects discoverable through: 1. Property inspection, including unrecorded rights of persons in possession 2. Examination of survey 3. Unrecorded liens not known of by policyholder	1. Defects and liens listed in policy 2. Defects known to buyer 3. Changes in land use brought about by zoning ordinances

would be revealed by examination of an accurate survey. The company does not agree to insure against any defects in or liens against the title found by the title examination and listed in the policy.

Upon completion of the examination the title company usually issues what may be called a *preliminary report* of title, or a *commitment* to issue a title policy or a *binder*. This report describes the policy that will be issued and gives the name of the insured party, the legal description of the real estate, the estate or interest covered, conditions and stipulations under which the policy is issued and a schedule of all exceptions, consisting of encumbrances and defects found in the public records, usually including unrecorded documents, unrecorded defects of which the policyholder has knowledge, rights of parties in possession and questions of survey. Under the contract the title insurance company promises to defend the title as insured and to pay any claims against the property if the title proves to be defective.

The *premium* for the policy is paid once for the life of the policy. The maximum loss for which the company may be liable cannot exceed the face amount of the policy (unless the amount of coverage has been extended by use of an *inflation rider*). When a title company makes a payment to settle a claim covered by a policy, the company acquires by the right of subrogation all the remedies and rights of the insured party against anyone responsible for the settled claim.

Title companies issue various forms of policies, the most common of which are the *owner's* title insurance policy, the *lender's* title insurance policy, the *leasehold* title insurance policy and the *certificate of sale* title insurance policy. As the names indicate, each of these policies is issued to insure specific interests. For example, a lender's title insurance policy insures a mortgage company or lender that it has a valid first lien against the property. A leasehold title insurance policy insures a lessee that he or she has a valid lease. A certificate of sale policy is issued to a purchaser in a court sale.

Title search. The examination undertaken by an abstractor or title insurance company to determine what, if any, defects exist in a property's chain of title is called a *title search*. The title searcher could begin the examination with the original source of title, which often dates from a government patent grant or award of title, or the search might begin with title records dating back no more than 30 or 40 years, or it might begin with the date of issuance of a prior title insurance policy. The searcher then checks the title in the recorder's office and searches the records in other governmental offices such as the tax offices and assessment offices (for sewer or special assessment liens that might be in effect).

In Practice . . .   *Before a lender will forward money on a loan secured by real estate, it will normally order a title search at the expense of the borrower to assure itself that there are no liens superior in priority to its mortgage on the property.*

In addition, in some states a preliminary title report is ordered upon acceptance of an offer to purchase, and copies are given to the buyers, agents and sellers. In fact the entire contract may depend on the buyers' written approval of this document within a certain number of days after receiving it. Sellers usually are also given a copy, to ensure that the correct property has been researched.

The Torrens System Under the **Torrens system** a written application to register a title to real estate is made with the clerk of the court of the county in which the real estate is located. If the applicant proves that he or she is the owner, the court enters an order to register the real estate and the *registrar of titles* is further directed to issue a certificate of title. At any time the Torrens original certificate of title in the registrar's office reveals the owner of the land and all mortgages, judgments and similar liens. It does not reveal federal or state taxes and some other items.

Uniform Commercial Code The **Uniform Commercial Code (UCC)** is a body of business law that has been adopted, wholly or in part, in all states. While this code generally does not apply directly to real estate, it governs the documents when personal property is the security for a loan.

For a lender to create a collateral interest, including chattels that will become fixtures, the code requires the use of a **security agreement,** which must contain a complete description of the items against which the lien applies. A short notice of this agreement, called a **financing statement** or UCC-1, which includes the identification of any real estate involved, must be filed for fixtures. The recording of the financing statement constitutes notice to subsequent purchasers and lenders of the security interest in chattels and fixtures on the real estate. Many lenders require the signing and recording of a financing statement when the collateral premises include chattels or readily removable fixtures (washers, dryers and the like) as part of the security for the debt.

Key Terms

abstract of title	evidence of title
actual notice	financing statement
American Land Title Association (ALTA) policy	marketable title
	recording
attorney's opinion of title	security agreement
caveat emptor	suit to quiet title
certificate of title	title insurance
chain of title	Torrens system
constructive notice	Uniform Commercial Code

Summary The purpose of the recording acts is to give legal, public and constructive notice to the world of parties' interests in real estate. The recording provisions have been adopted to create system and order in the transfer of real estate.

Possession of real estate is generally interpreted as conveying notice of the rights of the person in possession. Actual notice is knowledge acquired directly.

Title evidence shows whether or not a seller is conveying marketable title. Marketable title is generally one that is so free from significant defects that the purchaser can be assured against having to defend the title.

There are four forms of providing title evidence commonly used throughout the United States: abstract of title, certificate of title, Torrens certificate and title insurance policy.

The purpose of a deed is to transfer a grantor's interest in real estate to a grantee. It does not prove that the grantor has any interest at all.

A Torrens certificate, title insurance policy, certificate of title and abstract of title reveal the history of a title. Each must be later dated, or continued or reissued, to cover a more recent date.

Under the Uniform Commercial Code the recording of a financing statement gives notice to purchasers and mortgagees of the security interests in chattels and fixtures on the specific parcel of real estate.

—3

Questions

1. Public records may be inspected by:
   a. anyone.
   b. attorneys and abstractors only.
   c. attorneys, abstractors and real estate licensees only.
   d. anyone who obtains a court order under the Freedom of Information Act.

2. Which of the following statements *best* explains why instruments affecting real estate are recorded?
   a. Recording gives constructive notice to the world of the rights and interests in a particular parcel of real estate.
   b. The law requires that such instruments be recorded.
   c. The instruments must be recorded to comply with the terms of the statute of frauds.
   d. Recording proves the execution of the instrument.

3. A purchaser went to the county building to check the recorder's records. She found that the seller was the grantee in the last recorded deed and that no mortgage was on record against the property. The purchaser may assume which of the following?
   a. All taxes are paid and no judgments are outstanding.
   b. The seller has good title.
   c. The seller did not mortgage the property.
   d. No one else is occupying the property.

4. The date and time a document was recorded establish which of the following?
   a. Priority of filing   c. Subrogation
   b. Chain of title   d. Marketable title

5. The principle of *caveat emptor* states that if the buyer buys a parcel of real estate with a title problem the fault lies with the:
   a. buyer.   c. broker.
   b. seller.   d. lender.

6. P bought L's house, received a deed and moved into the residence but neglected to record the document. One week later L died, and his heirs in another city, unaware that the property had been sold, conveyed title to M, who recorded the deed. Who owns the property?
   a. P   c. L's heirs
   b. M   d. Both P and M

7. If a property has encumbrances, it:
   a. cannot be sold.
   b. can be sold only if title insurance is provided.
   c. cannot have a deed recorded without a survey.
   d. can be sold if a buyer agrees to take it subject to the encumbrances.

8. Which of the following is *not* acceptable proof of ownership?
   a. A Torrens certificate
   b. A title insurance policy
   c. An abstract and lawyer's opinion
   d. A deed signed by the last seller

9. *Chain of title* refers to which of the following?
   a. A summary or history of all documents and legal proceedings affecting a specific parcel of land
   b. A series of links measuring 7.92 inches each
   c. An instrument or a document that protects the insured parties (subject to specific exceptions) against defects in the examination of the record and hidden risks such as forgeries, undisclosed heirs, errors in the public records and so forth
   d. The succession of conveyances from some starting point whereby the present owner derives title

10. Proof of the kind of estate and all liens against an interest in a parcel of real estate can usually be found through:
    a. a recorded deed.
    b. a court suit for specific performance.
    c. one of the four evidences of title.
    d. a foreclosure suit.

11. The person who prepares an abstract of title for a parcel of real estate:

   a. writes a brief history of the title after inspecting the county records for documents affecting the title.

   b. insures the condition of the title.

   c. inspects the property.

   d. issues a certificate of title.

12. In locations where the abstract system is used, an abstract is usually examined by the:

   a. broker.

   b. abstract company.

   c. purchaser.

   d. attorney for the purchaser.

13. S is frantic because she cannot find her deed and now wants to sell the property. She:

   a. may need a suit to quiet title.

   b. will have to buy title insurance.

   c. does not need the deed to sell if it was recorded.

   d. should execute a replacement deed to herself.

14. Mortgage title policies protect which parties against loss?

   a. Buyers   c. Lenders

   b. Sellers   d. Buyers and lenders

15. When a title examination is completed, the title insurance company notifies the parties in writing of the condition of the title. This notification is referred to as:

   a. a chain of title.

   b. a preliminary report of title, binder or commitment for title insurance.

   c. a Torrens certificate.

   d. an abstract.

16. When a claim is settled by a title insurance company, the company acquires all rights and claims of the insured against any other person who is responsible for the loss. This is called:

   a. escrow.   c. subordination.

   b. abstract of title.   d. subrogation.

17. A title insurance policy with standard coverage generally covers all but which of the following?

   a. Forged documents

   b. Incorrect marital statements

   c. Rights of parties in possession

   d. Incompetent grantors

Real Estate
License Laws

All states, the District of Columbia and all Canadian provinces license and regulate the activities of real estate brokers and salespeople. Certain details of the laws vary from state to state, but the main provisions of many state laws are similar. In addition, uniform policies and standards in the fields of license law administration and enforcement are promoted by an organization of state license law officials known as NARELLO—the National Association of Real Estate License Law Officials.

Purposes of License Laws

The real estate license laws are intended to protect the public from dishonest or incompetent brokers and salespeople, to prescribe certain standards and qualifications for licensing brokers and salespeople and to maintain high standards in the real estate profession.

Each state and province has a licensing authority—a commission, department, division, board or agency—for real estate brokers and salespersons. (In this chapter the term *commission* will be used to mean any such licensing authority.) This authority has the power to issue licenses, make real estate information available to licensees and the public and enforce the statutory real estate law.

Each commission has also adopted a set of administrative **rules and regulations** that further define the statutory law, provide for its administration and set operating guidelines for its licensees. These rules and regulations have the same force and effect as the law. Both the law and the rules are usually enforced through the **denial, suspension or revocation of licenses,** although civil and criminal court actions can be brought against violators in some serious cases. Throughout this chapter the discussion of license law includes many typical provisions of commission rules and regulations.

Who Must Be Licensed

Generally the state license laws stipulate that a person must be licensed as a real estate broker if he or she, *for another and for compensation or the promise of compensation:*

1. lists real property;

2. sells it;

3. rents or leases it;

4. manages it;

5. exchanges it;

6. deals in real estate options;

7. offers to perform or negotiate one of these activities; or

8. represents that he or she engages in any of these activities.

In some states a person who performs these activities with regard to business opportunities must also be licensed as a real estate broker.

The specific provisions vary from state to state, and many states cite additional activities that a person must be licensed to perform. In some states, for example, a person who, *for others and for a fee,* auctions real estate, negotiates a mortgage loan or deals in cemetery lots may be required to have a broker's license. It is important to identify the specific requirements for your state.

Any person who performs any of the previously listed activities while employed by or associated with a real estate broker must be licensed as a real estate salesperson. In addition, some states have a special name or issue a special license for an individual who has qualified as a real estate broker and passed the broker's exam but is currently acting as a salesperson associated with and responsible to another licensed broker. Such person may be known as a broker-salesperson or an *associate broker.* A broker is authorized to operate his or her own real estate business; anyone licensed with a broker can operate only in the name of and under the supervision of that broker.

Exceptions

The real estate license laws *generally do not apply* to:

1. a person or firm that deals in his, her or its own property when this is not the person's or firm's principal vocation;

2. a person acting under a power of attorney;

3. a salaried employee of a property owner who acts on behalf of the property owner, when dealing in real estate is not the owner's principal vocation;

4. an attorney-at-law performing regular duties as part of a legal practice;

5. a receiver, trustee, guardian, administrator, executor or other person acting under court order;

6. an auctioneer performing regular duties (although, as previously mentioned, such person must be licensed in some states); or

7. a public official or employee performing regular duties of employment.

Licensing Procedure

While specific requirements for licensing vary, all states require applicants to be of legal age. In addition, applicants must not have had a real estate license or any other professional license revoked for a certain period of time in any state, must not have been convicted of a serious crime for a certain period of time and so forth. Some states also require fingerprint cards or FBI clearance or personal references. A broker applicant usually will be required to have a minimum amount of experience as a salesperson.

Educational Requirements

Many states require applicants to complete a certain number of hours of real estate education as a prerequisite to obtaining a license. These requirements vary from state to state, but generally broker applicants are required to complete more hours of classroom time than salesperson applicants. In addition, a number of states have enacted *continuing education* requirements that licensees must complete to qualify for license renewal.

Examinations

All states require license applicants to pass a written real estate examination prior to licensing. State requirements vary as to the length, manner and passing grade for such exams, but generally the broker's exam is more inclusive and longer than the salesperson's exam. The states also vary in their regulations regarding retests and appeals for applicants who have failed the exams.

Licensing of Nonresidents

Most state licensing authorities have reciprocity agreements with the commissions of certain other states. These agreements provide that out-of-state brokers will be allowed to operate within the state upon meeting certain requirements. Generally reciprocity agreements are made between states that have similar licensing requirements or states that adjoin each other. Some states require out-of-state brokers to take the local state real estate licensing exam; others do not. In addition, most states require nonresident brokers to file an irrevocable consent agreement or power of attorney with the state licensing agency. This document states that suits and actions may be brought against the out-of-state broker within the state in which the agreement is filed and that the outcome of such suits will be valid and binding.

Licensing of Corporations and Partnerships

In most cases a real estate brokerage may be established as a corporation if at least one officer of the corporation is a licensed real estate broker. All members of a partnership may be required to be brokers. Some states require that all officers or partners who are not participating in the business be registered as inactive brokers. The license laws usually provide that no officer or partner may be registered as a real estate salesperson.

Real Estate Recovery Fund

Many states have instituted a special **real estate recovery fund** from which members of the general public may collect if they have suffered financial loss as a result of the actions of a licensee. The fund is usually maintained by part of the fees that licensees must pay. Generally people who seek reimbursement from the fund can do so only after they have filed a court suit and obtained judgment against the licensee. If the aggrieved individual cannot collect the judgment from the licensee in any other way, he or she can apply for payment from the recovery fund. The broker or salesperson's license is usually suspended until the recovery fund is reimbursed with interest.

General Operation of a Real Estate Business

License laws regulate many of the everyday operations of real estate brokers and salespeople. Generally every resident real estate broker must maintain a definite place of business within the state and may operate one or more **branch offices.** The licenses of salespeople depend on that of their broker. Termination, suspension or revocation of the broker's license means that all activities of salespeople must cease.

In all transactions brokers must keep detailed accounting records and retain copies of the documents used for a specified period of time. In addition, many license laws include specific provisions regarding the contents of contracts and documents used in transactions. Each broker must also either maintain a special trust account for the deposit of funds belonging to clients and customers or make use of a neutral escrow depository.

Brokers must never *commingle* a client's funds with their own money. In some states, however, a broker is permitted to deposit a small amount of personal cash in a trust account to keep the account open.

Brokers cannot use any misleading or fraudulent advertising in the course of their business, and they cannot use blind ads (that is, advertising that does not specifically indicate that the advertiser of the property is a real estate broker). In addition, salespeople may advertise only in the name of their broker.

| **Suspension or Revocation of a Real Estate License** | Most state license laws detail the various violations of the license law and other reasons for which a real estate license may be suspended or revoked. Students should study the rules for their own state and know them thoroughly. |

Key Terms

branch office
denial, suspension or
   revocation of license

real estate recovery fund
rules and regulations

Summary

The real estate license laws were enacted by the states and Canadian provinces to protect the public from dishonest brokers and salespeople, prescribe certain licensing requirements and maintain high standards in the real estate profession.

Each state stipulates who must be licensed and who is exempt from licensing, sets forth certain operating standards to which brokers and salespersons must adhere and creates certain licensing procedures and requirements.

Note that each state law is different. You must know your own state license law. If you do not have a copy of your state real estate license law, obtain one immediately.

The analysis form that takes the place of questions in this chapter will help you determine and learn the requirements of your state law. Use it as a study device while you read through your state law and state supplement (where available) or as a testing device after studying the license law. (Be sure to check your answers against the provisions of the law.)

Remember, you will be operating and working under your state real estate license law—you must know it well.

Analysis Form: Real Estate Broker's and Salesperson's Law

State or province of _____

Instructions: After studying your state law, answer the questions and fill in the information. If the question or point does not apply in your state, indicate this fact by some statement such as *no, none, not required* or *does not apply*. If you complete this form carefully, the information will be valuable when you prepare for your state license examination.

1. When was your state law originally passed? _____

2. Has it been amended? _____ If so, when was the last amendment passed? _____

3. What are the requirements for licensure in your state?

	For Broker's License	For Salesperson's License
Minimum age	_____	_____
Apprenticeship	_____	_____
Education	_____	_____
Examination	_____	_____
Bond	_____	_____
Number and type of recommendations	_____	_____
Photograph	_____	_____
Fingerprints	_____	_____

4. Copy exactly the definition of a *broker* as given by your law. Know this definition and be able to list the activities that it includes.

_____

_____

_____

5. Copy exactly the definition of a *salesperson* as given by your law. Learn this definition.

_____

_____

_____

6. What persons or groups are *exempt* from licensure in your state?

_____

_____

_____

7. What fees are required in your state?

	For Broker	For Salesperson
Original license application fee	_____	_____
Examination fee	_____	_____
Periodic renewal fee	_____	_____
Recovery fund fee (if separate)	_____	_____

8. For what period is the license issued?   _____   _____

On what date does it expire?   _____   _____

What continuing education is required
for renewal?   _____   _____

9. The following are some of the reasons a state may discipline a licensee, refuse to issue a license or revoke or suspend a license. Place a check mark
in front of the reasons given in your state law. Cross out the reasons that do
not apply and add the reasons that are not listed here. When you have compiled your list, memorize it.

_____ Filing or recording any papers to cloud title as claim for commission

_____ Making false affidavits or committing perjury in any court proceeding

_____ Pursuing a continued and flagrant course of misrepresentation

_____ Making false promises through salespeople, advertising and the like

_____ Acting for more than one party without approval of all parties (dual
agency)

_____ Failing to remit or account for funds belonging to others

_____ Misleading by false advertising or advertising without the broker's
name

_____ Procuring a license by fraud, such as by filing a fraudulent application

_____ Willfully disregarding or violating provisions of the licensing law
or the commission rules and regulations

_____ Paying a commission to any unlicensed person in violation of the law

_____ Representing a broker other than one's employing broker

_____ Being convicted of embezzlement, fraud and similar crimes or state
or federal felonies

_____ Placing signs on property without proper authorization from the client

_____ Demonstrating negligence in one's capacity as a real estate licensee

_____ Not clearly explaining to a principal the duration of an exclusive listing agreement

_____ Engaging in conduct that constitutes bad faith or improper, incompetent, fraudulent or dishonest dealing

_____ Employing unlicensed salespeople

_____ Accepting a commission in violation of the licensing law

_____ Operating an office or branch office from an unregistered location

_____ Commingling funds or property of a principal with a broker's personal funds

_____ Failing to deposit the money of others in an escrow or trust account

_____ Other: _____

10. What penalties are provided in your state law for operating without a license?

	Individuals		Corporations	
	1st Offense	2nd Offense	1st Offense	2nd Offense
Fine	_____	_____	_____	_____
Imprisonment	_____	_____	_____	_____

Are other penalties or fines provided and, if so, for what offenses? _____

_____

11. What is the name of the state agency that is responsible for administering the real estate law in your state? _____

_____

12. If there is a real estate commission or advisory committee, how many members does it have? Are they appointed or elected? What is their term of office? _____

_____

13. What are the requirements for a broker's maintaining an office and a sign?

_____

14. What provisions and requirements are made for the discharge or termination of a real estate salesperson by a broker? _____

_____

15. List the main requirements for issuance of a license to a nonresident broker.

_____

16. Does your state have a real estate recovery fund? _____

_____

17. How long must a broker retain records of a real estate transaction in his or her office? _____

_____

14

Real Estate Financing: Principles

Mortgage Law

From their inception American courts of equity have considered a mortgage a voluntary lien on real estate, given to secure the payment of a debt or the performance of an obligation. Some states recognize a lender as the owner of mortgaged land. This ownership is subject to defeat upon full payment of the debt or performance of the obligation. These states are called **title theory** states. Under title theory a mortgagee (lender) has the right to possession of and rents from the mortgaged property immediately upon default by the mortgagor (borrower).

Those states that interpret a mortgage purely as a lien on real property are called **lien theory** states. In such states, if a mortgagor defaults, the lender may foreclose (generally through a court action), offer the property for sale and apply the funds received from the sale to reduce or extinguish the obligation. As protection to the borrower, some states allow a statutory redemption period during which a defaulted mortgagor can redeem the property.

Today a number of states have modified the strict interpretation of title and lien theories. These *intermediary*, or *modified lien theory*, states allow a lender to take possession of the mortgaged real estate upon default.

Security and Debt

Generally any interest in real estate that may be sold may be pledged as security for a debt. The basic principle of the property law, that a person cannot convey greater rights in property than he or she actually has, applies equally to the right to mortgage. So the owner of a fee simple estate can mortgage the fee, and the owner of a leasehold or subleasehold can mortgage that leasehold interest. For example, a large retail corporation renting space in a shopping center may mortgage its leasehold interest to finance some remodeling work.

As discussed in Chapter 7, the owner of a cooperative interest holds a personal property interest, not an interest in real estate. Although a cooperative owner has a leasehold interest, the nature of that leasehold is not generally acceptable to lenders as collateral. The owner of a condominium unit, however, does own a mortgageable interest.

Mortgage Loan Instruments

There are two parts to a mortgage loan—the debt itself and the security for the debt. When a property is to be mortgaged, the owner must execute, or sign, two separate instruments:

1. The **promissory note,** or *financing instrument,* is the written promise to repay a debt in definite installments.

2. The **mortgage,** or *security instrument,* is the document that creates the lien, or conveys the property to the mortgagee as *security* for the debt.

A mortgagor is a borrower who gives a mortgage to a lender (mortgagee).

Hypothecation is the term used to describe the pledging of property as security for payment of a loan without giving up possession of the property. A pledge of security—a mortgage—cannot be legally effective unless there is a debt to secure. *Both note and mortgage must be executed to create an enforceable mortgage loan.*

Deeds of trust. In some areas of the country and in certain situations, lenders prefer to use a three-party instrument known as a **deed of trust,** or trust deed, rather than a mortgage document. A trust deed conveys ''naked title'' or ''bare legal title'' (title without the right of possession) to the real estate as security for the loan to a third party, called the *trustee.* The trustee then holds title on behalf of the lender, known as the **beneficiary,** who is the legal owner and holder of the note. The wording of the conveyance sets forth actions that the trustee may take if the borrower, the *trustor,* defaults under any of the deed of trust terms. (See Figure 14.1 for a comparison of mortgages and deeds of trust.) In states where deeds of trust are generally preferred, foreclosure procedures for defaulted deeds of trust are usually simpler and faster than those for mortgage loans.

Figure 14.1
Mortgages and Deeds of Trust

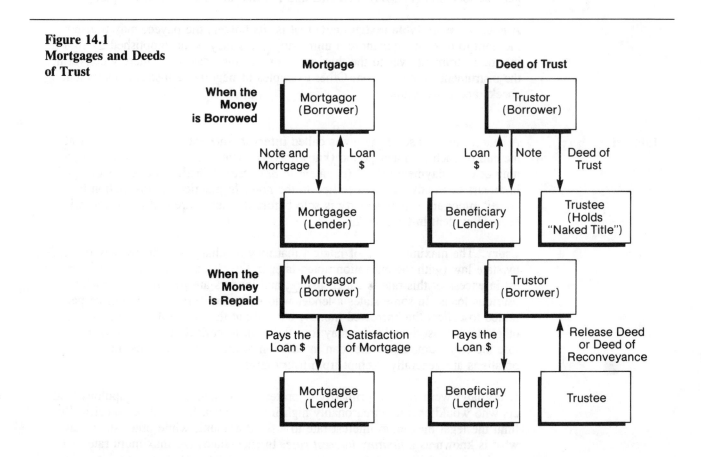

Usually the lender chooses the trustee and reserves the right to substitute trustees in the event of death or dismissal. State law usually dictates who may serve as trustee. Although the deed of trust is particularly popular in certain states, it is used all over the country. For example, in the financing of a commercial or industrial real estate venture that involves a large loan and several lenders, the borrower generally executes a single deed of trust to secure as many notes as are necessary.

Provisions of the Financing Instrument

In general the financing instrument executed by a borrower states the amount of the debt, the time and method of payment and the rate of interest. If a promissory note is used with a mortgage, the borrower (mortgagor) is the *maker* or *payor* and the lender (mortgagee) is the payee. If it is used with a deed of trust, the note may be made payable to the bearer. It may also refer to or repeat several of the clauses that appear in the mortgage document or deed of trust. The note, like the mortgage or deed of trust, should be signed by all parties who have an interest in the property. In states where dower and curtesy are in effect or where homestead or community property is involved, both spouses may have an interest in the property and both should sign the note.

Figure 14.2 is an example of a note commonly used with a mortgage. It is one of the standard forms used by lenders who may want to sell the loan to the Federal Home Loan Mortgage Corporation (FHLMC) or the Federal National Mortgage Association (FNMA). FHLMC and FNMA are discussed in Chapter 15.

A note is a **negotiable instrument;** that is, its holder, the payee, may transfer the right to receive payment to a third party. This may be accomplished by signing the instrument over to the third party or, in some cases, by merely delivering the instrument to that person. Other examples of negotiable instruments include checks and bank drafts.

Interest

A charge for the use of money is called **interest.** Interest may be due either at the end of each payment period (known as payment *in arrears*) or at the beginning of each payment period (payment *in advance*). Whether interest is charged in arrears or in advance is specified in the note. In practice the distinction becomes important if the property is sold before the debt is repaid in full, as will become evident in Chapter 23.

Usury. The maximum rate of interest that may be charged on loans may be set by state law (with the exception noted later in this discussion). Charging interest in excess of this rate is called **usury,** and lenders are penalized for making usurious loans. In some states a lender who makes a usurious loan will be permitted to collect the borrowed money, but only at the legal rate of interest. In other states a usurious lender may lose the right to collect any interest or may lose the entire amount of the loan in addition to the interest. Loans made to corporations are generally exempt from usury laws.

Usury laws were enacted primarily to protect consumers from unscrupulous lenders who would charge unreasonably high interest rates. Some states specifically limit the legal maximum interest rate to a fixed amount, while other states have what is known as a *floating interest rate*. In such states the maximum rate that may be charged is adjusted up or down at specific intervals based on a certain economic standard, such as the prime lending rate or the rate of return on government bonds.

Usury laws are state laws, but federal law specifically exempts from state interest limitations residential first mortgage loans made after March 31, 1980, by federally chartered institutions or insured or guaranteed by a federal agency. The exemption includes loans used to finance manufactured housing (the federal term for mobile homes) and the acquisition of stock in a cooperative housing corporation. The federal act effectively limits state usury laws to private lenders.

Discount points. The rate of interest that a lender charges for a mortgage loan might be less than the yield (true rate of return) required by an investor who would purchase that loan. For this reason the lender can charge **discount points** to make up the difference between the mortgage interest rate and the required investor yield. The number of points charged varies, depending both on the difference between the interest rate and the required yield, and on the average time the lender expects the loan to be outstanding. The average loan made for 30 years is in effect for seven to 12 years, and lenders calculate that it takes an average of five to eight discount points to increase the yield one percent, with eight points being the industry norm. Discount points can be charged on FHA-insured, VA-guaranteed and conventional loans.

One discount point equals one percent of the loan amount and is charged as prepaid interest at the closing. For example, three discount points charged on a $100,000 loan would be $3,000 ($100,000 × 3%). In this situation the lender would actually fund $97,000 (the $100,000 principal amount of the loan minus the $3,000 discount), but $100,000 would have to be repaid by the borrower, thereby increasing the investor's yield (a $97,000 loan receiving interest calculated on $100,000).

Discount points should not be confused with the loan origination fee charged by most lenders for generating the loan. Loan origination fees are not prepaid interest; they are an expense that must be paid to the lender, typically one percent of the loan amount regardless of any discount points that might also be charged.

In Practice . . .

As stated in Chapter 3 interest payments made under a mortgage loan secured by a first or second home are deductible for federal income tax purposes if the loan amount is not more than $1 million. This deduction in effect reduces the borrower's total cost of housing for the year. Interest deductions are limited, however, to the interest paid on an initial loan amount or refinancing no greater than the purchase price of the home plus capital improvements. Interest on home equity debt is deductible for loans of up to $100,000. Points (prepaid interest) paid at the time of financing a home purchase are fully deductible for the year paid. Points on a loan to finance property improvements are also fully deductible for the year paid. Points paid on loan refinancing are deductible, but only in portions each year over the stated term of the loan. If advance payments of the loan principal are made, there is no increase in the deduction. If the entire loan is repaid, however, any undeducted points may be deducted for that year.

Prepayment

When a loan is paid in installments over a long term, the total interest paid by the borrower can be larger than the principal amount of the loan. If such a loan is paid off ahead of its full term, the lender will collect less interest from the

Figure 14.2
Note

NOTE

.... April 12 ...., 19 90 ..   .. Chicago ...., ... Illinois ....
                                                                                     [City]   [State]

          222 Kelly Street, Chicago, Illinois 60601
....
                                                 [Property Address]

1. BORROWER'S PROMISE TO PAY

In return for a loan that I have received, I promise to pay U.S. $ 79,000.00 .... (this amount is called
"principal"), plus interest, to the order of the Lender. The Lender is .. First City Savings and Loan ....
..........Association of Chicago, Illinois .... I understand
that the Lender may transfer this Note. The Lender or anyone who takes this Note by transfer and who is entitled to
receive payments under this Note is called the "Note Holder."

2. INTEREST

Interest will be charged on unpaid principal until the full amount of principal has been paid. I will pay interest at a
yearly rate of .... 9.5 .... %.

The interest rate required by this Section 2 is the rate I will pay both before and after any default described in
Section 6(B) of this Note.

3. PAYMENTS

(A) Time and Place of Payments

I will pay principal and interest by making payments every month.

I will make my monthly payments on the .... 1st .. day of each month beginning on .... May 1 ....,
19.88.... I will make these payments every month until I have paid all of the principal and interest and any other charges
described below that I may owe under this Note. My monthly payments will be applied to interest before principal. If, on
.... April 1, 2018 ...., I still owe amounts under this Note, I will pay those amounts in full on that date,
which is called the "maturity date."

I will make my monthly payments at .... 130 North LaSalle Street, Chicago, Illinois ....
.... or at a different place if required by the Note Holder.

(B) Amount of Monthly Payments

My monthly payment will be in the amount of U.S. $.664.29 ....

4. BORROWER'S RIGHT TO PREPAY

I have the right to make payments of principal at any time before they are due. A payment of principal only is
known as a "prepayment." When I make a prepayment, I will tell the Note Holder in writing that I am doing so.

I may make a full prepayment or partial prepayments without paying any prepayment charge. The Note Holder
will use all of my prepayments to reduce the amount of principal that I owe under this Note. If I make a partial

**Figure 14.2
(continued)**

prepayment, there will be no changes in the due date or in the amount of my monthly payment unless the Note Holder agrees in writing to those changes.

5. LOAN CHARGES

If a law, which applies to this loan and which sets maximum loan charges, is finally interpreted so that the interest or other loan charges collected or to be collected in connection with this loan exceed the permitted limits, then: (i) any such loan charge shall be reduced by the amount necessary to reduce the charge to the permitted limit; and (ii) any sums already collected from me which exceeded permitted limits will be refunded to me. The Note Holder may choose to make this refund by reducing the principal I owe under this Note or by making a direct payment to me. If a refund reduces principal, the reduction will be treated as a partial prepayment.

6. BORROWER'S FAILURE TO PAY AS REQUIRED

(A) Late Charge for Overdue Payments

If the Note Holder has not received the full amount of any monthly payment by the end of ....fifteen.... calendar days after the date it is due, I will pay a late charge to the Note Holder. The amount of the charge will be ....5..% of my overdue payment of principal and interest. I will pay this late charge promptly but only once on each late payment.

(B) Default

If I do not pay the full amount of each monthly payment on the date it is due, I will be in default.

(C) Notice of Default

If I am in default, the Note Holder may send me a written notice telling me that if I do not pay the overdue amount by a certain date, the Note Holder may require me to pay immediately the full amount of principal which has not been paid and all the interest that I owe on that amount. That date must be at least 30 days after the date on which the notice is delivered or mailed to me.

(D) No Waiver By Note Holder

Even if, at a time when I am in default, the Note Holder does not require me to pay immediately in full as described above, the Note Holder will still have the right to do so if I am in default at a later time.

(E) Payment of Note Holder's Costs and Expenses

If the Note Holder has required me to pay immediately in full as described above, the Note Holder will have the right to be paid back by me for all of its costs and expenses in enforcing this Note to the extent not prohibited by applicable law. Those expenses include, for example, reasonable attorneys' fees.

7. GIVING OF NOTICES

Unless applicable law requires a different method, any notice that must be given to me under this Note will be given by delivering it or by mailing it by first class mail to me at the Property Address above or at a different address if I give the Note Holder a notice of my different address.

Any notice that must be given to the Note Holder under this Note will be given by mailing it by first class mail to the Note Holder at the address stated in Section 3(A) above or at a different address if I am given a notice of that different address.

MULTISTATE FIXED RATE NOTE—Single Family—**FNMA/FHLMC UNIFORM INSTRUMENT**   Form 3200 12/83

| **Math Concept: Discount Points and Investor Yields** | As a general rule it takes 8 discount points to change the interest rate 1%. From the standpoint of the borrower 1 discount point equals 1% of the loan amount.

To calculate the dollar value of 4 discount points (.04 as a decimal) on a $95,000 loan, multiply the loan amount by the number of points:

$$\$95,000 \times 4\% = \$95,000 \times .04 = \$3,800 \text{ discount}$$

To calculate the net amount of a $75,000 loan after a 3-point discount is taken, multiply the loan amount by 100% minus the discount:

$$\$75,000 \times (100\% - 3\%) = \$75,000 \times 97\% = \$75,000 \times .97 = \$72,750$$

Or, deduct the dollar amount of the discount from the loan:

$$\$75,000 - (\$75,000 \times 3\%) = \$75,000 - \$2,250 = \$72,750$$

From the standpoint of the investor 1 discount point received increases the yield on the loan by ⅛%. Two points would increase the yield by ¼%, 4 discount points would increase the yield by ½%, 6 points would increase the yield by ¾% and 8 points would increase the yield 1%.

For example, if a loan carried an interest rate of 9½% and a discount of 6 points, the yield to the investor would be calculated as follows:

6 discount points = ¾% increase in yield;

9½% interest per the contract + ¾% increase from the discount =

10¼% yield to the investor

If an investor requires a 10½% yield on a loan with a 10⅛% interest rate, the number of discount points needed would be calculated as follows:

10½% = 10⁴⁄₈%;   10⁴⁄₈% required yield − 10⅛% interest rate =

³⁄₈% difference;   ³⁄₈% = 3 discount points needed |

borrower. For this reason, some mortgage and deed of trust notes contain a *prepayment clause* requiring the borrower to pay a **prepayment penalty** against the unearned portion of the interest for any payments made ahead of schedule.

The premium charged may run from one percent of the balance due at the time of prepayment to all interest due for the first ten years of the loan. Some lenders allow the borrower to pay off 20 percent of the original loan in any one year without paying a premium, but if the loan is paid off in full the borrower may be charged a percentage of the principal paid in excess of that allowance. Some states either limit or do not permit a lender to charge a penalty on prepaid residential mortgage or deed of trust loans. Other states allow a lender to charge a prepayment penalty *only* if the loan is paid off with funds borrowed from another source.

Provisions of the Mortgage Document or Deed of Trust

The mortgage document or deed of trust refers to the terms of the note and clearly establishes that the property is security for the debt. It identifies the lender and borrower and includes an accurate legal description of the property. It should be signed by all parties who have an interest in the real estate.

Figure 14.3 is a sample mortgage; Figure 14.4 is a sample deed of trust. The documents shown are examples of FNMA/FHLMC uniform instruments. In every state using the documents, the first 18 clauses are exactly the same. Any differences between the states are included after clause 18.

Duties of the Mortgagor or Trustor

The borrower is required to fulfill many obligations, usually including:

1. payment of the debt in accordance with the terms of the note;

2. payment of all real estate taxes on the property given as security;

3. maintenance of adequate insurance to protect the lender if the property is destroyed or damaged by fire, windstorm or other hazard;

4. maintenance of the property in good repair at all times; and

5. lender authorization before making any major alterations on the property.

Failure to meet any of these obligations can result in a borrower's default on the note. When this happens, the loan documents may provide for a grace period (30 days, for example) during which the borrower can meet the obligation and cure the default. If the borrower does not do so, the lender has the right to foreclose the mortgage or deed of trust and collect on the note. The most frequent cause of default is the borrower's failure to meet monthly installments.

Provisions for Default

The mortgage or deed of trust typically includes an **acceleration clause** to assist the lender in foreclosure. If a borrower defaults, the lender has the right to accelerate the maturity of the debt—to declare the *entire* debt due and payable *immediately*. Without the acceleration clause the lender would have to sue the borrower every time a payment became overdue.

Other clauses in a mortgage or deed of trust enable the lender to take care of the property in the event of the borrower's negligence or default. If the borrower does not pay taxes or insurance premiums or make necessary repairs on the property, the lender may step in and do so to protect the security (the real estate). Any money advanced by the lender to cure such defaults is either added to the unpaid debt or declared immediately due from the borrower.

Assignment of the Mortgage

When a note is sold to a third party, the mortgagee will endorse the note to the third party and also execute an *assignment of mortgage* or an *assignment of deed of trust*. The assignee becomes the new owner of the debt and security instrument. This assignment must be recorded. Upon payment in full, or satisfaction of the debt, the assignee is required to execute the satisfaction, or release, of the security instrument as discussed in the following section.

Release of the Mortgage Lien

When all mortgage loan payments have been made and the note has been paid in full, the mortgagor wants the public record to show that the debt has been paid and the mortgage released. By the provisions of the **defeasance clause** in the usual mortgage document, when the note has been fully paid the mortgagee is required to execute a **satisfaction of mortgage,** also known as a *release of mortgage* or *mortgage discharge*. This document reconveys to the mortgagor all interest in the real estate that was conveyed to the mortgagee by the original recorded

Figure 14.3
Sample Mortgage

MORTGAGE

THIS MORTGAGE ("Security Instrument") is given on ....,
19......... The mortgagor is ....
.... ("Borrower"). This Security Instrument is given to ....
...., which is organized and existing
under the laws of ...., and whose address is ....
.... ("Lender").
Borrower owes Lender the principal sum of ....
.... Dollars (U.S. $...............................). This debt is evidenced by Borrower's note
dated the same date as this Security Instrument ("Note"), which provides for monthly payments, with the full debt, if not
paid earlier, due and payable on .... This Security Instrument
secures to Lender: (a) the repayment of the debt evidenced by the Note, with interest, and all renewals, extensions and
modifications; (b) the payment of all other sums, with interest, advanced under paragraph 7 to protect the security of this
Security Instrument; and (c) the performance of Borrower's covenants and agreements under this Security Instrument and
the Note. For this purpose, Borrower does hereby mortgage, grant and convey to Lender the following described property
located in .... County, Illinois:

which has the address of ...., ...,
                                                                    [Street]   [City]
Illinois .... ("Property Address");
                        [Zip Code]

TOGETHER WITH all the improvements now or hereafter erected on the property, and all easements, rights,
appurtenances, rents, royalties, mineral, oil and gas rights and profits, water rights and stock and all fixtures now or
hereafter a part of the property. All replacements and additions shall also be covered by this Security Instrument. All of the
foregoing is referred to in this Security Instrument as the "Property."

BORROWER COVENANTS that Borrower is lawfully seised of the estate hereby conveyed and has the right to
mortgage, grant and convey the Property and that the Property is unencumbered, except for encumbrances of record.
Borrower warrants and will defend generally the title to the Property against all claims and demands, subject to any
encumbrances of record.

THIS SECURITY INSTRUMENT combines uniform covenants for national use and non-uniform covenants with
limited variations by jurisdiction to constitute a uniform security instrument covering real property.

ILLINOIS—Single Family—**FNMA/FHLMC UNIFORM INSTRUMENT**   Form 3014 12/83

**Figure 14.3
(continued)**

UNIFORM COVENANTS. Borrower and Lender covenant and agree as follows:

1. Payment of Principal and Interest; Prepayment and Late Charges. Borrower shall promptly pay when due the principal of and interest on the debt evidenced by the Note and any prepayment and late charges due under the Note.

2. Funds for Taxes and Insurance. Subject to applicable law or to a written waiver by Lender, Borrower shall pay to Lender on the day monthly payments are due under the Note, until the Note is paid in full, a sum ("Funds") equal to one-twelfth of: (a) yearly taxes and assessments which may attain priority over this Security Instrument; (b) yearly leasehold payments or ground rents on the Property, if any; (c) yearly hazard insurance premiums; and (d) yearly mortgage insurance premiums, if any. These items are called "escrow items." Lender may estimate the Funds due on the basis of current data and reasonable estimates of future escrow items.

The Funds shall be held in an institution the deposits or accounts of which are insured or guaranteed by a federal or state agency (including Lender if Lender is such an institution). Lender shall apply the Funds to pay the escrow items. Lender may not charge for holding and applying the Funds, analyzing the account or verifying the escrow items, unless Lender pays Borrower interest on the Funds and applicable law permits Lender to make such a charge. Borrower and Lender may agree in writing that interest shall be paid on the Funds. Unless an agreement is made or applicable law requires interest to be paid, Lender shall not be required to pay Borrower any interest or earnings on the Funds. Lender shall give to Borrower, without charge, an annual accounting of the Funds showing credits and debits to the Funds and the purpose for which each debit to the Funds was made. The Funds are pledged as additional security for the sums secured by this Security Instrument.

If the amount of the Funds held by Lender, together with the future monthly payments of Funds payable prior to the due dates of the escrow items, shall exceed the amount required to pay the escrow items when due, the excess shall be, at Borrower's option, either promptly repaid to Borrower or credited to Borrower on monthly payments of Funds. If the amount of the Funds held by Lender is not sufficient to pay the escrow items when due, Borrower shall pay to Lender any amount necessary to make up the deficiency in one or more payments as required by Lender.

Upon payment in full of all sums secured by this Security Instrument, Lender shall promptly refund to Borrower any Funds held by Lender. If under paragraph 19 the Property is sold or acquired by Lender, Lender shall apply, no later than immediately prior to the sale of the Property or its acquisition by Lender, any Funds held by Lender at the time of application as a credit against the sums secured by this Security Instrument.

3. Application of Payments. Unless applicable law provides otherwise, all payments received by Lender under paragraphs 1 and 2 shall be applied: first, to late charges due under the Note; second, to prepayment charges due under the Note; third, to amounts payable under paragraph 2; fourth, to interest due; and last, to principal due.

4. Charges; Liens. Borrower shall pay all taxes, assessments, charges, fines and impositions attributable to the Property which may attain priority over this Security Instrument, and leasehold payments or ground rents, if any. Borrower shall pay these obligations in the manner provided in paragraph 2, or if not paid in that manner, Borrower shall pay them on time directly to the person owed payment. Borrower shall promptly furnish to Lender all notices of amounts to be paid under this paragraph. If Borrower makes these payments directly, Borrower shall promptly furnish to Lender receipts evidencing the payments.

Borrower shall promptly discharge any lien which has priority over this Security Instrument unless Borrower: (a) agrees in writing to the payment of the obligation secured by the lien in a manner acceptable to Lender; (b) contests in good faith the lien by, or defends against enforcement of the lien in, legal proceedings which in the Lender's opinion operate to prevent the enforcement of the lien or forfeiture of any part of the Property; or (c) secures from the holder of the lien an agreement satisfactory to Lender subordinating the lien to this Security Instrument. If Lender determines that any part of the Property is subject to a lien which may attain priority over this Security Instrument, Lender may give Borrower a notice identifying the lien. Borrower shall satisfy the lien or take one or more of the actions set forth above within 10 days of the giving of notice.

5. Hazard Insurance. Borrower shall keep the improvements now existing or hereafter erected on the Property insured against loss by fire, hazards included within the term "extended coverage" and any other hazards for which Lender requires insurance. This insurance shall be maintained in the amounts and for the periods that Lender requires. The insurance carrier providing the insurance shall be chosen by Borrower subject to Lender's approval which shall not be unreasonably withheld.

All insurance policies and renewals shall be acceptable to Lender and shall include a standard mortgage clause. Lender shall have the right to hold the policies and renewals. If Lender requires, Borrower shall promptly give to Lender all receipts of paid premiums and renewal notices. In the event of loss, Borrower shall give prompt notice to the insurance carrier and Lender. Lender may make proof of loss if not made promptly by Borrower.

Unless Lender and Borrower otherwise agree in writing, insurance proceeds shall be applied to restoration or repair of the Property damaged, if the restoration or repair is economically feasible and Lender's security is not lessened. If the restoration or repair is not economically feasible or Lender's security would be lessened, the insurance proceeds shall be applied to the sums secured by this Security Instrument, whether or not then due, with any excess paid to Borrower. If Borrower abandons the Property, or does not answer within 30 days a notice from Lender that the insurance carrier has offered to settle a claim, then Lender may collect the insurance proceeds. Lender may use the proceeds to repair or restore the Property or to pay sums secured by this Security Instrument, whether or not then due. The 30-day period will begin when the notice is given.

Unless Lender and Borrower otherwise agree in writing, any application of proceeds to principal shall not extend or postpone the due date of the monthly payments referred to in paragraphs 1 and 2 or change the amount of the payments. If under paragraph 19 the Property is acquired by Lender, Borrower's right to any insurance policies and proceeds resulting from damage to the Property prior to the acquisition shall pass to Lender to the extent of the sums secured by this Security Instrument immediately prior to the acquisition.

6. Preservation and Maintenance of Property; Leaseholds. Borrower shall not destroy, damage or substantially change the Property, allow the Property to deteriorate or commit waste. If this Security Instrument is on a leasehold, Borrower shall comply with the provisions of the lease, and if Borrower acquires fee title to the Property, the leasehold and fee title shall not merge unless Lender agrees to the merger in writing.

7. Protection of Lender's Rights in the Property; Mortgage Insurance. If Borrower fails to perform the covenants and agreements contained in this Security Instrument, or there is a legal proceeding that may significantly affect Lender's rights in the Property (such as a proceeding in bankruptcy, probate, for condemnation or to enforce laws or regulations), then Lender may do and pay for whatever is necessary to protect the value of the Property and Lender's rights in the Property. Lender's actions may include paying any sums secured by a lien which has priority over this Security Instrument, appearing in court, paying reasonable attorneys' fees and entering on the Property to make repairs. Although Lender may take action under this paragraph 7, Lender does not have to do so.

Any amounts disbursed by Lender under this paragraph 7 shall become additional debt of Borrower secured by this Security Instrument. Unless Borrower and Lender agree to other terms of payment, these amounts shall bear interest from the date of disbursement at the Note rate and shall be payable, with interest, upon notice from Lender to Borrower requesting payment.

Figure 14.3
(continued)

If Lender required mortgage insurance as a condition of making the loan secured by this Security Instrument, Borrower shall pay the premiums required to maintain the insurance in effect until such time as the requirement for the insurance terminates in accordance with Borrower's and Lender's written agreement or applicable law.

8. Inspection. Lender or its agent may make reasonable entries upon and inspections of the Property. Lender shall give Borrower notice at the time of or prior to an inspection specifying reasonable cause for the inspection.

9. Condemnation. The proceeds of any award or claim for damages, direct or consequential, in connection with any condemnation or other taking of any part of the Property, or for conveyance in lieu of condemnation, are hereby assigned and shall be paid to Lender.

In the event of a total taking of the Property, the proceeds shall be applied to the sums secured by this Security Instrument, whether or not then due, with any excess paid to Borrower. In the event of a partial taking of the Property, unless Borrower and Lender otherwise agree in writing, the sums secured by this Security Instrument shall be reduced by the amount of the proceeds multiplied by the following fraction: (a) the total amount of the sums secured immediately before the taking, divided by (b) the fair market value of the Property immediately before the taking. Any balance shall be paid to Borrower.

If the Property is abandoned by Borrower, or if, after notice by Lender to Borrower that the condemnor offers to make an award or settle a claim for damages, Borrower fails to respond to Lender within 30 days after the date the notice is given, Lender is authorized to collect and apply the proceeds, at its option, either to restoration or repair of the Property or to the sums secured by this Security Instrument, whether or not then due.

Unless Lender and Borrower otherwise agree in writing, any application of proceeds to principal shall not extend or postpone the due date of the monthly payments referred to in paragraphs 1 and 2 or change the amount of such payments.

10. Borrower Not Released; Forbearance By Lender Not a Waiver. Extension of the time for payment or modification of amortization of the sums secured by this Security Instrument granted by Lender to any successor in interest of Borrower shall not operate to release the liability of the original Borrower or Borrower's successors in interest. Lender shall not be required to commence proceedings against any successor in interest or refuse to extend time for payment or otherwise modify amortization of the sums secured by this Security Instrument by reason of any demand made by the original Borrower or Borrower's successors in interest. Any forbearance by Lender in exercising any right or remedy shall not be a waiver of or preclude the exercise of any right or remedy.

11. Successors and Assigns Bound; Joint and Several Liability; Co-signers. The covenants and agreements of this Security Instrument shall bind and benefit the successors and assigns of Lender and Borrower, subject to the provisions of paragraph 17. Borrower's covenants and agreements shall be joint and several. Any Borrower who co-signs this Security Instrument but does not execute the Note: (a) is co-signing this Security Instrument only to mortgage, grant and convey that Borrower's interest in the Property under the terms of this Security Instrument; (b) is not personally obligated to pay the sums secured by this Security Instrument; and (c) agrees that Lender and any other Borrower may agree to extend, modify, forbear or make any accommodations with regard to the terms of this Security Instrument or the Note without that Borrower's consent.

12. Loan Charges. If the loan secured by this Security Instrument is subject to a law which sets maximum loan charges, and that law is finally interpreted so that the interest or other loan charges collected or to be collected in connection with the loan exceed the permitted limits, then: (a) any such loan charge shall be reduced by the amount necessary to reduce the charge to the permitted limit; and (b) any sums already collected from Borrower which exceeded permitted limits will be refunded to Borrower. Lender may choose to make this refund by reducing the principal owed under the Note or by making a direct payment to Borrower. If a refund reduces principal, the reduction will be treated as a partial prepayment without any prepayment charge under the Note.

13. Legislation Affecting Lender's Rights. If enactment or expiration of applicable laws has the effect of rendering any provision of the Note or this Security Instrument unenforceable according to its terms, Lender, at its option, may require immediate payment in full of all sums secured by this Security Instrument and may invoke any remedies permitted by paragraph 19. If Lender exercises this option, Lender shall take the steps specified in the second paragraph of paragraph 17.

14. Notices. Any notice to Borrower provided for in this Security Instrument shall be given by delivering it or by mailing it by first class mail unless applicable law requires use of another method. The notice shall be directed to the Property Address or any other address Borrower designates by notice to Lender. Any notice to Lender shall be given by first class mail to Lender's address stated herein or any other address Lender designates by notice to Borrower. Any notice provided for in this Security Instrument shall be deemed to have been given to Borrower or Lender when given as provided in this paragraph.

15. Governing Law; Severability. This Security Instrument shall be governed by federal law and the law of the jurisdiction in which the Property is located. In the event that any provision or clause of this Security Instrument or the Note conflicts with applicable law, such conflict shall not affect other provisions of this Security Instrument or the Note which can be given effect without the conflicting provision. To this end the provisions of this Security Instrument and the Note are declared to be severable.

16. Borrower's Copy. Borrower shall be given one conformed copy of the Note and of this Security Instrument.

17. Transfer of the Property or a Beneficial Interest in Borrower. If all or any part of the Property or any interest in it is sold or transferred (or if a beneficial interest in Borrower is sold or transferred and Borrower is not a natural person) without Lender's prior written consent, Lender may, at its option, require immediate payment in full of all sums secured by this Security Instrument. However, this option shall not be exercised by Lender if exercise is prohibited by federal law as of the date of this Security Instrument.

If Lender exercises this option, Lender shall give Borrower notice of acceleration. The notice shall provide a period of not less than 30 days from the date the notice is delivered or mailed within which Borrower must pay all sums secured by this Security Instrument. If Borrower fails to pay these sums prior to the expiration of this period, Lender may invoke any remedies permitted by this Security Instrument without further notice or demand on Borrower.

18. Borrower's Right to Reinstate. If Borrower meets certain conditions, Borrower shall have the right to have enforcement of this Security Instrument discontinued at any time prior to the earlier of: (a) 5 days (or such other period as applicable law may specify for reinstatement) before sale of the Property pursuant to any power of sale contained in this Security Instrument; or (b) entry of a judgment enforcing this Security Instrument. Those conditions are that Borrower: (a) pays Lender all sums which then would be due under this Security Instrument and the Note had no acceleration occurred; (b) cures any default of any other covenants or agreements; (c) pays all expenses incurred in enforcing this Security Instrument, including, but not limited to, reasonable attorneys' fees; and (d) takes such action as Lender may reasonably require to assure that the lien of this Security Instrument, Lender's rights in the Property and Borrower's obligation to pay the sums secured by this Security Instrument shall continue unchanged. Upon reinstatement by Borrower, this Security Instrument and the obligations secured hereby shall remain fully effective as if no acceleration had occurred. However, this right to reinstate shall not apply in the case of acceleration under paragraphs 13 or 17.

Figure 14.3
(continued)

NON-UNIFORM COVENANTS. Borrower and Lender further covenant and agree as follows:

19. Acceleration; Remedies. Lender shall give notice to Borrower prior to acceleration following Borrower's breach of any covenant or agreement in this Security Instrument (but not prior to acceleration under paragraphs 13 and 17 unless applicable law provides otherwise). The notice shall specify: (a) the default; (b) the action required to cure the default; (c) a date, not less than 30 days from the date the notice is given to Borrower, by which the default must be cured; and (d) that failure to cure the default on or before the date specified in the notice may result in acceleration of the sums secured by this Security Instrument, foreclosure by judicial proceeding and sale of the Property. The notice shall further inform Borrower of the right to reinstate after acceleration and the right to assert in the foreclosure proceeding the non-existence of a default or any other defense of Borrower to acceleration and foreclosure. If the default is not cured on or before the date specified in the notice, Lender at its option may require immediate payment in full of all sums secured by this Security Instrument without further demand and may foreclose this Security Instrument by judicial proceeding. Lender shall be entitled to collect all expenses incurred in pursuing the remedies provided in this paragraph 19, including, but not limited to, reasonable attorneys' fees and costs of title evidence.

20. Lender in Possession. Upon acceleration under paragraph 19 or abandonment of the Property and at any time prior to the expiration of any period of redemption following judicial sale, Lender (in person, by agent or by judicially appointed receiver) shall be entitled to enter upon, take possession of and manage the Property and to collect the rents of the Property including those past due. Any rents collected by Lender or the receiver shall be applied first to payment of the costs of management of the Property and collection of rents, including, but not limited to, receiver's fees, premiums on receiver's bonds and reasonable attorneys' fees, and then to the sums secured by this Security Instrument.

21. Release. Upon payment of all sums secured by this Security Instrument, Lender shall release this Security Instrument without charge to Borrower. Borrower shall pay any recordation costs.

22. Waiver of Homestead. Borrower waives all right of homestead exemption in the Property.

23. Riders to this Security Instrument. If one or more riders are executed by Borrower and recorded together with this Security Instrument, the covenants and agreements of each such rider shall be incorporated into and shall amend and supplement the covenants and agreements of this Security Instrument as if the rider(s) were a part of this Security Instrument. [Check applicable box(es)]

☐ Adjustable Rate Rider   ☐ Condominium Rider   ☐ 2–4 Family Rider

☐ Graduated Payment Rider   ☐ Planned Unit Development Rider

☐ Other(s) [specify]

BY SIGNING BELOW, Borrower accepts and agrees to the terms and covenants contained in this Security Instrument and in any rider(s) executed by Borrower and recorded with it.

....(Seal)
—Borrower

....(Seal)
—Borrower

———————————————— [Space Below This Line For Acknowledgment] ————————————————

Figure 14.4
Deed of Trust

WHEN RECORDED MAIL TO

SPACE ABOVE THIS LINE FOR RECORDER'S USE

DEED OF TRUST

THIS DEED OF TRUST ("Security Instrument") is made on   The trustor
is

("Borrower").

The trustee is
("Trustee").

The beneficiary is

which is organized and existing under the laws of   , and
whose address is

("Lender").

Borrower owes Lender the principal sum of

Dollars (U.S. $). This debt is evidenced by Borrower's note dated the same date as this
Security Instrument ("Note"), which provides for monthly payments, with the full debt, if not paid earlier, due and
payable on   . This Security Instrument secures to Lender: (a) the repayment
of the debt evidenced by the Note, with interest, and all renewals, extensions and modifications; (b) the payment of
all other sums, with interest, advanced under paragraph 7 to protect the security of this Security Instrument; and (c)
the performance of Borrower's covenants and agreements under this Security Instrument and the Note. For this
purpose, Borrower irrevocably grants and conveys to Trustee, in trust, with power of sale, the following described
property located in   County, Arizona:

which has the address of

(Street)

, Arizona   ("Property Address");

(City)   (Zip Code)

TOGETHER WITH all the improvements now or hereafter erected on the property, and all easements, rights,
appurtenances, rents, royalties, mineral, oil and gas rights and profits, water rights and stock and all fixtures now or
hereafter a part of the property. All replacements and additions shall also be covered by this Security Instrument.
All of the foregoing is referred to in this Security Instrument as the "Property."

BORROWER COVENANTS that Borrower is lawfully seised of the estate hereby conveyed and has the right
to grant and convey the Property and that the Property is unencumbered, except for encumbrances of record.
Borrower warrants and will defend generally the title to the Property against all claims and demands, subject to any
encumbrances of record.

THIS SECURITY INSTRUMENT combines uniform covenants for national use and non-uniform covenants with
limited variations by jurisdiction to constitute a uniform security instrument covering real property.

ARIZONA — Single Family —   Page 1 of 5   Form 3003 12/83
FNMA/FHLMC UNIFORM INSTRUMENT   (8-89) T-11940-11

**Figure 14.4
(continued)**

UNIFORM COVENANTS. Borrower and Lender covenant and agree as follows:

1. **Payment of Principal and Interest; Prepayment and Late Charges.** Borrower shall promptly pay when due the principal of and interest on the debt evidenced by the Note and any prepayment and late charges due under the Note.

2. **Funds for Taxes and Insurance.** Subject to applicable law or to a written waiver by Lender, Borrower shall pay to Lender on the day monthly payments are due under the Note, until the Note is paid in full, a sum ("Funds") equal to one-twelfth of: (a) yearly taxes and assessments which may attain priority over this Security Instrument; (b) yearly leasehold payments or ground rents on the Property, if any; (c) yearly hazard insurance premiums; and (d) yearly mortgage insurance premiums, if any. These items are called "escrow items." Lender may estimate the Funds due on the basis of current data and reasonable estimates of future escrow items.

The Funds shall be held in an institution the deposits or accounts of which are insured or guaranteed by a federal or state agency (including Lender if Lender is such an institution). Lender shall apply the Funds to pay the escrow items. Lender may not charge for holding and applying the Funds, analyzing the account or verifying the escrow items, unless Lender pays Borrower interest on the Funds and applicable law permits Lender to make such a charge. A charge assessed by Lender in connection with Borrower's entering into this Security Instrument to pay the cost of an independent tax reporting service shall not be a charge for purposes of the preceding sentence. Borrower and Lender may agree in writing that interest shall be paid on the Funds. Unless an agreement is made or applicable law requires interest to be paid, Lender shall not be required to pay Borrower any interest or earnings on the Funds. Lender shall give to Borrower, without charge, an annual accounting of the Funds showing credits and debits to the Funds and the purpose for which each debit to the Funds was made. The Funds are pledged as additional security for the sums secured by this Security Instrument.

If the amount of the Funds held by Lender, together with the future monthly payments of Funds payable prior to the due dates of the escrow items, shall exceed the amount required to pay the escrow items when due, the excess shall be, at Borrower's option, either promptly repaid to Borrower or credited to Borrower on monthly payments of Funds. If the amount of the Funds held by Lender is not sufficient to pay the escrow items when due, Borrower shall pay to Lender any amount necessary to make up the deficiency in one or more payments as required by Lender.

Upon payment in full of all sums secured by this Security Instrument, Lender shall promptly refund to Borrower any Funds held by Lender. If under paragraph 19 the Property is sold or acquired by Lender, Lender shall apply, no later than immediately prior to the sale of the Property or its acquisition by Lender, any Funds held by Lender at the time of application as a credit against the sums secured by this Security Instrument.

3. **Application of Payments.** Unless applicable law provides otherwise, all payments received by Lender under paragraphs 1 and 2 should be applied: first to amounts payable under paragraph 2; second to interest; and last to principal.

4. **Charges; Liens.** Borrower shall pay all taxes, assessments, charges, fines and impositions attributable to the Property which may attain priority over this Security Instrument, and leasehold payments or ground rents, if any. Borrower shall pay these obligations in the manner provided in paragraph 2, or if not paid in that manner, Borrower shall pay them on time directly to the person owed payment. Borrower shall promptly furnish to Lender all notices of amounts to be paid under this paragraph. If Borrower makes these payments directly, Borrower shall promptly furnish to Lender receipts evidencing the payments.

Borrower shall promptly discharge any lien which has priority over this Security Instrument unless Borrower: (a) agrees in writing to the payment of the obligation secured by the lien in a manner acceptable to Lender; (b) contests in good faith the lien by, or defends against enforcement of the lien in, legal proceedings which in the Lender's opinion operate to prevent the enforcement of the lien or forfeiture of any part of the Property; or (c) secures from the holder of the lien an agreement satisfactory to Lender subordinating the lien to this Security Instrument. If Lender determines that any part of the Property is subject to a lien which may attain priority over this Security Instrument, Lender may give Borrower a notice identifying the lien. Borrower shall satisfy the lien or take one or more of the actions set forth above within 10 days of the giving of notice.

5. **Hazard Insurance.** Borrower shall keep the improvements now existing or hereafter erected on the Property insured against loss by fire, hazards included within the term "extended coverage" and any other hazards for which Lender requires insurance. This insurance shall be maintained in the amounts and for the periods that Lender requires. The insurance carrier providing the insurance shall be chosen by Borrower subject to Lender's approval which shall not be unreasonably withheld.

All insurance policies and renewals shall be acceptable to Lender and shall include a standard mortgage clause. Lender shall have the right to hold the policies and renewals. If Lender requires, Borrower shall promptly give to Lender all receipts of paid premiums and renewal notices. In the event of loss, Borrower shall give prompt notice to the insurance carrier and Lender. Lender may make proof of loss if not made promptly by Borrower.

Unless Lender and Borrower otherwise agree in writing, insurance proceeds shall be applied to restoration or repair of the Property damaged, if the restoration or repair is economically feasible and Lender's security is not lessened. If the restoration or repair is not economically feasible or Lender's security would be lessened, the insurance proceeds shall be applied to the sums secured by this Security Instrument, whether or not then due, with any excess paid to Borrower. If Borrower abandons the Property, or does not answer within 30 days a notice from Lender that the insurance carrier has offered to settle a claim, then Lender may collect the insurance proceeds. Lender may use the proceeds to repair or restore the Property or to pay sums secured by this Security Instrument, whether or not then due. The 30-day period will begin when the notice is given.

Unless Lender and Borrower otherwise agree in writing, any application of proceeds to principal shall not extend or postpone the due date of the monthly payments referred to in paragraphs 1 and 2 or change the amount of the payments. If under paragraph 19 the Property is acquired by Lender, Borrower's right to any insurance policies and proceeds resulting from damage to the Property prior to the acquisition shall pass to Lender to the extent of the sums secured by this Security Instrument immediately prior to the acquisition.

6. **Preservation and Maintenance of Property; Leaseholds.** Borrower shall not destroy, damage or substantially change the Property, allow the Property to deteriorate or commit waste. If this Security Instrument is on a leasehold, Borrower shall comply with the provisions of the lease, and if Borrower acquires fee title to the Property, the leasehold and fee title shall not merge unless Lender agrees to the merger in writing.

ARIZONA — Single Family —   **Page 2 of 5**   Form 3003 12/83
FNMA/FHLMC UNIFORM INSTRUMENT   (8-89) T-11940-12

**Figure 14.4
(continued)**

7. **Protection of Lender's Rights in the Property; Mortgage Insurance.** If Borrower fails to perform the covenants and agreements contained in this Security Instrument, or there is a legal proceeding that may significantly affect Lender's rights in the Property (such as a proceeding in bankruptcy, probate, for condemnation or to enforce laws or regulations), then Lender may do and pay for whatever is necessary to protect the value of the Property and Lender's rights in the Property. Lender's actions may include paying any sums secured by a lien which has priority over this Security Instrument, appearing in court, paying reasonable attorneys' fees and entering on the Property to make repairs. Although Lender may take action under this paragraph 7, Lender does not have to do so.

Any amounts disbursed by Lender under this paragraph 7 shall become additional debt of Borrower secured by this Security Instrument. Unless Borrower and Lender agree to other terms of payment, these amounts shall bear interest from the date of disbursement at the Note rate and shall be payable, with interest, upon notice from Lender to Borrower requesting payment.

If Lender required mortgage insurance as a condition of making the loan secured by this Security Instrument, Borrower shall pay the premiums required to maintain the insurance in effect until such time as the requirement for the insurance terminates in accordance with Borrower's and Lender's written agreement or applicable law.

8. **Inspection.** Lender or its agent may make reasonable entries upon and inspections of the Property. Lender shall give Borrower notice at the time of or prior to an inspection specifying reasonable cause for the inspection.

9. **Condemnation.** The proceeds of any award or claim for damages, direct or consequential, in connection with any condemnation or other taking of any part of the Property, or for conveyance in lieu of condemnation, are hereby assigned and shall be paid to Lender.

In the event of a total taking of the Property, the proceeds shall be applied to the sum's secured by this Security Instrument, whether or not then due, with any excess paid to Borrower. In the event of a partial taking of the Property, unless Borrower and Lender otherwise agree in writing, the sums secured by this Security Instrument shall be reduced by the amount of the proceeds multiplied by the following fraction: (a) the total amount of the sums secured immediately before the taking, divided by (b) the fair market value of the Property immediately before the taking. Any balance shall be paid to Borrower.

If the Property is abandoned by Borrower, or if, after notice by Lender to Borrower that the condemnor offers to make an award or settle a claim for damages, Borrower fails to respond to Lender within 30 days after the date the notice is given, Lender is authorized to collect and apply the proceeds, at its option, either to restoration or repair of the Property or to the sums secured by this Security Instrument, whether or not then due.

Unless Lender and Borrower otherwise agree in writing, any application of proceeds to principal shall not extend or postpone the due date of the monthly payments referred to in paragraphs 1 and 2 or change the amount of such payments.

10. **Borrower Not Released; Forbearance By Lender Not a Waiver.** Extension of the time for payment or modification of amortization of the sums secured by this Security Instrument granted by Lender to any successor in interest of Borrower shall not operate to release the liability of the original Borrower or Borrower's successors in interest. Lender shall not be required to commence proceedings against any successor in interest or refuse to extend time for payment or otherwise modify amortization of the sums secured by this Security Instrument by reason of any demand made by the original Borrower or Borrower's successors in interest. Any forbearance by Lender in exercising any right or remedy shall not be a waiver of or preclude the exercise of any right or remedy.

11. **Successors and Assigns Bound; Joint and Several Liability; Co-signers.** The covenants and agreements of this Security Instrument shall bind and benefit the successors and assigns of Lender and Borrower, subject to the provisions of paragraph 17. Borrower's covenants and agreements shall be joint and several. Any Borrower who co-signs this Security Instrument but does not execute the Note: (a) is co-signing this Security Instrument only to mortgage, grant and convey that Borrower's interest in the Property under the terms of this Security Instrument; (b) is not personally obligated to pay the sums secured by this Security Instrument; and (c) agrees that Lender and any other Borrower may agree to extend, modify, forbear or make any accommodations with regard to the terms of this Security Instrument or the Note without that Borrower's consent.

12. **Loan Charges.** If the loan secured by this Security Instrument is subject to a law which sets maximum loan charges, and that law is finally interpreted so that the interest or other loan charges collected or to be collected in connection with the loan exceed the permitted limits, then: (a) any such loan charge shall be reduced by the amount necessary to reduce the charge to the permitted limit; and (b) any sums already collected from Borrower which exceeded permitted limits will be refunded to Borrower. Lender may choose to make this refund by reducing the principal owed under the Note or by making a direct payment to Borrower. If a refund reduces principal, the reduction will be treated as a partial prepayment without any prepayment charge under the Note.

13. **Legislation Affecting Lender's Rights.** If enactment or expiration of applicable laws has the effect of rendering any provision of the Note or this Security Instrument unenforceable according to its terms, Lender, at its option, may require immediate payment in full of all sums secured by this Security Instrument and may invoke any remedies permitted by paragraph 19. If Lender exercises this option, Lender shall take the steps specified in the second paragraph of paragraph 17.

14. **Notices.** Any notice to Borrower provided for in this Security Instrument shall be given by delivering it or by mailing it by first class mail unless applicable law requires use of another method. The notice shall be directed to the Property Address or any other address Borrower designates by notice to Lender. Any notice to Lender shall be given by first class mail to Lender's address stated herein or any other address Lender designates by notice to Borrower. Any notice provided for in this Security Instrument shall be deemed to have been given to Borrower or Lender when given as provided in this paragraph.

15. **Governing Law; Severability.** This Security Instrument shall be governed by federal law and the law of the jurisdiction in which the Property is located. In the event that any provision or clause of this Security Instrument or the Note conflicts with applicable law, such conflict shall not affect other provisions of this Security Instrument or the Note which can be given effect without the conflicting provision. To this end the provisions of this Security Instrument and the Note are declared to be severable.

16. **Borrower's Copy.** Borrower shall be given one conformed copy of the Note and of this Security Instrument.

ARIZONA —Single Family—   Page 3 of 5   Form 3003 12/83
FNMA/FHLMC UNIFORM INSTRUMENT   (8–89) T–11940–13

Figure 14.4 (continued)

17. **Transfer of the Property or a Beneficial Interest in Borrower.** If all or any part of the Property or any interest in it is sold or transferred (or if a beneficial interest in Borrower is sold or transferred and Borrower is not a natural person) without Lender's prior written consent, Lender may, at its option, require immediate payment in full of all sums secured by this Security Instrument. However, this option shall not be exercised by Lender if exercise is prohibited by federal law as of the date of this Security Instrument.

If Lender exercises this option, Lender shall give Borrower notice of acceleration. The notice shall provide a period of not less than 30 days from the date the notice is delivered or mailed within which Borrower must pay all sums secured by this Security Instrument. If Borrower fails to pay these sums prior to the expiration of this period, Lender may invoke any remedies permitted by this Security Instrument without further notice or demand on Borrower.

18. **Borrower's Right to Reinstate.** If Borrower meets certain conditions, Borrower shall have the right to have enforcement of this Security Instrument discontinued at any time prior to the earlier of: (a) 5 days (or such other period as applicable law may specify for reinstatement) before sale of the Property pursuant to any power of sale contained in this Security Instrument; or (b) entry of a judgment enforcing this Security Instrument. Those conditions are that Borrower: (a) pays Lender all sums which then would be due under this Security Instrument and the Note had no acceleration occurred; (b) cures any default of any other covenants or agreements; (c) pays all expenses incurred in enforcing this Security Instrument, including, but not limited to, reasonable attorneys' fees; and (d) takes such action as Lender may reasonably require to assure that the lien of this Security Instrument, Lender's rights in the Property and Borrower's obligation to pay the sums secured by this Security Instrument shall continue unchanged. Upon reinstatement by Borrower, this Security Instrument and the obligations secured hereby shall remain fully effective as if no acceleration had occurred. However, this right to reinstate shall not apply in the case of acceleration under paragraphs 13 or 17.

NON-UNIFORM COVENANTS. Borrower and Lender further covenant and agree as follows:

19. **Acceleration; Remedies.** Lender shall give notice to Borrower prior to acceleration following Borrower's breach of any covenant or agreement in this Security Instrument (but not prior to acceleration under paragraphs 13 and 17 unless applicable law provides otherwise). The notice shall specify: (a) the default; (b) the action required to cure the default; (c) a date, not less than 30 days from the date the notice is given to Borrower, by which the default must be cured; and (d) that failure to cure the default on or before the date specified in the notice may result in acceleration of the sums secured by this Security Instrument and sale of the Property. The notice shall further inform Borrower of the right to reinstate after acceleration and the right to bring a court action to assert the non-existence of a default or any other defense of Borrower to acceleration and sale. If the default is not cured on or before the date specified in the notice, Lender at its option may require immediate payment in full of all sums secured by this Security Instrument without further demand and may invoke the power of sale and any other remedies permitted by applicable law. Lender shall be entitled to collect all expenses incurred in pursuing the remedies provided in this paragraph 19, including, but not limited to, reasonable attorneys' fees and costs of title evidence.

If Lender invokes the power of sale, Lender shall give written notice to Trustee of the occurrence of an event of default and of Lender's election to cause the Property to be sold. Trustee shall record a notice of sale in each county in which any part of the Property is located and shall mail copies of the notice as prescribed by applicable law to Borrower and to the other persons prescribed by applicable law. After the time required by applicable law and after publication and posting of the notice of sale, Trustee, without demand on Borrower, shall sell the Property at public auction to the highest bidder for cash at the time and place designated in the notice of sale. Trustee may postpone sale of the Property by public announcement at the time and place of any previously scheduled sale. Lender or its designee may purchase the Property at any sale.

Trustee shall deliver to the purchaser Trustee's deed conveying the Property without any covenant or warranty, expressed or implied. The recitals in the Trustee's deed shall be prima facie evidence of the truth of the statements made therein. Trustee shall apply the proceeds of the sale in the following order: (a) to all expenses of the sale, including, but not limited to, reasonable Trustee's and attorneys' fees; (b) to all sums secured by this Security Instrument; and (c) any excess to the person or persons legally entitled to it or to the clerk of the superior court of the county in which the sale took place.

20. **Lender in Possession.** Upon acceleration under paragraph 19 or abandonment of the Property, Lender (in person, by agent or by judicially appointed receiver) shall be entitled to enter upon, take possession of and manage the Property and to collect the rents of the Property including those past due. Any rents collected by Lender or the receiver shall be applied first to payment of the costs of management of the Property and collection of rents, including, but not limited to, receiver's fees, premiums on receiver's bonds and reasonable attorneys' fees, and then to the sums secured by this Security Instrument.

21. **Release.** Upon payment of all sums secured by this Security Instrument, Lender shall release this Security Instrument without charge to Borrower. Borrower shall pay any recordation costs.

22. **Substitute Trustee.** Lender may, for any reason or cause, from time to time remove Trustee and appoint a successor trustee to any Trustee appointed hereunder. Without conveyance of the Property, the successor trustee shall succeed to all the title, power and duties conferred upon Trustee herein and by applicable law.

23. **Time of Essence.** Time is of the essence in each covenant of this Security Instrument.

24. **Mailing Addresses.** Borrower's mailing address is the Property Address. Trustee's mailing address is

ARIZONA — Single Family —
FNMA/FHLMC UNIFORM INSTRUMENT

Page 4 of 5

Form 3003 12/83
(6—89) T-11940-14

Figure 14.4 (continued)

25. **Riders to this Security Instrument.** If one or more riders are executed by Borrower and recorded together with this Security Instrument, the covenants and agreements of each such rider shall be incorporated into and shall amend and supplement the covenants and agreements of this Security Instrument as if the rider(s) were a part of this Security Instrument. [Check applicable box(es)]

☐ Adjustable Rate Rider ☐ Condominium Rider ☐ 2-4 Family Rider
☐ Graduated Payment Rider ☐ Planned Unit Development Rider
☐ Other(s) [specify]

BY SIGNING BELOW, Borrower accepts and agrees to the terms and covenants contained in this Security Instrument and in any rider(s) executed by Borrower and recorded with it.

_________________ Borrower _________________ Borrower

_________________ Borrower _________________ Borrower

——— [Space Below This Line Reserved For Acknowledgement] ———

State of Arizona, County ss:

The foregoing instrument was acknowledged before me this (date)

by (person acknowledging)

My Commission expires:

_________________ Notary Public

ARIZONA – Single Family – FNMA/FHLMC UNIFORM INSTRUMENT Page 5 of 5 Form 3003 12/83′ (8–89) T–11940–15 mortgage document. By having this release entered in the public record, the owner shows that the mortgage lien has been removed from the property.

If a mortgage has been assigned by a recorded assignment, the release must be executed by the assignee/mortgagee.

When a real estate loan secured by a deed of trust has been completely repaid, the beneficiary requests in writing that the trustee convey the property back to the grantor. The trustee then executes and delivers a **release deed,** sometimes called a *deed of reconveyance,* to the trustor conveying the same rights and powers that the trustee was given under the trust deed. The release deed should be acknowledged and recorded in the public records of the county where the property is located.

Tax and Insurance Reserves

Many lenders require borrowers to provide a reserve fund, called an *impound* or *trust* or *escrow account,* to meet future real estate taxes and insurance premiums. When the mortgage or deed of trust loan is made, the borrower starts the reserve by depositing funds to cover the amount of unpaid real estate taxes. If a new insurance policy has just been purchased, the insurance premium reserve will be started with the deposit of one-twelfth of the annual tax and insurance premium liability. Thereafter the monthly loan payments required of the borrower will include principal, interest and tax and insurance reserves (PITI).

RESPA, the federal Real Estate Settlement Procedures Act (discussed in Chapter 23), limits the total amount of reserves that may be required by a lender.

Assignment of Rents

The borrower may make an assignment of rents to the lender, to be effective upon the borrower's default. The rent assignment may be included in the mortgage or deed of trust, or it may be made as a separate document. In either case the rent assignment should be drafted in language that clearly indicates that the parties intend to assign the rents and not merely to pledge them as security for the loan. In title theory states the lender is, in most cases, automatically entitled to any rents if the borrower defaults.

Buying Subject to or Assuming a Seller's Mortgage or Deed of Trust

A person who purchases real estate that has an outstanding mortgage or deed of trust on it may take the property *subject to* the mortgage or may *assume* it and agree to pay the debt. This technical distinction becomes important if the buyer defaults and the mortgage or deed of trust is foreclosed.

When the property is sold *subject to* the mortgage, the courts frequently hold that the purchaser is not personally obligated to pay the debt in full. The purchaser has bought the real estate knowing that he or she must make the loan payments and that, upon default, the lender will foreclose and the property will be sold by court order to pay the debt. If the sale does not pay off the entire debt, the purchaser is not liable for the difference; however, the original seller might still be liable for that difference. In contrast, when the grantee purchases the property and *assumes and agrees to pay* the seller's debt, the grantee becomes personally obligated for the payment of the *entire debt.* If the mortgage is foreclosed in such a case and the court sale does not bring enough money to pay the debt in full, a deficiency judgment against the assumer may be obtained for the unpaid balance of the note. Unless the lender agrees to the assumption, and a release of liability is given to the original borrower, that borrower will also be liable for the unpaid balance. Most states recognize this distinction.

Before a conventional mortgage may be assumed, most lending institutions require the assumer to qualify financially. The lender will usually charge a transfer fee to cover the costs of changing its records. This charge is customarily borne by the purchaser.

Alienation clause. Frequently when a conventional real estate loan is made, the lender wishes to prevent some future purchaser of the property from being able to assume that loan, particularly at its old rate of interest. For this reason some lenders include an **alienation clause** (also known as a *resale clause, due-on-sale clause* or *call clause*) in the note. An alienation clause provides that upon the sale of the property by the borrower to a buyer who wants to assume the loan the lender has the choice of either declaring the entire debt to be due immediately or permitting the buyer to assume the loan at current market interest rates.

Recording Mortgages and Deeds of Trust

The mortgage document or deed of trust must be recorded in the recorder's office of the county in which the real estate is located. The recordation gives constructive notice to the world of the borrower's obligations and establishes the lien's priority. If the property is registered in the Torrens system, notice of the lien must be entered on the original Torrens certificate on file.

First and Second Mortgages or Deeds of Trust

Mortgages and other liens normally have priority in the order in which they have been recorded. A mortgage or deed of trust on land that has no prior mortgage lien on it is a *first mortgage* or *first deed of trust*. When the owner of this land later executes another loan for additional funds, the new loan becomes a *second mortgage or deed of trust*, or a *junior lien*, when recorded. The second lien is subject to the first lien; the first has prior claim to the value of the land pledged as security. Because second loans represent a greater risk to the lender, they are usually issued at higher interest rates.

The priority of mortgage or deed of trust liens may be changed by the execution of a *subordination agreement*, in which the first lender subordinates his or her lien to that of the second lender. To be valid such an agreement must be signed by both lenders.

Provisions of Land Contracts (Installment Contracts or Contracts for Deed)

As discussed in Chapter 10, real estate can be purchased under *land contract*, also known as a *contract for deed*, or *installment contract*. Real estate is often sold on contract when mortgage financing is unavailable or too expensive or when the purchaser does not have a sufficient down payment to cover the difference between a mortgage or deed of trust loan and the selling price of the real estate.

Under a land contract the buyer (called the *vendee*) agrees to make a down payment and a monthly loan payment that includes interest and principal (and possibly real estate tax and insurance impounds). The seller (called the *vendor*) retains legal title to the property during the contract term, and the buyer is granted equitable title (see Chapter 10) and possession. At the end of the loan term the seller delivers clear title. The land contract usually includes a provision that if the buyer defaults, the seller can evict the buyer and retain any money paid by the buyer, which is construed to be rent. Many states now offer some legal protection to a defaulting buyer under a land contract.

Foreclosure

When a borrower defaults in making payments or fulfilling any of the obligations set forth in the mortgage or deed of trust, the lender can enforce his or her rights through a foreclosure. A **foreclosure** is a legal procedure whereby the property pledged as security in the mortgage document or deed of trust is sold to satisfy the debt. The foreclosure procedure brings the rights of the parties and all junior lienholders to a conclusion and passes title in the subject property to either the person holding the mortgage document or deed of trust or to a third party who purchases the realty at a *foreclosure sale*. Property thus sold is *free of the foreclosing mortgage and all junior liens*.

Methods of Foreclosure

There are three general types of foreclosure proceedings—judicial, nonjudicial and strict foreclosure. The specific provisions of these vary from state to state.

Judicial foreclosure. A judicial foreclosure proceeding provides that the property pledged as security may be sold by court order after the mortgagee has given sufficient public notice. Upon a borrower's default the lender may *accelerate* the due date of all remaining monthly payments. The lender's attorney can then file a suit to foreclose the lien. Upon presentation of the facts in court the property is ordered sold. A public sale is advertised and held, and the real estate is sold to the highest bidder.

Nonjudicial foreclosure. Other states allow nonjudicial foreclosure procedures to be used when a *power-of-sale clause* is contained in the security instrument. In those states that recognize deed of trust loans, the trustee is generally given the power of sale. Some states allow a similar power of sale to be used with a mortgage loan.

To institute a nonjudicial foreclosure the trustee (or mortgagee) must record a notice of default at the county recorder's office within a designated time period to give notice to the public of the intended auction. This official notice is generally accompanied by advertisements published in local newspapers that state the total amount due and the date of the public sale. The purpose of this notice is to publicize the sale. After selling the property the trustee (or mortgagee) may be required to file a copy of a notice of sale or an affidavit of foreclosure.

Strict foreclosure. Although the judicial and nonjudicial foreclosure procedures are the prevalent practices today, in some states it is still possible for a lender to acquire the mortgaged property by a strict foreclosure process. After appropriate notice has been given to the delinquent borrower and the proper papers have been prepared and filed, the court establishes a specific time period during which the balance of the defaulted debt must be paid in full. If this is not done, the court usually awards full legal title to the lender.

Deed in Lieu of Foreclosure

An alternative to foreclosure would be for the lender to accept a *deed in lieu of foreclosure* from the borrower. This is sometimes known as a *friendly foreclosure*, for it is carried out by agreement rather than by civil action. The major disadvantage of this manner of default settlement is that the mortgagee takes the real estate subject to all junior liens; foreclosure eliminates all such liens. Also, by accepting a deed in lieu of foreclosure the lender usually loses any rights pertaining to FHA insurance, VA guarantees or private mortgage insurance.

Redemption

Most states give defaulting borrowers a chance to redeem their property (see Chapter 9). Historically the right of redemption is inherited from the old common law proceedings in which the court sale ended the **equitable right of redemption.** Carried over to statutory law, this concept provides that if, during the course of a foreclosure proceeding but *before the foreclosure sale,* the borrower or any other person who has an interest in the real estate (such as another creditor) pays the lender the amount currently due, plus costs, the debt will be reinstated. In some cases the person who redeems may be required to repay the accelerated loan in full. If some person other than the mortgagor or trustor redeems the real estate, the borrower becomes responsible to that person for the amount of the redemption.

Certain states also allow defaulted borrowers a period in which to redeem their real estate *after the sale.* During this **statutory redemption** period (which may be as long as one year) the court may appoint a receiver to take charge of the property, collect rents, pay operating expenses and so forth. The mortgagor or trustor who can raise the necessary funds to redeem the property within the statutory period pays the redemption money to the court. Because the debt was paid from the proceeds of the sale, the borrower then can take possession free and clear of the former defaulted loan. Redemption is illustrated in Figure 14.5.

Deed to Purchaser at Sale

If redemption is not made or if no redemption period is allowed by state law, the successful bidder at the sale receives a deed to the real estate. This deed may be executed by a sheriff or master-in-chancery to *convey such title as the borrower had* to the purchaser at the sale. There are no warranties with such a deed; the title passes as is, but free of the former defaulted debt. It is possible to procure a title insurance policy in such a case, however.

Deficiency Judgment

If the foreclosure sale of the real estate secured by a mortgage or deed of trust does not produce a sufficient sales price to pay the loan balance in full after deducting expenses and accrued unpaid interest, the mortgagee may be entitled to a *personal judgment* against the maker of the note for the unpaid balance. Such a judgment is called a **deficiency judgment.** It may also be obtained against any endorsers or guarantors of the note and any owners of the mortgaged property

**Figure 14.5
Redemption**

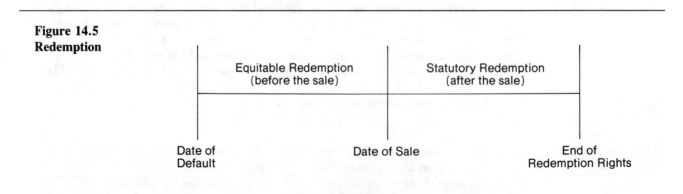

who may have assumed the debt by written agreement. If there are any surplus proceeds from the foreclosure sale after the debt and all junior liens (second mortgage, mechanic's lien and so on) are paid off and expenses and interest are deducted, these proceeds are paid to the borrower.

Key Terms	acceleration clause	lien theory
	alienation clause	mortgage
	beneficiary	negotiable instrument
	deed of trust	prepayment penalty
	defeasance clause	promissory note
	deficiency judgment	release deed
	discount point	satisfaction
	equitable right of redemption	statutory redemption
	foreclosure	title theory
	hypothecation	usury
	interest	

Summary

Some states recognize the lender as the owner of mortgaged property; these are known as title theory states. Others recognize the borrower as the owner of mortgaged property and are known as lien theory states. A few intermediary states recognize modified versions of these theories.

Mortgage and deed of trust loans provide the principal sources of financing for real estate operations. Mortgage loans involve a borrower, called the mortgagor, and a lender, the mortgagee. Deed of trust loans involve a third party, called the trustee, in addition to the borrower (the trustor) and the lender (the beneficiary).

After a lending institution has received, investigated and approved a loan application, it issues a commitment to make the mortgage loan. The borrower is required to execute a note, agreeing to repay the debt, and a mortgage or deed of trust placing a lien on the real estate to secure the note. The security instrument is recorded to give notice to the world of the lender's interest.

The mortgage document or deed of trust secures the debt and sets forth the obligations of the borrower and the rights of the lender. Payment in full of the note by its terms entitles the borrower to a satisfaction, or release, which is recorded to clear the lien from the public records. Default by the borrower may result in acceleration of payments, a foreclosure sale and, after the redemption period (if provided by state law), loss of title.

Questions

1. A charge of three discount points on a $120,000 loan is:
   a. $450. c. $4,500.
   b. $116,400. d. $3,600.

2. The person who obtains a real estate loan by signing a note and a mortgage is called the:
   a. mortgagor. c. mortgagee.
   b. beneficiary. d. vendor.

3. The borrower under a deed of trust is known as the:
   a. trustor. c. beneficiary.
   b. trustee. d. vendee.

4. Which of the following is true of a second mortgage?
   a. It has priority over a first mortgage.
   b. It cannot be used as a security instrument.
   c. It is not negotiable.
   d. It usually has a higher interest rate than a first mortgage.

5. All of the following would be true for the vendee in a contract for deed *except* that the vendee:
   a. is responsible for the real estate taxes on the property.
   b. must pay interest and principal.
   c. obtains possession at closing.
   d. obtains actual title at closing.

6. Laws that limit the amount of interest that can be charged to the borrower are called:
   a. Truth-In-Lending laws.
   b. usury laws.
   c. the statute of frauds.
   d. RESPA.

7. After the foreclosure sale a borrower who has defaulted on the loan seeks to pay off the debt plus any accrued interest and costs under the right of:
   a. equitable redemption.
   b. defeasance.
   c. usury.
   d. statutory redemption.

8. The clause in a note that gives the lender the right to have all future installments become due upon default is the:
   a. escalation clause.
   b. defeasance clause.
   c. alienation clause.
   d. acceleration clause.

9. What document is given to the mortgagor when the mortgage debt is completely repaid?
   a. Satisfaction of mortgage
   b. Defeasance certificate
   c. Deed of trust
   d. Mortgage estoppel

10. Under a land contract, when does the vendor give the deed to the vendee?
    a. When the contract is fulfilled
    b. At the closing
    c. When the contract for deed is approved by the parties
    d. After the first year's real estate taxes are paid

11. If a borrower must pay $2,700 for points on a $90,000 loan, how many points is the lender charging for this loan?
    a. Two c. Five
    b. Three d. Six

12. At the closing of a transaction involving an installment contract the vendor would *not*:
    a. provide financing for the vendee.
    b. still be liable for any senior financing.
    c. retain actual title.
    d. retain possession of the property.

13. Which of the following allows a mortgagee to proceed to a foreclosure sale without having to go to court first?
    a. Waiver of redemption right
    b. Power of sale
    c. Alienation clause
    d. Hypothecation

14. Pledging property for a loan without giving up possession is best described as:
    a. hypothecation.
    b. defeasance.
    c. alienation.
    d. novation.

15. Discount points on a mortgage are computed as a percentage of the:
    a. selling price.
    b. amount borrowed.
    c. closing costs.
    d. down payment.

15

Real Estate Financing: Practice

Financing Techniques

By altering the terms of the basic mortgage or deed of trust and note, a borrower and a lender can tailor financing instruments to suit the type of transaction and the financial needs of both parties. Note that, while the payment plans described in the following sections are commonly referred to as "mortgages," they are loans that may be secured by either a mortgage or a deed of trust.

Straight Loans

A mortgagor may choose a *straight mortgage plan* that calls for periodic payments of interest with the principal to be *paid in full at the end of the loan term*. This is known as a **straight,** or *term*, **loan.** Such plans are generally used for home improvement loans and second mortgages rather than for residential first mortgage loans. Prior to the 1930s the only form of mortgage loan available was the straight payment loan, payable after a relatively short term, such as three to five years. The high rate of foreclosure of such loans in the Depression years prompted the use of more manageable amortized loans.

Amortized Loans

Most mortgage and deed of trust loans are **amortized loans.** That is, regular payments are made—each payment being applied first to the interest owed and the balance to the principal amount—over a term of perhaps 15 to 30 years. At the end of the term the full amount of the principal and all interest due will be reduced to zero. Such loans are also called *direct reduction loans*.

Most amortized mortgage and deed of trust loans are paid in monthly installments; some, however, are payable quarterly or semiannually. These payments may be computed based on a number of payment plans, which tend alternately to gain and lose favor with lenders and borrowers as the cost and availability of mortgage money fluctuate.

The most frequently used plan, the *fully amortized mortgage,* requires the mortgagor to pay a *constant amount*, usually monthly. This may be referred to as a *level-payment* loan. The mortgagee credits each payment first to the interest due and then to the principal amount of the loan. Thus, while each payment is the same, the portion applied to repayment of the principal grows and the interest due declines as the unpaid balance of the loan is reduced (see Figure 15.1)

**Figure 15.1
Level-Payment
Amortized Loan**

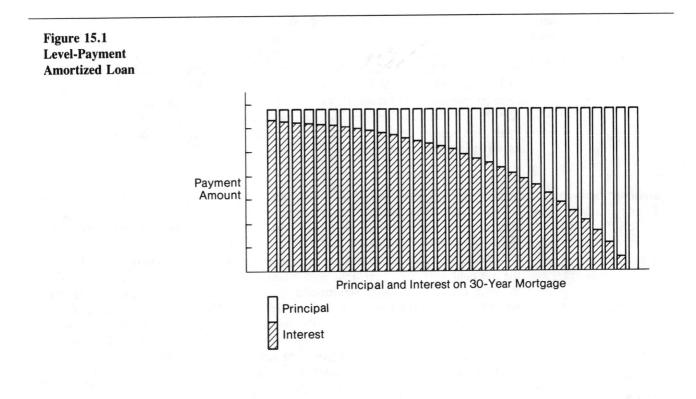

Payment
Amount

Principal and Interest on 30-Year Mortgage

☐ Principal

▨ Interest

**Adjustable-Rate
Mortgages (ARMs)**

Adjustable-rate mortgages are generally originated at one rate of interest, with the rate fluctuating up or down during the loan term based on a certain economic indicator. Because the interest may change, so may the mortgagor's loan payments. Details of how and when the rate of interest on the loan will change are included in the provisions of the note. Common components of an ARM include the following.

Index. The rate of the loan is tied to the movement of an index, such as the cost-of-funds index for federally chartered lenders. Most indexes are tied to U.S. Treasury securities.

Margin. Usually the interest rate on the loan is the index rate plus a premium called the *margin*. For example, the loan rate may be two percent over the U.S. Treasury bill rate.

Interest rate caps. Rate caps limit the amount the interest rate may change. Most ARMs have both periodic rate caps, which limit the amount the rate may increase at any one time, and aggregate rate caps, which limit the amount the rate may increase over the entire life of the loan.

Payment cap. The mortgagor is protected against the possibility of individual payments that he or she cannot afford by the payment cap, which sets a maximum amount for payments. With a payment cap, a rate increase could result in negative amortization—an increase in the loan balance.

Adjustment period. This establishes how often the loan rate may be changed. Common adjustment periods are monthly, quarterly and annually.

Graduated-Payment Mortgages (GPMs)

A *flexible-payment plan,* such as a **graduated-payment mortgage,** allows a mortgagor to make lower monthly payments for the first few years of the loan (typically the first five years) and larger payments for the remainder of the term, when the mortgagor's income is expected to have increased. Generally this type of loan is used to enable first-time buyers and buyers in times of high interest rates to purchase real estate. However, the monthly payments made generally are less than the interest due, resulting in negative amortization. As each payment is made, the unpaid interest is added to the principal balance, resulting in an increasing loan balance for the first few years.

Balloon Payment Loans

When a mortgage or deed of trust loan requires periodic payments that will not fully amortize the amount of the loan by the time the final payment is due, the final payment is larger than the others. This is called a **balloon payment,** and this type of loan is a *partially amortized loan.* For example, a loan made for $80,000 at 11½ percent interest may be computed on a 30-year amortization schedule but paid over a 20-year term with a final balloon payment due at the end of the 20th year. In this case each monthly payment would be $792.24 (the amount taken from a 30-year amortization schedule), with a final balloon payment of $56,340 (the amount of principal still owing after 20 years). It is frequently assumed that if the payments are made promptly the lender will extend the balloon payment for another limited term. The lender, however, is not legally obligated to grant this extension and can require payment in full when the note is due.

Growing-Equity Mortgages (GEMs)

The **growing-equity mortgage,** or *rapid-payoff mortgage,* makes use of a fixed interest rate, but payments of principal are increased according to an index or a schedule. The total payment thus increases, but the borrower's income is expected to keep pace, and the loan is paid off more quickly.

Shared-Appreciation Mortgages (SAMs)

In a **shared-appreciation mortgage** the lender originates a mortgage or deed of trust loan at a favorable interest rate (several points below the current rate) in return for a guaranteed share of the gain (if any) the borrower will realize when the property is eventually sold. This type of loan was originally made to developers of large real estate projects, but in times of expensive mortgage money it has appeared in the residential financing market. The specific details of the shared-appreciation agreement are set forth in the mortgage or deed of trust and note documents.

Reverse-Annuity Mortgages (RAMs)

With a **reverse-annuity mortgage** regular monthly payments are made *to the borrower,* based on the equity the homeowner has invested in the property given as security for the loan. A reverse loan allows senior citizens on fixed incomes to realize the equity buildup in their homes without having to sell. The borrower is charged a fixed rate of interest, and the loan is eventually paid from the sale of the property or from the borrower's estate upon his or her death.

Purchase-Money Mortgages (PMMs)

A **purchase-money mortgage** is given at the time of purchase to facilitate the sale. The term is used in two ways—to refer to *any* security instrument originating at the time of sale and (most often) to refer to the instrument *given by the purchaser to a seller who "takes back" a note for part or all of the purchase price.* It may be a first or second mortgage, and it becomes a lien on the property when the title passes.

Package Loans

A **package loan** includes not only the real estate but also *all fixtures and appliances installed on the premises*. In recent years this kind of loan has been used extensively in financing furnished condominium units. Such loans usually include the kitchen range, refrigerator, dishwasher, garbage disposal unit, washer and dryer, food freezer and other appliances, as well as furniture, drapes and carpets.

Blanket Loans

A **blanket loan** covers *more than one parcel or lot* and is usually used to finance subdivision developments (though it can be used to finance the purchase of improved properties as well). It usually includes a provision, known as a *partial release clause,* that the borrower may obtain the release of any one lot or parcel from the lien by repaying a definite amount of the loan. The lender issues a partial release for each parcel released from the mortgage lien. This release form includes a provision that the lien will continue to cover all other unreleased lots.

Wraparound Loans

A **wraparound loan,** also known as an *overriding* or *all-inclusive mortgage* or *deed of trust,* enables a borrower who is paying off an existing mortgage or deed of trust loan to obtain additional financing from a second lender. *The new lender assumes payment of the existing loan and gives the borrower a new, increased loan at a higher interest rate.* The total amount of the new loan includes the existing loan as well as the additional funds needed by the borrower. The borrower makes payments to the new lender on the larger loan, and the new lender makes the payments on the original loan.

For example, a buyer purchases a property for $100,000 with $15,000 down. The seller gives the buyer a wraparound note for $85,000 at 13 percent, and the buyer makes payments to the seller of $920.83. There is already a $50,000 mortgage at ten percent on the property with payments of $438.79. The seller continues to make these payments to the lender and realizes a net monthly income of $482.04 ($920.83 − $438.79).

A wraparound mortgage is frequently used as a method of refinancing real property or financing the purchase of real property when an existing mortgage cannot be prepaid. It is also used to finance the sale of real estate when the buyer wishes to put up a minimum of initial cash for the sale. The buyer executes a wraparound document to the seller, who will collect payments on the new loan and continue to make payments on the old loan. The buyer should require a protective clause in the document granting the right to make payments directly to the original lender in the event of a potential default on the old loan by the seller.

In Practice . . .

A wraparound loan is possible only if the original loan permits such a refinancing. An acceleration, alienation or due-on-sale clause in the original loan documents may prevent a sale under such terms.

Open-End Loans

The **open-end loan,** which is being used with increasing frequency, secures a *note* executed by the borrower to the lender as well as any future *advances* of funds made by the lender to the borrower or to the borrower's successors in title. The interest rate on the initial amount borrowed is fixed, but interest on future advances may be the market rate then in effect.

Open-end mortgages, or *equity lines of credit,* frequently are used by borrowers to obtain additional funds to improve their property. The borrower "opens" the mortgage or deed of trust to increase the debt to its original amount—after the debt has been reduced by payments over a period of time. The mortgage or deed of trust usually includes a statement of the maximum amount to be secured. The terms of an open-end mortgage usually limit the increase in debt to either the original amount of the debt or a stipulated amount set forth in the mortgage or deed of trust. The lender is not obligated to advance the additional funds.

Construction Loans

A construction loan is made to *finance the construction of improvements* on real estate (homes, apartments, office buildings and so forth). Under a construction loan the lender commits the full amount of the loan but makes partial *progress payments* as the building is being constructed.

Progress payments (also known as *draws*) are made to the *general contractor* for that part of the construction work that has been completed since the previous payment. Prior to each payment the lender inspects the work. The general contractor must provide the lender with adequate waivers of lien releasing all mechanic's lien rights for the work covered by the payment. This kind of loan generally bears a higher-than-market interest rate because of the risks assumed by the lender— inadequate releasing of mechanics' liens, possible delays in completing the building or financial failure of the contractor or subcontractors. This type of financing is generally *short-term,* or *interim, financing.* The borrower is expected to arrange for a permanent loan (also known as an *end loan* or *take-out loan*) that will repay or "take out" the construction financing lender when the work is completed.

Sale and Leaseback

Sale-and-leaseback arrangements are used as a means of financing large commercial or industrial plants. The land and building, usually used by the seller for business purposes, are sold to an investor, such as an insurance company. The real estate is then leased back by the buyer (the investor) to the seller, who continues to conduct business on the property as a tenant. The buyer becomes the lessor, and the original owner becomes the lessee. This enables a business firm that has money invested in a plant to free that money so it can be used as working capital.

In Practice . . .

Sale-and-leaseback arrangements involve complicated legal procedures, and their success is usually related to the effects the transaction has on the firm's tax situation. A real estate broker should advise the parties to consult with legal and tax experts when involved in this type of transaction.

Buydowns

In a **buydown** some of the mortgage loan interest is donated or "repaid" in advance to the lender on the borrower's behalf for the purpose of temporarily reducing the interest rate. That is, the original interest rate is effectively "bought down" for a period of time by the advance payment. Typical buydown arrangements provide for a reduced interest rate of one to three percent over the first one to three years of the loan term.

Common sources of buydown funds include home builders who wish to sell their stock of houses by offering the lower rate, parents or other relatives wanting to assist the buyers in purchasing a home and sellers seeking to help the buyers qualify for a loan at the lower interest rate, thus closing the sale on their property.

Home Equity Loans **Home equity loans** are a new source of funds for homeowners who wish to finance the purchase of expensive items, consolidate existing installment loans on credit card debt or pay for medical, educational, home improvement or other expenses. This type of financing has been used increasingly in the past few years, partly because recent tax laws have ended the deductibility of interest on debts not secured by real estate ("consumer interest"). Home equity loans are secured by the borrower's residence, and the interest charged is deductible up to a loan limit of $100,000.

A home equity loan can be taken out as a fixed loan amount or as an equity line of credit. With the home equity line of credit the lender extends a line of credit that the borrowers can use whenever they want. The borrowers can receive their money by a check sent to them, deposits made in a checking or savings account or a book of drafts the borrowers can use up to their credit limit.

FHA-Insured Loans The Federal Housing Administration (FHA) was created in 1934 under the National Housing Act to encourage improvement in housing standards and conditions, provide an adequate home financing system through insurance of housing credit and exert a stabilizing influence on the mortgage market. The FHA was the government's response to the lack of housing, excessive foreclosures and collapsed building industry that occurred during the Depression.

The FHA, which operates under the Department of Housing and Urban Development (HUD), neither builds homes nor lends money. Rather, *it insures loans on real property made by approved lending institutions*. It does not insure the property, but it does insure the lender against loss. The common term **FHA loan** refers to a loan that is not made by the agency but insured by it. The most popular FHA program is Title II, Section 203(b), which applies to loans on one- to four-family residences.

Technical requirements established under congressional authority must be met before the FHA will issue the insurance. Three of these requirements are as follows:

1. In addition to paying interest, the *borrower is charged a one-time mortgage insurance premium for the FHA insurance*. This amount may be paid at closing by the borrower or someone else, or it may be added to the loan amount.

2. The mortgaged real estate must be appraised by an *approved FHA appraiser*. The loan amount insured generally cannot exceed 97 percent on the first $25,000 of appraised value or purchase price, whichever is less, and 95 percent of the remainder. For a single-family owner-occupied house or condominium with a maximum appraised value or purchase price (whichever is less) of $50,000 (including closing costs), the maximum loan is 97 percent of the entire appraised value. For houses less than one year old and not insured prior to the beginning of construction, the loan ratio is 90 percent of the appraised value or selling price, whichever is less. If the purchase price exceeds the FHA-appraised value, the buyer may pay the difference in cash as part of the down payment. In addition, the FHA has set maximum loan amounts for various regions of the country.

3. The FHA regulations set minimum standards for the type and construction of buildings and the creditworthiness of borrowers.

Prepayment privileges. When a mortgage or deed of trust loan is insured by the FHA and the real estate given as security is a one- to four-family residence, the borrower may prepay the debt without penalty. The borrower must give the lender a notice of intention to exercise this privilege at least 30 days before the anticipated prepayment, or the lender has the option of charging up to 30 days' interest.

Assumption rules. The assumption rules for FHA-insured loans vary, depending on the date that the loan was originated:

• FHA loans originated prior to December 1986 generally have no restrictions on their assumption.

• For FHA loans originated since December 1, 1986, a creditworthiness review of the person proposing to assume is required. If the original loan was for the purchase of a principal residence, this review is required during the first 12 months of the loan's existence. If the original loan was for the purchase of an investment property, the review is required during the first 24 months of the loan.

• For FHA loans originated December 15, 1989, and thereafter, there are no assumptions without complete buyer qualification, and there are no longer any investor loans; all FHA loans made under the 203(b) program will be for owner-occupied properties only.

Discount points. The lender of an FHA-insured loan can charge discount points in addition to the one percent loan origination fee. The payment of points is a matter of negotiation between the seller and the buyer. However, if the seller pays more than six percent of the costs normally paid by the buyer (such as discount points, the loan origination fee, the mortgage insurance premium, buydown fees, prepaid items, impound or escrow amounts, etc.), the lender is to treat such payments as sales concessions and the price of the property for purposes of the loan will have to be reduced.

Interest rates. HUD and the FHA do not regulate the interest rates paid on FHA-insured loans. The rates fluctuate from lender to lender, and the buyer is responsible for trying to obtain the lowest interest rate possible.

Other FHA loan programs. In addition to loans made under Title II, Section 203(b), FHA loans are granted under the following programs:

1. Title I: Home improvement loans are covered under this title.

2. Title II, Section 234: Loans made to purchase condominiums are covered under this program, which in most respects is similar to the basic 203(b) program.

3. Title II, Section 245: This title covers five basic graduated-payment mortgage plans, which vary the rate of monthly payment increases and the number of years over which the payments increase.

4. Title II, Section 251: Adjustable-rate mortgages (ARMs) are allowed under this program. The interest rate cannot increase more than one percent per year or more than five percent from the initial rate of the loan.

VA-Guaranteed (GI) Loans

Under the Servicemen's Readjustment Act of 1944 and subsequent federal legislation the Department of Veteran Affairs is authorized to guarantee loans to purchase or construct homes for eligible veterans—those who have served a minimum of 181 days' active service since September 16, 1940 (90 days for veterans of World War II, the Korean War and the Viet Nam conflict; two full years for those enlisting for the first time after September 7, 1980). The VA also guarantees loans to purchase mobile homes and plots on which to place them. GI loans assist veterans in financing the purchase of homes with little or no down payments, at comparatively low interest rates. Rules and regulations are issued from time to time by the VA, setting forth the qualifications, limitations and conditions under which a loan may be guaranteed. (Table 15.1 is a comparison of VA and FHA loan programs.)

Like the term *FHA loan,* **VA loan** is something of a misnomer. The VA does not normally lend money; it guarantees loans made by lending institutions approved by the agency. The term *VA loan* refers to a loan that is not made by the agency but guaranteed by it.

There is no VA limit on the amount of the loan a veteran can obtain; this is determined by the lender. The VA does, however, set a limit on the amount of the loan that it will guarantee—currently 60 percent of the loan amount or $36,000 whichever is less, for the purchase, construction, repair or alteration of a house, condominium or farm residence. Note that the $36,000 figure (or 60 percent) is the amount of the guarantee and refers to the amount the lender would receive from the VA in the case of a default and foreclosure if the sale did not bring enough to cover the outstanding balance.

To determine what portion of a mortgage loan the VA will guarantee, the veteran must apply for a *certificate of eligibility.* This certificate does not mean that the veteran will automatically receive a mortgage. It merely sets forth the maximum guarantee the veteran is entitled to.

The VA will also issue a *certificate of reasonable value* (CRV) for the property being purchased, stating its current market value based on a VA-approved appraisal. The CRV places a ceiling on the amount of a VA loan allowed for the property; if the purchase price is greater than the amount cited in the CRV, the veteran may pay the difference in cash.

VA loans can be assumed by purchasers who do not quality as veterans. The original veteran borrower remains liable for the loan unless a release of the liability is approved by the VA. A release would be possible if, for example, another veteran used his or her own entitlement in assuming the loan.

Only in certain situations (such as in isolated rural areas) where financing is not reasonably available does the VA actually lend money; ordinarily a veteran obtains a loan from a VA-approved lending institution. The VA does not require a down payment. Although the VA guarantee is never more than $36,000, in practice the veteran may be able to obtain a 100 percent loan if the appraised valuation of the property is $144,000 or less and the veteran is entitled to a full $36,000 guarantee.

Maximum loan terms are 30 years for one- to four-family dwellings and 40 years for farm loans. The interest rate cannot exceed the rate set periodically by the VA. Residential property purchased with a VA loan must be owner-occupied.

Points. Points are generally not payable by a veteran, but the VA allows lenders to charge reasonable closing costs plus a loan origination fee that may not

Table 15.1 Comparison of FHA and VA Loan Programs	Federal Housing Administration	Veterans Administration
	1. Financing is available to veterans and nonveterans alike 2. Financing programs for owner-occupied only 3. Requires a larger down payment than VA 4. FHA valuation sets the maximum loan FHA will insure but does not limit the sales price 5. No prepayment penalty 6. Insures the loan by way of mutual mortgage insurance; mortgage insurance premiums (MIP) paid by borrower 7. Discount points can be charged, payable by either seller or buyer or split between them 8. Borrower is subject to one percent loan origination fee (can be paid by seller) 9. FHA loan can be assumed only with FHA approval	1. Financing available only to veterans and certain unremarried widows and widowers 2. VA financing limited to owner-occupied residential (one- to four-family) dwellings—must sign occupancy certificate 3. Does not normally require down payment, though lender may require small down payment 4. With regard to home loans, the VA loan may not exceed the appraised value of the home 5. No prepayment penalty 6. Borrower pays one percent loan origination fee to the lender 7. Guarantees up to 60 percent of the loan or $36,000, whichever is less 8. Borrower prohibited from paying discount points (except in refinancing and certain defined circumstances) 9. VA loan can be assumed by nonveteran with VA approval 10. Borrower must pay VA a funding fee of 1.25 percent of the loan amount if no down payment is made.

exceed one percent of the loan amount. There is also a 1.25 percent funding fee that the veteran pays the VA at closing.

Prepayment. As with an FHA loan, the borrower under a VA loan can prepay the debt at any time without penalty.

Conventional Loans

FHA-insured and VA-guaranteed loans are government-backed loans. In making **conventional loans,** lenders rely primarily on their own appraisal of the security and their own credit reports and information concerning the credit reliability of the prospective borrower. Because such loans are sold in the secondary mortgage market (discussed later), borrower qualifications are somewhat stricter.

However, under the provisions of **private mortgage insurance (PMI)** home purchasers can obtain conventional mortgage or deed of trust loans of up to 95 percent of the appraised property value at prevailing interest rates and reasonable insurance premium costs.

PMI insures only the top 20 or 25 percent of the loan. On a 95 percent loan the borrower is normally charged a fee of one percent of the loan at closing plus ¼ percent of the outstanding balance each year the insurance is in force. Because only the top portion of the loan is covered, once the loan-to-value ratio drops below a certain percentage (usually 75 or 80 percent), the lender may terminate the coverage.

Sources of Real Estate Financing—The Primary Mortgage Market

The funds used to finance the purchase of real estate come from a variety of sources that comprise the **primary mortgage market**—lenders who supply funds to borrowers as an investment. Lenders may originate loans for the purpose of selling them to other investors as part of what is termed the *secondary mortgage market* (discussed later).

Savings and Loan Associations

Savings and loan associations are active participants in the home loan mortgage market, specializing in long-term residential loans. A savings and loan earns money by paying less for the funds it receives than it charges for the loans it makes. Loan income includes more than interest, however—there are loan origination, loan assumption and other fees.

Traditionally savings and loan associations are the most flexible of all the lending institutions with regard to their mortgage lending procedures, and they are generally local in nature. In addition, they participate in FHA-insured and VA-guaranteed loans, though only to a limited extent.

All savings and loan associations must be chartered, either by the federal government or by the states in which they are located. The **Financial Institutions Reform, Recovery and Enforcement Act of 1989 (FIRREA),** enacted in response to the savings and loan association crisis of the 1980s, was intended to ensure the continued viability of the savings and loan industry. FIRREA restructured the savings and loan association regulatory system as well as the insurance system that protects its depositors. The **Federal Deposit Insurance Corporation (FDIC)** now manages the insurance funds for both savings and loan associations and commercial banks. Savings and loan deposits are insured through the **Savings Association Insurance Fund (SAIF),** and bank deposits are insured through the **Bank Insurance Fund (BIF).**

FIRREA also created the **Office of Thrift Supervision (OTS)** to monitor and regulate the savings and loan industry and the **Resolution Trust Corporation (RTC)** to liquidate the assets of failed savings and loan associations.

Because of their performance record of the 1980s, savings and loans are now subject to stricter capital requirements than before, as well as new housing loan requirements. Effective July 1, 1991, savings and loan associations are required to maintain 70 percent of their loan portfolios in housing-related loans, such as residential mortgage loans, residential construction loans and home equity loans.

Mutual Savings Banks

These institutions, which operate like savings and loan associations, are located primarily in the northeastern section of the United States. They issue no stock and are mutually owned by their investors. Although mutual savings banks do offer limited checking account privileges, they are primarily savings institutions and are highly active in the mortgage market, investing in loans secured by income property as well as residential real estate. In addition, because mutual savings banks usually seek low-risk loan investments, they often prefer to originate FHA-insured or VA-guaranteed loans.

Commercial Banks   Commercial banks are an important source of real estate financing. Bank loan departments primarily handle such short-term loans as construction, home improvement and mobile-home loans. In some areas, however, commercial banks are originating an increasing number of home mortgages. Commercial banks play a significant role in issuing VA and FHA loans. Like the savings and loan associations, banks must be chartered by the state or federal government.

Insurance Companies   Insurance companies amass large sums of money from the premiums paid by their policyholders. While a certain portion of this money is held in reserve to satisfy claims and cover operating expenses, much of it is invested in profit-earning enterprises, such as long-term real estate loans.

Most insurance companies like to invest their money in large, long-term loans that finance commercial and industrial properties. They also invest in residential mortgage and deed of trust loans by purchasing large blocks of FHA-insured and VA-guaranteed loans from the Federal National Mortgage Association and other agencies that warehouse such loans for resale in the secondary mortgage market (discussed later in this chapter).

In addition, many insurance companies seek to further ensure the safety of their investments by insisting on equity positions (known as *equity kickers*) in many projects they finance. This means that the company requires a partnership arrangement with, for example, a project developer or subdivider as a condition of making a loan. This is called *participation financing*.

Mortgage Banking Companies   Mortgage banking companies use money borrowed from other institutions and funds of their own to make real estate loans that may later be sold to investors (with the mortgage company receiving a fee for servicing the loans). Mortgage bankers are involved in all types of real estate loan activities and often serve as middlemen between investors and borrowers, but they are not mortgage brokers.

Mortgage banking companies are usually organized as stock companies. As a source of real estate financing they are subject to considerably fewer lending restrictions than are commercial banks or savings and loans.

Credit Unions   Credit unions are cooperative organizations in which members place money in savings accounts. In the past most credit unions made only short-term consumer and home improvement loans, but they have been branching out to originating longer-term first and second mortgage and deed of trust loans.

Mortgage Brokers   Mortgage brokers are not lenders but are often instrumental in obtaining financing. Mortgage brokers are individuals who are licensed to act as intermediaries in bringing borrowers and lenders together. They locate potential borrowers, process preliminary loan applications and submit the applications to lenders for final approval. Frequently they work with or for mortgage banking companies in these activities. They are not involved in servicing a loan once it is made. Many mortgage brokers are also real estate brokers who offer these financing services in addition to their regular brokerage activities.

Pension Funds   Pension funds have begun to participate actively in financing real estate projects. Most of the real estate activity for pension funds is handled through mortgage bankers and mortgage brokers.

Investment Group   Large real estate projects, such as high-rise apartment buildings, office com-
Financing   plexes and shopping centers, are often financed as a joint venture through group financing arrangements such as syndicates, limited partnerships and real estate investment trusts. These complex investment agreements are discussed in Chapter 22.

In Practice . . .   *Because interest rates and loan terms change frequently, you should check with local sources of real estate financing on a regular basis to learn of specific loan rates and terms. As a licensee you can better serve your customers—and thus more effectively sell your clients' properties—if you can knowledgeably refer buyers to local lenders offering the most favorable terms.*

Government   Aside from FHA-insured and VA-guaranteed loan programs, the federal govern-
Influence in   ment influences mortgage lending through the Federal Reserve System as well
Mortgage Lending   as through various federal agencies, such as the Farmer's Home Administration. It also deals in the secondary mortgage market through the Government National Mortgage Association, the Federal Home Loan Mortgage Corporation and the Federal National Mortgage Association.

Federal Reserve   The **Federal Reserve System ("the Fed")** operates to maintain sound credit
System   conditions, help counteract inflationary and deflationary trends and create a favorable economic climate. The Federal Reserve System divides the country into 12 federal reserve districts, each served by a federal reserve bank. All nationally chartered banks must join the Federal Reserve and purchase stock in its district reserve banks.

Through its member banks the Federal Reserve indirectly regulates the flow of money and interest rates in the marketplace by controlling the banks' *reserve requirements* and *discount rates*.

Reserve requirements. The Federal Reserve requires each member bank to keep a certain amount of its assets on hand as reserve funds unavailable for loans or any other use. This requirement was designed primarily to protect customer deposits, but it also provides a means of manipulating the flow of cash in the money market. By increasing its reserve requirements the Federal Reserve in effect limits the amount of money that member banks can use to make loans, thus causing interest rates to increase.

In this manner the government can slow down an overactive economy by limiting the number of loans that would have been directed toward major purchases of goods and services. The opposite is also true: by decreasing the reserve requirements the Federal Reserve can allow more loans to be made, thus increasing the amount of money circulated in the marketplace and causing interest rates to decline.

Discount rates. Federal Reserve member banks are permitted to borrow money from the district reserve banks to expand their lending operations. The interest rate that the district banks charge for the use of this money is called the *discount rate*. This rate is the basis on which the banks determine the percentage rate of interest that they, in turn, charge their loan customers. Theoretically, when the Federal Reserve discount rate is high, bank interest rates are high; therefore fewer loans will be made and less money will circulate in the marketplace. Conversely, a lower discount rate results in lower interest rates, more bank loans and more money in circulation.

Government Influence in the Secondary Market

Mortgage lending takes place in both the primary mortgage market, where loans are originated, and the **secondary mortgage market,** where loans are bought and sold only after they have been funded. A lender may wish to sell a number of loans to raise immediate funds when it needs more money to meet the mortgage demands in its area. Secondary market activity is especially desirable when money is in short supply, because it provides a great stimulant to the housing construction market as well as to the mortgage market.

When a loan has been sold, the original lender may continue to collect the payments from the borrower. The lender then passes the payments along to the investor who has purchased the loan and charges the investor a fee for servicing the loan.

A major source of secondary mortgage market activity is a warehousing agency, which purchases a number of mortgage loans and assembles them into one or more packages of loans for resale to investors. The major warehousing agencies are discussed in the following paragraphs.

Federal National Mortgage Association. The Federal National Mortgage Association (FNMA, "Fannie Mae"), is a quasi-governmental agency organized as a privately owned corporation that issues its own common stock and provides a secondary market for mortgage loans—conventional as well as FHA and VA loans. FNMA will buy a *block* or *pool* of mortgages from a lender in exchange for *mortgage-backed securities* that the lender may keep or sell. FNMA guarantees payment of all interest and principal to the holder of the securities.

Mortgage banking firms are generally actively involved with FNMA, originating loans and selling them to FNMA while retaining the servicing functions.

Government National Mortgage Association. The Government National Mortgage Association (GNMA, "Ginnie Mae") exists as a corporation without capital stock and is a division of HUD. GNMA is designed to administer special assistance programs and work with FNMA in secondary market activities. Fannie Mae and Ginnie Mae can join forces in times of tight money and high interest rates through their tandem plan. Basically the *tandem plan* provides that FNMA can purchase high-risk, low-yield (usually FHA) loans at full market rates, with GNMA guaranteeing payment and absorbing the difference between the low yield and current market prices.

Ginnie Mae also guarantees investment securities issued by private offerors (such as banks, mortgage companies and savings and loan associations) and backed by pools of FHA and VA mortgage loans. The *Ginnie Mae pass-through certificate* is a security interest in a pool of mortgages that provides for a monthly "pass-through" of principal and interest payments directly to the certificate holder. Such certificates are guaranteed by Ginnie Mae.

Federal Home Loan Mortgage Corporation. The **Federal Home Loan Mortgage Corporation (FHLMC, "Freddie Mac"),** provides a secondary market for mortgage loans, primarily conventional loans. Freddie Mac has the authority to purchase mortgages, pool them and sell bonds in the open market with the mortgages as security. Note, however, that FHLMC does not guarantee payment of Freddie Mac mortgages.

Many lenders use the standardized forms and follow the guidelines issued by Freddie Mac, because use of FHLMC forms is mandatory for lenders who wish to sell mortgages in the agency's secondary mortgage market. The standardized documents include loan applications, credit reports and appraisal forms.

Farmer's Home Administration

The **Farmer's Home Administration (FmHA)** is a federal agency of the Department of Agriculture. FmHA offers programs to help purchase or operate family farms. It also provides loans to help purchase or improve single-family homes in rural areas (generally areas with a population of fewer than 10,000). Loans are made to low- and moderate-income families, and the interest rate charged can be as low as one percent, depending on the borrower's income.

FmHA loan programs fall into two categories: guaranteed loans, made and serviced by a private lender and guaranteed for a specific percentage by the FmHA, and a direct loan program by the FmHA.

Financing Legislation

The federal government regulates the lending practices of mortgage lenders through the Truth-in-Lending Act, the Equal Credit Opportunity Act and the Real Estate Settlement Procedures Act.

Truth-in-Lending Act and Regulation Z

The National Consumer Credit Protection Act, referred to as the **Truth-in-Lending Act,** went into effect on July 1, 1969, under **Regulation Z** of the Federal Reserve Board. Regulation Z requires credit institutions to disclose to borrowers the true cost of obtaining credit so that the borrower can compare the costs of various lenders and avoid the uniformed use of credit. Regulation Z applies when credit is extended to individuals for personal, family or household uses and the amount of credit is $25,000 or less. Regardless of the amount, Regulation Z always applies when a credit transaction is secured by a residence. The regulation does not apply to business or commercial loans or to agricultural loans over $25,000.

The regulation requires that the consumer be fully informed of all finance charges, as well as the true annual interest rate, before a transaction is consummated. The finance charges must include any loan fees, finders' fees, service charges and points as well as interest. In the case of a mortgage loan made to finance the purchase of a dwelling the lender must compute and disclose the *annual percentage rate (APR)* but does not have to indicate the total interest payable during the term of the loan. Also, the lender does not have to include as part of the finance charge such actual costs as title fees, legal fees, appraisal fees, credit reports, survey fees and closing expenses.

Creditor. A *creditor,* for purposes of Regulation Z, is a person who extends consumer credit more than 25 times a year or more than five times a year if the transaction involves a dwelling as security. The credit must be subject to a finance charge or payable in more than four installments by written agreement.

Three-day right of rescission. In the case of most consumer credit transactions covered by Regulation Z the borrower has three days in which to rescind the transaction by merely notifying the lender. This right of rescission does not apply to residential purchase money or first mortgage or deed of trust loans. In an emergency the right to rescind may be waived in writing to prevent a delay in funding.

Advertising. Regulation Z provides strict regulation of real estate advertisements that include mortgage financing terms. General phrases like "liberal terms available" may be used, but if specifics are given they must comply with this act. By the provisions of the act the APR—which includes all charges—rather than the interest rate alone *must be stated.* The total finance charge must be specified as well.

Specific credit terms, such as down payment, monthly payment, dollar amount of the finance charge or term of the loan, may not be advertised unless the following information is set forth as well: cash price; required down payment; number, amounts and due dates of all payments; and annual percentage rate. The total of all payments to be made over the term of the mortgage must also be specified unless the advertised credit refers to a first mortgage or deed of trust to finance acquisition of a dwelling.

Penalties. Regulation Z provides penalties for noncompliance. The penalty for violation of an administrative order enforcing Regulation Z is $10,000 for each day the violation continues. A fine of up to $10,000 may be imposed for engaging in an unfair or deceptive practice. In addition, a creditor may be liable to a consumer for twice the amount of the finance charge, for a minimum of $100 and a maximum of $1,000, plus court costs, attorney's fees and any actual damages. Willful violation is a misdemeanor punishable by a fine of up to $5,000 or one year's imprisonment or both.

Federal Equal Credit Opportunity Act

The federal Equal Credit Opportunity Act (ECOA), in effect since 1975, prohibits lenders and others who grant or arrange credit to consumers from discriminating against credit applicants on the basis of race, color, religion, national origin, sex, marital status, age (provided the applicant is of legal age) or dependence on public assistance. In addition, lenders and other creditors must inform all rejected credit applicants, in writing, within 30 days, of the principal reasons for denial or termination of credit.

Real Estate Settlement Procedures Act

The federal Real Estate Settlement Procedures Act (RESPA) was created to ensure that the buyer and seller in a residential real estate transaction involving a new first mortgage loan have knowledge of all settlement costs. This important federal law is discussed in detail in Chapter 23.

Key Terms	adjustable-rate mortgage (ARM)	graduated-payment mortgage (GPM)
	amortized loan	growing-equity mortgage (GEM)
	balloon payment	home equity loan
	Bank Insurance Fund (BIF)	Office of Thrift Supervision (OTS)
	blanket loan	open-end loan
	buydown	package loan
	conventional loan	primary mortgage market
	Farmer's Home Administration (FmHA)	private mortgage insurance (PMI)
	Federal Deposit Insurance Corporation (FDIC)	purchase-money mortgage (PMM)
	Federal Home Loan Mortgage Corporation (FHLMC, "Freddie Mac")	Regulation Z
		Resolution Trust Corporation (RTC)
		reverse-annuity mortgage (RAM)
	Federal National Mortgage Association (FNMA, "Fannie Mae")	sale and leaseback
		Savings Association Insurance Fund (SAIF)
	Federal Reserve System (the "Fed")	secondary mortgage market
	FHA loan	shared-appreciation mortgage (SAM)
	Financial Institutions Reform, Recovery and Enforcement Act of 1989 (FIRREA)	straight loan
		Truth-in-Lending Act
		VA loan
	Government National Mortgage Association (GNMA, "Ginnie Mae")	wraparound loan

Summary

Types of loans include fully amortized and straight loans as well as adjustable-rate mortgages, graduated-payment mortgages, growing-equity mortgages, balloon-payment mortgages, shared-appreciation mortgages and reverse-annuity mortgages.

Other types of real estate financing include seller-financed purchase-money mortgages or deeds of trust, blanket mortgages, package mortgages, wraparound mortgages, open-end mortgages, construction loans, sale-and-leaseback agreements and home equity loans.

There are many types of mortgage and deed of trust loans, including conventional loans and those insured by the FHA or guaranteed by the VA. FHA and VA loans must meet certain requirements for the borrower to obtain the benefits of the government backing, which induces the lender to lend its funds. The interest rates for these loans may be lower than those charged for conventional loans. Lenders may also charge points.

The federal government affects real estate financing money and interest rates through the Federal Reserve Board's discount rate and reserve requirements; it also participates in the secondary mortgage market. The secondary market is generally composed of the investors who ultimately purchase and hold the loans as investments. These include insurance companies, investment funds and pension plans. Fannie Mae (Federal National Mortgage Association), Ginnie Mae (Government National Mortgage Association) and Freddie Mac (Federal Home Loan Mortgage Corporation) take an active role in creating a secondary market by regularly purchasing mortgage and deed of trust loans from originators and retaining, or warehousing, them until investment purchasers are available.

Regulation Z, implementing the federal Truth-in-Lending Act, requires lenders to inform prospective borrowers who use their homes as security for credit of all finance charges involved in such a loan. Severe penalties are provided for noncompliance. The federal Equal Credit Opportunity Act prohibits creditors from discriminating against credit applicants on the basis of race, color, religion, national origin, sex, marital status, age or dependence on public assistance. The Real Estate Settlement Procedures Act requires lenders to inform both buyers and sellers in advance of all fees and charges required for the settlement or closing of a residential real estate transaction.

Questions

1. The Ms are purchasing a lakefront summer home in a new resort development. The house is completely equipped, and the Ms have obtained a deed of trust loan that covers the purchase price of the residence, including furnishings and appliances. This kind of financing is called:

    a. a wraparound deed of trust.
    b. a package deed of trust.
    c. a blanket deed of trust.
    d. an unconventional deed of trust.

2. The Ds purchased a residence for $95,000. They made a down payment of $15,000 and agreed to assume the seller's existing mortgage, which had a current balance of $23,000. The Ds financed the remaining $57,000 of the purchase price by executing a mortgage and note to the seller. This type of loan, by which the seller becomes the mortgagee, is called a:

    a. wraparound mortgage.
    b. package mortgage.
    c. balloon note.
    d. purchase-money mortgage.

3. Which of the following is *not* a participant in the secondary market?

    a. FNMA   c. RESPA
    b. GNMA   d. FHLMC

4. F continues to live in the home she purchased 30 years ago, but she now receives monthly checks thanks to her:

    a. shared-appreciation mortgage.
    b. adjustable-rate mortgage.
    c. reverse-annuity mortgage.
    d. overriding deed of trust.

5. If buyers were seeking a mortgage on a single-family house, they would least likely obtain the mortgage from a:

    a. mutual savings bank.
    b. life insurance company.
    c. credit union.
    d. commercial bank.

6. Which of the following institutions does *not* deal with conventional loans?

    a. FHLMC   c. FIRREA
    b. FNMA   d. GNMA

7. A purchaser obtains a fixed-rate loan to finance a home. Which of the following characteristics is true of this type of loan?

    a. The amount of interest to be paid is predetermined.
    b. The loan cannot be sold in the secondary market.
    c. The monthly payment amount will fluctuate each month.
    d. The interest rate change may be based on an index.

8. All of the following statements are true regarding mutual savings banks *except:*

    a. they combine some of the characteristics of both banks and S&Ls.
    b. they are very prevalent in the eastern part of the country.
    c. they compete aggressively for savings deposits.
    d. they are primary lenders for real estate loans.

9. All of the following are government-owned institutions *except:*

    a. Fannie Mae.   c. FHA.
    b. Ginnie Mae.   d. Freddie Mac.

10. In a loan that requires periodic payments that do not fully amortize the loan balance by the final payment, what term best describes the final payment?

    a. Adjustment payment
    b. Acceleration payment
    c. Balloon payment
    d. Variable payment

11. A developer received a loan that covers five parcels of real estate and provides for the release of the mortgage lien on each parcel when certain payments are made on the loan. This type of loan arrangement is called a:
    a. purchase-money loan.
    b. blanket loan.
    c. package loan.
    d. wraparound loan.

12. Funds for Federal Housing Administration (FHA) loans are usually provided by:
    a. the Federal Housing Administration (FHA).
    b. the Federal Deposit Insurance Corporation (FDIC).
    c. qualified lenders.
    d. FNMA.

13. Under the provisions of the Truth-in-Lending Act (Regulation Z) the annual percentage rate (APR) of a finance charge includes all of the following components *except:*
    a. discount points.
    b. broker's commission.
    c. loan origination fee.
    d. loan interest rate.

14. An annual insurance fee of ¼ percent on the unpaid balance would most likely be used with which of the following types of mortgages?
    a. A privately insured conventional loan
    b. An FHA-insured loan
    c. A VA-guaranteed loan
    d. A purchase-money mortgage

15. A home is purchased using a fixed-rate, fully amortized mortgage loan. Which of the following is true regarding this mortgage?
    a. A balloon payment will be made at the end of the loan.
    b. Each payment amount is the same.
    c. Each payment reduces the principal by the same amount.
    d. The principal amount in each payment is greater than the interest amount.

16. Which of the following *best* defines the *secondary market?*
    a. Lenders who deal exclusively in second mortgages
    b. Where loans are bought and sold after they have been originated
    c. The major lender of residential mortgages and deeds of trust
    d. The major lender of FHA and VA loans

17. A borrower obtains a mortgage loan to make repairs on her home. The loan is not insured or guaranteed by a government agency, and the mortgage document secures the amount of the loan as well as any future funds advanced to the borrower by the lender. This borrower has obtained a(n):
    a. wraparound mortgage.
    b. conventional loan.
    c. open-end loan.
    d. growing-equity mortgage.

18. A graduated-payment mortgage:
    a. allows for smaller payments to be made in the early years of the loan.
    b. allows for the debt's interest rate to increase or decrease from time to time, depending on certain economic factors.
    c. is also called a growing-equity mortgage.
    d. must be insured by the Federal Housing Administration.

19. With a fully amortized mortgage or deed of trust loan:
    a. interest may be charged in arrears, meaning at the end of each period for which interest is due.
    b. the interest portion of each payment remains the same throughout the entire term of the loan.
    c. interest only is paid each period.
    d. the balloon payment will be the last payment made.

20. Freddie Mac:
    a. mortgages are guaranteed by the full faith and credit of the federal government.
    b. buys and pools blocks of conventional mortgages, selling bonds with such mortgages as security.
    c. can act in tandem with GNMA to provide special assistance in times of tight money.
    d. buys and sells VA and FHA mortgages.

21. The federal Equal Credit Opportunity Act prohibits lenders from discriminating against potential borrowers on the basis of all of the following *except:*

    a. race.
    b. sex.
    c. source of income.
    d. amount of income.

16

Leases

Leasing Real Estate

A **lease** is a contract between an owner of real estate (known as the *lessor*) and a tenant (the *lessee*) that transfers the rights to exclusive possession and use of the owner's property to the tenant for the specified period of time. This agreement sets forth the length of time the contract is to run, the amount to be paid by the lessee for the use of the property and other rights and obligations of the parties.

The lessor grants the lessee the right to occupy the premises and use them for purposes stated in the lease. In return the landlord receives payment for the use of the premises and retains a **reversionary right** to possession after the lease term has expired. The lessor's interest is called a *leased fee estate plus reversionary right*.

The statute of frauds in most states requires that to be enforceable an agreement to lease real estate be in writing if it is for more than one year or is for one year or less but cannot be performed within one year of its making. Generally verbal leases for one year or less that can be performed within a year of their making are enforceable. Written leases should be signed by both lessor and lessee.

In Practice . . .

Even though a particular lease may be enforceable if agreed to orally, such as a lease for one year commencing the day of agreement, it is always better practice to put lease agreements in writing and to have the writing signed by all parties to the agreement. The lease document should be as inclusive as possible.

Leasehold Estates

When a landowner leases real estate to a tenant, the tenant's right to occupy the land for the duration of the lease is called a **leasehold** (less-than-freehold) **estate.** A leasehold is generally considered personal property. However, when the contract is a lease for life or for more than 99 years, under which the tenant assumes many of the landowner's obligations, certain states give the tenant some of the benefits and privileges of ownership.

As there are several types of freehold (ownership) estates (covered in Chapter 6), there are also various leasehold estates (see Table 16.1).

Estate for Years

A leasehold that continues for a *definite period of time*, whether for years, months, weeks or even days, is an **estate for years.** An estate for years (sometimes

Table 16.1 Leasehold Estates	Type of Estate	Distinguishing Characteristic
	Estate for years	For definite period of time
	Estate from period to period	Automatically renews
	Estate at will	For indefinite period of time
	Estate at sufferance	Without landlord's consent

referred to as an *estate for term*) always has specific starting and ending times and does not automatically renew itself at the end of the lease period. When that period expires, the lessee is required to vacate the premises and surrender possession to the lessor. No notice is required to terminate the lease at the end of the lease period, because a specific expiration date is provided. A lease for years may be terminated prior to the expiration date by the mutual consent of both parties, but otherwise neither party may terminate without showing that the lease agreement has been breached. As is characteristic of all leases, it gives the lessee the right to occupy and use the leased property—subject to the terms and covenants contained in the lease agreement (which is generally written).

Estate from Period to Period

An **estate from period to period,** or *periodic tenancy,* is created when the landlord and tenant enter into an agreement that continues for a specific period, being *automatically renewed for an indefinite time without a specific ending date.* Rent is payable at definite intervals. Such a tenancy is generally created by agreement or operation of law to run for a certain amount of time, such as month to month, week to week or year to year. The agreement is automatically renewed for similar succeeding periods until one of the parties gives notice to terminate. In effect the payment and acceptance of rent extend the lease for another period.

A tenancy from period to period is usually created when a tenant with an estate for years remains in possession, or holds over, after the expiration of the lease term. If no new lease agreement has been made, the landlord may evict the tenant or treat the holdover tenant as under a periodic tenancy. Acceptance of rent is usually considered conclusive proof of the landlord's consent to a periodic tenancy.

A **month-to-month tenancy** is generally created when a tenant takes possession with no definite termination date and pays rent on a monthly basis. Some leases stipulate that in the absence of a renewal agreement a tenant who holds over does so as a month-to-month tenant. This is usually a valid agreement. In a few states a holdover tenancy is considered a tenancy at will (discussed below).

To *terminate* a periodic estate either the landlord or the tenant must give *proper notice.* The form of the notice and the time at which it must be given are usually set out in detail in state statutes. Normally to terminate an estate from week to week, one week's notice is required; to terminate an estate from month to month, one or two months' notice is required. Notices of termination for an estate from year to year vary widely and usually require a minimum of two months' and a maximum of six months' notice.

Estate at Will

An estate that gives the tenant the right to possess with the *consent of the landlord for a term of unspecified or uncertain duration* is an **estate at will,** or *tenancy* *at will.* It may be created by express agreement or by operation of law, and during its existence the tenant has all the rights and obligations of a lessor-lessee relationship, including the payment of rent at regular intervals.

For example, at the end of a lease period a landlord informs a tenant that in a few months the city is going to demolish the apartment building to make way for an expressway. The landlord gives the tenant the option to occupy the premises until demolition begins. If the tenant agrees to stay, a tenancy at will is created.

The term of an estate at will is indefinite, but the estate may be terminated by the landlord giving proper notice in accordance with the statutes of the state where the land is located. An estate at will is automatically terminated by the death of either the landlord or the tenant.

Estate at Sufferance

An **estate at sufferance,** or *tenancy at sufferance,* arises when a tenant who lawfully came into possession of real property continues, after his or her rights have expired, to hold possession of the premises *without the consent of the landlord.* An estate at sufferance exists when a tenant for years *fails to surrender* possession at the expiration of the lease or when a borrower, without consent of the purchaser, continues in possession after the foreclosure sale and expiration of the redemption period (the latter being a tenancy at sufferance *by operation of law*).

Standard Lease Provisions

Most states require no special wording to establish the landlord-tenant relationship. The lease may be written, oral or implied, depending on the circumstances and the requirements of the statute of frauds. The law of the state where the real estate is located must be followed to assure the validity of the lease. Figure 16.1 is an example of a typical residential lease.

Once a valid lease has been executed, the lessor, as the owner of the real estate, is usually bound by the **covenant of quiet enjoyment** implied by law. Under this covenant the lessor guarantees that the lessee may take possession of the leased premises and that the landlord will not interfere in the tenant's possession or use of the property.

The requirements for a valid lease are essentially the same as those for any other contract:

1. *Offer and acceptance.* The parties must reach a mutual agreement on all the terms of the contract.

2. *Consideration.* All leases, being contracts, must be supported by valid consideration. In leasing real estate, *rent* is the normal consideration granted for the right to occupy the leased premises; however, the payment of rent is not essential as long as consideration was granted in creation of the lease itself (sometimes, this consideration is labor performed on the property). The courts consider a lease a contract and not subject to subsequent changes in the rent or other terms unless these changes are in writing and executed in the same manner as the original lease.

3. *Capacity to contract.* The parties must have the legal capacity to contract.

4. *Legal objectives.* The objectives of the lease must be legal.

Figure 16.1
Sample Lease

GENERAL LEASE
COMMERCIAL OR RESIDENTIAL

THIS LEASE, made and entered into this _____ day of _____, 19_____, by and between

_____ the lessor, and

_____, the lessee

WITNESSETH: That the lessor, in consideration of the covenants of said lease hereinafter set forth, does by these presents lease to said lessee, under the terms and

conditions set forth, the premises described as follows: _____

_____

_____

1. TERMS
That the term of said lease is for a period of _____ years, commencing on the _____ day of _____ 19_____

and ending on the _____ day of _____, 19_____.

2. RENTS
That the total rents for said lease shall be the sum of $_____, payable in _____ installments of $_____

each, plus any excise, privilege or sales taxes levied by a political subdivision, for an additional sum of $_____ per _____

Total rents and applicable taxes, if any, equal the sum of $_____ per _____.

3. SECURITY DEPOSIT
Lessee has paid, upon the execution hereof, the amount of $_____, as security for the performance of the terms and conditions of this lease, which said sums shall be returned to lessee at the termination of this lease if the obligations of this lease have been fully discharged

4. USE OF PREMISES
The premises described above are leased to lessee for the sole purpose of _____
_____. And lessee agrees that the premises will be used only for such activity, complying fully with all applicable laws, ordinances or regulations regarding the use of the leased premises, including all sanitary and health regulations.

5. INSURANCE
a) Lessee shall obtain and continue in force during the term of this lease, a policy or policies of Insurance covering: (1) Loss or damages by fire or other perils to the appliances, contents, equipment, fixtures, furniture, interior motif or decor, and/or stock in trade, (2) Injury or death to any person or persons including lessee, (3) Vandalism, and/or malicious mischief.

b) Lessor shall obtain and continue in force during the term of this lease, a policy or policies of Insurance covering loss or damages to the premises by fire or other perils in the amount of the full replacement value thereof.

c) Lessee agrees to provide lessor with a memorandum copy of all Insurance Policies so obtained under this lease, and additionally name lessor as an additional assured party.

6. REPAIRS
a) Lessor agrees to make all necessary repairs to the exterior walls, doors, windows, roof and/or any other exterior features of the premises including air conditioning, heating and lighting equipment.

b) Lessee agrees to make all necessary repairs to the interior portions of the premises including any extraordinary damages to the electrical or plumbing facilities.

7. ALTERATIONS OR IMPROVEMENTS
Lessee may make improvements or other alterations in the interior of the leased premises at his (her) (its) own expense, provided, however, that prior to commencing any such work, lessee shall first obtain written consent from lessor. Such improvements or alterations shall remain the property of the **lessor** at the termination of this lease.

8. SERVICES/UTILITIES
Lessor agrees to provide the following utilities or other services to lessee, to wit: _____
_____

9. ASSIGNMENT/SUBLETTING
Lessee agrees that he (she) (it) will not assign or sublet in whole or part any portion of the leased premises without the prior written consent of lessor, which said consent will not be unreasonably withheld. Lessor may sell, transfer, or assign all or any part of his (her) (its) interest in the premises without the consent of the lessee.

10. INJURY OR LOSS
Lessor shall not be responsible or liable for any loss, theft, or damage to property or injury to, or death of, Lessee or any person on or about the leased premises, and Lessee agrees to indemnify, defend and hold Lessor harmless therefrom.

11. ENTRY OF LANDLORD
Lessor reserves the right to enter upon the leased premises at reasonable times for the purpose of inspecting the premises, and reserves the right, during the last two months of the term of the lease, to show the premises at reasonable times to prospective tenants, providing lessee has not tendered a written intent to Lessor of renewing said lease, or an intention to negotiate a new lease for the premises.

12. RENEWAL OF LEASE
Lessor agrees to entertain an intention by Lessee to renew this lease at its expiration thereof, provided the same is made at least ninety (90) days prior to the expiration of this lease. Such renewal shall be accomplished either by an addendum to this lease or the execution of a new lease upon such terms and conditions as may be required by Lessor

©1986, ALPHA ENTERPRISES OF ARIZONA — P.O. Box 26326 — Tucson, AZ 85726 FORM 101

Figure 16.1
(continued)

13. BREACH

a) The failure of either party to fully perform under any or all of the terms and conditions of this lease shall constitute a Breach of this lease, entitling the offended party to take any and all such action provided by law, including, but not limited to, one or more of the following: (1) Lock the doors to the leased premises, (2) Retain or take possession of any property on the premises pursuant to Lessor's Landlord Lien, (3) Enter the premises and remove all persons and property therefrom, (4) Declare the lease at an end and terminated, (5) Sue for the full balance due under the lease, and any damages sustained by Lessor.

b) Any breach alleged under this lease, shall be occasioned by a ten (10) day written notice of the same to the defaulting party. If at the end of such ten (10) days as provided in said notice, the defaulting party has not cured the breach, the offending party may take any and all such action provided by law, including an additional amount for Attorney's fees and cost.

14. SURRENDER OF PREMISES

Lessee shall, upon the expiration of the term of the Lease, or upon an earlier termination hereof, quit and surrender the premises in good order or condition and repair, reasonable wear and tear and acts of God excepted.

15. SIGNS/DECALS/POSTERS

Lessee agrees that he (she) (it) will not place, affix, or otherwise install any decals, posters, signs or other advertising, artistic, commemorative or communicative illustrations without the written consent of Lessor. If consent is so given, any such installations shall be at Lessee's expense.

16. SAVINGS CLAUSE

If any term or provision of this Lease or any application thereof shall be declared or held to be invalid or unenforceable, then the remaining terms and provisions of this Lease shall not be affected thereby.

17. OTHER CONDITIONS

_____

_____

_____

_____

18. NOTICES

a) Any notices or demands to be given hereunder shall be given to Lessor at _____

_____

b) The person or firm authorized to manage this property is _____

_____

IN WITNESS WHEREOF, the parties have hereunto set their hands, or caused this Lease to be executed by their authorized agent this _____ day of

_____, 19_____.

_____   _____
                LESSEE   LESSOR

_____   _____
                LESSEE   LESSOR

A copy of the foregoing Lease was received by Lessee/Authorized Agent this _____ day of _____, 19_____.

_____
                LESSEE

A description of the leased premises should be clearly stated. If the lease covers land, the legal description of the real estate should be used. If the lease is for a part of a building, such as office space or an apartment, the space itself or the apartment designation should be described clearly and carefully. If supplemental space is to be included, the lease should clearly identify it.

Use of Premises

A lessor may restrict a lessee's use of the premises through provisions included in the lease. Such restrictions are most important in leases for stores or commercial space. For example, a lease may provide that the leased premises are to be used *only* for the purpose of a real estate office *and for no other*. In the absence of such limitations a lessee may use the premises for any lawful purpose.

Term of Lease

The term of a lease is the period for which the lease will run, and it should be set out precisely. The date of the beginning of the term and the date of its ending should be stated together with a statement of the total period of the lease: for example, "for a term of 30 years beginning June 1, 1991, and ending May 31, 2021." Courts do not favor leases with an indefinite term and will hold that such perpetual leases are not valid unless the language of the lease and the surrounding circumstances clearly indicate that such is the intention of the parties. (Some states prohibit leases that run for more than 99 years.)

Security Deposit

Most leases require the tenant to provide some form of **security deposit** to be held by the landlord during the lease term and kept, wholly or partially, in the event of the tenant's default in payment of rent or destruction of the premises. State law may set maximum amounts for security deposits and specify how they must be handled. Some prohibit security deposits from being used for *both* nonpayment of rent and property damage. Some require that lessees receive annual interest on their security deposits.

Other safeguards against nonpayment of rent may include an advance rental payment, contracting for a lien on the tenant's property or requiring the tenant to have a third person guarantee payment.

In Practice . . .

A lease should specify whether a payment is a security deposit or an advance rental. If it is a security deposit, the tenant is usually not entitled to apply it to the final month's rent. If it is an advance rental, the landlord must treat it as income for tax purposes.

Legal Principles of Leases

Most states provide that leases can be filed for record in the county in which the property is located. But unless the lease is for a relatively long term, it *usually is not recorded*. Possession of the property by the lessee is notice to the world of his or her rights, and an inspection of the property will result in *actual notice* of the lessee's leasehold interest.

When a lease runs for *three years* or longer, recording is more common. The recording of a *long-term lease* places the world on notice of the rights of the lessee and is usually required if the lessee intends to mortgage the leasehold interest.

In some states only a *memorandum of lease* is filed for record. The terms of the lease are not disclosed to the public, but the objective of giving public notice of the rights of the lessee is still accomplished. The memorandum of lease must set forth the names of the parties and a description of the property being leased.

Possession of Leased Premises

As noted earlier, leases carry the implied covenant that the landlord will give the tenant enjoyment (possession) of the premises. If the premises are occupied by a holdover tenant, or adverse claimant, at the beginning of the new lease period, in most states it is the landlord's duty to bring whatever action is necessary to recover actual possession and to bear the expense of this action. In a few states, however, the landlord is bound only to give the tenant the right of possession; it is the tenant's obligation to bring any court action necessary to secure actual possession.

Improvements

Neither the landlord nor the tenant is required to make any improvements to the leased property. In the absence of an agreement to the contrary the tenant may make improvements with the landlord's permission. Any such alterations generally become the property of the landlord; that is, they become fixtures. However, as discussed in Chapter 2, a tenant may be given the right by the terms of the lease to install trade fixtures or chattel fixtures. It is customary to provide that such trade fixtures may be removed by the tenant before the lease expires, provided the tenant restores the premises to their previous condition.

Maintenance of Premises

Historically a landlord was not obligated to make any repairs to leased premises. However, many states now require a residential lessor to maintain dwelling units in a habitable condition and to make any necessary repairs to common elements, such as hallways, stairs or elevators, and to safety features, such as fire sprinklers and smoke alarms. The tenant does not have to make any repairs, but he or she must return the premises in the same condition they were received, with allowances for ordinary wear and tear.

Assignment and Subleasing

The lessee may assign the lease or may sublease if the lease terms do not prohibit it. A tenant who transfers all of his or her leasehold interests *assigns* the lease. One who transfers less than all of the leasehold interests by leasing them to a new tenant **subleases** (see Figure 16.2). In most cases the sublease or assignment of a lease does not relieve the original lessee of the obligation to make rental payments unless the landlord agrees to waive such liability. Most leases prohibit the lessee from assigning or subletting without the lessor's consent. The lessor thus retains control over the occupancy of the leased premises but must not unreasonably withhold consent. The sublessor's (original lessee's) interest in the real estate is known as a *sandwich lease*.

Options

Many leases contain an *option* that grants the lessee the privilege of *renewing* or extending the lease but requires that the lessee give *notice* on or before a specific date of intention to exercise the option. Some leases grant to the lessee the option to purchase the leased premises (discussed in Chapter 10 and later in this chapter).

**Figure 16.2
Assignment versus
Subletting**

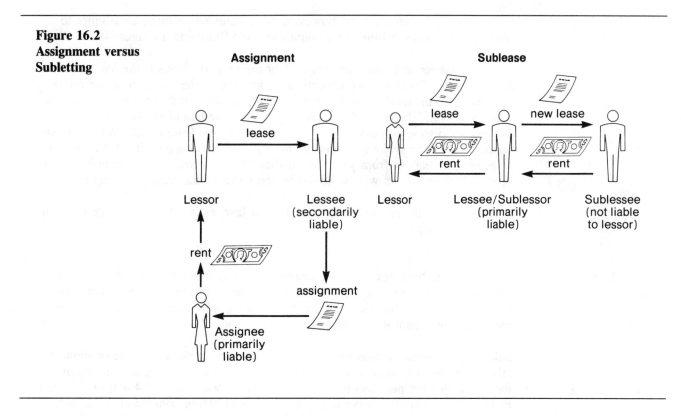

**Destruction of
Premises**

In land leases involving *agricultural land* the courts have held that damage to or destruction of the improvements, even if not the tenant's fault, does not relieve the tenant from the obligation to pay rent to the end of the term. This ruling has been extended in most states to include *ground leases* on which the tenant has constructed a building and, in many instances, leases that give possession of an entire building to the tenant. When the tenant leases an entire building, the courts have held that he or she is also leasing the land on which that building is located.

In those cases where the leased premises are only a part of the building (such as office or commercial space or an apartment in an apartment building), the tenant is *not* required to continue to pay rent upon destruction of the leased premises. In some states, if the property was destroyed as a result of the landlord's negligence the tenant can recover damages from the landlord.

In Practice . . .

All of these general statements concerning destruction of leased premises are controlled largely by terms of the lease. Printed lease forms and all carefully prepared leases usually include a provision covering the subject of destruction of the premises. Great care must be exercised in reading the entire lease document before signing it.

**Termination of
Lease**

In addition to the methods of lease termination mentioned earlier, the parties to a lease may mutually agree to cancel the lease. The tenant may offer to surrender the leasehold interest; if so, acceptance by the landlord will result in termination. A tenant who abandons leased property, however, remains liable for the terms of the lease—including the rent. The terms of the specific lease will usually indicate whether the landlord is obligated to try to rerent the space. If the landlord intends to sue for unpaid rent, however, most states will require an attempt to rerent the premises to limit the amount owed (to "mitigate damages").

When the owner of leased property dies or the property is sold, *the lease does not terminate*. There are two exceptions: a lease from the owner of a life estate terminates on the death of that person, and the death of either party terminates a tenancy at will. The heirs of a deceased landlord are bound by the terms of existing valid leases. *In addition, if a landlord conveys leased real estate, the new landlord takes the property subject to the rights of the tenants*. If a tenant under an estate for years or from year to year dies, the lease will remain in effect; the deceased lessee's heirs will be bound by the terms of the lease agreement.

A tenancy may be terminated by operation of law, as in a bankruptcy or condemnation proceeding.

Breach of Lease

When a tenant breaches any lease provision, the landlord may sue the tenant to obtain a judgment to cure the breach, such as to cover rent past due, damages to the premises or other defaults. Likewise, when a landlord breaches any lease provision, the tenant is entitled to certain remedies.

Suit for possession—actual eviction. When a tenant breaches a lease or improperly retains possession of leased premises, the landlord may regain possession through a **suit for possession.** This process is known as **actual eviction.** The law requires the landlord to serve *notice* on the tenant before commencing the suit. Most lease terms require at least a ten-day notice in case of a *default,* but in many states only a five-day notice must be given before filing a suit for possession based on a default in payment of rent. When a court issues a judgment for possession to a landlord, the tenant must peaceably leave and take all belongings, or the landlord can have the judgment enforced by a *bailiff* or other court officer, who will *forcibly remove* the tenant and the tenant's possessions.

Until such a judgment is issued on behalf of the landlord, he or she must be careful not to harass the tenant in any manner, such as by locking the tenant out of the property, impounding the tenant's possessions or disconnecting utility service (such as electricity and natural gas) so that the property becomes unusable.

Tenants' remedies—constructive eviction. If a landlord breaches any clause of a lease agreement, the tenant has the right to sue, claiming a judgment for damages against the landlord. If an action or omission on the landlord's part results in the leased premises becoming unusable for the purpose intended in the lease, the tenant may have the right to abandon the premises. This action, called **constructive eviction,** terminates the lease agreement if the tenant can prove that the premises have become unusable because of the conscious neglect of the landlord. To claim constructive eviction *the tenant must leave the premises* while the conditions that made the premises unusable exist.

For example, a lease requires the landlord to furnish heat; because of the landlord's failure to repair a defective heating plant, the heat is not provided. If this results in the leased premises become unusable, the tenant may abandon them. It should be noted that some leases provide that when failure to furnish heat is accidental and not the landlord's fault it is not grounds for constructive eviction.

Pro-Tenant Legislation

For the most part leases are drawn up primarily for the benefit of the landlord. However, consumer awareness has fostered the belief that a valid lease is dependent on both parties' fulfillment of certain obligations. To provide laws outlining such obligations several states have adopted some variation of the *Uniform Residential Landlord and Tenant Act*. This model law addresses such issues as the landlord's right of entry and maintenance of premises, the tenant's protection against retaliation by the landlord for complaints and the disclosure of the property owners' names and addresses to the tenants. The act further sets down specific remedies available to both the landlord and the tenant if a breach of the lease agreement occurs.

The federal Tenants' Eviction Procedures Act of 1976 establishes standardized eviction procedures for people living in *government-subsidized housing*. It requires the landlord to have a valid reason for evicting the tenant and to give the tenant proper notice of eviction. This act does not supersede state laws; however, it does provide recourse for tenants in states that have no such laws. The act applies only to multiunit residential buildings owned or subsidized by the Department of Housing and Urban Development and to buildings that have government-backed mortgages.

Types of Leases

The manner in which rent is determined indicates the type of lease that is in force (see Table 16.2).

In a **gross lease** the tenant is obligated to pay a *fixed rental,* and the landlord pays all taxes, insurance, repairs and the like connected with the property (usually called *property charges* or *operating expenses*). This type of lease is most often used for residential apartment rentals.

Net Lease

The **net lease** provides that in addition to the rent, the *tenant pays all or some of the property charges.* The monthly rental is net income for the landlord after operating costs have been paid. Leases for entire commercial or industrial buildings and the land on which they are located, ground leases (discussed later) and long-term leases are usually net leases.

In a *triple net lease,* or *net-net-net lease,* the tenant pays all operating and other expenses, such as taxes, insurance, assessments, maintenance and other charges.

Table 16.2 Types of Leases	Type of Lease	Lessee	Lessor
	Gross lease (residential)	Pays basic rent	Pays property charges (taxes, repairs, insurance, etc.)
	Net lease (commercial/industrial)	Pays basic rent plus all or most property charges	May pay some property charges
	Percentage lease (commercial/industrial)	Pays basic rent plus percent of gross sales (may pay property costs)	May pay some or all property charges

Math Concept: Calculating Percentage Lease Rents	Percentage leases usually call for a minimum monthly rent plus a percentage of gross sales income over a stated annual amount. For example, a lease might require minimum rent of $1,300 per month plus five percent of the business's sales over $160,000. On an annual sales volume of $250,000, the annual rent would be calculated as follows: $1,300 per month $\times$ 12 months = $15,600; $250,000 − $160,000 = $90,000; $90,000 $\times$ .05 (5%) = $4,500; $15,600 base rent + $4,500 percentage rent = $20,100 total rent

Percentage Lease

Either a gross lease or a net lease may be a **percentage lease**, which provides that the rental is based on a *percentage of the gross income* received by the tenant doing business on the leased property. This type of lease is usually used in the rental of retail business locations.

The percentage lease usually provides for a minimum fixed rental fee plus a percentage of that portion of the tenant's business income that exceeds a stated minimum. The percentage charged in such leases varies widely with the nature of the business and is negotiable between landlord and tenant. A tenant's bargaining power is determined by the volume of the business. Percentages vary with the location of the property and general economic conditions.

Other Lease Types

Several types of leases allow for increases in the rental charge during the lease period. Two of the more common ones are the *graduated lease,* which provides for increases in rent at set future dates in specified amounts, and the *index lease,* which allows rent to be increased or decreased periodically based on changes in the government cost-of-living index or some other index.

When a landowner leases land to a tenant who agrees to *erect a building* on the land, the lease is usually referred to as a **ground lease.** Ground leases usually involve separate ownership of land and building. Such a lease must be for a long enough term to make the transaction desirable to the tenant investing in the building. These leases are generally *net leases* that require the lessee to pay rent as well as real estate taxes, insurance, upkeep and repairs. Such leases often run for terms of 50 years or longer, and a lease for 99 years is not impossible.

When oil companies lease land to explore for oil and gas, a special lease agreement must be negotiated. Usually the landowner receives a cash payment for executing the lease. If no well is drilled within the period stated in the lease, the lease expires; however, most oil and gas leases provide that the oil company may continue its rights for another year by paying another flat rental fee. Such rentals may be paid annually until a well is produced. If oil and/or gas is found, the landowner usually receives one-eighth of its value as a royalty. In this case the lease will continue for as long as oil or gas is obtained in significant quantities.

A **lease option** allows the tenant the right to purchase the leased property at a predetermined price for a certain time period. Although it is not required, the owner frequently will give the tenant credit toward the purchase price for some of the rent paid. In a lease option the lease is the primary consideration and the option is secondary.

A **lease purchase** is used when the tenant wants to purchase the property and is unable to do so presently yet still needs the use of the leased facility. Common reasons for using a lease purchase are current inability to obtain favorable financing or obtain clear title and unfavorable tax consequences of a current purchase. Here the purchase agreement is the primary consideration and the lease is secondary.

Agricultural landowners often lease their land to tenant farmers, who provide the labor to produce and bring in the crop. The owner can be paid by the tenant in one of two ways: as an agreed-on rental amount in cash in advance (**cash rents**) or as a percentage of the profits from the sale of the crop when it is sold (**sharecropping**).

Key Terms

actual eviction	lease option
cash rent	lease purchase
constructive eviction	leasehold estate
covenant of quiet enjoyment	month-to-month tenancy
estate at sufferance	net lease
estate at will	percentage lease
estate for years	reversionary right
estate from period to period	security deposit
gross lease	sharecropping
ground lease	subletting
lease	suit for possession

Summary

A lease is an agreement that grants one person the right to use the property of another in return for consideration.

A leasehold estate that runs for a specific length of time creates an estate for years; one that runs for an indefinite number of terms creates an estate from period to period (year to year, month to month). An estate at will runs as long as the landlord permits, and an estate at sufferance is possession without the consent of the landlord. A leasehold estate is classified as personal property.

The requirements of a valid lease include offer and acceptance, consideration, capacity to contract and legal objectives. In addition, state statutes of frauds generally require that any lease that will not be completed within one year of the date of its making must be in writing to be enforceable in court. Most leases also include clauses relating to such rights and obligations of the landlord and tenant as the use of the premises, subletting, judgments, maintenance of the premises and termination of the lease period.

Leases may be terminated by the expiration of the lease period, the mutual agreement of the parties or a breach of the lease by either landlord or tenant. In most cases neither the death of the tenant nor the landlord's sale of the rental property terminates a lease.

Upon a tenant's default on any of the lease provisions a landlord may sue for a money judgment or for actual eviction in a case where a tenant has improperly retained possession of the premises. If the premises have become unusable due to the landlord's negligence, the tenant may have the right of constructive eviction, that is, the right to abandon the premises and refuse to pay rent until the premises are repaired.

There are several basic types of leases, including net leases, gross leases and percentage leases. These leases are classified according to the method used in determining the rental rate of the property.

− 6

Questions

1. A ground lease is usually:
   a. short-term.
   b. for 100 years or longer.
   c. long-term.
   d. a gross lease.

2. A percentage lease is a lease that provides for:
   a. a rental of a percentage of the value of a building.
   b. a definite periodic rent not exceeding a stated percentage.
   c. a definite monthly rent plus a percentage of the tenant's gross receipts in excess of a certain amount.
   d. a graduated amount due monthly and not exceeding a stated percentage.

3. If several tenants moved out of a rented store building because the building collapsed:
   a. this would be an actual eviction.
   b. the tenants would be liable for the rent until the expiration date of their leases.
   c. the landlord would have to provide substitute space.
   d. this would be a constructive eviction.

4. R's written five-year lease with monthly rental payments expired last month, but R has remained in possession and the landlord has accepted his most recent rent payment without comment. At this point:
   a. R is a holdover tenant.
   b. R's lease has been renewed for another five years.
   c. R's lease has been renewed for another month.
   d. R is a tenant at sufferance.

5. A lease for two years must be in writing because:
   a. either party may forget the terms.
   b. the tenant must sign the agreement to pay rent.
   c. the statute of frauds requires it.
   d. it is the customary procedure to protect the tenant.

6. A tenant who transfers the entire remaining term of the lease to a third party is:
   a. a sublessor.
   b. assigning the lease.
   c. automatically relieved of any further obligation under it.
   d. giving the third party a sandwich lease.

7. A tenant's lease has expired, the tenant has neither vacated nor negotiated a renewal lease and the landlord has declared that she does not want the tenant to remain in the building. The tenancy is called:
   a. an estate for years.
   b. a periodic estate.
   c. an estate at will.
   d. an estate at sufferance.

8. F has a lease that will expire in two weeks. At that time he will move into larger quarters on the other side of town. To terminate this agreement:
   a. F must give his landlord prior notice.
   b. the landlord must give F prior notice.
   c. nothing needs to be done—the agreement will terminate automatically.
   d. the agreement will terminate only after both parties renegotiate the original agreement.

9. When a tenant holds possession of a landlord's property without a current lease agreement and without the landlord's approval:
   a. the tenant is maintaining a gross lease.
   b. the landlord can file suit for possession.
   c. the tenant has no obligation to pay rent.
   d. the landlord may be subject to a constructive eviction.

10. Under the terms of a residential lease the landlord is required to maintain the water heater. If a tenant is unable to receive hot water because of a faulty water heater, all of the following remedies would be available to the tenant except that the tenant can:
    a. sue the landlord for damages.
    b. sue the landlord for back rent.
    c. abandon the premises under constructive eviction.
    d. terminate the lease agreement.

11. The leasehold interest that automatically renews itself at each expiration is the:

    a. tenancy for years.
    b. tenancy from period to period.
    c. tenancy at will.
    d. tenancy at sufferance.

12. K has leased space in her shopping center to B for B's dress store. However, B's business fails and she sublets the space to D. Should D not make her rental payments when they are due:

    a. K would have recourse against B only.
    b. K would have recourse against D only.
    c. K would have recourse against both B and D.
    d. D would have recourse against B.

13. Which of the following would most likely terminate a lease?

    a. The destruction of the property
    b. The sale of the property
    c. The failure of the tenant to pay the rent
    d. Constructive eviction

14. The type of lease generally constructed specifically for tax purposes is the:

    a. net lease.   c. percentage lease.
    b. lease option.   d. lease purchase.

15. Holdover tenancy is also referred to as:

    a. tenancy for years.
    b. periodic tenancy.
    c. tenancy at will.
    d. tenancy at sufferance.

Part Two
Practices

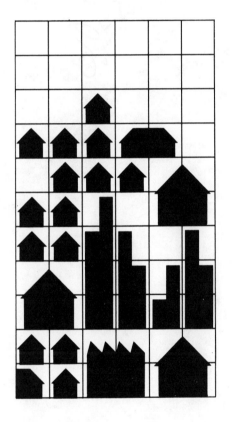

17

Property Management

In recent years the increased size of buildings; the technical complexities of construction, maintenance and repair; and the trend toward absentee ownership by individual investors and investment groups have led to the expanded use of professional property managers for both residential and commercial properties. Possible sources of management business include corporate owners, apartment and condominium associations, homeowners' associations, investment syndicates, trusts and absentee owners.

Property management has become so important that many brokerage firms maintain separate departments staffed by carefully selected, well-trained people. Corporate and institutional owners of real estate have also established property management departments. Many real estate investors still manage their own property, however, and thus must acquire the knowledge and skills of a property manager.

In most states property managers serving the public for a fee must be licensed real estate brokers. In others, property managers must be licensed specifically as property managers.

Responsibilities of the Property Manager

In the simplest terms a **property manager** is someone who *preserves the value of an investment property while generating income as an agent for the owners*. In this role the manager chooses the best possible means to carry out an agent's responsibilities—and has more authority and discretion than an employee. The property manager is expected to merchandise the property and control operating expenses so as to maximize income. He or she also should maintain and modernize the property to preserve and enhance the owner's capital investment. The manager carries out these objectives by securing suitable tenants, collecting the rents, caring for the premises, budgeting and controlling expenses, hiring and supervising employees, keeping proper accounts and making periodic reports to the owner.

In Practice . . .

In securing property management business, word of mouth is often the best advertising. A manager who consistently demonstrates the ability to increase property income over previous levels should have no difficulty finding new business.

The Management Agreement

The first step in taking over the management of any property is to enter into a **management agreement** with the owner (see Figure 17.1). This agreement creates an agency relationship between the owner and the property manager. A property manager is usually considered a *general agent*, whereas a real estate broker is usually considered a *special agent*. As agent a property manager is charged with the same agency responsibilities as a listing broker—care, obedience, accounting, loyalty and disclosure. After entering into an agreement with a property owner, a manager handles the property as the owner would. In all activities the manager's first responsibility is to *realize the highest return on the property that is consistent with the owner's instructions*.

The management agreement should be in writing and should cover the following points:

1. *Description* of the property.

2. *Time period* the agreement will cover.

3. *Definition of management's responsibilities*. All of the manager's duties should be stated in the contract; exceptions should be noted.

4. *Extent of manager's authority as an agent*. This provision should state what authority the manager is to have in such matters as hiring, firing and supervising employees, fixing rental rates for space, making expenditures and authorizing repairs within the limits established previously with the owner. (Repairs that exceed a certain expense limit may require the owner's written approval.)

5. *Reporting*. Agreement should be reached on the frequency and detail of the manager's periodic reports on operations and financial position. These reports serve as a means for the owner to monitor the manager's work and as a basis for both the owner and the manager to assess trends that can be used in shaping future management policy.

6. *Management fee*. The fee can be based on a percentage of gross or net income, a commission on new rentals, a fixed fee or a combination.

7. *Allocation of costs*. The agreement should state which of the property management expenses, such as custodial and other help, advertising, supplies and repairs, are to be charged to the property's expenses and paid by the owner.

Management Functions

A property manager must live up to both the letter and the spirit of the management agreement. The owner must be kept well informed on all matters of policy as well as on the financial condition of the property and its operation.

In Practice . . .

Before contracting to manage any property, the professional property manager should be certain that the building owner has realistic income expectations and is willing to spend money on necessary maintenance. Attempting to meet impossible owner demands by dubious methods can endanger the manager's reputation and prove detrimental to obtaining future business.

Budgeting Expenses

Before attempting to rent any property, a property manager should develop an operating budget based on anticipated revenues and expenses and reflecting the

**Figure 17.1
Sample Agreement
to Manage
Real Estate**

AGREEMENT TO MANAGE REAL ESTATE

Between _____, Owner

and

_____, Manager

THIS AGREEMENT dated as of the _____ day of _____,

19_____, by and between _____, as

principal (hereinafter collectively referred to as "Owner"), and _____,

a Corporation chartered in the State of _____, hereinafter referred to as

"Manager," as agent, shall be in effect for a period of _____ from date.

WITNESSETH

WHEREAS, Owner owns the tracts of real estate legally described in "Exhibit A" attached hereto and made a part hereof; and

WHEREAS, Owner desires to appoint Manager as Owner's agent to handle, manage and control the real estate described in said "Exhibit A," and also such other real estate as may be added to said "Exhibit A" from time to time by mutual agreement of the parties, hereinafter collectively called "THE PROPERTIES" in accordance with the terms and conditions hereinafter set out.

NOW THEREFORE, in consideration of the premises and the mutual promises and covenants herein contained, Owner and Manager agree as follows:

ARTICLE I

Powers and Duties of the Manager

1.01   Owner hereby appoints Manager as Owner's agent to handle, manage and control THE PROPERTIES and expressly authorizes and empowers Manager as follows:

(a) To advertise THE PROPERTIES for lease and to execute leases covering THE PROPERTIES, or any part thereof, for such rent and upon such terms and conditions as Manager may deem wise and proper, PROVIDED, HOWEVER, that Manager shall not enter into a lease for a period longer than five (5) years from the beginning date of such lease without Owner's written consent.

(b) To collect the rents and revenues from THE PROPERTIES.

Source: Floyd M. Baird, Tulsa, Oklahoma

Figure 17.1
(continued)

(c) To maintain and keep THE PROPERTIES in a reasonable state of repair and to expend such part of the rents and revenues from THE PROPERTIES, which it collects, as may be necessary in so doing; PROVIDED, HOWEVER, Manager shall not spend more than $_____ in repairing any one tract of real estate (or the improvements thereon) constituting THE PROPERTIES during any 12-month period unless and until first receiving the written consent of Owner to do so.

(d) To keep the improvements of THE PROPERTIES insured against the hazards normally covered by fire and extended-coverage insurance policies and rental income insurance and public liability insurance policies in such amounts as Manager may determine to be adequate to protect the interest of Owner.

(e) To pay ad valorem taxes and improvement assessments against THE PROPERTIES before same become delinquent.

(f) To maintain out of the rents and revenues collected from THE PROPERTIES such reserves as Manager may deem wise and proper.

(g) To employ such attorneys, agents, contractors and workmen as Manager may deem wise and proper in connection with the handling, managing and control of THE PROPERTIES.

(h) To adjust and compromise any claim that may be asserted with respect to THE PROPERTIES and/or which may arise in connection with the management of THE PROPERTIES and to give binding releases in connection therewith.

(i) Generally, to handle, manage and control THE PROPERTIES and to execute such agreements, contracts or other documents or do such other acts or things as Manager, from time to time, may deem wise and proper to carry out the duties stated in this Agreement.

1.02   Manager shall keep proper books of account of this agency, which said books shall be open to inspection by Owner during the regular business hours of the Manager. Manager need not maintain segregated bank accounts relating to THE PROPERTIES, but the books and records shall reflect at all times the rents and revenues received and the disbursements made as to each tract of real estate comprising THE PROPERTIES. Accounts shall be kept in compliance with all applicable state laws. At such periodic intervals as Owner shall request, but not more frequently than monthly, Manager shall furnish to Owner a statement showing the rents and revenues received, the disbursements made and the other transactions had with respect to THE PROPERTIES for the period indicated by Owner.

1.03   Manager may continue to hold THE PROPERTIES to be handled, managed and controlled in accordance with the terms and conditions of this Agreement without liability or depreciation or loss, and the liability of Manager shall be limited to reasonable diligence in exercising the powers and authorities herein granted.

**Figure 17.1
(continued)**

1.04   Manager is not authorized by this Agreement either to make any capital improvements on THE PROPERTIES or to sell any of the real estate constituting a part of THE PROPERTIES. Manager is not authorized to create any mortgages, liens or encumbrances against any of the real estate constituting a part of THE PROPERTIES, unless and until first instructed in writing by Owner to do so.

1.05   Owner agrees that Manager shall be under no duty to undertake any action, other than as herein specified, with respect to the handling, managing and controlling of THE PROPERTIES, unless and until specifically agreed to in writing by Manager.

1.06   Owner agrees that Manager shall have a lien against THE PROPERTIES to secure the payment of Manager's compensation and any advances Manager may make from other funds.

1.07   Owner's objectives in the management of this property are: _____

_____

_____

_____

_____

_____ .

Manager shall manage the properties accordingly.

ARTICLE II

Rights Reserved by the Parties

2.01   This Agreement may be altered, amended or modified at any time by a written mutual agreement signed by Owner and Manager.

2.02   This Agreement may be terminated by either Owner or Manager giving to the other at least _____ days written notice of intention to terminate this Agreement on a certain date specified in such notice; PROVIDED, HOWEVER, the termination of this Agreement shall not affect the right of Manager to receive leasing commissions or fees which have accrued on the date specified in such notice and have not been paid.

Figure 17.1
(continued)

ARTICLE III

Manager's Compensation and Right of Reimbursement

3.01   For service hereunder, Manager shall be entitled to receive and retain such compensation as is fair, reasonable and customary at the time such services are performed. Owner and Manager, however, may from time to time mutually agree in writing as to the amount of compensation that Manager may receive for services hereunder. Owner agrees to pay to Manager upon demand any fee for services rendered by Manager and/or out-of-pocket expenses incurred by Manager in the handling and managing of THE PROPERTIES where Manager does not have available funds from the rents and revenues from THE PROPERTIES from which to be reimbursed.

3.02   Owner promises and agrees to indemnify Manager and hold Manager harmless from and against any and all losses and liabilities incurred by Manager as a result of any action in good faith taken or not taken by Manager pursuant to the terms and conditions of this Agreement. The promise and agreement of Owner contained in this paragraph 3.02 shall survive any termination of this Agreement as to any such action taken or not taken by Manager prior to the receipt of Manager of written notice of such termination.

ARTICLE IV

Miscellaneous

4.01   This Agreement shall be binding upon and shall inure to the benefit of Owner and Manager and their respective heirs, executors, administrators, successors and assigns.

4.02   All notices authorized or required between the parties or required by any provisions of this Lease or by law shall be in writing and must be received by the parties or delivered by receipted means to the notification address of the receiving party, as set forth below, or to such other address as the parties may direct by notice given as herein provided. The effective date of any notice given hereunder shall be the date on which such notice is received or delivered as above set forth.

NOTIFICATION ADDRESSES

Owner	Manager
_____	_____
_____	_____
_____	_____

Figure 17.1
(continued)

ARTICLE V

Special Terms and Conditions

(Here insert any special provisions relating to this particular relationship and/or properties.)

ARTICLE VI

Distribution of Income

6.01   Manager shall distribute the "net income," as that term is hereinafter defined, derived from the handling, managing and controlling of THE PROPERTIES to Owner in accordance with the written instructions of Owner at such interval, not more frequently than monthly, as Owner may state in said written instructions. "Net income," as used in this paragraph, means gross rents and revenues derived from THE PROPERTIES after deducting proper expenses and amounts requisite for maintenance of authorized reserves.

IN WITNESS WHEREOF, Owner and Manager have executed this Agreement, as of the date first above written.

OWNER: _____

MANAGER: _____

_____

ATTEST:

_____   By: _____
Assistant Secretary   President

Owner Contact: _____
Name   Telephone

Manager Contact: _____
Name   Telephone

Figure 17.1
(continued)

"EXHIBIT A"

List of Owner's Properties to be Managed by Manager

*   *   *   *   *   *   *

(Normally this Agreement is not acknowledged. In event the parties desire that it be notarized, attach acknowledgments for both parties.)

---

long-term goals of the owner. In preparing a budget a manager should begin by allocating money for such continuous, fixed expenses as employees' salaries, real estate taxes, property taxes and insurance premiums. Although budgets should be as accurate an estimate of cost as possible, adjustments may sometimes be necessary, especially in the case of new properties.

Next the manager should establish a cash reserve fund for such variable expenses as repairs, decorating and supplies. The amount allocated for the reserve fund can be computed from the previous yearly costs of the variable expenses.

Capital expenditures. If an owner and a property manager decide that modernization or renovation of the property would enhance its value, the manager should budget money to cover the costs of remodeling. The property manager should be thoroughly familiar with the *principle of contribution* (discussed in Chapter 18) or seek expert advice when estimating any increase in value expected by an improvement. In the case of large-scale construction the expenses charged against the property's income should be spread over several years.

The cost of equipment to be installed in a modernization or renovation must be evaluated over its entire useful life. This is called **life cycle costing.** This term simply means that both the *initial* and the *operating* costs of equipment over its expected life must be measured to compare the total cost of one type of equipment with that of another.

Math Concept: **Rental Commissions**	Residential commissions are usually calculated based on the annualized rent from a property. For example, if an apartment unit rents for $475 per month and the commission payable is 8%, the commission would be calculated as follows:

$$\$475 \text{ per month} \times 12 \text{ months} = \$5,700; \$5,700 \times .08 \ (8\%) = \$456$$

Renting the Property

Effective rental of the property is essential to the success of a property manager. However, the role of the manager in managing a property should not be confused with that of a broker acting as a leasing agent and solely concerned with renting space. The property manager may use the services of a leasing agent, but that agent does not undertake the full responsibility of maintenance and management of the property.

Setting rental rates. In establishing rental rates for a property a basic concern must be that, in the long term, the income from the rental space cover the fixed charges and operating expenses and also provide a fair return on the investment. Consideration must also be given to the prevailing rates in comparable buildings and the current level of vacancy in the property to be rented—supply and demand. Following a detailed survey of the competitive space available in the neighborhood, prices should be noted and adjusted for differences between neighboring properties and the property being managed. Annual rent adjustments are usually warranted.

Note that while apartment rental rates are stated in monthly amounts on a unit basis, office and commercial space rentals are usually stated according to either the annual or the monthly rate per square foot of space.

If a high level of vacancy exists, the manager should immediately attempt to determine why. *A high level of vacancy does not necessarily indicate that rents are too high;* instead the problem may be inept management or defects in the property. The manager should attempt to identify and correct the problems first, rather than immediately lower rents. Conversely, *while a high percentage of occupancy may appear to indicate an effective rental program, it could also mean that rental rates are too low.* Whenever the occupancy level of an apartment house or office building exceeds 95 percent, serious consideration should be given to raising rents.

Tenant selection. Generally the highest rents can be secured from satisfied tenants. While a broker may sell a property and then have no further dealings with the purchaser, a building manager's success is greatly dependent on retaining sound, long-term relationships. The first and most important step is selection of tenants. In selecting prospective commercial or industrial tenants a manager should be sure that each person will ''fit the space'': that the *size of the space* meets the tenant's requirements, that the tenant will have the *ability to pay* for the space, that the *tenant's business will be compatible* with the building and the other tenants and that if the tenant is likely to expand in the future, *expansion space will be available.*

In selecting residential tenants the property manager must comply with all federal and local fair housing laws (see Chapter 21).

Collecting rents. The best way to minimize problems with rent collection is, again, to make a *careful selection* of tenants. The desire for a high level of occupancy should not override good judgment; a property manager should accept only those tenants who can be expected to meet their financial obligations to the property owner. The manager should investigate financial references given by the prospect, check with local credit bureaus and, when possible, interview the prospective tenant's former landlord.

The terms of rental payment should be spelled out in detail in the lease agreement. A *firm and consistent collection plan* with a sufficient system of notices and records should be established. In cases of delinquency every attempt must be made to make collections without resorting to legal action. For those cases in which it is required a property manager must be prepared to initiate and follow through with the necessary steps in conjunction with legal counsel.

Maintaining Good Relations with Tenants

The ultimate success of a property manager will depend greatly on the ability to maintain good relations with tenants. Dissatisfied tenants eventually vacate the property, and a high tenant turnover means greater expense for the owner in terms of advertising, redecorating and uncollected rents. The increased attention being given to landlord-tenant relationships by legal and judicial systems has added to the significance of this issue.

An effective property manager will establish a good communication system with tenants, use intangible as well as tangible benefits to keep tenants satisfied, ensure that maintenance and service requests are attended to promptly and enforce all lease terms and building rules. A good manager is tactful and decisive and will act to the benefit of both owner and occupants. The property manager must be able to handle residents who do not pay their rent on time or who break building regulations and breed dissatisfaction among other tenants. Careful record keeping will show whether rent is being remitted promptly and in the proper amount. Records of all lease renewal dates should be kept so that the manager can anticipate expiration and retain good tenants who might otherwise move when their leases end.

Maintaining the Property

One of the most important functions of a property manager is the supervision of property maintenance. A manager must learn to balance the services provided with the costs they entail so as to satisfy the tenants' needs while minimizing operating expenses.

Efficient property maintenance demands accurate assessment of the needs of the building and the number and kinds of personnel that will meet these needs. Staffing and scheduling requirements will vary with the type, size and regional location of the property, so owner and manager usually agree in advance on maintenance objectives for the property. In some cases the most viable plan may be to operate with a low rental schedule and minimal expenditures for services and maintenance. Another property may be more lucrative if kept in top condition and operated with all possible tenant services, because it can then command premium rental rates.

The manager must first *protect the physical integrity of the property* to ensure that the condition of the building and its grounds are kept at present levels over the long term. For example, preserving the property by repainting the exterior or replacing the heating system will help to keep the building functional and decrease routine maintenance costs.

Property maintenance falls into four areas: preventive maintenance, repair or corrective maintenance, routine maintenance and construction.

Preventive maintenance includes regularly scheduled activities, such as regular painting and periodic lubrication of gears and motors, that will maintain the structure so that the long-range value and physical integrity of the building are preserved. Most authorities agree this is the most critical but most neglected maintenance responsibility.

Repair or corrective maintenance involves the actual repairs that keep the building's equipment, utilities and amenities functioning as contracted for by the tenants. Repairing a boiler, fixing a leaky faucet and repairing a broken air-conditioning unit are acts of repair maintenance.

A property manager must also *supervise the routine cleaning and repairs* of the building, including such day-to-day duties as cleaning common areas, doing minor carpentry and plumbing and providing regularly scheduled upkeep of heating, air-conditioning and landscaping.

Last is new or renovative *construction*. Especially when dealing with commercial or industrial space, a property manager will be called on to make **tenant improvements**—alterations to the interior of the building to meet the functional demands of the tenant. These alterations range from repainting to completely gutting the interior and redesigning the space. Tenant improvements are especially important when renting new buildings, because the interior is usually left incomplete so that it can be adapted to the needs of the individual tenants.

Supervision of modernization or renovation of buildings that have become functionally obsolete and thus unsuited to today's building needs is also important. (See Chapter 18 for a definition of *functional obsolescence*.) The renovation of a building often increases the building's marketability and thus its possible income.

Hiring employees versus contracting for services. One of the major decisions a property manager faces is whether to contract for maintenance services from an outside firm or hire on-site employees to perform such tasks. This decision should be based on a number of factors, including size of the building, complexity of tenants' requirements and availability of suitable labor.

Handling Environmental Concerns

With the proliferation of federal and state laws and increasing local regulation environmental concerns have become a major responsibility of the property manager and will require an increasing amount of management time and attention in the future. While property managers are not expected to be experts in all of the disciplines necessary to operate a modern building, they are expected to be knowledgeable in many diverse subjects, most of which are technical in nature. Environmental concerns are one such subject.

The property manager must be able to respond to a variety of environmental problems. He or she may manage structures containing asbestos or radon, or be called on to arrange an environmental audit of a property. If hazardous wastes are produced by the manager's employer or tenants, the manager must see that they are properly disposed of. Even the normally nonhazardous waste of an office building must be controlled to avoid violation of laws requiring segregation of types of wastes. In areas where recycling is coming into practice, the property manager must provide the facilities and see that tenants sort their trash properly.

The Management Profession

Most metropolitan areas have local associations of building and property owners and managers that are affiliates of regional and national associations. The Institute of Real Estate Management was founded in 1933 and is one of the affiliates of the NATIONAL ASSOCIATION OF REALTORS®. The institute awards the designation of *Certified Property Manager* (CPM) to persons who have met certain requirements. The Building Owners and Managers Association International (BOMA International) is a federation of local associations of owners and managers, primarily of office buildings. Training courses leading to the designation *Real Property Administrator* (RPA), *Systems Maintenance Administrator* (SMA) and *Facilities Management Administrator* (FMA) are offered by the Building Owners and Managers Institute International (BOMI International), an independent institute affiliated with BOMA. In addition, there are many specialized professional organizations for apartment managers, community association managers, shopping center managers and others.

Risk Management

Because enormous monetary losses can result from certain occurrences, one of the most critical areas of responsibility for a property manager is the field of insurance. Awareness of the purposes of insurance coverage and how to make best use of the many types of insurance available are part of what is called **risk management.**

Risk management involves answering the question "What will happen if something goes wrong?" The perils of any risk must be evaluated in terms of options. In considering the possibility of a loss, the property manager must decide whether it is better to:

- *avoid it,* by removing the source of risk, such as a swimming pool;

- *retain it,* to a certain extent, by insuring with a large *deductible* (loss not covered by the insurer);

- *control it,* by installing sprinklers, fire doors and other preventive measures; or

- *transfer it,* by taking out an insurance policy.

When insurance is considered, a competent, reliable insurance agent familiar with the problems involved in the type of property involved should be selected to survey the property and make recommendations. Additional insurance surveys should be obtained if any questions remain. Final decisions, however, must be made by the property owner.

Types of Insurance Coverage

Some of the common types of insurance coverage available to income property owners and managers are as follows:

1. *Fire and hazard.* Fire insurance policies provide coverage against direct loss or damage to property from a fire on the premises. Standard fire coverage

can be extended to cover hazards such as windstorm, hail, smoke damage or civil insurrection.

2. *Consequential loss, use and occupancy.* Consequential loss insurance, which can include rent loss, covers the loss of revenue to a business that occurs if the business's property cannot be used.

3. *Contents and personal property.* Some insurance covers building contents and personal property during periods when they are not actually located on the business premises.

4. *Liability.* Public liability insurance covers the risks an owner assumes when the public enters the building. Payments under this coverage are used to pay claims for medical expenses by a person injured in the building as a result of the landlord's negligence. Another liability risk is that of medical or hospital payments for injuries sustained by building employees hurt in the course of their employment. These claims are covered by state laws known as **workers' compensation acts.** These laws require a building owner who is an employer to obtain a workers' compensation policy from a private insurance company.

5. *Casualty.* Casualty insurance policies include coverage against theft, burglary, vandalism, machinery damage and health and accident insurance. Casualty policies are usually written on specific risks, such as theft, rather than being all-inclusive.

6. *Surety bonds.* **Surety bonds** cover an owner against financial losses resulting from an employee's criminal acts or negligence while performing assigned duties.

Today many insurance companies offer **multiperil policies** for apartment and business buildings. These policies offer the property manager an insurance package that includes such standard types of commercial coverage as fire, hazard, public liability and casualty.

Claims

When a claim is made under a policy insuring a building or other physical object, there are two possible methods of determining the amount of the claim. One is the *depreciated* actual or cash value of the damaged property, and the other is current replacement cost. When purchasing insurance, a manager must assess whether the property should be insured at full replacement cost or at a depreciated cost. As with the homeowners' policies discussed in Chapter 3, commercial policies include *coinsurance clauses* that require the insured to carry fire coverage, usually in an amount equal to 80 percent of the building's replacement value.

Key Terms

life cycle costing	risk management
management agreement	surety bond
multiperil policies	tenant improvements
property manager	workers' compensation acts

Summary

Property management is a specialized service to owners of income-producing properties in which the managerial function may be delegated to an individual or a firm with particular expertise in the field. The manager, as agent of the owner, becomes the administrator of the project and assumes the executive functions required for the care and operation of the property.

A management agreement establishing the agency relationship between owner and manager must be prepared carefully to define and authorize the manager's duties and responsibilities.

Projected expenses, combined with the manager's analysis of the condition of the building and the rent patterns in the neighborhood, will form the basis on which rental rates for the property are determined. Once a rent schedule is established, the property manager is responsible for soliciting tenants whose needs are suited to the available space and who are financially capable of meeting the proposed rents. The manager is generally obligated to collect rents, maintain the building, hire necessary employees, pay taxes for the building and deal with tenant problems.

Maintenance includes safeguarding the physical integrity of the property and performing routine cleaning and repairs as well as making tenant improvements—adapting the interior space and overall design of the property to suit the tenants' needs and meet the demands of the market.

In addition, the manager is expected to secure adequate insurance coverage for the premises. The basic types of coverage applicable to commercial structures include fire and hazard insurance on the property and fixtures, consequential loss, use and occupancy insurance to protect the owner against revenue losses and casualty insurance to provide coverage against such losses as theft, vandalism and destruction of machinery. The manager should also secure public liability insurance to insure the owner against claims made by people injured on the premises and workers' compensation policies to cover the claims of employees injured on the job.

Questions

1. Which of the following types of insurance coverage insures the property owner against the claims of employees injured while on the job?
   a. Consequential loss
   b. Workers' compensation
   c. Casualty
   d. Surety bond

2. Apartment rental rates are usually expressed:
   a. in monthly amounts.
   b. on a per-room basis.
   c. in square feet per month.
   d. in square feet per year.

3. From a management point of view, apartment building occupancy that reaches as high as 98 percent would tend to indicate that:
   a. the building is poorly managed.
   b. the building has reached its maximum potential.
   c. the building is a desirable place to live.
   d. rents should be raised.

4. A guest slips on an icy apartment building stair and is hospitalized. A claim against the building owner for medical expenses may be paid under which of the following policies held by the owner?
   a. Workers' compensation
   b. Casualty
   c. Liability
   d. Fire and hazard

5. Which of the following should *not* be a consideration in selecting a tenant?

   a. The size of the space versus the tenant's requirements
   b. The tenant's ability to pay
   c. The racial and ethnic background of the tenant
   d. The compatibility of the tenant's business with other tenants' businesses

6. When a property manager chooses an insurance policy with a $250 deductible, the risk management technique being employed is:
   a. avoiding risk.   c. controlling risk.
   b. retaining risk.   d. transferring risk.

7. Tenant improvements are:
   a. fixtures.
   b. adaptations of space to suit tenants' needs.
   c. removable by the tenant.
   d. paid for by the landlord.

8. In preparing a budget, the property manager should set up for variable expenses:
   a. a control account.
   b. a floating allocation.
   c. a cash reserve fund.
   d. an asset account.

9. Rents should be determined by:
   a. rates prevailing in the area.
   b. the local apartment owners' association.
   c. HUD.
   d. a tenants' union.

10. What type of insurance covers a landlord against loss of rent if an occupied building is burned to the ground?
    a. Fire and hazard
    b. Liability
    c. Consequential loss, use and occupancy
    d. Casualty

11. Property manager J hires W as the full-time maintenance person for one of the buildings she manages. While repairing a faucet in one of the apartments, W steals a television set. J could protect the owner against this type of loss by purchasing:
    a. liability insurance.
    b. workers' compensation insurance.
    c. a surety bond.
    d. casualty insurance.

12. Which of the following might indicate rents are too low?
    a. A poorly maintained building
    b. Many "For Lease" signs in the area
    c. High building occupancy
    d. High vacancy level

13. Repairing a boiler is classified as which type of maintenance?
    a. Preventive   c. Routine
    b. Corrective   d. Construction

Real Estate Appraisal

Appraising

An **appraisal** is an estimate or opinion of value. Formal appraisal reports are relied on by mortgage lenders, investors, public utilities, governmental agencies, businesses and individuals. Home mortgage lenders, for instance, need to know a property's market value so that the loan-to-value ratio (the percentage of value to be loaned) will accurately reflect the property's value as collateral.

The tumultuous real estate market of the 1980s reinforced the need for competent appraisals. The collapse of many savings and loan associations as a result of the surge into unwise investments following enactment of the Depository Institutions Deregulation and Monetary Control Act of 1980 was at least partly the result of faulty property appraisals. With the passage of the Financial Institutions Reform, Recovery and Enforcement Act (FIRREA) in 1989, Congress took action to introduce appraisal regulation. As of July 1, 1991, appraisals performed as part of a federally related transaction *must* comply with state standards and be performed by a state-licensed or state-certified appraiser. State appraisal standards and appraiser licensing requirements must meet at least the minimum levels set by the Appraisal Standards Board and Appraiser Qualifications Board of the Appraisal Foundation, a national body composed of representatives of the major appraisal and related organizations.

The new federal regulations are the first attempt at compulsory appraiser regulation. Previously only a few states required appraisers to have even a real estate license. In recent years a few states have offered voluntary certification procedures to appraisers and/or established criteria for what could be called a "certified" appraisal.

The federal law will affect the majority of appraisers and appraisals performed nationwide. While a relatively low percentage of residential home loans have some government backing, most are packaged for sale in the federally regulated secondary mortgage market. Thus, as of July 1, 1991, lenders who wish to make use of that market must use only appraisers licensed or certified by the state in which the appraised property is located, and the appraisals must meet the federal criteria.

Not all estimates of real estate value are made by professional appraisers, however. Often a real estate agent must help a seller arrive at an asking price or a buyer determine an offering price for property without the aid of a formal appraisal report. Thus everyone engaged in the real estate business, even those who do not choose to be licensed in appraisal, must have at least a fundamental knowledge of real estate valuation.

Value	*Value* is an abstract word with many acceptable definitions. In a broad sense **value** may be defined as the relationship between an object desired and a potential purchaser. It is the power of a good or service to command other goods or services in exchange. In terms of real estate appraisal value may be described as the *present worth of future benefits arising from the ownership of real property.*

To have value in the real estate market property must have these characteristics:

1. *Demand.* The need or desire for possession or ownership backed up by the financial means to satisfy that need.

2. *Utility.* The capacity to satisfy human needs and desires.

3. *Scarcity.* A finite supply.

4. *Transferability.* The relative ease with which ownership rights are transferred from one person to another.

Market Value	A given parcel of real estate may have many different kinds of value at the same time, such as market value (used to estimate selling price), assessed value (used for property taxes), insured value, book value, mortgage value, salvage value, condemnation value and depreciated value. Generally the goal of an appraiser is to estimate *market value*. The market value of real estate is the most probable price that a property should bring in a competitive and open market, allowing a reasonable time to find a purchaser who knows all the uses to which it is adapted and for which it is capable of being used. Included in this definition are the following key points:

1. Market value is the *most probable* price a property will bring—not the average price or the highest price.

2. Payment must be made in *cash* or its equivalent.

3. Buyer and seller must be unrelated and acting without *undue pressure*.

4. A *reasonable length of time* must be allowed for the property to be exposed in the *open market*.

5. Both buyer and seller must be *well informed* of the property's use and potential, including its assets and defects.

The definition of market value used by many government agencies is shown in Figure 18.1.

Market value versus market price. Market value is an estimate based on an analysis of comparable sales and other pertinent market data. *Market price,* on the other hand, is what a property has *actually* sold for—its sales price. Theoretically the market price would be the same as market value. Market price can be taken as accurate evidence of current market value, however, only after considering all of the factors listed above. A sale from father to daughter, for instance, might well have been designed to favor one of the parties.

Basic Principles of Value	A number of economic principles can affect the value of real estate. The most important are defined as follows.

Figure 18.1
Market Value

DEFINITION OF MARKET VALUE: The most probable price which a property should bring in a competitive and open market under all conditions requisite to a fair sale, the buyer and seller, each acting prudently, knowledgeably and assuming the price is not affected by undue stimulus. Implicit in this definition is the consummation of a sale as of a specified date and the passing of title from seller to buyer under conditions whereby: (1) buyer and seller are typically motivated; (2) both parties are well informed or well advised, and each acting in what he considers his own best interest; (3) a reasonable time is allowed for exposure in the open market; (4) payment is made in terms of cash in U.S. dollars or in terms of financial arrangements comparable thereto; and (5) the price represents the normal consideration for the property sold unaffected by special or creative financing or sales concessions* granted by anyone associated with the sale.

*Adjustments to the comparables must be made for special or creative financing or sales concessions. No adjustments are necessary for those costs which are normally paid by sellers as a result of tradition or law in a market area; these costs are readily identifiable since the seller pays these costs in virtually all sales transactions. Special or creative financing adjustments can be made to the comparable property by comparisons to financing terms offered by a third party institutional lender that is not already involved in the property or transaction. Any adjustment should not be calculated on a mechanical dollar for dollar cost of the financing or concession but the dollar amount of any adjustment should approximate the market's reaction to the financing or concessions based on the appraiser's judgment.

Source: FHLMC Form 439 JUL 86/FNMA Form 1004 B July 86

Highest and best use. The most profitable single use to which the property may be adapted or the use that is likely to be in demand in the reasonably near future is its **highest and best use.** Highest and best use is noted in every appraisal but may also be the object of a more extensive analysis. For example, a highest-and-best-use study may show that a parking lot in a busy downtown area is not the highest and best use of that land.

Substitution. The principle of **substitution** states that the maximum value of a property tends to be set by the cost of purchasing an equally desirable and valuable replacement property.

Supply and demand. The principle of **supply and demand** states that the value of a property will increase if the supply decreases and the demand either increases or remains constant—and vice versa. For example, the last lot to be sold in a residential area where the demand for homes is high would probably be worth more than the first lot sold in that area.

Balance. Balance is achieved when adding improvements to land and structures will increase the property value.

Conformity. This means that maximum value is realized if the use of land conforms to existing neighborhood standards. In residential areas of single-family houses, for example, all buildings in a neighborhood should be similar in design, construction, size and age. Subdivision restrictions rely on the principle of **conformity** to ensure maximum future value.

Regression and progression. The principle that, between dissimilar properties, the worth of the better property is affected adversely by the presence of the lesser-quality property is known as **regression.** Thus, in a neighborhood of modest homes a structure that is larger, better maintained and/or more luxurious would tend to be valued in the same range as the others. Conversely, the principle of **progression** states that the worth of a lesser property tends to increase if it is located among better properties.

Anticipation. This principle holds that value can increase or decrease in **anticipation** of some future benefit or detriment affecting the property. For example, the value of a house may be affected if there are rumors that an adjacent parcel may be converted to commercial use in the near future.

Plottage. The principle of **plottage** holds that the merging or consolidation of adjacent lots held by separate landowners into one larger lot may produce a higher total land value than the sum of the two sites valued separately. For example, two adjacent lots may be valued at $35,000 each, but their total value if consolidated into one larger lot under a single use might be $90,000. The process of merging the two lots under one owner is known as **assemblage.**

Increasing and diminishing returns. Improvements to land and structures will eventually reach a point at which they will no longer have an effect on property value. As long as money spent on improvements produces an increase in income or value, the *law of increasing returns* is applicable. But beyond that point, when additional improvements will not produce a proportionate increase in income or value, the *law of diminishing returns* applies.

Contribution. According to the principle of **contribution** the value of any component of a property is what its addition contributes to the value of the whole or what its absence detracts from that value. For example, the cost of installing an air-conditioning system and remodeling an older office building may be greater than is justified by the increase in market value (a function of expected net rental increases) that may result from the improvement to the property.

Competition. This principle states that excess profits tend to attract **competition.** For example, the success of a retail store may induce investors to open similar stores in the area, which tends to mean less profit for all stores concerned unless the purchasing power in the area increases substantially.

Change. The principle of **change** states that no physical or economic condition remains constant. Real estate is subject to natural phenomena, such as tornadoes, fires and the routine wear and tear of the elements. The real estate business is also subject to the demands of its market, as is any business. It is an appraiser's job to be knowledgeable about the past and, therefore, perhaps predictable of the effects of natural phenomena and the behavior of the marketplace.

The Three Approaches to Value	To arrive at an accurate estimate of value appraisers traditionally use three basic valuation techniques: the sales comparison approach, the cost approach and the income capitalization approach. Each method serves as a check against the others and narrows the range within which the final estimate of value will fall. Each method is generally considered most reliable for specific types of property.
The Sales Comparison Approach	In the **sales comparison approach** (sometimes called the *market data approach*) an estimate of value is obtained by comparing the subject property (the property under appraisal) with recently sold comparable properties (properties similar to the subject). (A simplified version of this approach is the competitive market analysis, CMA, often used by brokers and salespeople helping a seller set a price for residential real estate in an active market.) Because no two parcels of real estate are exactly alike, the sales prices of the comparables must be adjusted for

any features dissimilar to the subject property. The principal factors for which adjustments must be made fall into four basic categories:

1. *Sales or financing concessions.* This consideration becomes important if a sale is not financed by a standard mortgage procedure.

2. *Date of sale.* An adjustment must be made if economic changes occur between the date of sale of the comparable property and the date of the appraisal.

3. *Location.* An adjustment may be necessary to compensate for locational differences. For example, similar properties might differ in price from neighborhood to neighborhood or even between locations within the same neighborhood.

4. *Physical features and amenities.* Physical features that may require adjustments include age of building, size of lot, landscaping, construction, number of rooms, square feet of living space, interior and exterior condition, presence or absence of a garage, fireplace or air conditioner and so forth.

After a careful analysis of the differences between comparable properties and the subject property, the appraiser assigns a dollar value to each of the differences noted. On the basis of their knowledge and experience appraisers estimate dollar adjustments that reflect actual values assigned in the marketplace. The value of a feature present in the subject property but not in the comparable property is *added* to the sales price of the comparable. This presumes that, all other features being equal, a property having a feature (such as a fireplace or wet bar) not present in the comparable property will tend to have a higher market value solely because of this feature. (The feature need not be a physical amenity; it may be a locational or an aesthetic feature.) Likewise the value of a feature present in the comparable but not the subject property is *subtracted* from the sales price of the comparable. The adjusted sales prices of the comparables represent the probable value range of the subject property. From this range a single market value estimate can be selected.

The sales comparison approach is essential in almost every appraisal of real estate. It is considered the most reliable of the three approaches in appraising residential property, where the amenities (intangible benefits) may be difficult to measure otherwise. An example of the sales comparison approach is shown in Table 18.1.

The Cost Approach

The **cost approach** to value is based on the principle of substitution. Sometimes called *appraisal by summation,* it consists of these steps:

1. Estimate the value of the land as if it were vacant and available to be put to its highest and best use.

2. Estimate the current cost of constructing the building(s) and site improvements.

3. Estimate the amount of accrued depreciation resulting from physical deterioration, functional obsolescence and/or external obsolescence.

4. Deduct accrued depreciation from the estimated construction cost of new building(s) and site improvements.

5. Add the estimated land value to the depreciated cost of the building(s) and site improvements to arrive at the total property value.

Table 18.1
Sales Comparison
Approach to Value

| | Subject Property | Comparables | | | | |
		A	B	C	D	E
Sale Price		$118,000	$112,000	$121,000	$116,500	$110,000
Financing Concessions	none	none	none	none	none	none
Date of Sale		current	current	current	current	current
Location	good	same	poorer +6,500	same	same	same
Age	6 years	same	same	same	same	same
Size of Lot	60′ × 135′	same	same	larger −5,000	same	larger −5,000
Landscaping	good	same	same	same	same	same
Construction	brick	same	same	same	same	same
Style	ranch	same	same	same	same	same
No. of Rooms	6	same	same	same	same	same
No. of Bedrooms	3	same	same	same	same	same
No. of Baths	1½	same	same	same	same	same
Sq. Ft. Living Space	1500	same	same	same	same	same
Other Space (basement)	full basement	same	same	same	same	same
Condition—Exterior	average	better −1,500	poorer +1000	better −1,500	same	poorer +2,000
Condition—Interior	good	same	same	better −500	same	same
Garage	2-car attached	same	same	same	same	none +5,000
Other Improvements	none	none	none	none	none	none
Net Adjustments		−1,500	+7,500	−7,000	-0-	+2,000
Adjusted Value		$116,500	$119,500	$114,000	$116,500	$112,000

Note: Because the value range of the properties in the comparison chart (excluding comparable B) is close, and comparable D required no adjustment, an appraiser would conclude that the indicated market value of the subject is $116,500.

Land value (step 1) is estimated by using the sales comparison approach; that is, the location and site improvements (presence of utilities, sewer lines and so on) of the subject property are compared to those of similar sites nearby, and adjustments are made for significant differences.

There are two ways to look at the construction cost of a building for appraisal purposes (step 2): reproduction cost and replacement cost. **Reproduction cost** is the construction cost at current prices of a duplicate of the subject property improvements, including both the benefits and the drawbacks of the property (such as hardwood flooring in a poorly designed floor plan). **Replacement cost** is the construction cost at current prices of improvements with utility or function similar to the subject property. This approach would permit the installation of less expensive hardwood kitchen cabinets instead of more expensive but outdated enameled steel cabinets. Replacement cost is used more frequently in appraising older structures because it eliminates obsolete features and takes advantage of current construction materials and techniques.

An example of the cost approach to value is shown in Table 18.2.

Table 18.2
Cost Approach to Value

Land Valuation: Size 60′ × 135′ @$450 per front foot		= $27,000
Plus site improvements: driveway, walks, landscaping, etc.		= 8,000
Total Land Valuation		$35,000

Building Valuation: Replacement Cost
1,500 sq. ft. @ $65 per sq. ft. = $97,500

Less Depreciation:
Physical depreciation,
  curable
    (items of deferred maintenance)

exterior painting	$4,000	
incurable (structural deterioration)	9,750	
Functional obsolescence	2,000	
External obsolescence	-0-	
Total Depreciation		−15,750

Depreciated Value of Building $ 81,750
Indicated Value by Cost Approach $116,750

Determining reproduction or replacement cost. An appraiser using the cost approach computes the reproduction or replacement cost of a building using one of the following methods:

1. **Quantity survey method.** An estimate is made of the quantities of raw materials needed to replace the subject structure (lumber, plaster, brick and so on), as well as of the current price of such materials and their installation costs. These factors are added to indirect costs (building permit, survey, payroll taxes, builder's profit) to arrive at the total replacement cost of the structure. Because it is so detailed and time-consuming, this method is usually used only in appraising historical and dedicated-use properties.

2. **Unit-in-place method.** The replacement cost of a structure is estimated based on the construction cost per unit of measure of individual building components, including material, labor, overhead and builder's profit. Most components are measured in square feet, although items like plumbing fixtures are estimated by unit cost.

3. **Square foot method.** The cost per square foot of a recently built comparable structure is multiplied by the number of square feet in the subject building; this is the most common method of cost estimation. The example in Table 18.2 uses the square foot method, which is also referred to as the *comparison method*. For some properties the cost per *cubic* foot of a recently built comparable structure is multiplied by the number of cubic feet in the subject structure.

4. **Index method.** A factor representing the percentage increase to the present time of construction costs is applied to the original cost of the subject property. Because it fails to take into account individual property variables, this method is useful only as a check of the estimate reached by one of the other methods.

Depreciation. In a real estate appraisal **depreciation** (step three) refers to any condition that adversely affects the value of an *improvement* to real property. Land usually does not depreciate, except in such rare cases as misused farmland, downzoned urban parcels or improperly developed land. For appraisal purposes (as opposed to depreciation for tax purposes, which is discussed in Chapter 22), depreciation is divided into three classes according to its cause:

1. **Physical deterioration**—*curable:* repairs that are economically feasible and would result in an increase in appraised value equal to or exceeding their cost. Routine maintenance, such as painting, falls into this category.

   Physical deterioration—incurable: repairs that are not economically feasible, such as installing expensive siding to repair the cosmetic appearance of the exterior of a building whose interior structure is otherwise unsound.

2. **Functional obsolescence**—*curable:* physical or design features that are no longer considered desirable by property buyers but could be replaced or redesigned at low cost. Outmoded fixtures, such as plumbing, are usually easily replaced. Room function might be redefined at no cost if the basic room layout allows for it. A bedroom adjacent to a kitchen, for instance, may be converted to a family room.

   Functional obsolescence—incurable: Currently undesirable physical or design features that could not be remedied easily. Many older multistory industrial buildings are considered less suitable than one-story buildings. An office building that cannot be air-conditioned suffers from functional obsolescence.

3. **External** *(environmental or economic)* **obsolescence**—*incurable only:* caused by factors not on the subject property so that this type of obsolescence cannot usually be considered curable. Proximity to a nuisance, such as a polluting factory, would be an unchangeable factor that could not be expected to be cured by the owner of the subject property.

In determining a property's depreciation most appraisers use the *breakdown method,* in which depreciation is broken down into all three classes, with separate estimates for curable and incurable factors in each class. Depreciation is difficult to measure, and the older the building, the more difficult depreciation is to estimate. The easiest but least precise way to determine depreciation is the **straight-line method,** also called the *economic age-life method.* Depreciation is assumed to occur at an even rate over a structure's **economic life,** the period during which it is expected to remain useful for its original intended purpose. The property's cost is divided by the number of years of its expected economic life to derive the amount of annual depreciation.

For example, a $120,000 property may have a land value of $30,000 and an improvement value of $90,000. If the improvements are expected to last 60 years, the annual straight-line depreciation would be $1,500 ($90,000 ÷ 60 years). Such depreciation can be calculated as an annual dollar amount or as a percentage of the property's replacement cost.

Much of the functional obsolescence and all of the external obsolescence, however, can be evaluated only by considering the actions of the buyers in the marketplace.

The cost approach is most helpful in the appraisal of special-purpose buildings such as schools, churches and public buildings. Such properties are difficult to appraise using other methods because there are seldom many local sales to use as comparables, and the properties do not ordinarily generate income.

**The Income
Capitalization
Approach**

The **income capitalization approach** to value is based on the present value of the rights to future income. It assumes that the income derived from a property will control the value of that property. The income capitalization approach is used for valuation of income-producing properties—apartment buildings, office buildings, shopping centers and the like. In using the income capitalization approach to estimate value an appraiser must take the following steps:

1. Estimate annual *potential gross income,* including both rental income and income from other sources, such as concessions and vending machines.

2. Based on market experience, deduct an appropriate allowance for vacancy and collection losses to arrive at *effective gross income.*

3. Based on appropriate operating standards, deduct the annual *operating expenses* of the real estate from the effective gross income to arrive at the annual *net operating income.* Management costs are always included as operating expenses, even if the current owner also manages the property. Mortgage payments, however (including principal and interest), are debt service and *not* considered operating expenses.

4. Estimate the price a typical investor would pay for the income produced by this particular type and class of property. This is done by estimating the rate of return (or yield) that an investor will demand for the investment of capital in this type of building. This rate of return is called the **capitalization** (or "cap") **rate** and is determined by comparing the relationship of net operating income to the sales prices of similar properties that have sold in the current market. For example, a comparable property that is producing an annual net income of $15,000 is sold for $187,500. The capitalization rate is $15,000 ÷ 187,500, or eight percent. If other comparable properties sold at prices that yield substantially the same rate, the appraiser should apply an eight percent rate to the subject property.

5. Finally the capitalization rate is applied to the property's annual net income, resulting in the appraiser's estimate of the property value.

With the appropriate capitalization rate and the projected annual net operating income, the appraiser can obtain an indication of value by the income capitalization approach in the following manner:

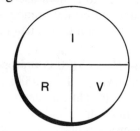

Net Operating Income ÷ Capitalization Rate = Value

Example: $18,000 income ÷ 9% cap rate = $200,000 value

This formula and its variations are important in dealing with income property.

$$\frac{\text{Income}}{\text{Rate}} = \text{Value} \qquad\qquad \frac{\text{Income}}{\text{Value}} = \text{Rate} \qquad\qquad \text{Value} \times \text{Rate} = \text{Income}$$

A very simplified version of the computations used in applying the income capitalization approach is illustrated in Table 18.3.

**Table 18.3
Income Capitalization
Approach to Value**

Potential Gross Annual Income		
Market Rent		$60,000
Income from other sources (vending machines and pay phones)		+600
		$60,600
Less vacancy and collection losses (estimated) @ 4%		−2,424
Effective Gross Income		$58,176
Expenses:		
Real estate taxes	$9,000	
Insurance	1,000	
Heat	2,800	
Maintenance	6,400	
Utilities, electricity, water, gas	800	
Repairs	1,200	
Decorating	1,400	
Replacement of equipment	800	
Legal and accounting	600	
Management	3,000	
Total Expenses		$27,000
Annual Net Operating Income		$31,176

Capitalization Rate = 10%

Capitalization of annual net income: $\dfrac{\$31,176}{.10}$

Indicated Value by Income Approach = $311,760

In Practice . . .

The most difficult step in the income capitalization approach to value is determining the appropriate capitalization rate for the property. This rate must be selected to recapture the original investment over the building's economic life, give the owner an acceptable rate of return on investment and provide for the repayment of borrowed capital. Note that an income property that carries with it a great deal of risk as an investment generally requires a higher rate of return than a property considered a safe investment.

Gross income multipliers. Certain properties, such as single-family homes and two-flat buildings, are not purchased primarily for their ability to generate income. As a substitute for a more elaborate income capitalization analysis, the **gross rent multiplier** (GRM) and **gross income multiplier** (GIM) are often used in the appraisal process. Each relates the sales price of a property to its expected income.

Because single-family residences usually produce only a rental income, the gross rent multiplier is used. This relates the sales price to *monthly* rental income. However, commercial and industrial properties generate income from many sources (rent, concessions, escalator clause income, etc.), and they are valued using their *annual* income from all sources.

The formulas are as follows:

$$\frac{\text{Sales Price}}{\text{Gross Income}} = \frac{\text{Gross Income Multiplier}}{\text{(GIM)}} \quad \text{or} \quad \frac{\text{Sales Price}}{\text{Gross Rent}} = \frac{\text{Gross Rent Multiplier}}{\text{(GRM)}}$$

For example, if a home recently sold for $82,000 and its monthly rental income was $650, the GRM for the property would be computed thus:

$$\frac{\$82,000}{\$650} = 126.2 \text{ GRM}$$

To establish an accurate GRM an appraiser should have recent sales and rental data from at least four properties similar to the subject property. The most appropriate GRM can then be applied to the estimated fair market rental of the subject property to arrive at its market value. The formula would then be:

Rental Income × GRM = Estimated Market Value

Table 18.4 shows some examples of GRM comparisons.

In Practice . . .   *Much skill is required to use multipliers accurately, because there is no fixed multiplier for all areas or all types of properties. Therefore many appraisers view the technique simply as a quick, informal way to check the validity of a property value obtained by one of the other appraisal methods.*

Reconciliation   If more than one of the three approaches to value are applied to the same property, they will normally produce different indications of value. **Reconciliation** is the art of analyzing and effectively weighing the findings from the different approaches used.

Although each approach may serve as an independent guide to value, whenever possible all three approaches should be used as a check on the final estimate of value. The process of reconciliation is more complicated than simply taking the average of the derived value estimates. An average implies that the data and logic applied in each of the approaches are equally valid and reliable and should therefore be given equal weight. In fact, however, certain approaches are more valid and reliable with some kinds of properties than with others.

For example, in appraising a home the income capitalization approach is rarely used, and the cost approach is of limited value unless the home is relatively new; therefore, the sales comparison approach is usually given greatest weight in valuing single-family residences. In the appraisal of income or investment property the income capitalization approach would normally be given the greatest weight. In the appraisal of churches, libraries, museums, schools and other special-use properties where there is little or no income or sales revenue, the cost approach

Table 18.4 Gross Rent Multiplier	Comparable No.	Sales Price	Monthly Rent	GRM
	1	$93,600	$650	144
	2	78,500	450	174
	3	95,500	675	141
	4	82,000	565	145
	Subject	?	625	?

Note: Based on an analysis of these comparisons, a GRM of 145 seems reasonable for homes in this area. In the opinion of an appraiser, then, the estimated value of the subject property would be $625 × 145, or $90,625.

would usually be assigned the greatest weight. From this analysis, or reconciliation, a single estimate of market value is produced.

The Appraisal Process

The key to an accurate appraisal lies in the methodical collection of data. The appraisal process is an orderly set of procedures used to collect and analyze data to arrive at an ultimate value conclusion. The data are divided into two basic classes:

1. *General data,* covering the nation, region, city and neighborhood. Of particular importance is the neighborhood, where an appraiser finds the physical, economic, social and political influences that directly affect the value and potential of the subject property.

2. *Specific data,* covering details of the subject property as well as comparative data relating to costs, sales and income and expenses of properties similar to and competitive with the subject property.

Figure 18.2 outlines the steps an appraiser takes in carrying out an appraisal assignment. The numbers in the following list correspond to the numbers on the flowchart.

1. *State the problem.* The kind of value to be estimated must be specified, and the valuation approach(es) most valid and reliable for the kind of property under appraisal must be selected.

2. *List the data needed and the sources.* Based on the approach(es) the appraiser will be using, the types of data needed and the sources to be consulted are listed.

3. *Gather, record and verify the necessary data.* Detailed information must be obtained concerning the economic, political and social conditions of the nation, region, city and neighborhood, and comments on the effects of these data on the subject property also must be obtained.

   Specific data about the subject site and improvements must be collected and verified.

   Depending upon the approach(es) used, comparative information relating to sales, income and expenses, and construction costs of comparable properties must be collected. All data should be verified, usually by checking the same information against two different sources. In the case of sales data, one source should be a person directly involved in the transaction.

4. *Determine highest and best use.* The appraiser analyzes market forces such as competition and current versus potential uses to determine the reasonableness of the property's present use in terms of its profitability.

5. *Estimate land value.* The features and sales prices of comparable sites are compared to the subject to determine the value of the land alone.

6. *Estimate value by each of the three approaches.* The *sales comparison, cost* and *income capitalization* approaches are used to estimate the value of the subject property.

7. *Reconcile estimated values for final value estimate.* The appraiser makes a definite statement of conclusions reached, usually in the form of a value estimate of the property.

Figure 18.2
The Appraisal Process

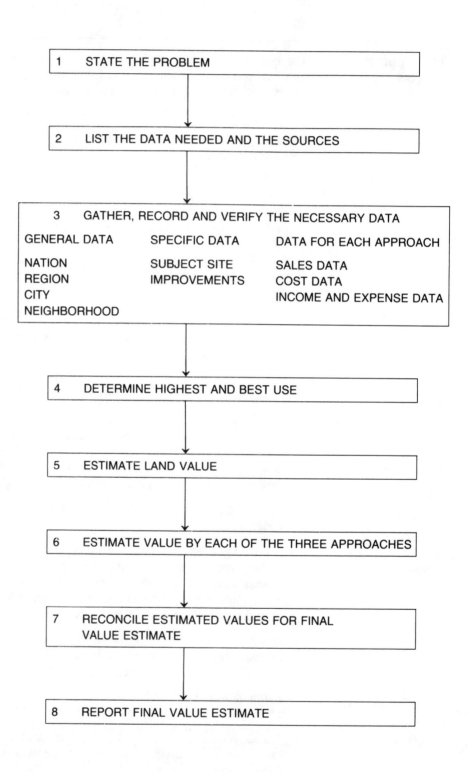

Source: *Fundamentals of Real Estate Appraisal,* Fifth Edition, by William L. Ventolo, Jr., and Martha R. Williams, p. 17, © 1990 by Dearborn Financial Publishing, Inc. Used with permission.

8. *Report final value estimate.* After the three approaches have been reconciled and an opinion of value has been reached, the appraiser prepares a formal written report for the client. The statement may be a completed *form,* a *letter* or a lengthy written *narrative.* The most complete appraisal report would contain:

a. the estimate of value and the date to which it applies;
b. the purpose for which the appraisal was made;
c. a description of the neighborhood and subject property;
d. factual data covering costs, sales and income and expenses of similar, recently sold properties;
e. an analysis and interpretation of the data collected;
f. a presentation of one or more of the three approaches to value in enough detail to support the appraiser's final value conclusion;
g. any qualifying conditions;
h. supportive material, such as charts, maps, photographs, floor plans, leases and contracts; and
i. the certification and signature of the appraiser.

Figure 18.3 is the **Uniform Residential Appraisal Report** form required by many governmental agencies. Note that, even in such a brief report, detailed descriptions of the neighborhood and property being appraised are required.

Key Terms

anticipation	income capitalization approach
appraisal	index method
assemblage	physical deterioration
balance	plottage
capitalization	progression
capitalization rate	quantity survey method
change	reconciliation
competition	regression
conformity	replacement cost
contribution	reproduction cost
cost approach	sales comparison approach
depreciation	square foot method
economic life	straight-line method
external obsolescence	substitution
functional obsolescence	supply and demand
gross income multiplier (GIM)	Uniform Residential Appraisal Report (URAR)
gross rent multiplier (GRM)	unit-in-place method
highest and best use	value

Summary

To appraise real estate means to estimate its value. Although there are many types of value, the most common objective of an appraisal is to estimate market value—the most probable sales price of a property. Basic to appraising are certain underlying economic principles, such as highest and best use, substitution, supply and demand, conformity, anticipation, increasing and diminishing returns, balance, regression, progression, plottage, contribution, competition and change.

A professional appraiser analyzes a property through three approaches to value. In the sales comparison approach the value of the subject property is compared

Figure 18.3
Residential Appraisal
Report

Property Description & Analysis   **UNIFORM RESIDENTIAL APPRAISAL REPORT**   File No.

SUBJECT				
Property Address		Census Tract		LENDER DISCRETIONARY USE
City	County	State	Zip Code	Sale Price $
Legal Description				Date
Owner/Occupant		Map Reference		Mortgage Amount $
Sale Price $	Date of Sale	PROPERTY RIGHTS APPRAISED		Mortgage Type
Loan charges/concessions to be paid by seller $		☐ Fee Simple		Discount Points and Other Concessions
R.E. Taxes $	Tax Year	HOA $/Mo.	☐ Leasehold	Paid by Seller $
Lender/Client			☐ Condominium (HUD/VA)	
			☐ De Minimis PUD	Source

NEIGHBORHOOD					
LOCATION	☐ Urban	☐ Suburban	☐ Rural	NEIGHBORHOOD ANALYSIS	Good Avg. Fair Poor
BUILT UP	☐ Over 75%	☐ 25-75%	☐ Under 25%	Employment Stability	☐ ☐ ☐ ☐
GROWTH RATE	☐ Rapid	☐ Stable	☐ Slow	Convenience to Employment	☐ ☐ ☐ ☐
PROPERTY VALUES	☐ Increasing	☐ Stable	☐ Declining	Convenience to Shopping	☐ ☐ ☐ ☐
DEMAND/SUPPLY	☐ Shortage	☐ In Balance	☐ Over Supply	Convenience to Schools	☐ ☐ ☐ ☐
MARKETING TIME	☐ Under 3 Mos.	☐ 3-6 Mos.	☐ Over 6 Mos.	Adequacy of Public Transportation	☐ ☐ ☐ ☐

PRESENT LAND USE %	LAND USE CHANGE	PREDOMINANT	SINGLE FAMILY HOUSING		
			PRICE $ (000)	AGE (yrs)	
Single Family	Not Likely	OCCUPANCY			Recreation Facilities	☐ ☐ ☐ ☐
2-4 Family	Likely ☐	Owner ☐			Adequacy of Utilities	☐ ☐ ☐ ☐
Multi-family	In process ☐	Tenant ☐	Low		Property Compatibility	☐ ☐ ☐ ☐
Commercial	To:	Vacant (0-5%) ☐	High		Protection from Detrimental Cond.	☐ ☐ ☐ ☐
Industrial		Vacant (over 5%) ☐	Predominant		Police & Fire Protection	☐ ☐ ☐ ☐
Vacant			—		General Appearance of Properties	☐ ☐ ☐ ☐
					Appeal to Market	☐ ☐ ☐ ☐

Note: Race or the racial composition of the neighborhood are not considered reliable appraisal factors.
COMMENTS: _____

SITE						
Dimensions				Topography		
Site Area		Corner Lot		Size		
Zoning Classification		Zoning Compliance		Shape		
HIGHEST & BEST USE: Present Use		Other Use		Drainage		
UTILITIES	Public Other	SITE IMPROVEMENTS Type	Public Private	View		
Electricity	☐	Street	☐ ☐	Landscaping		
Gas	☐	Curb/Gutter	☐ ☐	Driveway		
Water	☐	Sidewalk	☐ ☐	Apparent Easements		
Sanitary Sewer	☐	Street Lights	☐ ☐	FEMA Flood Hazard	Yes* ___ No ___	
Storm Sewer	☐	Alley	☐ ☐	FEMA* Map/Zone		

COMMENTS (Apparent adverse easements, encroachments, special assessments, slide areas, etc.): _____

IMPROVEMENTS				
GENERAL DESCRIPTION	EXTERIOR DESCRIPTION	FOUNDATION	BASEMENT	INSULATION
Units	Foundation	Slab	Area Sq. Ft.	Roof ☐
Stories	Exterior Walls	Crawl Space	% Finished	Ceiling ☐
Type (Det./Att.)	Roof Surface	Basement	Ceiling	Walls ☐
Design (Style)	Gutters & Dwnspts.	Sump Pump	Walls	Floor ☐
Existing	Window Type	Dampness	Floor	None ☐
Proposed	Storm Sash	Settlement	Outside Entry	Adequacy ☐
Under Construction	Screens	Infestation		Energy Efficient Items:
Age (Yrs.)	Manufactured House			
Effective Age (Yrs.)				

ROOM LIST												
ROOMS	Foyer	Living	Dining	Kitchen	Den	Family Rm.	Rec. Rm.	Bedrooms	# Baths	Laundry	Other	Area Sq. Ft.
Basement												
Level 1												
Level 2												

Finished area above grade contains: _____ Rooms; _____ Bedroom(s); _____ Bath(s); _____ Square Feet of Gross Living Area

Figure 18.3
(continued)

INTERIOR	SURFACES	Materials/Condition	HEATING		KITCHEN EQUIP.		ATTIC		IMPROVEMENT ANALYSIS	Good	Avg.	Fair	Poor
	Floors		Type		Refrigerator	☐	None	☐	Quality of Construction	☐	☐	☐	☐
	Walls		Fuel		Range/Oven	☐	Stairs	☐	Condition of Improvements	☐	☐	☐	☐
	Trim/Finish		Condition		Disposal	☐	Drop Stair	☐	Room Sizes/Layout	☐	☐	☐	☐
	Bath Floor		Adequacy		Dishwasher	☐	Scuttle	☐	Closets and Storage	☐	☐	☐	☐
	Bath Wainscot		COOLING		Fan/Hood	☐	Floor	☐	Energy Efficiency	☐	☐	☐	☐
	Doors		Central		Compactor	☐	Heated	☐	Plumbing-Adequacy & Condition	☐	☐	☐	☐
			Other		Washer/Dryer	☐	Finished	☐	Electrical-Adequacy & Condition	☐	☐	☐	☐
			Condition		Microwave	☐			Kitchen Cabinets-Adequacy & Cond.	☐	☐	☐	☐
	Fireplace(s) #		Adequacy		Intercom	☐			Compatibility to Neighborhood	☐	☐	☐	☐

CAR STORAGE: Garage ☐   Attached ☐   Adequate   House Entry   Appeal & Marketability ☐ ☐ ☐ ☐
No. Cars   Carport ☐   Detached ☐   Inadequate   Outside Entry   Estimated Remaining Economic Life _____ Yrs.
Condition   None ☐   Built-In ☐   Electric Door   Basement Entry   Estimated Remaining Physical Life _____ Yrs.

Additional features: _____

Depreciation (Physical, functional and external inadequacies, repairs needed, modernization, etc.): _____

General market conditions and prevalence and impact in subject/market area regarding loan discounts, interest buydowns and concessions: _____

Freddie Mac Form 70 10/86 **12Ch.** **AH**   Forms and Worms Inc.,° 315 Whitney Ave., New Haven, CT 06511 1(800) 243-4545   Item #111710   Fannie Mae Form 1004 10/86

Valuation Section   **UNIFORM RESIDENTIAL APPRAISAL REPORT**   **File No.**

Purpose of Appraisal is to estimate Market Value as defined in the Certification & Statement of Limiting Conditions.

COST APPROACH

BUILDING SKETCH (SHOW GROSS LIVING AREA ABOVE GRADE)
If for Freddie Mac or Fannie Mae, show only square foot calculations and cost approach comments in this space.

ESTIMATED REPRODUCTION COST – NEW – OF IMPROVEMENTS:

Dwelling _____ Sq. Ft. @ $ _____ = $ _____
_____ Sq. Ft. @ $ _____ = _____
Extras _____ = _____
_____ = _____
Special Energy Efficient Items _____ = _____
Porches, Patios, etc. _____ = _____
Garage/Carport _____ Sq. Ft. @ $ _____ = _____
Total Estimated Cost New .... = $ _____

	Physical	Functional	External
Less			

Depreciation _____ = $ _____
Depreciated Value of Improvements .... = $ _____
Site Imp. "as is" (driveway, landscaping, etc.) = $ _____
ESTIMATED SITE VALUE .... = $ _____
(If leasehold, show only leasehold value.)
INDICATED VALUE BY COST APPROACH .... = $ _____

(Not Required by Freddie Mac and Fannie Mae)
Does property conform to applicable HUD/VA property standards? ☐ Yes ☐ No
If No, explain: _____

Construction Warranty ☐ Yes ☐ No
Name of Warranty Program _____
Warranty Coverage Expires _____

The undersigned has recited three recent sales of properties most similar and proximate to subject and has considered these in the market analysis. The description includes a dollar adjustment, reflecting market reaction to those items of significant variation between the subject and comparable properties. If a significant item in the comparable property is superior to, or more favorable than, the subject property, a minus (−) adjustment is made, thus reducing the indicated value of subject; if a significant item in the comparable is inferior to, or less favorable than, the subject property, a plus (+) adjustment is made, thus increasing the indicated value of the subject.

Figure 18.3
(continued)

SALES COMPARISON ANALYSIS

ITEM	SUBJECT	COMPARABLE NO. 1		COMPARABLE NO. 2		COMPARABLE NO. 3	
Address							
Proximity to Subject							
Sales Price	$		$		$		$
Price/Gross Liv. Area	$ ☐	$ ☐		$ ☐		$ ☐	
Data Source							
VALUE ADJUSTMENTS	DESCRIPTION	DESCRIPTION	+ (-) $ Adjustment	DESCRIPTION	+ (-) $ Adjustment	DESCRIPTION	+ (-) $ Adjustment
Sales or Financing Concessions							
Date of Sale/Time							
Location							
Site/View							
Design and Appeal							
Quality of Construction							
Age							
Condition							
Above Grade Room Count	Total Bdrms Baths	Total Bdrms Baths		Total Bdrms Baths		Total Bdrms Baths	
Gross Living Area	Sq. Ft.	Sq. Ft.		Sq. Ft.		Sq. Ft.	
Basement & Finished Rooms Below Grade							
Functional Utility							
Heating/Cooling							
Garage/Carport							
Porches, Patio, Pools, etc.							
Special Energy Efficient Items							
Fireplace(s)							
Other (e.g. kitchen equip., remodeling)							
Net Adj. (total)		☐ + ☐ –	$	☐ + ☐ –	$	☐ + ☐ –	$
Indicated Value of Subject			$		$		$

Comments on Sales Comparison: ______

INDICATED VALUE BY SALES COMPARISON APPROACH .... $ ______
INDICATED VALUE BY INCOME APPROACH (If Applicable) Estimated Market Rent $ ______ /Mo. x Gross Rent Multiplier ______ = $ ______

RECONCILIATION

This appraisal is made ☐ "as is" ☐ subject to the repairs, alterations, inspections or conditions listed below ☐ completion per plans and specifications.

Comments and Conditions of Appraisal: ______

Final Reconciliation: ______

This appraisal is based upon the above requirements, the certification, contingent and limiting conditions, and Market Value definition that are stated in

☐ FmHA, HUD &/or VA instructions.

☐ Freddie Mac Form 439 (Rev. 7/86)/Fannie Mae Form 1004B (Rev. 7/86) filed with client ______ 19 ___ ☐ attached.

I (WE) ESTIMATE THE MARKET VALUE, AS DEFINED, OF THE SUBJECT PROPERTY AS OF ______ **19** ___ **to be $** ______

I (We) certify: that to the best of my (our) knowledge and belief the facts and data used herein are true and correct; that I (we) personally inspected the subject property, both inside and out, and have made an exterior inspection of all comparable sales cited in this report; and that I (we) have no undisclosed interest, present or prospective therein.

Appraiser(s) SIGNATURE ______ Review Appraiser SIGNATURE ______ ☐ Did ☐ Did Not
NAME ______ (if applicable) NAME ______ Inspect Property

Freddie Mac Form 70 10/86 **12Ch.** **Forms and Worms Inc.,® 315 Whitney Ave., New Haven, CT 06511 1(800) 243-4545** Fannie Mae Form 1004 10/86

with the values of others like it that have sold recently. Because no two properties are exactly alike, adjustments must be made to account for any differences. With the cost approach an appraiser calculates the cost of building a similar structure on a similar site. The appraiser then subtracts depreciation (loss in value), which reflects the differences between new properties of this type and present condition of the subject property. The income capitalization approach is an analysis based on the relationship between the rate of return that an investor requires and the net income that a property produces.

A special, informal version of the income approach, called the gross rent multiplier (GRM), is often used to estimate the value of single-family residential properties that are not usually rented but could be. The GRM is computed by dividing the sales price of a property by its gross monthly rent. For commercial or industrial property a gross income multiplier (GIM), based on annual income from all sources, may be used.

Normally the application of the different approaches will result in as many different estimates of value. In the process of reconciliation the validity and reliability of each approach are weighed objectively to arrive at the single best and most supportable conclusion of value.

Questions

1. Which of the following makes use of a rate of investment return?
   a. Sales comparison approach
   b. Cost approach
   c. Income capitalization approach
   d. Gross income multiplier method

2. The elements of value include which of the following?
   a. Competition   c. Anticipation
   b. Scarcity   d. Balance

3. The principle of value that states that two adjacent parcels of land combined into one larger parcel could have a greater value than the two parcels valued separately is called:
   a. substitution.   c. regression.
   b. plottage.   d. progression.

4. The amount of money a property commands in the marketplace is its:
   a. intrinsic value.
   b. market value.
   c. capitalization rate.
   d. a gross-income multiplier.

5. H has his "dream house" constructed for $100,000 in an area where most newly constructed houses are not as well equipped as his and typically sell for only $80,000. The value of H' house is likely to be affected by the principle of:
   a. progression.   c. change.
   b. assemblage.   d. regression.

6. In Question 5 the owners of the lesser-valued houses in H' immediate area may be affected by the principle of:
   a. progression.   c. competition.
   b. increasing returns. d. regression.

7. Accrued depreciation for appraisal purposes is not caused by which of the following?
   a. Functional obsolescence
   b. Physical deterioration
   c. External obsolescence
   d. Accelerated depreciation

8. *Reconciliation* refers to which of the following?
   a. Loss of value due to any cause
   b. Separating the value of the land from the total value of the property to compute depreciation
   c. Analyzing the results obtained by the different approaches to value to determine a final estimate of value
   d. The process by which an appraiser determines the highest and best use for a parcel of land.

9. One method an appraiser can use to determine a building's reproduction cost involves the estimated cost of the raw materials needed to build the structure, plus labor and indirect costs. This is called the:
   a. square foot method.
   b. quantity survey method.
   c. cubic foot method.
   d. unit-in-place method.

10. If a property's annual net income is $24,000 and it is valued at $300,000, what is its capitalization rate?
    a. 12.5 percent   c. 15 percent
    b. 10.5 percent   d. 8 percent

11. Certain figures must be determined by an appraiser before value can be computed by the income capitalization approach. Which one of the following is *not* required for this process?
    a. Annual net operating income
    b. Capitalization rate
    c. Accrued depreciation
    d. Annual gross income

12. The income capitalization approach would be given the most weight in the valuation of a(n):
    a. single-family residence.
    b. industrial property.
    c. strip shopping center.
    d. school.

13. The market value of a parcel of real estate is:
   a. an estimate of its future benefits.
   b. the amount of money paid for the property.
   c. an estimate of the most probable price it should bring.
   d. its value without improvements.

14. Capitalization is the process by which annual net operating income is used to:
   a. determine cost.
   b. estimate value.
   c. establish depreciation.
   d. determine potential tax value.

15. From the reproduction or replacement cost of a building the appraiser deducts depreciation, which represents:
   a. the remaining economic life of the building.
   b. remodeling costs to increase rentals.
   c. loss of value due to any cause.
   d. costs to modernize the building.

16. In the sales comparison approach to value the probable sales price of a building may be estimated by:
   a. capitalizing net operating income.
   b. considering sales of similar properties.
   c. deducting accrued depreciation.
   d. determining construction cost.

17. Which of the following factors would *not* be important in comparing properties under the sales comparison approach to value?
   a. Difference in dates of sale
   b. Difference in financing terms
   c. Difference in appearance and condition
   d. Difference in original cost

18. In the income capitalization approach to value:
   a. the reproduction or replacement cost of the building must be computed.
   b. the capitalization rate must be estimated.
   c. depreciation must be determined.
   d. sales of similar properties must be considered.

19. In the cost approach to value it is necessary to:
   a. determine a dollar value for depreciation.
   b. estimate future expenses and operating costs.
   c. check sales prices of recently sold homes in the area.
   d. reconcile differing value estimates.

20. The appraised value of a residence with four bedrooms and one bathroom would probably be reduced because of:
   a. external obsolescence.
   b. functional obsolescence.
   c. physical deterioration—curable.
   d. physical deterioration—incurable.

21. A factor representing the percentage increase in construction costs over time is used in the:
   a. square foot method.
   b. quantity survey method.
   c. unit-in-place method.
   d. index method.

19

Control of Land Use

Land use is controlled through public land-use controls, private land-use controls (deed restrictions) and public ownership of land.

Public Controls

The police power of the states, introduced in Chapter 6, is the inherent authority to create regulations necessary to protect the public health, safety and welfare. The states, in turn, allow counties, cities and towns to make regulations in keeping with general laws. The largely urban population and the increasing demands placed on finite natural resources have made it necessary for cities, towns and villages to increase their limitations on the private use of real estate. There are now controls over noise, air and water pollution as well as population density.

Privately owned real estate is regulated through:

1. planning;
2. zoning;
3. subdivision regulations;
4. codes that regulate building construction; and
5. environmental protection legislation.

The Master Plan

Local governments recognize development goals primarily through the formulation of a comprehensive **master plan,** also commonly referred to as a *general plan*. Cities and counties develop master plans to ensure that social and economic needs are balanced against environmental and aesthetic concerns.

The master plan is both a statement of policies and a presentation of how those policies can be implemented. As created by the city, county or regional *planning commission,* a typical master plan provides for:

• *land use,* including standards of population density and economic development;

• *public facilities,* including schools, civic centers and utilities;

• *circulation,* including public transportation and highways;

• *conservation* of natural resources; and

• *noise regulation*

Economic and physical surveys both are essential in preparing a master plan. Countywide plans also must coordinate numerous civic plans and developments to ensure orderly city growth with stabilized property values.

City plans are put into effect through enactment and enforcement of zoning ordinances.

Zoning

Zoning ordinances are local laws that regulate and control the use of land and structures within designated zones. Zoning regulates and affects such things as use of the land, lot sizes, types of structures permitted, building heights, setbacks (the minimum distance from streets or sidewalks that structures may be built) and density (the ratio of land area to structure area or population). The purpose of zoning is to implement a local master plan.

Zoning powers are conferred on municipal governments by state **enabling acts.** There are no nationwide zoning ordinances; zoning tends to be local in nature. State and federal governments may, however, regulate land use through special legislation, such as scenic easement and coastal management laws.

Zoning ordinances generally divide land use into residential, commercial, industrial, agricultural and special-purpose classifications. A use now included by many communities is *cluster zoning,* or *multiple-use zoning,* which permits planned unit developments.

To ensure adequate control, land-use areas are further divided into subclasses. For example, residential areas may be subdivided to provide for detached single-family dwellings, semidetached structures containing not more than four units, walk-up apartments, high-rise apartments and so forth. In addition, some communities require the use of **buffer zones**—such as landscaped parks and playgrounds—to separate and screen residential areas from nonresidential areas.

Adoption of zoning ordinances. Today almost all cities with populations in excess of 10,000 have enacted comprehensive zoning ordinances governing the utilization of land located *within corporate limits.* Many states have enacted legislation that provides that the use of land located *within one to three miles* of an incorporated area must receive the approval and consent of the incorporated area, even if the property is not adjacent to the village, town or city.

Zoning ordinances must not violate the rights of individuals and property holders (as provided under the due process provisions of the Fourteenth Amendment of the U.S. Constitution) or the various provisions of the state constitution of the state in which the real estate is located. If the means used to regulate the use of property are destructive, unreasonable, arbitrary or confiscatory, the legislation is usually considered void. *Tests* commonly applied in determining the validity of ordinances require that:

1. the power be exercised in a reasonable manner;

2. the provisions be clear and specific;

3. the ordinance be free from discrimination;

4. the ordinance promote public health, safety and general welfare under the police power concept; and

5. the ordinance apply to all property in a similar manner.

When land is taken for public use by the government's power of eminent domain, the owner must receive compensation. When *downzoning* occurs in an area—for instance, when land zoned for residential construction is rezoned for conservation or recreational purposes only—the state is ordinarily not responsible for compensating property owners for any resulting loss of value. However, if the courts find that a "taking" has occurred, then the downzoning will be held to be an unconstitutional attempt to use the power of eminent domain without providing fair compensation to the property owner.

Zoning laws are generally enforced through local requirements that building permits be obtained before property owners can build on their land. A permit will not be issued unless a proposed structure conforms to the permitted zoning, among other requirements.

Nonconforming use. In the enforcement of a zoning ordinance a frequent problem is the situation in which an improvement does not conform to the zoning use because it was erected prior to the enactment of the zoning law. This problem is most common in the case of sign ordinances. Such **nonconforming uses** may be allowed to continue for a specific number of years or until the improvements are destroyed or torn down, the current use is discontinued or the ownership of the property is transferred. If the nonconforming use is allowed to continue indefinitely, it is considered to be "grandfathered" into the new zoning.

Zoning boards of appeal. Zoning appeal boards have been established in most communities for the specific purpose of hearing complaints about the effects of zoning ordinances on specific parcels of property. Petitions may be presented to the appeal board for variances or exceptions in the zoning law.

Variances and conditional-use permits. Each time a plan is created or a zoning ordinance enacted, some owners are inconvenienced and want to change the use of a property. Generally such owners may appeal for either a **conditional-use permit** or a variance to allow a use that does not meet zoning requirements.

A **conditional-use permit** is usually granted to a property owner to allow a special use that is in the public interest, such as a church in a residential district. A **variance** may be sought to provide a deviation from an ordinance. For example, if an owner's lot is level next to a road but slopes steeply 30 feet away from the road, the zoning board may be willing to allow a variance so the owner can build closer to the road than the setback allows.

In addition, a property owner can change the zoning classification of a parcel of real estate by obtaining an *amendment* to the official *zoning map,* which is part of the original zoning ordinance for the area. The proposed amendment must be brought before a public hearing on the matter and approved by the governing body of the community.

When local officials fail to grant the desired relief from zoning regulations, the dissatisfied property owner can appeal to the courts.

Subdivision Regulations

Most communities have adopted subdivision regulations, often as part of a master plan. Subdivision regulations usually provide for:

1. location, grading, alignment, surfacing and widths of streets, highways and other rights-of-way;

2. installation of sewers and water mains;

3. minimum dimensions of lots and length of blocks;

4. building and setback lines;

5. areas to be reserved or dedicated for public use, such as parks or schools; and

6. easements for public utilities.

Subdivision regulations, like all other forms of zoning or building regulations, cannot be static. They must remain flexible to meet the ever-changing needs of society.

Building Codes

Most cities and towns have enacted ordinances to *specify construction standards* that must be met when repairing or erecting buildings. These are called **building codes,** and they set the requirements for kinds of materials, sanitary equipment, electrical wiring, fire prevention standards and the like.

Most communities require a property owner who wishes to build a structure or alter or repair an existing building within the municipality's corporate limits to obtain a **building permit** from the city clerk or other official. Through the permit requirement city officials are made aware of new construction or alterations and can verify compliance with building codes and zoning ordinances by examining the plans and inspecting the work. Once the completed structure has been inspected and found satisfactory, the city inspector issues a *certificate of occupancy*.

If the construction of a building or an alteration violates a deed restriction, the issuance of a building permit will *not* cure this violation. A building permit is merely evidence of the applicant's compliance with municipal regulations.

In Practice . . .

The subject of city planning, zoning and restriction of the use of real estate is extremely technical, and the interpretation of the law is not altogether clear. Questions concerning any of these subjects in relation to real estate transactions should be referred to legal counsel.

Environmental Protection Legislation

Federal and state legislators have passed a number of environmental protection laws in an attempt to respond to the growing public concern over the improvement and preservation of America's natural resources.

The various states have responded to the environmental issue by passing a variety of localized environmental protection laws regarding all forms of pollution—air, water, noise and solid waste disposal. For example, many states have enacted laws that prevent builders or private individuals from constructing septic tanks or other effluent-disposal systems in certain areas, particularly where public bodies of water—streams, lakes and rivers—are affected.

In addition to the states and federal government, cities and counties also frequently pass environmental legislation.

Private Land-Use Controls

When real estate is conveyed, its owner can include in the deed a deed restriction limiting the use of the property.

There is a distinction between restrictions on the grantee's right to *sell* and re-strictions on the grantee's right to *use*. In general a deed conveying a fee sim-ple estate may not restrict the grantee's right to sell, mortgage or convey it. Such restrictions attempt to limit the basic principle of the *free alienation (transfer) of property;* the courts consider them against public policy and therefore void and unenforceable.

A subdivider may establish restrictions on the right to *use* land through a **covenant** in a deed or by reference to a separate recorded declaration. When a lot in that subdivision is conveyed by an owner's deed, the deed refers to the plat or decla-ration of restrictions and incorporates these restrictions as limitations on the ti-tle conveyed by the deed. In this manner the restrictive covenants are included in the deed by reference and become binding on all grantees. Such covenants or restrictions usually relate to the type of building, the use to which the land may be put and the type of construction, height, setbacks and square footage.

These use restrictions are usually valid if they are reasonable restraints that bene-fit all property owners in the subdivision. If, however, such restrictions are too broad in their terms, they prevent the free transfer of property. If they are ''re-pugnant'' to the estate granted, such restrictions will probably not be enforce-able. If restrictive covenant or condition is considered ineffective by a court, the estate will then stand free from the invalid covenant or condition.

Deed restrictions may restrict an owner's use more severely than a zoning ordi-nance. The more restrictive of the two takes precedence.

Subdivision restrictions give each lot owner the right to apply to the court for an *injunction* to prevent a neighboring lot owner from violating the recorded re-strictions. If granted, the court injunction will direct the violator to stop or re-move the violation upon penalty of being in contempt of court. The court retains the power to punish the violator for failure to obey the court order. If adjoining lot owners stand idly by while a violation is being committed, they can *lose the right* to the court's injunction by their inaction; the court might claim their right was lost through **laches,** that is, loss of a right through undue delay or failure to assert it.

Conditions in a deed are different from restrictions or covenants. A grantor's deed of conveyance of land can be subject to certain stated conditions whereby the grantee's title may return to the grantor. For example, a seller conveys a lot to a buyer through a deed that includes a condition forbidding the sale, manufacture or giving away of intoxicating liquor on the lot. In case of violation the grantor has a right of reentry, that is, the right to retake possession of the property. If the grantee operates a tavern on the lot, the grantor can file suit and obtain title to the property.

| **Direct Public Ownership** | Over the years the government's general policy has been to encourage private own-ership of land. The government must, however, own a certain amount of land for such uses as municipal buildings, state legislative houses, schools and mili-tary stations. Such direct public ownership is a means of land control. |

There are other examples of necessary public ownership. Urban renewal efforts, especially government-owned housing, are one way that public ownership serves the public interest. Publicly owned streets and highways serve a necessary function for the entire population. In addition, public land is often used for such recreational purposes as parks. National and state parks and forest preserves create areas for public use and recreation and at the same time help to conserve our natural resources.

At present the federal government owns approximately 775 million acres of land, nearly one-third of the total area of the United States. At times the federal government has held title to as much as 80 percent of the nation's total land area.

Key Terms

buffer zone
building code
building permit
conditional-use permit
covenant
enabling acts

laches
master plan
nonconforming use
variance
zoning ordinances

Summary

The control of land use is exercised through public controls, private (or nongovernment) controls and direct public ownership of land.

Public controls are ordinances based on the states' police powers to protect the public health, safety and welfare. Through power conferred by state enabling acts local governments enact comprehensive master plans.

Zoning ordinances carrying out the provisions of the master plan segregate residential areas from business and industrial zones and control not only land use but also height and bulk of buildings and density of populations. Zoning enforcement problems involve boards of appeal, conditional-use permits, variances and exceptions, as well as nonconforming uses. Subdivision regulations are required to maintain control of the development of expanding community areas so that growth will be harmonious with community standards.

Building codes specify standards for construction, plumbing, sewers, electrical wiring and equipment.

In addition to land-use control on the local level the state and federal governments have occasionally intervened when necessary to preserve natural resources through environmental legislation.

Private controls are exercised by owners, generally subdividers, who control use of subdivision lots through carefully planned deed restrictions that apply to all lot owners. The usual recorded restrictions may be enforced by adjoining lot owners' obtaining a court injunction to stop a violator. Conditions are imposed by grantors, and their violation may allow the grantors or their heirs the right of reentry.

Public ownership is a means of land-use control that provides land for such public benefits as parks, highways, schools and municipal buildings.

Questions

1. A provision in a subdivision declaration used to force the grantee to live up to the terms under which he or she holds title is a:
   a. deed restriction.
   b. reverter.
   c. laches.
   d. conditional-use clause.

2. If a land owner wants to use property in a manner that is prohibited by a local zoning ordinance but would be of benefit to the community, the property owner can ask for which of the following?
   a. Variance
   b. Downzoning
   c. Conditional-use permit
   d. Dezoning

3. Public land-use controls include all of the following *except:*
   a. subdivision regulations.
   b. deed restrictions.
   c. environmental protection laws.
   d. master plan specifications.

4. The police power allows regulation of all of the following *except:*
   a. the number of buildings.
   b. the size of buildings.
   c. building ownership.
   d. building occupancy.

5. The purpose of a building permit is to:
   a. override a deed restriction.
   b. maintain municipal control over the volume of building.
   c. provide evidence of compliance with municipal regulations.
   d. show compliance with deed restrictions.

6. The goals of a city planning commission include all of the following *except:*
   a. formulation of policy.
   b. determination of land uses.
   c. conservation of natural resources.
   d. education of the public.

7. The grantor of a deed may place effective restrictions on:
   a. the right to sell the land.
   b. the use of the land.
   c. who the next purchaser will be.
   d. who may occupy the property.

8. Zoning powers are conferred on municipal governments:
   a. by state enabling acts.
   b. through police power.
   c. by eminent domain.
   d. through escheat.

9. Zoning boards of appeal are established to hear complaints about:
   a. restrictive covenants.
   b. the effects of a zoning ordinance.
   c. building codes.
   d. the effects of public ownership.

10. A new zoning code is enacted. A building that is permitted to continue in its former use even though that use does not conform to a new zoning ordinance is an example of:
    a. a nonconforming use.
    b. a variance.
    c. a special use.
    d. inverse condemnation.

11. To determine whether or not a location can be put to future use as a retail store one would examine the:
    a. building code.
    b. list of permitted nonconforming uses.
    c. housing code.
    d. zoning code.

12. Which of the following would probably *not* be included in a list of deed restrictions?
    a. Types of buildings that may be constructed
    b. Allowable ethnic origins of purchasers
    c. Activities that are not to be conducted at the site
    d. Minimum size of buildings to be constructed

13. A restriction in a seller's deed may be enforced by which of the following?
    a. Court injunction
    b. Zoning board of appeal
    c. City building commission
    d. State legislature

20

Property Development and Subdivision

Land Development	Land in large tracts must receive special attention before it can be converted into sites for homes, stores or other uses. As cities grow, additional land is required for their expansion. For such new areas to develop soundly the services of competent subdividers and land developers are required. A **subdivider** buys undeveloped acreage and divides it into smaller lots for sale to individuals or developers or for the subdivider's own use. A **developer** (who may also be a subdivider) builds homes or other buildings on the lots and sells them. Developing is generally a much more extensive activity than subdividing.
Regulation of Land Development	There is *no uniform planning and land development legislation that affects the entire country*. Laws governing subdividing and land planning are controlled by the state and local governing bodies where the land is located. Rules and regulations developed by governmental agencies have, however, provided certain minimum standards that serve as usable guides. Local regulations are by no means uniform throughout the country but reflect customs and local climate, health and hazard conditions. Many local governments have established standards for subdividers of land under their jurisdiction that are higher than the minimum standards.
	Although the recording of a plat of subdivision of land prior to public sale for residential or commercial use is usually required, land planning precedes the actual subdividing process. The land development plan must comply with the overall *master plan* adopted by the county, city, village or town. The basic city plan and zoning requirements are not inflexible, but long, expensive and frequently complicated hearings are usually required before alterations can be authorized. Approval of the subdivision plat is, however, a necessary step before recording.
	As discussed in Chapter 19, most villages, cities and other areas incorporated under state laws have *planning commissions*. Depending on how the particular group was organized, such committees or commissions may have only advisory status to the aldermen or trustees of the community. In other instances the commission has the authority to approve or disapprove plans. Communities establish strict criteria before approving new subdivisions. Frequently required are *dedication* of land for streets, schools and parks; assurance by *bonding* that sewer and street costs will be paid or such improvements will be completed before construction begins; and *compliance with zoning ordinances* governing use and lot size, along with fire and safety ordinances.

Because of the fear that they may pollute streams, rivers, lakes and underground water sources, septic systems are no longer authorized in most areas, and an approved sewage-disposal arrangement must be included in a land development plan. The shortage of water has caused great concern, and local authorities usually require land planners to submit information on how they intend to satisfy sewage-disposal and water-supply requirements. Development and/or septic tank installation may first require a *percolation test* of the soil's absorption and drainage capacities. Frequently a planner will also have to submit an *environmental impact report.*

Subdivision

The process of **subdivision** normally involves three distinct stages of development: the initial planning stage, the final planning stage and the disposition, or start-up.

During the *initial planning stage* the subdivider seeks out raw land in a suitable area. Once the land is located, the property is analyzed for its highest and best use, and preliminary subdivision plans are drawn up accordingly. As previously discussed, close contact is initiated between the subdivider and local planning and zoning officials. If the project requires zoning variances, negotiations begin along these lines. The subdivider also locates financial backers and initiates marketing strategies.

The *final planning stage* is basically a follow-up of the initial stage. Final plans are prepared, approval is sought from local officials, permanent financing is obtained, the land is purchased, final budgets are prepared and marketing programs are designed.

The *disposition,* or *start-up,* carries the subdividing process to a conclusion. Subdivision plans are recorded with local officials, and streets, sewers and utilities are installed. Buildings, open parks and recreational areas are constructed and landscaped if they are part of the subdivision plan. Marketing programs are then initiated, and title to the individual parcels of subdivided land is transferred as the lots are sold.

Subdivision Plans

In plotting out a subdivision according to local planning and zoning controls a subdivider usually determines the size as well as the location of the individual lots. The size of the lots, both in front footage and in depth, together with the total amount of square footage is generally regulated by local ordinances and must be considered carefully. Frequently ordinances regulate both the minimum and the maximum size of a lot.

The land itself must be studied, usually in cooperation with a surveyor, so that the subdivision can be laid out with consideration of natural drainage and land contours. A subdivider should provide for *utility easements* as well as easements for water and sewer mains.

Most subdivisions are laid out by use of *lots and blocks.* An area of land is designated as a block, and the area making up this block is divided into lots.

Although subdividers customarily designate areas reserved for schools, parks and future church sites, this is usually not considered good practice. Once a subdivision has been recorded, the purchasers of the lots have a vested interest in those areas reserved for schools, parks and churches. If for any reason in the future any such purpose is not appropriate, it will become difficult for the developer to abandon the original plan and use that property for residential purposes. To get around this situation many developers designate such areas as *out-lot A, out-lot B* and so forth. Such a designation does not vest any rights in these out-lots in the purchasers of the homesites. If one of these areas is to be used for church purposes, it can be so conveyed and so used. If, on the other hand, the out-lot is not to be used for such a purpose, it can be resubdivided into residential properties without the burden of securing the consent of the lot owners in the area.

Plat of subdivision. The subdivider's completed plat of subdivision must contain all necessary approvals of public officials and must be recorded in the county where the land is located.

Because the plat will be the basis for future conveyances, the subdivided land should be measured carefully, with all lot sizes and streets noted by the surveyor and entered accurately on the document. Survey monuments should be established, and measurements should be made from these monuments, with the location of all lots carefully marked.

Covenants and restrictions. Deed restrictions are originated and recorded by a subdivider as a means of *controlling and maintaining the desirable quality and character of the subdivision*. These restrictions can be included in the subdivision plat, or they may be set forth in a separate recorded instrument, commonly referred to as a *declaration of restrictions*.

Subdivision Density

Zoning ordinances control land use. Such controls often include minimum lot sizes and population density requirements for subdivisions and land developments. For example, a typical zoning restriction may set the minimum lot area on which a subdivider can build a single-family housing unit at 10,000 square feet. This means that the subdivider will be able to build four houses per acre. Many zoning authorities now establish special density zoning standards for certain subdivisions. **Density zoning** ordinances restrict the *average maximum number of houses per acre* that may be built within a particular subdivision. If the area is density-zoned at an average maximum of four houses per acre, for example, by *clustering* building lots the developer is free to achieve an open effect. Regardless of lot size or the number of units, the subdivider will be consistent with the ordinance as long as the average number of units in the development remains at or below the maximum density. This average is called *gross density*.

Street patterns. By varying street patterns and clustering housing units a subdivider can dramatically increase the amount of open and/or recreational space in a development. Two of these patterns are illustrated in Figure 20.1.

The gridiron pattern evolved out of the government rectangular survey system. Featuring large lots, wide streets and limited-use service alleys, the system works reasonably well up to a point. An overabundance of grid-patterned streets often results in monotonous neighborhoods, with all lots facing busy streets. In addition, sidewalks are usually adjacent to the streets, and the system provides for little or no open space.

**Figure 20.1
Street Patterns**

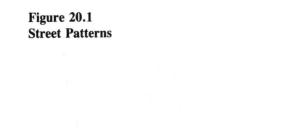
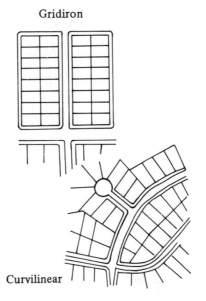

Gridiron

Curvilinear

The curvilinear system integrates major arteries of travel with smaller secondary and cul-de-sac streets carrying minor traffic. In addition, small parks are often provided at intersections.

Clustering for open space. By slightly reducing lot sizes and **clustering** them around varying street patterns a developer can house as many people in the same area as could be done using traditional subdividing plans but with substantially increased tracts of open space.

For example, compare the two illustrations in Figure 20.2. The first is a plan for a conventionally designed subdivision containing 368 housing units. It uses 23,200 linear feet of street and leaves only 1.6 acres open for park areas. Contrast this with the second subdivision pictured. Both subdivisions are equal in size and terrain. But when lots are reduced in size and clustered around limited-access cul-de-sac streets, the number of housing units remains nearly the same (366), with less street area (17,000 linear feet) and drastically increased open space (23.5 acres). In addition, with modern building designs this clustered plan could be modified to accommodate 550 patio homes or 1,100 town houses.

**Interstate Land
Sales Full
Disclosure Act**

To protect consumers from "overenthusiastic sales promotions" in interstate land sales Congress passed the **Interstate Land Sales Full Disclosure Act.** The law requires those engaged in the interstate sale or leasing of 25 or more lots to file a *statement of record* and *register* the details of the land with HUD.

The seller is also required to furnish prospective buyers a **property report** containing all essential information about the property, such as distance over paved roads to nearby communities, number of homes currently occupied, soil conditions affecting foundations and septic systems, type of title a buyer will receive and existence of liens. The property report must be given to a prospective purchaser at least three business days before any sales contract is signed.

Figure 20.2
Clustered Subdivision
Plan

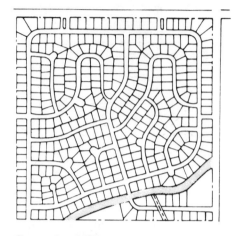 

Conventional Plan
12,500-square-foot lots
368 housing units
1.6 acres of parkland
23,200 linear feet of street

Cluster Plan
7,500-square-foot lots
366 housing units
23.5 acres of parkland
17,700 linear feet of street

Any contract to purchase a lot covered by this act may be revoked at the purchaser's option until midnight of the seventh day following the signing of the contract. If a contract is signed for the purchase of a lot covered by the act and a property report is not given to the purchaser, an action to revoke the contract may be brought by the purchaser within two years.

If the seller misrepresents the property in any sales promotion, a buyer induced by such a promotion is entitled to sue the seller for civil damages. Failure to comply with the law may also subject a seller to criminal penalties of fines and imprisonment.

State Subdivided-
Land Sales Laws

Many state legislatures have enacted their own subdivided-land sales laws. Some affect only the sale of land located outside the state to state residents, while others affect sales of land located both inside and outside the state. Generally these state land sales laws tend to be stricter and more detailed than the federal law.

Key Terms

clustering
density zoning
developer
Interstate Land Sales Full Disclosure Act

property report
subdivider
subdivision

Summary

A subdivider buys undeveloped acreage, divides it into smaller parcels and develops it or sells it. A developer builds homes on the lots and sells them, through the developer's own sales organization or through local real estate brokerage firms. City planners and land developers, working together, plan whole communities that are later incorporated into cities, towns or villages.

Land development must comply with the master plans adopted by counties, cities, villages or towns. This may entail approval of land-use plans by local planning committees or commissioners.

The process of subdivision includes dividing the tract of land into lots and blocks and providing for utility easements, as well as laying out street patterns and widths. A subdivider must generally record a completed plat of subdivision, with all necessary approvals of public officials, in the county where the land is located. Subdividers usually place restrictions on the use of all lots in a subdivision as a general plan for the benefit of all lot owners.

By varying street patterns and housing density and clustering housing units a subdivider can dramatically increase the amount of open and recreational space within a development.

Subdivided land sales are regulated on the federal level by the Interstate Land Sales Full Disclosure Act. This law requires developers engaged in interstate land sales or the leasing of 25 or more units to register the details of the land with HUD. At least three business days before any sales contract is signed, such developers must also provide prospective purchasers with a property report containing all essential information about the property. Subdivided land sales are also regulated by many states' laws.

Questions

1. To control and maintain the quality and character of a subdivision a developer will establish which of the following?
   a. Easements
   b. Deed restrictions
   c. Buffer zones
   d. Building codes

2. An owner of a large tract of land who, after adequate study of all facts, legally divides the land into lots of suitable size and location for the construction of residences, is known as a(an):
   a. subdivider.   c. land planner.
   b. developer.   d. urban planner.

3. A map illustrating the sizes and locations of streets and lots in a subdivision is called a:
   a. gridiron pattern.
   b. survey.
   c. plat of subdivision.
   d. property report.

4. *Gross density* refers to which of the following?
   a. The maximum number of residents that may, by law, occupy a subdivision
   b. The average maximum number of houses per acre that may, by law, be built in a subdivision
   c. The maximum size lot that may, by law, be built in a subdivision
   d. The minimum number of houses that may, by law, be built in a subdivision

5. The type of street pattern that is based on the rectangular survey system is called the:
   a. block plan.
   b. gridiron system.
   c. rectangular streets plan.
   d. cul-de-sac system.

6. Legal restrictions established by a recorded deed or subdivision plat, if permitted by public policy and not in violation of constitutional or statutory rights, are enforceable through:
   a. zoning ordinances.   c. covenants.
   b. court injunctions.   d. laches.

7. Soil absorption and drainage are measured by a:
   a. land survey.
   b. plat of subdivision.
   c. density test.
   d. percolation test.

8. All of the following items are usually designated on the plat for a new subdivision *except:*
   a. easements for sewer and water mains.
   b. land to be used for streets, schools and civic facilities.
   c. numbered lots and blocks.
   d. prices of residential and commercial lots.

9. A street pattern featuring housing units grouped into large cul-de-sac blocks is generally called a:
   a. cluster plan.
   b. curvilinear system.
   c. rectangular street system.
   d. gridiron system.

10. A subdivider can increase the amount of open and/or recreational space in a development by:
    a. varying street patterns.
    b. meeting local housing standards.
    c. scattering housing units.
    d. ignoring the zoning codes.

11. To protect the public from fraudulent interstate land sales a developer involved in interstate land sales of 25 or more lots must:
    a. provide each purchaser with a report of the details of the land, as registered with HUD.
    b. pay the prospective buyer's expenses to see the property involved.
    c. provide preferential financing.
    d. include deed restrictions.

21

Fair Housing and Ethical Practices

Equal Opportunity in Housing

Real estate licensees who offer *residential* property for sale must be aware of the federal, state and local laws pertaining to civil rights and nondiscrimination. These laws, under such titles as open housing, fair housing and equal opportunity housing, prohibit undesirable and discriminatory activities. Their provisions affect every phase of the real estate sales process, from listing to closing, and *all brokers and salespeople must comply with them.*

The goal of legislators who have enacted these laws and regulations is to create an unbiased housing market—one in which all home seekers have the opportunity to buy any home they choose, provided the home is within their financial means. As a potential licensee the student of real estate must be able to recognize illegal housing practices to avoid them. Failure to comply with fair housing practices is not only grounds for license revocation but also a criminal act.

In Practice . . .

State laws may be stricter than the federal requirements. It is imperative that licensees learn all pertinent state regulations.

Federal Fair Housing Laws

The efforts of the federal government to guarantee equal housing opportunities to all U.S. citizens began more than 100 years ago with the passage of the **Civil Rights Act of 1866.** This law, an outgrowth of the Fourteenth Amendment, prohibits any type of discrimination based on *race.* The law states "All citizens of the United States shall have the same right in every state and territory as is enjoyed by white citizens thereof to inherit, purchase, lease, sell, hold, and convey real and personal property." A summary of federal fair housing laws appears in Table 21.1.

Aside from a few isolated court decisions, there was little effort to enforce the principles of fair housing until 1962, when President John Kennedy issued *Executive Order No. 11063.* This order guaranteed nondiscrimination in all housing financed by FHA and VA loans. Because of the relatively small percentage of housing affected by Executive Order No. 11063, however, it had limited impact.

The scope of the federal government's fair housing regulation was expanded by the *Civil Rights Act of 1964,* which prohibited discrimination in any housing program that receives whole or partial federal funding. However, as only a very small percentage of housing in the United States is government-funded, this law also had little impact on the housing industry.

Fair Housing Act of 1968. In 1968 two major events greatly encouraged the progress of guaranteeing fair housing. The first of these was the passage of the **Federal Fair Housing Act,** which is contained in *Title VIII of the Civil Rights Act of 1968.* This law provides that it is unlawful to discriminate on the basis of *race, color, religion, or national origin* when selling or leasing residential property. (The second major event, the Supreme Court decision in *Jones v. Mayer,* is discussed on the following page.)

The **Housing and Community Development Act of 1974** added *sex* (gender) as a **protected class.** The **Fair Housing Amendments Act of 1988** then added as protected classes those with mental or physical *handicaps* and families with children *(familial status).*

Additional federal fair housing laws. Drug abusers are not protected as handicapped, nor are those who pose a threat to the health or safety of others. Housing intended for older persons is exempt if it is occupied solely by persons 62 and older or if 80 percent of its units are occupied by at least one person 55 or older and special facilities for the elderly are provided.

In Practice . . .

Individual states may name the same protected classes as the federal laws and may protect additional classes as well. Prospective licensees should be sure they are aware of all classes protected in their state.

The Federal Fair Housing Act (along with the 1974 and 1988 acts) covers houses and apartments as well as vacant land acquired for the construction of residential buildings, and it prohibits the following discriminatory acts:

1. Refusing to sell, rent or negotiate with any person or otherwise making a dwelling unavailable to any person

2. Changing terms, conditions or services for different individuals as a means of discrimination

3. Practicing discrimination through any statement or advertisement that restricts the sale or rental of residential property

Table 21.1
Summary of Federal
Fair Housing Laws

Law	Purpose
Civil Rights Act of 1866	Prohibits discrimination in housing based on race without exception
Executive Order No. 11063 (1962)	Prohibits discrimination in housing funded by FHA or VA loans
Civil Rights Act of 1964	Prohibits discrimination in federally funded housing programs
Title VIII of the Civil Rights Act of 1968 (Federal Fair Housing Act)	Prohibits discrimination in housing based on race, color, religion or national origin, with certain exceptions
Housing and Community Development Act of 1974	Extends prohibitions to discrimination in housing based on sex
Fair Housing Amendments Act of 1988	Extends protection to cover persons with handicaps and families with children, with certain exceptions

4. Representing to any person, as a means of discrimination, that a dwelling is not available for sale or rental

5. Making a profit by inducing owners of housing to sell or rent because of the prospective entry into the neighborhood of persons of a particular race, color, religion, national origin, handicap or familial status

6. Altering the terms or conditions for a home loan to any person who wishes to purchase or repair a dwelling or otherwise denying such a loan as a means of discrimination

7. Denying people membership or limiting their participation in any multiple-listing service, real estate brokers' organization or other facility related to the sale or rental of dwellings as a means of discrimination.

The following exemptions to the Federal Fair Housing Act are provided:

1. The sale or rental of a single-family home is exempted when the home is owned by an individual who does not own more than three such homes at one time and when a broker or salesperson is *not* used and discriminatory advertising is not used. If the owner is not living in the dwelling at the time of the transaction or was not the most recent occupant, only one such sale by an individual is exempt from the law within any 24-month period.

2. The rental of rooms or units is exempted in an owner-occupied one- to four-family dwelling.

3. Dwelling units owned by religious organizations may be restricted to people of the same religion if membership in the organization is not restricted on the basis of race, color, national origin, handicap or familial status.

4. A private club that is not open to the public may restrict the rental or occupancy of lodgings that it owns to its members as long as the lodgings are not operated commercially.

Jones v. Mayer. The second significant fair housing development of 1968 was the Supreme Court decision in the case of *Jones v. Alfred H. Mayer Company,* 392 U.S. 409 (1968). In its ruling the court upheld the Civil Rights Act of 1866, which ''prohibits all racial discrimination, private or public, in the sale and rental of property.''

The importance of this decision rests in the fact that while the 1968 federal law exempts individual homeowners and certain groups the 1866 law *prohibits all racial discrimination without exception.* So despite any exemptions in the 1968 law, an aggrieved person may seek a remedy for racial discrimination under the 1866 law against *any* homeowner, regardless of whether the owner employed a real estate broker and/or advertised the property. *Where race is involved, no exceptions apply.*

Equal Housing Poster. An amendment to the Federal Fair Housing Act of 1968 instituted the use of an equal housing opportunity poster, Figure 21.1. This poster, which can be obtained from the **Department of Housing and Urban Development (HUD),** features the equal housing opportunity slogan, an equal housing statement pledging adherence to the fair housing act and support of affirmative marketing and advertising programs, and the equal housing opportunity logo.

When HUD investigates a broker for discriminatory practices, it may consider failure to display the poster in the broker's place of business prima facie evidence of discrimination.

Equal Credit Opportunity Act. The federal **Equal Credit Opportunity Act (ECOA)** prohibits discrimination based on race, color, religion, national origin, sex, marital status or age (if the applicant has reached the age of contractual capacity) in the granting of credit. Credit applicants must be considered only by criteria based on income, net worth, job stability and credit rating.

Blockbusting and Steering

Blockbusting and steering are undesirable housing practices frequently discussed in connection with fair housing. **Blockbusting** means *inducing homeowners to sell by making representations regarding the entry or prospective entry of minority persons into the neighborhood.* The blockbuster frightens homeowners into selling and makes a profit by buying the homes cheaply and selling them at considerably higher prices to minority persons. The Federal Fair Housing Act specifically prohibits this practice.

Steering is the channeling of home seekers to particular areas on the basis of race, religion, country of origin or other protected class. On these grounds it is prohibited by the provisions of the Federal Fair Housing Act. Steering is often difficult to detect, however, because the steering tactics can be so subtle that the home seeker is unaware that his or her choices have been limited. Steering may be done unintentionally by agents who are not aware of their own unconscious assumptions.

Redlining

Refusing to make mortgage loans or issue insurance policies in specific areas without regard to the economic qualifications of the applicant is known as **redlining.** This practice, which often contributes to the deterioration of older, transitional neighborhoods, is frequently based on racial grounds rather than on any real objections to the applicant. However, a lending institution that refuses a loan solely on sound economic grounds cannot be accused of redlining.

Enforcement

A person who believes illegal discrimination has occurred has up to one year after the alleged act to file a charge with HUD or may bring a federal suit within two years. HUD will investigate, and if the department believes a discriminatory act has occurred it may issue a charge. Any party involved (or HUD) may choose to have the charge heard in a federal district court. If no one requests the court procedure, the charge will be heard by an administrative law judge within HUD itself.

The administrative judge has the authority to issue an *injunction.* The injunction would order the offender to do something—rent to the complaining party, for example—or to refrain from doing something. In addition, penalties can be imposed, ranging from $10,000 for a first violation to $25,000 for a second violation within five years and $50,000 for further violations within seven years. If the case is heard in federal court, an injunction, actual damages and punitive damages are possible, with no dollar limit. In addition to offended parties the Department of Justice may itself sue anyone who seems to show a pattern of illegal discrimination. Dollar limits on penalties in such cases are set at $50,000, with a $100,000 penalty for repeat violations.

Complaints brought under the Civil Rights Act of 1866 must be taken directly to a federal court. The only time limit for action would be the state's statute of limitation for *torts,* injuries done by one individual to another.

**Figure 21.1
Equal Housing
Opportunity Poster***

U.S.. Department of Housing and Urban Development

**EQUAL HOUSING
OPPORTUNITY**

**We Do Business in Accordance With the Federal Fair
Housing Law**
(The Fair Housing Amendments Act of 1988)

**It is Illegal to Discriminate Against Any Person
Because of Race, Color, Religion, Sex,
Handicap, Familial Status, or National Origin**

- In the sale or rental of housing or residential lots
- In advertising the sale or rental of housing
- In the financing of housing

- In the provision of real estate brokerage services
- In the appraisal of housing
- Blockbusting is also illegal

Anyone who feels he or she has been discriminated against may file a complaint of housing discrimination with the:

**U.S. Department of Housing and
Urban Development
Assistant Secretary for Fair Housing and
Equal Opportunity
Washington, D.C. 20410**

*Previous editions are obsolete.

Threats or Acts of Violence

The Federal Fair Housing Act of 1968 contains criminal provisions protecting the rights of those who seek the benefits of the open housing law as well as owners, brokers or salespeople who aid or encourage the enjoyment of open housing rights. Unlawful actions involving threats, coercion and intimidation are punishable by civil action. In such cases the victim should immediately report the incident to the local police and to the nearest office of the Federal Bureau of Investigation.

Implications for Licensees

To a large extent the laws place the burden of responsibility for effecting and maintaining fair housing on real estate licensees. The laws are clear and widely known. *The complainant does not have to prove guilty knowledge or specific intent—only the fact that discrimination occurred.*

When a broker is charged with discrimination, it is *no defense* that the offense was unintentional. Citing past service to members of the same minority group also is of little value as a defense. The licensee's best course is to study fair housing law, develop sensitivity on the subject and follow routine practices designed to reduce the danger of unintentionally hurting any member of the public. These practices include careful record keeping for each customer: financial analysis, properties suggested, houses shown, check-back phone calls. Using a standard form for all qualifying interviews is helpful. Special care should be taken to be on time for appointments and to follow through on returning all phone calls. Besides helping to avoid civil rights violations, these practices are simply good business and should result in increased sales.

In addition, besides the equal housing poster discussed earlier; HUD offers guidelines for nondiscriminatory language and illustrations for use in real estate advertising, to help licensees comply with the laws and make that policy known to the public.

From time to time real estate offices may be visited by testers or *checkers,* undercover volunteers who want to see whether customers and clients are being treated equally and are being offered the same free choice within a given price range. The courts have held that such practice is permissible as it is the only way to test compliance with the fair housing laws.

Code of Ethics

The National Association of REALTORS® adopted a Code of Ethics for its members in 1913. The NAR also publishes interpretations of the Code known as Standards of Practice. Because the real estate business is only as good as its reputation, and reputations are built on fair dealings with the public, licensees are obligated to conduct themselves in an ethical manner. The REALTORS® Code of Ethics and Standards of Practice appear in Figure 21.2.

Key Terms

blockbusting
Civil Rights Act of 1866
Department of Housing and Urban
    Development (HUD)
Equal Credit Opportunity Act (ECOA)
Fair Housing Amendments Act of 1988

Federal Fair Housing Act of 1968
Housing and Community Development
    Act of 1974
protected class
redlining
steering

Figure 21.2
REALTORS® Code of
Ethics

Code of Ethics and Standards of Practice

of the
NATIONAL ASSOCIATION OF REALTORS®

Where the word REALTOR® is used in this Code and Preamble, it shall be deemed to include REALTOR-ASSOCIATE®. Pronouns shall be considered to include REALTORS® and REALTOR-ASSOCIATE®s of both genders.

Preamble...

Under all is the land. Upon its wise utilization and widely allocated ownership depend the survival and growth of free institutions and of our civilization. The REALTOR® should recognize that the interests of the nation and its citizens require the highest and best use of the land and the widest distribution of land ownership. They require the creation of adequate housing, the building of functioning cities, the development of productive industries and farms, and the preservation of a healthful environment.

Such interests impose obligations beyond those of ordinary commerce. They impose grave social responsibility and a patriotic duty to which the REALTOR® should dedicate himself, and for which he should be diligent in preparing himself. The REALTOR®, therefore, is zealous to maintain and improve the standards of his calling and shares with his fellow REALTORS® a common responsibility for its integrity and honor. The term REALTOR® has come to connote competency, fairness, and high integrity resulting from adherence to a lofty ideal of moral conduct in business relations. No inducement of profit and no instruction from clients ever can justify departure from this ideal.

In the interpretation of this obligation, a REALTOR® can take no safer guide than that which has been handed down through the centuries, embodied in the Golden Rule, "Whatsoever ye would that men should do to you, do ye even so to them."

Accepting this standard as his own, every REALTOR® pledges himself to observe its spirit in all of his activities and to conduct his business in accordance with the tenets set forth below.

Articles 1 through 5 are aspirational and establish ideals the REALTOR® should strive to attain.

ARTICLE 1

The REALTOR® should keep himself informed on matters affecting real estate in his community, the state, and nation so that he may be able to contribute responsibly to public thinking on such matters.

ARTICLE 2

In justice to those who place their interests in his care, the REALTOR® should endeavor always to be informed regarding laws, proposed legislation, governmental regulations, public policies, and current market conditions in order to be in a position to advise his clients properly.

ARTICLE 3

The REALTOR® should endeavor to eliminate in his community any practices which could be damaging to the public or bring discredit to the real estate profession. The REALTOR® should assist the governmental agency charged with regulating the practices of brokers and salesmen in his state. (Amended 11/87)

ARTICLE 4

To prevent dissension and misunderstanding and to assure better service to the owner, the REALTOR® should urge the exclusive listing of property unless contrary to the best interest of the owner. (Amended 11/87)

ARTICLE 5

In the best interests of society, of his associates, and his own business, the REALTOR® should willingly share with other REALTORS® the lessons of his experience and study for the benefit of the public, and should be loyal to the Board of REALTORS® of his community and active in its work.

Articles 6 through 23 establish specific obligations. Failure to observe these requirements subjects the REALTOR® to disciplinary action.

ARTICLE 6

The REALTOR® shall seek no unfair advantage over other REALTORS® and shall conduct his business so as to avoid controversies with other REALTORS®. (Amended 11/87)

• Standard of Practice 6-1

The REALTOR® shall not misrepresent the availability of access to show or inspect a listed property. (Cross-reference Article 22.) (Amended 11/87)

ARTICLE 7

In accepting employment as an agent, the REALTOR® pledges himself to protect and promote the interests of the client. This obligation of absolute fidelity to the client's interests is primary, but it does not relieve the REALTOR® of the obligation to treat fairly all parties to the transaction.

• Standard of Practice 7-1

Unless precluded by law, government rule or regulation, or agreed otherwise in writing, the REALTOR® shall submit to the seller all offers until closing. Unless the REALTOR® and the seller agree otherwise, the REALTOR® shall not be obligated to continue to market the property after an offer has been accepted. Unless the subsequent offer is contingent upon the termination of an existing contract, the REALTOR® shall recommend that the seller obtain the advice of legal counsel prior to acceptance. (Cross-reference Article 17.) (Amended 5/87)

• Standard of Practice 7-2

The REALTOR®, acting as listing broker, shall submit all offers to the seller as quickly as possible.

• Standard of Practice 7-3

The REALTOR®, in attempting to secure a listing, shall not deliberately mislead the owner as to market value.

*The Code of Ethics is scheduled for revision in December, 1990.

**Figure 21.2
(continued)**

- **Standard of Practice 7-4**
  (Refer to Standard of Practice 22-1, which also relates to Article 7, Code of Ethics.)

- **Standard of Practice 7-5**
  (Refer to Standard of Practice 22-2, which also relates to Article 7, Code of Ethics.)

- **Standard of Practice 7-6**
  The REALTOR®, when acting as a principal in a real estate transaction, cannot avoid his responsibilities under the Code of Ethics.

ARTICLE 8
The REALTOR® shall not accept compensation from more than one party, even if permitted by law, without the full knowledge of all parties to the transaction.

ARTICLE 9
The REALTOR® shall avoid exaggeration, misrepresentation, or concealment of pertinent facts relating to the property or the transaction. The REALTOR® shall not, however, be obligated to discover latent defects in the property or to advise on matters outside the scope of his real estate license. (Amended 11/86)

- **Standard of Practice 9-1**
  The REALTOR® shall not be a party to the naming of a false consideration in any document, unless it be the naming of an obviously nominal consideration.

- **Standard of Practice 9-2**
  (Refer to Standard of Practice 21-3, which also relates to Article 9, Code of Ethics.)

- **Standard of Practice 9-3**
  (Refer to Standard of Practice 7-3, which also relates to Article 9, Code of Ethics.)

- **Standard of Practice 9-4**
  The REALTOR® shall not offer a service described as "free of charge" when the rendering of a service is contingent on the obtaining of a benefit such as a listing or commission.

- **Standard of Practice 9-5**
  The REALTOR® shall, with respect to the subagency of another REALTOR®, timely communicate any change of compensation for subagency services to the other REALTOR® prior to the time such REALTOR® produces a prospective buyer who has signed an offer to purchase the property for which the subagency has been offered through MLS or otherwise by the listing agency.

- **Standard of Practice 9-6**
  REALTORS® shall disclose their REALTOR® status when seeking information from another REALTOR® concerning real property for which the other REALTOR® is an agent or subagent.

- **Standard of Practice 9-7**
  The offering of premiums, prizes, merchandise discounts or other inducements to list or sell is not, in itself, unethical even if receipt of the benefit is contingent on listing or purchasing through the REALTOR® making the offer. However, the REALTOR® must exercise care and candor in any such advertising or other public or private representations so that any party interested in receiving or otherwise benefiting from the REALTOR®'s offer will have clear, thorough, advance understanding of all the terms and conditions of the offer. The offering of any inducements to do business is subject to the limitations and restrictions of state law and the ethical obligations established by Article 9, as interpreted by any applicable Standard of Practice. (Adopted 11/84)

- **Standard of Practice 9-8**
  The REALTOR® shall be obligated to discover and disclose adverse factors reasonably apparent to someone with expertise in only those areas required by their real estate licensing authority. Article 9 does not impose upon the REALTOR® the obligation of expertise in other professional or technical disciplines. (Cross-reference Article 11.) (Amended 11/86)

ARTICLE 10
The REALTOR® shall not deny equal professional services to any person for reasons of race, color, religion, sex, handicap, familial status, or national origin. The REALTOR® shall not be party to any plan or agreement to discriminate against a person or persons on the basis of race, color, religion, sex, handicap, familial status, or national origin. (Amended 11/89)

ARTICLE 11
A REALTOR® is expected to provide a level of competent service in keeping with the standards of practice in those fields in which the REALTOR® customarily engages.

The REALTOR® shall not undertake to provide specialized professional services concerning a type of property or service that is outside his field of competence unless he engages the assistance of one who is competent on such types of property or service, or unless the facts are fully disclosed to the client. Any person engaged to provide such assistance shall be so identified to the client and his contribution to the assignment should be set forth.

The REALTOR® shall refer to the Standards of Practice of the National Association as to the degree of competence that a client has a right to expect the REALTOR® to possess, taking into consideration the complexity of the problem, the availability of expert assistance, and the opportunities for experience available to the REALTOR®.

- **Standard of Practice 11-1**
  Whenever a REALTOR® submits an oral or written opinion of the value of real property for a fee, his opinion shall be supported by a memorandum in his file or an appraisal report, either of which shall include as a minimum the following:

  1. Limiting conditions
  2. Any existing or contemplated interest
  3. Defined value
  4. Date applicable
  5. The estate appraised
  6. A description of the property
  7. The basis of the reasoning including applicable market data and/or capitalization computation

  This report or memorandum shall be available to the Professional Standards Committee for a period of at least two years (beginning subsequent to final determination of the court if the appraisal is involved in litigation) to ensure compliance with Article 11 of the Code of Ethics of the NATIONAL ASSOCIATION OF REALTORS®.

- **Standard of Practice 11-2**
  The REALTOR® shall not undertake to make an appraisal when his employment or fee is contingent upon the amount of appraisal.

**Figure 21.2
(continued)**

- **Standard of Practice 11-3**

  REALTORS® engaged in real estate securities and syndications transactions are engaged in an activity subject to regulations beyond those governing real estate transactions generally, and therefore have the affirmative obligation to be informed of applicable federal and state laws, and rules and regulations regarding these types of transactions.

ARTICLE 12

The REALTOR® shall not undertake to provide professional services concerning a property or its value where he has a present or contemplated interest unless such interest is specifically disclosed to all affected parties.

- **Standard of Practice 12-1**

  (Refer to Standards of Practice 9-4 and 16-1, which also relate to Article 12, Code of Ethics.) (Amended 5/84)

ARTICLE 13

The REALTOR® shall not acquire an interest in or buy for himself, any member of his immediate family, his firm or any member thereof, or any entity in which he has a substantial ownership interest, property listed with him, without making the true position known to the listing owner. In selling property owned by himself, or in which he has any interest, the REALTOR® shall reveal the facts of his ownership or interest to the purchaser.

- **Standard of Practice 13-1**

  For the protection of all parties, the disclosures required by Article 13 shall be in writing and provided by the REALTOR® prior to the signing of any contract. (Adopted 2/86)

ARTICLE 14

In the event of a controversy between REALTORS® associated with different firms, arising out of their relationship as REALTORS®, the REALTORS® shall submit the dispute to arbitration in accordance with the regulations of their Board or Boards rather than litigate the matter.

- **Standard of Practice 14-1**

  The filing of litigation and refusal to withdraw from it by a REALTOR® in an arbitrable matter constitutes a refusal to arbitrate. (Adopted 2/86)

- **Standard of Practice 14-2**

  The obligation to arbitrate mandated by Article 14 includes arbitration requests initiated by the REALTOR®'s client. (Adopted 5/87)

- **Standard of Practice 14-3**

  Article 14 does not require a REALTOR® to arbitrate in those circumstances when all parties to the dispute advise the Board in writing that they choose not to arbitrate before the Board. (Adopted 5/88)

ARTICLE 15

If charged with unethical practice or asked to present evidence or to cooperate in any other way, in any disciplinary proceeding or investigation, the REALTOR® shall place all pertinent facts before the proper tribunal of the Member Board or affiliated institute, society, or council in which membership is held and shall take no action to disrupt or obstruct such processes. (Amended 11/89)

- **Standard of Practice 15-1**

  The REALTOR® shall not be subject to disciplinary proceedings in more than one Board of REALTORS® with respect to alleged violations of the Code of Ethics relating to the same transaction.

- **Standard of Practice 15-2**

  The REALTOR® shall not make any unauthorized disclosure or dissemination of the allegations, findings, or decision developed in connection with an ethics hearing or appeal. (Adopted 5/84)

- **Standard of Practice 15-3**

  The REALTOR® shall not obstruct the Board's investigative or disciplinary proceedings by instituting or threatening to institute actions for libel, slander or defamation against any party to a professional standards proceeding or their witnesses. (Adopted 11/87)

- **Standard of Practice 15-4**

  The REALTOR® shall not intentionally impede the Board's investigative or disciplinary proceedings by filing multiple ethics complaints based on the same event or transaction. (Adopted 11/88)

ARTICLE 16

When acting as agent, the REALTOR® shall not accept any commission, rebate, or profit on expenditures made for his principal-owner, without the principal's knowledge and consent.

- **Standard of Practice 16-1**

  The REALTOR® shall not recommend or suggest to a client or a customer the use of services of another organization or business entity in which he has a direct interest without disclosing such interest at the time of the recommendation or suggestion. (Amended 5/88)

- **Standard of Practice 16-2**

  When acting as an agent or subagent, the REALTOR® shall disclose to a client or customer if there is any financial benefit or fee the REALTOR® or the REALTOR®'s firm may receive as a direct result of having recommended real estate products or services (e.g., homeowner's insurance, warranty programs, mortgage financing, title insurance, etc.) other than real estate referral fees. (Adopted 5/88)

ARTICLE 17

The REALTOR® shall not engage in activities that constitute the unauthorized practice of law and shall recommend that legal counsel be obtained when the interest of any party to the transaction requires it.

ARTICLE 18

The REALTOR® shall keep in a special account in an appropriate financial institution, separated from his own funds, monies coming into his possession in trust for other persons, such as escrows, trust funds, clients' monies, and other like items.

ARTICLE 19

The REALTOR® shall be careful at all times to present a true picture in his advertising and representations to the public. The REALTOR® shall also ensure that his status as a broker or a REALTOR® is clearly identifiable in any such advertising. (Amended 11/86)

**Figure 21.2
(continued)**

- **Standard of Practice 19-1**

  The REALTOR® shall not submit or advertise property without authority, and in any offering, the price quoted shall not be other than that agreed upon with the owners.

- **Standard of Practice 19-2**

  (Refer to Standard of Practice 9-4, which also relates to Article 19, Code of Ethics.)

- **Standard of Practice 19-3**

  The REALTOR®, when advertising unlisted real property for sale in which he has an ownership interest, shall disclose his status as both an owner and as a REALTOR® or real estate licensee. (Adopted 5/85)

- **Standard of Practice 19-4**

  The REALTOR® shall not advertise nor permit any person employed by or affiliated with him to advertise listed property without disclosing the name of the firm. (Adopted 11/86)

- **Standard of Practice 19-5**

  Only the REALTOR®, as listing broker, may claim to have "sold" the property, even when the sale resulted through the cooperative efforts of another broker. However, after transactions have closed, the listing broker may not prohibit successful cooperating brokers from advertising their "cooperation," "participation," or "assistance" in the transaction, or from making similar representations.

  Only the listing broker is entitled to use the term "sold" on signs, in advertisements, and in other public representations. (Amended 11/89)

ARTICLE 20

The REALTOR®, for the protection of all parties, shall see that financial obligations and commitments regarding real estate transactions are in writing, expressing the exact agreement of the parties. A copy of each agreement shall be furnished to each party upon his signing such agreement.

- **Standard of Practice 20-1**

  At the time of signing or initialing, the REALTOR® shall furnish to the party a copy of any document signed or initialed. (Adopted 5/86)

- **Standard of Practice 20-2**

  For the protection of all parties, the REALTOR® shall use reasonable care to ensure that documents pertaining to the purchase and sale of real estate are kept current through the use of written extensions or amendments. (Adopted 5/86)

ARTICLE 21

The REALTOR® shall not engage in any practice or take any action inconsistent with the agency of another REALTOR®.

- **Standard of Practice 21-1**

  Signs giving notice of property for sale, rent, lease, or exchange shall not be placed on property without the consent of the owner.

- **Standard of Practice 21-2**

  The REALTOR® obtaining information from a listing broker about a specific property shall not convey this information to, nor invite the cooperation of a third party broker without the consent of the listing broker.

- **Standard of Practice 21-3**

  The REALTOR® shall not solicit a listing which is currently listed exclusively with another broker. However, if the listing broker, when asked by the REALTOR®, refuses to disclose the expiration date and nature of such listing; i.e., an exclusive right to sell, an exclusive agency, open listing, or other form of contractual agreement between the listing broker and his client, the REALTOR®, unless precluded by law, may contact the owner to secure such information and may discuss the terms upon which he might take a future listing or, alternatively, may take a listing to become effective upon expiration of any existing exclusive listing. (Amended 11/86)

- **Standard of Practice 21-4**

  The REALTOR® shall not use information obtained by him from the listing broker, through offers to cooperate received through Multiple Listing Services or other sources authorized by the listing broker, for the purpose of creating a referral prospect to a third broker, or for creating a buyer prospect unless such use is authorized by the listing broker.

- **Standard of Practice 21-5**

  The fact that a property has been listed exclusively with a REALTOR® shall not preclude or inhibit any other REALTOR® from soliciting such listing after its expiration.

- **Standard of Practice 21-6**

  The fact that a property owner has retained a REALTOR® as his exclusive agent in respect of one or more past transactions creates no interest or agency which precludes or inhibits other REALTORS® from seeking such owner's future business.

- **Standard of Practice 21-7**

  The REALTOR® shall be free to list property which is "open listed" at any time, but shall not knowingly obligate the seller to pay more than one commission except with the seller's knowledgeable consent. (Cross-reference Article 7.) (Amended 5/88)

- **Standard of Practice 21-8**

  When a REALTOR® is contacted by an owner regarding the sale of property that is exclusively listed with another broker, and the REALTOR® has not directly or indirectly initiated the discussion, unless precluded by law, the REALTOR® may discuss the terms upon which he might take a future listing or, alternatively, may take a listing to become effective upon expiration of any existing exclusive listing. (Amended 11/86)

- **Standard of Practice 21-9**

  In cooperative transactions a REALTOR® shall compensate the cooperating REALTOR® (principal broker) and shall not compensate nor offer to compensate, directly or indirectly, any of the sales licensees employed by or affiliated with another REALTOR® without the prior express knowledge and consent of the cooperating broker.

- **Standard of Practice 21-10**

  Article 21 does not preclude REALTORS® from making general announcements to property owners describing their services and the terms of their availability even though some recipients may have exclusively listed their property for sale or lease with another REALTOR®. A general telephone canvass, general mailing or distribution addressed to all property owners in a given geographical area or in a given profession, business, club, or organization, or other classification or group is deemed "general" for purposes of this standard.

**Figure 21.2
(continued)**

Article 21 is intended to recognize as unethical two basic types of solicitation:

First, telephone or personal solicitations of property owners who have been identified by a real estate sign, multiple listing compilation, or other information service as having exclusively listed their property with another REALTOR®; and

Second, mail or other forms of written solicitations of property owners whose properties are exclusively listed with another REALTOR® when such solicitations are not part of a general mailing but are directed specifically to property owners identified through compilations of current listings, "for sale" signs, or other sources of information required by Article 22 and Multiple Listing Service rules to be made available to other REALTORS® under offers of subagency or cooperation. (Adopted 11/83)

- **Standard of Practice 21-11**
  The REALTOR®, prior to accepting a listing, has an affirmative obligation to make reasonable efforts to determine whether the property is subject to a current, valid exclusive listing agreement. (Adopted 11/83)
- **Standard of Practice 21-12**
  The REALTOR®, acting as the agent of the buyer, shall disclose that relationship to the seller's agent at first contact. (Cross-reference Article 7.) (Adopted 5/88)
- **Standard of Practice 21-13**
  On unlisted property, the REALTOR®, acting as the agent of a buyer, shall disclose that relationship to the seller at first contact. (Cross-reference Article 7.) (Adopted 5/88)
- **Standard of Practice 21-14**
  The REALTOR®, acting as agent of the seller or as subagent of the listing broker, shall disclose that relationship to buyers as soon as practicable. (Adopted 5/88)
- **Standard of Practice 21-15**
  Article 21 does not preclude a REALTOR® from contacting the client of another broker for the purpose of offering to provide, or entering into a contract to provide, a different type of real estate service unrelated to the type of service currently being provided (e.g., property management as opposed to brokerage). However, information received through a Multiple Listing Service or any other offer of cooperation may not be used to target the property owners to whom such offers to provide services are made. (Adopted 2/89)
- **Standard of Practice 21-16**
  The REALTOR®, acting as subagent or buyer's agent, shall not use the terms of an offer to purchase to attempt to modify the listing broker's offer of compensation to subagents or buyer's agents nor make the submission of an executed offer to purchase contingent on the listing broker's agreement to modify the offer of compensation. (Adopted 2/89)

ARTICLE 22

In the sale of property which is exclusively listed with a REALTOR®, the REALTOR® shall utilize the services of other brokers upon mutually agreed upon terms when it is in the best interests of the client.

Negotiations concerning property which is listed exclusively shall be carried on with the listing broker, not with the owner, except with the consent of the listing broker.

- **Standard of Practice 22-1**
  It is the obligation of the selling broker as subagent of the listing broker to disclose immediately all pertinent facts to the listing broker prior to as well as after the contract is executed.
- **Standard of Practice 22-2**
  The REALTOR®, when submitting offers to the seller, shall present each in an objective and unbiased manner.
- **Standard of Practice 22-3**
  The REALTOR® shall disclose the existence of an accepted offer to any broker seeking cooperation. (Adopted 5/86)
- **Standard of Practice 22-4**
  The REALTOR®, acting as exclusive agent of the seller, establishes the terms and conditions of offers to cooperate. Unless expressly indicated in offers to cooperate made through MLS or otherwise, a cooperating broker may not assume that the offer of cooperation includes an offer of compensation. Entitlement to compensation in a cooperative transaction must be agreed upon between a listing and cooperating broker prior to the time an offer to purchase the property is produced. (Adopted 11/88)

ARTICLE 23

The REALTOR® shall not publicly disparage the business practice of a competitor nor volunteer an opinion of a competitor's transaction. If his opinion is sought and if the REALTOR® deems it appropriate to respond, such opinion shall be rendered with strict professional integrity and courtesy.

The Code of Ethics was adopted in 1913. Amended at the Annual Convention in 1924, 1928, 1950, 1951, 1952, 1955, 1956, 1961, 1962, 1974, 1982, 1986, 1987, and 1989.

EXPLANATORY NOTES (Revised 11/88)

The reader should be aware of the following policies which have been approved by the Board of Directors of the National Association:

In filing a charge of an alleged violation of the Code of Ethics by a REALTOR®, the charge shall read as an alleged violation of one or more Articles of the Code. A Standard of Practice may only be cited in support of the charge.

The Standards of Practice are not an integral part of the Code but rather serve to clarify the ethical obligations imposed by the various Articles. The Standards of Practice supplement, and do not substitute for, the Case Interpretations in *Interpretations of the Code of Ethics*.

Modifications to existing Standards of Practice and additional new Standards of Practice are approved from time to time. The reader is cautioned to ensure that the most recent publications are utilized.

Articles 1 through 5 are aspirational and establish ideals that a REALTOR® should strive to attain. Recognizing their subjective nature, these Articles shall not be used as the bases for charges of alleged unethical conduct or as the bases for disciplinary action.

NATIONAL ASSOCIATION
OF REALTORS®
430 North Michigan Avenue
Chicago, Illinois 60611

©1990, NATIONAL ASSOCIATION OF REALTORS®
All Rights Reserved

EQUAL HOUSING
OPPORTUNITY

Summary

Federal regulations regarding equal opportunity in housing are contained principally in two laws. The Civil Rights Act of 1866 prohibits all racial discrimination, and the Federal Fair Housing Act (Title VIII of the Civil Rights Act of 1968) prohibits discrimination on the basis of race, color, religion, national origin, sex (1974), handicap (1988) or the presence of children in a family (1988) in the sale or rental of residential property. Discriminatory actions include refusing to deal with an individual or a specific group, changing any terms of a real estate or loan transaction, changing the services offered for any individual or group, making statements or advertisements that indicate discriminatory restrictions or otherwise attempting to make a dwelling unavailable to any person or group because of membership in a protected class. Some exceptions apply to owners but none to brokers and none when the discriminatory act is based on race.

Complaints under the Federal Fair Housing Act may be reported to and investigated by the Department of Housing and Urban Development and may be taken to a U.S. district court. Complaints under the Civil Rights Act of 1866 must be taken to a federal court.

The law also prohibits steering, blockbusting and redlining. Compliance is occasionally monitored by undercover testers.

The National Association of REALTORS® Code of Ethics suggests a set of standards for all members to follow.

Questions

1. Which of the following acts is permitted under the Federal Fair Housing Act?

   a. Advertising property for sale only to a special group
   b. Altering the terms of a loan for a member of a minority group
   c. Refusing to sell a home to an individual because of a poor credit history
   d. Telling an individual that an apartment has been rented when in fact it has not

2. Complaints relating to the Civil Rights Act of 1866:

   a. must be taken directly to a federal court.
   b. are no longer reviewed in the courts.
   c. are handled by HUD.
   d. are handled by state enforcement agencies.

3. The Civil Rights Act of 1866 is unique because it:

   a. has been broadened to protect the aged.
   b. adds welfare recipients as a protected class.
   c. contains "choose your neighbor" provisions.
   d. provides no exceptions to racial discrimination.

4. "I hear they're moving in; there goes the neighborhood. Better sell to me today!" is an example of:

   a. steering.   c. redlining.
   b. blockbusting.   d. testing.

5. The act of channeling home seekers to a particular area either to maintain or to change the character of a neighborhood is:

   a. blockbusting.
   b. redlining.
   c. steering.
   d. permitted under the Fair Housing Act of 1968.

6. A lender's refusal to lend money to potential homeowners attempting to purchase property located in predominantly black neighborhoods is known as:

   a. redlining.   c. steering.
   b. blockbusting.   d. qualifying.

7. Which of the following would *not* be permitted under the Federal Fair Housing Act?

   a. The Harvard Club in New York will rent rooms only to graduates of Harvard who belong to the club.
   b. The owner of a 20-unit apartment building rents to women only.
   c. A Catholic convent refuses to furnish housing for a Jewish man.
   d. An owner refuses to rent the other side of her duplex home to families with children.

8. Under the federal law families with children may be refused rental or purchase in buildings where occupancy is reserved exclusively for those aged at least:

   a. 55.   c. 62.
   b. 60.   d. 65.

9. Guiding prospective buyers to a particular area because the agent feels they belong there may lead to:

   a. blockbusting.   c. steering.
   b. redlining.   d. bird-dogging.

10. A black real estate broker's practice of offering a special discount to black clients is:

    a. satisfactory.
    b. illegal.
    c. legal but ill advised.
    d. not important.

11. Under the Supreme Court decision in the case of *Jones v. Alfred H. Mayer Company:*

    a. racial discrimination is prohibited by any party in the sale or rental of real estate.
    b. sales by individual residential homeowners are exempted provided the owner does not employ a broker.
    c. laws against discrimination apply only to federally related transactions.
    d. persons with handicaps are a protected class.

12. The Federal Housing Amendments of 1988 added which of the following as new protected classes?

    a. Occupation and source of income
    b. Handicap and familial status
    c. Political affiliation and country of origin
    d. Prison record and marital status

13. The fine for a first violation of the Federal Fair Housing Act could be as much as:

    a. $500.   c. $5,000.
    b. $1,000.   d. $10,000.

14. Undercover investigation to see whether fair housing practices are being followed is sometimes made by:

    a. testers.   c. operatives.
    b. evaluators.   d. conciliators.

15. The seller who requests prohibited discrimination in the showing of a house should be told:

    a. "I'll need those instructions in writing to protect my company."
    b. "I'll do what I can, but I can't guarantee anything."
    c. "You'll have to clear that with my broker."
    d. "We are not allowed to obey such instructions."

Real Estate Investment

| **Investing in Real Estate** | Real estate licensees should possess an elementary knowledge of real estate investment so they can serve a variety of customer needs. Often, however, customers expect a licensee to act as an investment counselor. The licensee should always *refer an investor to a competent tax accountant, attorney or investment specialist* who can give expert advice regarding the investor's specific interest. |

Advantages of Real Estate Investment

In recent years real estate values have fluctuated widely in various regions of the country. As a result the ability of such investments to produce a return greater than the inflation rate (to serve as an "inflation hedge") has been impaired. This lack of potential profitability has made some real estate investments very unattractive to potential investors.

Still, real estate investments have shown an above-average *rate of return,* generally higher than the prevailing interest rate charged by mortgage lenders. Theoretically this means that an investor can use the *leverage* of borrowed money to finance a real estate purchase and feel relatively sure that, if held long enough, the asset will yield more money than it costs to finance the purchase.

Real estate investors also receive certain tax benefits. Both leveraging and taxes are discussed in full later in this chapter.

Disadvantages of Real Estate Investment

Unlike stocks and bonds, *real estate is not highly liquid* over a short period of time. This means that an investor cannot usually sell real estate quickly without taking some sort of loss. An investor in listed stocks need only call a stockbroker to liquidate such assets quickly when funds are needed. In contrast, even though a real estate investor may be able to raise a limited amount of cash by refinancing the property the investor may have to sell at a substantially lower price than desired to facilitate a quick sale.

In addition, *it is difficult to invest in real estate without some expert advice.* Investment decisions must be based on a careful study of all the facts, reinforced by a thorough knowledge of real estate and the manner in which it is affected by the marketplace.

Rarely can a real estate investor sit idly by and watch his or her money grow. *Management decisions must be made.* For example, can the investor effectively manage the property personally, or would it be preferable to hire a professional property manager? How much rent should be charged? How should repairs and tenant grievances be handled? "Sweat equity" (physical improvements accomplished by the investor personally) may be required to make the asset profitable.

Finally, and most important, *a high degree of risk* can be involved in real estate investment. There is always the possibility that an investor's property will decrease in value during the period it is held or that it will not generate an income sufficient to make it profitable.

The Investment

The most important form of real estate investment is *direct ownership*. Both individuals and corporations may own real estate directly and manage it for appreciation or cash flow (income). Property held for **appreciation** is generally expected to increase in value and to show a profit when sold at some future date. Income property is just that—property held for current income as well as a potential profit upon its sale.

Appreciation

Real estate is an avenue of investment open to those interested in holding property *primarily* for appreciation.

Two main factors affect appreciation: inflation and intrinsic value. **Inflation** is defined as the *increase in the amount of money in circulation, which results in a decline in its value coupled with a rise in wholesale and retail prices*. The **intrinsic value** of real estate is the result of a person's individual choices and preferences for a given geographical area, based on the features and amenities that the area has to offer. For example, property located in a well-kept suburb near business and shopping areas would have a greater intrinsic value to most people than similar property in a more isolated location. As a rule, the greater the intrinsic value, the more money a property can command upon its sale.

Unimproved land. Quite often investors speculate in purchases of either agricultural (farm) land or undeveloped (raw) land located in what is expected to be a major path of growth. In these cases, however, the property's intrinsic value and potential for appreciation are not easy to determine. Indeed this type of investment carries with it many inherent risks. How fast will the area develop? Will it grow sufficiently for the investor to make a good profit? Will the expected growth even occur? More importantly, will the profits eventually realized from the property be great enough to offset the costs (such as property taxes) of holding the land? Because these questions often cannot be answered with certainty, lending institutions are often reluctant to lend money for the purchase of raw land.

In addition, the Internal Revenue Service does not allow the depreciation (cost recovery) of land. Finally, such land may not be liquid (salable) at certain times under certain circumstances, because few people are willing to purchase raw or agricultural land on short notice. Despite all the risks land has historically been a good inflation hedge if held for a long term. It can also be a source of income to offset some of the holding costs. For example, agricultural land can be leased out for crops, timber production or grazing.

Investment in land ultimately is best left to experts, and even they frequently make bad land investment decisions.

Income

The wisest initial investment for a person who wishes to buy and personally manage real estate may be the purchase of rental income property.

Cash flow. The object of an investor's directing funds into income property is to generate spendable income, usually called *cash flow*. The **cash flow** is the total amount of money remaining after all expenditures have been paid, including taxes, operating costs and mortgage payments. The cash flow produced by any given parcel of real estate is determined by at least three factors: amount of rent received, operating expenses and method of debt repayment.

Generally the amount of *rent* (income) that a property may command depends on a number of factors, including location, physical appearance and amenities. If the cash flow from rents is not enough to cover all expenses, a *negative cash flow* will result.

To keep cash flow high an investor should attempt to *keep operating expenses reasonably low*. Such operating expenses include general maintenance of the building, repairs, utilities, taxes and tenant services (switchboard facilities, security systems and so forth).

In Practice . . .

With many of the tax advantages of real estate investment being reduced or withdrawn by Congress, licensees should advise investors to analyze each proposed purchase carefully with an accountant. It is more important than ever to be sure an investment will "carry itself by covering its own expenses." Where negative cash flow is anticipated, the investor's own tax bracket may be the deciding factor. (Income tax calculations are usually figured at the investor's marginal tax rate, that rate at which his or her top dollar of income is taxed.)

An investor often stands to make more money by investing borrowed money, usually obtained through a mortgage loan or deed of trust loan. *Low mortgage payments* spread over a long period of time result in a higher cash flow because they allow the investor to retain more income each month; conversely, higher mortgage payments would contribute to a lower cash flow.

Investment opportunities. Traditional income-producing property investments include apartment and office buildings, hotels, motels, shopping centers and industrial properties. Investors have historically found well-located, one- to four-family dwellings to be favorable investments. However, in recent years many communities have seen severe overbuilding of office space and shopping centers, with high vacancy rates.

Leverage

Leverage is the use of *borrowed money to finance the bulk of an investment*. As a rule an investor can receive a maximum return from the initial investment (the down payment and closing and other costs) by making a small down payment, paying a low interest rate and spreading mortgage payments over as long a period as possible.

The effect of leveraging for an investor is to provide, on a sale of the asset, a return that is a reflection of the effect of market forces on the entire amount of the original purchase price but is measured against only the actual cash invested. For example, if an investor spends $100,000 for rental property and makes a

$20,000 down payment, then sells that property five years later for $125,000, the return over five years is $25,000. Disregarding ownership expenses, the return is not 25 percent ($25,000 compared to $100,000), but 125 percent of the original amount invested ($25,000 compared to $20,000).

Risks are directly proportionate to leverage. A high degree of leverage gives the investor and lender a high degree of risk; lower leverage results in a lower risk. When values drop in an area or vacancy rates rise, the highly leveraged investor may be unable to pay even the financing costs of the property.

Equity buildup. Equity buildup is that portion of the payment directed toward the principal rather than the interest, *plus* any gain in property value due to appreciation. In a sense equity buildup is like money in the bank to the investor. Although this accumulated equity is not realized as cash unless the property is sold or refinanced, the equity interest may be sold, exchanged or mortgaged (refinanced) to be used as leverage for other investments.

Pyramiding through refinancing. By holding and refinancing using equity and appreciation buildup rather than selling or exchanging already-owned properties, an investor can increase his or her holdings without investing any additional capital. Through this practice, known as **pyramiding,** an investor who started out with a small initial cash down payment could end up owning heavily mortgaged properties worth hundreds of thousands or millions of dollars. With sufficient cash flow to cover all costs the income derived from such assets could pay off the various mortgage debts and produce a handsome profit.

Tax Benefits

One of the main reasons real estate investments were popular and profitable in the past is that federal law allowed investors to use losses generated by such investments to shelter income from other sources. Although tax laws have changed and some tax advantages of owning investment real estate are altered periodically by Congress, with professional tax advice the investor can still make a wise real estate purchase.

Capital Gains

The tax law no longer favors long-term investments by reducing taxable gain (profit) on their sale or exchange. Capital gain is defined as the difference between the adjusted basis of property and its net selling price. At various times tax law has excluded a portion of capital gains from income tax, in percentages ranging from zero to 50 percent.

Basis. A property's cost basis will determine the amount of gain to be taxed. The **basis** of the property is the investor's initial cost for the real estate. The investor adds to the basis the cost of any physical improvements subsequently made to the property and subtracts from the basis the amount of any depreciation claimed as a tax deduction (explained later) to derive the property's **adjusted basis.** When the property is sold by the investor, the amount by which the sale price exceeds the property's adjusted basis is the capital gain.

For example, an investor purchased a single-family dwelling for use as a rental property. The purchase price was $45,000. The investor is now selling the property for $100,000. Shortly before the sale date the investor made $3,000 worth of capital improvements to the home. Depreciation of $10,000 on the property

Must do this

improvements has been taken during the term of the investor's ownership. The investor will pay a broker's commission of seven percent of the sales price and will also pay closing costs of $600. The investor's capital gain is computed as follows:

Selling price:		$100,000
Less:		
7% commission	$7,000	
closing costs	+ 600	
	$7,600	−7,600
Net sales price:		$ 92,400
Basis:		
original cost	$45,000	
improvements	+3,000	
	$48,000	
Less:		
depreciation	−10,000	
Adjusted basis:	$38,000	−38,000
Total capital gain:		$ 54,400

Again, current law will specify what percentage of capital gains is taxable as income. To determine the taxable amount the investor multiplies the total capital gain by the current percentage (in decimal form).

Exchanges

Real estate investors can defer taxation of *capital gains* by making a property **exchange.** Even if property has appreciated greatly since its initial purchase, it may be exchanged for other property and the property owner will incur tax liability on the sale only if additional capital or property is also received. Note, however, that *the tax is deferred, not eliminated.* Whenever the investor sells the property, the capital gain will be taxed.

To qualify as a tax-deferred exchange, the properties involved must be of *like kind*—for example, apartment building for apartment building. Any additional capital or personal property included with the transaction to even out the exchange is considered **boot,** and the party receiving it is taxed at the time of the exchange. The value of the boot is added to the basis of the property with which it is given.

For example, investor A owns an apartment building with an adjusted basis of $225,000 and a market value of $375,000. Investor A exchanges the building plus $75,000 cash for another apartment building having a market value of $450,000. That building, owned by investor B, has an adjusted basis of $175,000. A's basis in the new building will be $300,000 (the $225,000 basis of the building exchanged plus the $75,000 cash boot paid), and A has no tax liability on the exchange. B must pay tax on the $75,000 boot received and has a basis of $175,000 (the same as the previous building) in the building now owned.

In Practice . . .

Tax-deferred exchanges are governed by strict federal requirements, and competent guidance from a tax professional is essential.

Depreciation (Cost Recovery)

Depreciation, or **cost recovery,** allows an investor to recover the cost of an income-producing asset by way of tax deductions over the period of the asset's useful life.

While investors rarely purchase property without the expectation that it will appreciate over time, the view of the Internal Revenue Service is that all physical structures will deteriorate and hence lose value over time. Cost recovery deductions may be taken only on personal property and improvements to land and only if they are used in a trade or business or for the production of income. Thus a cost recovery deduction cannot be claimed on an individual's personal residence, and *land cannot be depreciated*—technically it never wears out or becomes obsolete.

If depreciation is taken periodically in equal amounts over an asset's useful life, the method used is called *straight-line depreciation*. For certain property purchased before 1987 it was also possible to have used an *accelerated cost recovery system (ACRS)* to claim greater deductions in the early years of ownership, gradually reducing the amount deducted in each year of the useful life.

For property placed in service as of January 1, 1987, the Tax Reform Act of 1986 set the recovery period for residential rental property at 27.5 years and for nonresidential property at 31.5 years, using *only* the straight-line depreciation method.

Deductions and TRA '86

The Tax Reform Act of 1986 (TRA '86) limits the deductibility of losses from rental property. The first $25,000 of loss can be used to offset income from any source provided that the investor *actively participates* in the management and operation of the property and has taxable income of no more than $100,000 before the deduction is made. The deduction is reduced by $.50 for every dollar of income over $100,000 and is thus eliminated completely when income reaches $150,000. Two examples will help to illustrate the impact of this law.

1. Harvey has adjusted gross income of $130,000 and losses of $20,000 from three apartment buildings that he owns and personally manages. Harvey is entitled to a deduction of only $10,000 (because the $25,000 maximum is reduced by $.50 for every dollar of the $30,000 Harvey earned over $100,000), reducing his taxable income to $120,000.

2. Helen has adjusted gross income of $100,000 and losses of $20,000 from rental property that she actively manages. Helen is entitled to a deduction of the full $20,000 (her income does not exceed $100,000), reducing her taxable income to $80,000.

Active participation in management may be as great as personally managing the day-to-day operation of the rental property with no outside assistance or as minimal as simply making management decisions, such as the approval of new tenants and lease terms, while hiring others to provide services. A *passive activity*—one in which the investor is not an active participant—would include acting as a limited partner, that is, contributing investment monies but having no voice in the operation of the management.

The Tax Reform Act prevents an investor from using a loss from a passive activity to shelter active income (such as wages) or portfolio income (such as stock dividends, bank interest and capital gains). Generally a passive investor can offset investment losses only against investment income. If the passive investor has no other current investment income, the loss may be carried over to offset investment income in future years. If the investment is sold before the loss is used, it may offset what would otherwise be a taxable gain on the sale.

Tax credits. A **tax credit** is a direct reduction in tax due, rather than a deduction from income before tax is computed. A tax credit is therefore of far greater value.

Investors in older-building renovations and low-income housing projects may use designated tax credits to offset tax on up to $25,000 of other income. This is a major exception to the rule requiring active participation in the project; even passive investors can take advantage of tax credits. The maximum income level at which the credits can be taken is also higher. Investors with adjusted gross income of up to $200,000 are entitled to the full $25,000 offset, which is reduced by $.50 for every additional dollar of income and eliminated entirely for incomes above $250,000.

Since 1976 tax credits have been provided for taxpayers who renovate historic property. Historic property is property so designated by the Department of the Interior and listed in the *National Register of Historic Landmarks* or property of historic significance that is located in an area certified by a state as a historic district. The allowable credit is 20 percent of the money spent on renovation of historic property. The property can be depreciated, but the full amount of the tax credit must be subtracted from the basis derived by adding purchase cost and renovation expenses.

The work must be accomplished in accordance with federal historic property guidelines and certified by the Department of the Interior. After renovation the property must be used as a place of business or rented—it cannot be used as the personal residence of the person taking the tax credit.

Installment Sales

A taxpayer who sells real property and receives payment on an installment basis (periodically for at least two years) may report any profit on the transaction year by year as it is collected. Any accelerated depreciation previously taken, however, must be recaptured immediately. There are many complex provisions regarding **installment sales.**

Real Estate Investment Syndicates

A real estate investment syndicate is a form of business venture in which a group of people pool their resources to own and/or develop a particular piece of property. In this manner people with only modest capital can invest in large-scale operations such as high-rise apartment buildings and shopping centers. A certain amount of profit is realized from rents collected on the investment, but the main return usually comes when the syndicate sells the property.

Syndicate participation can take many different legal forms, from tenancy in common and joint tenancy to various kinds of partnerships, corporations and trusts. *Private syndication,* which generally involves a small group of closely associated or widely experienced investors, is distinguished from *public syndication,* which generally involves a much larger group of investors who may or may not be knowledgeable about real estate as an investment. Any pooling of individuals' funds raises questions of registration of securities under federal securities laws and state securities laws, commonly referred to as *blue-sky laws.*

To protect members of the public who are not sophisticated investors but may be solicited to participate, securities laws include provisions that control and regulate the offering and sale of securities. Real estate securities must be registered with state officials and the federal Securities and Exchange Commission (SEC) when they meet the defined conditions of a public offering. The number of prospects solicited, the total number of investors, the financial background and sophistication of the investors and the value or price per unit of investment are pertinent facts.

In Practice . . .   *Salespeople of such real estate securities may be required to obtain special licenses and state registration.*

Forms of Syndicates   A general partnership is organized so that *all members of the group share equally in the managerial decisions, profits and losses involved with the investment.* A certain member (or members) of the syndicate is designated to act as trustee for the group, holds title to the property and maintains it in the syndicate's name.

Under a limited partnership agreement *one party* (or parties), usually a developer or real estate broker, *organizes, operates and is responsible for the entire syndicate.* This person is called the *general partner.* The other members of the partnership are merely investors; they have no voice in the organization and direction of the operation. These *passive investors are called limited partners.*

The limited partners share in the profits and compensate the general partner out of such profits. The limited partners stand to lose only as much as they invest— nothing more. The general partner(s) is (are) totally responsible for any excess losses incurred by the investment. The sale of a limited partnership interest involves the sale of an *investment security* as defined by the SEC. Therefore such sales are subject to state and federal laws concerning the sale of securities. Unless exempt, the securities must be registered with the federal Securities and Exchange Commission and the appropriate state authorities.

Real Estate Investment Trusts   By directing their funds into **real estate investment trusts (REITs)** real estate investors can take advantage of the same tax benefits as mutual fund investors. A real estate investment trust does not have to pay corporate income tax as long as 95 percent of its income is distributed to its shareholders and certain other conditions are met. To qualify as a REIT at least 75 percent of the trust's income must come from real estate. The three types of investment trusts are discussed below.

Equity trusts. Much like mutual fund operations, equity REITs pool an assortment of large-scale income properties and sell shares to investors. In contrast a real estate syndicate pools its funds to purchase *one* particular property. An equity trust also differs from a syndicate in that the trust realizes and directs its main profits through the *income* derived from the various properties it owns rather than from the sale of those properties.

Mortgage trusts. Mortgage trusts operate similarly to equity trusts except that the mortgage trusts buy and sell real estate mortgages (usually short-term, junior instruments) rather than real property. A mortgage trust's major sources of income are mortgage interest and origination fees. Mortgage trusts may also make construction loans and finance land acquisitions.

Combination trusts. Combination trusts invest shareholders' funds in both real estate assets and mortgage loans. It has been predicted that these types of trusts will be best able to withstand economic slumps because they can balance their investments and liabilities more efficiently than can the other types of trusts.

Real Estate Mortgage Investment Conduits

The Tax Reform Act created a new tax entity that may issue multiple classes of investor interests (securities) backed by a pool of mortgages.

The **real estate mortgage investment conduit (REMIC)** has complex qualification, transfer and liquidation rules. Qualifications include the asset test (substantially all assets after a start-up period must consist of qualified mortgages and permitted investments) and the requirement that investors' interests consist of one or more classes of regular interests and a single class of residual interests. Holders of regular interests receive interest or similar payments based on either a fixed rate or a variable rate. Holders of residual interests receive distributions (if any) on a pro-rata basis.

Key Terms

adjusted basis	installment sale
appreciation	intrinsic value
basis	leverage
boot	pyramiding
cash flow	real estate investment trust (REIT)
cost recovery	real estate mortgage investment conduit (REMIC)
depreciation	syndicate
exchange	tax credit
inflation	

Summary

Traditionally real estate investment has offered an above-average rate of return while acting as an effective inflation hedge and allowing an investor to make use of other people's money through leverage. There may also be tax advantages to owning real estate. However, real estate is not a highly liquid investment and often carries with it a high degree of risk. Also, it is difficult to invest in real estate without expert advice, and a certain amount of involvement is usually required to establish and maintain the investment.

Investment property held for appreciation purposes is generally expected to increase in value to a point where its selling price is enough to cover holding costs and show a profit as well. The two main factors affecting appreciation are inflation and the property's present and future intrinsic value. Real estate held for income purposes is generally expected to generate a steady flow of income, called cash flow, and to show a profit upon its sale.

An investor hoping to use maximum leverage in financing an investment should make a small down payment, pay low interest rates and spread mortgage payments over as long a period as possible. By holding and refinancing properties, known as pyramiding, an investor may substantially increase investment holdings without contributing additional capital. The highly leveraged investor has correspondingly high risk.

By exchanging one property for another with an equal or greater selling value an investor can defer paying tax on the gain realized until a sale is made. A total tax deferment is possible only if the investor receives no cash or other incentive to even out the exchange. If received, such cash or property is called boot and is taxed.

Depreciation (cost recovery) is a concept that allows an investor to recover in tax deductions the basis of an asset over the period of its useful life. Only costs of improvements to land may be recovered, not costs for the land itself. The Tax Reform Act of 1986 greatly limited the potential for investment losses to shelter other income, but tax credits are still allowed for projects involving low-income housing and older buildings.

An investor may defer federal income taxes on a gain realized from the sale of an investment property through an installment sale of property.

Individuals may also invest in real estate through an investment syndicate; these generally include general and limited partnerships. Other forms of real estate investment are the real estate investment trust (REIT) and the real estate mortgage investment conduit (REMIC).

The real estate broker and salesperson should be familiar with the rudimentary tax implications of real property ownership but should refer clients to competent tax advisers for answers to specific questions.

Questions

1. The advantages of real estate investment include:
   - a. the illiquidity of the investment.
   - b. the need for expert advice.
   - c. the fact that the investment can be an inflation hedge.
   - d. the degree of risk involved.

2. Vacant land can be a good investment because:
   - a. it must appreciate enough to cover expenses.
   - b. it can have intrinsic value.
   - c. bank financing is easily arranged.
   - d. it may not be depreciated.

3. The increase of money in circulation, resulting in a sharp rise in prices and an equally sharp decline in the value of money, is called:
   - a. appreciation.
   - b. inflation.
   - c. negative cash flow.
   - d. recapture.

4. A small multifamily property generates $50,000 in rental income with expenses of $45,000 annually, including $35,000 in debt service. The property appreciates about $25,000 a year. On this property the cash flow is:
   - a. $5,000.
   - b. $15,000.
   - c. $25,000.
   - d. $35,000.

5. Leverage involves the extensive use of:
   - a. cost recovery.
   - b. borrowed money.
   - c. government subsidies.
   - d. alternative taxes.

6. A property's equity represents its current value less:
   - a. depreciation.
   - b. mortgage indebtedness.
   - c. physical improvements.
   - d. selling costs and depreciation.

7. An investor's marginal tax rate is the:
   - a. total tax bill divided by net taxable income.
   - b. extra tax if he has too many tax shelters.
   - c. top applicable income tax bracket.
   - d. percentage taxable on an installment sale.

8. The primary source of tax shelter in real estate investments comes from the accounting concept known as:
   - a. recapture.
   - b. boot.
   - c. depreciation.
   - d. net operating income.

9. For tax purposes the initial cost of an investment property plus the cost of any subsequent improvements to the property, less depreciation, represents the investment's:
   - a. adjusted basis.
   - b. capital gains.
   - c. basis.
   - d. salvage value.

10. The money left in an investor's pocket after expenses, including debt service, have been paid is known as:
    - a. net operating income.
    - b. gross income.
    - c. cash flow.
    - d. internal rate of return.

11. An investment syndicate in which all members share equally in the managerial decisions, profits and losses involved in the venture is an example of a:
    - a. real estate investment trust.
    - b. limited partnership.
    - c. real estate mortgage trust.
    - d. general partnership.

12. Shareholders in a real estate trust generally:
    - a. receive most of the trust's income each year.
    - b. take an active part in management.
    - c. find it difficult to sell their shares.
    - d. realize their main profit through sales of property.

13. In an installment sale of one's own home taxable gain is received and may be reported as income by the seller:
    - a. in the year the sale is initiated.
    - b. in the year the final installment payment is made.
    - c. in each year that installment payments are received.
    - d. at any one time during the period installment payments are received.

14. A separate license or registration may be required for the sale of:

    a. all investment property.
    b. real estate securities.
    c. installment property.
    d. boots.

15. A new tax entity that issues securities backed by a pool of mortgages is a:

    a. REIT.   c. TRA.
    b. REMIC.   d. general partnership.

23

Closing the Real Estate Transaction

The moment when a real estate transaction is finalized is known by many names, including *closing, settlement* and *transfer* (of title). In the Northeast, where the parties to the transaction sit around a single table and exchange a bewildering variety of documents, the process is known as *passing papers*. ("We passed papers on the new house Wednesday morning.") In the West, where buyer and seller may never meet and paperwork is handled by an escrow agent, the process is known as *closing escrow*. ("We're going to close escrow on the place next week.") Whether the closing occurs face-to-face or through escrow, main concerns are that the buyer receive the marketable title, that the seller receive the purchase price and that certain other items be adjusted properly between the two.

Though real estate licensees do not always conduct the proceedings at a closing, they usually attend and therefore should be thoroughly familiar with the process.

It is also obviously in the broker's interest that a transaction in which he or she has been instrumental be finalized successfully and smoothly. In addition, in some states a closing statement problem is part of the broker's licensing examination. Although the salesperson's examination does not usually include completion of a closing statement problem, most states require an applicant to compute prorations, and many include the completion of a sales contract and listing agreement from the description of a sample transaction.

Face-to-Face Closing	A face-to-face closing of a real estate transaction involves a gathering of interested parties at which the promises made in the *real estate sales contract* are kept, or *executed*. In many sales transactions two closings actually take place at this time: the closing of the buyer's loan—the disbursal of mortgage funds by the lender—and the closing of the sale.

As discussed in Chapter 10, a sales contract is the blueprint for the completion of a real estate transaction. Before completing the exchange of documents and funds the parties should assure themselves that the various stipulations of their sales contract have been met.

The buyer will want to be sure that the seller is delivering good title and that the property is in the promised condition. This involves inspecting the title evidence, the deed the seller will give, any documents representing the removal of undesired liens and encumbrances, the survey, the termite report and any leases if there are tenants on the premises. The seller will want to be sure that the buyer has obtained the stipulated financing and has sufficient funds to complete the sale. Both parties will wish to inspect the closing statement to make sure that all monies involved in the transaction have been accounted for properly. In many areas the parties are usually accompanied by their *attorneys*.

When the parties are satisfied that everything is in order, the exchange is made, and all pertinent documents are then recorded. The documents must be recorded in the correct order to avoid creating a defect in the title. For example, if the seller is paying off an existing loan and the buyer is obtaining a new loan, the seller's satisfaction of mortgage must be recorded before the seller's deed to the buyer. The buyer's new mortgage or deed of trust must then be recorded after the deed, because the buyers cannot pledge the property as security for the loan until they own it.

Where Closings Are Held and Who Attends

Face-to-face closings may be held at a number of locations, including the offices of the title insurance company, the lending institution, one of the parties' attorneys, the broker, the county recorder (or other local recording official) or the escrow company. Those attending a closing may include any of the following interested parties:

1. Buyer

2. Seller

3. Real estate licensees (brokers and salespeople)

4. Attorney(s) for the seller and/or buyer

5. Representatives of lending institutions involved with the buyer's new mortgage loan, the buyer's assumption of the seller's existing loan or the seller's payoff of an existing loan

6. Representative of the title insurance company

Closing agent. One person usually conducts the proceedings at a closing and calculates the official settlement, or division of incomes and expenses between the parties. In some areas real estate brokers preside, but more commonly the closing agent is an escrow agent, the buyer's or seller's attorney, a representative of the lender or a representative of a title company. Some title companies and law firms employ paralegal assistants, called *closers,* who conduct all closings for their firms. The closer is the person in such offices who arranges the closing with the parties involved, prepares the closing statements, compares figures with lenders and orders title evidence, surveys and other miscellaneous items needed.

Closing in Escrow

Although there are a few states where transactions are never closed in escrow, escrow closings are used to some extent in most states, especially in the West.

An **escrow** is a method of closing in which a disinterested third party is authorized to act as escrow agent and coordinate the closing activities. The escrow agent may also be called the *escrow holder*. The escrow agent may be an attorney, a title company, a trust company, an escrow company or the escrow department of a lending institution. While many brokerages do offer escrow services, a broker cannot be a disinterested party in a transaction from which he or she expects to collect a commission. Because the escrow agent is placed in a position of great trust, many states have laws regulating escrow agents and limiting who may serve in this capacity.

The Escrow Procedure

When a transaction will be closed in escrow, the buyer and seller choose an escrow agent and execute escrow instructions to the escrow agent after the sales contract is signed. Once the contract is signed, the broker turns over the earnest money to the escrow agent, who deposits it in a special trust, or escrow, account.

Buyer and seller deposit all pertinent documents and other items with the escrow agent before the specified date of closing. The seller will usually deposit:

1. the *deed* conveying the property to the buyer;

2. title *evidence* (abstract, title insurance policy or Torrens certificate);

3. existing hazard *insurance* policies;

4. a letter from the lender and an estoppel certificate stating the exact principal remaining if the buyer is assuming the seller's loan;

5. *affidavits of title* (if required);

6. a reduction certificate (payoff statement) if the seller's loan is to be paid off; and

7. other instruments or documents necessary to clear the title or to complete the transaction.

The buyer will deposit:

1. the balance of the *cash needed* to complete the purchase usually in the form of a certified check;

2. loan documents if the buyer is securing a new loan;

3. proof of hazard insurance, including, where required, flood insurance; and

4. other necessary documents.

The escrow agent is given the authority to examine the title evidence. When marketable title is shown in the name of the buyer and all other conditions of the escrow agreement have been met, the agent is authorized to disburse the purchase price—minus all charges and expenses—to the seller and record the deed and mortgage or deed of trust (if a new loan has been obtained by the purchaser).

If the escrow agent's examination of the title discloses liens against the seller or a lien for which the seller is responsible, the escrow instructions usually provide that a portion of the purchase price can be withheld from the seller and used to pay such liens as are necessary to clear the title so the transaction can be closed.

If the seller cannot clear the title, or if for any reason the sale cannot be consummated and the buyer will not accept the title as is, then the escrow instructions usually provide that the parties be returned to their former status. To accomplish this the purchaser reconveys title to the seller and the escrow agent restores all purchase money to the buyer. Because the escrow depends on specific conditions being met before the transfer becomes binding on the parties, the courts have held that the parties can be reinstated to their former status.

IRS Reporting Requirements

Every real estate transaction must be reported to the Internal Revenue Service by the closing agent on a form 1099. Information includes the sales price and the seller's social security number.

If the closing agent does not notify the IRS, the responsibility for filing the form 1099 then falls on the mortgage lender, although the brokers or the parties to the transaction ultimately could be held liable.

Broker's Role at Closing

Depending on the locality, the broker's role at a closing can vary from simply collecting the commission to conducting the proceedings. As discussed earlier in the text, a real estate broker is not authorized to give legal advice or otherwise engage in the practice of law. In some areas of the country, principally in some of the eastern states, this means that a broker's job is essentially finished when the sales contract is signed; at that point the attorneys take over. Even so, a broker's service generally continues after the contract is signed in that the broker advises the parties on practical matters and makes sure all the details are taken care of so that the closing can proceed smoothly. In this capacity the broker might make arrangements for such items as title evidence, surveys, appraisals, termite inspections and repairs or might recommend sources of these services to the parties.

Lender's Interest in Closing

Whether a buyer is obtaining new financing or assuming the seller's existing loan, the lender wants to protect its security interest in the property—to make sure that the buyer is getting good, marketable title and that tax and insurance payments are maintained so that there will be no liens with greater priority than the mortgage lien and the insurance will be paid up if the property is damaged or destroyed. For this reason the lender will frequently require a title insurance policy; a fire and hazard insurance policy, with receipt for the premium; additional information, such as a survey, a termite or other inspection report or a certificate of occupancy (for newly constructed buildings); establishment of a reserve, or escrow, account for tax and insurance payments; and possibly representation by its own attorney at the closing.

RESPA Requirements

The federal **Real Estate Settlement Procedures Act (RESPA),** was created to ensure that the buyer and seller in a residential real estate sale or transfer have knowledge of all settlement costs. In this context residential real estate includes one- to four-family homes, cooperatives and condominiums. *RESPA requirements apply when the purchase is financed by a federally related mortgage loan.* Federally related loans include those made by banks, savings and loan associations or other lenders whose deposits are insured by federal agencies (FDIC); those insured by the FHA or guaranteed by the VA; those administered by HUD and those intended to be sold by the lender to Fannie Mae, Ginnie Mae or Freddie Mac.

RESPA regulations apply only to transactions involving *new first mortgage loans.* A transaction financed solely by seller financing an installment contract (land contract, contract for deed) or the buyer's assumption of the seller's existing loan would *not* be covered by RESPA unless the terms of the assumed loan are modified or the lender imposes charges of more than $50 for the assumption. When a transaction is covered by RESPA, the following requirements must be complied with:

1. *Special information booklet:* Lenders must give a copy of the HUD booklet *Settlement Costs and You* to every person from whom they receive or for whom they prepare a loan application. This booklet provides the borrower with general information about settlement (closing) costs and explains the various RESPA provisions, including a line-by-line discussion of the Uniform Settlement Statement (see item 3).

2. *Good-faith estimate of settlement costs:* At the time of the loan application, or within three business days, the lender must provide the borrower with a good-faith estimate of the settlement costs the borrower is likely to incur. This estimate may be a specific figure or a range of costs based on comparable past transactions in the area. In addition, if the lender requires use of a particular attorney or title insurance company to conduct the closing, the lender must state whether it has any business relationship with that firm and must estimate the charges for this service.

3. *Uniform Settlement Statement (HUD Form 1):* RESPA provides that loan closing information must be prepared on a special HUD form, the **Uniform Settlement Statement** (Figure 23.1), designed to detail all financial particulars of a transaction. The completed statement must itemize all charges imposed by the lender. Charges incurred by the buyer and seller, contracted for separately and outside the closing, do not have to be disclosed. Items paid for prior to the closing must be marked clearly as such on the statement and are omitted from the totals. This statement must be made available for inspection by the borrower *at or before* the closing. Upon the borrower's request the closing agent must permit the borrower to inspect the settlement statement, to the extent that the figures are available, one business day before the closing. The Uniform Settlement Statement may be altered to allow for local custom, and certain lines may be deleted if they do not apply in the area.

4. *Prohibition against kickbacks:* RESPA explicitly prohibits the payment of kickbacks, or unearned fees, such as when an insurance agency pays a kickback to a lender for referring one of the lender's recent customers to the agency. This prohibition does *not* include fee splitting between cooperating brokers or members of multiple-listing services, brokerage referral arrangements or the division of a commission between a broker and his or her salespeople.

RESPA is administered by the U.S. Department of Housing and Urban Development (HUD).

The Title Procedure

The principle of caveat emptor requires the purchaser and the purchaser's lender to assure themselves that the seller's property and title comply with the contract requirements. The sales contract usually includes time limitations for the parties to obtain and present title evidence and remove any objections to the title. A contract that includes the provision "time is of the essence" expresses the agreement of the parties that all *time limitations are to be met as stated*.

The seller is usually required to show proof of ownership by producing a current *abstract* or *title commitment* from the title insurance company. When an abstract of title is used, the purchaser's attorney examines it and issues an opinion of title. This opinion, like the title commitment, sets forth the status of the seller's title, showing liens, encumbrances, easements, conditions or restrictions that appear on the record and to which the seller's title is subject.

On the date when the sale is actually completed (the date of delivery of the deed), the buyer has a title commitment or an abstract that was issued several days or weeks before the closing. For this reason the title or abstract company is usually required to make two searches of the public records. The first shows the status of the seller's title on the date of the sales contract; the seller usually pays the charges for this report. The second search is made after the closing and covers the date when the deed is recorded to the purchaser; the purchaser generally pays to "bring the title down" to the closing date.

In this later search the seller is usually required to execute an *affidavit of title*. This is a sworn statement in which the seller assures the title insurance company (and the buyer) that since the date of the title examination there have been no judgments, bankruptcies or divorces involving the seller, no unrecorded deeds or contracts made, no repairs or improvements that have not been paid for, and no defects in the title that the seller knows of; the seller also assures that he or she is in possession of the premises. This form is always required by the title insurance company before it will issue an owner's policy, particularly an extended-coverage policy, to the buyer. Through this affidavit the title insurance company obtains the right to sue the seller if his or her statements in the affidavit prove incorrect.

In some areas where real estate sales transactions are customarily closed through an escrow the escrow instructions usually include provision for an extended-coverage policy to be issued to the buyer as of the date of closing. In such cases there is no need for the seller to execute an affidavit of title.

Checking the Premises

It is important for the buyer to inspect the property to determine the interests of any parties in possession or other interests that cannot be determined from inspecting the public record. A *survey* is frequently required so that the purchaser will know the location and size of the property. The contract will specify who is to pay for this. It is usual for the survey to "spot" the location of all buildings, driveways, fences and other improvements located primarily on the premises being purchased, as well as any such improvements located on adjoining property that may encroach on the premises being bought. The survey also sets out, in full, any existing easements and encroachments.

Shortly before the closing takes place the buyer will usually make a *final inspection* of the property (often called the *walk-through*) with the broker. Through this inspection the buyer can make sure that necessary repairs have been made, that the property has been well maintained (both inside and outside), that all fixtures are in place and that there has been no unauthorized removal or alteration of any part of the improvements.

Releasing Existing Liens

When the purchaser is paying cash or is obtaining a new loan to purchase the property, the seller's existing loan is paid in full and released of record. To know the exact amount required to pay the existing loan the seller secures a current *payoff statement* from the lender. This payoff statement sets forth the unpaid amount of principal, interest due through the date of payment, the fee for issuing the certificate of satisfaction or release deed, credits (if any) for tax and insurance reserves and penalties that may be due because the loan is being prepaid before its maturity. The same procedure would be followed for any other liens that must be released before the buyer takes title.

When the buyer is assuming the seller's existing loan, the buyer will want to know the exact balance of the loan as of the closing date. In some areas it is customary for the buyer to obtain a **mortgage reduction certificate** (sometimes inaccurately referred to as an *estoppel certificate*) from the lender, stating the exact balance due and the last interest payment made.

Preparation of Closing Statements	A typical real estate transaction involves expenses for both parties in addition to the purchase price. These include items prepaid by the seller for which he or she must be reimbursed (such as, insurance premiums and prepaid taxes) and items of expense the seller has incurred but the buyer will be billed for (such as mortgage interest paid in arrears). The financial responsibility for these items must be prorated (adjusted or divided) between the buyer and the seller. In closing a transaction it is customary to account for all these items by preparing a written statement to determine how much money the buyer needs and how much the seller will net after expenses. There are many different formats of closing statements, or settlement statements, but all are designed to achieve the same results.

The broker should possess the necessary knowledge to prepare statements to give the seller an accurate estimate of sale costs. In addition, the buyer must be prepared with the proper amount of money to complete the purchase, and again, the broker should be able to assist by making a reasonably accurate estimate.

How the Closing Statement Works	The completion of a **closing statement** involves an accounting of the parties' debits and credits. A **debit** is a charge, an amount that the party being debited owes and must pay at the closing. A **credit** is an amount entered in a person's favor—either an amount that the party being credited has already paid, an amount that he or she must be reimbursed for or an amount the buyer promises to pay in the form of a loan.

To determine the amount the buyer needs at the closing the buyer's debits are totaled—any expenses and prorated amounts for items prepaid by the seller are added to the purchase price. Then the buyer's credits are totaled. These would include the earnest money (already paid), the balance of the loan the buyer is obtaining or assuming and the seller's share of any prorated items that the buyer will pay in the future. Finally the total of the buyer's credits is subtracted from the total amount the buyer owes (debits) to arrive at the actual amount of cash the buyer must bring to the closing. Usually the buyer brings a cashier's check or a certified check.

A similar procedure is followed to determine how much money the seller will actually receive. The seller's debits and credits are each totaled. The credits would include the purchase price, plus the buyer's share of any prorated items that the seller has prepaid. The seller's debits would include expenses, the seller's share of prorated items to be paid later by the buyer and the balance of any mortgage loan or other lien that the seller is paying off. Finally the total of the seller's charges is subtracted from the total credits to arrive at the amount the seller will receive.

Expenses

In addition to the payment of the sales price and the proration of taxes, interest and the like, a number of other expenses and charges may be involved in a real estate transaction.

Broker's commission. The broker's commission is usually paid by the seller because the broker is usually the seller's agent. When the buyer has employed the broker, the buyer pays the commission, unless other arrangements have been made.

Attorney's fees. If either of the parties' attorneys will be paid from the closing proceeds, that party will be charged with the expense in the closing statement.

Recording expenses. The charges for recording different types of documents vary widely. These charges are established by law and are based on the number of pages included in the instrument.

The *seller* usually pays for recording charges (filing fees) necessary to clear all defects and furnish the purchaser with a marketable title in accordance with the contract. Items customarily charged to the seller would include the recording of release deeds or satisfaction of mortgages, quitclaim deeds, affidavits and satisfaction of mechanic's lien claims. The *purchaser* pays for recording charges incidental to the actual transfer of title. Usually such items include recording the deed that conveys title to the purchaser and a mortgage or deed of trust executed by the purchaser.

Transfer tax. Most states require some form of transfer tax, conveyance fee or tax stamps on real estate conveyances. This expense is most often borne by the seller, although customs vary.

Title expenses. The responsibility for title expenses varies according to local custom. In most areas the seller is required to furnish evidence of good title and pay for the title search. If the buyer's attorney inspects the evidence or if the buyer purchases title insurance policies, the buyer is charged for these expenses.

Loan fees. When the purchaser is securing a new loan to finance the purchase, the lender will ordinarily charge a loan origination fee of one percent of the loan. The fee is usually paid by the purchaser at the time the transaction is closed. If the buyer is assuming the seller's existing financing, there may be an assumption fee.

The seller also may be charged fees by a lender if provided for in the contract. If the buyer finances the purchase with a VA loan, the seller may be required to pay discount points. Also, under the terms of some loans the seller may be required to pay a prepayment charge or penalty for paying off the existing loan in advance of its due date.

Tax reserves and insurance reserves (escrows or impound accounts). A *reserve* is a sum of money set aside to be used later for a particular purpose. The mortgage lender usually requires the borrower to establish and maintain a reserve so that the borrower will have sufficient funds to pay real estate taxes and renew hazard insurance policies when these items become due. To set up the reserve the borrower is required to make a lump-sum payment to the lender when the mortgage money is paid out (usually at the time of closing). Thereafter the borrower is required to pay into the reserve an amount equal to one month's portion of the *estimated* tax and insurance premium as part of the monthly payment made to the mortgage company (a PITI payment).

Appraisal fees. Either the seller or the purchaser pays the appraisal fees, depending on who orders the appraisal. When the buyer obtains a mortgage, it is customary for the lender to require an appraisal, which the buyer pays for.

Survey fees. The purchaser who obtains new mortgage financing customarily pays the survey fees. In some cases the sales contract may require the seller to furnish a survey.

Additional fees. An FHA borrower owes a lump sum for payment of the mortgage insurance premium (MIP) if it is not being financed as part of the loan. A VA mortgagor pays a one percent fee directly to the VA at closing. If a conventional loan carries private mortgage insurance, the buyer prepays one year's insurance premium at closing.

Prorations

Most closings involve the division of financial responsibility between the buyer and seller for such items as loan interest, taxes, rents, fuel and utility bills. These allowances are called **prorations.** Prorations are necessary to ensure that expenses are divided fairly between the seller and the buyer. For example, the seller may owe current taxes that have not been billed; the buyer would want this settled at the closing. In states where taxes must be paid in advance the seller would be entitled to a rebate at the closing. If the buyer assumes the seller's existing mortgage or deed of trust, the seller usually owes the buyer an allowance for accrued interest through the date of closing.

Accrued items are items to be prorated (such as water bills and interest on an assumed mortgage) that are owed by the seller but eventually will be paid by the buyer. The seller therefore gives the buyer credit for these items at closing.

Prepaid items are items to be prorated—such as fuel oil in a tank—that have been prepaid by the seller but not fully earned (not fully used up). They are therefore credits to the seller.

General rules for prorating. The rules or customs governing the computation of prorations for the closing of a real estate sale vary widely from state to state. In many states the real estate boards and the bar association have established closing rules and procedures. In some cases these rules and procedures control closings for the entire state; in others they merely affect closings within a given city, town or county.

Here are some general rules to guide you in studying the closing procedure and preparing the closing statement:

1. In most states the seller owns the property on the day of closing, and prorations or apportionments are usually made *to and including the day of closing*. In a few states, however, it is provided specifically that the buyer owns the

property on the closing date and that adjustments shall be made as of the day preceding the day on which title is closed.

2. Mortgage interest, real estate taxes, insurance premiums and similar expenses are usually computed by using *360 days in a year and 30 days in a month.* However, the rules in some areas provide for computing prorations on the basis of the actual number of days in the calendar month and year of closing. (The methods for calculating prorations are explained in full later in the chapter.)

3. Accrued *real estate* taxes that are not yet due are usually prorated at the closing (see the following section). When the amount of the current real estate tax cannot be determined definitely, the proration is usually based on the last obtainable tax bill. *Special assessments* for such municipal improvements as sewers, water mains or street paving are usually paid in annual installments over several years. As a general rule the municipality charges the property owner annual interest on the outstanding balance of future installments. In a sales transaction the seller pays the current installment and the buyer assumes all future installments. *The special assessment installment is generally not prorated at the closing;* some buyers, however, insist that the seller allow them a credit for the seller's share of the interest to the closing date.

4. *Rents* are usually adjusted on the basis of the *actual* number of days in the month of closing. It is customary for the seller to receive the rents for the day of closing and to pay all expenses for that day. If any rents for the current month are uncollected when the sale is closed, the buyer will often agree by a separate letter to collect the rents if possible and remit the pro-rata share to the seller.

5. *Security deposits* made by tenants to cover the last month's rent of the lease or to cover the cost of repairing damage caused by the tenant are generally transferred intact by the seller to the buyer. Some leases may require the tenant's consent to such a transfer of the deposit.

Real estate taxes. Proration of real estate taxes will vary widely, depending on how the taxes are paid in the area where the real estate is located. In some states real estate taxes are paid *in advance:* if the tax year runs from January 1 to December 31, taxes for the coming year are due on January 1. In that case the seller, who has prepaid a year's taxes, should be reimbursed for the portion of the year remaining after the buyer takes ownership of the tax-paid-up property. In other areas taxes are paid *in arrears,* on December 31 for the year just ended. In that case the buyer should be credited by the seller for the time the seller was occupying the property. Sometimes taxes are due during the tax year, partly in arrears and partly in advance; sometimes they are payable in installments. To compound the confusion city, state, school and other property taxes may start their tax years in different months. Whatever the case may be in a particular transaction, the licensee should understand how the taxes are to be prorated.

Mortgage loan interest. On almost every mortgage loan the interest is paid *in arrears,* so buyers and sellers must understand that the mortgage payment due on June 1, for example, includes interest due for the month of May. Thus the buyer who assumes a mortgage on May 31 and makes the June payment will be paying for the time the seller occupied the property and should be credited with a month's interest. On the other hand, the buyer who places a new mortgage loan on May 31 may be pleasantly surprised to hear that he or she will not need to make a mortgage payment until a month later.

Accounting for Credits and Charges

The items that must be accounted for in the closing statement fall into two general categories: prorations or other amounts due to either the buyer or seller (credit to) and paid for by the other party (debit to) and expenses or items paid by the seller or buyer (debit only). In the lists below the items marked by an asterisk (*) are not prorated; they are entered in full as listed.

Items credited to the buyer and debited to the seller. These items include:

1. the buyer's earnest money*;

2. the unpaid principal balance of an outstanding mortgage loan being assumed by the buyer*;

3. interest on an existing assumed mortgage not yet paid (accrued);

4. the unearned portion of current rent collected in advance;

5. an earned janitor's salary (and sometimes vacation allowance);

6. tenants' security deposits*;

7. a purchase-money mortgage; and

8. unpaid water and other utility bills.

The *buyer's earnest money,* while credited to the buyer, *is not usually debited to the seller.* The buyer receives a credit because he or she has already paid that amount toward the purchase price. Under the usual sales contract the money is held by the broker or attorney until the settlement, when it will be included as part of the total amount due the seller. If the seller is paying off an existing loan and the buyer is obtaining a new one, these two items are accounted for with a debit only to the seller for the amount of the payoff and a credit only to the buyer for the amount of the new loan.

Items credited to the seller and debited to the buyer. These items include:

1. the sales price*;

2. any fuel oil on hand, usually figured at current market price (prepaid);

3. an insurance and tax reserve (if any) when an outstanding mortgage loan is being assumed by buyer (prepaid);

4. a refund to the seller of prepaid water charge and similar expenses; and

5. any portion of general real estate tax paid in advance.

Accounting for expenses. Expenses paid out of the closing proceeds are debited only to the party making the payment. Occasionally an expense item—such as an escrow fee, a settlement fee or a transfer tax—may be shared by the buyer and the seller, and each party will be debited for one-half the expense.

The Arithmetic of Prorating

Accurate prorating involves four considerations: what the item being prorated is; whether it is an accrued item that requires the determination of an earned amount;

whether it is a prepaid item that requires the unearned amount—a refund to the seller—to be determined; and what arithmetic processes must be used. The information contained in the previous sections will assist in answering the first three questions.

The computation of a proration involves identifying a yearly charge for the item to be prorated, then dividing by 12 to determine a monthly charge for the item. It is usually also necessary to identify a daily charge for the item by dividing the monthly charge by the number of days in the month. These smaller portions are then multiplied by the number of months and/or days in the prorated time period to determine the accrued or unearned amount that will be figured in the settlement.

Using this general principle, there are two methods of calculating prorations:

1. The yearly charge is divided by a *360-day year* (commonly called a banking year), or 12 months of 30 days each.

2. The *yearly charge is divided by 365* (366 in a leap year) to determine the daily charge. Then the actual number of days in the proration period is determined, and this number is multiplied by the daily charge.

The final proration figure will vary slightly, depending on which computation method is used. The final figure will also vary according to the number of decimal places to which the division is carried. *All of the computations in this chapter are computed by carrying the division to three decimal places.* The third decimal place is rounded off to cents only after the final proration figure is determined.

Accrued Items

When the real estate tax is levied for the calendar year and is payable during that year or in the following year, the accrued portion is for the period from January 1 to the date of closing (or to the day before the closing in states where the sale date is excluded). If the current tax bill has not yet been issued, the parties must agree on an estimated amount based on the previous year's bill and any known changes in assessment or tax levy for the current year.

For example, assume a sale is to be closed on September 17, current real estate taxes of $1,200 are to be prorated accordingly and a 360-day year is being used. The accrued period, then, is eight months and 17 days. First determine the prorated cost of the real estate tax per month and day:

$$\frac{\$100 \text{ per month}}{12)\$1,200} \qquad \frac{3.333 \text{ per day}}{30)\$100.000}$$
$$\text{months} \qquad\qquad\qquad \text{days}$$

Next multiply these figures by the accrued period and add the totals to determine the prorated real estate tax:

$$
\begin{array}{lll}
\$100 & \$\ 3.333 & \$800.000 \\
\underline{\times\ 8 \text{ months}} & \underline{\times\quad 17 \text{ days}} & \underline{+\,56.661} \\
\$800 & \$56.661 & \$856.661
\end{array}
$$

Thus the accrued real estate tax for eight months and 17 days is $856.66 (rounded off to two decimal places after the final computation). This amount represents the seller's accrued *earned* tax; it will be *a credit to the buyer* and a *debit to the seller* on the closing statement.

To compute this proration using the actual number of days in the accrued period, the following method would be used: The accrued period from January 1 to September 17 runs 260 days (January's 31 days plus February's 28 days, and so on). A tax bill of $1,200 ÷ 365 days = $3.288 per day; $3.288 × 260 days = $854.880, or $854.88.

Prepaid Items

Assume that the water is billed in advance by the city without using a meter. The six months' billing is $8 for the period ending October 31. The sale is to be closed on August 3. Because the water is paid to October 31, the prepaid time must be computed. Using a 30-day basis, the time period is the 27 days left in August plus two full months: $8 ÷ 6 = $1.333 per month. For one day, divide $1.333 by 30, which equals $.044 per day. The prepaid period is two months and 27 days, so:

$$27 \text{ days} \times \$.044 = \$1.188$$
$$2 \text{ months} \times \$1.333 = \underline{\$2.666}$$
$$\$3.854, \text{ or } \$3.85$$

This is a prepaid item and is *credited to the seller* and *debited to the buyer* on the closing statement.

To figure this on the basis of the actual days in the *month* of closing, the following process would be used:

$$\$1.333 \text{ per month} \div 31 \text{ days in August} = \$.043 \text{ per day}$$
$$\text{August 4 through August 31} = 28 \text{ days}$$
$$28 \text{ days} \times \$.043 = \$1.204$$
$$2 \text{ months} \times \$1.333 = \$2.666$$
$$\$1.204 + \$2.666 = \$3.870, \text{ or } \$3.87$$

Sample Closing Statements

As stated previously, there are many possible formats for settlement computations. The remaining portion of this chapter illustrates two sample transactions, one using the HUD Uniform Settlement Statement in Figure 23.1 and the other using separate buyer's and seller's closing statements.

Uniform Settlement Statement

Basic information of offer and sale. John and Joanne Iuro listed their home at 3045 North Racine Avenue in Riverdale, Illinois, with the Open Door Real Estate Company. The listing price was $118,500, and possession could be given within two weeks after all parties had signed the contract. Under the terms of the listing agreement the sellers agreed to pay the broker a commission of six percent of the sales price.

On May 18, the Open Door Real Estate Company submitted a contract offer to the Iuros from Brook Redemann, a bachelor, presently residing at 22 King Court, Riverdale. Redemann offered $115,000, with earnest money/down payment of $23,000 and the remaining $92,000 of the purchase price to be obtained through a new conventional loan. No private mortgage insurance will be necessary as the loan-to-value ratio will not exceed 80 percent. The Iuros signed the contract on May 29. Closing was set for June 15 at the office of the Open Door Real Estate Company, 720 Main Street, Riverdale.

The unpaid balance of the Iuros' mortgage as of June 1, 19–– will be $57,700. Payments are $680 per month with interest at 11 percent per annum on the unpaid balance.

The sellers submitted evidence of title in the form of a title insurance binder at a cost of $10. The title insurance policy paid by the seller at the time of closing cost an additional $540, including $395 for lender's coverage and $145 for homeowner's coverage. Recording charges of $20 were paid for the recording of two instruments to clear defects in the sellers' title, and state transfer tax in the amount of $115 ($.50 per $500 of sale price or fraction thereof) were affixed to the deed. In addition, the sellers must pay an attorney's fee of $400 for preparation of the deed and for legal representation; this amount will be paid from the closing proceeds.

The buyer must pay an attorney's fee of $300 for examination of the title evidence and legal representation, as well as $10 to record the deed. These amounts will also be paid from the closing proceeds.

Real estate taxes in Riverdale are paid in arrears. Taxes for this year, estimated at last year's figure of $1,725, have not been paid. According to the contract, prorations are to be made on the basis of 30 days in a month.

Computing the prorations and charges. Following are illustrations of the various steps in computing the prorations and other amounts to be included in the settlement thus far.

1. *Closing date:* June 15

2. *Commission:* 6% × $115,000 (sales price) = $6,900

3. *Seller's mortgage interest:*
   11% × $57,700 (principal due after June 1 payment) = $6,347 interest per year
   $6,347 ÷ 360 days = $17.631 interest per day
   15 days of accrued interest to be paid by the seller
   15 × $17.631 = $264.465, or $264.47 interest owed by the seller
   $57,700 + $264.465 = $57,964.47 payoff of seller's mortgage

4. *Real estate taxes* (estimated at $1,725):
   $1,725.00 ÷ 12 months = $143.75 per month
   $ 143.75 ÷ 30 days = $ 4.792 per day
   The earned period is from January 1 to and including June 15, and equals 5 months, 15 days:
   $143.75 × 5 months = $718.750
   $4.792 × 15 days = $ 71.880
   $790.630, or $790.63 seller owes buyer

5. *Transfer tax* ($.50 per $500 of consideration or fraction thereof):
   $115,000 ÷ $500 = $230
   $230 × $.50 = $115.00 transfer tax owed by seller

The sellers' loan payoff is $57,964.47, and they must pay an additional $10 to record the mortgage release as well as $85 for a pest inspection. The buyer's new loan is from Thrift Federal Savings, 1100 Fountain Plaza, Riverdale, in the amount of $92,000 at ten percent interest. In connection with this loan he will be charged $125 to have the property appraised by Swift Appraisal and $60 for a credit report from the Acme Credit Bureau. (Because appraisal and credit reports

Figure 23.1
RESPA Uniform
Settlement Statement

A. SETTLEMENT STATEMENT U.S. DEPARTMENT OF HOUSING AND URBAN DEVELOPMENT HUD-1 Rev. 3/86		OMB NO. 2502-0265 (Exp. 12-31-86)

B. TYPE OF LOAN

1. ☐ FHA 2. ☐ FmHA 3. ☒ CONV. UNINS. 4. ☐ VA 5. ☐ CONV. INS.	6. File Number	7. Loan Number	8. Mortgage Insurance Claim Case Number

C. NOTE: *This form is furnished to give you a statement of actual settlement costs. Amounts paid to and by the settlement agent are shown. Items marked "(p.o.c.)" were paid outside the closing; they are shown here for informational purposes and are not included in the totals.*

D. NAME AND ADDRESS OF BORROWER:	E. NAME AND ADDRESS OF SELLER:	F. NAME AND ADDRESS OF LENDER:
Brook Redemann 22 King Court Riverdale, Illinois	John and Joanne Iuro 3045 North Racine Avenue Riverdale, Illinois	Thrift Federal Savings 1100 Fountain Plaza Riverdale, Illinois

G. PROPERTY LOCATION: 3045 North Racine Avenue Riverdale, Illinois	H. SETTLEMENT AGENT: Open Door Real Estate Company PLACE OF SETTLEMENT: Open Door Real Estate Company 720 Main Street, Riverdale, Illinois	I. SETTLEMENT DATE: June 15, 1988

J. SUMMARY OF BORROWER'S TRANSACTION		K. SUMMARY OF SELLER'S TRANSACTION	
100. GROSS AMOUNT DUE FROM BORROWER:		**400. GROSS AMOUNT DUE TO SELLER:**	
101. Contract sales price	$115,000.00	401. Contract sales price	$115,000.00
102. Personal property		402. Personal property	
103. Settlement charges to borrower (line 1400)	5,075.84	403.	
104.		404.	
105.		405.	
Adjustments for items paid by seller in advance		*Adjustments for items paid by seller in advance*	
106. City/town taxes to		406. City/town taxes to	
107. County taxes to		407. County taxes to	
108. Assessments to		408. Assessments to	
109.		409.	
110.		410.	
111.		411.	
112.		412.	
120. GROSS AMOUNT DUE FROM BORROWER	$120,075.84	**420. GROSS AMOUNT DUE TO SELLER**	$115,000.00
200. AMOUNTS PAID BY OR IN BEHALF OF BORROWER:		**500. REDUCTIONS IN AMOUNT DUE TO SELLER:**	
201. Deposit or earnest money	23,000.00	501. Excess deposit (see instructions)	
202. Principal amount of new loan(s)	92,000.00	502. Settlement charges to seller (line 1400)	8,080.00
203. Existing loan(s) taken subject to		503. Existing loan(s) taken subject to	
204.		504. Payoff of first mortgage loan	57,964.47
205.		505. Payoff of second mortgage loan	
206.		506.	
207.		507.	
208.		508.	
209.		509.	
Adjustments for items unpaid by seller		*Adjustments for items unpaid by seller*	
210. City/town taxes to		510. City/town taxes to	
211. County taxes 1/1/88 to 6/15/88	790.63	511. County taxes 1/1/88 to 6/15/88	790.63
212. Assessments to		512. Assessments to	
213.		513.	
214.		514.	
215.		515.	
216.		516.	
217.		517.	
218.		518.	
219.		519.	
220. TOTAL PAID BY/FOR BORROWER	$115,790.63	**520. TOTAL REDUCTION AMOUNT DUE SELLER**	$ 66,835.10
300. CASH AT SETTLEMENT FROM/TO BORROWER		**600. CASH AT SETTLEMENT TO/FROM SELLER**	
301. Gross amount due from borrower (line 120)	120,075.84	601. Gross amount due to seller (line 420)	115,000.00
302. Less amounts paid by/for borrower (line 220)	(115,790.63)	602. Less reductions in amount due seller (line 520)	(66,835.10)
303. CASH (☐ FROM) (☐ TO) BORROWER	$ 4,285.21	**603. CASH (☐ TO) (☐ FROM) SELLER**	$ 48,164.90

I have carefully reviewed the HUD-1 Settlement Statement and to the best of my knowledge and belief, it is a true and accurate statement of all receipts and disbursements made on my account or by me in this transaction. I further certify that I have received a copy of the HUD-1 Settlement Statement.

_____ _____
Borrower   Seller

_____ _____
Borrower   Seller

The HUD-1 Settlement Statement which I have prepared is a true and accurate account of this transaction. I have caused or will cause the funds to be disbursed in accordance with this statement.

_____ _____
Settlement Agent   Date

Warning: It is a crime to knowingly make false statements to the United States on this or any other similar form. Penalties upon conviction can include a fine and imprisonment. For details see: Title 18 U.S. Code Section 1001 and Section 1010.

2128 (6-86) 41b

Figure 23.1
(continued)

— 2 —

L. SETTLEMENT CHARGES

	PAID FROM BORROWER'S FUNDS AT SETTLEMENT	PAID FROM SELLER'S FUNDS AT SETTLEMENT
700. *TOTAL SALES/BROKER'S COMMISSION based on price* $ 115,000 @ 6 % =$6,900.00		
Division of Commission (line 700) as follows:		
701. $ to		
702. $ to		
703. Commission paid at Settlement		$6,900.00
704.		
800. *ITEMS PAYABLE IN CONNECTION WITH LOAN*		
801. Loan Origination Fee %	$ 920.00	
802. Loan Discount 2 %	$1,840.00	
803. Appraisal Fee $125.00 to Swift Appraisal	POC	
804. Credit Report $ 60.00 to ACME Credit Bureau	POC	
805. Lender's Inspection Fee		
806. Mortgage Insurance Application Fee to		
807. Assumption Fee		
808. Application Fee		
809. Wholesale Interest Differential Fee		
810. Underwriting Fee		
811. Buydown Fee		
812. Commitment Fee		
813.		
814. Messenger Service		
815. Shortfall		
816.		
817.		
818.		
819.		
900. *ITEMS REQUIRED BY LENDER TO BE PAID IN ADVANCE*		
901. Interest from 6/16/88 to 6/30/88 @ $ 25.556 /day	383.34	
902. Mortgage Insurance Premium for months to		
903. Hazard Insurance Premium for 1 years to Hite Insurance Co.	345.00	
904. One-Time FHA Insurance Premium		
905. VA Funding Fee		
906.		
907.		
1000. *RESERVES DEPOSITED WITH LENDER*		
1001. Hazard insurance 3 months @ $ 28.75 per month	86.25	
1002. Mortgage insurance months @ $ per month		
1003. City property taxes months @ $ per month		
1004. County property taxes 7 months @ $ 143.75 per month	1,006.25	
1005. Annual assessments months @ $ per month		
1006. months @ $ per month		
1007. months @ $ per month		
1008. months @ $ per month		
1100. *TITLE CHARGES*		
1101. Settlement or closing fee to		
1102. Abstract or title search to		
1103. Title examination to		
1104. Title insurance binder to		10.00
1105. Document preparation to		
1106. Notary fees to		
1107. Attorney's fees to	300.00	400.00
(includes above items numbers;)		
1108. Title insurance to		540.00
(includes above items numbers;)		
1109. Lender's coverage $ 395.00		
1110. Owner's coverage $ 145.00		
1111. Tax Service Contract Fee to		
1112. Amortization Schedule to		
1113.		
1114.		
1115.		
1116.		
1200. *GOVERNMENT RECORDING AND TRANSFER CHARGES*		
1201. Recording Fees: Deed $ 10.00 ; Mortgage $ 10.00 ; Releases $ 10.00	20.00	10.00
1202. City/county tax/stamps: Deed $; Mortgage $		
1203. State tax/Stamps: Deed $ 115.00 ; Mortgage $		115.00
1204. Record two documents to clear title		20.00
1205.		
1300. *ADDITIONAL SETTLEMENT CHARGES*		
1301. Survey to	175.00	
1302. Pest inspection to		85.00
1303.		
1304.		
1305.		
1400. TOTAL SETTLEMENT CHARGES (*enter on lines 103, Section J and 502, Section K*)	$5,075.84	$8,080.00

2128 (6-88) 41b Reverse   HUD-1 Rev. 5/76

are performed prior to loan approval, they are paid at the time of loan application, regardless of whether or not the transaction eventually closes. These items will be noted as POC—paid outside closing—on the settlement statement.) In addition, buyer Redemann will pay for interest on his loan for the remainder of the month of closing—15 days at $25.556 per day, or $383.34. His first full payment (including July's interest) will be due August 1. He must deposit $1,006.25, or 7/12 of the anticipated county real estate tax (of $1,725) into a tax reserve account. A one-year hazard insurance premium at $3 per $1,000 of appraised value ($115,000 ÷ 1,000 × 3 = 345) is paid in advance to Hite Insurance Company. An insurance reserve to cover the premium for three months is deposited with the lender. Redemann will have to pay an additional $10 to record the mortgage and $175 for a survey. He will also pay a loan origination fee of $920 and two discount points.

The Uniform Settlement Statement is divided into 12 sections. The most important information is included in Sections J, K and L. The borrower's and seller's summaries (J and K) are very similar to one another and are used as are the other formats of closing statements illustrated in this chapter. For example, in Section J, the summary of the borrower's transaction, the buyer/borrower's debits are listed in lines 100 through 112 and totaled on line 120 (gross amount due from borrower). The total of the settlement costs itemized in Section L of the statement is entered on line 103 as one of the buyer's charges. The buyer's credits are listed on lines 201 through 219 and totaled on line 220 (total paid by/for borrower). Then, the buyer's credits are subtracted from the charges to arrive at the cash due from the borrower to close (line 303).

In Section K the summary of the seller's transaction, the seller's credits are entered on lines 400 through 412 and totaled on line 420 (gross amount due to seller). The seller's debits are entered on lines 501 through 519 and totaled on line 520 (total reduction amount due seller). The total of the seller's settlement charges is on line 502. Then the debits are subtracted from the credits to arrive at the cash due to the sellers in order to close (line 603).

Section L is a summary of all the settlement charges for the transaction; the buyer's expenses are listed in one column and the sellers' expenses in the other. If an attorney's fee is listed as a lump sum in line 1107, the settlement should list by line number the services that were included in that total fee.

Buyer's and Seller's Closing Statements

Figure 23.2 details a buyer's closing statement and Figure 23.3 a seller's closing statement for the same transaction. The property is being purchased for $89,500, with $49,500 down and the seller taking back a mortgage for $40,000. Closing takes place on August 12.

Prorations. Taxes in this area are paid in advance. The buyer is taking over a house on which taxes have been paid, in one case until the end of the year. The buyer will therefore reimburse the seller for the time in which the buyer will be living in a tax-paid house. Specifically, the seller paid city and school taxes of $1,176.35 for the tax year that started July 1 and will receive a large portion of that back as a credit from the buyer. County taxes of $309.06 were paid January 1 for the year ahead, so the buyer will also credit the seller for the four months and 18 days remaining in the year, an adjustment of $118.52.

**Figure 23.2
Buyer's
Closing
Statement,
Closing on
August 12**

SELLER'S CREDITS

Sale Price _____ $ 89,500.00

ADJUSTMENT OF TAXES

School Tax 7/1/ to 6/30/   Amount $ 1176.35   Adj. 10 mos. 18 days $ 1,039.16

City, School Tax 7/1/ to 6/30/ Amount $_____ Adj. ____ mos. ____ days $_____

County Tax 19____   Amount $ 309.06   Adj. 4 mos. 18 days $ 118.52

Village Tax 6/1/ to 5/31/   Amount $_____ Adj. ____ mos. ____ days $_____

City Tax Embellishments   Amount $_____ Adj. ____ mos. ____ days $_____

_____

_____

_____

Total Seller's Credits $ 90,657.68

PURCHASER'S CREDITS

Deposit with ___Nothnagle_____ $ 500.00

(Assumed) (New) Mortgage with Seller $480.07 p/m ____ $ 40,000.00

beg. 9-12- , 12% int., 15 yrs. $_____

_____ $_____

_____ $_____

_____ $_____

_____ $_____

_____ $_____

_____ $_____

Total Purchaser's Credits $ 40,500.00

Cash (Rec'd) (Paid) at Closing $ 50,157.68

EXPENSES OF PURCHASER

Mortgage Tax .... $ 275.00

Recording Mortgage............... $ 11.00

Recording Deed................... $ 12.00

Bank Attorney Fee................. $_____

Points........................... $_____

Title Insurance.................. $_____

Interest......................... $_____

.... $_____

.... $_____

.... $_____

Legal Fee........................ $ 500.00

Total............................ $ 798.00

Cash paid to Seller: $ 50,157.68

Plus Purchaser's Expenses: $ 798.00

Total Disbursed: $ 50,955.68

EXPENSES OF SELLER

Title Search Fee .... $_____

Transfer Tax on Deed .... $_____

Filing of Gains Tax Affidavit .. $_____

Discharge Recording Fee ...... $_____

Mortgage Tax .... $_____

Surveyor's Fees .... $_____

Points .... $_____

Mortgage Payoff .... $_____

Real Estate Commission ...... $_____

Water Escrow .... $_____

.... $_____

.... $_____

.... $_____

.... $_____

Legal Fee.................... $_____

Total........................ $_____

Cash Received: $

Less Seller's Expenses: $

Net Proceeds: $

Figure 23.3 Seller's Closing Statement Closing on August 12

SELLER'S CREDITS

Sale Price _____ $ 89,500.00

ADJUSTMENT OF TAXES

School Tax 7/1/ to 6/30/   Amount $ 1176.35   Adj. 10 mos. 18 days $ 1,039.16

City/School Tax 7/1/ to 6/30/   Amount $ _____ Adj. _____ mos. _____ days $ _____

County Tax 19____   Amount $ 309.06 Adj. 4 mos. 18 days $ 118.52

Village Tax 6/1/ to 5/31/   Amount $ _____ Adj. _____ mos. _____ days $ _____

City Tax Embellishments   Amount $ _____ Adj. _____ mos. _____ days $ _____

Total Seller's Credits $ 90,657.68

PURCHASER'S CREDITS

Deposit with ___Nothnagle___ $ 500.00

(Assumed) (New) Mortgage with ___seller___ $ 40,000.00

12% interest, 15 years, payments $ _____

$ 480.07, beginning 9/12/ $ _____

$ _____

$ _____

$ _____

$ _____

Total Purchaser's Credits $ 40,500.00

Cash (Rec'd) (Paid) at Closing $ 50,157.68

EXPENSES OF PURCHASER		EXPENSES OF SELLER	
Mortgage Tax .... $ _____		Title Search Fee .... $ 220.00	
Recording Mortgage............... $ _____		Transfer Tax on Deed .... $ 358.00	
Recording Deed................... $ _____		Filing of Gains Tax Affidavit .. $ 1.00	
		Discharge Recording Fee ...... $ _____	
ESCROWS:		Mortgage Tax .... $ 100.00	
___ mos. insurance $ _____		Surveyor's Fees .... $ _____	
___ mos. school tax $ _____		Points .... $ _____	
___ mos. county tax $ _____		Mortgage Payoff .... $ _____	
___ mos. village tax $ _____		Real Estate Commission ...... $ 4870.00	
PMI FHA Insurance $ _____		Water Escrow .... $ _____	
Total: $ _____		19 - school tax ...... $ 1,182.14	
Bank Attorney Fee................. $ _____		Federal express .... $ 14.00	
Points........................... $ _____		.... $ _____	
Title Insurance................... $ _____		.... $ _____	
Interest.......................... $ _____		Legal Fee.................... $ 550.00	
.... $ _____		Total...................... $ 7,295.14	
.... $ _____			
.... $ _____		Cash Received: $ 50,157.68	
Legal Fee........................ $ _____		Less Seller's Expenses: $ 7,295.14	
Total............................ $ _____		Net Proceeds: $ 42,862.54	
Cash paid to Seller. $			
Plus Purchaser's Expenses: $ _____			
Total Disbursed: $			

The buyer owes the seller ("total seller's credits") the purchase price plus un-earned taxes, for a total of $90,657.68. Toward this sum the buyer receives credit for an earnest money deposit of $500 in a broker's escrow account. (The seller's attorney and the broker will later take this sum into consideration when the commission is paid.) The buyer also receives credit for the $40,000 bond and mortgage given to the seller at closing. The buyer therefore gives the seller cash (or a certified check) for the remaining sum, $50,157.68

The upper half of the closing statement accounts for the transaction between buyer and seller; the lower part details each one's individual expenses. The buyer pays to record the deed and mortgage and pays the mortgage tax. The buyer also pays his or her attorney.

The seller's expenses involve last-minute payment of the school tax (plus a small late-payment penalty) for which the seller is largely reimbursed, the required lender's share of the mortgage tax (seller/lender is a corporation), the remaining real estate commission, legal costs of proving title, transfer tax and incidental out-of-pocket expenses incurred by seller's attorney, who also deducts his or her own fee and turns over to the seller the net proceeds.

Key Terms

accrued item	prepaid items
closing statement	prorations
credit	Real Estate Settlement Procedures Act (RESPA)
debit	reduction certificate
escrow	Uniform Settlement Statement (HUD-I)

Summary

Closing a real estate sale involves both title procedures and financial matters. The broker, as agent of the seller, is often present at the closing to see that the sale is actually concluded and to account for the earnest money deposit.

Closings must be reported to the IRS on form 1099.

The federal Real Estate Settlement Procedures Act (RESPA) requires disclosure of all settlement costs when a residential real estate purchase is financed by a federally related mortgage loan. RESPA requires lenders to use a Uniform Settlement Statement to detail the financial particulars of a transaction.

The actual amount to be paid by the buyer at the closing is computed by preparation of a closing, or settlement, statement. This lists the sales price, earnest money deposit and all adjustments and prorations due between buyer and seller. The purpose of this statement is to determine the net amount due the seller at closing. The buyer reimburses the seller for prepaid items like unused taxes or fuel oil. The seller credits the buyer for bills the seller owes that will be paid by the buyer (accrued items), such as unpaid water bills.

Questions

1. Which of the following is true of real estate closings in most states?
   a. Closings are generally conducted by real estate salespeople.
   b. The buyer usually receives the rents for the day of closing.
   c. The buyer must reimburse the seller for any title evidence provided by the seller.
   d. The seller usually pays the expenses for the day of closing.

2. All encumbrances and liens shown on the report of title, other than those waived or agreed to by the purchaser and listed in the contract, must be removed so that the title can be delivered free and clear. The removal of such encumbrances is the duty of the:
   a. buyer.   c. broker.
   b. seller.   d. title company.

3. Legal title always passes from the seller to the buyer:
   a. on the date of execution of the deed.
   b. when the closing statement has been signed.
   c. when the deed is placed in escrow.
   d. when the deed is delivered.

4. Which of the following would a lender generally require to be produced at the closing?
   a. Title insurance policy
   b. Market value appraisal
   c. Application
   d. Credit report

5. When a transaction is to be closed in escrow, the seller generally deposits all but which of the following items with the escrow agent before the closing date?
   a. Deed to the property
   b. Title evidence
   c. Estoppel certificate
   d. Cash needed to complete the purchase

6. The RESPA Uniform Settlement Statement must be used to illustrate all settlement charges for:
   a. every real estate transaction.
   b. transactions financed by VA and FHA loans only.
   c. residential transactions financed by federally related mortgage loans.
   d. all transactions involving commercial property.

7. A mortgage reduction certificate is executed by a(n):
   a. abstract company.
   b. attorney.
   c. lending institution.
   d. grantor.

8. The principal amount of the purchaser's new mortgage loan is a:
   a. credit to the seller.
   b. credit to the buyer.
   c. debit to the seller.
   d. debit to the buyer.

9. The earnest money left on deposit with the broker is a:
   a. credit to the seller.
   b. credit to the buyer.
   c. debit to the seller.
   d. debit to the buyer.

10. The annual real estate taxes amount to $1,800 and have been paid in advance for the calendar year. If closing is set for June 15, which of the following is true?
    a. Credit seller $825; debit buyer $975.
    b. Credit seller $1,800; debit buyer $825.
    c. Credit buyer $975; debit seller $975.
    d. Credit seller $975; debit buyer $975.

11. The seller collected rent of $400, payable in advance, from the attic tenant on August 1. At the closing on August 15 the:
    a. seller owes the buyer $400.
    b. buyer owes the seller $400.
    c. seller owes the buyer $200.
    d. buyer owes the seller $200.

12. Security deposits should be listed on a closing statement as a credit to the:

   a. buyer.   c. lender.
   b. seller.   d. broker.

13. A building was bought for $50,000, with ten percent down and a loan for the balance. If the lender charged the buyer two discount points, how much cash did the buyer need to come up with?

   a. $6,900   c. $5,200
   b. $5,900   d. $90

14. A buyer of a $50,000 home has paid $2,000 as earnest money and has a loan commitment for 70 percent of the purchase price. How much more cash does the buyer need to complete the transaction?

   a. $10,000   c. $15,000
   b. $13,000   d. $35,000

15. At the closing the broker's commission will usually be shown as:

   a. credit to the seller.
   b. credit to the buyer.
   c. debit to the seller.
   d. debit to the buyer.

16. At the closing the seller's attorney gave credit to the buyer for certain accrued items. These items were:

   a. bills relating to the property that have already been paid by the seller.
   b. bills relating to the property that will have to be paid by the buyer.
   c. all of the seller's real estate bills.
   d. all of the buyer's real estate bills.

17. The Real Estate Settlement Procedures Act applies to the activities of:

   a. brokers selling commercial and office buildings.
   b. security salespersons selling limited partnerships.
   c. Ginny Mae or Fannie Mae when purchasing mortgages.
   d. lenders financing the purchase of a borrower's residence.

18. The purpose of RESPA (Real Estate Settlement Procedures Act) is to:

   a. make sure buyers do not borrow more than they can repay.
   b. make real estate brokers more responsive to buyers' needs.
   c. help buyers know how much money is required.
   d. see that buyers and sellers know all settlement costs.

Real Estate Mathematics Review

Mathematics plays an important role in the real estate business. Math is involved in nearly every aspect of a typical transaction, from the moment a listing agreement is filled out until the final monies are paid at the closing. Reflecting this, state licensing examinations contain a substantial number of questions that involve math.

This review is designed to explain some of the math formulas used most frequently in the computations required on licensing examinations. These computations are also important in day-to-day transactions. Some of this material has been covered in detail in the text. In these cases reference is made to the appropriate chapter. Additional help in working these problems may be found in *Mastering Real Estate Mathematics,* Fifth Edition, by Ventolo, Allaway and Irby, published by Real Estate Education Company.

Percentages

Many real estate computations are based on the calculation of percentages. A percentage expresses a portion of a whole (*percent* means "per hundred"). For example, 50 percent means 50 parts of the possible 100 parts that comprise the whole. Percentages greater than 100 percent contain more than one whole unit. Thus 163 percent is one whole and 63 parts of another whole. A whole is always expressed as 100 percent.

In problems involving percentages *the percentages must be converted to either decimals or fractions*. To convert a percentage to a decimal, place a decimal two places to the left and drop the percent sign. Thus,

$$60\% = .6 \qquad 7\% = .07 \qquad 175\% = 1.75$$

To change a percentage to a fraction, place the percentage over 100. For example:

$$50\% = \frac{50}{100} \qquad 115\% = \frac{115}{100}$$

These fractions may then be *reduced* to make it easier to work the problem. To reduce a fraction, determine the lowest number by which both numerator (top number) and denominator (bottom number) can be divided evenly and divide each of them by that number. For example:

$$25/100 = 1/4 \text{ (both numbers divided by 25)}$$
$$49/63 = 7/9 \text{ (both numbers divided by 7)}$$

Percentage problems contain three elements: *percentage, total* and *part.* To determine a specific percentage of a whole, multiply the total by the percentage. This is illustrated by the following formula:

$$\text{total} \times \text{percent} = \text{part}$$
$$200 \times 5\% = \mathbf{10}$$

This formula is used in calculating mortgage loan interest, brokers' commissions, loan origination fees, discount points, earnest money deposits and income on capital investments.

For example, a broker is to receive a seven percent commission on the sale of a $150,000 house. What will the broker's commission be?

$$.07 \times \$150,000 = \textbf{\$10,500 broker's commission}$$

A variation, or inversion, of the percentage formula is used to find the total amount when the part and percentage are known:

$$\text{total} = \frac{\text{part}}{\text{percent}}$$

For example, the Masterson Realty Company received a $4,500 commission for the sale of a house. The broker's commission was six percent of the total sales price. What was the total sales price of this house?

$$\frac{\$4,500}{.06} = \textbf{\$75,000 total sales price}$$

This formula is used to calculate the total sales price when the amount and percentage of commission or earnest money deposit are known. It also is used in computing the total mortgage loan principal still due if the monthly payment and interest rate are known, rent due if the monthly payment and interest rate are known and market value of property if the assessed value and the ratio (percentage) of assessed value to market value are known.

To determine the percentage when the amounts of the part and the total are known:

$$\text{percent} = \frac{\text{part}}{\text{total}}$$

This formula may be used to determine the tax rate when the taxes and assessed value are known or the commission rate when the sales price and commission amount are known.

You can use the following diagram as an aid in remembering the three formulas just discussed:

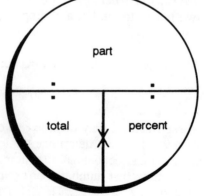

Rates

Property taxes, transfer taxes and insurance premiums are usually expressed as rates. A *rate* is the cost expressed as the amount of cost per unit. For example, tax might be computed at the rate of $5 per $100 of assessed value in a certain county. The formula for computing rates is:

$$\text{value} \times \text{rate} = \text{total}$$

For example, a house has been assessed at $90,000 and is taxed at an annual rate of $2.50 per $100 assessed valuation. What is the yearly tax?

$$\$90,000 \times \frac{\$2.50}{\$100} = \text{total annual tax}$$

$$\overset{900}{\cancel{\$90,000}} \times \frac{\$2.50}{\underset{1}{\cancel{100}}} = \text{total annual tax}$$

$$900 \times \$2.50 = \textbf{\$2,250 total annual tax}$$

See Chapter 9 for a further discussion of real estate tax computations.

Areas and Volumes

People in the real estate business must know how to compute the area of a parcel of land or figure the amount of living area in a house. To compute the area of a square or rectangular parcel, use the formula:

$$\text{length} \times \text{width} = \text{area}$$

Thus the area of a rectangular lot that measures 200 feet long by 100 feet wide would be:

$$200' \times 100' = \textbf{20,000 square feet}$$

Area is always expressed in square units. Table MR-1 shows the relationship of different units of measurement.

To compute the amount of surface in a triangular area, use the formula:

$$\text{area} = \tfrac{1}{2} (\text{base} \times \text{height})$$

The base of a triangle is the bottom, the side on which the triangle rests. The height is an imaginary straight line extending from the point of the uppermost angle straight down to the base:

For example, a triangle has a base of 50 feet and a height of 30 feet. What is its area?

$$\tfrac{1}{2} (50' \times 30') = \text{area in square feet}$$
$$\tfrac{1}{2} (1,500 \text{ square feet}) = \textbf{750 square feet}$$

To compute the area of an irregular room or parcel of land, divide the shape into regular rectangles, squares or triangles. Next, compute the area of each regular figure and add the areas together to obtain the total area.

Table MR-1
Units of Measurement

1 foot	12 inches
1 yard	3 feet or 36 inches
1 rod	16.5 feet
1 chain	66 feet
1 square foot	144 square inches
1 square yard	9 square feet
1 acre	43,560 square feet
1 cubic foot	1,728 cubic inches
1 cubic yard	27 cubic feet

For example, compute the area of the hallway shown below:

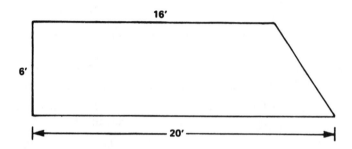

First make a rectangle and a triangle by drawing a single line through the figure as shown here:

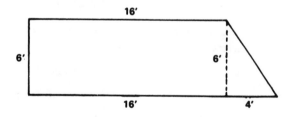

Compute the area of the rectangle:

$$\text{area} = \text{length} \times \text{width}$$
$$16' \times 6' = 96 \text{ square feet}$$

Compute the area of the triangle:

$$\text{area} = \frac{1}{2}(\text{base} \times \text{height})$$
$$\frac{1}{2}(4' \times 6') = \frac{1}{2}(24 \text{ square feet}) = 12 \text{ square feet}$$

Add the two areas:

$$96 + 12 = \textbf{108 square feet in total area}$$

The cubic capacity of an enclosed space is expressed as volume. Volume is used to describe the amount of space in any three-dimensional area. It would be used, for example, in measuring the interior airspace of a room to determine what capacity heating unit is required. The formula for computing cubic or rectangular volume is:

$$\text{volume} = \text{length} \times \text{width} \times \text{height}$$

Volume is always expressed in cubic units.

For example, the bedroom of a house is 12 feet long and 8 feet wide and has a ceiling height of 8 feet. How many cubic feet does the room enclose?

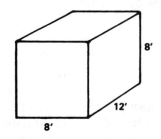

$$8' \times 12' \times 8' = \textbf{768 cubic feet}$$

To compute the volume of a triangular space, such as the airspace in an A-frame house, use the formula:

volume = ½ (base × height × width)

For example: What is the volume of airspace in the house shown below?

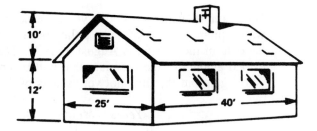

First, divide the house into two shapes, rectangular and triangular, as shown:

Find the volume of T:

volume = ½ (base × height × width)
½ (25' × 10' × 40') = ½ (10,000 cubic feet) = 5,000 cubic feet

Find the volume of R:

$$25' \times 40' \times 12' = 12,000 \text{ cubic feet}$$

Add volumes T and R:

$$5,000 + 12,000 = \textbf{17,000 cubic feet of airspace in the house}$$

Cubic measurements of volume are also used to compute the construction costs per cubic foot of a building and the amount of airspace being sold in a condominium unit.

Remember that when either area or volume is computed *all dimensions used must be given in the same unit of measure*. For example, you may not multiply 2 feet by 6 inches to get the area; you have to multiply 2 feet by ½ foot or 24 inches by 6 inches.

Prorations

As discussed in Chapter 23, the proration of taxes, insurance premiums and other items is customary when a real estate transaction is closed. Questions concerning closing statements generally appear in real estate brokers' examinations. They appear less often in salespersons' exams. Knowledge of the arithmetic of prorations is valuable to all real estate licensees in the course of their business.

When an item is to be prorated, the charge must first be broken down into yearly, monthly and daily amounts, depending on the type of charge. These smaller amounts are then multiplied by the number of years, months and days in the prorated time period to determine the accrued or unearned amount to be credited or debited at the closing. Depending on local custom, prorations may be made on the basis of a standard 30-day month (360-day year), a 365-day year or the actual number of days in the month of closing.

For example, using a 365-day year, consider a one-year prepaid insurance policy with a premium of $450. The policy became effective on March 1, 1991, and the date of the closing is August 9, 1991. The initial step in determining the unearned amount of the premium that will be credited to the seller at the closing is to figure out the time not yet used as of August 9, 1991, as follows:

	Years	Months	Days
		14	
	1	2̸	32
Expiration Date	199Z̸	3̸	1̸
Closing Date	1991	8	9
		6	23 or 6 months and 23 days unearned

Then the monthly and daily breakdowns of the premium amount are determined. (Remember to carry all computations to three decimal places until a final figure is reached, then round off to the nearest penny.)

First, divide the yearly charge by 12 to determine the monthly premium:

$$12\overline{)\$450.000} \quad \$\ 37.500 \text{ monthly premium}$$

Assuming your area computes such charges on the basis of a 30-day month, divide the monthly charge by 30 to arrive at the daily premium:

$$30\overline{)\$37.500} \quad \$1.250 \text{ daily premium}$$

Finally you must multiply the proper premium amounts by the appropriate number of months and days to determine the unearned amount to be prorated:

$$
\begin{array}{r}
\$\ 37.500 \\
\times \quad\quad 6 \\
\hline
\$225.000 \text{ for 6 months}
\end{array}
$$

$ 1.250
×   23
$ 28.750 for 23 days

$225.000
 28.750
$253.750, or $253.75 *unearned insurance premium*
(a credit to the seller and a debit to the buyer)

Similar computations are used to prorate other items, such as real estate taxes and mortgage interest. For a more detailed discussion of closing statement computations, refer to Chapter 23.

Questions

1. Broker S of Happy Valley Realty recently sold H's home for $79,500. S charged H a 6½ percent commission and will pay 30 percent of that amount to the listing salesperson and 25 percent to the selling salesperson. What amount of commission will the listing salesperson receive from the H sale?

   a. $5,167.50   c. $3,617.25
   b. $1,550.25   d. $1,291.87

2. L signed an agreement to purchase a condominium apartment from P. The contract stipulated that P replace the damaged bedroom carpet. The carpet L has chosen costs $16.95 per square yard plus $2.50 per square yard for installation. If the bedroom dimensions are as illustrated, how much will P have to pay for the job?

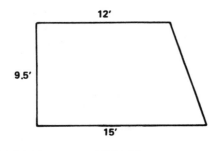

   a. $241.54   c. $277.16
   b. $189.20   d. $2,494.46

3. H, O, R and M decided to pool their savings and purchase a small apartment building for $125,000. If H invested $30,000 and O and R each contributed $35,000, what percentage of ownership was left for M?

   a. 20 percent   c. 28 percent
   b. 24 percent   d. 30 percent

4. D is curious to know how much money his son and daughter-in-law still owe on their mortgage loan. D knows that the interest portion of their last monthly payment was $391.42. If they are paying interest at the rate of 11½ percent, what was the outstanding balance of their loan before that last payment was made?

   a. $43,713.00   c. $36,427.50
   b. $40,843.83   d. $34,284.70

5. The Ns bought their home a year ago for $98,500. Property in their neighborhood is said to be increasing in value at a rate of five percent annually. If this is true, what is the current market value of Ns' real estate?

   a. $103,425   c. $104,410
   b. $93,575   d. $93,809

6. The Ds' home is valued at $95,000. Property in their area is assessed at 60 percent of its value, and the local tax rate is $2.85 per $100. What is the amount of the Ds' annual taxes?

   a. $2,451   c. $135.38
   b. $1,470.60   d. $1,624.50

7. The Fs are planning to construct a patio in their backyard. An illustration of the surface area to be paved appears here. If the cement is to be poured as a six-inch slab, how many cubic feet of cement will be poured into this patio?

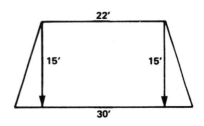

   a. 660 cubic feet   c. 330 cubic feet
   b. 450 cubic feet   d. 195 cubic feet

8. M receives a monthly salary of $1,000 plus three percent commission on all of his listings that sell and 2.5 percent on all of his sales. None of the listings that M took sold last month, but he received $4,175 in salary and commission. What was the value of the property M sold?

   a. $147,000   c. $122,500
   b. $127,000   d. $105,833

9. The Ps' residence has proved difficult to sell. Salesperson K suggests it might sell faster if they enclose a portion of the backyard with a privacy fence. If the area to be enclosed is as illustrated, how much would the fence cost at $6.95 per linear foot?

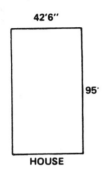

42'6"

95'

HOUSE

a. $1,911.25 c. $1,615.88
b. $1,654.10 d. $955.63

10. T leases the 12 apartments in the Overton Arms for a total monthly rental of $4,500. If this figure represents an eight percent annual return on T's investment, what was the original cost of the property?
a. $675,000 c. $54,000
b. $450,000 d. $56,250

For the following questions regarding closing statement prorations, base your calculations on a 30-day month. Carry all computations to three decimal places until the final solution.

11. A sale is to be closed on March 15. Real estate taxes for the current year have not been paid; taxes for last year amounted to $1,340. What is the amount of the real estate tax proration to be credited to the buyer?
a. $1,060.84 c. $223.33
b. $279.16 d. $1,116.60

12. The buyers are assuming an outstanding mortgage, which had an unpaid balance of $58,200 after the last payment on August 1. Interest at 12 percent per annum is paid in arrears each month; the sale is to be closed on August 11. What is the amount of mortgage interest proration to be debited to the seller at the closing?
a. $698.40 c. $368.60
b. $582.00 d. $213.40

13. In a sale of residential property real estate taxes for the current year amounted to $975 and have already been paid by the seller. The sale is to be closed on October 26; what is the amount of real estate tax proration to be credited the seller?
a. $173.33 c. $798.96
b. $162.50 d. $83.96

14. The buyer is assuming the seller's mortgage. The unpaid balance after the most recent payment (September 1) was $61,550. Interest is paid in arrears each month at 13 percent per annum. The sale is to be closed on September 22. What is the amount of mortgage interest proration to be credited to the buyer at the closing?
a. $666.97 c. $177.82
b. $488.97 d. $689.01

15. A 100-acre farm is divided into house lots. The streets require one-eighth of the whole farm, and there are 140 lots. How many square feet are there in each lot?
a. 35,004 c. 27,225
b. 31,114 d. 43,560

16. R's commission on a sale was $14,100, which was six percent of the sales price. What was the sales price?
a. $235,000 c. $846,000
b. $154,255.31 d. $234,500

Sample Examinations

The following sample exams contain the type of questions examinees might find on their licensing examinations. These questions are meant to provide prospective licensees with additional practice in preparing for the examination.

Sample Examination One

1. Which of the following is a lien on real estate?
   a. A recorded easement
   b. A recorded mortgage
   c. An encroachment
   d. A deed restriction

2. A contract agreed to under duress is:
   a. voidable.   c. discharged.
   b. breached.   d. void.

3. A broker receives a check for earnest money from a buyer and deposits the money in an escrow or trust account to protect herself from the charge of:
   a. commingling.   c. lost or stolen funds.
   b. novation.   d. embezzlement.

4. A mortgage loan that requires monthly payments of $875.70 for 20 years and a final payment of $24,095 is known as a(n):
   a. wraparound loan.   c. balloon loan.
   b. accelerated loan.   d. variable loan.

5. The borrower computed the interest he was charged for the previous month on his $60,000 loan balance as $412.50. What is his interest rate?
   a. 7.5 percent   c. 8.25 percent
   b. 7.75 percent   d. 8.5 percent

6. A lender may sell a loan originated by a bank in which of the following?
   a. Primary market   c. Mortgage market
   b. Secondary market   d. Investor market

7. The deed that contains five covenants is the:
   a. warranty deed.   c. grant deed.
   b. quitclaim deed.   d. deed in trust.

8. Steering is:
   a. leading prospective homeowners to or away from certain areas.
   b. refusing to make loans to persons residing in certain areas.
   c. a requirement to join a multiple-listing service.
   d. a practice of illegally setting commission rates.

9. H grants a life estate to her grandson and stipulates that upon the grandson's death the title to the property will pass to her son-in-law. This second estate is known as an:
   a. estate in remainder.
   b. estate in reversion.
   c. estate at sufferance.
   d. estate for years.

10. Under joint tenancy:
    a. a maximum of two people can own the real estate.
    b. the fractional interests can be different.
    c. additional owners can be added later.
    d. there is a right of survivorship.

11. A real estate salesperson may:

    a. write checks from his or her trust account.

    b. advertise the property in his or her own name.

    c. collect a commission directly from the principal.

    d. act under the supervision of the employing broker.

12. The states in which the lender is the owner of mortgaged real estate are known as:

    a. title theory states.

    b. lien theory states.

    c. statutory share states.

    d. strict forfeiture states.

13. What is a tenancy for years?

    a. A tenancy with the consent of the landlord

    b. A tenancy that expires on a specific date

    c. A tenancy created by the death of the owner

    d. A tenancy created by a testator

14. A residence with outmoded plumbing is suffering from:

    a. functional obsolescence.

    b. curable physical deterioration.

    c. incurable physical deterioration.

    d. external obsolescence.

15. K built a structure that has six stories. Several years later an ordinance was passed in that area banning any building six stories or higher. This instance represents:

    a. a nonconforming use.

    b. a situation in which the structure would have to be demolished.

    c. a conditional use.

    d. a violation of the zoning laws.

16. Assuming that the listing broker and the selling broker in a transaction split their commission equally, what was the sales price of the property if the commission rate was 6.5 percent and the listing broker received $2,593.50?

    a. $39,900   c. $79,800

    b. $56,200   d. $88,400

17. According to the statute of frauds, an oral lease for five years is:

    a. a long-term lease.   c. illegal.

    b. renewable.   d. unenforceable.

18. A mortgage lender intends to lend money at $9\frac{3}{4}$ percent, and if the lender intends to yield $10\frac{3}{8}$ percent, how many discount points must be charged on this loan?

    a. Eight   c. Four

    b. Five   d. One-half

19. The market value of a parcel of land:

    a. is an estimate of the present worth of future benefits.

    b. represents a measure of past expenditures.

    c. is what the seller wants for the property.

    d. is the same as the market price.

20. Police power includes all of the following *except:*

    a. zoning.

    b. deed restrictions.

    c. building codes.

    d. subdivision regulations.

21. The seller wants to net $65,000 from the sale of his house after paying the broker's fee of six percent. His gross sales price will be:

    a. $69,149.   c. $61,321.

    b. $68,900.   d. $61,100.

22. An acre contains:

    a. 360 degrees.   c. 160 square yards.

    b. 36 sections.   d. 43,560 square feet.

23. W is purchasing a condominium unit in a subdivision and obtaining financing from a local savings and loan association. In this situation, which of the following best describes W?

    a. Vendor   c. Grantor

    b. Mortgagor   d. Lessor

24. The current value of a property is $40,000. The property is assessed at 40 percent of its current value for real estate tax purposes, with an equalization factor of 1.5 applied to the assessed value. If the tax rate is $4 per $100 of assessed valuation, what is the amount of tax due on the property?

    a. $640   c. $1,600

    b. $960   d. $2,400

25. A building was sold for $60,000 with the purchaser putting ten percent down and obtaining a loan for the balance. The lending institution charged a one percent loan origination fee. What was the total cash used for the purchase?

    a. $540   c. $6,540
    b. $6,000   d. $6,600

26. After a snowstorm a property owner offers to pay $10 to anyone who will shovel his driveway. This is an example of:

    a. an implied contract.
    b. an executed contract.
    c. a bilateral contract.
    d. a unilateral contract.

27. Capitalization rates are:

    a. determined by the gross rent multiplier.
    b. the rates of return a property will produce.
    c. a mathematical value determined by the sales price.
    d. determined by the amount of depreciation in the property.

28. An eligible veteran made an offer of $50,000 to purchase a home to be financed with a VA-guaranteed loan. Four weeks after the offer was accepted a certificate of reasonable value (CRV) for $47,800 was issued for the property. In this case the veteran may:

    a. withdraw from the sale with a one percent penalty.
    b. purchase the property with a $2,200 down payment.
    c. not withdraw from the sale.
    d. withdraw from the sale upon payment of $2,200.

29. If a house was sold for $40,000 and the buyer obtained an FHA-insured mortgage loan for $38,500, how much money would be paid in discount points if the lender charged four points?

    a. $1,600   c. $1,500
    b. $1,540   d. $385

30. The commission rate is 7¾ percent on a sale of $50,000. What is the dollar amount of the commission?

    a. $3,500   c. $4,085
    b. $3,875   d. $4,585

31. All of the following will terminate an offer *except:*

    a. revocation of the offer before its acceptance.
    b. the death of the offeror before acceptance.
    c. a counteroffer by the offeree.
    d. an offer from a third party.

32. G is purchasing a home under a land contract. Until the contract is paid in full, G has:

    a. legal title to the premises.
    b. no interest in the property.
    c. a legal life estate in the premises.
    d. equitable title in the property.

33. F and K enter into an agreement wherein K will mow F's lawn every week during the course of the summer. Shortly thereafter K decides to go into a different business. V would like to assume K's duties mowing F's lawn. F agrees and enters into a new contract with V. F and K tear up their original agreement. This is known as:

    a. assignment.   c. substitution.
    b. novation.   d. rescission.

34. G borrowed $4,000 from a private lender, using the services of a mortgage broker. After deducting the loan costs, G received $3,747. What is the face amount of the note?

    a. $3,747   c. $4,253
    b. $4,000   d. $7,747

35. An offer to purchase real estate becomes a contract when it is signed by which of the following?

    a. Buyer   c. Seller
    b. Buyer and seller   d. Seller and broker

36. J has just made the final payment on his mortgage loan to his bank. Regardless of this fact, the lender will still hold a lien on J's mortgaged property until which of the following is recorded?

    a. A satisfaction of the mortgage document
    b. A reconveyance of the mortgage document
    c. A novation of the mortgage document
    d. An estoppel of the mortgage document

37. If the annual net income from a commercial property is $22,000 and the capitalization rate is eight percent, what is the value of the property using the income approach?

    a. $275,000   c. $183,000
    b. $200,000   d. $176,000

38. Broker N enters into a listing agreement with seller D wherein D will receive $120,000 from the sale of a vacant lot and N will receive any sale proceeds over that amount. This type of agreement is called a(n):

    a. exclusive-agency listing.
    b. net listing.
    c. exclusive-right-to-sell listing.
    d. multiple listing.

39. P, no longer needing her large house, decides to sell it and move into a cooperative apartment building. Under the cooperative form of ownership P will:

    a. become a stockholder in the corporation.
    b. not lose her apartment if she pays her share of the expenses.
    c. have to take out a new mortgage loan on her unit.
    d. receive a fixed-term lease for her unit.

40. A defect or a cloud on title to property may be cured by:

    a. obtaining quitclaim deeds from all interested parties.
    b. bringing an action to register the title.
    c. paying cash for the property at the settlement.
    d. bringing an action to repudiate the title.

41. Discount points on a real estate loan are a potential cost to both the seller and the buyer. The points are:

    a. set by FHA and VA for their loan programs.
    b. charged only on conventional loans.
    c. limited by government regulations.
    d. determined by the market for money.

42. Under the terms of a net lease the tenant would usually be responsible for paying all of the following *except:*

    a. maintenance expenses.
    b. mortgage debt service.
    c. fire and extended-coverage insurance.
    d. real estate taxes.

43. The Civil Rights Act of 1866 prohibits in all cases discrimination based on a person's:

    a. sex.   c. race.
    b. religion.   d. familial status.

44. What would it cost to put new carpeting in a den measuring 15 feet by 20 feet if the cost of the carpeting is $6.95 per square yard and the cost of laying it is an additional $250?

    a. $232   c. $610
    b. $482   d. $2,335

45. What is the difference between a general lien and a specific lien?

    a. A general lien cannot be enforced in court, while a specific lien can.
    b. A specific lien is held by only one person, while a general lien must be held by two or more.
    c. A general lien is a lien against personal property, while a specific lien is a lien against real estate.
    d. A specific lien is a lien against a certain parcel of real estate, while a general lien covers all of the debtor's property.

46. In an option to purchase real estate the optionee:

    a. must purchase the property but may do so at any time within the option period.
    b. is limited to a refund of the option consideration if the option is exercised.
    c. cannot obtain third-party financing on the property until after the option has expired.
    d. has no obligation to purchase the property during the option period.

47. An individual seeking to be excused from the dictates of a zoning ordinance should request a:

    a. building permit.
    b. certificate of alternative usage.
    c. variance.
    d. certificate of nonconforming use.

48. How many acres are there in the N ½ of the SW ¼ and the NE ¼ of the SE ¼ of a section?

    a. 20 acres   c. 80 acres
    b. 40 acres   d. 120 acres

49. Acceleration is a term associated with which of the following documents?

    a. Listings   c. Leases
    b. Mortgages   d. Purchase contracts

50. J's real estate loan indicates that if she sells the property the lender immediately must be paid in full. This clause is known as the:

    a. acceleration clause.
    b. alienation clause.
    c. subordination clause.
    d. habendum clause.

51. Broker H receives a deposit with a written offer that indicates that the offeror will leave the offer open for the seller's acceptance for ten days. On the fifth day, and prior to acceptance by the seller, the offeror notifies H that he is withdrawing his offer and demanding the return of his deposit. In this situation:

    a. the offeror cannot withdraw the offer—it must be held open for the full ten-day period.
    b. the offeror has the right to withdraw the offer and secure the return of the deposit at any time before he is notified of the seller's acceptance.
    c. the offeror can withdraw the offer, and the seller and the broker will each retain one-half of the forfeited deposit.
    d. the offeror can withdraw the offer, and the broker will declare the deposit forfeited and retain all of it in lieu of a commission.

52. C and L are joint tenants in a parcel of property. L sells her interest to F. What is the relationship between C and F regarding the property?

    a. They are joint tenants.
    b. They are tenants in common.
    c. They are tenants by the entirety.
    d. There is no relationship, because L cannot sell her joint tenancy interest.

53. S and W orally enter into a one-year lease. If W defaults, then S:

    a. may not bring a court action because of the parol evidence rule.
    b. may not bring a court action because of the statute of frauds.
    c. may bring a court action because one-year leases need not be in writing to be enforceable.
    d. may bring a court action because the statute of limitations does not apply to oral leases.

54. On Monday T offers to sell his vacant lot to K for $12,000. On Tuesday K counteroffers to buy the lot for $10,500. On Friday K withdraws his counteroffer and accepts T's original price of $12,000. Under these circumstances:

    a. there is a valid agreement, because K accepted T's offer exactly as it was made, regardless that it was not accepted immediately.
    b. there is a valid agreement, because K accepted before T advised him that the offer was withdrawn.
    c. there is no valid agreement, because T's offer was not accepted within 72 hours of its having been made.
    d. there is no valid agreement, because K's counteroffer was a rejection of T's offer, and once rejected, it cannot be accepted later.

55. The parcel of property over which an easement runs is known as the:

    a. dominant tenement.
    b. servient tenement.
    c. prescriptive tenement.
    d. eminent tenement.

56. If the quarterly interest at 7.5 percent is $562.50, what is the principal amount of the loan?

    a. $7,500   c. $30,000
    b. $15,000   d. $75,000

57. Assume a house is sold for $84,500 and the commission rate is seven percent. If the commission is split 60/40 between the selling broker and the listing broker, and each broker splits his share of the commission evenly with his salesperson, how much will the listing salesperson receive from this sale?

    a. $1,183   c. $2,366
    b. $1,775   d. $3,549

58. If the mortgage on a house is 80 percent of the appraised value and the mortgage interest rate of eight percent amounts to $460 per month, what is the appraised value of the house?

    a. $92,875   c. $71,875
    b. $86,250   d. $69,000

59. Local zoning ordinances often regulate all of the following *except:*

    a. the height of buildings in an area.
    b. the density of population.
    c. the appropriate use of the buildings.
    d. the market value of property.

60. Broker M took a listing and later discovered that her client had previously been declared incompetent by the court. The listing is now:

    a. unaffected, as M was acting in good faith as the owner's agent.
    b. of no value to M because the contract is void.
    c. the basis for recovery of a commission if M produces a buyer.
    d. renegotiable between M and her client.

61. P defaulted on his home mortgage loan payments, and the lender obtained a court order to foreclose on the property. At the foreclosure sale, however, P's property sold for only $64,000; the unpaid balance of the loan at the time of the foreclosure was $78,000. What must the lender do in an attempt to recover the $14,000 that P still owes?

    a. Sue for specific performance
    b. Sue for damages
    c. Seek a deficiency judgment
    d. Seek a judgment by default

62. All of the following are exemptions to the federal Fair Housing Act of 1986 *except:*

    a. the sale of a single-family home where the listing broker does not advertise the property.
    b. the restriction of noncommercial lodgings by a private club to members of the club.
    c. the rental of a unit in an owner-occupied three-family dwelling where an advertisement is placed in the paper.
    d. the restriction of noncommercial housing in a convent where a certified statement has not been filed with the government.

63. G purchases a $37,000 property, depositing $3,000 as earnest money. If he can obtain a 75 percent loan-to-value loan on the property and no additional items are prorated, how much more cash will he need at the settlement?

    a. $3,250   c. $5,250
    b. $3,500   d. $6,250

64. In the appraisal of a building constructed in the 1920s the cost approach would be the least accurate method because of difficulties in:

    a. estimating changes in material costs.
    b. obtaining 1920s building codes.
    c. estimating changes in labor rates.
    d. estimating depreciation.

65. G sold his property to W. In the deed of conveyance G's only guarantee was that the property was not encumbered during the time he owned it except as noted in the deed. The type of deed used in this transaction was a:

    a. general warranty deed.
    b. special warranty deed.
    c. bargain and sale deed.
    d. quitclaim deed.

66. S and T, who are not married, own a parcel of real estate. Each owns an undivided interest, with S owning one-third and T owning two-thirds. The form of ownership under which S and T own their property is:

    a. severalty.
    b. joint tenancy.
    c. tenancy at will.
    d. tenancy in common.

67. The Ls enter into a purchase contract with the Es to buy the Es' house for $84,500. The buyers pay $2,000 as earnest money and obtain a new mortgage loan for $67,600. The purchase contract provides for a March 15th settlement. The buyers and sellers prorate the previous year's real estate taxes of $1,880.96, which have been prepaid. The buyers have additional closing costs of $1,250, and the sellers have other closing costs of $850. How much cash must the buyers bring to the settlement?

    a. $19,638   c. $17,238
    b. $17,638   d. $16,388

68. On behalf of seller F Broker H had been offering F's house for sale at the price of $47,900. J, a Mexican, saw the house and was interested in it. When J asked H the price of the house, H told J $53,000. Under the federal Fair Housing Act of 1968 such a statement is:

   a. legal because all that is important is that J be given the opportunity to buy the house.
   b. legal because the representation was made by the broker and not directly by the owner.
   c. illegal because the difference in the offering price and the quoted price was greater than ten percent.
   d. illegal because the terms of the potential sale were changed for J.

69. A deed must be signed by which of the following?

   a. The grantor
   b. The grantee
   c. The grantor and the grantee
   d. The grantee and at least two witnesses

70. P has just been hired to prepare an appraisal report of a property for loan purposes. The property is an elegant old mansion that is now used as an insurance company office. Which approach to value would P give the greatest weight to when making this appraisal?

   a. Income approach
   b. Sales comparison approach
   c. Replacement cost approach
   d. Gross rent multiplier

71. Which of the following is true about a term mortgage loan?

   a. All of the interest is paid at the end of the term.
   b. The debt is partially amortized over the life of the loan.
   c. The length of the term is limited by state statutes.
   d. The entire principal amount is due at the end of the term.

72. J recently moved into a condominium. She has the use of many facilities there, including a swimming pool, putting green, and tennis courts. Under the typical condominium arrangement these facilities would be owned by:

   a. the association of homeowners in the condominium.
   b. the corporation in which J and the other owners hold stock.
   c. J and the other owners in the condominium in the form of divided interests.
   d. all of the condominium owners in the form of percentage undivided interests.

73. Which of the following is not usually prorated between the seller and the buyer at the settlement?

   a. Recording charges   c. Prepaid rents
   b. Real estate taxes   d. Utility bills

74. T believes that he has been the victim of an unfair discriminatory practice committed by a local real estate broker. In accordance with federal regulations, how long does T have to file his complaint against the broker?

   a. 90 days after the alleged discrimination
   b. 180 days after the alleged discrimination
   c. nine months after the alleged discrimination
   d. one year after the alleged discrimination

75. A real estate loan that uses both real estate and personal property as collateral is known as a:

   a. blanket loan.
   b. package loan.
   c. growing-equity loan.
   d. graduated-payment loan.

76. All of the following are true regarding the concept of adverse possession *except:*

   a. the person taking possession of the property must do so without the consent of the owner of the property.
   b. occupancy of the property by the person taking possession must be continuous over a specified period of time.
   c. the person taking possession of the property must compensate the owner at the end of the adverse possession period.
   d. the person taking possession of the property could ultimately end up owning the property.

77. What is the cost of constructing a fence six feet six inches high around a lot measuring 90 feet by 175 feet, if the cost of erecting the fence is $1.25 per linear foot and the cost of materials is $.825 per square foot of fence?

a. $1,752   c. $2,084
b. $2,054   d. $3,505

78. K, who desires to sell his house, enters into a listing agreement with broker E. Broker N obtains a buyer for the house, and E does not receive a commission. The listing agreement between K and E was probably a(n):

a. exclusive-right-to-sell listing.
b. open listing.
c. exclusive-agency listing.
d. multiple listing.

79. Antitrust laws prohibit all of the following *except:*

a. real estate companies agreeing on fees charged to sellers.
b. real estate brokers allocating markets based on the value of homes.
c. real estate companies allocating markets based on the location of commercial buildings.
d. real estate salespersons allocating markets based on the location of homes.

80. Under the concept of riparian rights the owners of property adjacent to navigable rivers or streams have the right to use the water and:

a. may erect a dam across the navigable river or stream if the owners on each side agree.
b. are considered to own the submerged land to the center point of the waterway.
c. are considered owners of the water adjacent to the land.
d. are considered to own the land to the edge of the water.

Sample Examination Two

1. The landlord of tenant D has sold his building to the state so that a freeway can be built. D's lease has expired, but the landlord is letting him remain until the time the building will be torn down. D continues to pay the same rent as prescribed in his lease. What is D's tenancy called?

a. Holdover tenancy
b. Month-to-month tenancy
c. Tenancy at sufferance
d. Tenancy at will

2. When a form of real estate sales contract has been agreed to and signed by the purchaser and spouse and then given to the seller's broker with an earnest money check:

a. this transaction constitutes a valid contract.
b. the purchasers can sue the seller for specific performance.
c. this transaction is considered to be only an offer.
d. the earnest money will be forfeited if the purchasers default.

3. A seller gives an open listing to several brokers, specifically promising that if one of the brokers finds a buyer for the seller's property, the seller will then be obligated to pay a commission to that broker. Which of the following best describes this offer by the seller?

a. Executed agreement
b. Discharged agreement
c. Unilateral agreement
d. Bilateral agreement

4. By paying his debt after a foreclosure sale the borrower has the right to regain his property under which of the following?

a. Acceleration
b. Redemption
c. Reversion
d. Recovery

5. In a sale-and-leaseback arrangement:

   a. the seller/vendor retains title to the real estate.

   b. the buyer/vendee gets possession of the property.

   c. the buyer/vendee is the lessor.

   d. this arrangement is disallowed in most states.

6. Fannie Mae and Ginnie Mae:

   a. work together as primary market lenders.

   b. are both federal agencies.

   c. are both privately owned entities.

   d. are both involved in the secondary market.

7. Q decided that he could make more money from his tree farm by dividing it into small parcels and selling the parcels to numerous individuals. Subsequently Q entered into a series of purchase agreements in connection with which he agreed to continue to operate the property and distribute proceeds from its income to the buyers of the parcels. Under these circumstances Q has sold:

   a. real estate, because the object of the sale was the land.

   b. securities, because the object of the purchase was the trees and the underlying land was merely incidental to the sale.

   c. real estate, because the property was subdivided before the sales ever took place.

   d. securities, because the buyers were investors relying on Q's activities to generate a profit from the premises purchased.

8. All of the following situations are in violation of the federal Fair Housing Act of 1968 *except:*

   a. the refusal of a property manager to rent an apartment to a Catholic couple who are otherwise qualified.

   b. the general policy of a loan company to avoid granting home improvement loans to individuals living in transitional neighborhoods.

   c. the intentional neglect of a broker to show an Asian family any property listings of homes in all-white neighborhoods.

   d. the insistence of a widowed woman on renting her spare bedroom only to another widowed woman.

9. If a storage tank that measures 12 feet by 9 feet by 8 feet was designed to store natural gas and the cost of the gas is $1.82 per cubic foot, what does it cost to fill the tank to one-half its capacity?

   a. $685   c. $864

   b. $786   d. $1,572

10. Assume the market interest rate is 10 percent, discount points are at six, and the mortgage lender must yield 10¾ percent. If points drop to four, the interest rate will:

   a. decrease by ½ percent.

   b. increase by ¼ percent.

   c. decrease by ¼ percent.

   d. increase by ½ percent.

11. When a buyer signs a purchase contract and the seller accepts, the buyer acquires an immediate interest in the property known as:

   a. legal title.   c. statutory title.

   b. equitable title.   d. defeasible title.

12. Which of the following requires that finance charges be stated as an annual percentage rate?

   a. Truth-in-Lending Act (Regulation Z)

   b. Real Estate Settlement Procedures Act

   c. Equal Credit Opportunity Act

   d. Federal Fair Housing Act

13. J owns an apartment building in a large city. After discussing the matter with his advisers, J decided to alter the type of occupancy in the building from rental to condominium status. This procedure is known as:

   a. amendment.   c. deportment.

   b. partition.   d. conversion.

14. In the preceding question, after checking the applicable laws, J discovered that in connection with the change to condominium status he must initially offer to sell each unit to the tenant who currently occupies the unit. If the tenant does not accept the offer, J may then offer the unit for sale to the general public. The requirement that J offer the property to the tenant in this situation is known as a:

   a. contingent restriction.

   b. conditional sales option.

   c. right of first refusal.

   d. covenant of prior acceptance.

15. Which of the following real estate documents is least likely to be recorded?

    a. A standard form deed
    b. A long-term lease
    c. An option agreement
    d. A purchase agreement

16. In a township of 36 sections, which of the following statements is true?

    a. Section 16 lies to the north of Section 21.
    b. Section 18 is by law set aside for school purposes.
    c. Section 6 lies in the northeast corner of the township.
    d. Section 31 lies to the east of Section 32.

17. Broker U represented the seller in a transaction. Her client informed her that he did not want to recite the actual consideration that was paid for the house. In this situation Broker U:

    a. must inform her client that only the actual price of the real estate may appear on the deed.
    b. may show the nominal consideration of only $10 on the deed.
    c. should inform the seller that either the full price should be stated in the deed or all references to consideration should be removed from it.
    d. may show a price on the deed other than the actual price, provided that the variance is not greater than ten percent of the purchase price.

18. Broker F obtained a listing agreement to act as the agent in the sale of seller H's house. A buyer has been found for the property, and all of the agreements have been signed. It is F's duty to assure herself that the buyer:

    a. will complete the loan application.
    b. has received copies of all documents.
    c. is qualified for the new mortgage loan.
    d. has thoroughly inspected the property.

19. G and M, co-owners of a corner parcel of vacant commercial property, have executed three open listing agreements with three brokers around town. All three brokers would like to place ''for sale'' signs on the sellers' property. Under these circumstances:

    a. a broker does not have to obtain the sellers' permission before placing a sign on the property.
    b. only one ''for sale'' sign may be placed on the property at one time.
    c. upon obtaining the sellers' written consent, all brokers can place their ''for sale'' signs on the property.
    d. the broker who obtained the first open listing must consent to all signs being placed on the property.

20. In estimating the value of real estate using the cost approach, the appraiser should:

    a. estimate the replacement cost of the improvements.
    b. deduct for the depreciation of the land and buildings.
    c. determine the original cost and adjust for inflation.
    d. review the sales prices of comparable properties.

21. The law that requires lenders to inform both buyers and sellers of all fees and charges is the:

    a. Equal Credit Opportunity Act.
    b. Truth-in-Lending Act (Regulation Z).
    c. Real Estate Settlement Procedures Act.
    d. Real Estate Investment Trust Act.

22. If the landlord of an apartment building breaches his lease with one of the tenants and her unit becomes uninhabitable, which of the following would be the most likely result?

    a. Suit for possession
    b. Constructive eviction
    c. Tenancy at sufferance
    d. Covenant of quiet enjoyment

23. When the title passes to a third party upon the death of the life tenant, what is the third party's interest in the property?

    a. Remainder interest
    b. Reversionary interest
    c. Pur autre vie interest
    d. Redemption interest

24. On the settlement statement the prorations for real estate taxes paid in arrears would be shown as a:

    a. credit to the seller and a debit to the buyer.
    b. debit to the seller and a credit to the buyer.
    c. credit to both the seller and the buyer.
    d. debit to both the seller and the buyer.

25. What type of lease establishes a set rental payment and requires the lessor to pay for the taxes, insurance, and maintenance on the property?

    a. A percentage lease
    b. A net lease
    c. An expense-only lease
    d. A gross lease

26. A conventional loan was closed on July 1st for $57,200 at 13.5 percent interest amortized over 25 years at $666.75 per month. On August 1st, what would the principal amount be after the monthly payment was made?

    a. $56,533.25   c. $57,065.35
    b. $56,556.50   d. $57,176.75

27. In the preceding problem, what would the interest payment be?

    a. $666.75   c. $620.25
    b. $643.50   d. $610.65

28. The requirements of the Real Estate Settlement Procedures Act apply to any residential real estate transaction that takes place:

    a. in a state that has adopted RESPA.
    b. involving a federally related mortgage loan.
    c. involving any mortgage financing less than $100,000.
    d. involving any purchase price less than $100,000.

29. Under the income approach to estimating the value of real estate the capitalization rate is:

    a. the rate at which the property will increase in value.
    b. the rate of return the property will earn as an investment.
    c. the rate of capital required to keep a property operating most efficiently.
    d. the maximum rate of return allowed by law on an investment.

30. On the settlement statement the cost of the lender's title insurance policy that would be required for a new loan would usually be shown as a:

    a. credit to the seller.
    b. credit to the buyer.
    c. debit to the seller.
    d. debit to the buyer.

31. An FHA-insured loan in the amount of $57,500 at 11½ percent for 30 years was closed on July 17th. The first monthly payment is due on September 1st. As interest is paid monthly in arrears, what was the amount of the interest adjustment the buyer had to make at the settlement?

    a. $6,612.50   c. $312.29
    b. $551.10   d. $257.18

32. If a home that originally cost $42,500 three years ago is now valued at 127 percent of its original cost, what is its current market value?

    a. $33,465   c. $58,219
    b. $53,975   d. $65,354

33. Failing to assert a right within a reasonable or statutory period of time might lead a court to determine that the right to assert it is now lost because of:

    a. laches.   c. rescission.
    b. novation.   d. revocation.

34. When searching the public record, which of the following documents would *always* be discovered?

    a. Encroachments
    b. Rights of parties in possession
    c. Inaccurate surveys
    d. Mechanics' liens

35. A rectangular lot has an apartment structure on it worth $193,600. This value is the equivalent of $4.40 per square foot. If one lot dimension is 200 feet, what is the other dimension?

    a. 110 feet   c. 400 feet
    b. 220 feet   d. 880 feet

36. Broker D listed widow K's property at an eight percent commission rate. After the property was sold and the settlement had occurred, K discovered that D had been listing similar properties at a six percent commission rate. Based on this information:

    a. broker D has done nothing wrong.
    b. broker D can lose his license.
    c. widow K can cancel the transaction.
    d. widow K is entitled to a refund.

37. A tenant on a long-term commercial lease is considering going out of business. Because the market rent is much greater than she is currently paying, she would most likely consider:

    a. assigning the lease.
    b. subletting the property.
    c. asking the owner to rescind the lease.
    d. surrendering the premises.

38. A broker would not have to show that he was the procuring cause in a(n):

    a. net listing.
    b. open listing.
    c. exclusive-agency listing.
    d. exclusive-right-to-sell listing.

39. The capitalization rate on a property considers which of the following factors?

    a. The risk of the investment
    b. The replacement cost of the improvements
    c. The real estate taxes
    d. The depreciation of the improvements

40. An investment property worth $180,000 was purchased seven years ago for $142,000. At the time of the purchase the land was valued at $18,000. Assuming a 31½-year life for straight-line depreciation purposes, what is the present book value of the property?

    a. $95,071   c. $114,444
    b. $113,071   d. $126,000

41. After N purchased a property from E, they both decided to rescind the recorded sale. To do this they must

    a. return the deed to E.
    b. record a notice of rescission.
    c. destroy the original deed.
    d. make a new deed from E to N.

42. A farmer owns the W ½ of the NW ¼ of the NW ¼ of a section. The adjoining property can all be purchased for $300 per acre. Owning all of the NW ¼ of the section would cost the farmer:

    a. $6,000.   c. $42,000.
    b. $12,000.   d. $48,000.

43. An offer to purchase real estate can be terminated by all of the following *except:*

    a. failure to accept the offer within a prescribed period.
    b. revocation by the offeror communicated to the offeree after acceptance.
    c. a conditional acceptance of the offer by the offeree.
    d. death of the offeror or offeree.

44. A property manager would least likely:

    a. handle new leases.
    b. arrange for repairs and improvements.
    c. resolve tenant disputes as to property use.
    d. prepare depreciation schedules for tax purposes.

45. The monthly rent on a warehouse was set at $1 per cubic yard. Assuming the warehouse was 36 feet by 200 feet by 12 feet high, what would the annual rent be?

    a. $3,200   c. $38,400
    b. $9,600   d. $115,200

46. A veteran wishes to refinance his home with a VA-guaranteed loan. The lender is willing but insists on 3½ discount points. In this situation the veteran:

    a. can refinance with a VA loan provided there are no discount points.
    b. can refinance with a VA loan provided the discount points do not exceed two.
    c. can be required to pay a maximum of one percent of the loan as an origination fee.
    d. can proceed with the refinance loan and pay the discount points.

47. All of the following are characteristics of a fee simple title *except* that it is:

    a. free from encumbrances.
    b. of indefinite duration.
    c. transferable with or without valuable consideration.
    d. transferable by will or intestacy.

48. A real estate transaction had a closing date of November 15th. The seller, who was responsible for costs up to and including the date of the settlement, had paid the property taxes of $1,116 for the calendar year. On the closing statement the buyer would be:

    a. debited for $139.50.
    b. debited for $976.50.
    c. credited for $139.50
    d. credited for $976.50.

49. An agreement that ends all future lessor-lessee obligations under a lease is known as a(n):

    a. assumption.   c. novation.
    b. surrender.   d. breach.

50. In depreciating a residential property an accountant would base the depreciable life on:

    a. age-life tables.
    b. the observed condition of the property.
    c. 27½ years.
    d. 31½ years.

51. A property manager leased a store for three years. The first year the store's rent was $1,000 per month and the rent was to increase ten percent per year thereafter. The broker received a seven percent commission for the first year, five percent for the second year and three percent for the balance of the lease. The total commission earned by the property manager was:

    a. $840   c. $1,936
    b. $1,613   d. $2,785

52. Against a recorded deed from the owner of record the party with the weakest position is a:

    a. party with a prior unrecorded deed who is not in possession.
    b. party in possession with a prior unrecorded deed.
    c. tenant in possession with nine months remaining on the lease.
    d. painter who is half-finished painting the house at the time of the sale and has not been paid.

53. J, age 58, sold the home he had purchased two years before and moved in with his daughter. He had purchased the property for $46,500 and sold it for $74,800. In computing his income tax, J would pay taxes on:

    a. $11,320   c. $28,300
    b. $16,980   d. nothing.

54. A man moved into an abandoned home, installing cabinets in the kitchen for his convenience and making extensive repairs. When the owner discovered the occupancy, he had the man ejected. What is the status of the kitchen cabinets?

    a. The man cannot get the cabinets back.
    b. The cabinets remain as they are trade fixtures.
    c. While the cabinets stay, the man is entitled to the value of the improvements.
    d. The man can get them back if they can be removed without damage to the real estate.

55. W, F and J are joint tenants. J sells his interest to L, and then F dies. As a result:

    a. F's heirs, L and W are joint tenants.
    b. F's heirs and W are joint tenants, but L is a tenant in common.
    c. W, L and F's heirs are tenants in common.
    d. W and L are tenants in common.

56. In a settlement statement the selling price will *always* be:

    a. a debit to the buyer.
    b. a debit to the seller.
    c. a credit to the buyer.
    d. greater than the loan amount.

57. The state wants to condemn a strip of land through a farm for a highway. The farm will decrease in value far more than the value of the condemned strip. The farmer should ask for:

    a. inverse condemnation.
    b. severance damages.
    c. nominal damages.
    d. an injunction.

58. A man willed his estate as follows: 54 percent to his wife, 18 percent to his daughter, 16 percent to his son and the remainder to his church. The church received $79,000. The daughter received:

    a. $105,333   c. $355,500
    b. $118,500   d. $658,333

59. An example of external obsolescence would be:

a. numerous pillars supporting the ceiling in a store.
b. roof leaks making premises unusable and therefore unrentable.
c. an older structure with massive cornices.
d. vacant and abandoned buildings in the area.

60. Which of the following phrases, when placed in a print advertisement, would comply with the requirements of the Truth-in-Lending Act (Regulation Z)?

a. ''12 percent interest''
b. ''12 percent annual percent''
c. ''12 percent annual interest''
d. ''12 percent annual percentage rate''

61. All of the following are true regarding capitalization rates *except:*

a. the rate increases when the risk increases.
b. an increase in rate means a decrease in value.
c. the net income is divided by the rate to estimate the value.
d. a decrease in rate results in a decrease in value.

62. The Equal Credit Opportunity Act makes it illegal for lenders to refuse credit or otherwise discriminate because an applicant is:

a. a single parent who cannot afford the payments and receives public assistance.
b. a new home buyer who does not have a credit history.
c. a single person.
d. unemployed.

63. When P died, a signed and acknowledged but unrecorded deed was found among his effects, giving his house to a local charity. His will, however, provided that his entire estate was to go to his nephew. In this situation the house most likely will go to:

a. the charity, because acknowledgment is a presumption of delivery.
b. the charity, because P's intent was clear.
c. the nephew, because P died while still owning the house.
d. the nephew, because the deed was not recorded.

64. The type of loan that features increasing payments with the increases being applied directly to the debt reduction is the:

a. SAM.   c. ARM.
b. GEM.   d. GPM.

65. After an offer is accepted, the seller finds out that the broker was the undisclosed agent for the buyer as well as the agent for the seller. The seller:

a. can withdraw without obligation to broker or buyer.
b. can withdraw but would be subject to liquidated damages.
c. can withdraw but only with the concurrence of the buyer.
d. would be subject to specific performance if he refused to sell.

66. To net the owner $90,000 after a six percent commission is paid, the list price would have to be:

a. $95,400   c. $95,906
b. $95,745   d. $96,000

67. Which of the following would most likely be legal under the provisions of the Civil Rights Act of 1968?

a. A lender refusing to make loans in areas with more than 25 percent blacks
b. A private country club where ownership of homes is tied to club membership but all members are white
c. A church, which excludes blacks from membership, renting its nonprofit housing to church members only
d. Directing prospective buyers away from areas where they are likely to feel uncomfortable because of their race

68. It is discovered after a sale that the land parcel is ten percent smaller than the owner represented it to be. The broker who passed the information on to the buyer is:

a. not liable as long as he only repeated the seller's data.
b. not liable if the misrepresentation was unintentional.
c. not liable if the buyer actually inspected what she was getting.
d. liable if he knew or should have known of the discrepancy.

69. On a residential lot 70 feet square the side yard building setbacks are ten feet, the front yard setback is 25 feet, and the rear yard setback is 20 feet. The maximum possible size for a single-story structure would be:
    a. 1,000 square feet.
    b. 1,200 square feet.
    c. 1,250 square feet.
    d. 4,900 square feet.

70. All of the following are violations of the Real Estate Settlement Procedures Act (RESPA) *except:*
    a. directing the buyer to a particular lender.
    b. accepting a kickback on a loan subject to RESPA requirements.
    c. requiring a particular title insurance company.
    d. accepting a fee or charging for services that were not performed.

71. The rescission provisions of the Truth-in-Lending Act aply to:
    a. home purchase loans.
    b. construction lending.
    c. business financing.
    d. consumer credit.

72. A property has a net income of $30,000. An appraiser decides to use a 12 percent capitalization rate rather than a ten percent rate on this property. The use of the higher rate results in:
    a. a two percent increase in the appraised value.
    b. a $50,000 increase in the appraised value.
    c. a $50,000 decrease in the appraised value.
    d. no change in the appraised value.

73. The section of a purchase contract that provides for the buyer forfeiting any earnest money if the buyer fails to complete the purchase is known as:
    a. liquidated damages.
    b. punitive damages.
    c. the safety clause.
    d. the subordination clause.

74. In one commercial building the tenant intends to start a health food shop using her life savings. In an identical adjacent building is a catalog store leased to a major national retailing chain. Both tenants have long-term leases with identical rents. Which of the following statements is correct?
    a. If the values of the buildings were the same before the leases, the values will be the same after they are leased.
    b. An appraiser would most likely use a higher capitalization rate for the store leased to the national retailing chain.
    c. The most accurate appraisal method to be used would be the sales comparison approach to value.
    d. The building with the health food shop will appraise for less than the other building.

75. An insurance company agreed to provide a developer financing for a shopping center at 11 percent interest plus an equity position. This type of arrangement is called a(n):
    a. package loan.   c. open-end loan.
    b. participation loan.   d. blanket loan.

76. A $100,000 loan at 12 percent could be amortized with monthly payments of $1,200.22 on a 15-year basis or payments of $1,028.63 on a 30-year basis. The 30-year loan results in total payments of what percent of the 15-year total payments?
    a. 146%   c. 171%
    b. 158%   d. 228%

77. A church has just purchased a large ranch that it intends to use for religious activities, including retreats and training. Which of the following can the owners of neighboring properties expect?
    a. An increase in value
    b. An increase in county services
    c. Lower real estate taxes
    d. Higher real estate taxes

78. "Naked legal title" best describes the interest of a:
    a. trustee under a deed of trust.
    b. vendee under a land contract.
    c. mortgagee under a mortgage.
    d. lessee under a lease.

79. At the settlement the lender requests $345, which will be kept in a trust account. This money is most likely:

    a. a security deposit.
    b. for taxes and insurance.
    c. to ensure against borrower default.
    d. to cover the expense of discount points.

80. An apartment has an annual gross income of $87,500. Annual expenses are: depreciation, $8,500; debt service, $34,000, including principal of $7,200; real estate taxes, $5,100; other operating costs, $14,100. The annual cash flow is:

    a. $25,800   c. $41,500
    b. $34,300   d. $57,400

Environmental Risks and the Real Estate Transaction*

Pollution and Environmental Risks in Real Estate Transactions

Environmental concern has come to the forefront of contemporary issues. Both actual and perceived pollution problems have the ability to stir anger, fear and other feelings. Indeed perhaps no other modern issue has a greater ability to elicit strong emotions. The increasing public awareness of and concern about pollution problems and their health and economic effects have had significant consequences on real estate sales and values.

Economically the actual dollar value of real property can be affected significantly by both real and perceived pollution. The desirability and salability of land and buildings may change drastically. Also, the cost of cleaning up and removing pollution may be much greater than the dollar value of the property before pollution.

The National Association of REALTORS® and the National Association of Environmental Risk Auditors report that in some areas of the United States mortgage and title insurance approval in many cases depend on inspection of the property for hazardous substances and proof of their absence.

For all of these reasons real estate professionals should be alert to the possibility of pollution and hazardous substances on property being sold. Knowledgeable real estate professionals should ask clients about the possibility of hazardous substances associated with a property. In addition, licensees can increasingly expect questions from customers concerned about pollution. Licensees should consider the consequences of potential liability in real estate transactions where hazardous substances may be involved.

Pollution is something in the environment that was not there originally and is impure or unclean. The simple act of throwing a piece of paper on the ground creates an unsightly, minor form of pollution. Major pollution problems can result from hazardous substances disposed by industrial and other activities, such as farming. Real estate licensees often, however, do not have the technical expertise required to determine if a hazardous material is present or near the property. Government agencies and private consulting firms may be contacted for information, guidance and detailed study. Brokers and salespersons must be scru-

---

*An addendum provided by the National Association of Environmental Risk Auditors.™ Based on materials written by Stephen J. Martin, Executive Director, and Nick A. Tillema, Attorney-at-Law, NAERA'S General Counsel.

pulous in considering environmental issues and must exercise a high degree of care in all real estate transactions.

Hazardous Substances of Concern to Real Estate Professionals

Radon Gas

Radon gas is an odorless radioactive gas produced by the decay of other radioactive materials in rocks under the surface of the earth. As radon is released from the rocks, it finds its way to the surface and is usually released in the general atmosphere. In some cases it is trapped by the buildings on top of the ground and builds up in concentration. The radon enters a house through cracks in the foundation or through the floor drains. It can become concentrated in the crawl space or in basements. Long-term exposure to radon gas is said to cause lung cancer.

Radon was identified as being a hazardous problem in homes in 1984. Since that time the U.S. Environmental Protection Agency has established levels of radon gas that are felt to be unsafe. Testing techniques have also been developed that allow homeowners to determine the exact quantity of radon gas in their homes.

Generally the elimination of radon gas from a home is a relatively simple matter. Radon is a potential health threat only if found in concentrated amounts. Therefore, proper ventilation systems or small exhaust fans can move the radon gas from the concentrated area into the general atmosphere.

If a home has been determined to have radon gas, the seller is obligated to find a way to eliminate such a hazard, whether or not the danger is actual or only perceived. The value of the property can be reduced dramatically under such conditions. Typically it would be reduced by the amount necessary to eliminate the problem.

Asbestos

Asbestos is a mineral that has been used for many years as insulation on plumbing pipes and heat ducts and as general insulation because it is a poor conductor of heat. It also has been used in floor tile and in roofing material.

Due to its heat-containing property and the fact that it is relatively inexpensive, asbestos has been used in the insulation of almost all types of buildings, especially public buildings such as libraries, schools and government buildings. Although it remains relatively harmless if not disturbed, it can become life-threatening when removed because of the accompanying dust.

Exposure to the dust can come through several methods. One is when the asbestos material gets old and starts to disintegrate. Remodeling projects that include the removal of asbestos shingles, roof tile or insulation can cause the dust to form in the air and expose people in the area to the health hazard.

Once a building has been determined to have an asbestos problem, the owner can take several approaches to eliminating the problem. One is to leave things well enough alone. Asbestos roofing, floor tile and insulation cannot expose someone to asbestos poisoning if they are not disturbed. The second alternative is to remove any asbestos material. Public laws have been passed that require all school buildings and other buildings that expose the general public to eliminate all such asbestos insulation. Removal can be accomplished only by professionals experienced and knowledgeable in this field.

The third approach is to encapsulate the material; in other words, if the exposure comes because of the dust in the air, it is possible to contain the dust by enclosing the insulation with a plastic or paint that does not allow the dust to reach the air. Again, such procedures should be carried out by a professional.

Urea Formaldehyde Foam Insulation

Urea formaldehyde foam insulation (UFFI) is a man-made material that has been used in insulation in many buildings. Typically it is pumped between the walls as a foam that later hardens and acts as an insulating material. It has been estimated that one-half million homes in the United States have been insulated with UFFI. UFFI also has been used as a caulking material to seal cracks in walls and in window frames.

UFFI becomes dangerous because of the gases released from the material after it hardens. Such gases have been known to escape into the interior of the building. The health effects can range from major diseases such as cancer to minor and short-term problems such as eye, nose and throat irritations. Many people that have a high sensitivity to allergens are especially at risk in such situations.

Generally the only way to correct a UFFI problem is through the total removal of the insulation. It is important that such removal not be attempted until an expert in the field is consulted.

Lead Poisoning

Lead is a mineral that has been used for many centuries because of its pliability and its ability to impede water flow. It has been used as an ingredient in paint to protect wood from damage by water and also has been used in the installation of water pipes. It becomes a health hazard when ingested. Once in the body, it can impair physical and mental development in young children and aggravate high blood pressure in adults.

Lead poisoning comes from two main sources. The first is peeling or flaking paint that is sometimes put into the mouths of small children. The second source is the plumbing system. Sometimes lead in connecting water pipes or in insulation for hot-water heaters contaminates the water that flows through them. Concentrated amounts of lead can lead to serious health effects.

Once the problem was defined, lead was immediately banned as an ingredient for any paint material. Other limitations have been imposed on all materials that include lead to keep the lead away from all materials that may be ingested. However, one can still be exposed to lead in many older homes.

Waste Disposal Sites

The American culture has become increasingly a ''throw-away'' society. Landfill operations have been the main receptacle for this type of garbage. A landfill is a specific site that has been excavated and lined with either a clay or a synthetic liner to prevent leakage of the waste material into the local water system. Garbage is then laid at the bottom of the excavation, and a layer of topsoil is then compacted onto the garbage. The procedure is used again and again until the excavation has been filled. Although there is no height limitation for the garbage, it is usually ''capped'' when it reaches several hundred feet. Capping a landfill means to layer from two to four feet of topsoil at the very top and then plant some type of vegetation. Completed landfills have been used for such purposes as parks and golf courses.

The construction and maintenance of a landfill operation is heavily regulated by state and federal authorities. Well-run landfill operations do not have to be a source of pollution. However, landfills at improper locations and improperly managed sites have been a source of major problems. Landfills constructed on the wrong type of soil will leak waste into nearby wells, causing major damage. Federal, state and local authorities and private industry have set up test wells around such landfill operations to constantly monitor the water in the local areas.

Radioactive waste is material that has accumulated from nuclear energy power plants and from various uses of radioactive material in medicine and scientific research. Emissions from the waste from such material can be extremely harmful, sometimes causing cancer or even death.

Radioactive material can have a life expectancy of thousands of years. Much is still to be learned about disposal techniques, and in most cases the only alternative is to put the material in some type of containment facility. The container is then either buried or dropped in the sea. The obvious problem is that sometimes these containers can leak or be damaged in transit.

Although waste disposal is heavily regulated, no one is interested in living next to a hazardous waste dump. Real estate professionals must be aware of such facilities within their area and take the appropriate action when dealing with potential clients.

Underground Storage Tanks

Underground storage tanks have been used in both residential and commercial settings for many years. It has been estimated that there are three to five million underground storage tanks in the United States that include hazardous substances, including gasoline. The risk comes when such containers become old and rust and start to leak. The toxic material then has the ability to enter the groundwater and contaminate wells and pollute the soil.

The most obvious source of such pollution is the millions of gas stations scattered around the United States. Older stations sometimes include steel tanks that develop leaks through the oxidation process (rusting). However, another major source of faulty storage tanks is the underground containers used to hold fuel oil for older homes. Many times the homeowner has converted the heating source to natural gas and has abandoned the use of the old oil tank. This, again, runs the risk of leakage and pollution of the general area.

Recent federal legislation has called for the removal of such tanks and all the polluted soil around them. The tank and the soil are then disposed of in a hazardous waste facility. Such a program is extremely expensive, sometimes costing hundreds of thousands of dollars to revamp a gas station, for instance.

Groundwater Contamination

The term *groundwater* is sometimes confusing to the general public. It consists not only of the runoff at ground level but also includes the underground water systems that are used as sources of wells for both private and public facilities. Underground streams are formed in the rocks, crevices and caves under the ground and flow just as dramatically as those rivers above the ground. This underground water table can be as shallow as two or three feet below the surface and range all the way down to several hundred feet.

Contamination of this water supply is a serious health threat. Many experts believe that water could someday become an extremely valuable asset, because this general contamination will make pure, clean water a scarce commodity.

Water can be contaminated from a number of sources, including waste disposal sites and underground storage tanks. It is also contaminated by the use of pesticides and herbicides that are typically found in farming communities. Heavy regulation in these areas is about the only protection the general public has against water contamination. Once a contamination has been identified, its source can be eliminated, but such a process is often time-consuming and extremely expensive. Many times freshwater wells must be relocated to provide water for residents and commercial establishments.

Legal Considerations

The majority of legislation dealing with environmental problems has been instituted within the last two decades. Although the Environmental Protection Agency has been created at the federal level to oversee such problems, there are several other federal agencies whose areas of concern generally overlap. The federal laws were also created in such a way as to encourage state and local governments to prepare legislation in their own areas. All of the legislation lies on a background of common law being established by the court systems that create liability for the seller, the buyer, the listing broker, the selling broker, the appraiser, lenders and anyone involved in the real estate business.

Federal environmental law is administered by such agencies as the United States Department of Transportation under the Hazardous Material Transportation Act; the Occupational Safety and Health Administration (OSHA) and the United States Department of Labor, which administers the standards for all employees working in the manufacturing sector; and the Environmental Protection Agency, which administers such laws as the Toxic Substance Control Act, the Federal Clean Water Act and the Resource Conservation and Recovery Act.

The following discussion is designed to give a broad overview and a historical background to those laws affecting real estate. Increases in technology and public awareness of the problem mean that this is a dynamic area of the law with many areas of liability still being defined.

Statutory Law

The need for federal legislation was recognized after the Love Canal situation developed in New York. A hazard waste leak created untold problems from both a physical health and property standpoint. The Resource Conservation and Recovery Act (RCRA) of 1976 consequently was created to regulate the generation, transportation, storage, use, treatment, disposal and cleanup of hazardous waste. However, it quickly became apparent that the legislation was not sufficiently comprehensive to cover all the situations that were quickly becoming a matter of concern.

The Comprehensive Environmental Response, Compensation, and Liability Act (CERCLA) was created in 1980. It established a fund of $9 billion, called the Super Fund, to clean up uncontrolled hazardous waste dumps and to respond to spills. It created a process for identifying liable parties and ordering them to take responsibility for the cleanup action. A landowner may become liable under this act when there has been a release or a threat of release of a hazardous substance. Regardless of whether the contamination is the result of the landowner's own actions or those of others, the owner could be held responsible for cleaning up any resulting contamination. The liability includes the cleanup of the landowner's property and any neighboring property that has been contaminated. A landowner who is not responsible for the contamination can seek recovery reimbursement for the cleanup cost from previous landowners, any other responsible party or the Super Fund.

In the event the Environmental Protection Agency has determined that there has been a release of hazardous material into the environment, the EPA is given the authority to begin remedial action. It will initially attempt to determine the responsible parties for the leak and approach these "potentially responsible parties" (PRP) to see if they will voluntarily cooperate in the cleanup. For a given site the potential responsible parties may include hundreds of industrial generators of waste, previous landowners and transporters. The potentially responsible parties must then decide whether and on what terms they can fund the cleanup. If this is not done, EPA will begin work through its own contractors and charge the responsible parties for this cost. If a court determines liability after the cleanup and the refusal to pay, the responsible parties could be required to pay triple damages.

Liability under the Super Fund is considered to be strict, joint and several, and retroactive. Strict liability means that the owner is responsible to the injured party without excuse. Joint and several liability means that each of the individual owners is personally responsible for the damages in whole. If only one of the owners is financially responsible enough to handle the total damage, then that owner will have to pay all and collect the proportionate share of the rest of the owners from them whenever possible. Retroactive liability means that the liability is not limited to the person who currently owns the property but also to people who have owned the site in the past. Basically the liability provision means that all owners and transporters of hazardous waste are liable for the resulting cleanup cost without regard to fault. Therefore, the EPA need not prove wrongdoing to complete the cleanup or obtain recovery costs.

Underground storage tanks. The underground chemical or petroleum storage tanks have been regulated under a 1984 amendment to the Resource Conservation and Recovery Act. A program was established called Leaking Underground Storage Tanks, which has come to be known under the acronym LUST. The new law governs for the first time on a nationwide scale installation, maintenance, monitoring and failure of underground storage tanks. The focus of this regulation is to protect groundwater in the United States through release prevention, detection and correction.

Basically the owners of commercial underground storage tanks and pipes must register the present tanks, meet standards for installation, make the tank leakproof for their entire lives, install leak detection systems, keep the required records and install no bare steel tanks in soils that will cause rust. Otherwise the tanks must be corrosion-proof. Owners must also take corrective actions on leaks and have funds available to cover potential damage from leaks.

The law generally exempts farm and residential tanks with fewer than 1,100 gallons of motor fuel that is used for noncommercial purposes, tanks storing heating oil at the premises where it is consumed and septic tanks. An important legal point is that LUST places the financial responsibility on the tank owner.

Super Fund Amendments and Reauthorization Act (SARA). In 1986 the United States Congress reauthorized the Super Fund. The amendment statute contains stronger cleanup standards for contaminated sites and five times the funding of the original Super Fund, which expired in September 1985.

The amendment also sought to clarify the obligation of the lenders. As previously mentioned, liability under the Super Fund extends to both the present and all previous owners of the contaminated site. Real estate lenders found themselves either as the present owner or somewhere in the chain of ownership through foreclosure proceedings. The new amendments sought to clarify the obligations of the lenders.

The amendments also created a concept called *innocent landowner immunity*. It was recognized that in certain cases a landowner in the chain of ownership had been completely innocent of all wrongdoing and therefore should not be held liable. The innocent landowner immunity clause established the criteria by which to judge if a person or business could be exempted from that liability. The criteria included that the pollution was caused by a third party, that the property was acquired after the fact, that the landowner had actual or constructive knowledge of the damage, that "due care" was exercised when the property was purchased (the landowner made a reasonable search to determine that there was no damage to the property) and that reasonable precautions were taken in the exercise of ownership rights.

Common Law

Common law, which is created by past court decisions, provides a backdrop for these federal, state and local statutes to catch those situations that do not specifically fall within the law. This common law offers an important remedy for damages for personal injury or property damage that is not covered under legislation.

A good example for this is the concept of negligence. This is a field of law that defines the duty that members of the public owe to each other to take reasonable care to avoid foreseeable harm. Negligence can be defined as the failure to use such care as a reasonably prudent and careful person would use to avoid harm to others that would be foreseeable. This doctrine can be used against all owners, whether public or private, of sites and facilities, who make mistakes resulting in hazardous waste being released into the environment. Negligent acts resulting in the release of chemicals to the environment are sometimes called "toxic torts." Such torts are said to carry strict liability.

One of the most far-reaching cases was the 1986 California case of *Easton v. Strassburger*. It involved the sale of a home that had been built on an improperly designed landfill. Both the selling and listing real estate agents involved in the transaction were held liable for not providing "reasonably discoverable facts" (those that should have been known) about the property. Subsequent legislation passed and was made law in California, requiring that all real estate agents conduct a "reasonably diligent and competent inspection" of the property for sale, examining for potential problems dealing with pollution. This inspection must be more thorough than both a casual examination of the property and a general inquiry of the seller. The law also requires and provides for the use of disclosure forms that must be presented to the prospective purchaser. Such laws appear to be a future trend for all states.

Implications of Environmental Law

The real estate professional must be aware of the exposure of all parties involved. The real estate broker, for instance, is often the central player in a real estate transaction. The other players in the transaction have little if any knowledge of environmental law, let alone the type of exposure that they might be subjected to.

Sellers, as mentioned earlier, often carry the majority of the exposure. Innocent landowners might be held responsible even though they did not know that the property had been exposed to environmental pollution.

It is also necessary to advise neighboring properties of the potential for risk. If the broker represents a seller whose property abuts a gas station, the broker must be aware of the possibility of a leak and make the appropriate disclosures. The trend of the legal system is such that all possible risk must be disclosed to the buyer in any situation in which there might be an environmental problem. Although the preceding example is rather blatant, sellers might also have exposure in terms of radon, asbestos and lead paint.

The entity with the greatest exposure from which the majority of lawsuits originate is the buyer. The days of "caveat emptor" (let the buyer beware) are long gone. Both the statutes and the courts are taking steps to protect the innocent buyer whenever possible. The real estate professional has no other choice but to help protect the buyer in all situations.

Liability of Real Estate Professionals

Additional exposure is created for the auxiliary functions to the transaction. For instance, the real estate appraiser must mention and make the proper adjustments in the estimate of market value. Most of the environmental problems associated with residential units can be cleaned up, and the adjustment to market value typically reflects the cost of that cleanup plus a factor of the "panic" that exists in the current market. Although the sales price can be affected dramatically, it is possible that the underlying market value would remain relatively equal to others in the neighborhood.

The real estate appraiser is at the forefront of liability with regard to the lender. Proper diagnosis by the appraiser or proper diagnosis coupled with the lender's determination to make the mortgage anyway can create specific liability of the lender. Again, the lender is protected under certain conditions through the 1986 amendments to the Super Fund Act. But in any event the lender must be notified of any potential problems existing with the property.

The last and certainly not least member of the group that might be affected by the transaction is the insurance carrier. The mortgage insurance companies will protect the lender in their investment of the mortgage and might be required to carry part of the ultimate responsibility in case of a loss. More importantly, the hazard insurance carrier might be directly responsible for the damages if such coverage was included in the initial policy.

Environmental law is a relatively new phenomenon. Although the statutes have defined many of the liabilities involved, common law is still being used to make definitive points. The real estate professional and all associated with the real estate transaction must be aware of both actual and potential liability.

All parties to the real estate transaction should be certain to ascertain that "due diligence" has been conducted on the property by having an environmental screening done prior to the purchase of the property. The environmental screening can take the form of the report found in Figures A.1 through A.5 or can become a complete environment audit with complete or engineering and scientific tests being conducted.

Modern computer technology is now allowing the various environmental data bases to be used to effectively "screen" properties for potential problems based on the "footprint" of information regarding the subject property. Nationally, one such system, VISTA Environmental Profiles, is an example of a screening system that can be utilized by the real estate professional to prevent any environmental surprises from occurring. This system, when used by qualified individuals, can provide a key element in the environmental assessment of a property in a matter of minutes. Techniques such as this will enable real estate professionals to become more knowledgeable regarding environmental factors relating to subject properties and also will prevent large amounts of time and capital from being expended on marketing only to find an environmental problem became a "deal killer" in the final stages of negotiation.

Figure A.1
Seller's Certification—
Environmental
Hazardous Substances

SELLER'S CERTIFICATION - ENVIRONMENTAL HAZARDOUS SUBSTANCES

Property Identification:

Address _____

City _____ State _____ Zip _____

Brief Description: _____

_____

_____

_____

Seller Identification:

Name of Owner(s) _____

Address _____

City _____ State _____ Zip _____

Telephone _____

Property Owned From _____ To _____

Seller's Certification:

I do hereby certify that to the best of my knowledge during and before my ownership of the above described property:

   a) The property was not used as a dump site or storage facility for hazardous substances.

   b) No one has received notification from a federal, state or local government in regard to pending or threatened Superfund or Superlien liability.

   c) To the best of my knowledge no environmental hazards have been identified on the subject property.

Exception to above: _____

_____

_____

_____

_____

I (we) do hereby certify that the above information is true to the best of my (our) knowledge and belief.

Date _____ Seller_____

Date _____ Seller_____

FW-70EH   Forms and Worms Inc., 315 Whitney Ave., New Haven, CT 06511   1 (800) 243-4545   Item #115200
National Association of Environmental Risk Auditors

**Figure A.2
Uniform
Environmental
History**

UNIFORM ENVIRONMENTAL HISTORY
Questionnaire and/or Certificate

File No. _____

Property Address _____

City _____ State _____ Zip _____

Name of Person Interviewed _____

Dates of Ownership From _____ To _____

Other Way Familiar With Property From _____ To _____

Interviewer _____ Date _____

Address _____

City _____ State _____ Zip _____

Telephone _____

This form is used to report the results of an interview with the current or former property owner or others familiar with the property about known Hazardous Substances or Detrimental Environmental Conditions on or around the subject property. When signed by the interviewer it becomes their certificate.

#		YES	NO	Comment on all "Yes's"
ASBESTOS				
1.	Are you aware of any asbestos on your property? Pipe covering Heating/Hot water unit covering Tile Siding Other			
2.	Are you aware of any asbestos survey being performed on your property?			
3.	Are you aware of any asbestos tests being conducted on materials from your property?			
PCBs (Polychlorinated Biphenyls)				
4.	Are you aware of any PCBs on your property?			
5.	Are you aware of any PCBs on neighboring properties that might contaminate your property?			
RADON				
6.	Are you aware of any radon tests made on the property?			
7.	If so, was radon test made more than 12 months ago?			
8.	Were the results over 4 pCi/l? (If so, report actual figures).			
9.	To the best of your knowledge do any properties within one mile have radon levels over 4 pCi/l.			
10.	Are you aware of any evidence that nearby structures have elevated indoor levels of radon or radon progeny?			
11.	Are you aware of any information that indicates the local water supplies have been found to have elevated levels of radon or radium?			
12.	Are you aware of any properties within one mile of your property of any sites that were or currently are used for uranium, thorium or radium extraction or for phosphate processing?			
UST'S (Underground Storage Tanks)				
13.	Are you aware of any underground storage tanks presently on the property?			
14.	Are you aware of any underground storage tanks which were previously removed from the property, (if so note date).			
15.	Are you aware of any site survey made by a qualified engineer which indicates the property is free of USTs.?			
WASTE DISPOSAL				
16.	Are you aware of any petroleum storage and/or delivery facilities (including gas stations) or chemical manufacturing plants located within one mile of the property?			

Page 1 of 2

FW-70EQ   Test Version   Forms and Worms, Inc.® 315 Whitney Ave., New Haven, CT 06511 1(800)243-4545   Item# 115250
            3A 1/90   Approved by The National Association of Environmental Risk Auditors

Figure A.2 (continued)

	#		Y E S	N O	File No. Comment on all "Yes's"
WASTE SITES	17.	Are you aware of any physical testing (including on-site sampling of soil and groundwater) to determine if the property is free of waste contamination?			
	18.	Do you know if the property was ever used for research, industrial or military purposes?			
	19.	Do you know if the property has ever been occupied by owners or commercial tenants who are likely to have used, transported or disposed of toxic chemicals (e.g. dry cleaners, print shops, service stations, etc.)?			
	20.	Do you know if there is any water provided to the property or from a well or private water company?			
	21.	Do you know if the property or any site within one mile, appears on any state or federal list of hazardous waste sites (e.g. CERCLIS, HWDMS, etc.)?			
	22.	Do you know of any visible evidence or documents that indicate there is or was dangerous waste handling on the property or neighboring sites (e.g. stressed vegetation, stained soil, open or leaking containers, foul fumes or smells, oily ponds, etc.)?			

UREA (Formaldehyde)

	#		YES	NO	
	23.	Do you know if the property contains UREA Formaldehyde Foam Insulation? (If yes, note location and amount).			

LEAD PAINT

	#		YES	NO	
	24.	Do you know if the property was tested for lead paint?			
	25.	Do you have any reason to believe that the property contains lead paint?			

DRINKING WATER	#		YES	NO	
	26.	Do you know if the drinking water was ever tested for lead? (If yes, note date and results).			
	27.	Do you know if any other tests were ever made on the drinking water? (If yes, describe and note results).			
	28.	Do you have any reason to believe there was or is any problem with the quality and quantity of drinking water available at the property?			

AIR POLLUTANTS

	#		YES	NO	
	29.	Do you know if the interior air was ever tested?			
	30.	Do you have any reason to believe there was or is any problem with the interior or exterior air of the property?			

OTHER ENVIRONMENTAL HAZARDS

	#		YES	NO	
	31.	Are you aware of any other hazardous substances or detrimental environmental conditions that effect the property?			

I certify that I have read the answers to the questions on this form and acknowledge that they are accurate to the best of my knowledge and belief.

Signatures   Current or former property owner(s)

_____   _____
                          Date   Date

_____   _____
                          Date   Date

Interviewer

FW-70EQ   Test Version   Forms and Worms, Inc.® 315 Whitney Ave., New Haven, CT 06511 1(800)243-4545
                    3A 1/90   Approved by The National Association of Environmental Risk Auditors   Item# 115250

**Figure A.3
Environmental Desk
Review**

ENVIRONMENTAL DESK REVIEW
Reviewer/Underwriter Certification
Hazardous Substances and Detrimental Environmental Conditions

Loan File No.: _____

Lender: _____

Property Identification

Address		
City	State	Zip
Type of Property		
Reviewer/Underwriter		

The following is a summary of how the property was screened for Hazardous Substances & Detrimental Environmental Conditions and the results of the screenings.

ASBESTOS   ☐ Screened   ☐ Not Screened

Name of Screener _____ Date Screened: _____
How Screened _____
Tests & Results _____

Screening Results: ☐ Acceptable   ☐ Acceptable: Requires O & M   ☐ Failed   ☐ Fail: Possible Remedy
☐ Additional Tests Required   ☐ Additional Inspections Required
Comments _____

PCBs (Polychlorinated Biphenyls)   ☐ Screened   ☐ Not Screened

Name of Screener _____ Date Screened: _____
How Screened _____
Tests & Results _____

Screening Results: ☐ Acceptable   ☐ Acceptable: Requires O & M   ☐ Failed   ☐ Fail: Possible Remedy
☐ Additional Tests Required   ☐ Additional Inspections Required
Comments _____

RADON   ☐ Screened   ☐ Not Screened

Name of Screener _____ Date Screened: _____
How Screened _____
Tests & Results _____

Screening Results: ☐ Acceptable   ☐ Acceptable: Requires O & M   ☐ Failed   ☐ Fail: Possible Remedy
☐ Additional Tests Required   ☐ Additional Inspections Required
Comments _____

USTs (Underground Storage Tanks)   ☐ Screened   ☐ Not Screened

Name of Screener _____ Date Screened: _____
How Screened _____
Tests & Results _____

Screening Results: ☐ Acceptable   ☐ Acceptable: Requires O & M   ☐ Failed   ☐ Fail: Possible Remedy
☐ Additional Tests Required   ☐ Additional Inspections Required
Comments _____

WASTE DISPOSAL   ☐ Screened   ☐ Not Screened

Name of Screener _____ Date Screened: _____
How Screened _____
Tests & Results _____

Screening Results: ☐ Acceptable   ☐ Acceptable: Requires O & M   ☐ Failed   ☐ Fail: Possible Remedy
☐ Additional Tests Required   ☐ Additional Inspections Required
Comments _____

WASTE SITES   ☐ Screened   ☐ Not Screened

Name of Screener _____ Date Screened: _____
How Screened _____
Tests & Results _____

Screening Results: ☐ Acceptable   ☐ Acceptable: Requires O & M   ☐ Failed   ☐ Fail: Possible Remedy
☐ Additional Tests Required   ☐ Additional Inspections Required
Comments _____

Page 1 of 2

**Figure A.3
(continued)**

UREA (Formaldehyde) ☐ Screened ■ Not Screened

Name of Screener _____ Date Screened: _____
How Screened _____
Tests & Results _____

Screening Results: ☐ Acceptable ☐ Acceptable: Requires O & M ☐ Failed ☐ Fail: Possible Remedy
                    ☐ Additional Tests Required ☐ Additional Inspections Required
Comments _____

LEAD PAINT ☐ Screened ■ Not Screened

Name of Screener _____ Date Screened: _____
How Screened _____
Tests & Results _____

Screening Results: ☐ Acceptable ☐ Acceptable: Requires O & M ☐ Failed ☐ Fail: Possible Remedy
                    ☐ Additional Tests Required ☐ Additional Inspections Required
Comments _____

DRINKING WATER ☐ Screened ■ Not Screened

Name of Screener _____ Date Screened: _____
How Screened _____
Tests & Results _____

Screening Results: ☐ Acceptable ☐ Acceptable: Requires O & M ☐ Failed ☐ Fail: Possible Remedy
                    ☐ Additional Tests Required ☐ Additional Inspections Required
Comments _____

AIR POLLUTANTS ☐ Screened ■ Not Screened

Name of Screener _____ Date Screened: _____
How Screened _____
Tests & Results _____

Screening Results: ☐ Acceptable ☐ Acceptable: Requires O & M ☐ Failed ☐ Fail: Possible Remedy
                    ☐ Additional Tests Required ☐ Additional Inspections Required
Comments _____

ADDITIONAL ENVIRONMENTAL HAZARDS ☐ Screened ■ Not Screened

Hazard(s) _____ Date Screened: _____
How Screened _____
Tests & Results _____

Screening Results: ☐ Acceptable ☐ Acceptable: Requires O & M ☐ Failed ☐ Fail: Possible Remedy
                    ☐ Additional Tests Required ☐ Additional Inspections Required
Comments _____

SUMMARY

I have reviewed the: (Check all that apply)
☐ Appraisal   ☐ Environmental Screenings   ☐ Test Results
☐ Seller's Certificate ☐ History   ☐ Other _____
Summary of Review _____
_____
_____
_____

They Do/Do not reveal any hazardous substances or detrimental environmental conditions,
☐ I recommend the property be accepted
☐ I recommend the following inspections, O & M and tests be conducted or reevaluated before the property is accepted
_____
_____

☐ I recommend the property not be accepted due to _____

Underwriter/Reviewer:
Signature _____ ☐ I inspected the property
Typed Name _____ ☐ I did not inspect the property
Date _____
Name of institution _____

Page 2 of 2

FW-70ER   Test Version   ©1989 Forms and Worms, Inc., 315 Whitney Ave., New Haven, CT 06511 1(800) 243-4545   Item #115350
              #3A 1/90   Approved by The National Association of Environmental Risk Auditors

Figure A.4
Phase 1
Environmental
Assessment

PHASE 1 ENVIRONMENTAL ASSESSMENT
Federal National Mortgage Association

File No. _____

REQUIRED FANNIE MAE PROPERTY LOG

Fannie Mae Loan # _____
Property Address _____
_____
_____
Borrower Address _____
_____
_____
Borrower Phone _____
Lender Company Name _____
Individual Lender _____
Environmental Underwriter _____
Individual Environmental
Consultant _____
Firm Name and Address _____
_____
Consultant Phone_____
Date Assessment Completed _____
Assessment Results _____

SUMMARY OF RESULTS AND RECOMMENDATION

1. Phase I Assessment Results (check applicable result for each hazard)

Hazard	Acceptable	Acceptable Requires O&M	Fail	Possible Remedy	Phase II Required
Asbestos	_____	_____	___	_____	_____
PCB	_____	_____	___	_____	_____
Radon	_____	_____	___	_____	_____
UST	_____	_____	___	_____	_____
Waste Sites	_____	_____	___	_____	_____
Other_____	_____	_____	___	_____	_____
_____	_____	_____	___	_____	_____
_____	_____	_____	___	_____	_____

2. Attach a brief explanation for each hazard requiring a Phase II assessment. List data deficiencies, test results etc., requiring further assessment.

3. Attach a brief explanation for each hazard that is acceptable but requires Operations and Maintenance (O & M) actions. What actions are required and how should they be performed?

4. Attach a brief explanation for each failed hazard that could be corrected with remedial actions. What actions are required and how should they be performed?

5. Other comments:

Signature: _____   Date: _____

INFORMATION CHECKLIST

The following checked items indicate overall sources used by the Field Observer to perform an assessment of the property to determine the existence of apparent hazardous materials and detrimental environmental conditions:

_____ Building Specifications
_____ Historical Aerial Photos
_____ Current Aerial Photos
_____ Title History
_____ Site Survey
_____ Interviews with Local
        Fire, Health, Land Use
        or Environmental Enforcement Officials

_____ Neighborhood Zoning Maps
_____ Neighborhood Land Use Maps
_____ List of Commercial Tenants On-site
_____ Verification of Public Water and Sewer
_____ Interviews with Builder, and/or Property Manager
_____ Other _____

2. Asbestos

_____ Dated Building Construction or Rehabilitation Specifications
_____ Report of: Engineer/Consultant/Asbestos
_____ Other _____

3. PCB's (Polychlorinated Biphenyls)

_____ Utility Transformer Records
_____ Site survey of Transformers
_____ Site Soil and Groundwater PCB Test Results
_____ Other _____

FW-70EA   Test Version   ©1989 Forms and Worms, Inc., 315 Whitney Ave., New Haven, CT 06511 1(800)243-4545   Item #115150
          3A-1/90   National Association of Environmental Risk Auditors

**Figure A.4
(continued)**

INFORMATION CHECKLIST (Continued)

4. Radon

_____ Water Utility Records
_____ Gas Utility Records
_____ On-Site Radon Test Results
_____ Other _____

5. USTs (Underground Storage Tanks)

_____ Oil, Motor Fuel and Waste Oil Systems Reports
_____ CERCLIS/HWDMS Results on Neighborhood (within radius of one mile)
_____ Site Soil and Groundwater Tests
_____ Site Tank Survey
_____ Other _____

6. Waste Sites

_____ CERCLIS/HWDMS Results on neighborhoods (within radius of one mile)
_____ State EPA site lists for neighborhoods (within radius of one mile)
_____ Site Soil and Groundwater Test Results
_____ Other _____

7. Additional Hazards

_____ Urea Formaldehyde Foam Insulation Survey
_____ Interior Air Test Results
_____ Lead Paint Survey
_____ Lead in Drinking Water Test Results
_____ Other _____

ASBESTOS

Required Fannie Mae Phase 1 Environmental Assessment questions and signature:	YES	NO	UNKNOWN
1. Was the building constructed prior to 1979?	☐	☐	☐
2. Does a site walk through reveal any visible evidence of asbestos?	☐	☐	☐
3. Is there any documented evidence of asbestos?	☐	☐	☐

Note: If the answer to all three of the above questions is "no", then stop, the property is acceptable for asbestos. If the answer to any of the questions is "yes" or "unknown", answer the questions below.

	YES	NO	UNKNOWN
4. Is there an asbestos survey by a certified, independent firm performed since 1979?	☐	☐	☐

Note: If the answer to question 4 is "yes", answer the question below. Otherwise, stop, a Phase II assessment is required.

	YES	NO	UNKNOWN
5. Did the survey find the building to be free of treated or untreated ACM?	☐	☐	☐

Note: If the answer to question 5 is "yes", then stop, the property is acceptable for asbestos. Otherwise, either the building fails or a Phase II assessment is required.

6. Comments of: Underwriter/Appraiser/Inspector _____

7. Phase I Assessment Results (circle one):
   Acceptable   Acceptable Requires O & M   Fail   Fail, Possible Remedy   Phase II Required

8. Signature of: Underwriter/Appraiser/Inspector _____ Date_____

PCBs (Polychlorinated Biphenyls)

Required Fannie Mae Phase 1 Environmental Assessment questions and signature:	YES	NO	UNKNOWN
1. Are there any fluorescent light ballasts containing PCBs in the building?	☐	☐	☐
2. Are there any transformers or capacitors containing PCBs anywhere on the property?	☐	☐	☐
3. Is there any visible or documented evidence of soil or groundwater contamination from PCBs on the property?	☐	☐	☐

Note: If the answer to all three questions is "no", then stop, the property is acceptable for PCBs. If the answer to any question is "unknown", then stop, a Phase II assessment is required. Otherwise, answer the questions below.

	YES	NO	UNKNOWN
4. (If question 1 above is "yes") Are any of the lights damaged or leaking?	☐	☐	☐
5. (If question 2 above is "yes") Are any of the capacitors or transformers inside residential buildings?	☐	☐	☐
6. (If question 2 above is "yes") Are any of the transformers or capacitors not clearly marked, well maintained or secure?	☐	☐	☐
7. (If question 2 above is "yes") Is there any evidence of leakage on or around the transformers or capacitors?	☐	☐	☐
8. (If question 3 above is "yes") Have PCB concentrations of 50ppm or greater been found in contaminated soils or groundwater?	☐	☐	☐

Note: If the answers to question 4, 5, 6, 7, and 8 are all "no", then the property is acceptable for PCBs. Otherwise, the property either fails or requires a Phase II assessment.

9. Comments of: Underwriter/Appraiser/Inspector _____

10. Phase I Assessment Results (circle one):
   Acceptable   Acceptable Requires O & M   Fail   Fail, Possible Remedy   Phase II Required

11. Signature of: Underwriter/Appraiser/Inspector _____ Date_____

FW-70EA   Test Version   ©1989 Forms and Worms, Inc., 315 Whitney Ave., New Haven, CT 06511 1(800)243-4545   Item #115150
                2A-9/89   National Association of Environmental Risk Auditors

**Figure A.4
(continued)**

File No.
_____

Required Fannie Mae Phase 1 Environmental Assessment questions and signature:	YES	NO	UNKNOWN

RADON

1. Were the results of an EPA approved short-term radon test, performed in the basement within the last six months, at/or below 4 pCi/l or 0.02 WL?   ☐ ☐ ☐
   Note: If the answer is "no" or "unknown", then stop, a Phase II assessment is required. If the answer is "yes", answer the questions below.
2. Is there any evidence that nearby structures have elevated indoor levels of radon or radon progeny?   ☐ ☐ ☐
3. Have local water supplies been found to have elevated levels of radon or radium?   ☐ ☐ ☐
4. Is the property located on or near sites that currently are or formerly were used for uranium, thorium, or radium extraction or for phosphate processing?   ☐ ☐ ☐
   Note: If the answer to questions 2, 3 or 4 is "yes", then a Phase II assessment is required. If the answer to questions 2, 3 and 4 is "no", then the property is acceptable for radon. A property may be acceptable for radon with a "unknown" answer for questions 2, 3 or 4 but the underwriter must justify the decision.
5. Comments of: Underwriter/Appraiser/Inspector _____
   _____
6. Phase I Assessment Results (circle one):
   Acceptable   Acceptable Requires O & M   Fail   Fail, Possible Remedy   Phase II Required
7. Signature of: Underwriter/Appraiser/Inspector _____   Date_____

Required Fannie Mae Phase 1 Environmental Assessment questions and signature:	YES	NO	UNKNOWN

USTs (Underground Storage Tanks)

1. Is there a current site survey performed by a qualified engineer which indicates that the property is free of any UST's?   ☐ ☐ ☐
2. Is there any visible or documented evidence of soil or groundwater contamination on the property?   ☐ ☐ ☐
3. Are there any petroleum storage and/or delivery facilities (including gas stations) or chemical manufacturing plants located on adjacent properties?   ☐ ☐ ☐
   Note: If the answer to question 1 is "yes", and the answers to questions 2 and 3 are "no", the property is acceptable for UST's skip to next section. Otherwise, answer the questions below.
4. (If "yes" to question 3) Have these facilities been maintained in accordance with sound industry standards (e.g. API Bulletins 1621 and 1623; NFPA Bulletins 329, 70, 77 etc.)?   ☐ ☐ ☐
   Note: If the answer to 4 is "no", skip to question 7 below. If the answer to 4 is "unknown", the property fails or a Phase II assessment is required. If the answer to both questions 3 and 4 is "yes", answer the questions below.
5. Are any of the tanks more than 10 years old?   ☐ ☐ ☐
6. Have any of the tanks that are more than 10 years old not been successfully tested for leaks within the last year using an API approved test?   ☐ ☐ ☐
   Note: If the answer to question 6 is "no", answer the questions below. If the answer to question 6 is "yes" or "unknown", the property fails or a Phase II assessment is required.
7. Are there any deactivated UST's on the property?   ☐ ☐ ☐
8. (If "yes" to question 7) Were all of the tanks deactivated in accordance with sound industry practices (e.g. API Bulletins #1604 and #2202 or NFPA Bulletin #30)?   ☐ ☐ ☐
   Note: If the answer to question 7 is "no", or if the answer to question 8 is "yes" then the property is acceptable for UST's. If the answer to question 7 is "yes" or "unknown" or if the answer to question 8 is "no" or "unknown" then the property fails or a Phase II assessment is required.
9. Comments of: Underwriter/Appraiser/Inspector _____
   _____
10. Phase I Assessment Results (circle one):
    Acceptable   Acceptable: Requires O & M   Fail   Fail: Possible Remedy   Phase II Required
11. Signature of: Underwriter/Appraiser/Inspector _____   Date_____

FW-70EA   Test Version   ©1989 Forms and Worms, Inc., 315 Whitney Ave., New Haven, CT 06511   1(800)243-4545   Item #115150
                 2A-9/89   National Association of Environmental Risk Auditors

Figure A.4 (continued)

File No. _____

WASTE DISPOSAL FACILITIES

Required Fannie Mae Phase 1 Environmental Assessment questions and signature:	YES	NO	UNKNOWN
1. Are there results of physical testing (including on-site sampling of soil and groundwater meeting all regulatory standards and sound industry practice) indicating that the property is free of waste contamination and is being operated in an environmentally safe manner?	☐	☐	☐
2. Are there any obvious high risk neighbors in adjacent properties engaged in producing, storing or transporting hazardous waste, chemicals or substances?	☐	☐	☐

Note: If the answer to question 1 is "yes" and the answer to question 2 is "no", then stop, the property is acceptable for waste disposal facilities. Otherwise, answer questions below.

	YES	NO	UNKNOWN
3. Was the site ever used for research, industrial or military purposes during the last 30 years?	☐	☐	☐
4. Has any of the site space ever been leased to commercial tenants who are likely to have used, transported or disposed of toxic chemicals (e.g. dry cleaner, print shop, service station, etc.)?	☐	☐	☐
5. Is water for the building provided either by a private company or directly from a well on the property?	☐	☐	☐
6. Does the property or any site within 1 mile, appear on any state or federal list of hazardous waste sites (e.g. CERCLIS, HWDMS etc.)?	☐	☐	☐
7. Is there any documented or visible evidence of dangerous waste handling on the subject property or neighboring sites (e.g. stressed vegetation, stained soil, open or leaking containers, foul fumes or smells, oily ponds etc.)?	☐	☐	☐

Note: If the answer to any of questions 2 through 6 are "yes" or "unknown", then either the property fails or a Phase II assessment is required. If the answer to all questions 2 through 6 are "no", then the property is acceptable for waste disposal facilities.

8. Comments of: Underwriter/Appraiser/Inspector _____

_____

9. Phase I Assessment Results (circle one):

    Acceptable   Acceptable: Requires O & M   Fail   Fail: Possible Remedy   Phase II Required

10. Signature of: Underwriter/Appraiser/Inspector _____ Date _____

ADDITIONAL HAZARDS

Required Fannie Mae Phase 1 Environmental Assessment questions and signature:	YES	NO	UNKNOWN
1. Is there any visible or documented evidence of peeling lead paint on the floors, walls or ceilings of tenant or common areas?	☐	☐	☐

Note: If the answer to question 1 is "no", the property is acceptable for lead paint. If the answer is "yes" or "unknown", the property fails. The application may continue, but remedial actions to remove or cover all peeling lead paint must be taken prior to Commitment by Fannie Mae.

	YES	NO	UNKNOWN
2. Do the tenant areas contain Urea Formaldehyde Foam Insulation that was installed less than a year ago?	☐	☐	☐
3. (If the answer to question 2 is "yes" or "unknown") Did the current HVAC system meet ASHRAE standards when it was installed?	☐	☐	☐

Note: If the answer to question 2 is "no", or if the answer to question 3 is "yes", then the property is acceptable for UFFI. If the answer to question 3 is "no" or "unknown", then the property fails. The application may continue, but the Lender must demonstrate prior to Commitment by Fannie Mae that the ventilation system currently meets ASHRAE standards.

	YES	NO	UNKNOWN
4. Does the drinking water in the project contain lead at levels above 50ppb?	☐	☐	☐

Note: If the answer to question 4 is "yes" or "unknown", the property fails. Action must be taken prior to Commitment by Fannie Mae to reduce the lead content of the drinking water. Otherwise, the property is acceptable for lead in drinking water.

5. Comments of: Underwriter/Appraiser/Inspector _____

_____

6. Phase I Assessment Results (circle one):

    Acceptable   Acceptable: Requires O & M   Fail   Fail: Possible Remedy   Phase II Required

7. Signature of: Underwriter/Appraiser/Inspector _____ Date _____

FW-70EA   Test Version 2A-9/89   ©1989 Forms and Worms Inc., 315 Whitney Ave., New Haven, CT 06511 1(800)243-4545
National Association of Environmental Risk Auditors   Item #115150

Figure A.5
Sample Environmental
Profile

```
                    VISTA ENVIRONMENTAL PROFILE

                         SUMMARY PROFILE


                                                    Page 1

     Prepared For:                          Customer#: 012465

     L & A Engineering Associates              Date: 10/06/90
     ================================================================
     Facility:   Diaz Chemical Corp.     VISTA Number:   000000219
                 40 Jackson St.          Latitude:       43:13:25
                 Holley, NY  14470       Longitude:      78:01:49.0
                 (718) 638-6321          Latest update:  09/27/90
     ================================================================

     NATURE OF BUSINESS & INDUSTRY

     Industry Description               SIC  %Reporting*   RIO**

     Cyclical Organics and Intermediates  2965    71%       142
     Pharmaceutical Preparations          2965    73%       191
     Chemicals N.E.C.                     2899    67%       172
     Pesticides & Agricultural Chemicals  2879    82%       201


     * Percentage of firms in this line of business which have any
     environmental reported record or permit.

     **Relative Incident Occurence (RIO) is the relative industry risk
     of having a reported environmental incident ( a spill, a violation
     or improper use of hazardous materials). 100 = average risk.



     ENVIRONMENTAL CONCERNS WITHIN THIS ZIP CODE

           National Priority List sites............................0
           Other CERCLIS hazardous sites...........................0
           Hazardous waste treatment/storage/disposal facilities...1
           Sanitary landfills/incinerators transfer stations.......0
           Hazardous waste generators..............................2
           Underground storage tank sites..........................4
           Leaking underground storage tanks.......................0
           Toxic Release Inventory (TRI) reporters.................2
           Chemical producers......................................3
           Radioactive materials handlers..........................1
           Public drinking water systems (PDWS)....................0
           PDWS in significant non-compliance......................0
           Other permitted sites...................................1
           Look-a-Like sites.......................................7


     ================================================================
              © VISTA Environmental Information, Inc.
                   For more information call:
                       1 (800) 733-7606
```

Figure A.5
(continued)

```
=====================================================================
Diaz Chemical Corp.                                           Page 2

Date: 10/06/90                                Customer#:    046851

=====================================================================

ENVIRONMENTAL CONCERNS AT THIS SITE

Existing Contamination:                                          RIO

        Facility is on the National Priority List............ 150
        CERCLIS hazardous site requiring clean-up............ 206
        Active hazardous waste disposal site on premises..... 187
        Inactive hazardous waste disposal site on premises... 725
        Active sanitary landfill on premises................. 146
    x   Leaking underground storage tank reported............ 204


Manufacturing or Storage Operations:

    x   Produces toxic chemicals.............................  71
        Manufactures or processes pesticides.................  98
    x   Employs toxic chemicals in manufacturing process.....  40
    x   Stores toxic chemicals in major quantities........... 135
        Handles radioactive materials........................  67
    x   Utilizes  4  underground storage tanks .............. 182
    x   Utilizes  2  above ground storage tanks............. 170
    x   Generates hazardous waste............................ 167
    x   Processes hazardous waste on-site.................... 231
        Stores hazardous waste in large quantities........... 256
    x   Discharges waste into surface water.................. 183
        Discharges waste using underground injection......... 112
    x   Produces hazardous air emissions..................... 125
    x   Operates a drinking water system serving 200 people..  32


Commercial Operations:
                                                                RIO
        Commercial handler of hazardous waste................ 121
    x   Commercial transporter of hazmat with  2  trucks..... 165
        Commercial storage of hazardous waste................ 100
        Registered PCB handler...............................  40
        Registered hospital waste handler....................  64


RESPONSIBILITY BEYOND THIS SITE

    The operations at this site are named as a Potentially
    Responsible Party at   6   CERCLIS sites.


=====================================================================
          ©      VISTA Environmental Information, Inc.
                     For more information call:
                        1 (800) 733-7606
```

**Figure A.5
(continued)**

```
=====================================================================
Diaz Chemical Corp.                                        Page 3

Date:  10/06/90                              Customer#:  046851

=====================================================================
HISTORY OF ENVIRONMENTAL COMPLIANCE

Air Emissions:
    Number of Months reporting for compliance............ 24
    Number of months in compliance....................... 22
    Number of months out of compliance...................  2
    Significant violator flag (Y/N).......................  N

Water Discharge:

    Number of quarters reporting for compliance..........  8
    Number of quarters in compliance.....................  8
    Number of quarters out of compliance.................  0

Drinking Water:

    In significant non-compliance at least once.......... NA
    Number of violations................................. NA

Hazardous Waste:

    Number of RCRA Class One Violations..................  3
    Total penalties (000's of dollars)...................426

Toxic Substance Control Act:

    Number of TOSCA violations...........................  0
    Total penalties (000's of dollars)...................  0

Federal Insecticide, Fungicide and Rodenticide Act:

    Number of FIFRA violations........................... NA
    Total penalties (000's of dollars)................... NA

Emergency Planning and Community Right-to-Know Act:

    Number of EPCRA violations...........................  1
    Total penalties (000's of dollars)...................210

Occupational Safety and Health Act:

    Number of willful OSHA violations....................  2
    Number of serious OSHA violations....................  1
    Number of repeat OSHA violations.....................  0
    Total penalties (000's of dollars)...................640

=====================================================================
               ©    VISTA Environmental Information, Inc.
                       For more information call:
                          1 (800) 733-7606
```

Figure A.5
(continued)

```
=====================================================================
Diaz Chemical Corp.                                        Page 4

Date:  10/06/90                              Customer#: 046851

=====================================================================
HISTORY OF ENVIRONMENTAL COMPLIANCE (con't)

Civil and Judicial Actions taken by EPA:

   Number of actions taken............................. 1
   Clean-up cost recovery  (000's of dollars)........... 0
   Total penalties (000's of dollars).................. 14

HISTORY OF REPORTED SPILLS

Emergency Response Notification System (ERNS):

   Number of spills/releases reported.................... 2
   Number of deaths........................................ 0
   Number of injuries...................................... 1
   Total pounds releases............................21,345
   Damages (000's of dollars)............................ 0

Department of Transportation HAZMAT System:

   Number of spills/releases reported.................... 0
   Number of major injuries.............................. 0
   Number of minor injuries.............................. 0
   Number of deaths........................................ 0
   Dollars of damages (000's of dollars)................. 0

State Spill Reporting System:

   Number  of spills/releases reported.................. 3

LIMITATIONS OF INFORMATION

This report is not a substitute for a thorough environmental
risk audit performed by a qualified environmental engineer or
scientist. It is provided under a subscription agreement with
VISTA Environmental Information Inc. and is subject to all the
terms, conditions and limitations thereof.

VISTA does not warrant the accuracy, timeliness, merchantability,
completeness or usefulness of any information furnished, and the
subscriber accepts any and all risks resulting from decisions
made based solely or in part on VISTA information.

=====================================================================
           Other VISTA Environmental Profiles on this site:
     Summary Profile       x  Zip Code Area Profile
   x  Detailed Profile

            ©     VISTA Environmental Information, Inc.
                    For more information call:
                      1 (800) 733-7606
```

Residential Construction Appendix

The illustrations included in this appendix are designed to introduce the reader to basic residential construction techniques and terminology. Specifically, diagrams depicting various architectural styles, roof designs, roof framing systems, exterior structural walls and framing and a cutaway view of a typical house—illustrating all major components—are featured.

For a more detailed treatment of these and other important construction techniques and terminology, consult *The Complete Home Inspection Kit* by William L. Ventolo, Jr., available from Real Estate Education Company.

Figure A.1
Architectural Styles

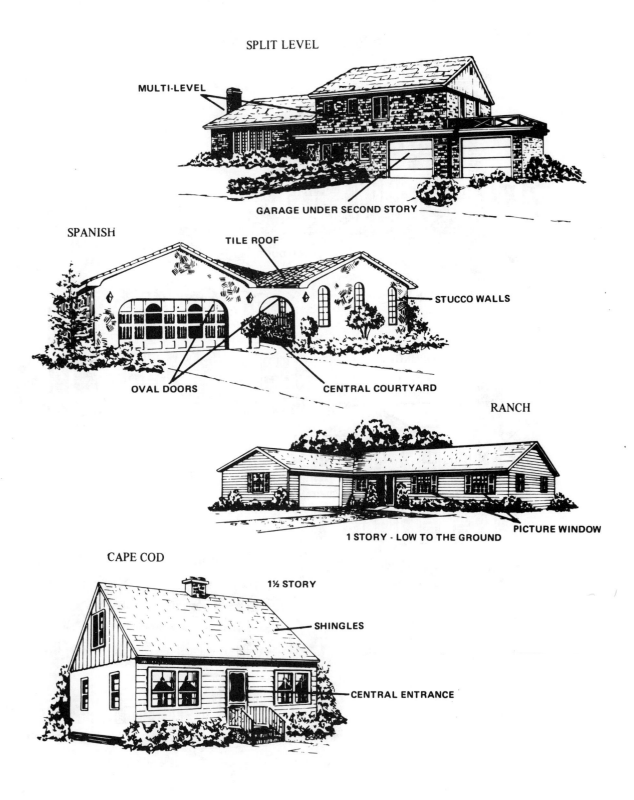

SPLIT LEVEL

MULTI-LEVEL

GARAGE UNDER SECOND STORY

SPANISH

TILE ROOF

STUCCO WALLS

OVAL DOORS

CENTRAL COURTYARD

RANCH

1 STORY - LOW TO THE GROUND

PICTURE WINDOW

CAPE COD

1½ STORY

SHINGLES

CENTRAL ENTRANCE

Figure A.1 (continued)

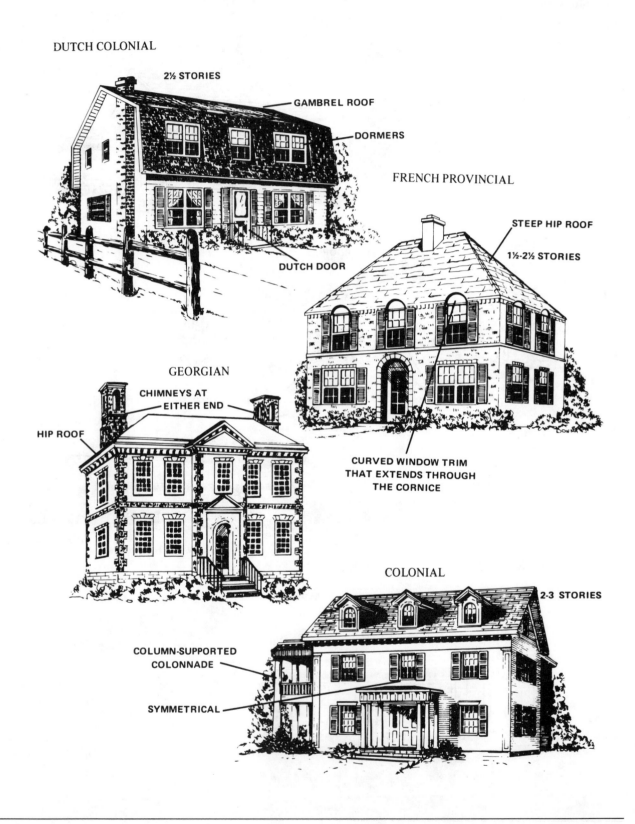

Figure A.2
Roof Designs

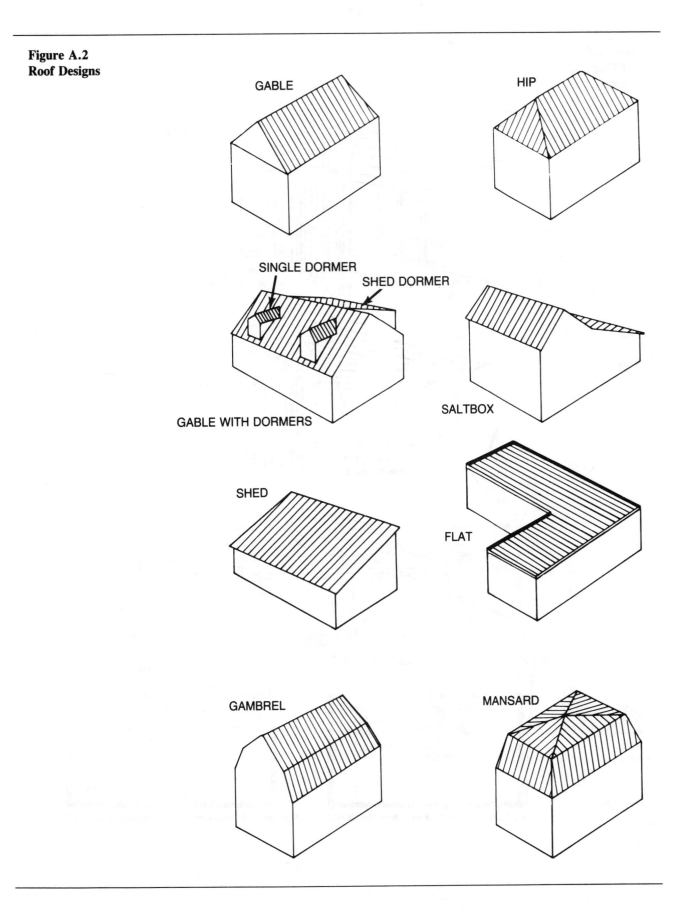

Figure A.3
Roof Framing
Systems

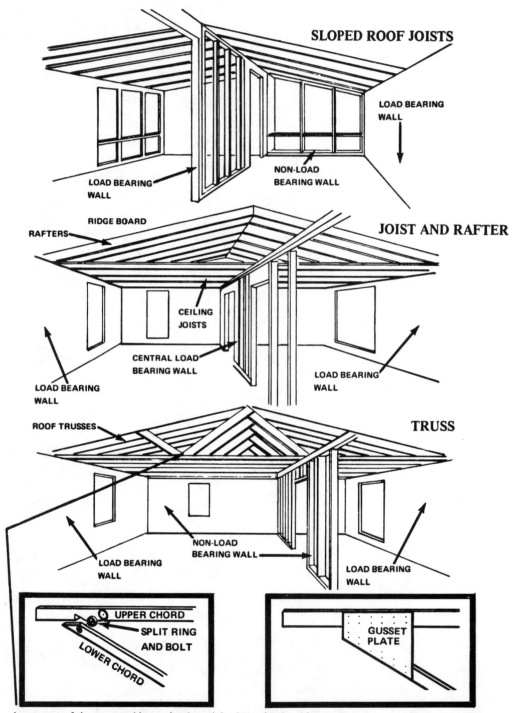

In a truss roof the upper and lower chords are joined together by either a gusset plate or a split ring and bolt.

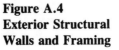

**Figure A.4
Exterior Structural
Walls and Framing**

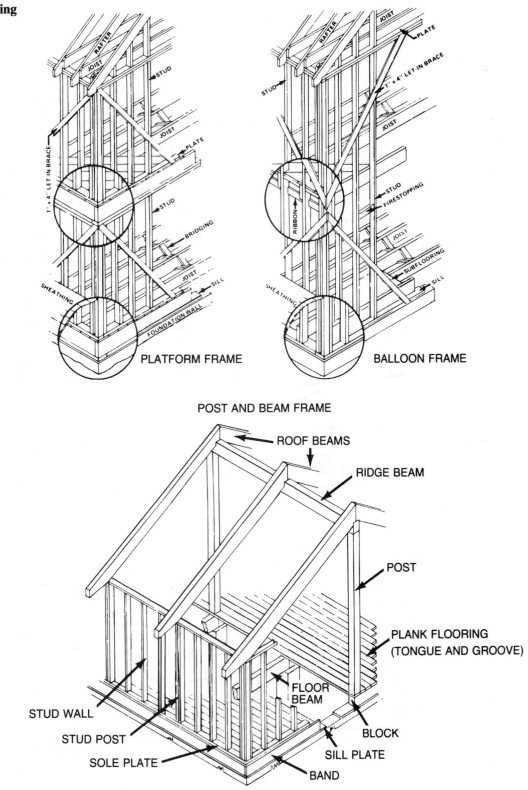

PLATFORM FRAME

BALLOON FRAME

POST AND BEAM FRAME

Figure A.4 (continued)

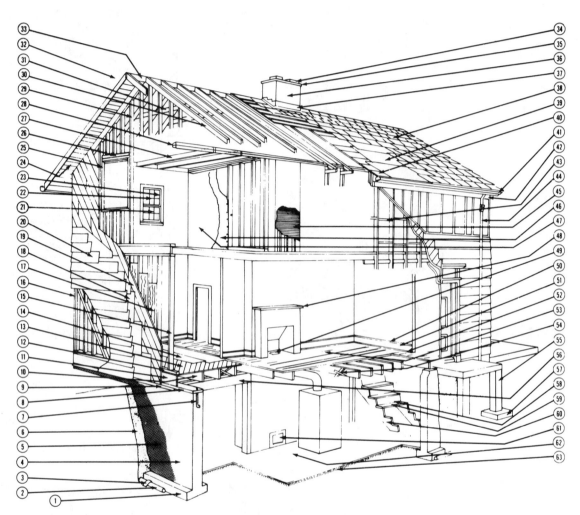

1. FOOTING	22. MUNTIN	43. FIRESTOP
2. FOUNDATION DRAIN TILE	23. WINDOW SASH	44. DOWNSPOUT
3. FELT JOINT COVER	24. EAVE (ROOF PROJECTION)	45. LATHS
4. FOUNDATION WALL	25. WINDOW JAMB TRIM	46. PLASTER BOARD
5. DAMPPROOFING OR WEATHERPROOFING	26. DOUBLE WINDOW HEADER	47. PLASTER FINISH
	27. CEILING JOIST	48. MANTEL
6. BACKFILL	28. DOUBLE PLATE	49. ASH DUMP
7. ANCHOR BOLT	29. STUD	50. BASE TOP MOULDING
8. SILL	30. RAFTERS	51. BASEBOARD
9. TERMITE SHIELD	31. COLLAR BEAM	52. SHOE MOULDING
10. FLOOR JOIST	32. GABLE END OF ROOF	53. FINISH MOULDING
11. BAND OR BOX SILL	33. RIDGE BOARD	54. BRIDGING
12. PLATE	34. CHIMNEY POTS	55. PIER
13. SUBFLOORING	35. CHIMNEY CAP	56. GIRDER
14. BUILDING PAPER	36. CHIMNEY	57. FOOTING
15. WALL STUD	37. CHIMNEY FLASHING	58. RISER
16. DOUBLE CORNER STUD	38. ROOFING SHINGLES	59. TREAD
17. INSULATION	39. ROOFING FELTS	60. STRINGER
18. BUILDING PAPER	40. ROOF SHEATHING	61. CLEANOUT DOOR
19. WALL SHEATHING	41. EAVE TROUGH OR GUTTER	62. CONCRETE BASEMENT FLOOR
20. SIDING	42. FRIEZE BOARD	63. CINDER FILL
21. MULLION		

Glossary of Real Estate Terms

Abstract of title The condensed history of a title to a particular parcel of real estate, consisting of a summary of the original grant and all subsequent conveyances and encumbrances affecting the property and a certification by the abstractor that the history is complete and accurate.

Acceleration clause The clause in a mortgage or deed of trust that can be enforced to make the entire debt due immediately if the borrower defaults on an installment payment or other covenant.

Accession Acquiring title to additions or improvements to real property as a result of the annexation of fixtures or the accretion of alluvial deposits along the banks of streams.

Accretion The increase or addition of land by the deposit of sand or soil washed up naturally from a river, lake or sea.

Accrued items On a closing statement, items of expense that are incurred but not yet payable, such as interest on a mortgage loan or taxes on real property.

Acknowledgment A formal declaration made before a duly authorized officer, usually a notary public, by a person who has signed a document.

Actual eviction The legal process that results in the tenant's being physically removed from the leased premises.

Actual notice Express information or fact; that which is known; direct knowledge.

Adjustable-rate mortgage (ARM) A loan characterized by a fluctuating interest rate, usually one tied to a bank or savings and loan association cost-of-funds index.

Adjusted basis *See* Basis.

Ad valorem tax A tax levied according to value, generally used to refer to real estate tax. Also called the *general tax*.

Adverse possession The actual, open, notorious, hostile and continuous possession of another's land under a claim of title. Possession for a statutory period may be a means of acquiring title.

Affidavit of title A written statement, made under oath by a seller or grantor of real property and acknowledged by a notary public, in which the grantor (1) identifies himself or herself and indicates marital status, (2) certifies that since the examination of the title on the date of the contracts no defects have occurred in the title and (3) certifies that he or she is in possession of the property (if applicable).

Agency The relationship between a principal and an agent, usually a property owner and a real estate broker.

Agency coupled with an interest An agency relationship in which the agent is given an estate or interest in the subject of the agency (the property).

Agent One who acts or has the power to act for another. A fiduciary relationship is created under the *law of agency* when a property owner, as the principal, executes a listing agreement or management contract authorizing a licensed real estate broker to be his or her agent.

Air lot A designated airspace over a piece of land. An air lot, like surface property, may be transferred.

Air rights The right to use the open space above a property, usually allowing the surface to be used for another purpose.

Alienation The act of transferring property to another. Alienation may be voluntary, such as by gift or sale, or involuntary, as through eminent domain or adverse possession.

Alienation clause The clause in a mortgage or deed of trust that states that the balance of the secured debt becomes immediately due and payable at the lender's option if the property is sold by the borrower. In effect this clause prevents the borrower from assigning the debt without the lender's approval.

Allodial system A system of land ownership in which land is held free and clear of any rent or service due to the government; commonly contrasted to the feudal system. Land is held under the allodial system in the United States.

American Land Title Association (ALTA) policy A title insurance policy that protects the interest in a collateral property of a mortgage lender who originates a new real estate loan.

Amortized loan A loan in which the principal as well as the interest is payable in monthly or other periodic installments over the term of the loan.

Anticipation The appraisal principle that holds that value can increase or decrease based on the expectation of some future benefit or detriment produced by the property.

Antitrust laws Laws designed to preserve the free enterprise of the open marketplace by making illegal certain private conspiracies and combinations formed to minimize competition. Most violations of antitrust laws in the real estate business involve either *price-fixing* (brokers conspiring to set fixed compensation rates) or *allocation of customers or markets* (brokers agreeing to limit their areas of trade or dealing to certain areas or properties).

Appraisal An estimate of the quantity, quality or value of something. The process through which conclusions of property value are obtained; also refers to the report that sets forth the process of estimation and conclusion of value.

Appreciation An increase in the worth or value of a property due to economic or related causes, which may prove to be either temporary or permanent; opposite of depreciation.

Assemblage The combining of two or more adjoining lots into one larger tract to increase their total value.

Assignment The transfer in writing of interest in a bond, mortgage, lease or other instrument.

Assumption of mortgage Acquiring title to property on which there is an existing mortgage and agreeing to be personally liable for the terms and conditions of the mortgage, including payments.

Attachment The act of taking a person's property into legal custody by writ or other judicial order to hold it available for application to that person's debt to a creditor.

Attorney's opinion of title An abstract of title that an attorney has examined and has certified to be, in his or her opinion, an accurate statement of the facts concerning the property ownership.

Automatic extension A clause in a listing agreement that states that the agreement will continue automatically for a certain period of time after its expiration date. In many states, use of this clause is discouraged or prohibited.

Avulsion The sudden tearing away of land, as by earthquake, flood, volcanic action or the sudden change in the course of a stream.

Balance The appraisal principle that states that the greatest value in a property will occur when the type and size of the improvements are proportional to each other as well as the land.

Balloon payment A final payment of a mortgage loan that is considerably larger than the required periodic payments because the loan amount was not fully amortized.

Bargain and sale deed A deed that carries with it no warranties against liens or other encumbrances but that does imply that the grantor has the right to convey title. The grantor may add warranties to the deed at his or her discretion.

Base line The main imaginary line running east and west and crossing a principal meridian at a definite point, used by surveyors for reference in locating and describing land under the rectangular (government) survey system of legal description.

Basis The financial interest that the Internal Revenue Service attributes to an owner of an investment property for the purpose of determining annual depreciation and gain or loss on the sale of the asset. If a property was acquired by purchase, the owner's basis is the cost of the property plus the value of any capital expenditures for improvements to the property, minus any depreciation allowable or actually taken. This new basis is called the *adjusted basis*.

Benchmark A permanent reference mark or point established for use by surveyors in measuring differences in elevation.

Beneficiary (1) The person for whom a trust operates or in whose behalf the income from a trust estate is drawn. (2) A lender in a deed of trust loan transaction.

Bilateral contract *See* Contract.

Blanket loan A mortgage covering more than one parcel of real estate, providing for each parcel's partial release from the mortgage lien upon repayment of a definite portion of the debt.

Blockbusting The illegal practice of inducing homeowners to sell their properties by making representations regarding the entry or prospective entry of persons of a particular race or national origin into the neighborhood.

Blue-sky laws Common name for those state and federal laws that regulate the registration and sale of investment securities.

Boot Money or property given to make up any difference in value or equity between two properties in an *exchange*.

Branch office A secondary place of business apart from the principal or main office from which real estate business is conducted. A branch office usually must be run by a licensed real estate broker working on behalf of the broker who operates the principal office.

Breach of contract Violation of any terms or conditions in a contract without legal excuse; for example, failure to make a payment when it is due.

Broker One who acts as an intermediary on behalf of others for a fee or commission.

Brokerage The bringing together of parties interested in making a real estate transaction.

Buffer zone A strip of land, usually used as a park or designated for a similar use, separating land dedicated to one use from land dedicated to another use (e.g., residential from commercial).

Building code An ordinance that specifies minimum standards of construction for buildings to protect public safety and health.

Building permit Written governmental permission for the construction, alteration or demolition of an improvement, showing compliance with building codes and zoning ordinances.

Bulk transfer *See* Uniform Commercial Code.

Bundle of legal rights The concept of land ownership that includes *ownership of all legal rights to the land*—for example, possession, control within the law and enjoyment.

Buydown A financing technique used to reduce the monthly payments for the first few years of a loan. Funds in the form of discount points are given to the lender by the builder or seller to buy down or lower the effective interest rate paid by the buyer, thus reducing the monthly payments for a set time.

Capital gain Profit earned from the sale of an asset.

Capitalization A mathematical process for estimating the value of a property using a proper rate of return on the investment and the annual net income expected to be produced by the property. The formula is expressed:

$$\frac{\text{Income}}{\text{Rate}} = \text{Value}$$

Capitalization rate The rate of return a property will produce on the owner's investment.

Cash flow The net spendable income from an investment, determined by deducting all operating and fixed expenses from the gross income. If expenses exceed income, a *negative cash flow* is the result.

Cash rent In an agricultural lease, the amount of money given as rent to the landowner at the outset of the lease, as opposed to sharecropping.

Caveat emptor A Latin phrase meaning "Let the buyer beware."

Certificate of sale The document generally given to the purchaser at a tax foreclosure sale. A certificate of sale does not convey title; normally it is an instrument certifying that the holder received title to the property after the redemption period passed and that the holder paid the property taxes for that interim period.

Certificate of title A statement of opinion on the status of the title to a parcel of real property based on an examination of specified public records.

Chain of title The succession of conveyances, from some accepted starting point, whereby the present holder of real property derives title.

Change The appraisal principle that holds that no physical or economic condition remains constant.

Chattel *See* Personal property.

Closing statement A detailed cash accounting of a real estate transaction showing all cash received, all charges and credits made and all cash paid out in the transaction.

Cloud on title Any document, claim, unreleased lien or encumbrance that may impair the title to real property or make the title doubtful; usually revealed by a title search and removed by either a quitclaim deed or suit to quiet title.

Clustering The grouping of homesites within a subdivision on smaller lots than normal, with the remaining land used as common areas.

Codicil A supplement or an addition to a will, executed with the same formalities as a will, that normally does not revoke the entire will.

Coinsurance clause A clause in insurance policies covering real property that requires the policyholder to maintain fire insurance coverage generally equal to at least 80 percent of the property's actual replacement cost.

Commingling The illegal act by a real estate broker of placing client or customer funds with personal funds. By law brokers are required to maintain a separate *trust account* for other parties' funds held temporarily by the broker.

Commission Payment to a broker for services rendered, such as in the sale or purchase of real property; usually a percentage of the selling price of the property.

Common elements Parts of a property that are necessary or convenient to the existence, maintenance and safety of a condominium or are normally in common use by all of the condominium residents. Each condominium owner has an undivided ownership interest in the common elements.

Common law The body of law based on custom, usage and court decisions.

Community property A system of property ownership based on the theory that each spouse has an equal interest in the property acquired by the efforts of either spouse during marriage. A holdover of Spanish law, found predominantly in western states; the system was unknown under English common law.

Comparables Properties used in an appraisal report that are substantially equivalent to the subject property.

Competition The appraisal principle that states that excess profits generate competition

Competitive market analysis (CMA) A comparison of the prices of recently sold homes that are similar to a listing seller's home in terms of location, style and amenities.

Condemnation A judicial or administrative proceeding to exercise the power of eminent domain, through which a government agency takes private property for public use and compensates the owner.

Conditional-use permit Written governmental permission allowing a use inconsistent with zoning but necessary for the common good, such as locating an emergency medical facility in a predominantly residential area.

Condominium The absolute ownership of a unit in a multiunit building based on a legal description of the airspace the unit actually occupies, plus an undivided interest in the ownership of the common elements, which are owned jointly with the other condominium unit owners.

Conformity The appraisal principle that holds that the greater the similarity among properties in an area, the better they will hold their value.

Consideration (1) That received by the grantor in exchange for his or her deed. (2) Something of value that induces a person to enter into a contract.

Constructive eviction Actions of a landlord that so materially disturb or impair a tenant's enjoyment of the leased premises that the tenant is effectively forced to move out and terminate the lease without liability for any further rent.

Constructive notice Notice given to the world by recorded documents. All people are charged with knowledge of such documents and their contents, whether or not they have actually examined them. Possession of property is also considered constructive notice that the person in possession has an interest in the property.

Contingency A provision in a contract that requires a certain act to be done or a certain event to occur before the contract becomes binding.

Contract A legally enforceable promise or set of promises that must be performed and for which, if a breach of the promise occurs, the law provides a remedy. A contract may be either *unilateral*, by which only one party is bound to act, or *bilateral*, by which all parties to the instrument are legally bound to act as prescribed.

Contribution The appraisal principle that states that the value of any component of a property is what it gives to the value of the whole or what its absence detracts from that value.

Conventional loan A loan that is not insured or guaranteed by a government source.

Cooperating broker *See* Listing broker.

Cooperative A residential multiunit building whose title is held by a trust or corporation that is owned by and operated for the benefit of persons living within the building, who are the beneficial owners of the trust or stockholders of the corporation, each possessing a proprietary lease.

Corporation An entity or organization, created by operation of law, whose rights of doing business are essentially the same as those of an individual. The entity has continuous existence until it is dissolved according to legal procedures.

Correction lines Provisions in the rectangular survey (government survey) system made to compensate for the curvature of the earth's surface. Every fourth township line (at 24-mile intervals) is used as a correction line on which the intervals between the north and south range lines are remeasured and corrected to a full six miles.

Cost approach The process of estimating the value of a property by adding to the estimated land value the appraiser's estimate of the reproduction or replacement cost of the building, less depreciation.

Cost recovery An Internal Revenue Service term for *depreciation.*

Counteroffer A new offer made as a reply to an offer received. It has the effect of rejecting the original offer, which cannot be accepted thereafter unless revived by the offeror.

Covenant A written agreement between two or more parties in which a party or parties pledge to perform or not perform specified acts with regard to property; usually found in such real estate documents as deeds, mortgages, leases and contracts for deed.

Covenant of quiet enjoyment The covenant implied by law by which a landlord guarantees that a tenant may take possession of leased premises and that the landlord will not interfere in the tenant's possession or use of the property.

Credit On a closing statement, an amount entered in a person's favor—either an amount the party has paid or an amount for which the party must be reimbursed.

Curtesy A life estate, usually a fractional interest, given by some states to the surviving husband in real estate owned by his deceased wife.

Datum A horizontal plane from which heights and depths are measured.

Debit On a closing statement, an amount charged; that is, an amount that the debited party must pay.

Decedent A person who has died.

Dedication The voluntary transfer of private property by its owner to the public for some public use, such as for streets or schools.

Deed A written instrument that, when executed and delivered, conveys title to or an interest in real estate.

Deed in trust An instrument that grants a trustee under a land trust full power to sell, mortgage and subdivide a parcel of real estate. The beneficiary controls the trustee's use of these powers under the provisions of the trust agreement.

Deed of trust *See* Trust deed.

Deed of trust lien *See* Trust deed lien.

Deed restrictions Clauses in a deed limiting the future uses of the property. Deed restrictions may impose a vast variety of limitations and conditions—for example, they may limit the density of buildings, dictate the types of structures that can be erected or prevent buildings from being used for specific purposes or even from being used at all.

Default The nonperformance of a duty, whether arising under a contract or otherwise; failure to meet an obligation when due.

Defeasance clause A clause used in leases and mortgages that cancels a specified right upon the occurrence of a certain condition, such as cancellation of a mortgage upon repayment of the mortgage loan.

Defeasible fee estate An estate in which the holder has a fee simple title that may be divested upon the occurrence or nonoccurrence of a specified event.

There are two categories of defeasible fee estates: fee simple on condition precedent (fee simple determinable) and fee simple on condition subsequent.

Deficiency judgment A personal judgment levied against the borrower when a foreclosure sale does not produce sufficient funds to pay the mortgage debt in full.

Demand The amount of goods people are willing and able to buy at a given price; often coupled with *supply*.

Denial, suspension or revocation of license The potential penalties for licensees who violate real estate statutes or rules and regulations.

Density zoning Zoning ordinances that restrict the maximum average number of houses per acre that may be built within a particular area, generally a subdivision.

Depreciation (1) In appraisal, a loss of value in property due to any cause, including physical deterioration, *functional obsolescence* and *external obsolescence*. (2) In real estate investment, an expense deduction for tax purposes taken over the period of ownership of income property.

Descent Acquisition of an estate by inheritance in which an heir succeeds to the property by operation of law.

Developer One who attempts to put land to its most profitable use through the construction of improvements.

Devise A gift of real property by will. The donor is the devisor, and the recipient is the devisee.

Discount point A unit of measurement used for various loan charges; one point equals one percent of the amount of the loan.

Dominant tenement A property that includes in its ownership the appurtenant right to use an easement over another person's property for a specific purpose.

Dower The legal right or interest, recognized in some states, that a wife acquires in the property her husband held or acquired during their marriage. During the husband's lifetime the right is only a possibility of an interest; upon his death it can become an interest in land.

Dual agency Representing both parties to a transaction. This is unethical unless both parties agree to it, and it is illegal in many states.

Duress Unlawful constraint or action exercised upon a person whereby the person is forced to perform an act against his or her will. A contract entered into under duress is voidable.

Earnest money Money deposited by a buyer under the terms of a contract, to be forefeited if the buyer defaults but applied to the purchase price if the sale is closed.

Easement A right to use the land of another for a specific purpose, such as for a right-of-way or utilities; an incorporeal interest in land.

Easement by necessity An easement allowed by law as necessary for the full enjoyment of a parcel of real estate; for example, a right of ingress and egress over a grantor's land.

Easement by prescription An easement acquired by continuous, open and hostile use of the property for the period of time prescribed by state law.

Easement in gross An easement that is not created for the benefit of any *land* owned by the owner of the easement but that attaches *personally to the easement owner*. For example, a right granted by Eleanor Franks to Joe Fish to use a portion of her property for the rest of his life would be an easement in gross.

Economic life The number of years during which an improvement will add value to the land.

Emblements Growing crops, such as grapes and corn, that are produced annually through labor and industry; also called *fructus industriales*.

Eminent domain The right of a government or municipal quasi-public body to acquire property for public use through a court action called *condemnation*, in which the court decides that the use is a public use and determines the compensation to be paid to the owner.

Employee Someone who works as a direct employee of an employer and has employee status. The employer is obligated to withhold income taxes and social security taxes from the compensation of employees. *See also* Independent contractor.

Employment contract A document evidencing formal employment between employer and employee or between principal and agent. In the real estate business this generally takes the form of a listing agreement or management agreement.

Enabling acts State legislation that confers zoning powers on municipal governments.

Encroachment A building or some portion of it—a wall or fence for instance—that extends beyond the land of the owner and illegally intrudes on some land of an adjoining owner or a street or alley.

Encumbrance Anything—such as a mortgage, tax, or judgment lien, an easement, a restriction on the use of the land or an outstanding dower right—that may diminish the value of a property.

Equalization The raising or lowering of assessed values for tax purposes in a particular county or taxing district to make them equal to assessments in other counties or districts.

Equalization factor A factor (number) by which the assessed value of a property is multiplied to arrive at a value for the property that is in line with statewide tax assessments. The *ad valorem tax* would be based on this adjusted value.

Equitable lien *See* Statutory lien.

Equitable right of redemption The right of a defaulted property owner to recover the property prior to its sale by paying the appropriate fees and charges.

Equitable title The interest held by a vendee under a contract for deed or an installment contract; the equitable right to obtain absolute ownership to property when legal title is held in another's name.

Equity The interest or value that an owner has in property over and above any mortgage indebtedness.

Erosion The gradual wearing away of land by water, wind and general weather conditions; the diminishing of property by the elements.

Escheat The reversion of property to the state or county, as provided by state law, in cases where a decedent dies intestate without heirs capable of inheriting, or when the property is abandoned.

Escrow The closing of a transaction through a third party called an *escrow agent,* or *escrowee,* who receives certain funds and documents to be delivered upon the performance of certain conditions outlined in the escrow instructions.

Escrow instructions A document that sets forth the duties of the escrow agent, as well as the requirements and obligations of the parties, when a transaction is closed through an escrow.

Estate at sufferance The tenancy of a lessee who lawfully comes into possession of a landlord's real estate but who continues to occupy the premises improperly after his or her lease rights have expired.

Estate at will An estate that gives the lessee the right to possession until the estate is terminated by either party; the term of this estate is indefinite.

Estate for years An interest for a certain, exact period of time in property leased for a specified consideration.

Estate from period to period An interest in leased property that continues from period to period—week to week, month to month or year to year.

Estate in land The degree, quantity, nature and extent of interest a person has in real property.

Estate taxes Federal taxes on a decedent's real and personal property.

Estoppel Method of creating an agency relationship in which someone states incorrectly that another person is his or her agent, and a third person relies on that representation.

Estoppel certificate A document in which a borrower certifies the amount owed on a mortgage loan and the rate of interest.

Eviction A legal process to oust a person from possession of real estate.

Evidence of title Proof of ownership of property; commonly a certificate of title, an abstract of title with lawyer's opinion or a Torrens registration certificate.

Exchange A transaction in which all or part of the consideration is the transfer of *like-kind* property (such as real estate for real estate).

Exclusive-agency listing A listing contract under which the owner appoints a real estate broker as his or her exclusive agent for a designated period of time to sell the property, on the owner's stated terms, for a commission. The owner reserves the right to sell without paying anyone a commission if he or she sells to a prospect who has not been introduced or claimed by the broker.

Exclusive-right-to-sell listing A listing contract under which the owner appoints a real estate broker as his or her exclusive agent for a designated period of time, to sell the property on the owner's stated terms, and agrees to pay the broker a commission when the property is sold, whether by the broker, the owner or another broker.

Executed contract A contract in which all parties have fulfilled their promises and thus performed the contract.

Execution The signing and delivery of an instrument. Also, a legal order directing an official to enforce a judgment against the property of a debtor.

Executory contract A contract under which something remains to be done by one or more of the parties.

Express agreement An oral or written contract in which the parties state the contract's terms and express their intentions in words.

Express contract *See* Express agreement.

External obsolescence Reduction in a property's value caused by outside factors (those that are off the property).

Fee simple absolute The maximum possible estate or right of ownership of real property, continuing forever.

Fee simple defeasible *See* Defeasible fee estate.

Feudal system A system of ownership usually associated with precolonial England, in which the king or other sovereign is the source of all rights. The right to possess real property was granted by the sovereign to an individual as a life estate only. Upon the death of the individual title passed back to the sovereign, not to the decedent's heirs.

FHA loan A loan insured by the Federal Housing Administration and made by an approved lender in accordance with the FHA's regulations.

Fiduciary One in whom trust and confidence is placed; usually a reference to a broker employed under the terms of a listing contract.

Fiduciary relationship A relationship of trust and confidence, as between trustee and beneficiary, attorney and client or principal and agent.

Financing statement *See* Uniform Commercial Code.

Fixture An item of personal property that has been converted to real property by being permanently affixed to the realty.

Foreclosure A legal procedure whereby property used as security for a debt is sold to satisfy the debt in the event of default in payment of the mortgage note or default of other terms in the mortgage document. The foreclosure procedure brings the rights of all parties to a conclusion and passes the title in the mortgaged property to either the holder of the mortgage or a third party who may purchase the realty at the foreclosure sale, free of all encumbrances affecting the property subsequent to the mortgage.

Fractional section A parcel of land less than 160 acres, usually found at the edge of a rectangular survey.

Fraud Deception intended to cause a person to give up property or a lawful right.

Freehold estate An estate in land in which ownership is for an indeterminate length of time, in contrast to a *leasehold estate.*

Functional obsolescence A loss of value to an improvement to real estate arising from functional problems, often caused by age or poor design.

Future interest A person's present right to an interest in real property that will not result in possession or enjoyment until some time in the future, such as a reversion or right of reentry.

Gap A defect in the chain of title of a particular parcel of real estate; a missing document or conveyance that raises doubt as to the present ownership of the land.

General agent One who is authorized by a principal to represent the principal in a specific range of matters.

General lien The right of a creditor to have all of a debtor's property—both real and personal—sold to satisfy a debt.

General partnership *See* Partnership.

General warranty deed A deed in which the grantor fully warrants good clear title to the premises. Used in most real estate deed transfers, a general warranty deed offers the greatest protection of any deed.

Government check The 24-mile-square parcels composed of 16 townships in the rectangular (government) survey system of legal description.

Government lot Fractional sections in the rectangular (government) survey system that are less than one quarter-section in area.

Government survey system *See* Rectangular (government) survey system.

Graduated-payment mortgage (GPM) A loan in which the monthly principal and interest payments increase by a certain percentage each year for a certain number of years and then level off for the remaining loan term.

Grantee A person who receives a conveyance of real property from a grantor.

Granting clause Words in a deed of conveyance that state the grantor's intention to convey the property at the present time. This clause is generally worded as "convey and warrant," "grant," "grant, bargain and sell" or the like.

Grantor The person transferring title to or an interest in real property to a grantee.

Gross income multiplier A figure used as a multiplier of the gross annual income of a property to produce an estimate of the property's value.

Gross lease A lease of property according to which a landlord pays all property charges regularly incurred through ownership, such as repairs, taxes, insurance and operating expenses. Most residential leases are gross leases.

Gross rent multiplier (GRM) The figure used as a multiplier of the gross monthly income of a property to produce an estimate of the property's value.

Ground lease A lease of land only, on which the tenant usually owns a building or is required to build as specified in the lease. Such leases are usually long-term net leases; the tenant's rights and obligations continue until the lease expires or is terminated through default.

Growing-equity mortgage (GEM) A loan in which the monthly payments increase annually, with the increased amount being used to reduce directly the principal balance outstanding and thus shorten the overall term of the loan.

Habendum clause That part of a deed beginning with the words, "to have and to hold," following the granting clause and defining the extent of ownership the grantor is conveying.

Heir One who might inherit or succeed to an interest in land under the state law of descent when the owner dies without leaving a valid will.

Highest and best use The possible use of a property that would produce the greatest net income and thereby develop the highest value.

Holdover tenancy A tenancy whereby a lessee retains possession of leased property after the lease has expired and the landlord, by continuing to accept rent, agrees to the tenant's continued occupancy as defined by state law.

Holographic will A will that is written, dated and signed in the testator's handwriting.

Home equity loan A loan (sometimes called a *line of credit*) under which a property owner uses his or her residence as collateral and can then draw funds up to a prearranged amount against the property.

Homeowner's insurance policy A standardized package insurance policy that covers a residential real estate owner against financial loss from fire, theft, public liability and other common risks.

Homestead Land that is owned and occupied as the family home. In many states a portion of the area or value of this land is protected or exempt from judgments for debts.

Hypothecation The pledge of property as security for a loan.

Implied agreement A contract under which the agreement of the parties is demonstrated by their acts and conduct.

Implied contract *See* Implied agreement.

Improvement (1) Any structure, usually privately owned, erected on a site to enhance the value of the property—for example, building a fence or a driveway. (2) A publicly owned structure added to or benefiting land, such as a curb, sidewalk, street or sewer.

Income capitalization approach The process of estimating the value of an income-producing property through capitalization of the annual net income expected to be produced by the property during its remaining useful life.

Incorporeal right A nonpossessory right in real estate; for example, an easement or a right-of-way.

Independent contractor Someone who is retained to perform a certain act but who is subject to the control and direction of another only as to the end result and not as to the way in which the act is performed. Unlike an employee, an independent contractor pays for all expenses and social security and income taxes and receives no employee benefits. Most real estate salespeople are independent contractors.

Index method The appraisal method of estimating building costs by multiplying the original cost of the property by a percentage factor to adjust for current construction costs.

Inflation The gradual reduction of the purchasing power of the dollar, usually related directly to the increases in the money supply by the federal government.

Inheritance taxes State-imposed taxes on a decedent's real and personal property.

Installment contract A contract for the sale of real estate whereby the purchase price is paid in periodic installments by the purchaser, who is in possession of the property even though title is retained by the seller until a future date, which may be not until final payment. Also called a *contract for deed* or *articles of agreement for warranty deed*.

Installment sale A transaction in which the sales price is paid in two or more installments over two or more years. If the sale meets certain requirements, a taxpayer can postpone reporting such income until future years by paying tax each year only on the proceeds received that year.

Interest A charge made by a lender for the use of money.

Interim financing A short-term loan usually made during the construction phase of a building project (in this case often referred to as a *construction loan*).

Intestate The condition of a property owner who dies without leaving a valid will. Title to the property will pass to the decedent's heirs as provided in the state law of descent.

Intrinsic value An appraisal term referring to the value created by a person's personal preferences for a particular type of property.

Investment Money directed toward the purchase, improvement and development of an asset in expectation of income or profits.

Involuntary alienation *See* Alienation.

Involuntary lien A lien placed on property without the consent of the property owner.

Joint tenancy Ownership of real estate between two or more parties who have been named in one conveyance as joint tenants. Upon the death of a joint tenant, the decedent's interest passes to the surviving joint tenant or tenants by the *right of survivorship*.

Joint venture The joining of two or more people to conduct a specific business enterprise. A joint venture is similar to a partnership in that it must be created by agreement between the parties to share in the losses and profits of the venture. It is unlike a partnership in that the venture is for one specific project only, rather than for a continuing business relationship.

Judgment The formal decision of a court upon the respective rights and claims of the parties to an action or suit. After a judgment has been entered and recorded with the county recorder, it usually becomes a general lien on the property of the defendant.

Junior lien An obligation, such as a second mortgage, that is subordinate in right or lien priority to an existing lien on the same realty.

Laches An equitable doctrine used by courts to bar a legal claim or prevent the assertion of a right because of undue delay or failure to assert the claim or right.

Land The earth's surface, extending downward to the center of the earth and upward infinitely into space, including things permanently attached by nature, such as trees and water.

Land contract *See* Installment contract.

Law of agency *See* Agency.

Lease A written or oral contract between a landlord (the lessor) and a tenant (the lessee) that transfers the right to exclusive possession and use of the landlord's real property to the lessee for a specified period of time and for a stated consideration (rent). By state law leases for longer than a certain period of time (generally one year) must be in writing to be enforceable.

Leasehold estate A tenant's right to occupy real estate during the term of a lease, generally considered to be a personal property interest.

Lease option A lease under which the tenant has the right to purchase the property either during the lease term or at its end.

Lease purchase The purchase of real property, the consummation of which is preceded by a lease, usually long-term. Typically done for tax or financing purposes.

Legacy A disposition of money or personal property by will.

Legal description A description of a specific parcel of real estate complete enough for an independent surveyor to locate and identify it.

Legally competent parties People who are recognized by law as being able to contract with others; those of legal age and sound mind.

Lessee *See* Lease.

Lessor *See* Lease.

Leverage The use of borrowed money to finance the bulk of an investment.

Levy To assess; to seize or collect. To levy a tax is to assess a property and set the rate of taxation. To levy an execution is to officially seize the property of a person in order to satisfy an obligation.

License (1) A privilege or right granted to a person by a state to operate as a real estate broker or salesperson. (2) The revocable permission for a temporary use of land—a personal right that cannot be sold.

Lien A right given by law to certain creditors to have their debts paid out of the property of a defaulting debtor, usually by means of a court sale.

Lien theory Some states interpret a mortgage as being purely a lien on real property. The mortgagee thus has no right of possession but must foreclose the lien and sell the property if the mortgagor defaults.

Life cycle costing In property management, comparing one type of equipment to another based on both purchase cost and operating cost over its expected useful lifetime.

Life estate An interest in real or personal property that is limited in duration to the lifetime of its owner or some other designated person or persons.

Life tenant A person in possession of a life estate.

Limited partnership *See* Partnership.

Liquidated damages An amount predetermined by the parties to a contract as the total compensation to an injured party should the other party breach the contract.

Liquidity The ability to sell an asset and convert it into cash, at a price close to its true value, in a short period of time.

Lis pendens A recorded legal document giving constructive notice that an action affecting a particular property has been filed in either a state or a federal court.

Listing agreement A contract between an owner (as principal) and a real estate broker (as agent) by which the broker is employed as agent to find a buyer for the owner's real estate on the owner's terms, for which service the owner agrees to pay a commission.

Listing broker The broker in a multiple-listing situation from whose office a listing agreement is initiated, as opposed to the *cooperating broker,* from whose office negotiations leading up to a sale are initiated. The listing broker and the cooperating broker may be the same person.

Littoral rights (1) A landowner's claim to use water in large navigable lakes and oceans adjacent to his or her property. (2) The ownership rights to land bordering these bodies of water up to the high-water mark.

Lot-and-block (recorded plat) system A method of describing real property that identifies a parcel of land by reference to lot and block numbers within a subdivision, as specified on a recorded subdivision plat.

Management agreement A contract between the owner of income property and a management firm or individual property manager that outlines the scope of the manager's authority.

Market A place where goods can be bought and sold and a price established.

Marketable title Good or clear title, reasonably free from the risk of litigation over possible defects.

Market value The most probable price property would bring in an arm's-length transaction under normal conditions on the open market.

Master plan A comprehensive plan to guide the long-term physical development of a particular area.

Mechanic's lien A statutory lien created in favor of contractors, laborers and materialmen who have performed work or furnished materials in the erection or repair of a building.

Meridian One of a set of imaginary lines running north and south and crossing a base line at a definite point, used in the rectangular (government) survey system of property description.

Metes-and-bounds description A legal description of a parcel of land that begins at a well-marked point and follows the boundaries, using directions and distances around the tract, back to the place of beginning.

Mill One-tenth of one cent. Some states use a mill rate to compute real estate taxes; for example, a rate of 52 mills would be $0.052 tax for each dollar of assessed valuation of a property.

Minor Someone who has not reached the age of majority and therefore does not have legal capacity to transfer title to real property.

Month-to-month tenancy A periodic tenancy under which the tenant rents for one month at a time. In the absence of a rental agreement (oral or written) a tenancy is generally considered to be month to month.

Monument A fixed natural or artificial object used to establish real estate boundaries for a metes-and-bounds description.

Mortgage A conditional transfer or pledge of real estate as security for the payment of a debt. Also, the document creating a mortgage lien.

Mortgagee A lender in a mortgage loan transaction.

Mortgage lien A lien or charge on the property of a mortgagor that secures the underlying debt obligations.

Mortgagor A borrower in a mortgage loan transaction.

Multiperil policies Insurance policies that offer protection from a range of potential perils, such as those of a fire, hazard, public liability, and casualty.

Multiple-listing clause A provision in an exclusive listing for the additional authority and obligation on the part of the listing broker to distribute the listing to other brokers in the multiple-listing organization.

Multiple-listing service (MLS). A marketing organization composed of member brokers who agree to share their listing agreements with one another in the hope of procuring ready, willing and able buyers for their properties more quickly than they could on their own. Most multiple-listing services accept only exclusive-right-to-sell listings from their member brokers, although any broker can sell a property listed in an MLS.

Negotiable instrument A written promise or order to pay a specific sum of money that may be transferred by endorsement or delivery. The transferee then has the original payee's right to payment.

Net lease A lease requiring the tenant to pay not only rent but also costs incurred in maintaining the property, including taxes, insurance, utilities and repairs.

Net listing A listing based on the net price the seller will receive if the property is sold. Under a net listing the broker can offer the property for sale at the highest price obtainable to increase the commission. This type of listing is illegal in many states.

Nonconforming use A use of property that is permitted to continue after a zoning ordinance prohibiting it has been established for the area.

Nonhomogeneity A lack of uniformity; dissimilarity. Because no two parcels of land are exactly alike, real estate is said to be nonhomogeneous.

Note *See* Promissory note.

Novation Substituting a new obligation for an old one or substituting new parties to an existing obligation.

Nuncupative will An oral will declared by the testator in his or her final illness, made before witnesses and afterward reduced to writing.

Offer and acceptance Two essential components of a valid contract; a "meeting of the minds."

Open-end loan A mortgage loan that is expandable by increments up to a maximum dollar amount, the full loan being secured by the same original mortgage.

Open listing A listing contract under which the broker's commission is contingent on the broker's producing a ready, willing and able buyer before the property is sold by the seller or another broker.

Option An agreement to keep open for a set period an offer to sell or purchase property.

Option listing Listing with a provision that gives the listing broker the right to purchase the listed property.

Ostensible agency A form of implied agency relationship created by the actions of the parties involved rather than by written agreement or document.

Package loan A real estate loan used to finance the purchase of both real property and personal property, such as in the purchase of a new home that includes carpeting, window coverings and major appliances.

Parol evidence rule A rule of evidence providing that a written agreement is the final expression of the agreement of the parties, not to be varied or contradicted by prior or contemporaneous oral or written negotiations.

Partition The division of co-tenants' interests in real property when the parties do not all voluntarily agree to terminate the co-ownership; takes place through court procedures.

Partnership An association of two or more individuals who carry on a continuing business for profit as co-owners. Under the law a partnership is regarded as a group of individuals rather than as a single entity. A *general partnership* is a typical form of joint venture in which each general partner shares in the administration, profits and losses of the operation. A *limited partnership* is a business arrangement whereby the operation is administered by one or more general partners and funded, by and large, by limited or silent partners, who are by law responsible for losses only to the extent of their investments.

Party wall A wall that is located on or at a boundary line between two adjoining parcels of land and is used or is intended to be used by the owners of both properties.

Patent A grant or franchise of land from the United States government.

Payoff statement *See* Reduction certificate.

Percentage lease A lease, commonly used for commercial property, whose rental is based on the tenant's gross sales at the premises; it usually stipulates a base monthly rental plus a percentage of any gross sales above a certain amount.

Periodic estate *See* Estate from period to period.

Personal property Items, called *chattels,* that do not fit into the definition of real property; movable objects.

Physical deterioration A reduction in a property's value resulting from a decline in physical condition; can be caused by action of the elements or by ordinary wear and tear.

Planned unit development (PUD) A planned combination of diverse land uses, such as housing, recreation and shopping, in one contained development or subdivision.

Plat map A map of a town, section or subdivision indicating the location and boundaries of individual properties.

Plottage The increase in value or utility resulting from the consolidation (*assemblage*) of two or more adjacent lots into one larger lot.

Point of beginning (POB) In a metes-and-bounds legal description, the starting point of the survey, situated in one corner of the parcel; all metes-and-bounds descriptions must follow the boundaries of the parcel back to the point of beginning.

Police power The government's right to impose laws, statutes and ordinances, including zoning ordinances and building codes, to protect the public health, safety and welfare.

Power of attorney A written instrument authorizing a person, the *attorney-in-fact,* to act as agent for another person to the extent indicated in the instrument.

Prepaid items On a closing statement, items that have been paid in advance by the seller, such as insurance premiums and some real estate taxes, for which he or she must be reimbursed by the buyer.

Prepayment penalty A charge imposed on a borrower who pays off the loan principal early. This penalty compensates the lender for interest and other charges that would otherwise be lost.

Price-fixing *See* Antitrust laws.

Primary market *See* Secondary mortgage market.

Principal (1) A sum loaned or employed as a fund or an investment, as distinguished from its income or profits. (2) The original amount (as in a loan) of the total due and payable at a certain date. (3) A main party to a transaction—the person for whom the agent works.

Principal meridian The main imaginary line running north and south and crossing a base line at a definite point, used by surveyors for reference in locating and describing land under the rectangular (government) survey system of legal description.

Prior appropriation A concept of water ownership in which the landowner's right to use available water is based on a government-administered permit system.

Priority The order of position or time. The priority of liens is generally determined by the chronological order in which the lien documents are recorded; tax liens, however, have priority even over previously recorded liens.

Private mortgage insurance (PMI) Insurance provided by any private carrier that protects a lender against a loss in the event of a foreclosure and deficiency.

Probate A legal process by which a court determines who will inherit a decedent's property and what the estate's assets are.

Procuring cause The effort that brings about the desired result. Under an open listing the broker who is the procuring cause of the sale receives the commission.

Progression An appraisal principle that states that, between dissimilar properties, the value of the lesser-quality property is favorably affected by the presence of the better-quality property.

Promissory note A financing instrument that states the terms of the underlying obligation, is signed by its maker and is negotiable (transferable to a third party).

Property manager Someone who manages real estate for another person for compensation. Duties include collecting rents, maintaining the property and keeping up all accounting.

Property reports The mandatory federal and state documents compiled by subdividers and developers to provide potential purchasers with facts about a property prior to their purchase.

Prorations Expenses, either prepaid or paid in arrears, that are divided or distributed between buyer and seller at the closing.

Protected class Any group of people designated as such by the Department of Housing and Urban Development (HUD) in consideration of federal and state civil rights legislation. Currently includes ethnic minorities, women, religious groups, the handicapped and others.

Puffing Exaggerated or superlative comments or opinions.

Pur autre vie For the life of another. A life estate pur autre vie is a life estate that is measured by the life of a person other than the grantee.

Purchase-money mortgage (PMM) A note secured by a mortgage or deed of trust given by a buyer, as borrower, to a seller, as lender, as part of the purchase price of the real estate.

Pyramiding The process of acquiring additional properties by refinancing properties already owned and investing the loan proceeds in additional properties.

Quantity survey method The appraisal method of estimating building costs by calculating the cost of all of the physical components in the improvements, adding the cost to assemble them and then including the indirect costs associated with such construction.

Quitclaim deed A conveyance by which the grantor transfers whatever interest he or she has in the real estate, without warranties or obligations.

Range A strip of land six miles wide, extending north and south and numbered east and west according to its distance from the principal meridian in the rectangular (government) survey system of legal description.

Ratification Method of creating an agency relationship in which the principal accepts the conduct of someone who acted without prior authorization as the principal's agent.

Ready, willing and able buyer One who is prepared to buy property on the seller's terms and is ready to take positive steps to consummate the transaction.

Real estate Land; a portion of the earth's surface extending downward to the center of the earth and upward infinitely into space, including all things permanently attached to it, whether naturally or artificially.

Real estate investment syndicate *See* Syndicate.

Real estate investment trust (REIT) Trust ownership of real estate by a group of individuals who purchase certificates of ownership in the trust, which in turn invests the money in real property and distributes the profits back to the investors free of corporate income tax.

Real estate license law State law enacted to protect the public from fraud, dishonesty and incompetence in the purchase and sale of real estate.

Real estate mortgage investment conduit (REMIC) A tax entity that issues multiple classes of investor interests (securities) backed by a pool of mortgages.

Real estate recovery fund A fund established in some states from real estate license revenues to cover claims of aggrieved parties who have suffered monetary damage through the actions of a real estate licensee.

Real property The interests, benefits and rights inherent in real estate ownership.

REALTOR® A registered trademark term reserved for the sole use of active members of local REALTOR® boards affiliated with the National Association of REALTORS®.

Reconciliation The final step in the appraisal process, in which the appraiser combines the estimates of value received from the sales comparison, cost and income approaches to arrive at a final estimate of market value for the subject property.

Reconveyance deed A deed used by a trustee under a deed of trust to return title to the trustor.

Recording The act of entering or recording documents affecting or conveying interests in real estate in the recorder's office established in each county. Until it is recorded, a deed or mortgage ordinarily is not effective against subsequent purchasers or mortgagees.

Rectangular (government) survey system A system established in 1785 by the federal government, providing for surveying and describing land by reference to principal meridians and base lines.

Redemption The right of a defaulted property owner to recover his or her property by curing the default.

Redemption period A period of time established by state law during which a property owner has the right to redeem his or her real estate from a foreclosure or tax sale by paying the sales price, interest and costs. Many states do not have mortgage redemption laws.

Redlining The illegal practice of a lending institution denying loans or restricting their number for certain areas of a community.

Reduction certificate (payoff statement) The document signed by a lender indicating the amount required to pay a loan balance in full and satisfy the debt; used in the settlement process to protect both the seller's and the buyer's interests.

Regression An appraisal principle that states that, between dissimilar properties, the value of the better-quality property is affected adversely by the presence of the lesser-quality property.

Regulation Z Implements the Truth-in-Lending Act requiring credit institutions to inform borrowers of the true cost of obtaining credit.

Release deed A document, also known as a *deed of reconveyance*, that transfers all rights given a trustee under a deed of trust loan back to the grantor after the loan has been fully repaid.

Remainder interest The remnant of an estate that has been conveyed to take effect and be enjoyed after the termination of a prior estate, such as when an owner conveys a life estate to one party and the remainder to another.

Rent A fixed, periodic payment made by a tenant of a property to the owner for possession and use, usually by prior agreement of the parties.

Rent schedule A statement of proposed rental rates, determined by the owner or the property manager or both, based on a building's estimated espenses, market supply and demand and the owner's long-range goals for the property.

Replacement cost The construction cost at current prices of a property that is not necessarily an exact duplicate of the subject property but serves the same purpose or function as the original.

Reproduction cost The construction cost at current prices of an exact duplicate of the subject property.

Reverse-annuity mortgage (RAM) A loan under which the homeowner receives monthly payments based on his or her accumulated equity rather than a lump sum. The loan must be repaid at a prearranged date or upon the death of the owner or the sale of the property.

Reversionary interest The remnant of an estate that the grantor holds after granting a life estate to another person.

Reversionary right The return of the rights of possession and quiet enjoyment to the lessor at the expiration of a lease.

Right of survivorship *See* Joint tenancy.

Riparian rights An owner's rights in land that borders on or includes a stream, river or lake. These rights include access to and use of the water.

Risk management Evaluation and selection of appropriate property and other insurance.

Rules and regulations Real estate licensing authority orders that govern licensees' activities; they usually have the same force and effect as statutory law.

Sale and leaseback A transaction in which an owner sells his or her improved property and, as part of the same transaction, signs a long term lease to remain in possession of the premises.

Sales comparison approach The process of estimating the value of a property by examining and comparing actual sales of comparable properties.

Salesperson A person who performs real estate activities while employed by or associated with a licensed real estate broker.

Satisfaction of mortgage A document acknowledging the payment of a mortgage debt.

Secondary mortgage market A market for the purchase and sale of existing mortgages, designed to provide greater liquidity for mortgages; also called the *secondary money market*. Mortgages are first originated in the *primary mortgage market*.

Section A portion of township under the rectangular (government) survey system. A township is divided into 36 sections, numbered one through 36. A section is a square with mile-long sides and an area of one square mile, or 640 acres.

Security agreement *See* Uniform Commercial Code.

Security deposit A payment by a tenant, held by the landlord during the lease term and kept (wholly or partially) on default or destruction of the premises by the tenant.

Separate property Under community property law, property owned solely by either spouse before the marriage, acquired by gift or inheritance after the marriage or purchased with separate funds after the marriage.

Servient tenement Land on which an easement exists in favor of an adjacent property (called a *dominant estate*); also called a *servient estate*.

Setback The amount of space local zoning regulations require between a lot line and a building line.

Severalty Ownership of real property by one person only, also called *sole ownership*.

Severance Changing an item of real estate to personal property by detaching it from the land; for example, cutting down a tree.

Sharecropping In an agricultural lease, the agreement between the landowner and the tenant farmer to split the crop or the profit from its sale, actually sharing the crop.

Shared-appreciation mortgage (SAM) A mortgage loan in which the lender, in exchange for a loan with a favorable interest rate, participates in the profits (if any) the borrower receives when the property is eventually sold.

Situs The personal preference of people for one area over another, not necessarily based on objective facts and knowledge.

Special agent One who is authorized by a principal to perform a single act or transaction; a real estate broker is usually a special agent authorized to find a ready, willing and able buyer for a particular property.

Special assessment A tax or levy customarily imposed against only those specific parcels of real estate that will benefit from a proposed public improvement like a street or sewer.

Special warranty deed A deed in which the grantor warrants, or guarantees, the title only against defects arising during the period of his or her tenure and ownership of the property and not against defects existing before that time, generally using the language, "by, through or under the grantor but not otherwise."

Specific lien A lien affecting or attaching only to a certain, specific parcel of land or piece of property.

Specific performance A legal action to compel a party to carry out the terms of a contract.

Square foot method The appraisal method of estimating building costs by multiplying the number of square feet in the improvements being appraised by the cost per square foot for recently constructed similar improvements.

Statute of frauds That part of a state law that requires certain instruments, such as deeds, real estate sales contracts and certain leases, to be in writing to be legally enforceable.

Statute of limitations That law pertaining to the period of time within which certain actions must be brought to court.

Statutory lien A lien imposed on property by statute—a tax lien, for example—in contrast to an *equitable lien*, which arises out of common law.

Statutory redemption The right of a defaulted property owner to recover the property after its sale by paying the appropriate fees and charges.

Steering The illegal practice of channeling home seekers to particular areas, either to maintain the homogeneity of an area or to change the character of an area to create a speculative situation.

Straight-line method A method of calculating depreciation for tax purposes, computed by dividing the adjusted basis of a property by the estimated number of years of remaining useful life.

Straight loan A loan in which only interest is paid during the term of the loan, with the entire principal amount due with the final interest payment.

Subagent One who is employed by a person already acting as an agent. Typically a reference to a salesperson licensed under a broker (agent) who is employed under the terms of a listing agreement.

Subdivider One who buys undeveloped land, divides it into smaller, usable lots and sells the lots to potential users.

Subdivision A tract of land divided by the owner, known as the *subdivider*, into blocks, building lots and streets according to a recorded subdivision plat, which must comply with local ordinances and regulations.

Sublease *See* Subletting.

Subletting The leasing of premises by a lessee to a third party for part of the lessee's remaining term. *See also* Assignment.

Subordination Relegation to a lesser position, usually in respect to a right or security.

Subordination agreement A written agreement between holders of liens on a property that changes the priority of mortgage, judgment and other liens under certain circumstances.

Subrogation The substitution of one creditor for another, with the substituted person succeeding to the legal rights and claims of the original claimant. Subrogation is used by title insurers to acquire from the injured party rights to sue in order to recover any claims they have paid.

Substitution An appraisal principle that states that the maximum value of a property tends to be set by the cost of purchasing an equally desirable and valuable substitute property, assuming that no costly delay is encountered in making the substitution.

Subsurface rights Ownership rights in a parcel of real estate to the water, minerals, gas, oil and so forth that lie beneath the surface of the property.

Suit for possession A court suit initiated by a landlord to evict a tenant from leased premises after the tenant has breached one of the terms of the lease or has held possession of the property after the lease's expiration.

Suit to quiet title A court action intended to establish or settle the title to a particular property, especially when there is a cloud on the title.

Supply The amount of goods available in the market to be sold at a given price. The term is often coupled with *demand*.

Supply and demand The appraisal principle that follows the interrelationship of the supply of and demand for real estate. As appraising is based on economic concepts, this principle recognizes that real property is subject to the influences of the marketplace just as is any other commodity.

Surety bond An agreement by an insurance or bonding company to be responsible for certain possible defaults, debts or obligations contracted for by an insured party; in essence, a policy insuring one's personal and/or financial integrity. In the real estate business a surety bond is generally used to ensure that a particular project will be completed at a certain date or that a contract will be performed as stated.

Surface rights Ownership rights in a parcel of real estate that are limited to the surface of the property and do not include the air above it *(air rights)* or the minerals below the surface *(subsurface rights)*.

Survey The process by which boundaries are measured and land areas are determined; the on-site measurement of lot lines, dimensions and position of a house on a lot, including the determination of any existing encroachments or easements.

Syndicate A combination of people or firms formed to accomplish a business venture of mutual interest by pooling resources. In a *real estate investment syndicate* the parties own and/or develop property, with the main profit generally arising from the sale of the property.

Tacking Adding or combining successive periods of continuous occupation of real property by adverse possessors. This concept enables someone who has not been in possession for the entire statutory period to establish a claim of adverse possession.

Taxation The process by which a government or municipal quasi-public body raises monies to fund its operation.

Tax credit An amount by which tax owed is reduced directly.

Tax deed An instrument, similar to a certificate of sale, given to a purchaser at a tax sale. *See also* Certificate of sale.

Tax lien A charge against property, created by operation of law. Tax liens and assessments take priority over all other liens.

Tax sale A court-ordered sale of real property to raise money to cover delinquent taxes.

Tenancy by the entirety The joint ownership, recognized in some states, of property acquired by husband and wife during marriage. Upon the death of one spouse the survivor becomes the owner of the property.

Tenancy in common A form of co-ownership by which each owner holds an undivided interest in real property as if he or she were sole owner. Each individual owner has the right to partition. Unlike joint tenants, tenants in common have right of inheritance.

Tenant One who holds or possesses lands or tenements by any kind of right or title.

Tenant improvements Alterations to the interior of a building to meet the functional demands of the tenant.

Testate Having made and left a valid will.

Testator A person who has made a valid will. A woman often is referred to as a testatrix, although testator can be used for either gender.

Tier (township strip) A strip of land six miles wide, extending east and west and numbered north and south according to its distance from the base line in the rectangular (government) survey system of legal description.

Time is of the essence A phrase in a contract that requires the performance of a certain act within a stated period of time.

Time-sharing A form of ownership interest that may include an estate interest in property and which allows use of the property for a fixed or variable time period.

Title (1) The right to or ownership of land. (2) The evidence of ownership of land.

Title insurance A policy insuring the owner or mortgagee against loss by reason of defects in the title to a parcel of real estate, other than encumbrances, defects and matters specifically excluded by the policy.

Title theory Some states interpret a mortgage to mean that the lender is the owner of mortgaged land. Upon full payment of the mortgage debt the borrower becomes the landowner.

Torrens system A method of evidencing title by registration with the proper public authority, generally called the *registrar,* named for its founder, Sir Robert Torrens.

Township The principal unit of the rectangular (government) survey system. A township is a square with six-mile sides and an area of 36 square miles.

Township strips *See* Tier.

Trade fixture An article installed by a tenant under the terms of a lease and removable by the tenant before the lease expires.

Transfer tax Tax stamps required to be affixed to a deed by state and/or local law.

Trust A fiduciary arrangement whereby property is conveyed to a person or institution, called a *trustee,* to be held and administered on behalf of another person, called a *beneficiary.* The one who conveys the trust is called the *trustor.*

Trust deed An instrument used to create a mortgage lien by which the borrower conveys title to a trustee, who holds it as security for the benefit of the note holder (the lender); also called a *deed of trust.*

Trust deed lien A lien on the property of a trustor that secures a deed of trust loan.

Trustee The holder of bare legal title in a deed of trust loan transaction.

Trustee's deed A deed executed by a trustee conveying land held in a trust.

Trustor A borrower in a deed of trust loan transaction.

Undivided interest *See* Tenancy in common.

Unenforceable contract A contract that has all the elements of a valid contract, yet neither party can sue the other to force performance of it. For example, an unsigned contract is generally unenforceable.

Uniform Commercial Code A codification of commercial law, adopted in most states, that attempts to make uniform all laws relating to commercial transactions, including chattel mortgages and bulk transfers. Security interests in chattels are created by an instrument known as a *security agreement.* To give notice of the security interest, a *financing statement* must be recorded. Article 6 of the code regulates *bulk transfers*—the sale of a business as a whole, including all fixtures, chattels and merchandise.

Unilateral contract A one-sided contract wherein one party makes a promise so as to induce a second party to do something. The second party is not legally bound to perform; however, if the second party does comply, the first party is obligated to keep the promise.

Unit-in-place method The appraisal method of estimating building costs by calculating the costs of all of the physical components in the structure, with the cost of each item including its proper installation, connection, etc.; also called the *segregated cost method*.

Unity of ownership The four unities that are traditionally needed to create a joint tenancy—unity of title, time, interest and possession.

Usury Charging interest at a higher rate than the maximum rate established by state law.

Valid contract A contract that complies with all the essentials of a contract and is binding and enforceable on all parties to it.

VA loan A mortgage loan on approved property made to a qualified veteran by an authorized lender and guaranteed by the Department of Veteran Affairs in order to limit the lender's possible loss.

Value The power of a good or service to command other goods in exchange for the present worth of future rights to its income or amenities.

Variance Permission obtained from zoning authorities to build a structure or conduct a use that is expressly prohibited by the current zoning laws; an exception from the zoning ordinances.

Vendee A buyer, usually under the terms of a land contract.

Vendor A seller, usually under the terms of a land contract.

Voidable contract A contract that seems to be valid on the surface but may be rejected or disaffirmed by one or both of the parties.

Void contract A contract that has no legal force or effect because it does not meet the essential elements of a contract.

Voluntary alienation *See* Alienation.

Voluntary lien A lien placed on property with the knowledge and consent of the property owner.

Waste An improper use or an abuse of a property by a possessor who holds less than fee ownership, such as a tenant, life tenant, mortgagor or vendee. Such waste ordinarily impairs the value of the land or the interest of the person holding the title or the reversionary rights.

Will A written document, properly witnessed, providing for the transfer of title to property owned by the deceased, called the *testator*.

Workers' compensation acts Laws that require an employer to obtain insurance coverage to protect his or her employees who are injured in the course of their employment.

Wraparound loan A method of refinancing in which the new mortgage is placed in a secondary, or subordinate, position; the new mortgage includes both the unpaid principal balance of the first mortgage and whatever additional sums are advanced by the lender. In essence it is an additional mortgage in which another lender refinances a borrower by lending an amount over the existing first mortgage amount without disturbing the existence of the first mortgage.

Zoning ordinance An exercise of police power by a municipality to regulate and control the character and use of property.

Answer Key

Following are the correct answers to the review questions included in each chapter of the text (except Chapter 13, which has no questions). In parentheses following the correct answers are references to the pages where the question topics are discussed or explained. If you have answered a question incorrectly, be sure to go back to the page or pages noted and restudy the material until you understand the correct answer.

Chapter 1
The Real Estate Business
1. b (5)
2. b (5)
3. d (6)
4. b (5)

Chapter 2
Real Property and the Law
1. c (13)
2. b (15)
3. c (10)
4. c (10)
5. d (10)
6. d (13)
7. a (14–15)
8. a (9)
9. a (15)
10. c (10)
11. c (14)

Chapter 3
Concepts of Home Ownership
1. d (21)
2. b (22)
3. a (20)
4. b (25)
5. c (22)
6. b (19)
7. b (23)
8. d (23)
9. d (24–25)

Chapter 4
Real Estate Brokerage
1. a (30)
2. d (30)
3. a (30)
4. a (29–30)
5. b (35)
6. c (34)
7. b (31)
8. d (31–33)

9. b (35)
10. d (29–30)
11. b (37)
12. a (35)
13. d (37)
14. a (32)
15. c (32)
16. d (36)

Chapter 5
Listings Agreements
1. a (42)
2. c (42–43)
3. c (44)
4. a (43)
5. c (46)
6. d (44)
7. b (47, 50–51)
8. c (45)
9. a (42)
10. c (43)
11. b (44)
12. a (43)
13. b (42)
14. b (45)
15. a (46)

Chapter 6
Interests in Real Estate
1. b (55)
2. a (56)
3. c (56)
4. d (68)
5. c (61, 65)
6. a (58)
7. d (60)
8. d (63)
9. c (66)
10. a (55)
11. b (58)
12. b (61)
13. a (60)
14. b (59)

15. b (64)
16. c (60)
17. d (64)
18. a (61)
19. d (56)

Chapter 7
How Ownership Is Held
1. d (73)
2. b (72)
3. a (72, 76)
4. b (79)
5. b (76)
6. d (75)
7. b (75)
8. a (76)
9. b (80)
10. c (81)
11. d (72, 78)
12. d (72)
13. d (72)
14. b (81)
15. b (75)
16. c (79)
17. b (79)
18. b (75–76)
19. d (79)
20. a (76)

Chapter 8
Legal Descriptions
1. b (90–91)
2. d (89)
3. d (90–91)
4. b (86)
5. b (90, 92)
6. b (90, 92)
7. d (90, 92)
8. c (90, 92)
9. a (90, 92)
10. b (98)
11. d (92)
12. c (90)

13. d (92)
14. c (89)
15. d (92)
16. b (92)
17. b (99)
18. b (92)
19. b (98)
20. b (98)
21. b (91)
22. b (98)
23. c (91)
24. d (99)
25. b (90)
26. c (86)

Chapter 9
Real Estate Taxes
and Other Liens
 1. d (103)
 2. b (104)
 3. b (108)
 4. c (103)
 5. b (108, 110)
 6. c (106–7)
 7. c (105)
 8. c (109)
 9. b (106)
10. c (108)
11. d (110)
12. d (110)
13. c (108)
14. b (108)
15. b (108–9)
16. d (109)
17. d (107)
18. a (105)
19. b (105)
20. d (105)

Chapter 10
Real Estate Contracts
 1. c (117)
 2. b (116)
 3. d (116)
 4. d (116)
 5. b (116–17)
 6. c (117)
 7. a (118)
 8. d (118)
 9. d (120)
10. d (118–19)
11. d (120)
12. a (123–24)
13. a (125–26)

14. d (125–26)
15. b (126)
16. d (130)
17. d (130)
18. c (118)
19. b (123)
20. b (122)
21. a (119)
22. b (122)

Chapter 11
Transfer of Title
 1. a (134)
 2. a (134)
 3. d (135)
 4. a (136)
 5. b (137)
 6. c (135)
 7. d (138)
 8. d (140)
 9. b (139)
10. c (134, 137)
11. b (135)
12. b (136)
13. b (137)
14. c (140–41)
15. b (141–42)
16. d (140–42)
17. a (141)
18. c (140)
19. b (142–143)
20. d (143)
21. a (142)
22. c (143)

Chapter 12
Title Records
 1. a (148)
 2. a (148)
 3. c (148)
 4. a (148)
 5. a (149)
 6. a (149)
 7. d (150)
 8. d (150)
 9. d (150)
10. c (150)
11. a (150)
12. d (151)
13. c (148)
14. c (151)
15. b (152)
16. d (152)
17. c (151)

Chapter 14
Real Estate Financing:
Principles
 1. d (167)
 2. a (171)
 3. a (165)
 4. d (182)
 5. d (182)
 6. b (166)
 7. d (184)
 8. d (171)
 9. a (171)
10. a (182)
11. b (170)
12. d (182)
13. b (183)
14. a (165)
15. b (167)

Chapter 15
Real Estate Financing:
Practice
 1. b (191)
 2. d (190)
 3. c (200–1)
 4. c (190)
 5. b (198)
 6. c (197)
 7. a (188)
 8. a (197)
 9. a (200)
10. c (190)
11. b (191)
12. c (193)
13. b (201)
14. a (196)
15. b (188)
16. b (200)
17. c (191)
18. a (190)
19. a (188)
20. b (201)
21. d (202)

Chapter 16
Leases
 1. c (218)
 2. c (218)
 3. d (216)
 4. a (209)
 5. c (208)
 6. b (214)
 7. d (210)
 8. c (208)

9. b (216)
10. b (216)
11. b (209)
12. a (214)
13. a (213)
14. d (219)
15. d (210)

Chapter 17
Property Management
1. b (237)
2. a (233)
3. d (233)
4. c (237)
5. c (233)
6. b (236)
7. b (235)
8. c (232)
9. a (233)
10. c (237)
11. c (237)
12. c (233)
13. b (235)

Chapter 18
Real Estate Appraisal
1. c (248)
2. b (241)
3. b (243)
4. b (241)
5. d (242)
6. a (242)
7. d (247)
8. c (250)
9. b (246)
10. d (248–49)
11. c (249)
12. c (248)
13. c (241)
14. b (248)
15. c (245)
16. b (243)
17. d (245)
18. b (248)
19. a (246)
20. b (247)
21. d (246)

Chapter 19
Control of Land Use
1. a (264)
2. c (262)
3. b (260)
4. c (260)
5. c (263)
6. d (260)
7. b (264)
8. a (261)
9. b (262)
10. a (262)
11. d (262)
12. b (264)
13. a (264)

Chapter 20
Property Development
and Subdivision
1. b (270)
2. a (268)
3. c (270)
4. b (270)
5. b (270)
6. b (264)
7. d (269)
8. d (270)
9. a (271)
10. a (270)
11. a (271)

Chapter 21
Fair Housing and
Ethical Practices
1. c (276–78)
2. a (275, 278)
3. d (275)
4. b (278)
5. c (278)
6. a (278)
7. b (276)
8. c (276)
9. c (278)
10. b (276)
11. a (277)
12. b (276)
13. d (278)

14. a (280)
15. d (280)

Chapter 22
Real Estate Investment
1. c (289)
2. b (290)
3. b (290)
4. a (291)
5. b (291)
6. b (292)
7. c (291)
8. c (293)
9. a (292)
10. c (291)
11. d (296)
12. a (296)
13. c (295)
14. b (297)
15. b (297)

Chapter 23
Closing the Real Estate
Transaction
1. d (311)
2. b (307)
3. d (306)
4. a (306)
5. d (303)
6. c (304)
7. c (307)
8. b (311)
9. b (311)
10. d (312, 311)
11. c (311)
12. a (311)
13. b (318)
14. b (318)
15. c (308)
16. b (309)
17. d (304)
18. d (304)

Mathematics Review

1. $79,500 sales price × 6½% commission =
   $79,500 × .065 = $5,167.50, Happy Valley's commission
   $5,167.50 × 30% or $5,167.50 × .30 = $1,550.25, listing
   salesperson's commission

   b. $1,550.25

2.

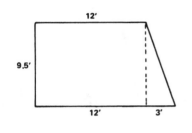

   12′ × 9.5′ = 114 square feet, area of rectangle
   ½ (3′ × 9.5′) = ½ (28.5) = 14.25 square feet, area of triangle
   114 + 14.25 = 128.25 square feet
   To convert square feet to square yards divide by 9:
   128.25 ÷ 9 = 14.25 square yards
   $16.95 carpet + $2.50 installation = $19.45 cost per square yard
   $19.45 × 14.25 square yards = $277.1625 rounded to $277.16

   c. $277.16

3. $30,000 Peters + $35,000 Gamble + $35,000 Clooney = $100,000
   $125,000 – $100,000 = $25,000, Considine's contribution
   $$\frac{\text{part}}{\text{total}} = \text{percent}$$
   $25,000 ÷ $125,000 = .20 or 20%

   a. 20%

4. $391.42 × 12 = $4,697.04, annual interest
   $$\frac{\text{part}}{\text{percent}} = \text{total}$$
   $4,697.04 ÷ 11½% or $4,697.04 ÷ .115 = $40,843.826
   rounded to $40,843.83

   b. $40,843.83

5. $98,500 × 5% = $98,500 × .05 = $4,925, annual increase in value
   $98,500 + $4,925 = $103,425, current market value

   a. $103,425

6. $95,000 × 60% = $95,000 × .60 = $57,000 assessed value
   Divide by 100 because tax rate is stated per hundred dollars:
   $57,000 ÷ 100 = $570
   $570 × $2.85 = $1,624.50, annual taxes

   d. $1,624.50

7.

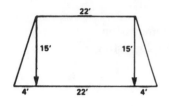

22′ × 15′ = 330 square feet, area of rectangle
½ (4′ × 15′) = ½ (60) = 30 square feet, area of each triangle
30 × 2 = 60 square feet, area of two triangles
330 + 60 = 390 square feet, surface area to be paved
6″ deep = ½ foot
390 × ½ = 195 cubic feet, cement needed for patio   **d. 195 cubic feet**

8. $4,175 – $1,000 salary = $3,175 commission on sales
$3,175 ÷ 2.5% = $3,175 ÷ .025 = $127,000, value of property sold   **b. $127,000**

9. two sides of 95′ plus one side of 42′6″
95′ × 2 = 190 feet
42′6″ = 42.5 feet
190 + 42.5 = 232.5 linear feet
232.5 × $6.95 = $1,615.875 rounded to $1,615.88   **c. $1,615.88**

10. $4,500 × 12 = $54,000 annual rental
$54,000 ÷ 8% = $54,000 ÷ .08 = $675,000, original cost of property   **a. $675,000**

11. $1,340 ÷ 12 months = $111.667/month
$111.667 ÷ 30 days = $3.722/day
$111.667 × 2 months = $223.334
$3.722 × 15 days = $55.83
$223.334 + $55.83 = $279.164 rounded to $279.16   **b. $279.16**

12. $58,200 × 12% = $58,200 × .12 = $6,984
$6,984 ÷ 12 months = $582/month
$582 ÷ 30 days = $19.40/day
$19.40 per day × 11 days = $213.40   **d. $213.40**

13. $975 ÷ 12 months = $81.25/month
$81.25 ÷ 30 days = $2.708
$81.25 × 2 months = $162.500
$2.708 × 4 days = $10.832
$162.500 + $10.832 = $173.332 rounded to $173.33   **a. $173.33**

14. $61,550 × 13% = $61,550 × .13 = $8,001.500
$8,001.500 ÷ 12 months = $666.792/month
$666.792 ÷ 30 days = $22.226/day
$22.226 × 22 days = $488.972 rounded to $488.97   **b. $488.97**

15. 43,560 sq. ft./acre × 100 acres = 4,356,000 sq. ft.
    4,356,000 total sq. ft. × ⅛ = 544,500 sq. ft. for streets
    4,356,000 − 544,500 = 3,811,500 sq. ft. for lots
    3,811,500 sq. ft. ÷ 140 lots = 27,225 sq. ft./lot

    c. 27,225

16. $14,100 commission ÷ 6% commission rate =
    $14,100 ÷ .06 = $235,000 sales price

    a. $235,000

Sample Examination One

1. b	43. c	4. b
2. a	44. b	5. c
3. a	45. d	6. d
4. c	46. d	7. d
5. c	47. c	8. d
6. b	48. d	9. b
7. a	49. b	10. b
8. a	50. b	11. b
9. a	51. b	12. a
10. d	52. b	13. d
11. d	53. c	14. c
12. a	54. d	15. d
13. b	55. b	16. a
14. a	56. c	17. b
15. a	57. a	18. b
16. c	58. b	19. c
17. d	59. d	20. a
18. b	60. b	21. c
19. a	61. c	22. b
20. b	62. a	23. a
21. a	63. d	24. b
22. d	64. d	25. d
23. b	65. b	26. d
24. b	66. d	27. b
25. c	67. b	28. b
26. d	68. d	29. b
27. b	69. a	30. d
28. b	70. a	31. d
29. b	71. d	32. b
30. b	72. d	33. a
31. d	73. a	34. d
32. d	74. b	35. b
33. b	75. b	36. a
34. b	76. c	37. b
35. b	77. d	38. d
36. a	78. b	39. a
37. a	79. d	40. c
38. b	80. d	41. b
39. a		42. c
40. a	**Sample Examination Two**	43. b
41. d		44. d
42. b	1. d	45. c
	2. c	46. d
	3. c	47. a

48.	a	59.	d	70.	a
49.	b	60.	d	71.	d
50.	c	61.	d	72.	c
51.	c	62.	c	73.	a
52.	a	63.	c	74.	d
53.	c	64.	b	75.	b
54.	a	65.	a	76.	c
55.	d	66.	b	77.	d
56.	a	67.	b	78.	a
57.	b	68.	d	79.	b
58.	b	69.	c	80.	b

Index